# MASTERIN

# SPANISH

LEVEL 1

**Hear It • Speak It • Write It • Read It**

Developed for the
FOREIGN SERVICE INSTITUTE,
DEPARTMENT OF STATE

by Robert P. Stockwell, J. Donald Bowen, and Ismael Silva-Fuenzalida

SECOND EDITION

This course was developed for the Foreign Service Institute, Department of State.



*All inquiries should be addressed to:*
Barron's Educational Series, Inc.
250 Wireless Boulevard
Hauppauge, New York 11788
http://www.barronseduc.com

ISBN-10: 0-7641-2371-8
ISBN-13: 978-0-7641-2371-9

**Library of Congress Cataloging-in-Publication Data**
Stockwell, Robert P.
Mastering Spanish : hear it, speak it, write it, read it / developed for the Foreign Service Institute, Department of State by Robert P. Stockwell, J. Donald Bowen, Ismael Silva-Fuenzalida.—2nd ed.
p. cm.
ISBN 0-7641-2371-8 (alk. paper)
1. Spanish language—Textbooks for foreign speakers—English. 2. Spanish language—Conversation and phrase books—English. I. Bowen, J. Donald (Jean Donald), 1922– II. Silva-Fuenzalida, Ismael III. Title

PC4129.E5 S755 2003
468.2'421—dc21 2002027923

**A large part of the text of this book is recorded on the accompanying tapes or CDs. Their contents are described in the accompanying booklet.**

On the tapes and CDs, selected statements about life and customs in Spanish-speaking countries are adapted from *Spanish at a Glance* by Heywood Wald and *Learn Spanish the Fast and Fun Way* by Gene Hammitt.

PRINTED IN THE UNITED STATES OF AMERICA

20 19 18 17 16 15 14 13 12 11 10 9

# INTRODUCTION

The materials in this book have been developed to present Spanish as a spoken language, and the skills of understanding and speaking are accordingly emphasized. The method of presentation will likely be new to students acquainted with more traditional methods of language teaching. In order to understand the materials, one must first understand the method upon which they are built.

## Method of Teaching

The method is known as GUIDED IMITATION. There are two very important aspects of this method. First, learning a relatively small body of material so well that it requires very little effort to produce it. This is OVERLEARNING. The second aspect is learning to manipulate the sounds, sequences, and patterns of the language authentically. The important implication here is the reality of both the model and the imitation. The model (teacher, recording, etc.) must provide Spanish as people really speak it in actual conversations, and the student must be helped to an accurate imitation.

## Pronunciation

The first two units are focused primarily on pronunciation problems. Drills on other aspects of the language are deliberately postponed because of the importance of developing good pronunciation habits from the very beginning of the course. Pronunciation is extremely important. It is the basis of all real fluency.

## Aids to Listening

If speakers of English were not so highly literate, it might be possible to teach effectively without reference to any written symbolization, but most students are much more comfortable if some kind of representation of what they are imitating is also available for visual reference. There is, of course, a traditional writing system for Spanish which is used in all parts of the Spanish speaking world. It is a very adequate system for its purpose, which might be stated as providing visual cues for persons who already speak the language. For pedagogical purposes, a respelling, or phonetic representation of Spanish is also provided as a means of reminding the student of important features of the pronunciation which the traditional spelling system does not provide, such as significant sound distinctions, word groupings, intonation patterns, etc. The phonetic symbolization may at first look unfamiliar and somewhat foreboding, but this very unfamiliarity is a healthy reminder that none of the English sounds (which are so easily associated with the familiar letters of the alphabet) are exact duplications of the Spanish sounds to be mastered. This is also, of course, true in the respelling when familiar symbols are used: the appearance of the letter t does not mean the familiar English t-sound is indicated.

The intonations are marked in the respelling by a system of dots and accents placed at relative heights over the vowels. The patterns recorded in this way are not necessarily the only possibilities in spoken Spanish, but they are all normal patterns which have been thoroughly and widely tested.

The symbolization in the respelling will allow for a consistent interpretation of the pronunciation of any dialect area of the Spanish speaking world. For example, the /ş/ symbol is to be interpreted as a sound similar to the 's' of 'sink' in Spanish America, but as the 'th' of 'think' in Central Spain. Other regional pronunciation features are similarly marked.

The acquisition of a good pronunciation is first of all the result of careful listening and imitation plus whatever help can be obtained from initial pronunciation drills and description, and from the cues provided for continuing reference by the aids to listening.

Every unit (after the first two) is organized in the same way: part one is the basic dialog with a few pertinent notes; part two is grammar drills and discussion; part three is a set of recombination narratives and dialogs.

## Basic Dialogs

The basic dialogs are the core of each unit. These dialogs are recreations of the real situations a student is most likely to encounter, and the vocabulary and sentences are those he or she is most likely to need. The dialogs are set in a mythical country called *Surlandia,* which is described as a typical Latin American republic, insofar as it is possible to extract common features from so diverse an area.

In the first part of the book new vocabulary is introduced mainly in the basic dialogs. Occasionally, in the illustrations of grammar points, new words are introduced in order to fill out patterns needed to do the exercises. New words are always clearly indicated by placing them on a line themselves, indented between the lines that are complete sentences. Since each new word is introduced in this fashion only once, the student should take pains to be sure he or she learns each word as it is presented. Careful pains have been taken to see that each word introduced will reappear many times later in the course to help the student assimilate each word in a variety of contexts.

The student should very carefully learn both the literal meanings of each individual word or phrase that is given on an indented line and the meaning that appears in the full sentences. It should not be cause for concern if the meaning in context is strikingly different from the literal meaning. In the construction of each dialog, the Spanish was written first, and the corresponding English is its closest equivalent and not a literal translation. It is therefore not at all surprising if the Spanish does not seem to 'follow' the English.

## Drills and Grammar

Each unit can in some ways be likened to a musical theme with variations. The basic dialogs are the theme, and the drills provide the variations. Patterns of the structure of the language which have been learned in the basic sentences are expanded and manipulated in the drills.

There are four kinds of drills in each unit (three before Unit 6). Of these, two are designed to vary selected basic sentences within the structure and vocabulary the student has already learned. And two are oriented toward the structure of the language to provide a systematic coverage of all important patterns.

All of these drills are planned to be easily and rapidly answered. If a drill is found to be hard, the difficulty probably reflects inadequacy in the mastery of the dialogs and earlier drills.

Pattern drills are presented in a format which provides both practice and explanation. First appears a presentation of the pattern to be drilled, then various kinds of drills, and finally a more detailed discussion of the pattern.

The presentation consists of a listing of basic sentences (and a few new sentences when necessary) which illustrate the grammar point to be drilled. Then there is an extrapolation which shows the relationships involved in the pattern in a two-dimensional chart, which is further explained by a short note or two. This presentation should provide sufficient clues to enable the student to understand and use the pattern correctly in the drills that follow. These drills are mainly exercises making substitutions, responses, and translations, highlighting the grammar points covered. They are devised for oral answers to oral stimuli.

After the drills there is a more detailed discussion of the pattern drilled. While an effort was made to keep these discussions clear and readable, it has to be recognized that a description of a language is a technical subject.

The student may notice slight differences in the respelling used in the aids to listening and in the grammar charts and discussions. The respelling useful as a guide to pronunciation for an English speaking student records more details than a respelling to be used in grammar discussions where comparisons are made between Spanish forms, not between English and Spanish pronunciation.

## Conversation

The conversation section of each unit is designed to help bridge the gap between the more or less mechanical stimulus-response activity of the drills and the skill of free conversation which is the ultimate aim of the course. These recombination monologues and dialogs extend the abilities of the student into ever more natural situations.

# PREFACE

*Mastering Spanish* is part of a series of language courses being presented by Barron's Educational Series, Inc. This course is intended for the serious language student who wishes to speak Spanish fluently. The course book and accompanying CDs or tapes present Spanish as a spoken language, emphasizing pronunciation and verbal comprehension.

This course was developed by the Foreign Service Institute of the Department of State to train government officers who needed to speak Spanish fluently. In addition to being an excellent choice for those who wish to teach themselves Spanish, this course can be of great help to the student of Spanish who can read the language or is currently studying it in school but would like to achieve greater fluency.

# Table of Contents

# 1.1 BASIC SENTENCES

## Useful phrases

| English Spelling | Aid to Listening | Spanish Spelling |
|---|---|---|
| Good morning. | bwénȯzđíȧs ↓ | Buenos días. |
| Good morning, sir. | bwénȯzđíȧs \| sėn̦yór ↓ | Buenos días, señor. |
| Good afternoon, ma'am. | bwénȧstárđės \| sėn̦yórȧ ↓ | Buenas tardes, señora. |
| Good evening, miss. | bwénȧznóchės \| sėn̦yȯrítȧ ↓ | Buenas noches, señorita. |
| how | kómȯ ↓ | cómo |
| are (to be) | ėstá ↓ ėstár ↓ | está (estar) |
| you | u̇stéđ ↓ | usted |
| How are you? | kómo̯ėstáu̯stéđ ↓ | ¿Cómo está usted? |
| (I) am (to be) | ėstóy ↓ ėstár ↓ | estoy (estar) |
| well | byén ↓ | bien |
| thanks | grás̯yȧs ↓ | gracias |
| and | í ↓ | y |
| I'm fine, thanks. How are *you?* | ėstóyƀyéŋ \| grás̯yȧs \| i̯u̇stéđ ↑ | Estoy bien, gracias, ¿y usted? |

| | | |
|---|---|---|
| very | múy ↓ | muy |
| Very well, thanks. | mu̇yƀyéŋ \| gráşyȧs ↓ | Muy bien, gracias. |
| hello, hi | ólȧ ↓ | hola |
| what such | ké-tál ↓ | qué tal |
| Hi! How goes it? (1) | ólȧ ↓ kétál ↓ | ¡Hola! ¿Qué tal? |
| (it) goes (to go) | bá ↓ ír ↓ | va (ir) |
| to you (it) goes | lė-ƀá ↓ | le va |
| How are you getting along? | kómȯleƀá ↓ | ¿Como le va? |
| Fine, thanks. | byéŋ \| gráşyȧs ↓ | Bien, gracias. |
| with | kón ↓ | con |
| the permission | ėl-pėrmísȯ ↓ | el permiso |
| Excuse me. (2) | kȯmpėrmísȯ ↓ | Con permiso. |
| no, not | nó ↓ | no |
| Certainly. | kómȯnó ↓ | Cómo no. |
| excuse (to excuse) | dispénsė ↓ dispėnsár ↓ | dispense (dispensar) |
| Excuse me. (3) | dispénsėmė ↓ | Dispénseme. |

| | | |
|---|---|---|
| it (I) regret (to regret, to feel) | lȯ-syéntȯ ↓ sėntír ↓ | lo siento (sentir) |
| much, lots, too much | múchȯ ↓ | mucho |
| I'm very sorry. | lȯsyéntȯmúchȯ ↓ | Lo siento mucho. |
| That's okay. | ėstáƀyén ↓ | Está bien. |
| many (f.pl.) (4) | múchȧs ↓ | muchas |
| Thanks a lot. | múchȧzgrá̩syȧs ↓ | Muchas gracias. |
| of, from | dé ↓ | de |
| nothing | náđȧ ↓ | nada |
| You're welcome. | dėnáđȧ ↓ | De nada. |
| there is, there are (there to be) | áy ↓ ȧƀér ↓ | hay (haber) |
| Don't give it a thought. (5) | no̩áyđėké ↓ | No hay de qué. |
| (I) want (to want) | kyérȯ ↓ kėrér ↓ | quiero (querer) |
| to present | prėsėntár ↓ | presentar |
| to present to you | prėsėntárlė ↓ | presentarle |

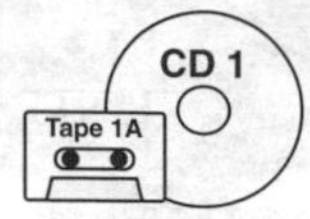




| | | |
|---|---|---|
| to | á ↓ | a |
| the (m. sg.) | él ↓ | el |
| to the | ál ↓ | al |
| I'd like to present Mr. Molina to you. | kyérȯ \| prėsėntárlȩ \| ȧlsėn̦yórmȯlínȧ ↓ | Quiero presentarle al señor Molina. |
| the (f.sg.) | lá ↓ | la |
| I'd like to present Mrs. Molina to you. | kyérȯ \| prėsėntárlȩ \| ȧlȧsėn̦yórȧđėmȯlínȧ ↓ | Quiero presentarle a la señora de Molina. |
| the pleasure | ėl-gústȯ ↓ | el gusto |
| Glad to meet you. | múchȯgústȯ ↓ | Mucho gusto. |
| equally (equal) | igwálméntė ↓ igwál ↓ | igualmente (igual) |
| Same here, thanks. | igwálméntė \| grásyȧs ↓ | Igualmente, gracias. |
| enchanted (to enchant) | ėŋkȧntáđȯ ↓ eŋkȧntár ↓ | encantado (encantar) |
| to meet, get acquainted, to know | kȯnȯsér ↓ | conocer |
| to meet you (f.) | kȯnȯsérlȧ ↓ | conocerla |

| | | |
|---|---|---|
| Delighted to meet you. (6) | ėŋkȧntáđȯ \| đėkȯnȯs̯érlȧ ↓ | Encantado de conocerla. |
| to meet you (m.) | kȯnȯs̯érlȯ ↓ | conocerlo |
| Glad to meet you. (6) | múchȯg̯ústȯ \| đėkȯnȯs̯érlȯ ↓ | Mucho gusto de conocerlo. |
| Goodbye. | ȧđyós ↓ | Adiós, |
| until | ástȧ ↓ | hasta |
| tomorrow | mȧŋ̯yánȧ ↓ | mañana |
| See you tomorrow. | ȧstȧmȧŋ̯yánȧ ↓ | Hasta mañana. |
| then, later | lwég̯ȯ ↓ | luego |
| So long. | ȧstȧlwég̯ȯ ↓ | Hasta luego. |

## 1.10 Notes on the basic sentences

(l) /óla ↓ kétál ↓ / *¡Hola! ¿Qué tal?* is a greeting generally used with a person whom you already know more than casually, and who occupies a status approximately equivalent to yours.

(2) /kompermíso ↓ / *Con permiso* is used to excuse yourself when, for example, you are on an elevator and need to squeeze between other people who are in front of you in order to get out; or, when you want to excuse yourself from a group you are talking with. It is not ordinarily interchangeable with /dispénseme ↓ / *dispénseme*.

(3) /dispénseme ↓ / *dispénseme* is used as apology for a minor breach of etiquette, to interrupt a conversation to ask about something, etc.

(4) Note that /múchas ↓ / *muchas* 'many' is simply the feminine plural of a word /múcho ↓ / *mucho* 'much' that you also met in the phrase /múchogústo ↓ / *mucho gusto*. The / —s / is the plural part, while the /—a/ before the /–s/ is the feminine marker.

(5) /nọáydeké ↓ / *No hay de qué* is used when the other person thanks you for some small favor you have done for him; it is about the same as /denáda ↓ / *De nada*.

(6) /enkantádo | dekonoșérla ↓ / *Encantado de conocerla* is regularly used only when you are introduced to a woman (if you are a man). If you are a woman, a different form is used and you should not learn this sentence to use yourself. /múchogústo | dekonoșérlo ↓ / *Mucho gusto de conocerlo* is what you say (if you are a man) to another man, or else just the short form /muchogústo ↓ /*Mucho gusto*. In Spain, instead of /—lo/ you say /—le/.

## 1.2 DRILLS ON PRONUNCIATION

### 1.21 Vowel contrasts in weak-stessed syllables

In learning the basic sentences in the first section of this unit, you should have been repeatedly corrected for your pronunciation of the underlined vowels in such phrases as these:

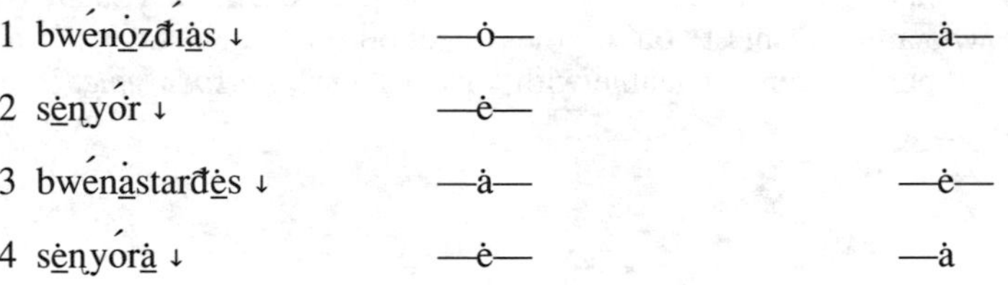

| | | | |
|---|---|---|---|
| 1 | bwénọzđías ↓ | —ȯ— | —ȧ— |
| 2 | sėnyór ↓ | —ė— | |
| 3 | bwénạstarđės ↓ | —ȧ— | —ė— |
| 4 | sėnyórȧ ↓ | —ė— | —ȧ |

| | | | |
|---|---|---|---|
| 5 bwénȧ̲znóchė̲s ↓ | —ȧ— | | —ė— |
| 6 grás̯yȧ̲s ↓ | —ȧ— | | |
| 7 di̲spénsė̲mė̲ ↓ | —i— | —ė— | —ė |
| 8 múchȧ̲zgrás̯yȧ̲s ↓ | —ȧ— | | —ȧ— |
| 9 prė̲sė̲ntárlė̲ ↓ | —ė— | —ė— | —ė |
| 10 mȯ̲línȧ̲ ↓ | —ȯ— | | —ȧ |
| 11 ástȧ̲mȧ̲n̯yánȧ̲ ↓ | —ȧ— | —ȧ— | —ȧ |
| 12 ástȧ̲lwégȯ̲ ↓ | —ȧ— | | —ȯ |

It is perfectly normal for you to have trouble with these vowels, because, as the dots over them indicate, *they are all under weak stress* in positions where such vowels *do not occur under weak stress in English.*

While it is normal to make these mistakes at first, they constitute a *very serious error* which must be corrected early in your efforts to form Spanish habits of pronunciation. The following lists are for the purpose of helping you to master these *vowels under weak stress*. They are arranged in *pairs of words* such that the *only* difference between the members of each pair is in the pronunciation of one weak-stressed vowel: such a pair of words is called a *minimally contrasting pair.*

Practice repeating these after your instructor until you can make the contrast *easily,* just as he does, and insist that he continue practicing them with you until they *do* come easily.

## 1.21.1 Exercises on minimal vowel contrasts under weak stress

/a/ and /e/ in contrast under weak stress

| | | | |
|---|---|---|---|
| séđȧ̲ ↓ | séđė̲ ↓ | pȧ̲lón ↓ | pė̲lón ↓ |
| sápȧ̲ ↓ | sápė̲ ↓ | fȧ̲tál ↓ | fė̲tál ↓ |
| lótȧ̲ ↓ | lótė̲ ↓ | tȧ̲n̯yír ↓ | tė̲n̯yír ↓ |
| mésȧ̲s ↓ | mésė̲s ↓ | pȧ̲pítȯ ↓ | pė̲pítȯ ↓ |
| bóchȧ̲ ↓ | bóchė̲ ↓ | dȧ̲đítȯ ↓ | dė̲đítȯ ↓ |
| tíntȧ̲ ↓ | tíntė̲ ↓ | ėskúpȧ̲ ↓ | ėskúpė̲ ↓ |
| chínchȧ̲ ↓ | chínchė̲ ↓ | s̯ȯkétȧ̲ ↓ | s̯ȯkétė̲ ↓ |
| kórtȧ̲ ↓ | kórtė̲ ↓ | ȧlúmbrȧ̲ ↓ | ȧlúmbrė̲ ↓ |
| sóƀrȧ̲s ↓ | sóƀrė̲s ↓ | frȧns̯ésȧ̲s ↓ | frȧns̯ésė̲s ↓ |
| bȧ̲sár ↓ | bė̲sár ↓ | kȧntórȧ̲s ↓ | kȧntórė̲s ↓ |
| mȧ̲nár ↓ | mė̲nár ↓ | birrétȧ̲ ↓ | birrétė̲ ↓ |
| mȧ̲chón ↓ | mė̲chón ↓ | sėn̯yórȧ̲s ↓ | sėn̯yórė̲s ↓ |
| tȧ̲chár ↓ | tė̲chár ↓ | pȧstórȧ̲s ↓ | pȧstórė̲s ↓ |
| tȧ̲chón ↓ | tė̲chón ↓ | mȧ̲rkáđȯ ↓ | mė̲rkáđȯ ↓ |
| pȧ̲nál ↓ | pė̲nál ↓ | ȧpȧ̲gár ↓ | ȧpė̲gár ↓ |
| tȧ̲hón ↓ | tė̲hón ↓ | pȯrtu̇gésȧ̲s ↓ | pȯrtu̇gésė̲s ↓ |

/a/ and /i/ in contrast under weak stress

| | | | |
|---|---|---|---|
| lȧ̲ƀár ↓ | li̲ƀár ↓ | pȧ̲n̮yál ↓ | pi̲n̮yál ↓ |
| pȧ̲tón ↓ | pi̲tón ↓ | mȧ̲sítȧ ↓ | mi̲sítȧ ↓ |
| nȧ̲đár ↓ | ni̲đár ↓ | lȧ̲térȧ ↓ | li̲térȧ ↓ |
| mȧ̲táđ ↓ | mi̲táđ ↓ | sȧ̲lérȯ ↓ | si̲lérȯ ↓ |
| chȧ̲rlár ↓ | chi̲rlár ↓ | pȧ̲kétė ↓ | pi̲kétė ↓ |
| pȧ̲nşón ↓ | pi̲nşón ↓ | fȧ̲hárȯn ↓ | fi̲hárȯn ↓ |
| pȧ̲sándȯ ↓ | pi̲sándȯ ↓ | mȧ(l)y̧ȧ̲đór ↓ | mȧ(l)y̧i̲đór ↓ |

/a/ and /o/ in contrast under weak stress

| | | | |
|---|---|---|---|
| árȧ̲ ↓ | árȯ̲ ↓ | kúƀȧ̲ ↓ | kúƀȯ̲ ↓ |
| tíȧ̲ ↓ | tíȯ̲ ↓ | kókȧ̲ ↓ | kókȯ̲ ↓ |
| şérȧ̲ ↓ | şérȯ̲ ↓ | kárȧ̲ ↓ | kárȯ̲ ↓ |
| pésȧ̲ ↓ | pésȯ̲ ↓ | párȧ̲ ↓ | párȯ̲ ↓ |
| pásȧ̲ ↓ | pásȯ̲ ↓ | chínȧ̲ ↓ | chínȯ̲ ↓ |
| málȧ̲ ↓ | málȯ̲ ↓ | kántȧ̲ ↓ | kántȯ̲ ↓ |
| mésȧ̲ ↓ | mésȯ̲ ↓ | mántȧ̲ ↓ | mántȯ̲ ↓ |
| máy̧ȧ̲ ↓ | máy̧ȯ̲ ↓ | şórrȧ̲ ↓ | şórrȯ̲ ↓ |
| bólȧ̲ ↓ | bólȯ̲ ↓ | | |

| | | | |
|---|---|---|---|
| sántȧ̲ ↓ | sántȯ̲ ↓ | dėréchȧ̲ ↓ | dėréchȯ̲ ↓ |
| swégrȧ̲ ↓ | swégrȯ̲ ↓ | şigárrȧ̲ ↓ | şigárrȯ̲ ↓ |
| négrȧ̲ ↓ | négrȯ̲ ↓ | mȧ̲ríȧ ↓ | mȯ̲ríȧ ↓ |
| pálmȧ̲ ↓ | pálmȯ̲ ↓ | şȧpátȧ̲ ↓ | şȧpátȯ̲ ↓ |
| pástȧ̲ ↓ | pástȯ̲ ↓ | ėrmánȧ̲ ↓ | ėrmánȯ̲ ↓ |
| trómpȧ̲ ↓ | trómpȯ̲ ↓ | mimósȧ̲ ↓ | mimósȯ̲ ↓ |
| rrémȧ̲ ↓ | rrémȯ̲ ↓ | pȧréhȧ̲ ↓ | pȧréhȯ̲ ↓ |
| kóƀrȧ̲ ↓ | kóƀrȯ̲ ↓ | mȧréȧ̲ ↓ | mȧréȯ̲ ↓ |
| nyétȧ̲ ↓ | nyétȯ̲ ↓ | tėrnérȧ̲ ↓ | tėrnérȯ̲ ↓ |
| índyȧ̲ ↓ | índyȯ̲ ↓ | şėrésȧ̲ ↓ | şėrésȯ̲ ↓ |
| kȧ̲lór ↓ | kȯ̲lór ↓ | (l)y̧ȧmáđȧ̲ ↓ | (l)y̧ȧmáđȯ̲ ↓ |
| ėspósȧ̲ ↓ | ėspósȯ̲ ↓ | lȧkónikȧ̲ ↓ | lȧkónikȯ̲ ↓ |

/a/ and /u/ in contrast under weak stress

| | | | |
|---|---|---|---|
| pȧ̲hár ↓ | pu̲̇hár ↓ | lȧ̲nérȯ ↓ | lu̲̇nérȯ ↓ |
| tȧ̲rón ↓ | tu̲̇rón ↓ | kȧ̲rákȧs ↓ | ku̲̇rákȧs ↓ |
| sȧ̲ƀíđȯ ↓ | su̲̇ƀíđȯ ↓ | bȧ̲rrítȧ ↓ | bu̲̇rrítȧ ↓ |
| pȧ̲pítȧ ↓ | pu̲̇pítȧ ↓ | pȧ̲rgítȧ ↓ | pu̲̇rgítȧ ↓ |

CD 1 Tape 1A

| | | | |
|---|---|---|---|
| mȧ̲láṣȯ ↓ | mu̲̇láṣȯ ↓ | kȧ̲ṇyáđȯ ↓ | ku̲̇ṇyáđȯ ↓ |
| kȧ̲nítȧ ↓ | ku̲̇nítȧ ↓ | mȧ̲rṣyánȯ ↓ | mu̲̇rṣyánȯ ↓ |
| lȧ̲nítȧ ↓ | lu̲̇nítȧ ↓ | pȧ̲liđéṣ ↓ | pu̲̇liđéṣ ↓ |
| mȧ̲lítȧ ↓ | mu̲̇lítȧ ↓ | mȧ̲tȧđór ↓ | mu̲̇tȧđór ↓ |

/e/ and /i/ in contrast under weak stress

| | | | |
|---|---|---|---|
| pė̲nár ↓ | pi̲nár ↓ | pė̲sáđȯ ↓ | pi̲sáđȯ ↓ |
| pė̲tón ↓ | pi̲tón ↓ | pė̲rítȧ ↓ | pi̲rítȧ ↓ |
| pė̲lón ↓ | pi̲lón ↓ | pė̲sáđȧ ↓ | pi̲sáđȧ ↓ |
| tė̲lón ↓ | ti̲lón ↓ | pė̲sárȯn ↓ | pi̲sárȯn ↓ |
| rrė̲már ↓ | rri̲már ↓ | mė̲(l)y̲ár ↓ | mi̲(l)y̲ár ↓ |
| mė̲sérȧ ↓ | mi̲sérȧ ↓ | pė̲ṇyítȧ ↓ | pi̲ṇyítȧ ↓ |

/e/ and /o/ in contrast under weak stress

| | | | |
|---|---|---|---|
| pásė̲ ↓ | pásȯ̲ ↓ | pépė̲ ↓ | pépȯ̲ ↓ |
| tómė̲ ↓ | tómȯ̲ ↓ | tírė̲ ↓ | tírȯ̲ ↓ |
| fúmė̲ ↓ | fúmȯ̲ ↓ | káƀė̲ ↓ | káƀȯ̲ ↓ |
| bínė̲ ↓ | bínȯ̲ ↓ | bíƀė̲ ↓ | bíƀȯ̲ ↓ |

| | | | |
|---|---|---|---|
| léchė̲ ↓ | léchȯ̲ ↓ | lė̲syón ↓ | lȯ̲syón ↓ |
| tráhė̲ ↓ | tráhȯ̲ ↓ | mė̲sítȧ ↓ | mȯ̲sítȧ ↓ |
| déhė̲ ↓ | déhȯ̲ ↓ | bė̲lítȧ ↓ | bȯ̲lítȧ ↓ |
| téhė̲ ↓ | téhȯ̲ ↓ | bė̲táđȯ ↓ | bȯ̲táđȯ ↓ |
| kyérė̲ ↓ | kyérȯ̲ ↓ | pė̲sáđȧ ↓ | pȯ̲sáđȧ ↓ |
| péynė̲ ↓ | péynȯ̲ ↓ | ė̲rmítȧ ↓ | ȯ̲rmítȧ ↓ |
| kóƀrė̲ ↓ | kóƀrȯ̲ ↓ | gė̲rrítȧ ↓ | gȯ̲rrítȧ ↓ |
| kántė̲ ↓ | kántȯ̲ ↓ | kȯntéstė̲ ↓ | kȯntéstȯ̲ ↓ |
| (l)y̯éƀė̲ ↓ | (l)y̯éƀȯ̲ ↓ | tė̲rnérȯ ↓ | tȯ̲rnérȯ ↓ |
| mándė̲ ↓ | mándȯ̲ ↓ | s̬ė̲rrítȯ ↓ | s̬ȯ̲rrítȯ ↓ |
| kámbyė̲ ↓ | kámbyȯ̲ ↓ | kȯmfórmė̲ ↓ | kȯmfórmȯ̲ ↓ |
| kómprė̲ ↓ | kómprȯ̲ ↓ | ėklípsė̲ ↓ | ėklípsȯ̲ ↓ |
| pė̲lár ↓ | pȯ̲lár ↓ | trȧƀáhė̲ ↓ | trȧƀáhȯ̲ ↓ |
| mė̲ntón ↓ | mȯ̲ntón ↓ | prė̲pȯsis̬yón ↓ | prȯ̲pȯsis̬yón ↓ |

/e/ and /u/ in contrast under weak stress

| | | | |
|---|---|---|---|
| tė̲mór ↓ | tu̲̇mór ↓ | s̬ė̲rrár ↓ | s̬u̲̇rrár ↓ |
| lė̲gár ↓ | lu̲̇gár ↓ | lė̲chón ↓ | lu̲̇chón ↓ |
| lė̲chár ↓ | lu̲̇chár ↓ | fė̲stín ↓ | fu̲̇stín ↓ |

| | | | |
|---|---|---|---|
| sė̱kşyón ↓ | su̱̇kşyón ↓ | pė̱nsáđȯ ↓ | pu̱̇nşáđȯ ↓ |
| pė̱nşyón ↓ | pu̱̇nşyón ↓ | tė̱ndérȯ ↓ | tu̱̇ndérȯ ↓ |
| mė̱şítȧ ↓ | mu̱̇şítȧ ↓ | pė̱chérȯ ↓ | pu̱̇chérȯ ↓ |
| lė̱lítȯ ↓ | lu̱̇lítȯ ↓ | pė̱rítȧ ↓ | pu̱̇rítȧ ↓ |
| şė̱rkáđȯ ↓ | su̱̇rkáđȯ ↓ | rrė̱tínȧ ↓ | rru̱̇tínȧ ↓ |
| tė̱rkítȯ ↓ | tu̱̇rkítȯ ↓ | ȧnė̱lár ↓ | ȧnu̱̇lár ↓ |

/i/ and /o/ in contrast under weak stress

| | | | |
|---|---|---|---|
| ti̱mó ↓ | tȯ̱mó ↓ | mi̱ráđȧ ↓ | mȯ̱ráđȧ ↓ |
| fi̱gón ↓ | fȯ̱gón ↓ | pi̱kítȯ ↓ | pȯ̱kítȯ ↓ |
| li̱sár ↓ | lȯ̱sár ↓ | pi̱sáđȧ ↓ | pȯ̱sáđȧ ↓ |
| mi̱rár ↓ | mȯ̱rár ↓ | ti̱rítȯ ↓ | tȯ̱rítȯ ↓ |
| mi̱syón ↓ | mȯ̱şyón ↓ | i̱hítȯ ↓ | ȯ̱hítȯ ↓ |
| tri̱ŋkár ↓ | trȯ̱ŋkár ↓ | i̱mítȯ ↓ | ȯ̱mítȯ ↓ |
| mi̱(l)y̱ár ↓ | mȯ̱(l)y̱ár ↓ | ti̱ntísimȯ ↓ | tȯ̱ntísimȯ ↓ |

/i/ and /u/ in contrast under weak stress

| | | | |
|---|---|---|---|
| li̱gár ↓ | lu̱̇gár ↓ | mi̱rár ↓ | mu̱̇rár ↓ |
| mi̱rón ↓ | mu̱̇rón ↓ | pi̱n̦yón ↓ | pu̱̇n̦yón ↓ |

| | | | |
|---|---|---|---|
| bi̱(l)y̨ár ↓ | bu̱̇(l)y̨ár ↓ | mi̱nítȧ ↓ | mu̱̇nítȧ ↓ |
| pi̱ns̨ón ↓ | pu̱̇ns̨ón ↓ | chi̱nchérȯ ↓ | chu̱̇nchérȯ ↓ |
| pi̱ntár ↓ | pu̱̇ntár ↓ | ni̱đósȯ ↓ | nu̱̇đósȯ ↓ |
| fi̱syón ↓ | fu̱̇syón ↓ | pi̱đyéndȯ ↓ | pu̱̇đyéndȯ ↓ |
| fi̱ŋhír ↓ | fu̱̇ŋhír ↓ | rri̱mítȧ ↓ | rru̱̇mítȧ ↓ |
| mi̱sítȧ ↓ | mu̱̇sítȧ ↓ | mi̱ráhės ↓ | mu̱̇ráhės ↓ |
| i̱mítȯ ↓ | u̱̇mítȯ ↓ | pi̱ntáđȧ ↓ | pu̱̇ntáđȧ ↓ |
| mi̱lítȧ ↓ | mu̱̇lítȧ ↓ | rri̱kítȧ ↓ | rru̱̇kítȧ ↓ |
| li̱nósȯ ↓ | lu̱̇nósȯ ↓ | bi̱rlađór ↓ | bu̱̇rlađór ↓ |
| ti̱nérȯ ↓ | tu̱̇nérȯ ↓ | pi̱rítȧ ↓ | pu̱̇rítȧ ↓ |
| fi̱lérȧ ↓ | fu̱̇lérȧ ↓ | li̱nárės ↓ | lu̱̇nárės ↓ |
| s̨i̱rkítȯ ↓ | s̨u̱̇rkítȯ ↓ | | |

/o/ and /u/ in contrast under weak stress

| | | | |
|---|---|---|---|
| tȯ̱pé ↓ | tu̱̇pé ↓ | ȯ̱mítȯ ↓ | u̱̇mítȯ ↓ |
| bȯ̱kál ↓ | bu̱̇kál ↓ | mȯ̱nítȧ ↓ | mu̱̇nítȧ ↓ |
| ȯ̱látė ↓ | u̱̇látė ↓ | plȯ̱mérȯ ↓ | plu̱̇mérȯ ↓ |
| trȯ̱ŋkár ↓ | tru̱̇ŋkár ↓ | mȯ̱s̨ítȧ ↓ | mu̱̇sítȧ ↓ |
| lȯ̱nítȧ ↓ | lu̱̇nítȧ ↓ | rrȯ̱kítȧ ↓ | rru̱̇kítȧ ↓ |

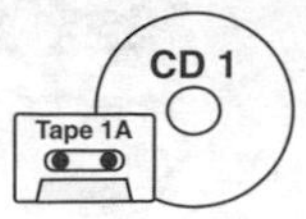




| | | | |
|---|---|---|---|
| sȯ̲tánȧ ↓ | su̲̇tánȧ ↓ | mȯ̲tilár ↓ | mu̲̇tilár ↓ |
| pȯ̲rítȯ ↓ | pu̲̇rítȯ ↓ | ȧkȯ̲sár ↓ | ȧku̲̇sár ↓ |

## 1.21.2 Discussion of minimal vowel contrasts under weak stress

English speakers of course also distinguish words in this same minimal way—*pit, pet, pat, pot, putt, put,* for example—but only rarely *under weak stress.* That is, English has similar differences only in syllables that are noticeably *louder* than any of the Spanish syllables you have been practicing. The underlined vowels in the following English words are all the same vowel sound in actual speech, no matter how they are spelled.

| | | | | | |
|---|---|---|---|---|---|
| presi̲dent | prece̲dent | botto̲m | plot'e̲m | warde̲n | pardo̲n |

They would *not* be the same in Spanish.

By careful repetition of these Spanish words after a native speaker, and by observing closely the point of difference between each pair, you can begin to *hear* and, having *heard,* to *imitate* differenees of a type and frequency that are quite strange to an English speaker's way of talking.

In learning the basic sentences you were probably also corrected for placing too much stress on some syllables, too little stress on others. There are only *two levels of stress* in Spanish (English has four, as we will discover). These two levels are indicated in the 'Aids to Listening' by an acute accent /ˊ/ over the vowels that have louder stress and a dot /˙/ over the vowels that have softer stress. We will call these STRONG STRESS and WEAK STRESS.

## 1.22 The stress system in Spanish

There are two things that are important about stress. One is to get the two stresses placed on the right syllables. The other is to make each of them the right strength. Let us examine these two aspects one at a time.

The following pairs of words differ only in the placement of stress, and, as you can see, the difference in meaning that results is considerable.

### 1.22.1 Exercises on minimal stress contrasts

| | | | |
|---|---|---|---|
| 1. éstà ↓ | 'this' | èstá ↓ | 'is' |
| 2. ı́ŋglès ↓ | 'groins' | ìŋglés ↓ | 'English' |
| 3. pésò ↓ | 'monetary unit' | pèsó ↓ | 'he weighed' |
| 4. pérnò ↓ | 'bolt' | pèrnó ↓ | 'a kind of wine' |
| 5. pı́kò ↓ | 'peak' | pìkó ↓ | 'he stung' |
| 6. báldè ↓ | 'bucket' | bàldé ↓ | 'I crippled' |
| 7. lı́ƀrò ↓ | 'book' | lìƀró ↓ | 'he freed' |
| 8. árà ↓ | 'altar' | àrá ↓ | 'he will do' |
| 9. áƀrà ↓ | 'open' | àƀrá ↓ | 'there will be' |

### 1.22.2 Discussion of minimal stress contrasts

In short, you can be rather drastically misunderstood if you fail to place the stresses correctly when you speak. This, of course, is also true in English, but not so obviously true in view of the greater complexity of the English stress system. We have in English also a fair number of items which can have the stresses arranged in more than one way:

áddrèss ↓ or àddréss ↓ Càribbéàn ↓ or Cárıbbèàn ↓

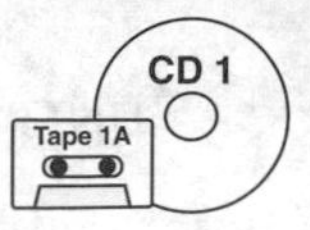




Chílèàn ↓ or Chiléàn ↓ Nèw Órlèàns ↓ or Nèw Órléàns ↓

Since we do not have as many nice neat minimal pairs in English as there are in Spanish (like /ésta—/está/), we may at first be deceived into thinking that Spanish uses stress in a way that English does not, but this is not true.

The other important thing to learn in drilling on stress is to stress syllables with the right amount of force or strength. It is at this point that the four stresses of English interfere with the *two* stresses of Spanish. Let us first learn what the four stresses of English are. Listen to yourself say this phrase:

<u>elevator</u> — <u>operator</u>

Which syllable is loudest? el— in elevator. Let us indicate this by writing an acute accent over the <u>e</u>:

<u>élevator</u> — <u>operator</u>

Which syllable is next loudest? op— in operator. We'll write it with a circumflex accent:

<u>élevator</u> — <u>ôperator</u>

Then we can hear that —vat— and —rat— are about equally loud, but softer than <u>op</u>—, so we will write a grave accent:

<u>élevàtor</u> — <u>ôperàtor</u>

The syllables that are left over are the weakest, so we write:

élĕvàtŏr — ôpĕràtŏr

In doing this we have marked four levels of stress, which we can label:

primary— el— secondary— <u>ôp</u>—

tertiary— <u>vàt</u>— <u>ràt</u>— weak— <u>ĕ</u>— <u>ŏr</u>— <u>ĕ</u>— <u>ŏr</u>

This represents a great many different levels of stress, but every English speaker (native) uses all four quite regularly and unconsciously every time he makes an utterance.

Now, how do these four English stresses affect your Spanish? If we remember that Spanish only has TWO stresses, then it seems likely that you will get your FOUR mixed up with these two, with the result that you will put too much stress on some syllables, not enough on others. The correspondence between the English stresses and those of Spanish is roughly this:

| <u>English</u> | | <u>Spanish</u> |
|---|---|---|
| Primary | /´/ | Strong /´/ |
| Secondary | /ˆ/ | |
| Tertiary | /`/ | Weak /˙/ |
| Weak | /˘/ | |

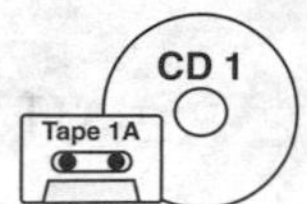




Let us look back now at the basic sentences and see if any of the difficulties you had with them can be traced to this difference between the two languages.

| | RIGHT | YOUR PROBABLE ERROR |
|---|---|---|
| 1 | kȯmpėrmíṡȯ ↓ | kòmpėrmísȯ ↓ |
| 2 | dispénsėmė ↓ | dispénsėmè ↓ |
| 3 | prėsėntárlė ↓ | prèsėntárlė ↓ |
| 4 | làsėn̥yóráđėmȯlíná ↓ | làsėn̥yôráđèmȯlíná ↓ |
| 5 | igwálméntė ↓ | ìgwȧlméntė ↓ |
| 6 | ėŋkȧntáđȯ ↓ | èŋkȧntáđȯ ↓ |
| 7 | ȧstȧmȧn̥yánȧ ↓ | âstȧmȧn̥yánȧ ↓ |

Now because we consider this a very important point indeed, and because it is a point which is rarely drilled elsewhere, we have put together the following long list, arranged according to the number of syllables and placement of stress. Until you can say these using only the two stresses that are marked instead of the four of English you cannot expect to go on and learn complex utterances successfully. Time spent practicing these, therefore, will be very well spent.

## 1.22.3 Exercises on contrasting stress patterns

| ´ ˙ ↓ | | ˙ ´ ↓ | |
|---|---|---|---|
| rróhȧ ↓ | kómȯ ↓ | ėstá ↓ | kȯlór ↓ |
| múchȯ ↓ | gústȯ ↓ | kȧlór ↓ | ustéđ ↓ |
| tántȯ ↓ | bwénȯ ↓ | ėstóy ↓ | ȧđyós ↓ |
| ástȧ ↓ | lwégȯ ↓ | sėn̥yór ↓ | kȯrtés ↓ |
| dóndė ↓ | frásės ↓ | rrȧșón ↓ | fumár ↓ |

fúmȯ ↓
bán̦yȯ ↓
téŋgȧ ↓
án̦yȯ ↓
tárđė ↓

ábrȧ ↓
bísȧ ↓
táksi ↓
y̧élȯ ↓
şérkȧ ↓

pȧsár ↓
ȧƀrír ↓
dėşír ↓
şyủđáđ ↓
sėrƀír ↓

fȧƀór ↓
pėrđón ↓
bisté ↓
tȧmbyén ↓
şerrár ↓

_́ _̇ _̇ ↓

rrápiđȯ ↓
lástimȧ ↓
fósfȯrȯ ↓
syéntėsė ↓
déhėmė ↓
únikȯ ↓
bárƀȧrȯ ↓
méđikȯ ↓
myérkȯlés ↓
sáƀȧđȯ ↓
şéntimȯ ↓

_̇ _́ _̇ ↓

trȧƀáhȧ ↓
sȧlúđȯs ↓
mȧn̦yánȧ ↓
sėn̦yórȧ ↓
difíşil ↓
mȯléstȧ ↓
ėskúchė ↓
bėntánȧ ↓
minútȯs ↓
tikétės ↓
şėntáƀȯs ↓

_̇ _̇ _́ ↓

trȧƀȧhár ↓
ȯrȧşyón ↓
ėntėndér ↓
ėspȧn̦yól ↓
ȧwtȯƀús ↓
ėstȧşyón ↓
kȯrȧşón ↓
sȧlủđár ↓
rrėgủlár ↓
kȯnȯşér ↓
pȧrȧgwáy ↓

| | | |
|---|---|---|
| sáŋw̱ichė ↓ | bȯlétȯs ↓ | u̇ru̇gwáy ↓ |
| últimȯ ↓ | sȧƀémȯs ↓ | sȧlbȧđór ↓ |
| próksimȯ ↓ | (l)y̱ėg̱áđȧ ↓ | kȯntėstár ↓ |

**End of Tape 1A**

| _́ _̇ _̇ _̇ ↓ | _̇ _́ _̇ _̇ ↓ | _̇ _̇ _́ _̇ ↓ | _̇ _̇ _̇ _́ ↓ |
|---|---|---|---|
| dígȧmėlȯ ↓ | tėléfȯnȯ ↓ | tėlėgrámȧ ↓ | trȧƀȧhárė ↓ |
| préstėsėlȯ ↓ | simpátikȯ ↓ | inmėđyátȧ ↓ | kȧswȧliđáđ ↓ |
| tómėsėlȯ ↓ | dėșíđȧsė ↓ | dėspėđíđȧs ↓ | liƀėrȧșyón ↓ |
| tráyg̱ȧmėlȯ ↓ | mȧgnífikȯ ↓ | ȧbsȯlútȯ ↓ | ȧƀiliđáđ ↓ |
| béȧsėlȯ ↓ | mu̇chísimȯ ↓ | su̇fișyéntė ↓ | kȯmu̇nikár ↓ |
| kwéntėmėlȯ ↓ | prȯpósitȯ ↓ | prėsėntárlė ↓ | fėrrȯkȧrríl ↓ |
| dándȯmėlȯ ↓ | fȧnátikȯ ↓ | sėṉyȯrítȧ ↓ | mėntȧliđáđ ↓ |
| byéndȯsėlȯ ↓ | pėrđónėmė ↓ | kȯnȯșyéndȯ ↓ | ȧgrikųltór ↓ |
| kámbyėmėlȯ ↓ | ȧltímėtrȯ ↓ | ȧđėlántė ↓ | ėntȯnȧșyón ↓ |
| sákėsėlȯ ↓ | figúrėsė ↓ | dėmȧsyáđȯ ↓ | ėŋkȯntrárȧ ↓ |
| mwéƀȧsėlȯ ↓ | ȧmérikȧ ↓ | pȧnórȧmȧ ↓ | kȧminárė ↓ |
| súƀȧmėlȧs ↓ | milésimȯ ↓ | mȯnȯgrámȧ ↓ | ȧmȧrișár ↓ |
| kómȧsėlȯ ↓ | tȧntísimȯ ↓ | ėntėndíđȯ ↓ | ȧmȧnėșér ↓ |
| búskȧmėlȯ ↓ | bwėnísimȯ ↓ | kȯmfu̇ndíđȯ ↓ | fȧșilitár ↓ |

. . ´ . . . ↓

kȯnos̯yéndȯsė ↓

ȧs̯ėrkándȯsė ↓

prės̯yȯsísimȯ ↓

prėsėntándȯlė ↓

primėrísimȯ ↓

ėŋkȯntrándȯlȧ ↓

. . . . ´ . ↓

prėsėntȧs̯yónės ↓

ȧmėrikánȯ ↓

lȧbȯrȧtóryȯ ↓

kȯmbėrsȧs̯yónės ↓

kȯnsėrƀátoryȯ ↓

kȧmisėríȧ ↓

. . . . . ´ ↓

ȧntėryȯriđáđ ↓

pȯstėryȯriđáđ ↓

kristȧlis̯ȧs̯yón ↓

kȯmu̇nikȧs̯yón ↓

nȧs̯yȯnȧliđáđ ↓

ȧrgu̇mėntȧs̯yón ↓

. . . . . . ´ ↓

hėnėrȧlis̯ȧs̯yón ↓

iđėntifikȧs̯yón ↓

nȧturȧlis̯ȧs̯yón ↓

rrėkȧpitu̇lȧs̯yón ↓

kȧpitȧlis̯ȧs̯yón ↓

ėspės̯yȧlis̯ȧs̯yón ↓

dėkȯntȧminȧs̯yón ↓

rrėspȯnsȧƀiliđáđ ↓

rrėspėtȧƀiliđáđ ↓

irrėgu̇lȧriđáđ ↓

. . . . . . . ´ ↓

institu̇s̯yȯnȧliđáđ ↓

imprėsyȯnȧbiliđáđ ↓

kȯnstitu̇s̯yȯnȧliđáđ ↓

su̇pėrnȧtu̇rȧliđáđ ↓

dėskȧpitȧlis̯ȧs̯yón ↓

dėznȧtu̇rȧlis̯ȧs̯yón ↓

impėrsȯnȧlis̯ȧs̯yón ↓

ȧgriku̇ltu̇ris̯ȧs̯yón ↓

ȧmėrikȧnis̯ȧs̯yón ↓

su̇pėrȧlimėntȧs̯yón ↓

. ´ ´ . ↓

igwálméntė ↓

u̇swálméntė ↓

ȧktwálméntė ↓

kȯrđyálméntė ↓

. . ´ ´ . ↓

hėnėrálméntė ↓

litėrálméntė ↓

mȧtėryálméntė ↓

ėlsėn̯yórkártėr ↓

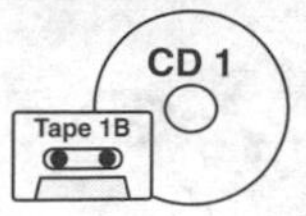




| | | | |
|---|---|---|---|
| sėn̯yórkártėr ↓ | sėn̯yórkástrȯ ↓ | ȧlsėn̯yórkástrȯ ↓ | ėspėşyálméntė ↓ |
| dȯktórkámpȯs ↓ | ȧsíđíşė ↓ | inmȯrálméntė ↓ | ėlkȯlórnégrȯ ↓ |
| kȯlórƀérđė ↓ | ȧ(l)y̧áƀyénė ↓ | imfȯrmálméntė ↓ | ėlsėn̯yórƀárgȧs ↓ |

## 1.22.4 Discussion of contrasting stress patterns

You probably noticed, in listening to and imitating these items, that they seem to be pronounced faster than English words of similar length. Actually they are not, but there is a big difference in *rhythm* which makes it *seem* that they are. This difference in rhythm can be indicated something like this, using longer lines to indicate longer syllables and shorter lines to indicate shorter syllables:

**English Speaker**

<u>Where</u> <u>do</u> <u>you</u> <u>think</u> <u>it'</u>ll <u>be</u> <u>found</u>?

**Spanish Speaker**

W<u>here</u> <u>do</u> <u>you</u> th<u>in</u>k <u>it</u> w<u>ill</u> <u>be</u> f<u>ou</u>nd?

Thus the Spanish way is to make every syllable almost equally long, giving a machine-gun effect, whereas the English way is to make the louder syllables longer. The two languages divide up their time differently.

## 1.23 The intonation system in Spanish

Up to this point we have discussed two errors you were corrected for in learning the basic sentences: UNSTRESSED VOWELS and SYLLABLE STRESS. The third problem which occurs from the very beginning and will be with you to mar your Spanish for a very long time is INTONATION: the rise and fall of the pitch of the voice. We have indicated this by placing our accent marks at *three different heights* over the vowel:

Low pitch: directly over the vowel /ȧ ȯ/

Middle pitch: one space above the vowel /ȧ ó/

High pitch: two spaces above the vowel /ȧ ó/

All three in sequence look like this: /a ȧ ȧ/ /á á á/

These are analogous to steps in a musical scale:

In addition to these various levels of pitch, there may be a slight rise / ↑ / or a slight fall at / ↓ / after the last pitch, or it may remain level / | / .

Now let us return to the basic sentences and see what you were corrected on.

| RIGHT | YOUR PROBABLE ERROR |
|---|---|
| 1 bwénȯzđías \| sėn̦yór ↓ | bwénȯzđías \| sėn̦yór ↑ |
| 2 bwénȧstárđės \| sėn̦yórȧ ↓ | bwénȧstárđės \| sėn̦yórȧ ↑ |
| 3 bwénȧznóchės \| sėn̦yȯrítȧ ↓ | bwénȧznóchės \| sėn̦yȯrítȧ ↑ |
| 4 kómo̯ėstáu̯stéđ ↓ | kómo̯ėstáu̯stéđ ↓ |
| 5 mu̇yƀyéŋ \| grás̯yȧs ↓ | mu̇yƀyéŋ \| grás̯yȧs ↑ |
| 6 kómȯlėƀá ↓ | kómȯlėƀá ↓ |
| 7 kómȯnó ↓ | kómȯnó ↓ |

| | |
|---|---|
| 8 múchȧzgrás̯yȧs ↓ | múchȧzgras̯yȧs ↓ |
| 9 dėnáđȧ ↓ | dėnáđȧ ↑ |
| 10 no̯áyđėké ↓ | no̯áyđėké ↑ |
| 11 igwálméntė \| grás̯yȧs ↓ | igwȧlméntė \| grás̯yȧs ↑ |
| 12 ȧđyós ↓ | ȧđyós ↑ |
| 13 ȧstȧmȧn̯yánȧ ↓ | ȧstamȧn̯yánȧ ↑ |
| 14 ȧstȧlwégȯ ↓ | ȧstȧlwégȯ ↑ |

It will be evident to you that all of the mistaken patterns of the right-hand column above are attributable to some very common pattern that such utterances have in English. A few of the common non-Spanish interference patterns that English sets up are these:

| | |
|---|---|
| 1 Goȯd mórnĭng \| Bíll ↑ | 5 Gôod byė́ ↑ |
| 2 Fínė \| thánks ↑ | 6 Gôod býe ↑ |
| 3 Hôw are yȯú ↓ | 7 Mâny thánks ↓ |
| 4 Hôw ȧre yóu ↓ | |

The only way to get these (and other) English patterns out of your way in talking Spanish is by the correct repetition of Spanish patterns so often that they automatically replace the English ones when they are supposed to. The following exercise is directed toward that end.

## 1.23.1 Exercises on contrasting intonation patterns

Group 1

All of a 'falling' pattern

1 béngàká ↓
2 klárókèsí ↓
3 sónlàstrés ↓
4 (l)yégạènàbyón ↓
5 nólókréò ↓
6 nómẹimpórtà ↓
7 byénèmàn̦yánà ↓
8 (l)yègómàríà ↓
9 àkísèbáylà ↓
10 kómọèstá ↓
11 dóndèstá ↓
12 kómólèbá ↓
13 kyénè(s)són ↓
14 kélèpásà ↓
15 kwándò(l)yégà ↓

16 kwántȯkwéstȧ ↓

17 kékȯmémȯs ↓

18 dėđóndėsón ↓

19 pȧrȧđóndėƀán ↓

20 pȯrkésėfwé ↓

21 pȯrkwántȯtyémpȯ ↓

22 ȧkwánto̯ėstámȯs ↓

Group 2

All of a 'rising' pattern

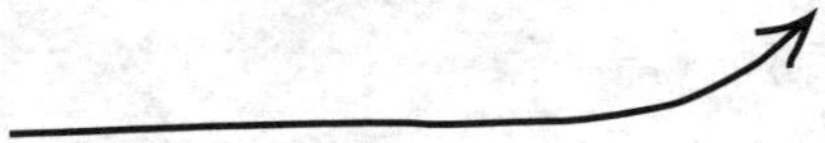

1 y̯ásėƀá ↑

2 kyérėkȧfé ↑

3 bínȯkȯnụ̇stéđ ↑

4 kȯmyérȯny̯á ↑

5 tyéne̯u̇nlápi̇s̯ ↑

6 sėbákȯnmígȯ ↑

7 lėgu̇stómȧríȧ ↑

8 lėy̯óe̯ldyáryȯ ↑

9 tyénėnọ́trȯ ↑

10 lėpȧsólȧléchė ↑

11 tráhȯsu̇kárrȯ ↑

12 lėgústȧsu̇trȧƀáhȯ ↑

1 grásyȧs | sėn̪yór ↓

2 mu̇yƀyéŋ | grásyȧs ↓

3 sí | sėn̪yórȧ ↓

4 nó | sėn̪yȯrítȧ ↓

5 nóay | ómbrė ↓

6 béŋgȧ | mȧríȧ ↓

7 nó | múchȧzgrásyȧs ↓

8 nȯƀyénė | ėntónsės ↓

9 sí | pȧpá ↓

10 nó | mȧmá ↓

11 ȧđyós | sėn̪yórės ↓

12 ȧstȧmȧn̪yánȧ | sėn̪yórės ↓

Group 3

All ending in a low level pattern

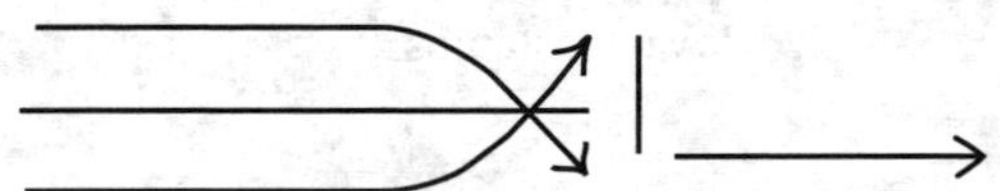

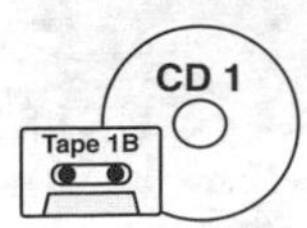




# 2.1 BASIC SENTENCES

## Useful phrases

| English Spelling | Aid to Listening | Spanish Spelling |
|---|---|---|
| ahead, forward | ȧđėlántė ↓ | adelante |
| Come on in. | ȧđėlántė ↓ | ¡Adelante! |
| seat (to seat) | syéntė ↓ sėntár ↓ | siente (sentar) |
| seat yourself (to seat oneself) | syéntėsė ↓ sėntársė ↓ | siéntese (sentarse) |
| Sit down. | syéntėsė ↓ | Siéntese. |
| (you) have (to have) | tyénė ↓ tėnér ↓ | tiene (tener) |
| a, an (one) | ún ↓ únȯ ↓ | un (uno) |
| the pencil | ėl-lápiṣ ↓ | el lápiz |
| Do you have a pencil? | tyénẹunlápiṣ ↓ | ¿Tiene un lápiz? |
| (I) have (to have) | téŋgȯ ↓ tėnér ↓ | tengo (tener) |
| No, I don't. | nó ↓ notéŋgȯ ↓ | No, no tengo. |
| yes | sí ↓ | sí |

| | | |
|---|---|---|
| Yes, I do. | sí ↓ sítéŋgȯ ↓ | Sí, sí tengo. |
| repeat (to repeat) | rrėpítȧ ↓ rrėpėtír ↓ | repita (repetir) |
| Say it again. | rrėpítȧ ↓ | Repita. |
| translate (to translate) | trȧđúşkȧ ↓ trȧđůşír ↓ | traduzca (traducir) |
| Translate. | trȧđúşkȧ ↓ | Traduzca. |
| another | ótrȧ ↓ | otra |
| the time | lȧ-ƀéş ↓ | la vez |
| again | ótrȧ-ƀéş ↓ | otra vez |
| for | pór ↓ | por |
| the favor | ėl-fȧƀór ↓ | el favor |
| please | pȯr-fȧƀór ↓ | por favor |
| Again, please. | ótrȧƀéş \| pȯrfȧƀór ↓ | Otra vez, por favor. |
| the pardon | ėl-pėrđón ↓ | el perdón |
| (you) say (to say) | díşė ↓ dėşír ↓ | dice (decir) |
| Excuse me, what did you say? [1] | pėrđón ↓ kómođíşęústéđ ↓ | Perdón. ¿Cómo dice usted? |
| give (to give) | dé ↓ dár ↓ | dé (dar) |
| to me | mé ↓ | me |

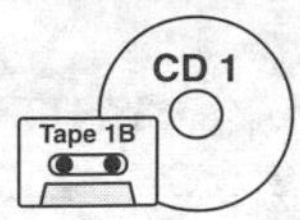




| | | |
|---|---|---|
| the pen | lȧ-plúmȧ ↓ | la pluma |
| Give me the pen. | déṁelaplúmȧ ↓ | Déme la pluma. |
| pass (to pass, to hand) | pásė ↓ pȧsár ↓ | pase (pasar) |
| pass me | pásėmė ↓ | páseme |
| the book | ėl-líƀrȯ ↓ | el libro |
| Pass me the book. | páseṁe(l)líƀrȯ ↓ | Páseme el libro. |
| is (to be) | és ↓ sér ↓ | es (ser) |
| that | ésȯ ↓ | eso |
| What's that? | késẹ́sȯ ↓ | ¿Qué es eso? |
| this | éstȯ ↓ | esto |
| the ashtray | ėl-s̥ėnis̥érȯ ↓ | el cenicero |
| This is an ashtray. | éstọ \| ės̥ụns̥ėnis̥érȯ ↓ | Esto es un cenicero. |
| wants (to want) | kyérė ↓ kėrér ↓ | quiere (querer) |
| to say | dės̥ír ↓ | decir |
| (it) means | kyérė-đės̥ír ↓ | quiere decir |

| | | |
|---|---|---|
| What does *cenicero* mean? | kékyéređéșır \| șenișéró ↓ | Qué quiere decir *cenicero?* |
| It means *ashtray.* | kyéređéșır \| ǽshtréy ↓ | Quiere decir *ashtray.* |
| says itself, is said (to say) | sė-đíșė ↓ đėșír ↓ | se dice (decir) |
| in | én ↓ | en |
| the Spanish | ėl-ėspȧnyól ↓ | el español |
| How do you say *table* in Spanish? | kómosėđíșė \| téybil \| ėṇėspȧnyól ↓ | ¿Cómo se dice *table* en español? |
| the table | lȧ-mésȧ ↓ | la mesa |
| You say *mesa.* (2) | sėđíșė \| mésȧ ↓ | Se dice *mesa.* |
| the English | ėl-iŋglés ↓ | el inglés |
| the chair | lȧ-sí(l)y̭ȧ ↓ | la silla |
| How do you say *silla* in English? | kómosėđíșė \| sí(l)y̭a̭ \| ėṇiŋglés ↓ | ¿Cómo se dice *silla* en inglés? |
| You say *chair.* | sėđíșė \| chéhr ↓ | Se dice *chair.* |
| where | dóndė ↓ | dónde |
| the embassy | la̭-ėmbȧháđȧ ↓ | la embajada |
| American | ȧmėrikánȧ ↓ | americana |

| | | |
|---|---|---|
| Where's the American Embassy? | dóndėstá \| la̯ėmbȧhȧđȧmėrıkánȧ ↓ | ¿Dónde está la Embajada Americana? |
| the bathroom | ėl-báṇyȯ ↓ | el baño |
| Where's the bathroom? | dóndėstá \| e̯lbáṇyȯ ↓ | ¿Dónde está el baño? |
| there | ȧí ↓ | ahí |
| at, to | á ↓ | a |
| the left | la̯-iṣkyérđȧ ↓ | la izquierda |
| There to the left. | ȧí \| ȧla̯iṣkyérđȧ ↓ | Ahí a la izquierda. |
| the right | lȧ-đėréchȧ ↓ | la derecha |
| There to the right. | ȧí \| ȧlađėréchȧ ↓ | Ahí a la derecha. |
| There straight ahead. | ȧí \| ȧđėlánte ↓ | Ahí adelante. |
| take, carry (to take) | (l)y̯ébė ↓ (l)y̯ėƀár ↓ | lleve (llevar) |
| take us | (l)y̯éƀėnȯs ↓ | llévenos |
| the center (of town) | ėl-ṣéntrȯ ↓ | el centro |
| Take us downtown. | (l)y̯ébėnȯs \| ȧlṣéntrȯ ↓ | Llévenos al centro. |
| are (to be) | ėstán ↓ ėstár ↓ | están (estar) |

| | | |
|---|---|---|
| the (m. pl.) | lós ↓ | los |
| Where're the books? | dóndėstán \| lȯzlíƀrȯs ↓ | ¿Dónde están los libros? |
| take me | (l)y̬éƀėmė ↓ | lléveme |
| the hotel | ėt-ȯtél ↓ | el hotel |
| Take me to the hotel. | (l)y̬éƀėme̯ \| ȧlȯtél ↓ | Lléveme al hotel. |
| (it) goes down (to go down) | súƀė \| sủƀír ↓ | sube (subir) |
| or | ó ↓ | o |
| (it) goes down (to go down) | báhȧ \| bȧhár ↓ | baja (bajar) |
| Going up or down? (3) | súƀe̯ȯƀáhȧ ↓ | ¿Sube o baja? |
| how much | kwántȯ ↓ | cuánto |
| How much is it? | kwánto̯ės ↓ | ¿Cuánto es? |

| | | | | | |
|---|---|---|---|---|---|
| one | únȯ ↓ | uno | six | séys ↓ | seis |
| two | dós ↓ | dos | seven | syétė ↓ | siete |
| three | trés ↓ | tres | eight | óchȯ ↓ | ocho |
| four | kwátrȯ ↓ | cuatro | nine | nwéƀė ↓ | nueve |
| five | s̯íŋkȯ ↓ | cinco | ten | dyés̯ ↓ | diez |

| eleven | ónşė ↓ | once | fifteen | kínşė ↓ | quince |
|---|---|---|---|---|---|
| twelve | dóşė ↓ | doce | sixteen | dyėşiséys ↓ | dieciséis |
| thirteen | tréşė ↓ | trece | twenty | béyntė ↓ | veinte |
| fourteen | kȧtórşė ↓ | catorce | twenty-one | bėynti̯únȯ ↓ | veintiuno |

## 2.10 Notes on the basic sentences

(1) Instead of using the entire phrase 'What did you say?', the Spanish speaker frequently uses only the first word, i.e. /kómo ↑/, just as we may say only 'What?'

(2) Note that here, and in the other phrases above and below which also have the form /se—díşe ↓ / in them, that the idea of 'someone' actually *saying* the word is not given: rather, the word *says itself,* which makes this construction *impersonal,* and which is translated into English as 'is said' or 'you say'. The Spanish construction used is the *reflexive* construction, which will be examined in detail in Unit 24.

(3) More literally, 'Does it (the elevator) go up or does it go down?'

# 2.2 DRILLS ON PRONUNCIATION

In the first unit we examined the vowels under weak stress, the stress system, the intonation system, and the resulting rhythmic effect.

Before going on to an examination of consonants, and vowels under strong stress, notice in the lists below how in words which sound familiar, you are liable to make some rather serious mistakes because of the very familiarity of the words.

## 2.21 Typical errors from English vowel influence in similar-sounding words

| Correct | Your Probable Error | Familiar English Pronunciation | English Spelling |
|---|---|---|---|
| ȯfişı́nȧ ↓ | ȧ̲fişı́nȧ ↓ | áfis ↓ — ə́fis ↓ | office |
| dȯktór ↓ | dȧ̲któr ↓ | dáktə̇r ↓ | doctor |
| ȯpȯrtu̇niđáđ ↓ | ȧ̲pə̲rtu̇niđáđ ↓ | ȧpə̇rtúwnɨtiy ↓ | opportunity |
| kȯŋgrésȯ ↓ | kȧ̲ŋgrésȯ ↓ | káŋgrɨs ↓ | congress |
| kȯmfėrénşyȧ ↓ | kȧ̲mfėrénşyȧ ↓ | kánfə̇rɨns ↓ | conference |
| trȯpikál ↓ | trȧ̲pikál ↓ | trápɨkə̇l ↓ | tropical |
| ȧtómikȧ ↓ | ȧtá̲mikȧ ↓ | ə̇támik ↓ | atomic |
| ȯndúrȧs ↓ | ȧ̲ndúrȧs ↓ | hȧndúrɨs ↓ | Honduras |
| kȯmbėrsȧşyón ↓ | kȧ̲mbėrsȧşyón ↓ | kànvə̇rséyšɨn ↓ | conversation |
| ȯspitál ↓ | ȧ̲spitál ↓ | háspitɨl ↓ | hospital |
| kȯntrátȯ ↓ | kȧ̲ntrátȯ ↓ | kántræ̀kt ↓ | contract |
| pȯsı́ɓlė ↓ | pȧ̲sı́ɓlė ↓ | pásɨbɨl ↓ | possible |

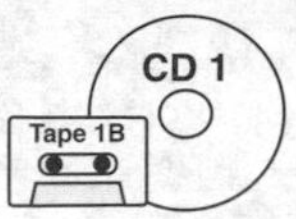

CD 1
Tape 1B



| | | | |
|---|---|---|---|
| bȯmbȧrđéȯ ↓ | ba̲mbȧrđéȯ ↓ | bàmbárdmɨnt ↓ | bombardment |
| próntȯ ↓ | prá̲ntȯ ↓ | prántòw ↓ | pronto |
| próksimȧ ↓ | prá̲ksimȧ ↓ | ə̇práksimɨt ↓ | approximate |
| fósfȯrȯ ↓ | fá̲sfȯrȯ ↓ | fásfə̇rə̇s ↓ | phosphorous |
| kóstȯ ↓ | ká̲stȯ ↓ | kást ↓ — kɔ́st ↓ | cost |
| | | | |
| bláŋkȧ ↓ | blǽ̲ŋkȧ ↓ | blǽŋk ↓ | blank |
| kánsȧs ↓ | kǽ̲nsȧs ↓ | dǽnzɨz ↓ | Kansas |
| pásė ↓ | pǽ̲sė ↓ | pǽs ↓ | pass |
| klásė ↓ | klǽ̲sė ↓ | klǽs ↓ | class |
| gráṣyȧs ↓ | grǽ̲ṣyȧs ↓ | grǽs ↓ | grass |
| lástimȧ ↓ | lǽ̲stimȧ ↓ | lǽst ↓ | last |
| ėspȧn̲yól ↓ | ėspæ̲̇n̲yól ↓ | spǽniš ↓ | Spanish |
| ȧƀsȯlútȯ ↓ | æ̲̇ƀsȯlútȯ ↓ | ǽbsəlùwt ↓ | absolute |

From these examples it is no doubt clear that many words which *look* easy, because they seem very much like English words, are in fact the most misleading because of their similarity. If you are alert to the possibility of this error, however, it is a relatively easy one to correct.

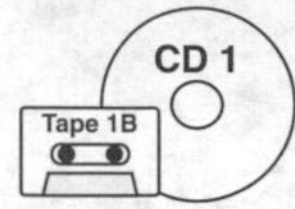




## 2.22 Voiced stop consonants

### 2.22.1 /d/ in Spanish

The problem that arises from /d/ is that it has two varieties of pronunciation which are, from the point of view of English speakers, actually different sounds; but from the point of view of Spanish speakers, they are one and the same sound.

How can there be such a difference in point of view? A sound is, one would think, either the same as another or it isn't. But this is an instance where the 'common sense' viewpoint does not hold. From infancy speakers of Spanish are taught to ignore the difference between [d] and [đ]. English speakers are taught to respect that difference but ignore others (such as the puff of air that comes after the /p/ of *pill* but does not come after the /p/ of *spill).*

The symbol [d] represents the initial sound of English *den, do, die, dare,* etc., but the tip of the tongue actually touches the back side of the upper teeth when this sound is produced in Spanish, whereas in English it touches somewhat further back.

The symbol [đ] represents the initial sound of English *then, thee, the, those, that, there,* etc., or the middle sound of *either, mother, other, father,* etc., or the final sound of *lathe, bathe*. However, it must be distinguished carefully from the *other* sound which English writes with *th,* the initial sound of *thin, thick, thistle,* or the middle sound of *ether, Ethel,* or the final sound of *bath*. This other sound is written [ş] in this book, and it has no connection with /d/.

Examples of the two /d/ sounds are below.

| | |
|---|---|
| dáđȯ ↓ | ȧđóndė ↓ |
| déđȯ ↓ | ȧndáđȯ ↓ |
| du̇đár ↓ | sȯldáđȯ ↓ |
| du̇đósȯ ↓ | tildáđȯ ↓ |
| gwȧrđáđȯ ↓ | dėzđėn̦yáđȯ ↓ |
| kȧrđáđȯ ↓ | dėzđicháđȯ ↓ |

You will of course notice that both kinds of /d/ appear here, and wonder how you can tell which variety to expect. The rule is reasonably clear and consistent, though in some dialect areas, slight variations may occur:

| | pause | /n/ | /l/ | /↓/ | /↑/ | vowels | /y/ | /w/ | other consonants |
|---|---|---|---|---|---|---|---|---|---|
| [d] appears after | x | x | x | x | x | | | | |
| [đ] appears after | | | | | | x | x | x | x |

The real importance of producing the right variety of /d/ at the right time becomes evident upon examination of the contrasts below, where the use of [d] instead of [đ] ín the left-hand column will cause the word to be misinterpreted as being the one in the right-hand column.

### 2.22.11 Exercise on /d/ and /r/ between vowels

| | | | |
|---|---|---|---|
| óđȧ ↓ | órȧ ↓ | píđȧ ↓ | pírȧ ↓ |
| tóđȯ ↓ | tórȯ ↓ | lóđȯ ↓ | lórȯ ↓ |
| káđȧ ↓ | kárȧ ↓ | kóđȯ ↓ | kórȯ ↓ |
| séđȧ ↓ | sérȧ ↓ | múđȯ ↓ | múrȯ ↓ |
| móđȯ ↓ | mórȯ ↓ | áđȧ ↓ | árȧ ↓ |
| míđȧ ↓ | mírȧ ↓ | | |

### 2.22.2 /b/ in Spanish

The problem of /b/ is similar to that of /d/. There are two varieties which are the *same* from the Spanish point of view but noticeably different from the English point of vew.

The symbol [ b] represents the initial sound of English words like *bee, bill, buy, borrow,* the middle sound in *baby, tabby, tubby,* the final sound in *tub, hub, rub, flub.*

The symbol [ƀ] represents a sound which does not exist in English. It is produced by bringing the lips close to each other, but not allowing them to touch, so that the air passes through them with a slight friction noise. The result sounds like a cross between a *b, v,* and *w.* The easiest way to learn to produce it is to start out as though to make a [b] in a word like *about,* but not allow the lips to touch so that the resulting sound is *v*-like in character (but remember that it is *not* a *v*).

Examples of [b] and [ƀ] follow:

bėƀér ↓

biƀír ↓

bȧƀór ↓

bȧƀósȧ ↓

s̬u̇mbáƀȧ ↓

kȧmbyáƀȧ ↓

silbáƀȧ ↓

sȧlbáƀȧ ↓

ėnėrƀáƀȧ ↓

ėrƀáƀȧ ↓

ėzƀȯs̬áƀȧ ↓

ėzƀóƀȯ ↓

| | pause | /m/ | /l/ | /↓/ | /↑/ | vowels | /y/ | /w/ | other consonants |
|---|---|---|---|---|---|---|---|---|---|
| [b] appears after | x | x | x | x | x | | | | |
| [ƀ] appears after | | | | | | x | x | x | x |

To make a mistake in the production of /b/ is not as serious as with the /d/, but errors can lead to misunderstanding. More important, there is no *v* sound in Spanish, even though it is in the writing system. The Spanish sound which Americans may hear as *v* in a word like *Havana* is actually the [ƀ] sound.

### 2.22.3 /g/ in Spanish

The problem of /g/ is similar to that of /d/ and /b/. There are two varieties which are the same from the Spanish point of view but noticeably different from the English point of view.

The symbol [g] represents the initial sound of English words like *go, get, got, guess,* the middle sound in *ago, again,* the final sound in *tug, tag, tog*.

The symbol [ǥ] represents a sound which is heard only rarely in English, in a word like *sugar.* It is produced by raising the back part of the tongue up towards the roof of the mouth as though to make a [g] but without allowing the tongue to touch, so that the air is free to pass through with a slight friction noise.

Examples of [g] and [ǥ] follow:

| | |
|---|---|
| gálgȯ ↓ | ėstėǥálgȯ ↓ |
| gáǥȧ ↓ | ėlgáǥȯ ↓ |
| grėǥóryȯ ↓ | lȧǥȧrgántȧ ↓ |
| gȧǥérȧ ↓ | lȧǥórǥȧ ↓ |
| ȧgriŋgáđȯ ↓ | ėzgrėǥóryȯ ↓ |
| ȧǥȧŋgrėnársė ↓ | ėzǥȧǥérȧ ↓ |

As with /d/ and /b/, the distribution of two varieties of /g/ is fairly clear and consistent:

| | pause | /ŋ/ | /l/ | /↓/ | /↑/ | vowels | /y/ | /w/ | other consonants |
|---|---|---|---|---|---|---|---|---|---|
| [g] appears after | x | x | x | x | x | | | | |
| [ǥ] appears after | | | | | | x | x | x | x |

To make a mistake in the production of /g/ is not serious, but unless you learn to produce the [ǥ] variety you will find that it is difficult to identify when you are listening to a Spanish speaker. So for the purpose of comprehension it is worth the trouble to master it.

## 2.23 Vibrants / r / and / rr / in Spanish

Even though we write these sounds with the letter *r,* the student should take special note of the very important fact that these /r/—sounds do not even vaguely resemble the /r/—sounds that occur in most varieties of English. Any attempt to transfer one's English /r/ over into Spanish will result in utter failure to produce a satisfactory imitation of the Spanish sound.

You have already (2.22.11) gone through a session of drill-work on the difference between /r/ and the variety of /d/ that appears between vowel contrasts like [tóđȯ ↓] - [tórȯ ↓] . Now it is necessary to distinguish this *single* /r/ (the one which is so much like English *tt* or *d* or *dd* in words like *Betty, cottage, lettuce, better, wader, waiter, shutter, shudder)* from the *double* /rr/. The /rr/ is a rapid trill of the tongue-tip, and it can usually be learned only by careful imitation. The following drill is to help you hear and learn to reproduce the difference between the two kinds of /r/.

### 2.23.1 Exercise on /r/ and /rr/ between vowels

| | |
|---|---|
| pérȯ ↓ | pérrȯ ↓ |
| kárȯ ↓ | kárrȯ ↓ |
| párȧ ↓ | párrȧ ↓ |
| bárȧ ↓ | bárrȧ ↓ |
| kórȯ ↓ | kórrȯ ↓ |
| ṣérȯ ↓ | ṣérrȯ ↓ |
| y̯érȯ ↓ | y̯érrȯ ↓ |
| fórȯ ↓ | fórrȯ ↓ |
| fyérȯ ↓ | fyérrȯ ↓ |
| ȧmárȧ ↓ | ȧmárrȧ ↓ |

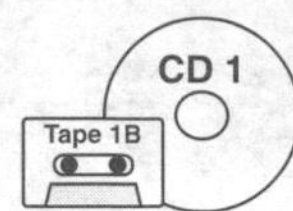

Not only is the Spanish /r/ quite different from the English *r* when it occurs between vowels, as in the preceding drill; it is also quite different in association with consonants. Take the Spanish word [tárđė ↓] for example. Your first attempt will probably sound something like the English words *tar day*. If you will try to make it sound more like *totter-they* (spoken rapidly), you will come pretty close to the Spanish pronunciation.

The following drill will allow you to practice /r/ in all combinations with other consonants.

## 2.23.2 Excercise on /r/ before and after consonants

| | | | |
|---|---|---|---|
| próntȯ ↓ | kwérpȯ ↓ | grándė ↓ | ȧmárgȯ ↓ |
| prímȯ ↓ | tórpė ↓ | fríȯ ↓ | mȧrfíl ↓ |
| trés ↓ | kártȧ ↓ | frásė ↓ | pėrfíl ↓ |
| trátȯ ↓ | pwértȧ ↓ | | fársȧ ↓ |
| krúđȯ ↓ | ṣérkȧ ↓ | | írsė ↓ |
| kréȯ ↓ | párkė ↓ | | ȧrhėntínȧ ↓ |
| brȧsíl ↓ | árƀȯl ↓ | | su̇rhyó ↓ |
| brómȧ ↓ | kúrƀȧ ↓ | | dȯrmí ↓ |
| drámȧ ↓ | tárđė ↓ | | ármȧ ↓ |
| drógȧ ↓ | gwárđȧ ↓ | | byérnės ↓ |
| gráṣyȧs ↓ | gȧrgántȧ ↓ | | órnȯ ↓ |

CD 1
Tape 1B

Whenever /r/ occurs at the very end of an utterance (*not* the end of a word, but the end just before pause), and especially when that final syllable is a *stressed* syllable, it has a different pronunciation from what is heard elsewhere. It is more like /rr/, but the vocal cords do not vibrate during it. The effect is almost like combining /r/ with /s/ except that the tongue-tip remains *up* at the end. This sound can be practiced by imitation of the following words.

### 2.23.3 Exercise on Spanish /r/ at the end of an utterance

| | |
|---|---|
| sėn̯yór ↓ | ȧs̯úkȧr ↓ |
| ȧƀlár ↓ | nákȧr ↓ |
| mėtér ↓ | étėr ↓ |
| kȧnsár ↓ | káns̯ėr ↓ |
| rrėƀȯlbér ↓ | rrėƀólbėr ↓ |
| pȧrtír ↓ | mártir ↓ |
| fȧƀór ↓ | bȯlíƀȧr ↓ |

In the preceding pages the *gross* differences in the pronunciation of sounds that are similar in Spanish and English have been illustrated and discussed. These are the differences which if unmastered will cause great difficulty and misunderstanding in an attempt to communicate in Spanish, and their mastery is therefore of the utmost importance to a student. However, there are other pronunciation features that should be understood and learned, to reduce the 'gringo accent' that will inevitably distract the listener's attention and thus impair the communication efficiency. The following lists of similar sounding words pronounced by a Spanish speaker and an English speaker respectively will illustrate important differences in the pronunciation of what might be considered the same vowels. Note especially that the English vowels seem to be more prolonged, more drawn out, and especially note that they do *not* seem to maintain the same quality from the beginning to the end of the vowel, whereas the Spanish vowel *does*.

**End of Tape 1B**

**End of CD 1**

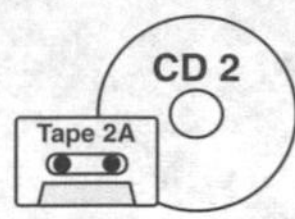


## 2.24 Vowel nuclei in Spanish

### 2.24.1 English /ey/ and Spanish /e/

| | |
|---|---|
| day | dé˙ ↓ |
| Kay | ké˙ ↓ |
| say | sé˙ ↓ |
| bay | bé˙ ↓ |
| Fay | fé˙ ↓ |
| May | mé˙ ↓ |
| lay | lé˙ ↓ |

### 2.24.2 English /ow/ and Spanish /o/

| | |
|---|---|
| no | nó˙ ↓ |
| low | ló˙ ↓ |
| yoe | yó˙ ↓ |
| so | só˙ ↓ |

### 2.24.3 English /iy/ and Spanish /i/

| | |
|---|---|
| me | mí ↓ |
| tea | tí ↓ |
| see | sí ↓ |
| bee | bí ↓ |
| Dee | dí ↓ |
| knee | ní ↓ |

### 2.24.4 English /uw/ and Spanish /u/

| | |
|---|---|
| too | tú ↓ |
| sue | sú ↓ |
| pooh | pú ↓ |
| coo | kú ↓ |
| boo | bú ↓ |
| moo | mú ↓ |

Generally if you are imitating a native or near-native pronunciation at full normal colloquial speed, errors of the type illustrated above are not likely to be obtrusive. Probably the most important detail to remember is to say words which contain these vowels without allowing the quality to change in the course of producing them. For /u/ and /o/, this means rounding the lips during the production of the preceding consonant so that the lips are properly rounded in anticipation of the rounding required for the vowel.

## 2.25 Lateral —/l/ in Spanish

/l/ in English is a sound that is produced by raising the tip of the tongue up to touch the roof of the mouth in such a way that the air column is forced to pass around either side of it: this way of producing a sound is called *lateral* (i.e., 'side') *articulation.*

In Spanish, the /l/ is actually a *laterally released* [d], and it has a *very* different sound from the English /l/. If you will try to follow by manipulating your own tongue, a technical description will be helpful: produce a [d] as in the word *did.* Notice that to make the [d], you release the whole tip of the tongue so that the air can flow suddenly out across the top of it. Now instead of releasing the entire tongue downward, keep the tip locked in its [d] position at the end of the word *did* but release the air through one side as though you were going to say the word *diddle,* but without lowering the back part of the tongue as you would in *diddle.* If you have followed these instructions, you are producing a Spanish /l/.

Compare the following pairs which are approximately alike except for the /l/-sounds and try to imitate the difference.

### 2.25.1 Exercise on Spanish /l/

| | | | | | |
|---|---|---|---|---|---|
| feel | fíl ↓ | dell | dél ↓ | coal | kól ↓ |
| hotel | òtél ↓ | tall | tál ↓ | tool | túl ↓ |
| el | él ↓ | | | | |

## 2.26 Voiceless stops

### 2.26.1 /p/ in Spanish

It was mentioned earlier that in English there are at least two conspicuously different kinds of *p*-sounds: the *p* of *pin, pill,* which has the puff of air called *aspiration,* and the *p* of *spin, spill,* which has no aspiration.

The Spanish /p/ is always produced *without* aspiration. One way for an American to get at the mastery of it is by thinking of an *s* before Spanish words that begin with /p/ in order to transfer the English pattern of producing unaspirated *p* after *s*.

The following list will give you a basis for comparing the *p*-sound in the two languages and learning to reproduce the difference.

#### 2.26.11 Exercise on Spanish /p/

| | |
|---|---|
| pace | pé͘s̜ ↓ |
| Peru | pėrú͘ ↓ |
| pawn | pá͘n ↓ |
| par | pá͘r ↓ |
| pore | pó͘r ↓ |
| pone | pó͘n ↓ |
| pooh | pú͘ ↓ |
| plan | plá͘n ↓ |

## 2.26.2 /t/ in Spanish

The /t/ problem is like the /p/ problem: in English it is aspirated, in Spanish it is not. In addition, the tongue touches a point that is more forward in the mouth to produce a Spanish /t/: it literally touches the back side of the upper teeth, which it does not do in English.

### 2.26.21 Exercise on Spanish /t/

| | |
|---|---|
| tea | tí̇ ↓ |
| ten | té̇n ↓ |
| toss | tá̇s ↓ |
| taboo | tȧƀú̇ ↓ |

## 2.26.3 /k/ in Spanish

If you have mastered /p/ and /t/, /k/ will be a breeze since it involves again the aspiration problem.

### 2.26.31 Exercise on Spanish /k/

| | |
|---|---|
| kilo | kílȯ ↓ |
| Kay | ké̇ ↓ |
| call | ká̇l ↓ |
| can | ká̇n ↓ |
| cafe | kȧfé̇ ↓ |

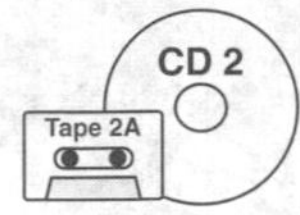




## 2.27 Voiceless spirants

### 2.27.1 /s/ in Spanish

Spanish has an [s] and a [z] , but unlike English they are considered as variants of a single sound, /s/. That is to say, two Spanish words are never distinguished solely by the difference [s—z ] as are the English words 'seal' and 'zeal'. Note the following pairs of words in Spanish which have partly similar sequences of sounds.

#### 2.27.11 Exercise on the distribution of the variants of /s/

| | |
|---|---|
| ėzƀóṣȯ ↓ | ėspósȯ ↓ |
| rrȧzgár ↓ | rrȧskár ↓ |
| ėzƀéltȧ ↓ | ėspéltȧ ↓ |
| áznȯ ↓ | áskȯ ↓ |
| mízmȯ ↓ | místȯ ↓ |
| hu̇z̨gár ↓ | bu̇skár ↓ |
| dėzđėn̯yár ↓ | dėstėn̯yír ↓ |
| dizgústȯ ↓ | diskúrsȯ ↓ |
| dézđė ↓ | déstė ↓ (de̯ éstė) |
| ézđė ↓ (éz dė) | éstė ↓ |

#### 2.27.12 Discussion of the distribution of the variants of /s/

You will notice that the [z] occurs in Spanish only in a syllable-final position before a *voiced consonant,* namely [b, d, g, m, n, l, r]. Anywhere else, [s] occurs, except before semi-vowels /y/ and /w/ where both [s] and [z] occur, depending on

whether the syllable begins with the /s/ or with the semi-vowel. Since there is no choice on the part of the speaker—only one or the other occurs in any given situation, but not both—they are *not in contrast* and belong to only one basic sound unit, /s/.

But in some dialects and styles of speaking Spanish, another variety of [s] occurs. Note these pronunciations of some Caribbean and South American dialects.

bwénȧ$^{h}$nóchė$^{h}$ ↓ múchȧ$^{h}$grásyȧ$^{h}$ ↓

kómo̯ė$^{h}$táu̯$^{h}$té ↓ á$^{h}$tȧmȧn̯yánȧ ↓

ke̯óra̯é$^{h}$ ↓ éso̯é$^{h}$ ↓

The /s/ is not dropped entirely in these dialects. Actually there are some rather complex differences in distribution from one dialect to another, so that Argentineans may say that Chileans 'eat their s's', and Colombians will say the Argentineans eat *their* s's, and so on, without any of these stereotypes reflecting the facts. Thus, for example, since the Chileans use the [$^{h}$] variety of /s/ in all syllable-final occurrences, they are accused of eating their s's by Argentineans who use the [$^{h}$] variety only in those syllable-final ocurrences that are followed by a syllable which begins with a consonant. Such details are not pertinent to the development of your pronunciation, since in any case you should imitate your instructor's pronunciation. But you may hear other varieties some day, and it is well to understand the patterns they follow. Remember that in *no* dialect does the syllable-initial /s/ appear as [$^{h}$].

There are certain groups of words in which the /s/ will bother you more than elsewhere, because the words sound familiar and lead you back into English /z/—channels. Such are the words listed below.

### 2.27.13 Typical errors from English /z/—influence on Spanish /s/

| Correct | Your Probable Error | Familiar English Pronunciation | English Spelling |
|---|---|---|---|
| kánsȧs ↓ | kánz̲ȧs ↓ | kǽnzɨs ↓ | Kansas |
| imflwénşȧ ↓ | imflwénz̲ȧ ↓ | ìnflůwénzə̇ ↓ | influenza |
| bėnėşwélȧ ↓ | bėnėz̲wélȧ ↓ | vènɨzůwélə̇ ↓ | Venezuela |
| ėksámėnės ↓ | ėgz̲ámėnės ↓ | ėgzǽmz ↓ | exams |
| rrȧşón ↓ | rrȧz̲ón ↓ | ríyzɨn ↓ | reason |
| diƀisyón ↓ | diƀiz̲yón ↓ | dɨvížɨn ↓ | division |
| prȯpósitȯ ↓ | prȯpóz̲itȯ ↓ | pràpə̇zíšɨn ↓ | proposition |
| prėsiđéntė ↓ | prėziđéntė ↓ | prézɨdɨnt ↓ | president |
| prėséntė ↓ | prėz̲éntė ↓ | priyzént ↓ | present |
| prėsėntár ↓ | prėz̲ėntár ↓ | prézɨnt ↓ | present |
| prėsėntȧşyónės ↓ | prėz̲ėntȧşyónės ↓ | prèzintéyšɨn ↓ | presentation |
| bisitár ↓ | biz̲itár ↓ | vízit ↓ | visit |
| sántȧrrósȧ ↓ | sántȧrróz̲ȧ ↓ | sǽntə̇ rówzə̇ ↓ | Santa Rosa |
| rrȯsȧlíndȧ ↓ | rrȯz̲ȧlíndȧ ↓ | ròwzə̇líndə̇ ↓ | Rosalinda |

### 2.27.14 American Spanish /s/ and Castilian /s̯/

In Castilian Spanish, a dialect used in some areas of Spain, but having a prestige status that far outweighs its geographical distribution, the sounds /s/ and /s̯/ are different. The /s/ is pronounced with the tongue-tip raised toward the top of the mouth, so that an effect like a very slight lisp is noticeable. The /s̯/ is pronounced something like the *th* of the English word *thin*. Thus words like the following, which are alike in other dialects, are distinguished in Castilian Spanish.

| | | | |
|---|---|---|---|
| kásȧ ↓ | kás̯ȧ ↓ | lásȯ ↓ | lás̯ȯ ↓ |
| ás ↓ | ás̯ ↓ | másȧ ↓ | más̯ȧ ↓ |
| pésės ↓ | pés̯ės ↓ | lósȧ ↓ | lós̯ȧ ↓ |
| kȯsér ↓ | kȯs̯ér ↓ | pásȯ ↓ | pás̯ȯ ↓ |
| pósȯ ↓ | pós̯ȯ ↓ | ásȧ ↓ | ás̯ȧ ↓ |

This distinction can be ignored by anyone who expects to use Spanish among speakers of American Spanish dialects.

## 2.27.2 /h/ in Spanish

Another consonant that marks an American accent is the /h/. The following lists of similar sounding words pronounced by an English speaker and a Spanish speaker will illustrate the difference between English *h* and Spanish /h/.

### 2.27.21 Exercise on Spanish /h/

| | |
|---|---|
| heater | hírȧ ↓ |
| hurrah | hu̇rár ↓ |
| holly | hálė ↓ |
| hotter | hárȧ ↓ |
| hoosegow | hu̇z̯gađȯ ↓ |

| | |
|---|---|
| Hilda | hı́ldȧ ↓ |
| junta | húntȧ ↓ |
| aha | ȧhá̇ ↓ |
| Mohican | mȯhı́kȧ ↓ |

#### 2.27.22 Discussion of Spanish /h/

When you produce *h* in English your tongue is relaxed and low in your mouth, so that you merely breathe easily across it before beginning the vowel that follows. For a Spanish /h/, the tongue must be tenser and higher in the mouth, near the roof but not touching it, so that more friction noise is created when air is forced past. It is especially difficult for an English speaker to produce Spanish /h/ between vowels and after a stressed syllable as in /méhiko ↓ déheme/, etc. Though always stronger than English *h* Spanish /h/ carries more or less friction noise depending on the area of the Spanish speaking world. Listen carefully and imitate what you hear to the best of your ability.

## 2.28 Nasals and palatals

### 2.28.1 /n/ in Spanish

Spanish /n/ differs from English *n* in that it is usually produced against the back of the upper teeth, instead of on the gum ridge above the teeth. In this respect it is similar to Spanish /t/ and /d/. The correct articulation of /n/ is not too difficult for English speakers, but there are a couple of combinations of /n/ plus another consonant that create problems.

#### 2.28.11 The cluster /nt/ in Spanish

| | |
|---|---|
| quantity | kȧntiđá̇đ ↓ |
| Tonto | tántȯ ↓ |
| lentil | léntė ↓ |

| | |
|---|---|
| canto | kántȯ ↓ |
| antidote | ȧntíđȯtȯ ↓ |
| Tantalus | tántȧlȯ ↓ |
| pinto | píntȯ ↓ |
| junta | húntȧ ↓ |
| Santa Mónica | sántȧ–mónikȧ ↓ |

The close yoking of *nt* in English in words like the ones above, especially when not pronounced slowly and in expressions like 'I wanta' does not happen in the pronunciation of Spanish /nt/, where the /n/ is clearly resonated through the nose before the /t/ begins.

## 2.28.2 /n̦y/ and /ny/ in Spanish

Speakers from practically all dialect areas can, when they try, make a difference between forms with /n̦y/ and those with /ny/. It seems, however, that this difference is unimportant from the point of view of its limited usefulness, since the distinction is frequently obscured at normal utterance speed. It is somewhat like the difference between medial *tt* and *dd* after stress in words like *shutter* and *shudder:* the difference is there, and we can make it if we try to, but we usually do not. In the hierarchy of importance of the various details of learning Spanish pronunciation, this is one of the last.

### 2.28.21 English /niy/ , /ny/ and Spanish /n̦y/ , /ny/

| 1 | 2 | 3 | 4 |
|---|---|---|---|
| uranium | | u̇rán̦yȯ ↓ | u̇ránỵȯ ↓ |
| lineal | | ȧlín̦yȧ ↓ | ȧlínyȧ ↓ |
| matrimonial | | món̦yȯ ↓ | mȧtrimónyȯ ↓ |

| | | | |
|---|---|---|---|
| Antonio | | ȯtóṇyȯ ↓ | ȧntónyȯ ↓ |
| linear | vineyard | lȧ–ƀíṇyȧ ↓ | lȧƀínyȧ ↓ |
| | minion | míṇyȯ ↓ | mínyȯ ↓ |
| | onion | dė–móṇyȯ ↓ | dėmónyȯ ↓ |
| | Hispania | ėspáṇyȧ ↓ | ispányȧ ↓ |
| | Hispaniola | ėspȧṇyólȧ ↓ | ispȧnyólȧ ↓ |
| | canyon | ėskáṇyȯ ↓ | ȧskányȯ ↓ |
| | annual | áṇyȯ ↓ | hėrányȯ ↓ |
| | pinion, piñon | piṇyón ↓ | opinyón ↓ |

The English and Spanish pronunciations of /n/ and /y/ together (colums 2 and 4) do not sound alike largely because in English, the syllable division is *after* the /n/, but in Spanish it is *before* the /n/. Column 3 really hardly needs to be given except that purists would be uncomfortable if we failed to indicate that the contrast can be, and sometimes is, made.

## 2.28.3 /ly/, /(l)y/, and /y/ in Spanish

### 2.28.31 English /liy/, /ly/ and Spanish /ly/, /(l)y/, and /y/

| | | | | |
|---|---|---|---|---|
| Balearic | dahlia | bályȧ ↓ | bá(l)y̱ȧ ↓ | báy̱ȧ ↓ |
| polio | pavilion | pólyȯ ↓ | pó(l)y̱ȯ ↓ | póy̱ȯ ↓ |
| alias | stallion | ályȧs ↓ | á(l)y̱ȧs ↓ | áy̱ȧs ↓ |

| | | | | |
|---|---|---|---|---|
| malleable | Amelia | ȧmályȧ ↓ | ȧmá(l)y̠ȧ ↓ | ȧmáy̠ȧ ↓ |
| oleo | collier | ólyȯ ↓ | ó(l)y̠ȯ ↓ | óy̠ȯ ↓ |
| oleography | goliard | ȯlyár ↓ | ȯ(l)y̠ár ↓ | ȯy̠ár ↓ |
| Ilion | million | ilyón ↓ | mi(l)y̠ón ↓ | mi–y̠ó ↓ |
| alien | billion | élyȯ ↓ | é(l)y̠ȯ ↓ | |
| Quintilian | quintillion | fílyȯ ↓ | fí(l)y̠ȯ ↓ | |

The preceding lists are not so much for drill as for illustration of an important and widespread dialect difference. To distinguish the important dialect difference, the [l] of the forms in column 4 is placed in parentheses, /(l)y/, since it drops in all dialects except in some parts of Castile in Spain, in upland Colombia, Ecuador, Bolivia, Paraguay, and a few other areas. In most of these dialects the minimal difference between /ly/ and /(l)y/ (the similar forms in columns 3 and 4) can be made, but has the same limited usefulness as the /ny/ — /n̦y/ distinction. For all the other dialect areas, the similar forms of columns 4 and 5 are not distinguished; both have the [y̠] variant of /y/, described below.

## 2.28.4 /y/ in Spanish

/y/ has two variants which are obvious to the English ear because they are like two entirely separate sounds in English. We write these variants with [y] for the one that is the y of *yea, yes, bay, buy, yacht,* etc., and with [y̠] for the one that varies all the way from [y] to (j) as in *judge*. In the English words below, either of the two words on each line begins with a sound that is equally likely to occur in the Spanish items of the right-hand column.

### 2.28.41 English *y* and *j* and Spanish [y̠]

| | | |
|---|---|---|
| yes | Jess | y̠ésȯ ↓ |
| yellow | jello | y̠élȯ ↓ |

| | | |
|---|---|---|
| yah | jaw | y̭á ↓ |
| yoe | Joe | y̭ó ↓ |
| uke | juke | y̭úgo ↓ |
| yearn | germ | y̭érno ↓ |
| yabber | jabber | y̭ába ↓ |
| yea | jay | y̭é ↓ |

In Spanish these are variants of the same sound. It often puzzles an English speaker to hear both variants because he does not know which one to imitate. Actually both Spanish variants may be used by a single speaker. The significant difference in English is no longer significant, and you must learn to ignore it.

Not all /y/'s in Spanish can be pronounced both ways: only those which are syllable initial, and especially those which are utterance initial. Another way of saying this is that Spanish [y] will appear at the end of a word or before or after consonants within a word, pretty much like the English *y*. In other positions the Spanish /y/ varies from a [y], to sounds English speakers would interpret as the *z* in *azure* or the *j* of *judge*. As you have probably noticed, we have transcribed this latter variant as [y̭], to distinguish it from the [y] which cannot be pronounced like English *j*.

## 2.29 Conclusion

There are, be it admitted, other difficulties in the pronunciation of Spanish than those which have been pointed out here. One is the handling of juncture—that is, the way words run together in a sequence. We call attention to this by the way in which we transcribe utterances in the text (without spaces separating words). Another is the problem of pronouncing various unfamiliar consonant sequences like /bw/, /trw/, /yw/ etc. These we are inclined to leave to the correction of the pronunciation of complete phrases as they happen to turn up—not on the assumption that they are less important, but because there are no drills which will help the student learn them except repetition of the utterances themselves. If the student has learned to make all the contrasts described in the foregoing material, and to avoid the most serious pitfalls that have also been described, he is well on his way toward accurate pronunciation of Spanish and should find that mastery of the utterances comes much easier than it otherwise would.

# 2.3 DRILLS AND GRAMMAR

## 2.31 Pattern drills

### 2.31.1 Some demonstratives

A. PRESENTATION OF PATTERN (1)

*ILLUSTRATIONS*

| | | |
|---|---|---|
| ______________ | 1 kéṣésȯ ↓ | ¿Qué es *eso?* |
| ______________ | 2 éstọ ėṣu̇nṣėniṣérȯ ↓ | *Esto* es un cenicero. |
| What's this? | 3 kéṣéstȯ ↓ | ¿Qué es *esto?* |
| a, an (f.) | únȧ ↓ | una |
| That's a chair. | 4 ésọ ėṣu̇nȧsí(l)yȧ ↓ | *Eso* es una silla. |

(1) The 'presentation of pattern' is a device that will be used here and in subsequent pattern drills to briefly explain the grammar principles and chart the illustrative forms that make up the pattern. It will usually consist of three parts: illustrations, extrapolation, and notes.

The illustrations are a group of sentences, some of which have previously appeared as basic sentences and some of which have not. New sentences can be identified by the appearance of an English translation in the left hand column. These 'structural filler' sentences contain forms needed to fill out the pattern of the point being drilled and should be memorized just as basic sentences. In these sentences the forms to be drilled are underlined or italicized.

The extrapolation is an arrangement of the forms to be drilled that shows the relationships between these forms. These relationships are analytically 'extrapolated' and shown in a chart for the benefit of those who can grasp the relationships more easily when they are presented visually in a spatial configuration.

The notes, when they occur, are designed to very briefly explain the extrapolation.

A fuller discussion of the pattern is presented after the drills in Section B, entitled 'discussion of pattern'. Further explanation and correlation with other grammar points can be found in the appendix.

| | | |
|---|---|---|
| That's good. | 5 ésǫėzƀwénȯ ↓ | *Eso* es bueno. |
| Translate this. | 6 tràđúsk̯ą̑éstȯ ↓ | Traduzca *esto*. |
| Repeat that. | 7 rrèpítą̑ésȯ ↓ | Repita *eso*. |

*EXTRAPOLATION*

| | |
|---|---|
| ésto | this |
| éso | that |

*NOTES*

a. English 'this' and 'that' can sometimes be translated /ésto/ and /éso/ in Spanish.

## 2.31.11 RESPONSE DRILL (1)

(1) This and subsequent response drills are made up of four groups of questions which are designed to elicit answers that require the use of the grammar point previously illustrated, but at the same time to insure answers that are completely natural in their most probable contexts. The four groups are: (1) choice questions, which normally require full sentence replies. (2) Information questions, the answers to which are listed and can be given *sotto voce* just before the questions. These will also normally require full sentence replies. (3) Yes-no questions to be answered 'no'. The correct answer is listed and can be given *sotto voce* just before the questions. These too will normally require full sentence replies. (4) Yes-no questions to be answered 'yes'. These will normally require just /sí ↓/ or a partial sentence reply.

The student's cue for the kind of answer he should give is the presence or absence of a *sotto voce* prompting before the question and whether the question has an intonation ending with a /↓/ or /↑/. The first and second groups end with /↓/ and require answers which are chosen by the student in group one and suggested *sotto voce* by the instructor in group two. The third and fourth groups end with /↑/ and require /nó ↓/ with a correction which is given *sotto voce* by the instructor in group three and /sí ↓/ with or without additional elaboration, usually in the form of a partial sentence, in group four.

The student should not need to look at the materials to do this drill orally.

Model Problem:

1 ėṣésto̯ėspȧn̯yól ↑ o̯iŋglés ↓

[ėls̯éntrȯ ↓] 2 keṣésȯ ↓

[ủnsyétė ↓] 3 ėṣéṣto̯ủnwéƀė ↑

4 ėṣéṣo̯ủntrés ↑

Model Answer:

1 ésȯ ↑ éṣėspȧn̯yól ↓

2 ésȯ ↑ éṣėls̯éntrȯ ↓

3 éstȯ ↑ nó ↓ éṣủnsyétė ↓

4 éstȯ ↑ sí ↓ éṣủntrés ↓

---

Model Problem:

1 ¿Es esto español o inglés?

(el centro) 2 ¿Qué es eso?

(un siete) 3 ¿Es esto un nueve?

4 ¿Es eso un tres?

Model Answer:

1 ¿Eso? En español.

2 ¿Eso? Es el centro.

3 ¿Esto? No, es un siete.

4 ¿Esto? Sí, es un tres.

| | | |
|---|---|---|
| | 1 ėṣésto̯u̇nlápış ↑ o̯u̇nȧplúmȧ ↓ | ésȯ ↑ éṣu̇nȧplúmȧ ↓ |
| | 2 ėṣésto̯u̇nȧsí(l)y̠ȧ ↑ o̯u̇nȧmésȧ ↓ | éstȯ ↑ éṣu̇nȧmésȧ ↓ |
| [u̇nlíƀrȯ ↓] | 3 keṣéstȯ ↓ | ésȯ ↑ éṣu̇nlíƀrȯ ↓ |
| [u̇nşėnişérȯ ↓] | 4 keṣésȯ ↓ | éstȯ ↑ éṣu̇nşėnişérȯ ↓ |
| [u̇nlápiş ↓] | 5 ėṣéso̯u̇nȧplúmȧ ↑ | éstȯ ↑ nó ↓ éṣu̇nlápiş ↓ |
| [u̇nȧplúmȧ ↓] | 6 ėṣésto̯u̇nlápiş ↑ | ésȯ ↑ nó ↓ éṣu̇nȧplúmȧ ↓ |
| | 7 ėṣéso̯u̇nȯtél ↑ | ésȯ ↑ sí ↓ éṣu̇nȯtél ↓ |
| | 8 ėṣésto̯u̇nşėnişérȯ ↑ | ésȯ ↑ sí ↓ éṣu̇nşėnişérȯ ↓ |
| | 9 ėṣéso̯u̇nȧsí(l)y̠ȧ ↑ | éstȯ ↑ sí ↓ éṣu̇nȧsí(l)y̠ȧ ↓ |

---

| | | |
|---|---|---|
| | 1 ¿Es esto un lápiz o una pluma? | ¿Eso? Es una pluma. |
| | 2 ¿Es esto una silla o una mesa? | ¿Esto? Es una mesa. |
| (un libro) | 3 ¿Qué es esto? | ¿Eso? Es un libro. |
| (un cenicero) | 4 ¿Qué es eso? | ¿Esto? Es un cenicero. |
| (un lápiz) | 5 ¿Es eso una pluma? | ¿Esto? No, es un lápiz. |
| (una pluma) | 6 ¿Es esto un lápiz? | ¿Eso? No, es una pluma. |
| | 7 ¿Es eso un hotel? | ¿Eso? Si, es un hotel. |
| | 8 ¿Es esto un cenicero? | ¿Eso? Si, es un cenicero. |
| | 9 ¿Es eso una silla? | ¿Esto? Si, es una silla. |

## 2.31.12 TRANSLATION DRILL [1]

| | | | |
|---|---|---|---|
| 1 | That's good. | éso̮ \| ézƀwénȯ ↓ | Eso es bueno. |
| 2 | This isn't Spanish. | éstȯ \| no̮éṣėspȧn̮yól ↓ | Esto no es español. |
| 3 | How's that going? | kėtál \| báésȯ ↓ | ¿Qué tal va eso? |
| 4 | What's that? | kéṣésȯ ↓ | ¿Qué es eso? |
| 5 | What's this? | kéṣéstȯ ↓ | ¿Qué es esto? |
| 6 | That's too much. | éso̮ėzmúchȯ ↓ | Eso es mucho. |
| 7 | I don't want that until tomorrow. | nókyéro̮éso̮ \| ástȧmȧn̮yánȧ ↓ | No quiero eso hasta mañana. |
| 8 | I want that later. | kyéro̮ésȯ \| lwégȯ ↓ | Quiero eso luego. |
| 9 | I regret this very much. | syéntȯmúcho̮ \| éstȯ ↓ | Siento mucho esto. |
| 10 | This is going very well. | éstȯƀá \| múyƀyén ↓ | Esto va muy bien. |
| 11 | The young lady wants this. | lȧsėn̮yȯrítȧ \| kyéréstȯ ↓ | La señorita quiere esto. |

(1) Translate the English sentences to Spanish. The student should cover the Spanish answers while doing this drill orally.

## B. DISCUSSION OF PATTERN [1]

Basically, /éso/ is used to refer to an object which is relatively nearer the person being addressed than it is to the person speaking, whereas /ésto/ refers to an object relatively nearer to the person speaking. Roughly, then, they correspond to the English words *that* and *this,* but in Spanish the ending /—o/ on these two words indicates that the speaker does not know what the Spanish word for the object is (as when asking the question 'What is this?'), or that the speaker is answering a question in which /ésto/ or /éso/ is used, or that the speaker is referring to a situation or set of circumstances instead of to an object (as in /éso̭esbwéno ↓ /. Otherwise the speaker would choose these forms with other endings, which will be presented in Unit 7.

(1) This and subsequent discussions of pattern are not designed for use in the classroom. They are explanations of the structural patterns of the drills for the orientation of students who feel that such explanations are helpful to their efforts to master the language. Classroom time should be reserved for drilling the language itself, leaving grammar explanations largely for home study or special grammar sessions of the class.

# 3.1 BASIC SENTENCES

## White's arrival in Surlandia

John White, an American arriving for the first time in Surlandia, a country south of the United States, has been met at the airport and seen through customs to his hotel by American friends. They leave him at the hotel, where he checks in at the desk and then is accompanied to his room by the porter carrying his bags. He arrives in the room.

| English Spelling | Aid to Listening | Spanish Spelling |
|---|---|---|
| to you | lé ↓ | le |
| (it) pleases, is pleasing (to please) | gústȧ ↓ gůstár ↓ | gusta (gustar) |
| to you is pleasing | lė—gústȧ ↓ | le gusta |
| the room | ėl—kwártȯ ↓ | el cuarto |
| *PORTER* | | *MOZO* |
| Do you like the room? (1) | lėgústa̭ėlkwártȯ ↑ | ¿Le gusta el cuarto? |
| to me is pleasing | mė—gústȧ ↓ | me gusta |
| *WHITE* | | *WHITE* |
| Yes, I do. | sí \| mėgústȧ ↓ | Sí, me gusta. |
| (you) want (to want) | kyérė ↓ kėrér ↓ | quiere (querer) |
| the water | ėl—ágwȧ ↓ | el agua (f.) |
| mineral | minėrál ↓ | mineral |
| soda water | ágwȧ—minėrál ↓ | agua mineral |

| | | |
|---|---|---|
| *PORTER* | | *MOZO* |
| Do you want soda water? (2) | kyérḙustéđ \| ágwàminèrál ↑ | ¿Quiere usted agua mineral? |
| rise, bring up (to go up) | súƀà ↓ sùƀír ↓ | suba (subir) |
| it | lá ↓ | la (f.) |
| bring it up to me (3) | súƀàmèlà ↓ | súbamela |
| later | dèspwés ↓ | después |
| *WHITE* | | *WHITE* |
| Yes. Bring it up to me later. | sí ↓ súƀàmèlà \| đèspwés ↓ | Sí. Súbamela después. |
| (you) need (to need) | nèșèsítà ↓ nèșèsitár ↓ | necesita (necesitar) |
| anything, something | álgò ↓ | algo |
| else | más ↓ | más |
| anything else | álgò—más ↓ | algo más |
| *PORTER* | | *MOZO* |
| Do you need anything else? | nèșèsítàlgòmás ↑ | ¿Necesita algo más? |
| near (4) | șérkà ↓ | cerca |
| near to | șérkà—đè ↓ | cerca de |
| here | àkí ↓ | aquí |

| | | |
|---|---|---|
| *WHITE* | | *WHITE* |
| Yes. Is the American Embassy | sí ↓ èstálạèmbàháđàmèrìkánà \| | Sí. ¿Está la Embajada |
| near here? | ṣérkàđẹàkí ↑ | Americana cerca de aquí? |
| far | léhòs ↓ | lejos |
| the avenue | lạ—àƀènídà ↓ | la avenida |
| Columbus | kòlón ↓ | Colón |
| *PORTER* | | *MOZO* |
| No. It's quite a distance. | nó ↓ èstálehòs ↓ | No. Está lejos. |
| On Columbus Avenue. | ènlàƀènídà \| đèkòlón ↓ | En la avenida de Colón. |
| that | ké ↓ | que |
| there is that, it's necessary (5) | áy—kè ↓ | hay que |
| to take | tòmár ↓ | tomar |
| the taxi | èl—táksi ↓ | el taxi |
| It's necessary to take a taxi. | áykètòmáruntáksi ↓ | Hay que tomar un taxi. |
| *WHITE* | | *WHITE* |
| Thanks. Here you are. | gráṣyàs ↓ àkítyéné ↓ | Gracias. Aquí tiene. |
| *PORTER* | | *MOZO* |
| Thank you very much, sir. | múchàzgráṣyàs \| sèṇyór ↓ | Muchas gracias, señor. |
| the elevator | èl—às(ṣ)ènsór ↓ | el ascensor |

| | | |
|---|---|---|
| Are you going down in the elevator? | báhạen̤elás(ṣ)ėnsór ↑ | ¿Baja en el ascensor? |
| now | ȧórȧ ↓ | ahora |
| same | mízmȯ ↓ | mismo |
| right now | ȧórȧ—mízmȯ ↓ | ahora mismo |
| *WHITE* | | *WHITE* |
| Yes. Right now. | sí ↓ ȧóramízmȯ ↓ | Sí, ahora mismo. |
| the box, the cashier's desk | lȧ—káhȧ ↓ | la caja |
| Where's the cashier's desk? | dóndėstálakáhȧ ↓ | ¿Dónde está la caja? |
| first | primér ↓ primérȯ ↓ | primer (primero) |
| the floor | ėl—písȯ ↓ | el piso |
| the entrance | lạ—ėntrádȧ ↓ | la entrada |
| *PORTER* | | *MOZO* |
| On the first floor to the right of the entrance. | ėn̤ėlprimérpísọ \| ȧlȧđėrécha \| đėlạentrádȧ ↓ | En el primer piso, a la derecha de la entrada. |

**End of Tape 2A**

(Mr. White goes down on the elevator and up to the cashier's window.)

| | | |
|---|---|---|
| (you) can (to be able) | pwéđė ↓ pȯđér ↓ | puede (poder) |
| to change, exchange | kȧmbyár ↓ | cambiar |
| to change for me | kȧmbyármė ↓ | cambiarme |

| | | |
|---|---|---|
| some, a few | únȯs ↓ | unos |
| the dollar | ėl—dólȧr ↓ | el dólar |
| some dollars | únȯz—đólȧrės ↓ | unos dólares |
| *WHITE* | | *WHITE* |
| Can you change a few dollars for me? | pwéđė \| kȧmbyármḙ \| u̇nȯzđólȧrės ↑ | ¿Puede cambiarme unos dólares? |
| *CASHIER* | | *CAJERO* |
| Yes. How many? | sí ↓ kwántȯs ↓ | Sí. ¿Cuántos? |
| how, at what | ȧ—kómȯ ↓ | a cómo |
| the change, exchange | ėl—kámbyȯ ↓ | el cambio |
| *WHITE* | | *WHITE* |
| Ten. What's the rate of exchange? | dyéṣ ↓ ȧkómoḙstá \| ḙlkámbyȯ ↓ | Diez. ¿A cómo está el cambio? |
| the bill | ėl—bi(l)y̱étė ↓ | el billete |
| the bills | lȯz—ƀi(l)y̱étės ↓ | los billetes |
| the check | ėl—chékė ↓ | el cheque |
| *CASHIER* | | *CAJERO* |
| In bills or in a check? | ėmbi(l)y̱étes \| o̯enchékė ↓ | ¿En billetes o en cheque? |
| this | éstė ↓ | este |
| traveler | byȧhérȯ ↓ | viajero |
| *WHITE* | | *WHITE* |
| This traveler's check. | éstėchékė \| ƀyȧhérȯ ↓ | Este cheque viajero. |

| | | |
|---|---|---|
| then | ėntónșės ↓ | entonces |
| *CASHIER* | | *CAJERO* |
| Five to one, then. | àșíŋkȯpȯrúno̯ \| ėntónșės ↓ | A cinco por uno, entonces. |
| it | ló ↓ | lo (m.) |
| How do you want it? | kómȯlȯkyérė ↓ | ¿Cómo lo quiere? |
| the coin, the change | là—mȯnéđà ↓ | la moneda |
| *WHITE* | | *WHITE* |
| Eight in bills and two in change. | óchoėmbí(l)yétės ↑ iđóșėnmȯnéđà ↓ | Ocho en billetes y dos en moneda. |
| (it) costs (to cost) | kwéstà ↓ kȯstár ↓ | cuesta (costar) |
| How much does a taxi to the American Embassy cost? | kwántokwéstaùntáksį \| àlaėmbàháđàmėríkánà ↓ | ¿Cuánto cuesta un taxi a la Embajada Americana? |
| the peso | ėl—pésȯ ↓ | el peso |
| the pesos | lȯs—pésȯs ↓ | los pesos |
| less | ménȯs ↓ | menos |

| *CASHIER* | | *CAJERO* |
|---|---|---|
| Two pesos more or less. | dóspésòz ǀ máṣòménòs ↓ | Dos pesos más o menos. |
| for, in exchange for | pór ↓ | por |
| the information | là—imfòrmàṣyón ↓ | la información |
| *WHITE* | | *WHITE* |
| Thanks for the information. | gráṣyàs ǀ pòrla̯imfòrmàṣyón ↓ | Gracias por la información. |

## 3.10 Notes on the basic sentences

(1) As can be seen by comparing the literal translation in the build-up with the free translation given in this sentence, there is simply not any literal way to equate the English idea of 'liking' something with a word in Spanish which takes an object as the English word *like* does. Rather, one has to say that the object which he likes is 'pleasing' to him. Thus 'I like it' becomes 'It's pleasing to me'.

(2) *Agua mineral,* which literally means 'mineral water', may be carbonated 'soda water' or it may simply be purified drinking water. The terms used for purified drinking water differ from one area to another. Sometimes such water is called by the trade name of the company that distributes it, such as 'Agua Güitig' in Ecuador, or 'Agua Chuquitanta' in Peru. At other times it is called *agua cristal.* At any rate, one should be certain that he finds out *what* to ask for, since the public water supply is safe in only a very few places in the Spanish-speaking world.

(3) The forms /me/ and /la/ in the utterance /súbamela/ are called *clitic pronouns,* or, for short, just *clitics*. They will be discussed in detail beginning with Unit 10.

(4) Note that the word /ṣérka/ 'near' modifies a verb, but does not function as a phrase relator. The *English* word *near,* however, functions in both capacities. That is, in English we can say 'He didn't even get *near*' or 'He didn't even get near the house.' The Spanish equivalent of near is /ṣérka/, in the first example, but /ṣérka/ *plus* /de/, 'near of, near to', in the second.

(5) This idiom is especially useful to bear in mind. It is the equivalent of several English expressions. The closest is 'It is necessary to...', but the most frequent is 'You've got to...' or 'You have to...' or 'Ya gotta...', in all three of which the *you* does not refer to you personally, but really means something like 'One should...' or 'One ought to...'.

# 3.2 DRILLS AND GRAMMAR

## 3.21 Pattern drills

### 3.21.1 Gender of singular nouns and adjectives

A. PRESENTATION OF PATTERN

*ILLUSTRATIONS*

| | | |
|---|---|---|
| ______________ | 1 pásėme̯ė(l)líƀrȯ ↓ | Páseme *el libro.* |
| ______________ | 2 démėlȧplúmȧ ↓ | Déme *la pluma.* |
| ______________ | 3 tyéne̯ėunlápiṣ̯ ↑ | ¿Tiene *un lápiz?* |
| Do you have a pen? | 4 tyéneėunȧplúmȧ ↑ | ¿Tiene *una pluma?* |
| ______________ | 5 múchȯgústȯ ↓ | *Mucho gusto.* |
| (it) has (to have) | tyénė ↓ tėnér ↓ | tiene (tener) |
| ______________ | 6 tyénėmúchágwȧ ↑ | ¿Tiene *mucha agua?* |
| ______________ | 7 éstėchékėƀyȧhérȯ ↓ | Este *cheque viajero.* |
| ______________ | 8 dóndėstá \| la̯ėmbȧháđȧmėrikánȧ ↓ | ¿Dónde está *la Embajada Americana?* |

*EXTRAPOLATION*

| | Masculine article | Masculine noun | Feminine article | Feminine noun | |
|---|---|---|---|---|---|
| Definite | el | líbro | la | mésa | 'the' |
| Indefinite | un | líbro | una | mésa | 'a(n)' |

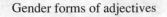

Gender forms of adjectives

| Masculine | Feminine |
|---|---|
| ........ o | ........ a |
| ........ e | |
| ........ C | |

*NOTES*

a. All Spanish nouns can be divided into two groups, or subclasses, called 'masculine' and 'feminine'.

b. Spanish articles, like many other Spanish adjectives, have distinct masculine and feminine forms.

c. The masculine form of adjectives appears only with masculine nouns, the feminine form with feminine nouns.

d. Many Spanish adjectives have gender marking endings (distinct masculine and feminine forms /múcho – múcha/); others, primarily those ending in /—e/ or in a consonant /minerál, trés, syéte/, etc.), do not have different endings when used with masculine or feminine nouns.

## 3.21.11 SUBSTITUTION DRILL (1)

Item substitution

Model Problem:

| Aid to Listening | Spanish Spelling |
|---|---|
| éstoesunlápis ↓ | Esto es un lápiz. |
| ____________ senisérò ↓ | ____________ cenicero. |

Model Answer:

| | |
|---|---|
| éstoesunsenisérò ↓ | Esto es un cenicero. |

(1) This and subsequent substitution drills are designed to elicit from the student slight variations on given sentences. These variations concern the structural relationships within the grammar point being drilled, such as the agreement between articles and nouns in the present drill. The model problem and answer are given only this once. All subsequent substitution drills are to be carried out in the same way.

The student should not need to look at the materials to do this drill orally. Both the *Aids to Listening* and the *Spanish Spelling* are given for all drills (on top half and bottom half of page, respectively); they are for the instructor to use in class and for the student to use in home study, not in class.

1 éso̯ėṣunȧplúmȧ

| | |
|---|---|
| _________ ȯtél ↓ | éso̯ėṣunȯtél ↓ |
| _________ bı̇(l)y̯étė ↓ | éso̯eṣumbı(l)y̯étė ↓ |
| _________ mésȧ ↓ | éso̯ėṣunȧmésȧ ↓ |
| _________ líƀrȯ ↓ | éso̯ėṣunlíƀrȯ ↓ |

2 ėṣésto̯u̇nȧƀėníđȧ ↑

| | |
|---|---|
| _________ mȯnéđȧ ↑ | ėṣésto̯u̇nȧmȯnéđȧ ↑ |
| _________ kwártȯ ↑ | ėṣésto̯u̇ŋkwártȯ ↑ |
| _________ sí(l)y̯ȧ ↑ | ėṣésto̯u̇nȧsí(l)y̯ȧ ↑ |
| _________ pésȯ ↑ | ėṣésto̯u̇mpésȯ ↑ |

---

1 Eso es una pluma.

| | |
|---|---|
| __________ hotel. | Eso es un hotel. |
| __________ billete. | Eso es un billete. |
| __________ mesa. | Eso es una mesa |
| __________ libro. | Eso es un libro. |

2 ¿Es esto una avenida?

| | |
|---|---|
| ¿ ______________ moneda? | ¿Es esto una moneda? |
| ¿ ______________ cuarto? | ¿Es esto un cuarto? |
| ¿ ______________ silla? | ¿Es esto una silla? |
| ¿ ______________ peso? | ¿Es esto un peso? |

3 dóndėstá | lȧkáhȧ ↓

| | |
|---|---|
| __________ sėn̯yór ↓ | dóndėstá \| e̯lsėn̯yór ↓ |
| __________ sėn̯yȯrítȧ ↓ | dóndėstá \| lȧsėn̯yȯrítȧ ↓ |
| __________ ėmbȧháđȧ ↓ | dóndėstá \| la̯embȧháđȧ ↓ |
| __________ ȧs(s̩)ėnór ↓ | dóndėstá \| e̯lȧs(s̩)ėnór ↓ |

4 grás̩yȧs | pȯrlȧplúmȧ ↓

| | |
|---|---|
| ___________ s̩ėnis̩érȯ ↓ | grás̩yȧs \| pȯrels̩ėnis̩érȯ ↓ |
| ___________ ımformȧs̩yón ↓ | grás̩yȧs \| pȯrla̯imfȯrmȧs̩yón ↓ |
| ___________ lápis̩ ↓ | grás̩yȧs \| pȯrė(l)lápis̩ ↓ |
| ___________ chékė ↓ | grás̩yȧs \| pȯrelchékė ↓ |

---

3 ¿Dónde está la caja?

| | |
|---|---|
| ¿ ___________ señor? | ¿Dónde está el señor? |
| ¿ ___________ señorita? | ¿Donde está la señorita? |
| ¿ ___________ Embajada? | ¿Dónde está la Embajada? |
| ¿ ___________ ascensor? | ¿Dónde está el ascensor? |

4 Gracias por la pluma.

| | |
|---|---|
| ___________ cenicero. | Gracias por el cenicero. |
| ___________ información. | Gracias por la información. |
| ___________ lápiz. | Gracias por el lápiz. |
| ___________ cheque. | Gracias por el cheque. |

5 ȧı́e̯stáe̯lágwȧ ↓

| | |
|---|---|
| __________ sėn̯yórȧ ↓ | ȧı́e̯stálasėn̯yórȧ ↓ |
| __________ mésȧ ↓ | ȧı́e̯stálamésȧ ↓ |
| __________ ėntráđȧ ↓ | ȧı́e̯stála̯ėntráđȧ ↓ |
| __________ táksi ↓ | ȧı́e̯stáe̯ltáksi ↓ |

6 dóndėstá | lȧsėn̯yóramėrıkánȧ ↓

| | |
|---|---|
| __________ sėn̯yór __________ ↓ | dóndėstá | e̯lsėn̯yóramėrıkánȯ ↓ |
| __________ sėn̯yȯrı́tȧ __________ ↓ | dóndėstá | lȧsėn̯yȯrı́tamėrıkánȧ ↓ |
| __________ ȯtél __________ ↓ | dóndėstá | e̯lȯtélamėrıkánȯ ↓ |
| __________ mȯnéđȧ__________ ↓ | dóndėstá | lȧmȯnéđamėrıkánȧ ↓ |

---

5 Ahí está el agua.

| | |
|---|---|
| __________ señora. | Ahí está la señora. |
| __________ mesa. | Ahí está la mesa. |
| __________ entrada. | Ahí está la entrada. |
| __________ taxi. | Ahí está el taxi. |

6 ¿Dónde está la señora americana?

| | |
|---|---|
| ¿ __________ señor __________ ? | ¿Dónde está el señor americano? |
| ¿ __________ señorita __________ ? | ¿Dónde está la señorita americana? |
| ¿ __________ hotel __________ ? | ¿Dónde está el hotel americano? |
| ¿ __________ moneda __________ ? | ¿Dónde está la moneda americana? |

| | | |
|---|---|---|
| 7 | ȧ́ıe̯stá \| lȧmízmȧsí(l)y̱ȧ ↓ | |
| | ____________ s̯ėnis̯éṙo ↓ | ȧ́ıe̯stá \| e̯lmízmȯs̯ėnis̯éṙo ↓ |
| | ____________ plúmȧ ↓ | ȧ́ıe̯stá \| lȧmízmȧplúmȧ ↓ |
| | ____________ sėn̯yór ↓ | ȧ́ıe̯stá \| e̯lmízmȯsėn̯yór ↓ |
| | ____________ sėn̯yórȧ ↓ | ȧ́ıe̯stá \| lȧmízmȧsėn̯yórȧ ↓ |
| 8 | ȧ́ıe̯stá \| e̯lótrȯchékė ↓ | |
| | ____________ ėntráđȧ ↓ | ȧ́ıe̯stá \| la̯ótra̯ėntráđȧ ↓ |
| | ____________ táksi ↓ | ȧ́ıe̯stá \| e̯lótrȯtáksi ↓ |
| | ____________ mésȧ ↓ | ȧ́ıe̯stá \| la̯ótrȧmésȧ ↓ |
| | ____________ líƀrȯ ↓ | ȧ́ıe̯stá \| e̯lótrȯlíƀrȯ ↓ |

---

| | | |
|---|---|---|
| 7 | Ahí está la misma silla. | |
| | ____________ cenicero. | Ahí está el mismo cenicero. |
| | ____________ pluma. | Ahí está la misma pluma. |
| | ____________ señor. | Ahí está el mismo señor. |
| | ____________ señora. | Ahí está la misma señora. |
| 8 | Ahí está el otro cheque. | |
| | ____________ entrada. | Ahí está la otra entrada. |
| | ____________ taxi. | Ahí está el otro taxi. |
| | ____________ mesa. | Ahí está la otra mesa. |
| | ____________ libro. | Ahí está el otro libro. |

9 tyéne̯ | u̇nȧplúmaƀwénȧ ↓

| | | |
|---|---|---|
| ____________ lápı̇s̯ ______________ ↓ | | tyéne̯ \| u̇nlápı̇z̯ƀwénȯ ↓ |
| ____________ sı̇(l)y̯ȧ ____________ ↓ | | tyéne̯ \| u̇nȧsı̇(l)y̯ȧƀwénȧ ↓ |
| ____________ lı́ƀrȯ ______________ ↓ | | tyéne̯ \| u̇nlı́ƀrȯƀwénȯ ↓ |
| ____________ mésȧ ______________ ↓ | | tyéne̯ \| u̇nȧmésȧƀwénȧ ↓ |

10 téŋgȯ | trézđı́azmás ↓

| | | |
|---|---|---|
| ____________ tárđėz ____________ ↓ | | téŋgȯ \| trésťárđėzmás ↓ |
| ____________ bı(l)y̯étėz __________ ↓ | | téŋgȯ \| trézƀı(l)y̯étėzmás ↓ |
| ____________ nóchėz ____________ ↓ | | téŋgȯ \| tréznóchėzmás ↓ |
| ____________ đólarėz ____________ ↓ | | téŋgȯ \| trézđólarėzmás ↓ |

---

9 Tiene una pluma buena.

| | | |
|---|---|---|
| ____________ lápiz ______________ . | | Tiene un lápiz bueno. |
| ____________ silla ______________ . | | Tiene un libro bueno. |
| ____________ mesa ______________ . | | Tiene una mesa buena. |

10 Tengo tres días más.

| | | |
|---|---|---|
| ____________ tardes ______________ . | | Tengo tres tardes más. |
| ____________ billetes ____________ . | | Tengo tres billetes más. |
| ____________ noches ____________ . | | Tengo tres noches más. |
| ____________ dólares ____________ . | | Tengo tres dólares más. |

| | |
|---|---|
| 11 tyénė \| ṣıŋkȯnóchėzmás ↓ | |
| ______ đíȧz ______ ↓ | tyénė \| ṣıŋkȯđíȧzmás ↓ |
| ______ tárđėz ______ ↓ | tyénė \| ṣıŋkȯtárđėzmás ↓ |
| ______ bı̇(l)y̯étėz ______ ↓ | tyénė \| ṣıŋkȯbı̇(l)y̯étėzmás ↓ |
| ______ đólȧrėz ______ ↓ | tyénė \| ṣıŋkȯđólȧrėzmás ↓ |

## 3.21.12 RESPONSE DRILL

| | |
|---|---|
| 1 ėstála̯ėntráđa̯ \| ȧlȧđėréchȧ ↑ o̯ala̯ıṣkyérđȧ ↓ | ėstálȧđėréchȧ ↓ |
| 2 kyére̯u̇nlápıṣ ↑ o̯u̇nȧplúmȧ ↓ | kyéro̯u̇nȧplúmȧ ↓ |
| 3 kyére̯u̇nlíbrȯ ↑ o̯u̇nchékė ↓ | kyéro̯u̇nchékė ↓ |

---

| | |
|---|---|
| 11 Tiene cinco noches más. | |
| ______ días ______ . | Tiene cinco días más. |
| ______ tardes ______ . | Tiene cinco tardes más. |
| ______ billetes ______ . | Tiene cinco billetes más. |
| ______ dólares ______ . | Tiene cinco dólares más. |

| | |
|---|---|
| 1 ¿Está la entrada a la derecha o a la izquierda? | Está a la derecha. |
| 2 ¿Quiere un lápiz o una pluma? | Quiero una pluma. |
| 3 ¿Quiere un libro o un cheque? | Quiero un cheque. |

| | | | |
|---|---|---|---|
| | 4 | tyéne̯umbi(l)y̯éte ↑ o̯únamonéđa ↓ | téŋgo̯unamonéđa ↓ |
| | 5 | áiayunseny̯ór ↑ o̯únaseny̯óra ↓ | áyunaseny̯óra ↓ |
| [enelkwárto] | 6 | dóndestálasí(l)y̯a ↓ | está̯enelkwárto ↓ |
| [enelsentro] | 7 | dónde̯áyunotél ↓ | áyunotel \| enelséntro ↓ |
| [laplúma] | 8 | legústa̯e(l)lápis ↑ | nó ↓ megústalaplúma ↓ |
| [enelséntro] | 9 | estalaseny̯óra \| đemolínakí ↑ | nó ↓ está \| e̯nelséntro ↓ |
| [unlápis] | 10 | tyéne̯unaplúma ↑ | nó ↓ téŋgo̯unlápis ↓ |
| | 11 | legústa̯elséntro ↑ | sí ↓ megústamúcho ↓ |
| | 12 | estálaseny̯órakí ↑ | sí ↓ si̯estákí ↓ |
| | 13 | áyunamésaí ↑ | sí ↓ siáy ↓ |

---

| | | | |
|---|---|---|---|
| | 4 | ¿Tiene un billete o una moneda? | Tengo una moneda. |
| | 5 | ¿Ahí hay un señor o una señora? | Hay una señora. |
| (en el cuarto) | 6 | ¿Dónde está la silla? | Está en el cuarto. |
| (en el centro) | 7 | ¿Dónde hay un hotel? | Hay un hotel en el centro. |
| (la pluma) | 8 | ¿Le gusta el lápiz? | No, me gusta la pluma. |
| (en el centro) | 9 | ¿Está la señora de Molina aquí? | No, está en el centro. |
| (un lápiz) | 10 | ¿Tiene una pluma? | No, tengo un lápiz. |
| | 11 | ¿Le gusta el centro? | Sí, me gusta mucho. |
| | 12 | ¿Está la señora aquí? | Sí, sí está aquí. |
| | 13 | ¿Hay una mesa ahí? | Sí, sí hay. |

## 3.21.13 TRANSLATION DRILL

| | | |
|---|---|---|
| 1 That's a coin. | ésoėsụnamonéđȧ ↓ | Eso es una moneda. |
| 2 No, this is not a bill. | nó ↓ éstònoės \| ùmbi(l)yétė ↓ | No, esto no es un billete. |
| 3 The young lady is at the Embassy. | làsėnyórıtạ \| ėstáenlaėmbȧháđȧ ↓ | La señorita está en la embajada. |
| 4 Do you want a chair? | kyéreunasí(l)yȧ ↑ | ¿Quiere una silla? |
| 5 Do you have the check or not? | tyénėlchéke ↑ ònó ↓ | ¿Tiene el cheque o no? |
| 6 The teller's window is to the left. | làkáha \| ėstálaiskyérđȧ ↓ | La caja está a la izquierda. |
| 7 The Embassy is not far from here. | laėmbȧháđȧ \| nóestáléhȯz \| đeàkí ↓ | La embajada no está lejos de aquí. |
| 8 I want you to meet a young lady. | kyéropresėntárle \| aùnàsėnyórıtà ↓ | Quiero presentarle a una señorita. |
| 9 Do you like Columbus Avenue? | lėgústȧ \| làbėníđȧkólȯn ↑ | ¿Le gusta la Avenida Colón? |
| 10 The bathroom is to the right. | ėlbányo \| ėstálađėréchȧ ↓ | El baño está a la derecha. |
| 11 I have a room in the hotel. | téŋgouŋkwárto \| ėnėlòtél ↓ | Tengo un cuarto en el hotel. |
| 12 Do you want a pencil? | kyéreunlápıs ↑ | ¿Quiere un lápiz? |
| 13 Do you need a pen? | nėsėsítaunaplúmȧ ↑ | ¿Necesita una pluma? |
| 14 Where's there a chair? | dóndeáy \| ùnasí(l)yȧ ↓ | ¿Dónde hay una silla? |
| 15 Is the hotel downtown? | ėstáelótel \| ėnėlséntrȯ ↑ | ¿Está el hotel en el centro? |

## B. DISCUSSION OF PATTERN

In Spanish there is a large class of words to which the label *noun* can be applied. A noun can be identified by the fact that it can have endings added to it to change its reference from one to more than one (as explained in Unit 4) and by the fact that it belongs to one of two subclasses, called *masculine* and *feminine*. While a noun can change for nunber, it has only one gender or the other, which is inherent and does not change. The terms masculine and feminine are convenient but more or less arbitrary tags to represent grammatical categories and have nothing to do with gender or sex in the real world. Nouns that have appeared so far include /el—gústo, el—lápış, la—béş, el—lĭbro, el—şenışéro, el—espaṉyól, la—sí(l)ya, la—embaháda, el—báṉyo, el—şéntro, el—otél, el—kwárto, el—ágwa, la—abenída, el—táksı, el—as(ş)ensór, la—káha, el—píso, la—entráda, el—chéke, el—dolar, el—kámbyo, el—bi(l)yéte, la—monéda, la—imformaşyón/.

You will notice that the word /el/ or the word /la/ precedes each noun. These are the singular forms of the definite article: /el/ is masculine, and /la/ is feminine. When memorizing each noun it is well to memorize its gender at the same time. Usually this can be done by memorizing the appropriate form of the definite article with the noun. ( /el—ágwa/ is an exception, since it is actually feminine.) The words /el/ and /la/, called *definite articles,* are usually the equivalent of English 'the'. The words /un/ and /una/, called *indefinite articles,* are usually the equivalent of English 'a' or 'an'.

The articles, and other adjectives which change for gender, *must appear in the same gender category as the noun* with which they are associated. This is called *gender agreement,* and the associated adjective is said to *agree with* the noun. Thus adjectives differ from nouns in having two gender forms in order to agree with nouns from either subclass.

There are two subclasses of adjectives—those which show a gender change, and those for which distinct gender forms are only potential. In certain circumstances the latter subclass *can* show a change (see Unit 39 for a discussion of diminutives) but usually they have the same endings for masculine or feminine agreement. Usually the forms which change have a final /—o/ for masculine and /—a/ for feminine forms, though sometimes the masculine form may end in a consonant, as /espaṉyól – espaṉyóla, ınglés – ınglésa/ when these are used as adjectives.

Other adjectives, like /minerál, séys, syéte/, which end in /—e/ or in a consonant do not change. Thus:

| | |
|---|---|
| múcho-gústo | múcha-imformaşyón |
| ménos-gústo | ménos-imformaşyón |

Note that in Spanish adjectives usually *follow* the noun modified /embaháda—amerikána, chéke—byahéro/ etc. Some adjectives, like the articles /el, la/, etc. always precede: /lạ—abenída, dós—pésos/, etc. These are usually 'number' or 'limiting' adjectives. Some adjectives, however, may follow or precede the noun: /plúma—bwéna, bwéna—plúma/.

## 3.22 REPLACEMENT DRILLS (1)

Model Problem:

tyéne̯u̇nlápis̯ ↑

__________ plúmȧ ↑

kyére̯ __________ ↑

Model Answer:

tyéne̯u̇nȧplúmȧ ↑

kyére̯u̇nȧplúmȧ ↑

---

Model Problem:

¿Tiene un lápiz?

¿ __________ pluma?

¿Quiere __________ ?

Model Answer:

¿Tiene una pluma?

¿Quiere una pluma?

(1) This and subsequent replacement drills are designed as a fast moving substitution-type drill on selected basic sentences, with the substitutions occurring in different parts of the sentence, each being a single change—plus any obligatory associated change(s)—of the sentence immediately preceding.

The student should not need to look at the materials to do this drill orally.

A kómȯe̯stáu̯stéđ ↓

| | |
|---|---|
| 1 _________ lȧsėn̯yórȧ ↓ | kómȯe̯stá ǀ lȧsėn̯yórȧ ↓ |
| 2 _________ sėn̯yór ↓ | kómȯe̯stá ǀ e̯lsėn̯yór ↓ |
| 3 dóndė _________ ↓ | dóndėstá ǀ e̯lsėn̯yór ↓ |
| 4 _________ sėn̯yȯrítȧ ↓ | dóndėstá ǀ lȧsėn̯yȯrítȧ ↓ |
| 5 kómȯ _________ ↓ | kómȯe̯stá ǀ lȧsėn̯yȯrítȧ ↓ |
| 6 _________ e̯lsėn̯yórhwáyt ↓ | kómȯe̯stá ǀ e̯lsėn̯yórhwáyt ↓ |
| 7 dóndė _________ ↓ | dóndėstá ǀ e̯lsėn̯yórhwáyt ↓ |

---

A ¿Cómo está usted?

| | |
|---|---|
| 1 ¿ _________ la señora? | ¿Cómo está la señora? |
| 2 ¿ _________ señor? | ¿Cómo está el señor? |
| 3 ¿Dónde _________ ? | ¿Dónde está el señor? |
| 4 ¿ _________ señorita? | ¿Dónde está la señorita? |
| 5 ¿Cómo _________ ? | ¿Cómo está la señorita? |
| 6 ¿ _________ el Sr. White? | ¿Cómo está el Sr. White? |
| 7 ¿Dónde _________ ? | ¿Dónde está el Sr. White? |

B kyéreustéđ | ágwàminèrál ↑

| | |
|---|---|
| 1 ________________ álgòmás ↑ | kyéreustéđ \| álgòmás ↑ |
| 2 _______ èlsènyórhwáyt \| _______ ↑ | kyérèlsènyórhwáyt \| álgòmás ↑ |
| 3 nèsèsíta _____________________ ↑ | nèsèsítaèlsènyórhwáyt \| álgòmás ↑ |
| 4 __________ ùstéđ _____________ ↑ | nèsèsítaùstéđ \| álgòmás ↑ |
| 5 ________________ álgò ↑ | nèsèsítaùstéđ \| álgò ↑ |
| 6 díse _____________________ ↑ | díseùstéđ \| álgò ↑ |
| 7 __________________ ƀwénòzđías ↑ | díseùstéđ \| ƀwénòzđías ↑ |

---

B ¿Quiere usted agua mineral?

| | |
|---|---|
| 1 ¿ _____________________ algo más? | ¿Quiere usted algo más? |
| 2 ¿ _________ el Sr. White _________ ? | ¿Quiere el Sr. White algo más? |
| 3 ¿Necesita _____________________ ? | ¿Necesita el Sr. White algo más? |
| 4 ¿ ___________ usted ___________ ? | ¿Necesita usted algo más? |
| 5 ¿ _________________________ algo? | ¿Necesita usted algo? |
| 6 ¿Dice ________________________ ? | ¿Dice usted algo? |
| 7 ¿ _________________ 'buenos días'? | ¿Dice usted 'buenos días'? |

CD 2
Tape 2B

C nėṣėsíta̯ | álgȯmás ↑

1 ________ únȯ ________ ↑ nėṣėsíta̯ | únȯmás ↑

2 tyéne̯ ________________ ↑ tyéne̯ | únȯmás ↑

3 ________ đóz ________ ↑ tyéne̯ | đózmás ↑

4 kyérė ________________ ↑ kyérė | đózmás ↑

5 ________________ ménȯs ↑ kyérė | đózménȯs ↑

6 áy ________________ ↑ áyđózménȯs ↑

7 __________ tréz _______ ↑ áy | trézménȯs ↑

---

C ¿Necesita algo más?

1 ¿ ________ uno ________ ? ¿Necesita uno más?

2 ¿Tiene ________________ ? ¿Tiene uno más?

3 ¿ ________dos __________? ¿Tiene dos más?

4 ¿Quiere ______________ ? ¿Quiere dos más?

5 ¿ ________________ menos? ¿Quiere dos menos?

6 ¿Hay ________________ ? ¿Hay dos menos?

7 ¿ ________ tres ________ ? ¿Hay tres menos?

D ėstȧ́ | le̯embȧhȧ́đȧmėrikȧ́nȧ | ṣérkȧđe̯ȧkı́ ↑

1 _______ e̯lȯtél _______________ ↑ — ėstȧ́ | e̯lȯtėlȧmėrikȧ́nȯ | ṣérkȧđe̯ȧkı́ ↑

2 _________ ıŋglés ___________ ↑ — ėstȧ́ | e̯lȯtėlıŋglés | ṣérkȧđe̯ȧkı ↑

3 ___________ léhȯz __________ ↑ — ėstȧ́ | e̯lȯtėlıŋglés | léhȯzđe̯ȧkı́ ↑

4 __________________ đe̯ȧı́ ↑ — ėstȧ́ | e̯lȯtėlıŋglés | léhȯzđe̯ȧı́ ↑

5 _______ le̯embȧhȧ́đȧ ___________ ↑ — ėstȧ́ | le̯embȧhȧ́đȧıŋglésȧ | léhȯzđe̯ȧı ↑

6 _________ ėspȧṇyólȧ _________ ↑ — ėstȧ́ | le̯embȧhȧ́đe̯ȧespȧṇyólȧ | léhȯzđe̯ȧı́ ↑

7 _______ ȯtél _______________ ↑ — ėstȧ́ | e̯lȯtėlėspȧṇyól | léhȯzđe̯ȧı́ ↑

---

D ¿Está la Embajada Americana cerca de aquí?

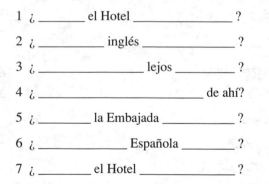

1 ¿ _______ el Hotel _______________ ? — ¿Está el Hotel Americano cerca de aquí?

2 ¿ _________ inglés _____________ ? — ¿Está el Hotel Inglés cerca de aquí?

3 ¿ ______________ lejos ________ ? — ¿Está el Hotel Inglés lejos de aquí?

4 ¿ ______________________ de ahí? — ¿Está el Hotel Inglés lejos de ahí?

5 ¿ _______ la Embajada __________ ? — ¿Está la Embajada Inglesa lejos de ahí?

6 ¿ ____________ Española _______ ? — ¿Está la Embajada Española lejos de ahí?

7 ¿ _______ el Hotel _____________ ? — ¿Está el Hotel Español lejos de ahí?

E dóndėstálȧkáhȧ ↓

1 ___________ ȯtél ↓ — dóndėstá͜elȯtél ↓

2 ___________ sėn͜yórȧ ↓ — dóndėstálȧsėn͜yórȧ ↓

3 kómȯ ____________ ↓ — kómȯ͜estálȧsėn͜yórȧ ↓

4 ___________ u̇stéđ ↓ — kómȯ͜está͜ustéđ ↓

5 ____________ hwán ↓ — kómȯ͜estáhwán ↓

6 dóndė ___________ ↓ — dóndėstáhwán ↓

7 __________ la͜ėntráđȧ ↓ — dóndėstála͜ėntráđȧ ↓

---

E ¿Dónde está la caja?

1 ¿ ______________ hotel? — ¿Dónde está el hotel?

2 ¿ _____________ señora? — ¿Dónde está la señora?

3 ¿Cómo _____________ ? — ¿Cómo está la señora?

4 ¿ ____________ usted? — ¿Cómo está usted?

5 ¿ ____________ Juan? — ¿Cómo está Juan?

ó ¿Dónde _____________ ? — ¿Dónde está Juan?

7 ¿ ___________ la entrada? — ¿Dónde está la entrada?

F kómȯlȯkyérė ↓

| | |
|---|---|
| 1 ______________ đís̯ė ↓ | kómȯlȯđís̯ė ↓ |
| 2 _________________ nės̯ėsítȧ ↓ | kómȯlȯnės̯ėsítȧ ↓ |
| 3 dóndė ___________________ ↓ | dóndėlȯnės̯ėsítȧ ↓ |
| 4 kóŋké ___________________ ↓ | kóŋkélȯnės̯ėsítȧ ↓ |
| 5 ___________________ kyérė ↓ | kóŋkélȯkyérė ↓ |
| 6 dóndė __________________ ↓ | dóndėlȯkyérė ↓ |
| 7 ___________________ tyénė ↓ | dóndėlȯtyénė ↓ |

---

F ¿Cómo lo quiere ?

| | |
|---|---|
| 1 ¿ ________________ dice? | ¿Cómo lo dice? |
| 2 ¿ ________________ necesita? | ¿Cómo lo necesita? |
| 3 ¿Dónde ________________ ? | ¿Dónde lo necesita? |
| 4 ¿Con qué ________________ ? | ¿Con qué lo necesita? |
| 5 ¿ __________________ quiere? | ¿Con qué lo quiere? |
| 6 ¿Dónde ________________ ? | ¿Dónde lo quiere? |
| 7 ¿ __________________ tiene? | ¿Dónde lo tiene? |

## 3.23 VARIATION DRILLS [1]

A démėlȧplúmȧ ↓ — Déme la pluma.

| | | |
|---|---|---|
| 1 Give me the book. | démė(l)líƀrȯ ↓ | Déme el libro. |
| 2 Pass me the pen. | pásėmėlȧplúmȧ ↓ | Páseme la pluma. |
| 3 Give us the book. | dénȯṣe(l)líƀrȯ ↓ | Dénos el libro. |
| 4 Give us that. | dénȯṣésȯ ↓ | Dénos eso. |
| 5 Take us downtown. | (l)y̯éƀėnȯṣalṣéntrȯ ↓ | Llévenos al centro. |
| 6 Take me downtown. | (l)y̯éƀėme̯alṣéntrȯ ↓ | Lléveme al centro. |
| 7 Take me to the hotel. | (l)y̯éƀėme̯alȯtél ↓ | Lléveme al hotel. |

(1) This and subsequent variation drills consist of translations of sentences similar to and within the basic structural frame of selected basic sentences.

The student should cover the Spanish answers while doing this drill orally.

| | | | |
|---|---|---|---|
| B | lėgústa̯elkwártȯ ↑ | | ¿Le gusta el cuarto? |
| | 1 Do you like the book? | lėgústa̯ė(l)líƀrȯ ↑ | ¿Le gusta el libro? |
| | 2 Do you like the hotel? | lėgústa̯ėlótėl ↑ | ¿Le gusta el hotel? |
| | 3 Do you like the Embassy? | lėgústala̯ėmbaháđȧ ↑ | ¿Le gusta la embajada? |
| | 4 Do you like the avenue? | lėgústalȧƀėníđȧ ↑ | ¿Le gusta la avenida? |
| | 5 Do you like (the) Spanish? | lėgústa̯ėlėspanyól ↑ | ¿Le gusta el español? |
| | 6 Do you like (the) English? | lėgústa̯ėliŋglés ↑ | ¿Le gusta el inglés? |
| | 7 Do you like (the) Miss Molina? | lėgústalasėnyorítamolínȧ ↑ | ¿Le gusta la señorita Molina? |
| C | nó ↓ ėstaléhȯs ↓ | | No, está lejos. |
| | 1 No, it's near. | nó ↓ ėstasérkȧ ↓ | No, está cerca. |
| | 2 No, it's to the right. | nó ↓ ėstálȧđėréchȧ ↓ | No, está a la derecha. |
| | 3 No, it's to the left. | nó ↓ ėstála̯iskyérđȧ ↓ | No, está a la izquierda. |
| | 4 No, it's up ahead. | nó ↓ ėstáđėlántė ↓ | No, está adelante. |

| | | | |
|---|---|---|---|
| | 5 Yes, it's at the entrance. | sí ↓ ėstálạėntráđȧ ↓ | Sí, está a la entrada. |
| | 6 Yes, it's here. | sí ↓ ėstakí ↓ | Sí, está aquí. |
| | 7 Yes, it's there. | sí ↓ ėstaí ↓ | Sí, está ahí. |
| D | áykėtomár ǀ ùntáksı ↑ | | ¿Hay que tomar un taxi? |
| | 1 Is it necessary to take a room? | áykėtomár ǀ ùŋkwártȯ ↑ | ¿Hay que tomar un cuarto? |
| | 2 Is it necessary to take the elevator? | áykėtomár ǀ ėlás(ș)ėnsór ↑ | ¿Hay que tomar el ascensor? |
| | 3 Is it necessary to take anything else? | áykėtomár ǀ álgomás ↑ | ¿Hay que tomar algo más? |
| | 4 Is it necessary to say that? | áykėđėșír ǀ ésȯ ↑ | ¿Hay que decir eso? |
| | 5 Is it necessary to translate that? | áykėtrȧđușír ǀ ésȯ ↑ | ¿Hay que traducir eso? |
| | 6 Is it necessary to cash a check? | áykėkȧmbyár ǀ ùnchékė ↑ | ¿Hay que cambiar un cheque? |
| | 7 Is it necessary to have traveler's checks? | áykėtėnér ǀ chékezƀyȧhérȯs ↑ | ¿Hay que tener cheques viajeros? |

| | | |
|---|---|---|
| **E** | pwéđė \| kȧmbyármȩ \| éstėchékė ↑ | ¿Puede cambiarme este cheque? |
| 1 Can you break this bill for me? | pwéđė \| kȧmbyármȩ \| éstėƀi(l)yétė ↑ | ¿Puede cambiarme este billete? |
| 2 Can you change one dollar for me? | pwéđė \| kȧmbyármȩ \| úndólȧr ↑ | ¿Puede cambiarme un dólar? |
| 3 Can you change the pen for me? | pwéđė \| kȧmbyármȩ \| lȧplúmȧ ↑ | ¿Puede cambiarme la pluma? |
| 4 Can you take me to the hotel? | pwéđė \| (l)y̯ėƀármȩ \| ȧlòtél ↑ | ¿Puede llevarme al hotel? |
| 5 Can you introduce Mr. Molina to me? | pwéđė \| prėsėntármȩ \| ȧlsėn̯yórmólınȧ ↑ | ¿Puede presentarme al señor Molina? |
| 6 Can you tell me that? | pwéđė \| đėșírmȩ \| ésȯ ↑ | ¿Puede decirme eso? |
| 7 Can you repeat that for me? | pwéđė \| rrėpėtírmȩ \| ésȯ ↑ | ¿Puede repetirme eso? |

| | | |
|---|---|---|
| **F** | kwántȯkwéstạuntáksı̯ \| ȧlạėmbȧháđȧmėrıkánȧ ↓ | ¿Cuánto cuesta un taxi a la Embajada Americana? |
| 1 How much does a taxi to the Embassy cost? | kwántȯkwéstạuntáksı̯ \| ȧlạėmbȧháđȧ ↓ | ¿Cuánto cuesta un taxi a la Embajada? |
| 2 How much does a taxi to the hotel cost? | kwántȯkwéstạuntáksı̯ \| ȧlȯtél ↓ | ¿Cuánto cuesta un taxi al hotel? |

| | | |
|---|---|---|
| 3 How much does a taxi to Columbus Avenue cost? | kwántȯkwésta̯u̇ntáksı̯ \| ȧlȧƀėníđȧkȯlón ↓ | ¿Cuánto cuesta un taxi a la Avenida Colón? |
| 4 How much does a taxi downtown cost? | kwántȯkwésta̯u̇ntáksı̯ \| ȧlşéntrȯ ↓ | ¿Cuánto cuesta un taxi al centro? |
| 5 How much does the book cost? | kwántȯkwésta̯ė(l)líƀrȯ ↓ | ¿Cuánto cuesta el libro? |
| 6 How much does the room cost? | kwántȯkwésta̯ėlkwártȯ ↓ | ¿Cuánto cuesta el cuarto? |
| 7 How much does it cost? | kwántȯkwéstȧ ↓ | ¿Cuánto cuesta? |

## 3.3 CONVERSATION STIMULUS (1)

### NARRATIVE 1

| | | |
|---|---|---|
| 1 Mr. White is at the Columbus Hotel. | ėlsėn̥yórhwáyt ǀ ėstá ǀ e̯ṇėlȯtélkȯlón ↓ | El Sr. White está en el Hotel Colón. |
| 2 He has a room there. | tyéne̯uŋkwártọ ǀ àí ↓ | Tiene un cuarto ahí. |
| 3 He likes his room. | lėgústa̯ ǀ ėlkwártȯ ↓ | Le gusta el cuarto. |

(1) This and subsequent conversation stimuli are designed to help bridge the gap between pattern-drill sentence practice and actual conversation. They are divided into one, two, or more combinations of narratives and dialogs. The narrative part is a translation drill of sentences in a sequence context, which sets the stage for the dialog following. The dialog is elicited from the participants by the teacher, acting as a prompter for players who have not learned their lines very well. He tells each what he should say (until such time as the lines are memorized), making sure that the participants address each other, talk naturally and meaningfully, and fully understand what they are saying.

The student should cover the Spanish answers while doing the narratives orally. He should not need to look at the materials to do the dialogs orally.

The following expressions are necessary for the prompting or direction of the dialogs.

| | | |
|---|---|---|
| Tell him (that)... | dígalė ǀ kė... | Dígale que ... |
| Answer him (that)... | kȯntéstėlė ǀ kė... | Contéstele que ... |
| Ask him if... | prėgúntėlė ǀ si... | Pregúntele si.... |
| Tell him again (that)... | rrėpítalė ǀ kė... | Repítale que... |

| | | |
|---|---|---|
| 4 He needs something. | nèsèsítálgò ↓ | Necesita algo. |
| 5 He needs to change a twenty dollar bill. | nèsèsítákámbyár \| ùmbi(l)yétè \| đèbéyntèđólàrès ↓ | Necesita cambiar un billete de veinte dólares. |
| 6 The cashier's desk is to the right. | làkáha \| èstáláđèréchà ↓ | La caja está a la derecha. |

## DIALOG 1

| | | |
|---|---|---|
| Juan, dígale 'buenos días' a la señorita. | bwénózđíàs \| sènyòrítà ↓ | Juan: Buenos días, señorita. |
| Srta., contéstele 'buenos dias' al Sr. White y pregúntele si le gusta el cuarto. | bwénózđíàs \| sènyórhwáyt ↓ | Srta.: Buenos días, Sr. White. |
| | lègústaélkwártò ↑ | ¿Le gusta el cuarto? |
| Juan, contéstele que sí, que le gusta mucho, y que gracias. | sí ↓ mègústámúchò \| grásyàs ↓ | Juan: Sí, me gusta mucho, gracias. |
| Srta., pregúntele si necesita algo. | nèsèsítálgo ↑ | Srta.: ¿Necesita algo? |
| Juan, dígale que sí, que Ud. quiere cambiar un billete de veinte dólares. Pregúntele que dónde está la caja. | sí ↓ kyérókàmbyár \| ùmbi(l)yétè \| đèbéyntèđólàrès ↓ dóndèstálàkáhà ↓ | Juan: Sí, quiero cambiar un billete de veinte dólares. ¿Dónde está la caja? |

| | | |
|---|---|---|
| Srta., digale que está abí, a la derecha. | ėstaí \| àlàđėréchà ↓ | Srta.: Está ahí, a la derecha. |
| Juan, digale que muchas gracias. | múchȧzgrás̥yȧs ↓ | Juan: Muchas gracias. |

## NARRATIVE 2

| | | |
|---|---|---|
| 1 He goes there. | baí ↓ | Va ahí. |
| 2 The rate of exchange is three to one. | ėlkámbyo̯ėstá \| a̯trésporúnȯ ↓ | El cambio está a tres por uno. |
| 3 He wants to change twenty dollars. | kyérėkȧmbyár \| ƀeyntėđólȧrės ↓ | Quiere cambiar veinte dólares. |
| 4 And how does he want it? | ikómolȯkyérė ↑ | Y ¿cómo lo quiere? |
| 5 He wants two twenties and two tens. | kyérė \| đózđėƀeyntė̯ \| iđózđėđyés̥ ↓ | Quiere dos de veinte y dos de diez. |

## DIALOG 2

| | | |
|---|---|---|
| Juan, dígale al cajero que dispense y pregúntele que a cómo está el cambio. | dispénsė ↓ ȧkómȯ ǀ e̯stáe̯lkámbyȯ ↓ | Juan: Dispense, ¿a cómo está el cambio? |
| Cajero, contéstele que está a tres por uno. | ėstátrésporúnȯ ↓ | Caj: Está a tres por uno. |
| Juan, pregúntele si puede cambiarle este billete. | pwéđėkȧmbyármésteƀı(l)y̯étė ↑ | Juan: ¿Puede cambiarme este billete? |
| Cajero, pregúntele que de cuánto es. | dėkwánto̯és ↓ | Caj: ¿De cuánto es? |
| Juan, contéstele que es de veinte dólares. | ézđėƀéyntėđólȧrės ↓ | Juan: Es de veinte dólares. |
| Cajero, dígale que con mucho gusto, y pregúntele que cómo lo quiere. | kónmúchȯgústȯ ↓ kómȯlȯkyérė ↓ | Caj: Con mucho gusto. ¿Cómo lo quiere? |
| Juan, dígale que dos de veinte y dos de diez, por favor. | dózđėƀéyntė ↑ iđózđėđyés̯ ǀ pȯrfȧƀór ↓ | Juan: Dos de veinte y dos de diez, por favor. |
| Cajero, contéstele que cómo no, que aquí tiene. | kómȯnó ↓ ȧkítyénė ↓ | Caj: Cómo no, aquí tiene. |

## NARRATIVE 3

| | | |
|---|---|---|
| 1 He goes to the American Embassy in a taxi. | bála̯èmbàháđàmèrikána̯ \| èntáksi ↓ | Va a la Embajada Americana en taxi. |
| 2 The Embassy isn't far. | la̯èmbàháđànóe̯stáléhòs ↓ | La Embajada no está lejos. |
| 3 It's on Columbus Avenue. | èstá \| e̯nlàƀèníđàkòlón ↓ | Está en la Avenida Colón. |
| 4 The taxi costs two and a quarter. | èltáksı \| kwéstà \| đózƀéyntıs̯íŋkò ↓ | El taxi cuesta dos veinticinco. |

## DIALOG 3

| | | |
|---|---|---|
| Juan, dígale al chofer que lo lleve a la Embajada Americana. | (l)yéƀème̯ \| àla̯èmbàháđàmèrıkánà ↓ | Juan: Lléveme a la Embajada Americana. |
| Chofer, dígale que perdón, que cómo dice. | pèrđón ↓ kómòđís̯e ↑ | Chof: Perdón, ¿cómo dice? |
| Juan, repítale que a la Embajada Americana, y pregúntele si está muy lejos de aquí. | àla̯èmbàháđàmèrikánà ↓ èstámùyléhòz \| đe̯ákı ↑ | Juan: A la Embajada Americana. ¿Está muy lejos de aquí? |
| Chofer, contéstele que no mucho, que está en la Avenida Colón. | nómúchò ↓ èstá \| e̯nlàbènídàkòlón ↓ | Chof: No mucho, está en la Avenida Colón. |

| | | |
|---|---|---|
| Juan, pregúntele que cuánto es. | kwántọ̑és ↓ | Juan: ¿Cuánto es? |
| Chofer, dígale que dos veinticinco. | dózƀéyntịsíŋkȯ ↓ | Chof: Dos veinticinco. |
| Juan, dígale que aquí tiene, que gracias. | ȧkítyénė ↓  grásỵȧs ↓ | Juan: Aquí tiene, gracias. |
| Chofer, dígale que gracias a él. | grásỵȧsạ̑ủstéđ \| sėnỵór ↓ | Chof: Gracias a usted, señor. |

**End of Tape 2B**

**End of CD 2**

# 4.1 BASIC SENTENCES

## White meets Molina at the Embassy

Mr. White arrives at the Embassy by taxi and pays the driver.

<table>
<tr><th>English Spelling</th><th>Aid to Listening</th><th>Spanish Spelling</th></tr>
<tr><td>(I) owe (to owe)</td><td>déƀȯ ↓ dėƀér ↓</td><td>debo (deber)</td></tr>
<tr><td>to you (I) owe</td><td>lė—đéƀȯ ↓</td><td>le debo</td></tr>
<tr><td>WHITE</td><td></td><td>WHITE</td></tr>
<tr><td>How much do I owe you?</td><td>kwántȯlėđéƀȯ ↓</td><td>¿Cuánto le debo?</td></tr>
<tr><td>(they) are (to be)</td><td>són ↓ sér ↓</td><td>son (ser)</td></tr>
<tr><td>the chauffeur</td><td>ėl—chȯfér ↓</td><td>el chofer</td></tr>
<tr><td>TAXI DRIVER</td><td></td><td>CHOFER DE TAXI</td></tr>
<tr><td>It's four pesos.</td><td>sóŋkwátrȯpésȯs ↓</td><td>Son cuatro pesos.</td></tr>
<tr><td>(they) told, said (to tell, to say) (1)</td><td>dihérȯn ↓ dėṣír ↓</td><td>dijeron (decir)</td></tr>
<tr><td>to me (they) told</td><td>mė—đihérȯn ↓</td><td>me dijeron</td></tr>
<tr><td>they would be (to be)</td><td>sėrían ↓ sér ↓</td><td>serían (ser)</td></tr>
<tr><td>WHITE</td><td></td><td>WHITE</td></tr>
<tr><td>At the hotel they told me it'd be two. (2)</td><td>ėnẹlȯtél | mėđihérȯŋ | kė sėríandós ↓</td><td>En el hotel me dijeron que serían dos.</td></tr>
</table>

| | | |
|---|---|---|
| (I) give (to give) | dóy ↓ dár ↓ | doy (dar) |
| to you (I) give (3) | lė—đóy ↓ | le doy |
| the tip | lȧ—prȯpínȧ ↓ | la propina |
| I'll give you three. One for a tip. | lėđóytrés ↓ únȯđeprȯpínȧ ↓ | Le doy tres. Uno de propina. |
| good, OK | bwénȯ ↓ | bueno |

*TAXI DRIVER* — *CHOFER DE TAXI*

| | | |
|---|---|---|
| O.K. Thank you, sir. | bwénȯ ↓ gráṣyȧs \| sėṇyór ↓ | Bueno, gracias, señor. |

(Mr. White enters the Embassy and goes to the Administrative Office. He is taken to the consular section where he is going to work and introduced to one of the young local employees with whom he is going to be associated.)

*ADMINISTRATIVE OFFICER* — *OFICIAL ADMINISTRATIVO*

| | | |
|---|---|---|
| Mr. Molina, this is Mr. White.(4) | sėṇyórmȯlínȧ ↑ ésteṣelsėṇyórhwáyt ↓ | Señor Molina, éste es el señor White. |
| (he) goes (to go) | bá ↓ ír ↓ | va (ir) |
| to work | trȧƀȧhár ↓ | trabajar |
| we, us | nȯsótrȯs ↓ | nostros |
| He is going to work with us. | bátrȧƀȧhár \| kȯ(n)nȯsótrȯs ↓ | Va a trabajar con nosotros. |
| so much | tántȯ ↓ | tanto |
| to know him (5) | kȯnȯṣérlȯ ↓ | conocerlo |

| | | |
|---|---|---|
| *MOLINA* | | *MOLINA* |
| I'm very glad to know you, Mr. White. | tántogústo \| đėkónoṣérlo \| sėṇyórhwáyt ↓ | Tanto gusto de conocerlo, señor White. |
| mine | mío ↓ | mío |
| *WHITE* | | *WHITE* |
| The pleasure's mine. | ėlgústọėzmío ↓ | El gusto es mío. |
| since | dézđė ↓ | desde |
| when | kwándo ↓ | cuando |
| *MOLINA* | | *MOLINA* |
| How long have you been here? | dézđėkwándọ \| ėstákí ↓ | ¿Desde cuándo está aquí? |
| yesterday | ȧyér ↓ | ayer |
| *WHITE* | | *WHITE* |
| Since yesterday. | dézđẹȧyér ↓ | Desde ayer. |
| such | tál ↓ | tal |
| how, how goes it | ké—tál ↓ | qué tal |
| the trip | ėl—byáhė ↓ | el viaje |
| *MOLINA* | | *MOLINA* |
| How was the trip? | kétálėlbyáhė ↓ | ¿Qué tal el viaje? |

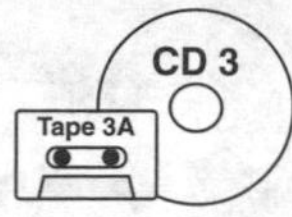




| | | |
|---|---|---|
| excellent | ėks(s̹)ėlénte ↓ | excelente |
| *WHITE* | | *WHITE* |
| Excellent. | ėks(s̹)ėlénte ↓ | Excelente. |
| the movement | ėl—mȯƀimyénto ↓ | el movimiento |
| the section | lȧ—sėks̹yón ↓ | la sección |
| consular | kȯnsulár ↓ | consular |
| Is there much activity in the consular section here? | áy \| múchomȯƀimyénto̰ \| ėnlȧsėks̹yóŋ \| kȯnsuláraki ↑ | ¿Hay mucho movimiento en la sección consular aquí? |
| almost | kási ↓ | casi |
| always | syémpre ↓ | siempre |
| (we) are (to be) | ėstámȯs ↓ ėstár ↓ | estamos (estar) |
| busy (to occupy) | ȯkupáđȯs ↓ ȯkupár ↓ | ocupados (ocupar) |
| *MOLINA* | | *MOLINA* |
| Yes. We're almost always very busy. | sí ↓ kásisyémprestámȯz \| múyȯkupáđȯs ↓ | Sí. Casi siempre estamos muy ocupados. |
| (you) speak (to speak) | áƀlȧ ↓ aƀlár ↓ | habla (hablar) |
| *WHITE* | | *WHITE* |
| Do you speak English, Mr. Molina? | áƀla̯ustéđiŋgles \| sėn̯yórmȯlínȧ ↓ | ¿Habla usted inglés, señor Molina? |

<table>
<tr><td>(I) speak (to speak)</td><td>áƀlȯ ↓ ȧƀlár ↓</td><td>hablo (hablar)</td></tr>
<tr><td>little</td><td>pókȯ ↓</td><td>poco</td></tr>
<tr><td>a little</td><td>u̇m—pókȯ ↓</td><td>un poco</td></tr>
<tr><td>MOLINA</td><td></td><td>MOLINA</td></tr>
<tr><td>Yes. I speak a little.</td><td>sí ↓ áƀlo̯u̇mpókȯ ↓</td><td>Sí, hablo un poco.</td></tr>
<tr><td>but</td><td>pérȯ ↓</td><td>pero</td></tr>
<tr><td>(you) must, ought (must, ought)</td><td>déƀė ↓ dėƀér ↓</td><td>debe (deber)</td></tr>
<tr><td>to practice</td><td>prȧktikár ↓</td><td>practicar</td></tr>
<tr><td>But you ought to practice your Spanish.</td><td>pėro̯u̇stéđ | đéƀėprȧktikár |<br>ėlėspȧn̯yól ↓</td><td>Pero usted debe practicar<br>el español.</td></tr>
<tr><td>the purpose</td><td>ėl—prȯpósitȯ ↓</td><td>el propósito</td></tr>
<tr><td>by the way</td><td>ȧ—prȯpósitȯ ↓</td><td>a propósito</td></tr>
<tr><td>(you) pronounce (to pronounce)</td><td>prȯnúnșyȧ ↓ prȯnu̇nșyár ↓</td><td>pronuncia (pronunciar)</td></tr>
<tr><td>(you) learned (to learn) (6)</td><td>ȧprėndyó ↓ ȧprėndér ↓</td><td>aprendió (aprender)</td></tr>
<tr><td>By the way.</td><td>ȧprȯpósitȯ ↓</td><td>A propósito.</td></tr>
<tr><td>You speak it and pronounce it very well.</td><td>lo̯áƀla̯ | ilȯprȯnúnșyȧ | múyƀyén ↓</td><td>Lo habla y lo pronuncia muy bien.</td></tr>
<tr><td>Where did you learn it?</td><td>dóndėlo̯ȧprėndyó ↓</td><td>¿Dónde lo aprendió?</td></tr>
</table>

| | | |
|---|---|---|
| the school | la̯—ėskwélȧ ↓ | la escuela |
| the language, tongue | lȧ—léŋgwȧ ↓ | la lengua |
| school of languages | ėskwélȧ—đė—léŋgwȧs ↓ | escuela de lenguas |
| the state | ėl—ėstáđȯ ↓ | el estado |
| united (to unite) | u̇níđȯ ↓ u̇nír ↓ | unido (unir) |
| the United States | lȯs—ėstáđȯs—u̇níđȯs ↓ | los Estados Unidos |
| *WHITE* | | *WHITE* |
| At a language school in the States. | ėnụ́na̯ėskwélȧđėléŋgwȧs \| ėnlȯsẹstáđȯsụníđȯs ↓ | En una escuela de lenguas en los Estados Unidos. |
| the thing | lȧ—kósȧ ↓ | la cosa |
| say (to say) [7] | dígȧ dėṣír ↓ | diga (decir) |
| not to me say | nó—mė—đígȧ ↓ | no me diga |
| *MOLINA* | | *MOLINA* |
| Another thing. Don't call me Mr. Molina. | ótrȧkósȧ ↓ noméđígȧ \| sėṇyórmȯlínȧ ↓ | Otra cosa. No me diga señor Molina. |
| my (mine) | mí ↓ míȯ ↓ | mi (mío) |
| the name | ėl—nómbrė ↓ | el nombre |
| My name is Joe. | minómbrėshȯsé ↓ | Mi nombre es José. |
| oh | á ↓ | ah |
| the mine | ėl—míȯ ↓ | el mío |
| *WHITE* | | *WHITE* |
| Oh. All right. Mine is John. | á ↓ múyƀyén ↓ ėlmíȯ̯ėshwán ↓ | Ah, muy bien. El mío es Juan. |

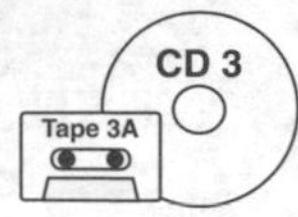




## 4.10 Notes on the basic sentences

(1) /dıhéron/ *dijeron* is a Past I tense form of a fairly irregular type which will not be drilled in detail until Unit 23.

(2) Notice that in the English translation the word /ke/ 'that' is left untranslated, even though we can also say 'They told me that it'd be two.' This omission in English is very common, but *it never happens in Spanish.* While there will be drills on this matter later in this text, it would be well for the student to fix in his mind here and now the fact that the verb /deşír/ 'to say, to tell' always requires /ke/ 'that' after it if there is another verb being introduced by it.

(3) Notice that the word /le/ *le* is '(to) you' in the context of the complete utterance. Formal usage in contexts that mean 'you' is actually the same as in those that mean 'him, her'. The sentence /ledóytrés ↓ / *le doy tres* can be translated either 'I'll give you three', 'I'll give him three', or 'I'll give her three', and only the context will distinguish which translation is appropriate.

(4) One of the *very* common uses of the definite article in Spanish where it is never used in English is in *talking about* a person whose name is cited with /seŋyór/ or /seŋyoríta/ or /seŋyóra/: 'The Mister White', 'The Mrs. Smith', etc.

(5) The form /lo/ *lo* which appears here in the literal meaning 'him', but referring to the person being addressed (that is, 'you'—see note (3) above), often has the form /le/ *le* in Spain. For this reason a person who plans to go to Spain should practice saying /konoşérle/ *conocerle* as well as /konoşérlo/ *conøcerlo.* We will not bother to point out this difference throughout this book, since the teacher can readily point out which form he himself uses ( /le/ or /lo/ ), and that is the one the student should imitate. It may be noted here that the difference between Spain and Latin America on this point is easily stated by rule: the form /le/ is used in Latin America *only* as an indirect clitic form but in Spain it occurs also as the direct clitic form if the reference is to a male human being where /lo/ would be used in Latin America.

(6) /aprendyó/ *aprendió* is a regular Past I tense form which will be drilled in Unit 17.

(7) The form /díga/ *diga* is a command form which will be drilled, along with others of the type, in Unit 27. As in the present sentence, it can be used with the meaning 'call'.

# 4.2 DRILLS AND GRAMMAR

## 4.21 Pattern drills

### 4.21.1 Number in nouns and adjectives

A. PRESENTATION OF PATTERN

*ILLUSTRATIONS*

| | | |
|---|---|---|
| Hand me the books. | 1 pásemelozlíƀros ↓ | Páseme *los libros.* |
| Give me the pens. | 2 démelasplúmas ↓ | Déme *las plumas.* |
| ________________ | 3 pwéđe \| kambyárme \| unozđólares ↑ | ¿Puede cambiarme *unos dólares ?* |
| Give me some pens. | 4 démeunasplúmas ↓ | Déme *unas plumas.* |
| ________________ | 5 bwénozđías \| señyór ↓ | *Buenos dias,* señor. |
| ________________ | 6 bwénaznóches \| señyoríta ↓ | *Buenas noches,* señorita. |
| ________________ | 7 múchazgrásyas \| señyór ↓ | *Muchas gracias,* señor. |

## *EXTRAPOLATION*

### Nouns and adjectives

| singular | plural |
|---|---|
| ...........vowel | ...........vowel —s |
| .....consonant | .....consonant —es |

### Partially irregular patterns of articles

Indefinite articles

| | sg | pl |
|---|---|---|
| m | un | unos |
| f | una | unas |

Definite articles

| | sg | pl |
|---|---|---|
| m | el | los |
| f | la | las |

## *NOTES*

a. Spanish nouns, like English nouns, have different forms in the plural.

b. Spanish adjectives, *unlike* most English adjectives, also have different forms in the plural.

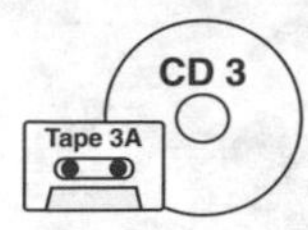




## 4.21.11 SUBSTITUTION DRILL (1)

Number substitution

Model Problem:

ȧkí | áyu̇nọtélbwénȯ ↓

Model Answer:

ȧkí | áyu̇nȯsọtélėzƀwénȯs ↓

1 téŋgo̯u̇nȧplúma̯ėks(s̯)ėléntė ↓ — téŋgo̯u̇nȧplúmȧṣėks(s̯)ėléntės ↓

2 tyénėlmízmȯlíƀrȯ ↓ — tyénėlȯzmízmȯzlíƀrȯs ↓

3 kyéro̯ėlótrȯđólȧr ↓ — kyérȯlȯṣótrȯzđólȧrės ↓

---

Model Problem:

Aquí hay un hotel bueno.

Model Answer:

Aquí hay unos hoteles buenos.

1 Tengo una pluma excelente. — Tengo unas plumas excelentes.

2 Tiene el mismo libro. — Tiene los mismos libros.

3 Quiero el otro dólar. — Quiero los otros dólares.

(1) Number substitution involves a change between singular and plural forms. In the present drill these forms are nouns; change the singular nouns (and any associated adjectives) to plural and plural nouns (with any associated adjectives) to singular.

| | |
|---|---|
| 4 téngo̮ùnchékėƀyȧhérȯ ↓ | téngo̮ùnȯschékėzƀyȧhérȯs ↓ |
| 5 áƀlȯ \| kȯnlȧsėn̨yȯrítȧ̮ėspȧn̨yólȧ ↓ | áƀlȯ \| kȯnlȧ(s)sėn̨yȯrítȧṣėspȧn̨yólȧs ↓ |
| 6 nėṣėsítȧ̮ùnȧmésȧƀwénȧ ↓ | nėṣėsítȧ̮ùnȧzmésȧzƀwénȧs ↓ |
| 7 áƀlȧ \| kȯnẹlmízmo̮ȧmėrıkánȯ ↓ | áƀlȧ \| kȯnlȯzmízmȯṣȧmėrıkánȯs ↓ |

---

| | |
|---|---|
| 4 Tengo un cheque viajero. | Tengo unos cheques viajeros. |
| 5 Hablo con la señorita española. | Hablo con las señoritas españolas. |
| 6 Necesita una mesa buena. | Necesita unas mesas buenas. |
| 7 Habla con el mismo americano. | Habla con los mismos americanos. |

## 4.21.12 RESPONSE DRILL

| | | |
|---|---|---|
| | 1 kyérėpóḱágwa̯ ↑ ȯmúchȧ ↓ | kyérȯpóḱȧ ↓ |
| | 2 áƀla̯ustéđ ǀ kȯṇėlmízmȯsėɲyór ↑ ȯkȯṇótrȯ ↓ | áƀlȯ ǀ kȯṇėlmízmȯ ↓ |
| | 3 tyéne̯ ǀ ótrȧplúma̯ ↑ ȯlȧmízmȧ ↓ | téŋgótrȧ ↓ |
| | 4 áƀla̯ȧustéđ ǀ múcho̯ėspȧɲyól ↑ ȯpókȯ ↓ | áƀlȯpókȯ ↓ |
| | 5 tyéne̯ ǀ ótrȯzlíƀrȯs ↑ ȯlȯzmízmȯs ↓ | téŋgȯ ǀ lȯzmízmȯs ↓ |
| [ėṇėls̯éntrȯ ↓] | 6 dóndėstá ǀ lȧsėɲyórıta̯ėspȧɲyólȧ ↓ | lȧsėɲyórıta̯ėspȧɲyóla̯ ǀ ėstáe̯n ėls̯éntrȯ ↓ |
| [ėnlȧmésȧ ↓] | 7 dóndėstá ǀ lȧmȯnéđȧmėrıkánȧ ↓ | lȧmȯnéđȧmėrikána̯ ǀ ėstáe̯nlȧmésȧ ↓ |

---

| | | |
|---|---|---|
| | 1 ¿Quiere poca agua o mucha? | Quiero poca. |
| | 2 ¿Habla Ud. con el mismo señor o con otro? | Hablo con el mismo. |
| | 3 ¿Tiene otra pluma o la misma? | Tengo otra. |
| | 4 ¿Habla usted mucho español o poco? | Hablo poco. |
| | 5 ¿Tiene otros libros o los mismos? | Tengo los mismos. |
| (en el centro) | 6 ¿Dónde está la señorita española? | La señorita española está en el centro. |
| (en la mesa ) | 7 ¿Dónde está la moneda americana? | La moneda americana está en la mesa. |

| | | |
|---|---|---|
| [ȧkí ↓] | 8 dóndėstá ǀ e̯(l)líbrȯbwénȯ ↓ | ė(l)líbróbwéno̯ ǀ ėstákí ↓ |
| [kȯnlȧ(s)sėn̯yórȧs ↓] | 9 áblau̯stéd ǀ kȯnlȯ(s)sėn̯yórėsiŋglésės ↑ | nó ↓ áblȯ ǀ kȯnlȧ(s)sėn̯yórȧs̯iŋglésȧs ↓ |
| [ėlmízmȯ ↓] | 10 tyéne̯ústéd ǀ ótrolíbro ↑ | nó ↓ téŋgo̯ėlmízmȯ ↓ |
| [pókȯ ↓] | 11 áblau̯stéd ǀ múcho̯ėspán̯yól ↑ | nó ↓ áblȯpókȯ ↓ |
| | 12 áy ǀ múchȯs̯ótėlézbwénȯs ǀ ȧkí ↑ | sí ↓ áymúchȯs ↓ |
| | 13 tyéné(l)y̯ȧ ǀ múchȧzmȯnédȧs ǀ ȧmėrikánȧs ↑ | sí ↓ tyénėmúchȧs ↓ |
| | 14 áy ǀ múchȯmȯbimyénto̯ ǀ ėnlȧsėks̯yóŋ kȯnsulár ↑ | sí ↓ áymúchȯ ↓ |
| | 15 nės̯ėsíta̯ ǀ ȧnȯschékėzbyȧhérȯs ↑ | sí ↓ nės̯ėsíto̯únȯs ↓ |

---

| | | |
|---|---|---|
| (aquí) | 8 ¿Dónde está el libro bueno? | El libro bueno está aqui. |
| (con las señoras) | 9 ¿Habla usted con los señores ingleses? | No, hablo con las señoras inglesas. |
| (el mismo) | 10 ¿Tiene usted otro libro? | No, tengo el mismo. |
| (poco) | 11 ¿Habla usted mucho español? | No, hablo poco. |
| | 12 ¿Hay muchos hoteles buenos aquí? | Sí, hay muchos. |
| | 13 ¿Tiene ella muchas monedas americanas? | Sí, tiene muchas. |
| | 14 ¿Hay mucho movimiento en la sección consular? | Sí, hay mucho. |
| | 15 ¿Necesita unos cheques viajeros? | Sí, necesito unos. |

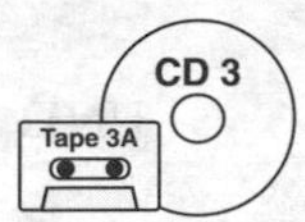




## 4.21.13 TRANSLATION DRILL

| | | |
|---|---|---|
| 1 There're many good schools here. | ȧkíáy \| múchȧs̩ėskwélȧzƀwénȧs ↓ | Aquí hay muchas escuelas buenas. |
| 2 There's an excellent school there. | ȧíȧy \| ùnḁėskwélḁėks(s̩)ėléntė ↓ | Ahí hay una escuela excelente. |
| 3 I always speak with the same ladies. | syémpre̯áƀlȯ \| kȯnlȧzmızmá(s)sėn̩yóràs ↓ | Siempre hablo con las mismas señoras. |
| 4 Can you change some American coins for me? | pwéđėkȧmbyȧrme̯ \| ùnȧzmȯnéđȧs̩ȧmérikánȧs ↑ | ¿Puede cambiarme unas monedas americanas? |
| 5 I haven't got the other dollars now. | nótéŋgȯ \| lȯs̩ótrȯzđólȧrės \| ȧórȧ ↓ | No tengo los otros dólares ahora. |
| 6 I have very few bills. | téŋgȯ \| múypókȯzƀı(l)y̩étės ↓ | Tengo muy pocos billetes. |
| 7 Hand me another pencil. | pásėme̯ \| ótrȯlápis̩ ↓ | Páseme otro lápiz. |
| 8 Give me the other checks. | démė \| lȯs̩ótrȯschékės ↓ | Déme los otros cheques. |
| 9 I always leave good tips. | syémpređóy \| prȯpínȧzƀwénȧs ↓ | Siempre doy propinas buenas. |

## B. DISCUSSION OF PATTERN [(1)]

Both English and Spanish use the concept of *number,* which distinguishes *one* (singular) from *more than one* (plural). English nouns regularly add an ending for plural forms, e.g., the endings of the words 'cats, dogs, horses', the particular ending that appears depending on what sound the singular form ends with. In Spanish the plural ending also depends on the last sound of the singular form, though with a different formula: word sending with a vowel add /—s/, with a consonant, /—es/, as /mésa — mésas, otel—oteles/.

Adjectives in English do not usually change in form when modifying plural nouns: '*the* boy - *the* boys, *good* book - *good* books'. However, the indefinite article a (a special kind of adjective) can appear only with singular nouns: 'a boy' but '*some* boys'; and the demonstratives (another special kind of adjective, often used when pointing) genuinely change when modifying plural nouns: *this* boy - *these* boys, that book - *those* books'.

Almost *all* Spanish adjectives change forms for singular and plural in the same way nouns do; that is, add /—s/ if the word ends in a vowel, /—es/ if in a consonant.

The patterns of pluralization of the articles (the special adjectives, equivalent to 'a, an, some, the' in English, used before nouns to limit their application, definitely or indefinitely) are slightly irregular. The irregularities are charted in the presentation of pattern that began this section,with irregular elements underlined.

(1) There are irregular forms. See appendix for presentation of them.

## 4.21.2 The irregular verb /estár/

### A. PRESENTATION OF PATTERN

*ILLUSTRATIONS*

| | | |
|---|---|---|
| ________________ | 1 ėstóyƀyéŋ ǀ grás̯yȧs ↓ | *Estoy* bien, gracias. |
| I | yó ↓ | yo |
| I'm in the bathroom. | 2 yo̯estóy ǀ ėne̯lbáŋyȯ ↓ | Yo *estoy* en el baño. |
| you (fam.) | tú ↓ | tú |
| (you) are (to be) | ėstás ↓ ėstár ↓ | estás (estar) |
| How are you? | 3 kómo̯ėstástú ↓ | ¿Cómo *estás* tú? |
| ________________ | 4 kómo̯ėstáu̯stéđ ↓ | ¿Cómo *está* usted? |
| he | él ↓ | él |
| How is he? | 5 kómo̯ėstáél ↓ | ¿Cómo *está* él? |
| she | é(l)yȧ ↓ | ella |
| How is she? | 6 kómo̯ėstáé(l)yȧ ↓ | ¿Cómo *está* ella? |
| ________________ | 7 kásisyémprėstámȯz ǀ múyȯkupáđȯs ↓ | Casi siempre *estamos* muy ocupados. |
| (you) are (pl.) (to be) | ėstán ↓ ėstár ↓ | están (estar) |

| | | |
|---|---|---|
| you (pa.) | u̇stéđės ↓ | ustedes |
| How are you all? | 8 kómo̯ėstánụ̇stéđės ↓ | ¿Cómo *están* ustedes? |
| they (m.) | é(l)y̰ȯs ↓ | ellos |
| How are they? | 9 kómo̯ėstánẹ́(l)y̰ȯs ↓ | ¿Cómo *están* ellos? |

*EXTRAPOLATION*

<table>
<tr><th></th><th>sg</th><th>pl</th></tr>
<tr><td>lst person</td><td>estóy</td><td>estámos</td></tr>
<tr><td>2nd person familiar</td><td>estás</td><td rowspan="3">están</td></tr>
<tr><td>2nd person formal</td><td rowspan="2">está</td></tr>
<tr><td>3rd person</td></tr>
</table>

*NOTES*

a. Spanish verbs change to agree with their subject for singular and plural, for first person (I), second person (you), and third person (he or anything else).

b. Second person is further distinguished for familiar or formal.

c. Second person formal and third person take the same verb form in the singular; all second and third person take the same form in the plural.

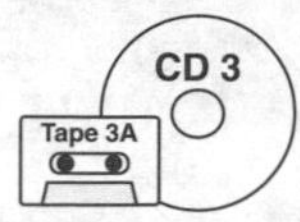




## 4.21.21 SUBSTITUTION DRILLS

Number substitution

Model Problem:

ėstámȯsẹnẹlȯtél ↓

Model Answer:

ėstóyėnẹlȯtél ↓

| | |
|---|---|
| 1 ėstánạí ↓ | ėstáí ↓ |
| 2 ėstámȯzƀyén ↓ | ėstóyƀyén ↓ |

---

Model Problem:

Estamos en el hotel.

Model Answer:

Estoy en el hotel.

| | |
|---|---|
| 1 Están ahi. | Está ahi. |
| 2 Estamos bien. | Estoy bien. |

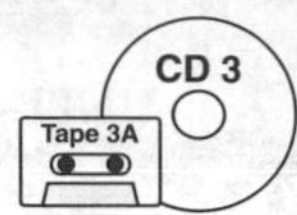




3 ėstámbyén | ȧkí ↓
ėstáƀyén | ȧkí ↓

4 ėstá | e̯nla̯ėskwélȧ ↓
ėstán | ėnla̯ėskwélȧ ↓

5 ėstóy | ėnla̯ėmbȧháđȧ ↓
ėstámȯs | ėnla̯ėmbȧháđȧ ↓

6 nóe̯stáƀyén | ȧí ↓
nóe̯stámbyén | ȧí ↓

7 ėstámȯs | ėne̯ls̯éntrȯ ↓
ėstóyėne̯ls̯éntrȯ ↓

---

3 Están bien aquí.
Está bien aquí.

4 Está en la escuela.
Están en la escuela.

5 Estoy en la Embajada.
Estamos en la Embajada.

6 No está bien ahí.
No están bien ahí.

7 Estamos en el centro.
Estoy en el centro.

Person - number substitution

Model Problem:

àntónyọ / èstáẹnẹlṣéntrò ↓

ùstéđes __________________ ↓

Model Answer:

èstánẹnẹlṣéntrò ↓

1 yóẹstóy | múyƀyénạkí ↓

àlíṣyạ __________________ ↓ èstá | múyƀyénạkí ↓

nòsótròs __________________ ↓ èstámòz | múyƀyénạkí ↓

àlíṣyạiàntónyọ __________________ ↓ èstán | múyƀyénạkí ↓

ùstéđ __________________ ↓ èstá | múyƀyénạkí ↓

---

Model Problem:

*Antonio* está en el centro.

Ustedes __________________

Model Answer:

Están en el centro.

1 *Yo* cstoy muy bien aquí.

Alicia __________________ Está muy bien aquí.

Nosotros __________________ Estamos muy bien aquí.

Alicia y Antonio __________________ Están muy bien aquí.

Usted __________________ Está muy bien aquí.

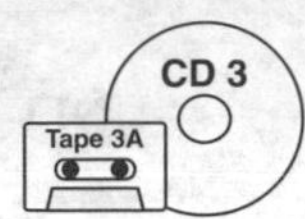




2 páblo | èstáenlaèmbaháđà ↓

| | |
|---|---|
| yó ______________ ↓ | èstóyènlaèmbàháđà ↓ |
| àntónyo ______________ ↓ | èstáenlaèmbàháđà ↓ |
| lòsènyórès ______________ ↓ | èstánenlaèmbàháđà ↓ |
| làsènyòríta ______________ ↓ | èstáenlaèmbàháđà ↓ |

3 àlísyàiyó | estámòsènèlòtél ↓

| | |
|---|---|
| yó ______________ ↓ | èstóyènèlòtél ↓ |
| ùstéđès ______________ ↓ | èstánènèlòtél ↓ |
| élìàntónyo ______________ ↓ | èstánènèlòtél ↓ |
| é(l)ya ______________ ↓ | èstáenèlòtél ↓ |

---

2 *Pablo* está en la Embajada.

| | |
|---|---|
| Yo ______________ | Estoy en la Embajada. |
| Antonio ______________ | Está en la Embajada. |
| Los señores ______________ | Están en la Embajada. |
| La señorita ______________ | Está en la Embajada. |

3 *Alicia y yo* estamos en el hotel.

| | |
|---|---|
| Yo ______________ | Estoy en el hotel. |
| Ustedes ______________ | Están en el hotel. |
| El y Antonio ______________ | Están en el hotel. |
| Ella ______________ | Está en el hotel. |

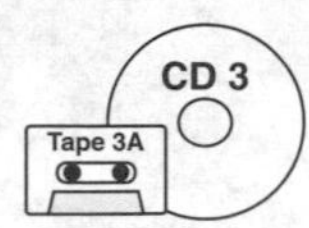



## 4.21.22 RESPONSE DRILL

| | | |
|---|---|---|
| | 1 ėstálasėnyóra̰ \| ėnėlótél ↑ | |
| | o̯ėnla̯ėmbȧháđȧ ↓ | ėstáe̯nla̯ėmbȧháđȧ ↓ |
| | 2 ėstánlȯzƀı(l)yétės \| ȧkí ↑ o̯aí ↓ | ėstánȧkí ↓ |
| | 3 ėstánu̯stéđės \| ėnla̯ėskwélȧ ↑ | |
| | o̯ėnėlȯtél ↓ | ėstámȯsėnla̯ėskwélȧ ↓ |
| | 4 ėstánlȯ(s)sėnyórės \| ȧkí ↑ | ėstánėnėlsėntrȯ ↓ |
| | o̯ėnėlséntrȯ ↓ | |
| [byén ↓] | 5 kómo̯ėstáu̯stéđ ↓ | ėstóyƀyéŋ \| grásyȧs ↓ |
| [ėnėlséntrȯ ↓] | 6 dóndėstáe̯lȯtél ↓ | ėstáe̯nėlséntrȯ ↓ |
| [byén ↓] | 7 kómo̯ėstánu̯stéđės ↓ | ėstámȯzƀyéŋ \| grásyȧs ↓ |

---

| | | |
|---|---|---|
| | 1 ¿Está la señora en el hotel o en la Embajada? | Está en la Embajada. |
| | 2 ¿Están los billetes aquí o ahí? | Están aquí. |
| | 3 ¿Están Uds. en la escuela o en el hotel? | Estamos en la escuela. |
| | 4 ¿Estan los señores aquí o en el centro? | Están en el centro. |
| (bien) | 5 ¿Cómo está usted? | Estoy bien. Gracias. |
| (en el centro) | 6 ¿Dónde está el hotel? | Está en el centro. |
| (bien) | 7 ¿Cómo están ustedes? | Estamos bien. Gracias. |

| | | |
|---|---|---|
| [şérkȧ ↓] | 8 ėstálaėmbȧháđȧ ǀ léhȯzđėlşéntrȯ ↑ | nó ↓ ėstáşérkȧ ↓ |
| [ėnėlşéntrȯ ↓] | 9 ėstánló(s)sėnyórės ǀ ȧkí ↑ | nó ↓ ėstánėnėlşéntrȯ ↓ |
| [ėnlaėmbȧháđa ↓] | 10 ėstáustéđ ǀ ėnėlȯtél ↑ | nó ↓ ėstóyėnlaėmbȧháđȧ ↓ |
| | 11 ėstáné(l)yȧz ǀ ƀyénȧkí ↑ | sí ↓ ėstánmúyƀyén ↓ |
| | 12 ėstánustéđės ǀ ȯkủpáđȯs ↑ | sí ↓ ėstámȯzmúy ǀ ȯkủpáđȯs ↓ |
| | 13 ėstáustéđ ǀ ȯkủpáđȯ ↑ | sí ↓ ėstóymúy ǀ ȯkủpáđȯ ↓ |

---

| | | |
|---|---|---|
| (cerca) | 8 ¿Está la Embajada lejos del centro? | No, está cerca. |
| (en el centro) | 9 ¿Están los señores aquí? | No, están en el centro. |
| (en la Embajada) | 10 ¿Está usted en el hotel? | No, estoy en la Embajada. |
| | 11 ¿Están ellas bien aquí? | Sí, están muy bien. |
| | 12 ¿Están ustedes ocupados? | Sí, estamos muy ocupados. |
| | 13 ¿Está usted ocupado? | Sí, estoy muy ocupado. |

## 4.21.23 TRANSLATION DRILL

| | | | |
|---|---|---|---|
| 1 | The books are on the table. | lòzlíƀròs \| èstánènlàmésà ↓ | Los libros están en la mesa. |
| 2 | We're in a hotel a long way from here. | èstámòs \| ènu̯nòtél \| léhòzđe̯àkí ↓ | Estamos en un hotel lejos de aquí. |
| 3 | How are you? | kómo̯èstáu̯stéđ ↓ | ¿Cómo está usted? |
| 4 | Are you busy? | èstáu̯stéđ \| òkùpáđò ↓ | ¿Está usted ocupado? |
| 5 | The elevator is to the left. | èlàs(s̥)ènsór \| èstála̯ìs̥kyérđà ↓ | El ascensor está a la izquierda. |
| 6 | Where's the cashier? | dóndèstá \| làkáhà ↓ | ¿Dónde está la caja? |
| 7 | Columbus Avenue is very near here. | làbèníđàkòlón \| èstámúys̥érkà \| de̯àkí ↓ | La Avenida Colón está muy cerca de aquí. |
| 8 | They're very busy. | é(l)y̯òs \| èstánmúyòkùpáđòs ↓ | Ellos están muy ocupados. |
| 9 | Good evening. How are you? | bwénàznóchès ↓ kómo̯èstáu̯stéđ ↓ | Buenas noches. ¿Cómo está usted? |

## B. DISCUSSION OF PATTERN

The following discussion needs the prior clarification of two concepts:

*verb* — a word identified in English by the endings it can occur with, as: 'work, works, worked, working', or some internal modification, as: 'sing, sings, sang, sung, singing.' Spanish verbs are similary identified by comparable (though more numerous and complex) endings and changes. Verbs in English and Spanish commonly express action, occurrence, etc.

*pronoun* — one of a relatively small group of words which contain the categories of person, number, and case. The following chart lists the English pronouns which can occur as subjects of verbs:

| | sg | pl |
|---|---|---|
| 1st person | I | we<br>(you and I)<br>(Bill and I) |
| 2nd person | you | you<br>(you and he)<br>(you and Bill) |
| 3rd person | he<br>she<br>it<br>(the book) | they<br>(he and she)<br>(Bill and he)<br>(the books) |

The concept of *person* exists in English pronouns, but has a very limited application to English verbs. Most verbs in English occur with an ending in what might be called the 3rd person singular forms: 'I hit — he hits, I dig — he digs, I miss — he misses'. In Spanish there are usually five (1) widely used forms, which accompany and agree with different pronoun subjects, showing person and number distinctions. The following chart gives examples of these forms, with the verb /estár/.

| | | | |
|---|---|---|---|
| yó | estóy | nosótros | estámos |
| tú | estás | | |
| ustéd | | ustédes | |
| él | está | é(l)yos | están |
| é(l)ya | | é(l)yas | |

Second and third person verb forms are identical, except that the concept of *familiarity* makes a distinction between second person singular *familiar* and second person singular *formal* forms. In Spanish, two persons addressing each other will select one of two subject pronouns, i.e. /ustéd/ or /tú/. Automatically, the accompanying verb will take specific endings depending on which pronoun has been selected. Thus, the sentence 'How are you?' can be translated either as /kómo̯—está—u̯stéd ↓/ or /kómo̯—estás—tú ↓/.

This selection involves a pattern of personal relationships which is by no means simple or even the same throughout the Spanish speaking world. Furthermore, it implies that the speaker *must* select one set of forms or the other when addressing another individual depending on their personal relationship. For the sake of brevity, the distinctions involved have been termed *formal* /ustéd/ and *familiar* /tú/, and in a general way correspond to the usage of 'Sir' or 'Mister' and first names in English. However, the Spanish and English usages do not correlate one hundred percent, and in Spanish there is a finer gradation from formality to familiarity in which *both* the selection of /ustéd/ or /tú/ and the use of titles, first names, and last names play an important part. Thus, in greeting Mr. Juan Molina, there are the following possibilities:

| | |
|---|---|
| ¿Cómo está usted, señor Molina? | ¿Cómo está usted, Juan? |
| ¿Cómo está usted, Molina? | ¿Cómo estás tú, Juan? |

(1) Two other forms exist: /bosótros/, a 2nd person familiar plural form, is still used in parts of Spain, though considered archaic in other dialect areas; and /bós/, a 2nd person familiar singular form, used in some areas in place of or alongside /tú/, the more common form. Both /bosótros/ and /bós/ require separate and distinct equivalent verb forms. See Appendix.

It does *not* follow that in his answer to a greeting, Mr. Molina is automatically going to use the *same* set of forms selected by the first speaker. The status of personal relationships between two individuals depends on such factors as their difference in age, period of mutual acquaintance, sex, rank, and family relationship.

There are no rules of thumb which can guide the student in his selection of *usted* or *tú* forms. Rather, it is a question of feeling for differences which he will develop as he adjusts to the cultural patterns of the individuals in any specific Spanish speaking area.

Spanish verbs, unlike English (except in the case of commands), can appear with no accompanying pronoun or noun subject with no loss of meaning content, i.e., they contain their pronominal reference. Indeed they most frequently *do* appear alone, unless the pronouns are present for special emphasis or contrast or unless (as is possible with 3rd person forms) the context does not make the reference clear. Thus the following translation correlations are usually correct.

| | | | |
|---|---|---|---|
| /estóy/ | I am | /yó estóy/ | *I* am |
| /estás/ | you are | /tú estás/ | *you* are |
| /está/ | he (she) is (you are) | /él está/ | *he* is |
| /estámos/ | we are | /nosótros estámos/ | *we* are |
| /están/ | they (you) are | /é(l)yos están/ | *they* are |

The verb /estár/ has certain irregularities in its pattern, namely the addition of /—y/ to the first person singular form and the occurrence of stress on the endings of all singular and second-third person plural forms. These irregularities will become more obvious by contrast with the regular pattern which will be presented in Unit 6.

**End of Tape 3A**

## 4.22 REPLACEMENT DRILLS

A sȯŋkwátrȯpésȯs ↓

| | |
|---|---|
| 1 ______________ sėn̥yȯrítȧs ↓ | sȯŋkwátrȯsėn̥yȯrítȧs ↓ |
| 2 ______ únȧ ______________ ↓ | ėṣúnȧsėn̥yȯrítȧ ↓ |
| 3 __________________ sėn̥yór ↓ | ėṣúnsėn̥yór ↓ |
| 4 ______ óchȯ ____________ ↓ | sȯnọ́chȯsėn̥yórės ↓ |
| 5 __________________đólȧrės ↓ | sȯnọ́chȯđólȧrės ↓ |
| 6 déƀȯ____________________ ↓ | déƀóchȯđólȧrės ↓ |
| 7 téŋgȯ ________________ ↓ | téŋgóchȯđólȧrės ↓ |

---

A Son cuatro pesos.

| | |
|---|---|
| 1 ________________ señoritas. | Son cuatro señoritas. |
| 2 _______ una______________ . | Es una señorita. |
| 3 ____________________ señor. | Es un señor. |
| 4 _______ ocho ____________ . | Son ocho señores. |
| 5 ___________________ dolares. | Son ocho dólares. |
| 6 Debo____________________ . | Debo ocho dólares. |
| 7 Tengo __________________ . | Tengo ocho dólares. |

B dézđėkwándo̯ | ėstákí ↓

| | |
|---|---|
| 1 ástȧ ________________ ↓ | ástȧkwándo̯ | ėstákí ↓ |
| 2 _______ ėstámȯs _______ ↓ | ástȧkwándo̯ | ėstámȯs̯akí ↓ |
| 3 ______________ȯkȯpáđȯs ↓ | ástȧkwándo̯ | ėstámȯs̯ȯkȯpáđȯs ↓ |
| 4 dézđė ________________ ↓ | dézđėkwándo̯ | ėstámȯs̯ȯkȯpáđȯs ↓ |
| 5 _______ ėnlȯs̯ėstáđȯs̯uníđȯs ↓ | dézđėkwándo̯ | ėstámȯs | ėnlȯs̯ėstáđȯs̯uníđȯs ↓ |
| 6 _______ ėstóy __________ ↓ | dézđėkwándo̯ | ėstóy | ėnlȯs̯ėstáđȯs̯uníđȯs ↓ |
| 7 _______ ėstá __________ ↓ | dézđėkwándo̯ | ėstá | e̯nlȯs̯ėstáđȯs̯uníđȯs ↓ |

---

B ¿Desde cuándo está aquí?

| | |
|---|---|
| 1 ¿Hasta ________________? | ¿Hasta cuándo está aquí? |
| 2 ¿_________ estamos ______? | ¿Hasta cuándo estamos aquí? |
| 3 ¿______________ocupados? | ¿Hasta cuándo estamos ocupados? |
| 4 ¿Desde ________________? | ¿Desde cuándo estamos ocupados? |
| 5 ¿ _____ en los Estados Unidos? | ¿Desde cuándo estamos en los Estados Unidos? |
| 6 ¿ _______ estoy _________? | ¿Desde cuándo estoy en los Estados Unidos? |
| 7 ¿ _______ está __________? | ¿Desde cuándo está en los Estados Unidos? |

C áymúchȯ | mȯƀımyéntǫ | ėnlȧsėkṣyóŋkȯnsúlár ↑

1 ____________________ ȧkí ↑ — áymúchȯ | mȯƀımyéntǫ | ȧkí ↑

2 ________ kósȧs__________ ↑ — áymúchȧs | kósȧs | ȧkí ↑

3 ____________________ ȧórȧ ↑ — áymúchȧs | kósȧs | ȧórȧ ↑

4 _______ pókȧs __________ ↑ — áypókȧs | kósȧs | ȧórȧ ↑

5 ______________________ ȧí ↑ — áypókȧs | kósȧs | ȧí ↑

6 ________ líƀrȯs __________ ↑ — áypókȯz | líƀrȯs | ȧí ↑

7 ________ mésȧs __________ ↑ — áypókȧz | mésȧs | ȧí ↑

---

C ¿Hay mucho movimiento en la Sección Consular?

1 ¿____________________aquí? — ¿Hay mucho movimiento aquí?

2 ¿_________cosas__________? — ¿Hay muchas cosas aquí?

3 ¿___________________ahora? — ¿Hay muchas cosas ahora?

4 ¿_______ pocas ___________? — ¿Hay pocas cosas ahora?

5 ¿_____________________ahí? — ¿Hay pocas cosas ahí?

6 ¿_________ libros ________? — ¿Hay pocos libros ahí?

7 ¿_________ mesas ________? — ¿Hay pocas mesas ahí?

D sí ↓ kásisyémpre̯ | ėstámȯṣȯku̇pádȯs ↓

1 ____________________ ȧkí ↓ — sí ↓ kásisyémpre̯ | ėstámȯṣȧkí ↓

2 __________ ėstóy ________ ↓ — sí ↓ kásisyémpre̯ | ėstóyȧkí ↓

3 _____ únȧzƀé̯sės __________ ↓ — sí ↓ únȧzƀé̯sės | ėstóyȧkí ↓

4 ________________ȯku̇páđȯ ↓ — sí ↓ únȧzƀé̯sės | ėstóyȯku̇páđȯ ↓

5 _____ ótrȧzƀé̯sės__________ ↓ — sí ↓ ótrȧzƀé̯sės | ėstóyȯku̇páđȯ ↓

6 __________ėstámȯs ______ ↓ — sí ↓ ótrȧzƀé̯sės | ėstámȯṣȯku̇páđȯs ↓

7 _____ kásisyémpre̯ ________ ↓ — sí ↓ kásisyémpre̯ | ėstámȯṣȯku̇páđȯs ↓

---

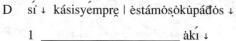

D Sí, casi siempre estamos ocupados.

1 ____________________ aquí. — Sí, casi siempre estamos aquí.

2 __________ estoy ________ . — Sí, casi siempre estoy aquí.

3 ______ unas veces _________ . — Sí, unas veces estoy aquí.

4 _________________ocupado. — Sí, unas veces estoy ocupado.

5 ______ otras veces_________ . — Sí, otras veces estoy ocupado.

6 _________ estamos _______ . — Sí, otras veces estamos ocupados.

7 _____ casi siempre ________ . — Sí, casi siempre estamos ocupados.

E áƀla̯ustéđiŋglés | sėṇyórmȯlínȧ ↑

1 és ____________________ ↑     éṣu̇stéđiŋglés | sėṇyórmȯlínȧ ↑

2 ______ ȧmėrikánȯ | __________ ↑     éṣu̇stéđȧmėrikánȯ | sėṇyórmȯlínȧ ↑

3 ________ | sėṇyȯrítȧ __________ ↑     éṣu̇stéđȧmėrikánȧ | sėṇyȯrítamȯlínȧ ↑

4 _______ ėspȧṇyólȧ | __________ ↑     éṣu̇stéđėspȧṇyólȧ | sėṇyȯrítamȯlínȧ ↑

5 áƀla̯ ____________________ ↑     áƀla̯ustéđespȧṇyól | sėṇyȯrítamȯlínȧ ↑

6 _______ yó ________________ ↑     áƀlȯyóe̯spȧṇyól | sėṇyȯrítamȯlínȧ ↑

7 ________ ƀyén | ____________ ↑     áƀlȯyóƀyén | sėṇyȯrítamȯlínȧ ↑

---

E ¿Habla usted inglés, señor Molina?

1 ¿Es____________________?     ¿Es usted inglés, Sr. Molina?

2 ¿________ americano ________?     ¿Es usted americano, Sr. Molina?

3 ¿__________ señorita________?     ¿Es usted americana, Srta. Molina?

4 ¿________ española __________?     ¿Es usted española, Srta. Molina?

5 ¿Habla __________________?     ¿Habla usted español, Srta. Molina?

6 ¿_______ yo ________________?     ¿Hablo yo español, Srta. Molina?

7 ¿_________ bien ___________?     ¿Hablo yo bien, Srta. Molina?

F minómbrėshȯsé ↓

| | |
|---|---|
| 1 ____________________ ı̇ŋglés ↓ | minómbrėsı̣ŋglés ↓ |
| 2 ____________________ éstė ↓ | minómbrėsẹ́stė ↓ |
| 3 _______ lı́b̄ro̯ ______________ ↓ | milı́b̄ro̯ėsẹ́stė ↓ |
| 4 _______________ ėks(s̥)ėléntė ↓ | milı́b̄ro̯ėsẹks(s̥)ėléntė ↓ |
| 5 ________ lı́b̄rȯs ____________ ↓ | mizlı́b̄rȯ(s)sȯnẹk(s̥)éléntės ↓ |
| 6 ____________________bwénȯs ↓ | mizlı́b̄rȯ(s)sȯmbwénȯs ↓ |
| 7 ________ plúmȧs ___________ ↓ | misplúmȧ(s)sȯmbwénȧs ↓ |

---

F Mi nombre es José.

| | |
|---|---|
| 1 ______________________ inglés. | Mi nombre es inglés. |
| 2 _______________________ éste. | Mi nombre es éste. |
| 3 ________ libro ______________ . | Mi libro es éste. |
| 4 ___________________ excelente. | Mi libro es excelente. |
| 5 _______ libros ______________ . | Mis libros son excelentes. |
| 6 ____________________ buenos. | Mis libros son buenos. |
| 7 _______ plumas ____________ . | Mis plumas son buenas. |

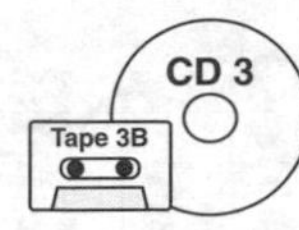




## 4.23 VARIATION DRILLS

| | | |
|---|---|---|
| A kwántȯlėđéƀȯ ↓ | | ¿Cuánto le debo? |
| 1 What do I owe you? | kélėđéƀȯ ↓ | ¿Qué le debo? |
| 2 What are you telling him? | kélėđíşė ↓ | ¿Qué le dice? |
| 3 What did they tell him? | kélėđihérȯn ↓ | ¿Qué le dijeron? |
| 4 When did they tell him? | kwándȯlėđihérȯn ↓ | ¿Cuándo le dijeron? |
| 5 Where did they tell him? | dóndėlėđihérȯn ↓ | ¿Dónde le dijeron? |
| 6 How did they tell him? | kómȯlėđihérȯn ↓ | ¿Cómo le dijeron? |
| 7 How is he getting along? | kómȯlėƀá ↓ | ¿Cómo le va? |

| | | |
|---|---|---|
| B lėđóytrés ↓ únȯđėprȯpínȧ ↓ | | Le doy tres, uno de propina. |
| 1 Here are four, two for a tip. | lėđóykwátrȯ ↓ dózđėprȯpínȧ ↓ | Le doy cuatro, dos de propina. |
| 2 Here are twenty, ten for a tip. | lėđóyƀéyntė ↓ dyéz̧đėprȯpínȧ ↓ | Le doy veinte, diez de propina. |
| 3 Here are ten, five for a tip. | lėđóyđyéş ↓ şíŋkȯđėprȯpínȧ ↓ | Le doy diez, cinco de propina. |

| | | |
|---|---|---|
| 4 Here are eleven, one for a tip. | lėđóyónṣė ↓ únȯđėprȯpínȧ ↓ | Le doy once, uno de propina. |
| 5 Here's a dollar and no tip. | lėđóyúndólȧr ↓ náđȧđėprȯpínȧ ↓ | Le doy un dólar, nada de propina. |
| 6 Here's this, that's for a tip. | lėđóyéstȯ ↓ ésȯđėprȯpínȧ ↓ | Le doy esto, eso de propina. |
| 7 I'll give you this, not that. | lėđóyéstȯ ↓ ésȯnó ↓ | Le doy esto, eso no. |

| | | |
|---|---|---|
| C | bátrȧbȧhár \| kȯ(n)nȯsótrȯs ↓ | Va a trabajar con nosotros. |
| 1 He's going to work with you all. | bátrȧƀȧhár \| kȯnụstéđės ↓ | Va a trabajar con ustedes. |
| 2 She's going to work here. | bátrȧƀȧhár \| ȧkí ↓ | Va a trabajar aquí. |
| 3 She's going to speak Spanish. | báƀlár \| ėspȧṇyól ↓ | Va a hablar español. |
| 4 He's going to learn English. | báprėndér \| iŋglés ↓ | Va a aprender inglés. |
| 5 He's going to say something. | báđėṣírálgȯ ↓ | Va a decir algo. |
| 6 She's going to translate the name. | bátrȧđụṣír \| ėlnómbrė ↓ | Va a traducir el nombre. |
| 7 You're going to be very busy. | báe̯stár \| múyȯkụpáđȯ ↓ | Va a estar muy ocupado. |

| | | | |
|---|---|---|---|
| D | | sí ↓ yo̯áƀlo̯ùmpókȯ ↓ | Sí, yo hablo un poco. |
| | 1 Yes, I speak a lot. | sí ↓ yo̯áƀlȯmúchȯ ↓ | Sí, yo hablo mucho. |
| | 2 Yes, you speak more. | sí ↓ ùstéđáƀlȧmás ↓ | Sí, usted habla más. |
| | 3 Yes, he speaks less. | sí ↓ éláƀlȧménȯs ↓ | Sí, él habla menos. |
| | 4 Yes, I have five dollars. | sí ↓ yótéŋgȯs̯íŋkȯđólȧrės ↓ | Sí, yo tengo cinco dolares. |
| | 5 Yes, you have fifteen. | sí ↓ ùstéđtyénėkíns̯ė ↓ | Sí, usted tiene quince. |
| | 6 No, I don’t have much. | nó ↓ yónȯtéŋgȯmúchȯ ↓ | No, yo no tengo mucho. |
| | 7 No, I don’t owe much. | nó ↓ yónȯđéƀȯmúchȯ ↓ | No, yo no debo mucho. |
| E | | péro̯ùsté \| đéƀėpràktikár \| èlėspàn̯yól ↓ | Pero usted debe practicar el español. |
| | 1 But you ought to practice English. | péro̯ùsté \| đéƀėpràktikár \| èliŋglés ↓ | Pero usted debe practicar el inglés. |
| | 2 But you ought to say something. | péro̯ùsté \| đéƀėđės̯írálgȯ ↓ | Pero usted debe decir algo. |
| | 3 But you ought to take a taxi. | péro̯ùsté \| đéƀėtȯmár \| ùntáksi ↓ | Pero usted debe tomar un taxi. |

| | | | |
|---|---|---|---|
| | 4 But you ought to speak less. | pérǫùsté \| đéƀḙàƀláṛménòs ↓ | Pero usted debe hablar menos. |
| | 5 But you ought to speak more. | pérǫùsté \| đéƀḙàƀláṛmás ↓ | Pero usted debe hablar más. |
| | 6 But you ought to go to the Embassy. | pérǫùsté \| đéƀḙír \| àlạèmbàháđà ↓ | Pero usted debe ir a la Embajada. |
| | 7 But you ought to go up in the elevator. | pérǫùsté \| đéƀèsùƀír \| èṇèlàs(ṣ)ènsór ↓ | Pero usted debe subir en el ascensor. |
| F | óstrakósà ↓ nómeđígà \| sèṇyórmòlínà ↓ | | Otra cosa, no me diga Sr. Molina. |
| | 1 Another thing, don't tell me that. | ótrakósà ↓ nómèđígạésò ↓ | Otra cosa, no me diga eso. |
| | 2 Another thing, don't repeat that to me. | ótrakósà ↓ nómèrrèpítạésò ↓ | Otra cosa, no me repita eso. |
| | 3 Another thing, don't translate that for me. | ótrakósà ↓ nómètràđúṣkạésò ↓ | Otra cosa, no me traduzca eso. |
| | 4 Another thing, don't give me a tip. | ótrakósà ↓ nómèđéprópínà ↓ | Otra cosa, no me dé propina. |
| | 5 Another thing, don't pass me the book. | ótrakósà ↓ nómèpásè(l)líƀrò ↓ | Otra cosa, no me pase el libro. |

| | | |
|---|---|---|
| 6 Another thing, don't take me to the hotel. | ótrȧkósȧ ↓ nómė(l)yébẹȧlȯtél ↓ | Otra cosa, no me lleve al hotel. |
| 7 Another thing, don't take me to the Embassy. | ótrȧkósȧ ↓ nómė(l)yébẹȧlạėmbȧhádȧ ↓ | Otra cosa, no me lleve a la Embajada. |

## 4.3 CONVERSATION STIMULUS

### NARRATIVE 1

| | | |
|---|---|---|
| 1 Mr. Smith and Mr. White are at the Embassy. | ėlsėn̦yórsmíṣ \| ı̯ėlsėn̦yórhwáyt \| ėstánẹ̇nlạėmbȧháđȧ ↓ | El Sr. Smith y el Sr. White están en la Embajada. |
| 2 Mr. Smith wants him to meet Mr. Molina. | ėlsėn̦yórsmíṣ \| kyérėprėsėntárlẹ \| ȧl sėn̦yórmȯlínȧ ↓ | El Sr. Smith quiere presentarle al Sr. Molina. |
| 3 Mr. White speaks Spanish very well. | ėlsėn̦yórhwáyt \| áƀlȧmúyƀyén \| ėspȧn̦yól ↓ | El Sr. White habla muy bien español. |
| 4 He learned it in school. | lọȧprėndyó \| ẹnlạėskwélȧ ↓ | Lo aprendió en la escuela. |
| 5 Mr. Molina speaks English a little, not much. | ėlsėn̦yórmȯlínạ \| áƀlạiŋglés \| ůmpókȯ ↓ nómúchȯ ↓ | El Sr. Molina habla inglés un poco, no mucho. |

## DIALOG 1

Sr. Smith, dígale a Juan que Ud. quiere presentarle al Sr. Molina.

hwán ↓ kyéṛȯprėsėntárlẹ̑ | ȧlsėṇyórmȯlínȧ ↓

Smith: Juan, quiero presentarle al Sr. Molina.

José, déle su nombre—José Molina— y dígale que mucho gusto.

hȯsémȯlínȧ ↓ múchȯgústȯ ↓

José: José Molina, mucho gusto.

Juan, dígale que igualmente y déle su nombre—John White.

igwálméntė ↓ ǰáŋhwáyt ↓ kómȯsė

Juan: Igualmente, John White.

Pregúntele que cómo se dice John en español, que si Juan.

đísẹ̇ | ǰán | ėnẹ̇spȧṇyól ↓ hwán ↑

¿Cómo se dice 'John' en español?, ¿Juan?

José, dígale que sí, que Juan y dígale que él habla muy bien el español.

sí ↓ hwán ↓ ȯstéđáƀlȧ | múyƀyén |

ėlėspȧṇyól ↓

José: Sí, Juan. Usted habla muy bien el español.

Juan, dígale que muchas gracias.

múchȧzgráṣyȧs ↓

Juan: Muchas gracias.

José, pregúntele que dónde lo aprendió.

dóndėlọ̑ȧprėndyó ↓

José: Dónde lo aprendió?

Juan, dígale que en la escuela. Pregúntele si él habla inglés.

ėnlạ̑ėskwélȧ ↓ ị̑ȯstéđ ↓

áƀlạ̑ȧiŋglés ↑

Juan: En la escuela. Y usted ¿habla inglés?

José, contéstele que Ud. habla un poco, no más.

áƀlọ̑ȯmpókȯ | nȯmás ↓

José: Hablo un poco, no más.

## NARRATIVE 2

| | | |
|---|---|---|
| 1 John's been here since yesterday. | hwánẹstákı \| đézđẹayér ↓ | Juan está aquí desde ayer. |
| 2 He's going to work in the Consular Section. | bátràƀàhár \| ènlàsèkṣyóŋkònsùlár ↓ | Va a trabajar en la Sección Consular. |
| 3 The Consular Section is on the main floor. | làsèkṣyóŋkònsùlár ↓ èstáẹnẹlprimérpísò ↓ | La Sección Consular está en el primer piso. |
| 4 It's to the right of the entrance. | èstálàđèréchà \| đèlạèntráđà ↓ | Está a la derecha de la entrada. |
| 5 Most of the time they're very busy in the Consular Section. | kásisyémprẹ \| èstánmúyòkùpáđòs \| ènlàsèkṣyóŋkònsùlár ↓ | Casi siempre están muy ocupados en la Sección Consular. |
| 6 But right now there isn't much doing there. | pérọàóràmízmò \| nọáymúchò mòƀimyéntọ \| àí ↓ | Pero ahora mismo no hay mucho movimiento ahí. |

## DIALOG 2

| | | |
|---|---|---|
| José, pregúntele al Sr. White que ¿desde cuando está aquí? | dézđèkwándọ \| èstákí \| sènyórhwáyt ↓ | José: ¿Desde cuándo está aquí, Sr. White? |
| Juan, dígale que no le diga 'Sr. White', que le diga 'John' o 'Juan'. | nómèđígà \| sènyórhwáyt ↓ dígàmẽján \| òhwán ↓ | Juan: No me diga 'Sr. White'. Dígame 'John' o 'Juan'. |

| | | |
|---|---|---|
| José, dígale que está bien, y otra vez pregúntele que ¿desde cuándo está aquí? | èstáƀyéŋ \| hwán ↓ dézđèkwándo̯ \| èstákí ↓ | José: Está bien, Juan. ¿Desde cuándo está aquí? |
| Juan, dígale que desde ayer. | dézđe̯àyér ↓ | Juan: Desde ayer. |
| José, dígale que a Ud. le dijeron que él va a trabajar con ustedes. | mèđihéròŋ \| kèƀátràƀàhár \| kò(n)nòsótròs ↓ | José: Me dijeron que va a trabajar con nosotros. |
| Juan, dígale que sí, y pregúntele que dónde está la Sección Consular. | sí ↓ dóndèstá \| làsèkṣyóŋkònsùlár ↓ | Juan: Sí. ¿Dónde está la Sección Consular? |
| José, dígale que en el primer piso, a la derecha de la entrada. | ènẹlprimérpísò ↓ àlàđeréchà đèla̯entráđà ↓ | José: En el primer piso, a la derecha de la entrada. |
| Juan, pregúntele si hay mucho movimiento ahí ahora. | áy \| múchòmòƀimyénto̯ \| áia̯órà ↑ | Juan: ¿Hay mucho movimiento ahí ahora? |
| Jose, contéstele que casi siempre ustedes están muy ocupados, pero que ahora mismo no hay mucho movimiento. | kásisyémpre̯ \| èstámòz \| múyòkùpáđòs ↓ péro̯àóràmízmò ↑ no̯áymúchòmòƀimyéntò ↓ | José: Casi siempre estamos muy ocupados, pero ahora mismo no hay mucho movimiento. |

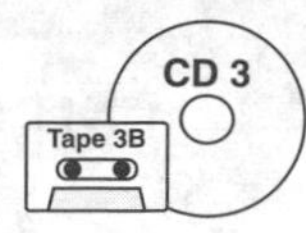




# 5.1 BASIC SENTENCES

## White's first day at work

In their office, John White and José Molina begin to get better acquainted.

| English Spelling | Aid to Listening | Spanish Spelling |
|---|---|---|
| to be | sér ↓ | ser |
| your (yours) | sú ↓ súyȯ ↓ | su (suyo) |
| the desk | ėl—ėskritóryȯ ↓ | el escritorio |
| *MOLINA* | | *MOLINA* |
| John, this is going to be your desk. | hwán ↓ éstėƀásér \| su̯ėskritóryȯ ↓ | Juan, éste va a ser su escritorio. |
| whatever | kwȧlkyér ↓ kwȧlkyérȧ ↓ | cualquier (cualquiera) |
| that (you) may need (to need) [1] | kė—nėşėsítė ↓ nėşėsitár ↓ | que necesite (necesitar) |
| notify (to notify) | ȧƀísė ↓ ȧƀisár ↓ | avise (avisar) |
| notify me | ȧƀísėmė ↓ | avíseme |
| Whatever you need, let me know. | kwȧlkyérkósȧ \| kėnėşésítė ↑ ȧƀísėmė ↓ | Cualquier cosa que necesite, avíseme. |
| very much (much) | mu̇chísimȯs ↓ múchȯ ↓ | muchísimos (mucho) |
| *WHITE* | | *WHITE* |
| O. K. Thanks a lot. | múyƀyén ↓ mu̇chísimázgráşyȧs ↓ | Muy bien. Muchísimas gracias. |

| | | |
|---|---|---|
| the part | là—pártè ↓ | la parte |
| *MOLINA* | | *MOLINA* |
| What part of the States are you from? | dèképàrtè \| đèlòsèstáđòsùníđòs \| èsùstéđ ↓ | ¿De qué parte de los Estados Unidos es usted? |
| (I) am (to be) | sóy ↓ sér ↓ | soy (ser) |
| *WHITE* | | *WHITE* |
| I'm from San Francisco, California. | sóy \| đèsàmfrànsískò \| kàlifórnyà ↓ | Soy de San Francisco, California. |
| Where are you from? | ìustéđèđóndés ↓ | Y usted, ¿de dónde es? |
| *MOLINA* | | *MOLINA* |
| I'm from here. | sóyđèakí ↓ | Soy de aquí. |
| (you) came (to come) | bínò ↓ bènír ↓ | vino (venir) |
| the family | là—fàmílyà ↓ | la familia |
| Did you come with your family? | bínòustéđ \| kònsùfàmílyà ↑ | ¿Vino usted con su familia? |
| bachelor | sòltérò ↓ | soltero |
| *WHITE* | | *WHITE* |
| No, I'm a bachelor. | nó ↓ sóy \| sòltérò ↓ | No, soy soltero. |
| married (to marry) | kàsáđò ↓ kàsár ↓ | casado (casar) |

| | | |
|---|---|---|
| What about you? Are you married? | ʌùstéđ ↓ éskàsáđȯ ↑ | Y usted, ¿es casado? |
| also, too | tàmbyén ↓ | también |
| *MOLINA* | | *MOLINA* |
| No, I'm a bachelor, too. | nó ↓ sóysòltérȯ \| tàmbyén ↓ | No, soy soltero también. |
| the hour | la̯—órà ↓ | la hora |
| *WHITE* | | *WHITE* |
| What time is it? | ke̯óra̯és ↓ | ¿Qué hora es? |
| the quarter | ėl—kwártȯ ↓ | el cuarto |
| *MOLINA* | | *MOLINA* |
| It's a quarter to twelve. | sónlàzđóse̯ \| ménȯskwártȯ ↓ | Son las doce menos cuarto. |
| it is that | és—kė ↓ | es que |
| already | yá ↓ | ya |
| the hunger | ėl—ámbrė ↓ | el hambre (f) |
| to be hungry | tėnér—ámbrė ↓ | tener hambre |
| Are you hungry already? | és \| kėy̯átyéne̯ámbrė ↑ | ¿Es que ya tiene hambre? |
| enough, quite (a bit) | bàstántė ↓ | bastante |
| good | bwén ↓ bwénȯ ↓ | buen (bueno) |
| the restaurant | ėl—rrėstòrán ↓ | el restorán |

| | | |
|---|---|---|
| *WHITE* | | *WHITE* |
| Yes, quite hungry. Is there a good restaurant near here? | sí ↓ bȧstántė ↓ áyůmbwén rrėstórȧn \| s̯érkȧđe̯ȧkí ↑ | Sí, bastante. ¿Hay un buen restorán cerca de aquí? |
| the turn | lȧ—ƀwéltȧ ↓ | la vuelta |
| around the corner | ȧ—lȧ—ƀwéltȧ ↓ | a la vuelta |
| cheap, inexpensive | bȧrátȯ ↓ | barato |
| *MOLINA* | | *MOLINA* |
| Yes, there's one around the corner that's good and inexpensive. | sí ↓ áyúno̯ \| ȧlȧƀwéltȧ \| kézƀwéno̯iƀárátȯ ↓ | Sí, hay uno a la vuelta que es bueno y barato. |
| (we) can (to be able) | pȯđémȯs ↓ pȯđér ↓ | podemos (poder) |
| to lunch | ȧlmȯrs̯ár ↓ | almorzar |
| together | húntȯs ↓ | juntos |
| (it) seems (to seem) | pȧrés̯ė ↓ pȧrės̯ér ↓ | parece (parecer) |
| to you (it) seems | lė—pȧrés̯ė ↓ | le parece |
| We can have lunch together. | pȯđémȯs̯ȧlmȯrs̯ár \| húntȯs ↓ | Podemos almorzar juntos. |
| O. K. with you? | lėpȧrés̯ėƀyén ↑ | ¿Le parece bien? |
| let's go, we go (to go) | bámȯs ↓ ír ↓ | vamos (ir) |
| *WHITE* | | *WHITE* |
| Sure. Let's go. | kómȯnó ↓ bámȯs ↓ | Cómo no. Vamos. |

## 5.10 Notes on the basic sentences

(1) /neṣesíte/ *necesite* is an example of a verb form which has no exact equivalent in English. Forms of this type are called 'subjunctive.' The particular use of a subjunctive construction illustrated in the present sentence will be drilled in Unit 40. Subjunctive forms will be designated in English by the translation device 'that (you) may...'

# 5.2 DRILLS AND GRAMMAR

## 5.21.1 Pattern drills

## 5.21.1 The irregular verb /sér/

### A. PRESENTATION OF PATTERN

*ILLUSTRATIONS*

| | | |
|---|---|---|
| ______________ | 1 nó ↓ sóysòltérò ↓ | No, *soy* soltero. |
| (you) are (to be) | érès ↓ sér ↓ | eres (ser) |
| And you, are you married? | 2 itú ↓ érèskàsáđȯ ↑ | Y tú, ¿*eres* casado? |
| ______________ | 3 i̯ùstéđ ↓ éskàsáđȯ ↑ | Y usted, ¿*es* casado? |
| ______________ | 4 minómbrẹ \| ėshòsé ↓ | Mi nombre *es* José. |
| (we) are (to be) | sómòs ↓ sér ↓ | somos (ser) |
| No, we're single. | 5 nó ↓ sómò(s)sòltéròs ↓ | No, *somos* solteros. |
| (you) (pl.) are (to be) | són ↓ sér ↓ | son (ser) |

| | | |
|---|---|---|
| And are you all married? | 6 ı̯ùstéđės ↓ sóŋkȧsáđȯs ↑ | Y ustedes, ¿*son* casados? |
| ________________ | 7 són \| lȧzđós̯ėménȯskwártȯ ↓ | *Son* las doce menos cuarto. |

## *EXTRAPOLATION*

<table>
<tr><th colspan="2"></th><th>sg</th><th>pl</th></tr>
<tr><td>1</td><td></td><td>sóy</td><td>sómos</td></tr>
<tr><td>2</td><td>fam</td><td>éres</td><td rowspan="2">són</td></tr>
<tr><td>2-3</td><td>for</td><td>és</td></tr>
</table>

## *NOTES*

a. Spanish has two verbs which translate English ‘to be’:

/estár/, presented in Unit 4, and /sér/, presented in this unit.

## 5.21.11 SUBSTITUTION DRILLS

Number substitution

| | |
|---|---|
| 1 sóyàmèrikánò ↓ | sómòṣàmèrikánòs ↓ |
| 2 sóŋkàsáđòs ↓ | éskàsáđò ↓ |
| 3 sómò(s)sòltéròs ↓ | sóysòltérò ↓ |
| 4 sónde̯àkí ↓ | ézđe̯àkí ↓ |
| 5 ézđèkàlifórnyà ↓ | sóndèkàlifórnyà ↓ |
| 6 sóyđe̯àkí ↓ | sómòzđe̯àkí ↓ |
| 7 éṣàmèrikánò ↓ | sóṇàmèrikánòs ↓ |

---

| | |
|---|---|
| 1 Soy americano. | Somos americanos. |
| 2 Son casados. | Es casado. |
| 3 Somos solteros. | Soy soltero. |
| 4 Son de aquí. | Es de aquí. |
| 5 Es de California. | Son de California. |
| 6 Soy de aquí. | Somos de aquí. |
| 7 Es americano. | Son americanos. |

Person - number substitution

1 àntónyọèzđèchílè ↓

yó ______________ ↓ sóyđèchílè ↓

páƀlọ ______________ ↓ ézđèchílè ↓

àntónyò | ịàlíṣyà ______________ ↓ sóndèchílè ↓

ùstéđ ______________ ↓ ézđèchílè ↓

2 nòsótrò(s)sómòs | àmèrikánòs ↓

àlíṣyạ ______________ ↓ éṣamèrıkánà ↓

ùstéđès ______________ ↓ sónạmèrikánòs ↓

---

1 *Antonio* es de Chile.

Yo ______________ . Soy de Chile.

Pablo ______________ . Es de Chile.

Antonio y Alicia ______________ . Son de Chile.

Usted ______________ . Es de Chile.

2 *Nosotros* somos americanos.

Alicia ______________ . Es americana.

Ustedes ______________ . Son americanos.

| | |
|---|---|
| y̯ó ____________________ ↓ | sóyȧmėrıkánȯ ↓ |
| é(l)y̯ȯs ____________________ ↓ | són̯ȧmėrıkánȯs ↓ |

3 ȧlíşy̯ȧė(s)sȯltérȧ ↓

| | |
|---|---|
| páblo̯ıy̯ó ____________________ ↓ | sómȯ(s)sȯltérȯs ↓ |
| él̯ıantónyȯ ____________________ ↓ | sónsȯltérȯs ↓ |
| é(l)y̯ȧ ____________________ ↓ | é(s)sȯltérȧ ↓ |
| y̯ó ____________________ ↓ | sóysȯltérȯ ↓ |

---

| | |
|---|---|
| Yo ____________________ . | Soy americano. |
| Ellos ____________________ . | Son americanos. |

3 *Alicia* es soltera.

| | |
|---|---|
| Pablo y yo ____________________ . | Somos solteros. |
| El y Antonio ____________________ . | Son solteros. |
| Ella ____________________ . | Es soltera. |
| Yo ____________________ . | Soy soltero. |

## 5.21.12 RESPONSE DRILL

| | | |
|---|---|---|
| | 1 àlíşyạė(s)sòltérạ ↑ òkàsáđà ↓ | é(s)sòltérà ↓ |
| | 2 ėşùstéđàmėrikánȯ ↑ ọėspàn̦yól ↓ | sóyàmėrikánȯ ↓ |
| | 3 sòn̦é(l)y̦òzđėchílẹ ↑ òđėlòşėstáđòşùníđòs ↓ | són I dėlòşėstáđòşùníđòs ↓ |
| [lòşėstáđòşùníđòs] | 4 dėđóndėsónùstéđės ↓ | sómòz I đėlòşėstáđòşùníđòs ↓ |
| [sámfrànşískò] | 5 dėđóndėşùstéđ ↓ | sóyđėsámfrànşískò ↓ |
| [làúnà] | 6 kẹóràés ↓ | ėzlạúnà ↓ |
| [kàlifórnyà] | 7 dėképártėşé(l)y̦à ↓ | ézđėkàlifórnyà ↓ |

---

| | | |
|---|---|---|
| | 1 ¿Alicia es soltera o casada? | Es soltera. |
| | 2 ¿Es usted americano o español? | Soy americano. |
| | 3 ¿Son ellos de Chile o de los Estados Unidos? | Son de los Estados Unidos. |
| (los Estados Unidos) | 4 ¿De dónde son ustedes? | Somos de los Estados Unidos. |
| (San Francisco) | 5 ¿De dónde es usted? | Soy de San Francisco. |
| (la una ) | 6 ¿Qué hora es? | Es la una. |
| (California) | 7 ¿De que parte es ella? | Es de California. |

| | | |
|---|---|---|
| [lȯs̩ėstáđȯs̩ùnı́đȯs] | 8 ės̩éldėchı́lė ↑ | nó ↓ ézđėlȯs̩ėstáđȯs̩ùnı́đȯs ↓ |
| [lȧzđós̩ė] | 9 sónlȧzđós̩ė \| ménȯskwártȯ ↑ | nó ↓ sónlȧzđós̩ė ↓ |
| [kȧsáđȯ] | 10 és̩ùstéđsȯltérȯ ↑ | nó ↓ sóykȧsáđȯ ↓ |
| [ȧmėrikánȯs] | 11 sónùstéđės \| ėspȧnyólės ↑ | nó ↓ sómȯs̩ȧmėrikánȯs ↓ |
| | 12 és̩ùstéđkȧsáđȯ ↑ | sí ↓ sóykȧsáđȯ ↓ |
| | 13 sónẹ́(l)yȯs̩ȧmėrikánȯs ↑ | sí ↓ sónȧmėrikánȯs ↓ |

---

| | | |
|---|---|---|
| (los Estados Unidos) | 8 ¿Es él de Chile? | No, es de los Estados Unidos. |
| (las 12) | 9 ¿Son las doce menos cuarto? | No, son las doce. |
| (casado) | 10 ¿Es usted soltero? | No, soy casado. |
| (americanos) | 11 ¿Son ustedes españoles? | No, somos americanos. |
| | 12 ¿Es usted casado? | Sí, soy casado. |
| | 13 ¿Son ellos americanos? | Sí, son americanos. |

**End of Tape 3B**
**End of CD 3**

## 5.21.13 TRANSLATION DRILL

| | | | |
|---|---|---|---|
| 1 | We're from San Francisco. | sómȯz \| dėsámfrànșískȯ ↓ | Somos de San Francisco. |
| 2 | She's married, too. | é(l)y̯ȧėskȧsáđȧ \| tȧmbyén ↓ | Ella es casada también. |
| 3 | The hotels are excellent. | lȯșȯtélės \| sȯnẹks(ș)ėléntės ↓ | Los hoteles son excelentes. |
| 4 | Where's the lady from? | dėképártẹ \| ėzlȧsėny̯órȧ ↓ | ¿De qué parte es la señora? |
| 5 | Where're you from? | dėđóndeșȯustéđ ↓ | ¿De dónde es usted? |
| 6 | My name is Pancho. | minómbrėspánchȯ ↓ | Mi nombre es Pancho. |
| 7 | I'm (an) American. | sóyȧmėrikánȯ ↓ | Soy americano. |
| 8 | How much is the tip? | kwántọėzlȧprȯpínȧ ↓ | ¿Cuánto es la propina? |
| 9 | They're from the Consular Section. | é(l)yȯs \| sóndėlȧsėkșyóŋkȯnsulár ↓ | Ellos son de la sección consular. |
| 10 | When is the trip? | kwándọėșėlbyáhė ↓ | ¿Cuándo es el viaje? |
| 11 | The pleasure is mine. | ėlgústọėzmíȯ ↓ | El gusto es mio. |
| 12 | We're married, too. | sómȯskȧsáđȯs \| tȧmbyén ↓ | Somos casados tambien. |
| 13 | The restaurants are not expensive. | lȯzrrėstȯránės \| sómbȧrátȯs ↓ | Los restoranes son baratos. |

## B. DISCUSSION OF PATTERN

The verb /sér/ is highly irregular in the present tense, as will be seen by comparing it to regular verb patterns presented in Unit 7.

Both /estár/ and /sér/ translate the English verb 'be'. They are not, however, equivalent. Rather they divide an area of meaning which is included in the content of a single English concept, named by the verb 'be'. Therefore a confusion between the two cannot be thought of as a relatively minor mistake simply because they express aspects of what is considered 'the same thing' in English; in Spanish /sér/ and /estár/ are as genuinely different as any other two verbs, and the use of one when the other is expected is painfully obvious.

The difference between /sér/ and /estár/ can perhaps best be generalized by other English concepts: /sér/ is the link of *identity,* (the essential, inherent or permanent), /estár/ the link of *association,* (the casual, accidental or temporary). This generalization is more useful descriptively in some cases than in others. Thus when a noun follows the linking verb to express complete identity, /sér/ is always selected.

| | |
|---|---|
| /hwán ǀ ésmi̯ermáno ↓/ | John is my brother. |

When an adjective follows the linking verb, one has to decide whether the link of identity or the link of association is appropriate. The choice may often seem quite arbitrary to Americans, but when identity is involved (/sér/) , there seems to be a more inherent connection between the noun and the quality; when association is involved (/estár/), the connection is more or less incidental.

Thus even though /sér/ and /estár/ appear in utterances which show no other difference, the two utterances will never have the same 'meaning'. If a person describes a house with an adjective like pretty, saying 'The house is pretty', he cannot, in Spanish, express only this much of the idea. He must also say either that the house is intrinsically pretty,

/lakása̯ ǀ esboníta ↓/

or that it presents an unusually attractive appearance on a specific occasion (looks pretty),

/lakása̯ ǀ estáboníta ↓/

There is no way to make the incomplete statement (from the Spanish point of view) that the house 'is' pretty; additional refinements in meaning are obligatory in the choice of /sér/ or /estár/. Through this choice the Spanish speaker indicates the circumstances he considers *identity* and distinguishes them from those he considers *association.*

The distinction is, to be sure, forced by the structure of the language (the divided linking verb), but it is no less real to the speaker of Spanish, who never hesitates to select the correct form. It is only the American, whose background lacks the experience of making a meaning distinction, nonsignificant in English but highly significant in Spanish, who experiences a confusion between the two forms. In a very real sense, using /sér/ and /estár/ correctly involves an entire way of life, and an American seeking proficiency in spoken Spanish needs to acquire a 'feel' for the distinction by making a large number of sentences his own through memorization in meaningful contexts.

When a verb modifier appears with the linking verb, association is generally selected (/estár/), though not exclusively. Notice the following contrasts, most of which are illustrated in basic sentences:

| /estár/ | association | /sér/ | identity |
|---|---|---|---|
| /kómo̯estámaría ↓/ | How's Mary? | /kómo̯ésmaría ↓/ | What's Mary like? |
| /dóndestásu̯espósó ↓/ | Where's your husband? | /dedóndé(s)su̯espóso ↓/ | Where's your husband from? |
| /dóndestálafyésta ↓/ | Where's the party? | /dóndéslafyésta ↓/ | Where's the party being held? |

Other classifications and examples can be found in the appendix.

## 5.22 REPLACEMENT DRILLS

A dėképártė | đėlòṣėstáđòṣùníđòs | ėṣùstéđ ↓

| | |
|---|---|
| 1 ______________________ é(l)y̰òs ↓ | dėképártė \| đėlòṣėstáđòṣùníđòs \| sónẹ́(l)y̰òs ↓ |
| 2 _______________ ės _________ ↓ | dėképártė \| đėlòṣėstáđòṣùníđòs \| ėṣél ↓ |
| 3 ________ kȧlifórnyạ _________ ↓ | dėképártė \| đėkȧlifórnyȧ \| ėṣél ↓ |
| 4 ________________ lȧ(s)sėn̰yórȧs ↓ | dėképártė \| đėkȧlifórnyȧ \| sónlȧ(s)sėn̰yórȧs ↓ |
| 5 ______ đóndė _______________ ↓ | dėđóndėsón \| lȧ(s)sėn̰yórȧs ↓ |
| 6 ______________________ ùstéđ ↓ | dėđóndẹ \| ėṣùstéđ ↓ |
| 7 _____________ sómȯz _______ ↓ | dėđóndė \| sómȯznȯsótrȯs ↓ |

---

A ¿De qué parte de los Estados Unidos es usted?

| | |
|---|---|
| 1 ¿______________________ellos? | ¿De qué parte de los Estados Unidos son ellos? |
| 2 ¿__________________es ______? | ¿De qué parte de los Estados Unidos es él? |
| 3 ¿__________California ________? | ¿De qué parte de California es él? |
| 4 ¿__________________las señoras? | ¿De qué parte de California son las señoras? |
| 5 ¿______ dónde______________? | ¿De dónde son las señoras? |
| 6 ¿______________________ usted? | ¿De dónde es usted? |
| 7 ¿___________ somos ________? | ¿De dónde somos nosotros? |

B bı́nȯ | kȯnsu̇famı́lyȧ ↑

| | |
|---|---|
| 1 ________ mı ________ ↑ | bı́nȯ \| kȯnmıfamı́lyȧ ↑ |
| 2 báhȧ ________________ ↑ | báhȧ \| kȯnmıfamı́lyȧ ↑ |
| 3 ________ lȧ ________ ↑ | báhȧ \| kȯnlȧfamı́lyȧ ↑ |
| 4 ________________ famı́lyȧs ↑ | báhȧ \| kȯnlȧsfamı́lyȧs ↑ |
| 5 ________________ sėn̯yór ↑ | báhȧ \| kȯnẹlsėn̯yór ↑ |
| 6 trȧƀáhȧ ________________ ↑ | trȧƀáhȧ \| kȯnẹlsėn̯yór ↑ |
| 7 ________ lȯs ________ ↑ | trȧƀáhȧ \| kȯnlo(s)sėn̯yóres ↑ |

---

B ¿Vino con su familia?

| | |
|---|---|
| 1 ¿ ________ mi ________ ? | ¿Vino con mi familia? |
| 2 ¿Baja ________________ ? | ¿Baja con mi familia? |
| 3 ¿ ________ la ________ ? | ¿Baja con la familia? |
| 4 ¿ ________________ familias? | ¿Baja con las familias? |
| 5 ¿ ________ señor ________ ? | ¿Baja con el señor? |
| 6 ¿Trabaja ________________ ? | ¿Trabaja con el señor? |
| 7 ¿ ________ los ________ ? | ¿Trabaja con los señores? |

C nó̇ ↓ sóysȯlté̇rȯ ↓

| | | |
|---|---|---|
| 1 | __________ sómȯs __________ ↓ | nó̇ ↓ sómȯ(s)sȯlté̇rȯs ↓ |
| 2 | ______________________ ṣɪŋkȯ ↓ | nó̇ ↓ sómȯs(ṣ)ɪ́ŋkȯ ↓ |
| 3 | __________ són __________ ↓ | nó̇ ↓ sónṣɪ́ŋkȯ ↓ |
| 4 | ______________________ bwé̇nȧs ↓ | nó̇ ↓ sómbwé̇nȧs ↓ |
| 5 | ______________________ má̇s ↓ | nó̇ ↓ sónmá̇s ↓ |
| 6 | __________ áy __________ ↓ | nó̇ ↓ áymá̇s ↓ |
| 7 | __________ kyérȯ __________ ↓ | nó̇ ↓ kyérȯmá̇s ↓ |

---

C No, soy soltero.

| | | |
|---|---|---|
| 1 | __________ somos __________ . | No, somos solteros. |
| 2 | ______________________ cinco. | No, somos cinco. |
| 3 | __________ son __________ . | No, son cinco. |
| 4 | ______________________ buenas. | No, son buenas. |
| 5 | ______________________ más. | No, son más. |
| 6 | __________ hay __________ . | No, hay más. |
| 7 | __________ quiero __________ . | No, quiero más. |

D i̯ùstéđ ↓ éskàsáđò ↑

| | | |
|---|---|---|
| 1 | ____________ sóŋ ____________ ↑ | i̯ùstéđès ↓ sóŋkàsáđòs ↑ |
| 2 | ______________________ sòltéròs ↑ | i̯ùstéđès ↓ sónsòltéròs ↑ |
| 3 | _____ é(l)y̯a̯ __________________ ↑ | i̯é(l)y̯a̯ ↓ é(s)sòltérà ↑ |
| 4 | ____________ sóy _____________ ↑ | iy̯ó ↓ sóysòltérò ↑ |
| 5 | ______________________ sòltéràs ↑ | i̯é(l)y̯às ↓ sónsòltéràs ↑ |
| 6 | ____ nòsótròs _________________ ↑ | inòsótròs ↓ sómò(s)sòltéròs ↑ |
| 7 | ___________________ àmèrikánòs ↑ | inòsótròs ↓ sómòṣàmèrikánòs ↑ |

---

D Y usted, ¿es casado?

| | | |
|---|---|---|
| 1 | ____________ ¿son ____________ ? | Y ustedes, ¿son casados? |
| 2 | _____________ ¿________ solteros? | Y ustedes, ¿son solteros? |
| 3 | ______ ella, ¿ ________________ ? | Y ella, ¿es soltera? |
| 4 | ___________ ¿soy ____________ ? | Y yo, ¿soy soltero? |
| 5 | ___________ ¿__________solteras? | Y ellas, ¿son solteras? |
| 6 | _____ nosotros ¿ ______________ ? | Y nosotros, ¿somos solteros? |
| 7 | __________ ¿ _______ americanos? | Y nosotros, ¿somos americanos? |

E áy | u̇nrrėstȯrán | s̯ėrkȧđe̯ȧkí ↑

| | |
|---|---|
| 1 ________ ȯtél ________________ ↑ | áy \| u̇no̯tél \| s̯érkȧđe̯ȧkí ↑ |
| 2 _______ múchos ______________ ↑ | áy \| múchȯs̯ȯtélės \| (s̯)érkȧđe̯ȧkí ↑ |
| 3 __________ aƀéníđȧs _________ ↑ | áy \| múchas̯aƀėníđas \| (s̯)érkȧđe̯ȧkí ↑ |
| 4 __________________________ aí ↑ | áy \| múchas̯aƀėníđas \| (s̯)érkȧđe̯aí ↑ |
| 5 ________ ƀȧstántės ____________ ↑ | áy \| ƀastántes̯aƀėníđas \| (s̯)érkȧđe̯aí ↑ |
| 6 ______________táksıs __________ ↑ | áy \| ƀȧstántėstáksıs \| (s̯)érkȧđe̯aí ↑ |
| 7 ___________________la̯ėmbȧháđȧ ↑ | áy \| ƀȧstántėstáksıs \| (s̯)érkȧđela̯ėmbȧháđȧ ↑ |

---

E ¿Hay un restorán cerca de aquí?

| | |
|---|---|
| 1 ¿ _________ hotel _____________ ? | ¿Hay un hotel cerca de aquí? |
| 2 ¿ _______ muchos _____________ ? | ¿Hay muchos hoteles cerca de aquí? |
| 3 ¿ _________ avenidas __________ ? | ¿Hay muchas avenidas cerca de aquí? |
| 4 ¿ __________________________ ahí? | ¿Hay muchas avenidas cerca de ahí? |
| 5 ¿ _______ bastantes ____________ ? | ¿Hay bastantes avenidas cerca de ahi? |
| 6 ¿ ____________ taxis___________ ? | ¿Hay bastantes taxis cerca de ahí? |
| 7 ¿ __________________la Embajada? | ¿Hay bastantes taxis cerca de la Embajada? |

F pȯđémȯs | ȧlmȯrs̥ár | húntȯs ↓

| | |
|---|---|
| 1 ____________________ ȯtrȧƀés̥ ↓ | pȯđémȯs | ȧlmȯrs̥ár | ȯtrȧƀés̥ ↓ |
| 2 kyéro̯ ____________________ ↓ | kyéro̯ | ȧlmȯrs̥ár | ȯtrȧƀés̥ ↓ |
| 3 ________ ír ________________ ↓ | kyéro̯ír | ȯtrȧƀés̥ ↓ |
| 4 ________________________ ȧí ↓ | kyéro̯íraí ↓ |
| 5 pwéđe̯ ____________________ ↓ | pwéđe̯íraí ↓ |
| 6 __________________ tȧmbyén ↓ | pwéđe̯ír | tȧmbyén ↓ |
| 7 nės̥ėsítḁ __________________ ↓ | nės̥ėsítḁír | tȧmbyén ↓ |

---

F Podemos almorzar juntos.

| | |
|---|---|
| 1 ____________________ otra vez. | Podemos almorzar otra vez. |
| 2 Quiero ____________________ . | Quiero almorzar otra vez. |
| 3 ______ ir __________________ . | Quiero ir otra vez. |
| 4 ________________________ ahí. | Quiero ir ahí. |
| 5 Puede ____________________ . | Puede ir ahí. |
| 6 ____________________ también. | Puede ir también. |
| 7 Necesita ____________________ . | Necesita ir también. |

## 5.23 VARIATION DRILLS

| | | | |
|---|---|---|---|
| A | | ɪùstéđ ↓ dėđóndés ↓ | Y usted, ¿de dónde es? |
| 1 | And where's the gentleman from? | ɪėlsėnyór ↓ dėđóndés ↓ | Y el señor, ¿de dónde es? |
| 2 | And where's Mrs. Molina from? | ilàsėnyóramòlínà ↓ dėđóndés ↓ | Y la señora Molina, ¿de dónde es? |
| 3 | And where's the taxi driver from? | ɪėlchòférđėtáksi ↓ dėđóndés ↓ | Y el chofer de taxi, ¿de dónde es? |
| 4 | And where's the waiter from? | ɪėlmóșò ↓ dėđóndés ↓ | Y el mozo, ¿de dónde es? |
| 5 | And where's the cashier from? | ɪėlkàhérò ↓ dėđóndés ↓ | Y el cajero, ¿de dónde es? |
| 6 | And where're John and Joseph from? | ihwánɪhòsé ↓ dėđóndėsón ↓ | Y Juan y José, ¿de dónde son? |
| 7 | And where're the Molinas from? | ilòzmòlínà ↓ dėđóndėsón ↓ | Y los Molina, ¿de dónde son? |

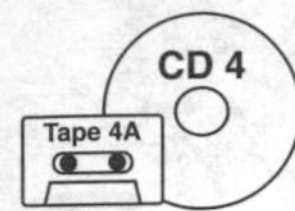




| | | | |
|---|---|---|---|
| B | sóyđèsàmfràns̯ískò \| kàlifórnyà ↓ | | Soy de San Francisco, California. |
| | 1 I'm from the United States. | sóy \| đèlòs̯èstáđòs̯ùníđòs ↓ | Soy de los Estados Unidos. |
| | 2 I'm from Florida. | sóyđèflòríđà ↓ | Soy de Florida. |
| | 3 I'm from here. | sóyđe̯àkí ↓ | Soy de aquí. |
| | 4 I'm a bachelor. | sóysòltérò ↓ | Soy soltero. |
| | 5 I'm a taxi driver. | sóychòférđètáksi ↓ | Soy chofer de taxi. |
| | 6 We're married. | sómòskàsáđòs ↓ | Somos casados. |
| | 7 We're single. | sómò(s)sòltéròs ↓ | Somos solteros. |
| C | ke̯óra̯és ↓ | | ¿Qué hora es? |
| | 1 What day is it? | kéđía̯és ↓ | ¿Qué día es? |
| | 2 What language is it? | kéléŋgwa̯és ↓ | ¿Qué lengua es? |

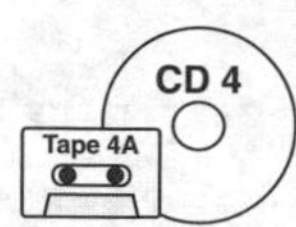




| | | | |
|---|---|---|---|
| | 3 What hotel is it? | kéo̯télés ↓ | ¿Qué hotel es? |
| | 4 What school is it? | késkwélaa̯és ↓ | ¿Qué escuela es? |
| | 5 What tables are they? | kémésȧ(s)són ↓ | ¿Que mesas son? |
| | 6 What books are they? | kélíƀrȯ(s)són ↓ | ¿Qué libros son? |
| | 7 What (kind of a) thing is it? | kékósa̯és ↓ | ¿Qué cosa es? |
| D | són I lázđóşėménȯskwártȯ ↓ | | Son las doce menos cuarto. |
| | 1 It's fifteen to twelve. | són I lȧzđóşėménȯskínşė ↓ | Son las doce menos quince. |
| | 2 It's ten to eleven | són I lȧşónşėménȯzđyéş ↓ | Son las once menos diez. |
| | 3 It's twenty to seven. | són I lȧ(s)syétėménȯzƀéyntė ↓ | Son las siete menos veinte. |
| | 4 It's five to nine. | són I lȧznwéƀėménȯ(s)şíŋkȯ ↓ | Son las nueve menos cinco. |
| | 5 It's a quarter to eight. | són I lȧşóchȯménȯskwártȯ ↓ | Son las ocho menos cuarto. |

| | | |
|---|---|---|
| 6 It's six. | són \| lȧ(s)séẏs ↓ | Son las seis. |
| 7 It's one. | éz \| la̯únȧ ↓ | Es la una. |

| | | |
|---|---|---|
| E | y̯átyéne̯ámbrė ↑ | ¿Ya tiene hambre? |
| 1 Have you got the dollars already? | yátyénė \| lȯzđólȧrės ↑ | ¿Ya tiene los dólares? |
| 2 Have you got the check already? | yátyéne̯ \| ėlchékė ↑ | ¿Ya tiene el cheque? |
| 3 Has she got a room already? | yátyéne̯ \| u̇ŋkwártȯ ↑ | ¿Ya tiene un cuarto? |
| 4 Has she got a table already? | yátyéne̯ \| u̇nȧmésȧ ↑ | ¿Ya tiene una mesa? |
| 5 Has he got twenty dollars already? | yátyénė \| ƀéyntėđólȧrės ↑ | ¿Ya tiene veinte dólares? |
| 6 Does he have a hotel? | tyéne̯u̇nọ́tel ↑ | ¿Tiene un hotel? |
| 7 Does he have a taxi? | tyéne̯u̇ntáksı ↑ | ¿Tiene un taxi? |

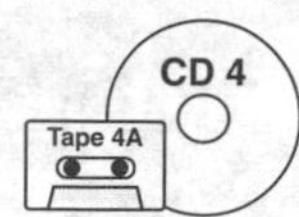




F sí ↓ áyúno̯ | àlàƀwélta | kèzƀwéno̯iƀàráto ↓ — Sí, hay uno a la vuelta que es bueno y barato.

| | | | |
|---|---|---|---|
| 1 | Yes, there's one here that's very good. | sí ↓ áyúno̯ \| àkí \| kèzmúyƀwéno ↓ | Sí, hay uno aquí que es muy bueno. |
| 2 | Yes, there's one here that's excellent. | sí ↓ áyúno̯ \| àkí \| kèsèks(s̯)èlénte ↓ | Sí, hay uno aquí que es excelente. |
| 3 | Yes, there's one there, but it costs a lot. | sí ↓ áyúno̯ \| àí \| péròkwéstàmúcho ↓ | Sí, hay uno ahí, pero cuesta mucho. |
| 4 | Yes, there's one at the Embassy but it's busy. | sí ↓ áyúno̯ \| ènla̯èmbàháđa \| péro̯ èstáo̯kùpáđo ↓ | Sí, hay uno en la Embajada pero está ocupado. |
| 5 | Yes, there's one on the first floor who is an American. | sí ↓ áyúno̯ \| èn̯èlprimérpíso \| kès̯àmèrikáno ↓ | Sí, hay uno en el primer piso que es americano. |
| 6 | No, there's not another one to the left. | nó ↓ no̯áyótro̯ \| àla̯is̯kyérđa ↓ | No, no hay otro a la izquierda. |
| 7 | No, there's not another school of languages. | nó ↓ no̯áyótra̯ \| èskwélàđèléŋgwàs ↓ | No, no hay otra escuela de lenguas. |

# 5.3 CONVERSATION STIMULUS

## NARRATIVE 1

| | | |
|---|---|---|
| 1 It's almost twelve o'clock. | sóŋkásilȧzđós̯ė ↓ | Son casi las doce. |
| 2 Jose is going to have lunch with John. | hȯsé \| ƀálmȯrs̯ár \| kȯŋhwán ↓ | José va a almorzar con Juan. |
| 3 John isn't very hungry. | hwán \| nótyénė \| múchámbrė ↓ | Juan no tiene mucha hambre. |
| 4 There's a good restaurant around the corner. | áyúmbwénrrėstȯrán \| ȧlȧƀwéltȧ ↓ | Hay un buen restorán a la vuelta. |
| 5 The restaurant is quite inexpensive. | ėlrrėstorán \| ėzbȧstántėƀȧrátȯ ↓ | El restorán es bastante barato. |

## DIALOG 1

| | | |
|---|---|---|
| José, preguntele a Juan si no va a almorzar. | nóƀálmȯrs̯ár \| hwán ↑ | José: ¿No va a almorzar, Juan? |
| Juan, contéstele que Ud. no tiene mucha hambre y preguntele que qué hora es. | nótéŋgȯmúchámbrė ↓  ke̯óra̯és ↓ | Juan: No tengo mucha hambre. ¿Qué hora es? |

| | | |
|---|---|---|
| José, dígale que son casi las doce, y pregúntele si pueden almorzar juntos. | sóŋkásilȧzđóṣė ↓ pȯđémȯs<br>ȧlmȯrṣár \| húntȯs ↑ | José: Son casi las doce. ¿Podemos almorzar juntos? |
| Juan, contéstele que muy bien, que vayan, y pregúntele que adónde pueden ir. | múyƀyém ↓ bámȯs ↓ ȧđóndė<br>pȯđémȯsír ↓ | Juan: Muy bien, vamos. ¿A dónde podemos ir? |
| José, dígale que a la vuelta, que hay un buen restorán ahí. | ȧlȧƀwéltȧ ↓ áy \| ȗm<br>bwénrrėstȯrán \| ȧí ↓ | José: A la vuelta. Hay un buen restorán ahí. |
| Juan, preguntele si es barato. | ézƀȧrátȯ ↑ | Juan: ¿Es barato? |
| José, dígale que sí, que es bastante barato. | sí ↓ ézƀȧstántėƀȧrátȯ ↓ | José: Sí, es bastante barato. |

## NARRATIVE 2

| | | |
|---|---|---|
| 1 Carmen del Valle is in the restaurant. | kármėndėlbá(l)y̯e̯ \| ėstáe̯nėlrrėstȯrán ↓ | Carmen del Valle está en el restorán. |
| 2 John wants to meet her. | hwáŋkyérėkȯnȯṣérlȧ ↓ | Juan quiere conocerla. |
| 3 She is at a table on the left. | é(l)y̯a̯ėstá \| e̯nụnȧmésȧla̯iṣkyérđȧ ↓ | Ella está en una mesa a la izquierda. |
| 4 Carmen speaks English very well. | kármėn \| ábla̯iŋgléz \| múyƀyén ↓ | Carmen habla inglés muy bien. |

| | | |
|---|---|---|
| 5 She learned it in school, in the States. | lo̯àprèndyó \| e̯nla̯èskwélà ↓ ènlòs̯èstáđòs̯uníđòs ↓ | Lo aprendió en la escuela, en los Estados Unidos. |

## DIALOG 2

| | | |
|---|---|---|
| José, dígale a Juan que ahí está Carmen del Valle. Pregúntele si quiere conocerla. | áie̯stá \| kármèndèlbá(l)y̯è ↓ kyérèkònòs̯érlà ↑ | José: Ahí está Carmen del Valle. ¿Quiere conocerla? |
| Juan, contestele que si, que cómo no. Pregúntele que dónde está. | sí ↓ kómònó ↓ dóndèstá ↓ | Juan: Sí, cómo no. ¿Dónde está? |
| José, dígale que está ahí a la izquierda. | èstáí ↓ àla̯is̯kyérđà ↓ | José: Está ahí, a la izquierda. |
| Juan, pregúntele a José si Carmen habla inglés. | áƀla̯iŋgléskármèn ↑ | Juan: ¿Habla inglés Carmen? |
| José, contéstele que sí, que lo habla muy bien, que lo aprendió en los Estados Unidos en la escuela. | sí ↓ lo̯áblàmúyƀyén ↓ lo̯àprèndyó \| e̯nlòs̯èstáđòs̯uníđòs \| ènla̯èskwélà ↓ | José: Sí, lo habla muy bien. Lo aprendió en los Estados Unidos en la escuela. |

## NARRATIVE 3

| | | |
|---|---|---|
| 1 John is delighted to meet Carmen. | hwán \| èstáe̯ŋkàntáđò \| đèkònòşérà kármèn ↓ | Juan está encantado de conocer a Carmen. |
| 2 He talks with her in English and then in Spanish. | ábla \| kòne̥(l)ya̯èniŋglés ↑ ilwégo̯ èn̥èspàn̥yól ↓ | Habla con ella en inglés y luego en español. |
| 3 He says that he is from California. | éldíşè \| kézđèkàlifórnyà ↓ | El dice que es de California. |
| 4 No, he isn't from San Francisco, he's from San Diego. | nó ↓ élno̯ézđèsamfrànşískò ↓ ézđèsàndyégò ↓ | No, él no es de San Francisco, es de San Diego. |
| 5 He arrived yesterday. | bíno̯ayér ↓ | Vino ayer. |
| 6 He didn't come with his family. | nóbínòkònláfamílyà ↓ | No vino con la familia. |
| 7 He's single. | é(s)sòltérò ↓ | Es soltero. |

## DIALOG 3

| | | |
|---|---|---|
| José, dígale hola a Carmen y pregúntele que qué tal. | ólȧ ǀ kármėn ↓ ketál ↓ | José: Hola, Carmen, ¿qué tal? |
| Carmen, dígale hola también y pregúntele que qué tal, que cómo le va. | ólȧ ǀ hȯsé ↓ ketál ↓ kȯmȯlėƀá ↓ | Carmen: Hola, José ¿qué tal? ¿Cómo le va? |
| José, contéstele que bastante bien, que gracias, y dígale que quiere presentarle al Sr. White, Juan White. | bȧstántėƀyéŋ ǀ grás̥yȧs ↓<br>kármėn ↓ kyérȯprėsėntárlẹ ǀ<br>ȧlsėn̥yórhwáyt ↓ hwáŋhwáyt ↓ | José: Bastante bien, gracias. Carmen, quiero presentale al Sr. White, Juan White. |
| Carmen, dígale a Juan que mucho gusto. | múchȯgústȯ ǀ sėn̥yór ↓ | Carmen: Mucho gusto, señor. |
| Juan, dígale a la señorita que encantado de conocerla. | ėŋkȧntáđođėkȯnȯs̥érlȧ ǀ sėn̥yȯrítȧ ↓ | Juan: Encantado de conocerla, señorita. |
| Jose, pregúntele a Carmen si pueden almorzar con ella. | pȯđémȯs ǀ ȧlmȯrs̥ár ǀ kȯn̥ustéđ ǀ kármėn ↑ | José: ¿Podemos almorzar con usted, Carmen? |
| Carmen, contéstele que sí, cómo no, que encantada. Dígales a los dos que se sienten. | sí ↓ kómȯnó ↓ ėŋkȧntáđȧ ↓ syéntėnsė ↓ | Carmen: Sí, cómo no, encantada. Siéntense. |
| Jose, dígale a Carmen que Juan es de California. | hwánẹzđėkȧlıfórnyȧ ǀ kármėn ↓ | José: Juan es de California, Carmen. |

| | | |
|---|---|---|
| Carmen, dígale que dispense, que cómo dice. | dispénsė ↓ kómȯđíșė ↑ | Carmen: Dispense, ¿cómo dice? |
| José, repítale que Juan es de California. | kėhwánėzđėkalifórnyȧ ↓ | José: Que Juan es de California. |
| Carmen, diga ¿ah, sí? y pregúntele a Juan que de qué parte, si de San Francisco. | á \| sí ↑ dėképártė ↓ dėsȧmfrȧnșískȯ ↑ | Carmen: ¿Ah, sí? ¿De qué parte? ¿De San Francisco? |
| Juan, contéstele que no, que Ud. es de San Diego. | nó ↓ sóyđėsȧndyégȯ ↓ | Juan: No, soy de San Diego. |
| Carmen, pregúntele que cuándo vino. | kwándȯƀínȯ ↓ | Carmen: ¿Cuándo vino? |
| Juan, contéstele que ayer. | ȧyér ↓ | Juan: Ayer. |
| Carmen, pregúntele si vino con la familia. | bínȯ \| kȯnlȧfamílyȧ ↑ | Carmen: ¿Vino con la familia? |
| Juan, contéstele que no, que Ud. no tiene familia, que es soltero. | nó ↓ yónȯtéŋgȯfamílyȧ ↓ sóysȯltérȯ ↓ | Juan: No, yo no tengo familia, soy soltero. |

**End of Tape 4A***

*Tape 4A actually ends on page 178 of this book because it covers the dialogues for listening and learning of Unit 6. However, Tape 4B starts on page 174 and covers the dialogue for fluency of the same Unit.

# 6.1 BASIC SENTENCES

## White and Molina have lunch together

John White and Jose Molina enter the restaurant.

| English Spelling | Aid to Listening | Spanish Spelling |
|---|---|---|
| there (in that place) | ȧ(l)y̯í ↓ | allí |
| empty (to vacate, empty) | dėsȯkůpáđȯ ↓ dėsȯkůpár ↓ | desocupado (desocupar) |
| *JOSE MOLINA* | | *JOSE MOLINA* |
| There's an empty table over there. | ȧ(l)y̯íáy \| ůnȧmésȧ \| đėsȯkůpáđȧ ↓ | Allí hay una mesa desocupada. |
| to seat | sėntár ↓ | sentar |
| ourselves | nós ↓ | nos |
| to seat ourselves (to seat oneself, to sit down) | sėntárnȯs ↓ sėntársė ↓ | sentarnos (sentarse) |
| *JOHN WHITE* | | *JOHN WHITE* |
| Let's sit down. | bámȯsa̦sėntárnȯs ↓ | Vamos a sentarnos. |
| let's see (to see) | bėámȯs ↓ bér ↓ | veamos (ver) |
| the menu | ėl—mėnú ↓ | el menú |
| *JOSE MOLINA* | | *JOSE MOLINA* |
| Let's see the menu. | bėámȯse̦lmėnú ↓ | Veamos el menú. |
| (you) wish (to wish) | dėséȧn ↓ dėsėár ↓ | desean (desear) |

| *WAITER* | | *MESERO* |
|---|---|---|
| What will you have, gentlemen? | kéđèséanụstéđès \| sèṇyórès ↓ | ¿Qué desean ustedes, señores? |
| the sandwich | èl—sáŋw̱ich ↓ | el sandwich |
| the ham | èl—hàmón ↓ | el jamón |
| *JOHN WHITE* | | *JOHN WHITE* |
| I want a ham sandwich. | y̱ókyérọunsáŋw̱ich \| đèhàmón ↓ | Yo quiero un sandwich de jamón. |
| the salad | lạ—ènsàláđà ↓ | la ensalada |
| the lettuce | là—lèchúgà ↓ | la lechuga |
| the tomato | èl—tòmátè ↓ | el tomate |
| Also a lettuce and tomato salad. | tàmbyén \| ènsàláđà \| đèlèchúgạitòmátè ↓ | También ensalada de lechuga y tomate. |
| the beer | là—ṣèrƀéṣà ↓ | la cerveza |
| And a beer. | ịúnàṣèrƀésà ↓ | Y una cerveza. |
| to me | à—mí ↓ | a mí |
| bring (to bring) | tráygà ↓ trạér ↓ | traiga (traer) |
| bring me | tráygàmè ↓ | tráigame |

| | | |
|---|---|---|
| the soup | lȧ—sópȧ ↓ | la sopa |
| the vegetable | lȧ—lėgúmbrė ↓ | la legumbre |
| the chop | lȧ—chu̇létȧ ↓ | la chuleta |
| the pork, pig | ėl—şérđȯ ↓ | el cerdo |
| the wine | ėl—bínȯ ↓ | el vino |
| *JOSE MOLINA* | | *JOSE MOLINA* |
| Bring *me* vegetable soup, pork chops and wine. (1) | ȧmí \| tráygȧmėsópȧ \| đėlėgúmbrės ↑ chu̇létȧzđėşérđọibínȯ ↓ | A mí tráigame sopa de legumbres, chuletas de cerdo y vino. |
| the dessert | ėl—póstrė ↓ | el postre |
| of (for) dessert | dė—póstrė ↓ | de postre |
| (you) want (to want) | kyérėn ↓ kėrér ↓ | quieren (querer) |
| *WAITER* | | *MESERO* |
| What'll you have for dessert? | dėpóstrė \| kékyérėn ↓ | De postre, ¿qué quieren? |
| the pie | ėl—pȧstél ↓ | el pastel |
| the apple | lȧ—mȧnşánȧ ↓ | la manzana |
| There's some apple pie, that's very good. | áy \| u̇mpȧstéldėmȧnşánȧ \| kėzmúyƀwénȯ ↓ | Hay un pastel de manzana que es muy bueno. |
| (we) try (to try, to taste) | prȯƀámȯs ↓ prȯƀár ↓ | probamos (probar) |
| *JOHN WHITE* | | *JOHN WHITE* |
| Shall we try it? | lȯprȯƀámȯs ↑ | ¿Lo probamos? |

| | | |
|---|---|---|
| (I) have (to have) | é ↓ ȧƀér ↓ | he (haber) |
| eaten (to eat) | kȯmíđȯ ↓ kȯmér ↓ | comido (comer) |
| (I) have eaten (2) | ė—kȯmíđȯ ↓ | he comido |
| *JOSE MOLINA* | | *JOSE MOLINA* |
| I've already had it. It's excellent. | yóyálọėkȯmíđȯ ↓ ézƀwénȯ ↓ | Yo ya lo he comido. Es bueno. |
| for | párȧ ↓ | para |
| Bring us both some. | tráyg̣apȧrȧlozđós ↓ | Traiga para los dos. |
| if | sí ↓ | si |
| to treat | trȧtár ↓ | tratar |
| ourselves (we) treat of you (to address as) | nós—trȧtámȯz—đė—tú ↓<br>trȧtársė—đė ↓ | nos tratamos de tú (tratarse de) |
| What do you say if we just use 'tú' ? (3) | kėlėpȧréṣė \| sınȯstrȧtámȯz \| đėtú ↓ | ¿Qué le parece si nos tratamos de tú? |
| (you) have (to have) | tyénės ↓ tėnér ↓ | tienes (tener) |
| the reason | lȧ—rrȧṣón ↓ | la razón |
| *JOHN WHITE* | | *JOHN WHITE* |
| You're right. Good idea. | tyénėzrrȧṣón ↓ múyƀyén ↓ | Tienes razón. Muy bien. |
| (you) go (to go) | bás ↓ ír ↓ | vas (ir) |

<table>
<tr><td>to live</td><td>biƀír ↓</td><td>vivir</td></tr>
<tr><td>JOSE MOLINA</td><td></td><td>JOSE MOLINA</td></tr>
<tr><td>Are you going to live at the hotel?</td><td>básạƀiƀír | ènẹlòtél ↑</td><td>¿Vas a vivir en el hotel?</td></tr>
<tr><td>(I) think (to think)</td><td>pyénsò ↓ pènsár ↓</td><td>pienso (pensar)</td></tr>
<tr><td>to look for (4)</td><td>bùskár ↓</td><td>buscar</td></tr>
<tr><td>the apartment</td><td>èl—àpàrtàméntò ↓</td><td>el apartamento</td></tr>
<tr><td>JOHN WHITE</td><td></td><td>JOHN WHITE</td></tr>
<tr><td>No, I plan to look for an apartment.</td><td>nó ↓ pyénsò | ƀùskárùnạpàrtàméntò ↓</td><td>No, pienso buscar un apartamento.</td></tr>
<tr><td>easy</td><td>fáṣil ↓</td><td>fácil</td></tr>
<tr><td>to find</td><td>èŋkòntrár ↓</td><td>encontrar</td></tr>
<tr><td>Is it easy to find one here?</td><td>ésfáṣil | dèŋkòntrárákí ↑</td><td>¿Es fácil de encontrar aquí?</td></tr>
<tr><td>(I) believe (to believe)</td><td>kréò ↓ krẹér ↓</td><td>creo (creer)</td></tr>
<tr><td>JOSE MOLINA</td><td></td><td>JOSE MOLINA</td></tr>
<tr><td>I think so.</td><td>y̯ókréò | kèsí ↓</td><td>Yo creo que sí.</td></tr>
<tr><td>(you fam.) want (to want)</td><td>kyérès ↓ kèrér ↓</td><td>quieres (querer)</td></tr>
<tr><td>you, to you (fam)</td><td>té ↓</td><td>te</td></tr>
<tr><td>(I) can (to be able)</td><td>pwéđò ↓ pòđér ↓</td><td>puedo (poder)</td></tr>
<tr><td>to help</td><td>àyùđár ↓</td><td>ayudar</td></tr>
<tr><td>If you want, I can help you.</td><td>sikyérès ↑ y̯ó | tèpwéđòạyùđár ↓</td><td>Si quieres, yo te puedo ayudar.</td></tr>
<tr><td>the check, the bill</td><td>là—kwéntà ↓</td><td>la cuenta</td></tr>
<tr><td>Waiter! The check.</td><td>móṣò ↓ làkwéntà ↓</td><td>¡Mozo! La cuenta.</td></tr>
</table>

### 6.10 Notes on the basic sentences

(1) The Spanish equivalent of 'bring *me*' in this sentence is [ amí | tráygame] *a mi tráigame* 'to me bring me'. The reason why *a mi* is present is to indicate contrast with what the other person is having. This is shown in English by extra stress on the word *me,* but in Spanish one cannot make the contrast by placing stress on the *me* of [ tráygame].

(2) Note that there are two verbs meaning 'have' in Spanish. You have already had *tener,* which means 'have' in the sense of 'possess'. This new verb, *haber,* means 'have,' the auxiliary verb form in verb constructions like 'have gone, have been,' etc. Constructions with *haber* will be drilled and explained in detail in Unit 9.

(3) This is the first occurrence in the dialogs of the use of the verb and pronoun forms that are ordinarily called the *familiar forms*. They are in contrast with the *formal forms* that go with the pronouns *usted* and *ustedes*. As explained in Unit 4, the problem of when to use *tú* and when to use *usted* is a very complex one indeed, and you should observe throughout all the remainder of the text which people use the *tú* forms with each other and which ones use *usted*.

(4) Notice that the single word [buskár] *buscar* means 'to look for', not just 'to look' —that is, no preposition is needed to translate the 'for' part of 'look for'.

## 6.2 DRILLS AND GRAMMAR

### 6.21 Pattern drills

### 6.21.1 Present tense forms of regular /—ár/ verbs

A. PRESENTATION OF PATTERN

*ILLUSTRATIONS*

| | | |
|---|---|---|
| ________________ | 1 sí ↓ áƀlo̯u̇mpókȯ ↓ | Si, *hablo* un poco. |
| I ('ll) help you. | 2 y̰óte̯ȧy̰úđȯ ↓ | Yo te *ayudo*. |
| Do you speak English? | 3 áƀlȧṣiŋglés ↑ | ¿*Hablas* inglés? |
| Are you looking for an apartment? | 4 búskȧs \| u̇nạpȧrtȧméntȯ ↑ | ¿*Buscas* un apartamento? |

| | | |
|---|---|---|
| ________________ | 5 áƀla̯u̇stéđi̇ŋglés ↑ | ¿*Habla* usted inglés? |
| ________________ | 6 nėʂėsítálgȯmás ↑ | ¿*Necesita* algo más? |
| John works with us. | 7 hwántrȧƀáhȧ ǀ kȯ(n)nȯsótrȯs ↓ | Juan *trabaja* con nosotros. |
| ________________ | 8 nȯstrȧtámȯzđėtú ↑ | ¿Nos *tratamos* de 'tú'? |
| Yes, we speak a little. | 9 sí ↓ ȧƀlámȯṣu̇mpókȯ ↓ | Sí, *hablamos* un poco. |
| ________________ | 10 kéđėséȧṇu̇stéđės ǀ sėn̨yórės ↓ | ¿Qué *desean* ustedes, señores? |
| The gentlemen take a taxi. | 11 lȯ(s)sėn̨yórės ǀ tómȧṇu̇ntáksi ↓ | Los señores *toman* un taxi. |
| The ladies practice a lot. | 12 lȧ(s)sėn̨yórȧs ǀ prȧktíkȧnmúchȯ ↓ | Las señoras *practican* mucho. |

## *EXTRAPOLATION*

| | sg | pl |
|---|---|---|
| 1 | —o | —ámos |
| 2 fam | —as | |
| 2-3 | —a | —an |

## *NOTES*

a. Spanish regular verbs can be grouped into *theme classes*. Which set of endings a verb takes depends on which theme class the verb belongs to.

b. Regular /—ár/ verbs have the theme /a/ recurring in the endings of all present tense forms except 1 sg.

## 6.21.11 SUBSTITUTION DRILLS

Number substitution

1 tràƀáhò | nwéƀe̯óràs ↓ — tràƀàhámòz | nwéƀe̯óràs ↓

2 áƀlànè̩spànyól ↓ — áƀla̯èspànyól ↓

3 nónèse̯sítà(n)náđà ↓ — nónèse̯sítànádà ↓

4 tràƀàhámòzmúchò ↓ — tràƀáhòmúchò ↓

5 áƀlàni̩ŋglés ↓ — áƀla̯iŋglés ↓

6 nótràƀáhàna̩í ↓ — nótràƀáhaí ↓

7 nèse̯sítótròlíbrò ↓ — nèse̯sitámòsótròlíbrò ↓

---

1 Trabajo nueve horas. — Trabajamos nueve horas.

2 Hablan español. — Habla español.

3 No necesitan nada. — No necesita nada.

4 Trabajamos mucho. — Trabajo mucho.

5 Hablan inglés. — Habla inglés.

6 No trabajan ahí. — No trabaja ahí.

7 Necesito otro libro. — Necesitamos otro libro.

Person - number substitution

1 nȯsótrȯstrȧƀahámȯṣakí ↓

y̯ó ____________________ ↓ trȧƀáho̯ȧkí ↓

ȧlíṣya̯i̯ȧntónyȯ ____________ ↓ trȧƀáhȧṇakí ↓

él ____________________ ↓ trȧƀáhȧkí ↓

u̇stéđės ______________ ↓ trȧƀáhȧṇakí ↓

2 y̯o̯áblȯpóko̯ėspȧn̯yól

é(l)y̯a̯ _________________ ↓ áƀlȧpóko̯ėspȧn̯yól ↓

ȧntónyo̯ı̇páƀlo̯ ____________ ↓ áƀlȧmpóko̯ėspȧn̯yól ↓

---

1 *Nosotros* trabajamos aquí.

Yo ____________________ . Trabajo aquí.

Alicia y Antonio ___________ . Trabajan aquí.

El ____________________ . Trabaja aquí.

Ustedes ________________ . Trabajan aquí.

2 *Yo* hablo poco español.

Ella __________________ . Habla poco español.

Antonio y Pablo ___________ . Hablan poco español.

| | |
|---|---|
| àlı́s̯yaiyó ________________ ↓ | àb̶lámòspokòespàn̯yól ↓ |
| ùsted̶ ________________ ↓ | áblàpokòespàn̯yól ↓ |

3 àlı́s̯ya | nónès̯èsı́tàpèrmísò ↓

| | |
|---|---|
| yó ________________ ↓ | nónès̯èsı́topèrmísò ↓ |
| nòsótròz ________________ ↓ | nónès̯èsitámòspèrmísò ↓ |
| é(l)yàz ________________ ↓ | nónès̯èsı́tampèrmíso ↓ |
| ùstéd̶èz ________________ ↓ | nónès̯èsı́tampèrmísò ↓ |

---

| | |
|---|---|
| Alicia y yo ________________ . | Hablamos poco español. |
| Usted ________________ . | Habla poco español. |

3 *Alicia* no necesita permiso.

| | |
|---|---|
| Yo ________________ . | No necesito permiso. |
| Nosotros ________________ . | No necesitamos permiso. |
| Ellas ________________ . | No necesitan permiso. |
| Ustedes ________________ . | No necesitan permiso. |

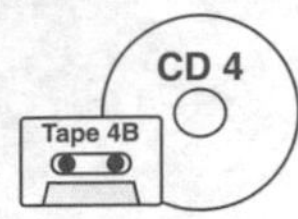



## 6.21.12 RESPONSE DRILL

| | | |
|---|---|---|
| | 1 tràƀáhaùstéđàkí ↑ o̯eŋkàlifórnyà ↓ | tràƀáho̯àkí ↓ |
| | 2 áƀlànùstéđèzƀyén \| èlèspàn̰yól ↑ o̯èlìŋglès ↓ | àƀlámòzƀyén \| èliŋglés ↓ |
| | 3 tràƀáha̯él \| ènla̯èmbàhádà ↑ o̯àkí ↓ | tràƀáhàkí ↓ |
| | 4 nèṣèsíta̯ùstéđ \| ùnlápɪṣ ↑ o̯ùnàplúmà ↓ | nèṣèsíto̯ùnàplúmà ↓ |
| [èspàn̰yól ↓] | 5 ke̯áƀlàn \| é(l)y̯òṣàkí ↓ | áƀlàn̰èspàn̰yól ↓ |
| [àkí ↓] | 6 dóndètràƀáha̯ \| ùstéđ ↓ | tràƀáho̯àkí ↓ |
| [èspàn̰yól ↓] | 7 ke̯áƀla̯ \| ùstéđàkí ↓ | áƀlo̯èspàn̰yól ↓ |

---

| | | |
|---|---|---|
| | 1 ¿Trabaja usted aquí o en California? | Trabajo aquí. |
| | 2 ¿Hablan ustedes bien el español o el inglés? | Hablamos bien el inglés. |
| | 3 ¿Trabaja él en la Embajada o aquí? | Trabaja aquí. |
| | 4 ¿Necesita usted un lápiz o una pluma? | Necesito una pluma. |
| (español) | 5 ¿Qué hablan ellos aquí? | Hablan español. |
| (aquí) | 6 ¿Dónde trabaja usted? | Trabajo aquí. |
| (español) | 7 ¿Qué habla usted aquí? | Hablo español. |

| | | |
|---|---|---|
| [séys ↓] | 8 kwántaṣórȧs \| trȧƀȧhámȯznȯsótrȯs ↓ | trȧƀȧhámȯs \| séyṣórȧs ↓ |
| [sı́(l)y̧ȧs ↓] | 9 nėṣėsı́tanụstéđez \| mázmésȧs ↑ | nó ↓ nėṣėsitámȯzmá(s)sı́(l)y̧ȧs ↓ |
| [ȧkí ↓] | 10 trȧƀahạéleŋkalı́fornyȧ ↑ | nó ↓ trȧƀáhȧkí ↓ |
| [iŋglés ↓] | 11 áƀlạustéđbyén \| ėléspȧṇyól ↑ | nó ↓ áƀlȯƀyénẹliŋglés ↓ |
| | 12 ȧƀlámȯṣélıyọ \| éspȧṇyól ↑ | sí ↓ ȯstéđes \| áƀlȧnėspȧṇyól ↓ |
| | 13 trȧƀahạustéđbȧstánte ↑ | sí ↓ trȧƀáhȯƀȧstántė ↓ |

---

| | | |
|---|---|---|
| (seis) | 8 ¿Cuántas horas trabajamos nosotros? | Trabajamos seis horas. |
| (sillas) | 9 ¿Necesitan ustedes más mesas? | No, necesitamos más sillas. |
| (aquí) | 10 ¿Trabaja él en California? | No, trabaja aquí. |
| (inglés) | 11 ¿Habla usted bien el español? | No, hablo bien el inglés. |
| | 12 ¿Hablamos él y yo español? | Sí, ustedes hablan español. |
| | 13 ¿Trabaja usted bastante? | Sí, trabajo bastante. |

## 6.21.13 TRANSLATION DRILL

| | | | |
|---|---|---|---|
| 1 | I don't pronounce very well. | nóprònúns̯yȯ \| mùyƀyén ↓ | No pronuncio muy bien. |
| 2 | We don't speak much Spanish. | no̯áƀlámȯz \| múcho̯ėspȧn̯yól ↓ | No hablamos mucho español. |
| 3 | When do you all need the desk? | kwándȯnės̯ėsítȧṇùstéđės \| ėlėskritóryȯ ↓ | ¿Cuándo necesitan ustedes el escritorio? |
| 4 | She doesn't need anything now. | é(l)y̯ȧ \| nónės̯ėsítȧ \| náđȧórȧ ↓ | Ella no necesita nada ahora. |
| 5 | I always take a taxi. | syémprė \| tómo̯ùntáksi ↓ | Siempre tomo un taxi. |
| 6 | Where do you work? | dóndėtrȧƀáha̯ \| ùstéđ ↓ | ¿Dónde trabaja usted? |
| 7 | Do you all speak Spanish? | áƀlȧṇùstéđės \| ėspȧn̯yól ↑ | ¿Hablan ustedes español? |
| 8 | I haven't worked since yesterday. | nótrȧƀáhȯ \| đėzđe̯ȧy̯ér ↓ | No trabajo desde ayer. |
| 9 | Do I pronounce well? | prònúns̯yȯyó \| ƀyén ↑ | ¿Pronuncio yo bien? |
| 10 | We'll cash the check later. | dėspwés \| kȧmbyámȯzlȯschékės ↓ | Después cambiamos los cheques. |
| 11 | They almost always speak in Spanish. | é(l)y̯ȯs \| kásisyémpre̯ \| áƀlȧṇėṇėspȧn̯yól ↓ | Ellos casi siempre hablan en español. |

| | | |
|---|---|---|
| 12 We work in a language school. | tráƀàhámȯs ǀ ėṇu̇naẹ̇skwélȧđėléŋgwȧs ↓ | Trabajamos en una escuela de lenguas. |
| 13 Do you speak Spanish? | áƀla̯u̇séđ ǀ ėspȧṇyól ↑ | ¿Habla usted español? |

## B. DISCUSSION OF PATTERN

Determining which verbs are *regular* and which are *irregular* in a language like Spanish is a matter of statistics. When one examines all the verbs in the lexicon, the largest group which has similar changes within a patterned frame is considered regular; other verb patterns are most economically described in terms of their deviation from this established norm.

An examination of Spanish verbs shows that the *infinitive* forms (traditionally the 'center' or 'point of beginning' in the verb pattern) can be divided into three groups, according to what vowel precedes the final /—r/. The three groups can be referred to as /—ár/, /—ér/, and /—ír/ verbs. The identifying vowel is called the *theme vowel,* since it recurrs in many of the conjugated forms of the verb. That part of the infinitive which remains when the /—Vr/ *(vowels* plus /r/ ) is removed is known as the *stem.*

From among these three subclasses of verbs, the present discussion describes those of the /—ár/ theme class which are regular in the present tense.

One of the characteristics of regular verbs in Spanish is that person, number, and tense categories are signalled by changes in the *endings*. In regular verbs (and in some irregular verbs) there are no changes in the stem other than the occurrence or non-occurrence of strong stress, which is shifted to the ending for 1 pl forms in the present tense:

| | sg | pl |
|---|---|---|
| 1 | _́ o | —ámos |
| 2 fam | _́ as | |
| 2-3 | _́ a | _́ an |

The importance of the correct placement of strong stress cannot be over-emphasized. As other tense forms are presented where the only difference from some of the forms above is a different placement of the strong stress, it will be seen that this feature carries the entire burden of distinguishing the otherwise identical forms. A mistake in stress placement will more likely lead to misunderstanding than a malpronunciation of several sounds. The results will be every bit as striking as 'Abbot' ~ 'a bat'

are in English when stress (and a structurally obligatory, corresponding vowel substitution characteristic of the English phonological pattern) is shifted from the first to the second syllable.

In the Spanish pattern the /—o/ ending of the 1 sg form is distinct. In the other endings the theme vowel /a/ appears, followed by /—s, —mos, —n/. These are the regular signals of 2 sg fam, 1 pl, and 2 - 3 pl respectively; these endings recur in other theme class and tense form patterns.

## 6.21.2 The semantic differences between /está(n)/ and /áy/

### A. PRESENTATION OF PATTERN

*ILLUSTRATIONS*

| | | |
|---|---|---|
| ______________________ | 1 dóndestáelbáṇyȯ ↓ | ¿Dónde *está* el baño? |
| Where is (there) a bathroom? | 2 dóndeáyumbáṇyȯ ↓ | ¿Dónde *hay* un baño? |

*EXTRAPOLATION*

| | |
|---|---|
| Definite | está el... |
| Indefinite | áy un... |

*NOTES*

a. /está/ translates 'is'.

b. /áy/ translates 'there is' or 'is there?'

## 6.21.21 SUBSTITUTION DRILL

1 dóndeayúnotél ↓

_____ el _____ ↓ dóndestáelotél ↓

2 àkíestáe(l)líbrò ↓

_____ un _____ ↓ àkíayúnlíbrò ↓

3 àíayúnasenyorítà ↓

_____ la _____ ↓ àíestálasenyorítà ↓

4 dóndeayúna(s)sí(l)yàs ↓

_____ las _____ ↓ dóndestánla(s)sí(l)yàs ↓

5 àkíestánlozlápisès ↓

_____ unoz _____ ↓ àkíayúnozlápisès ↓

---

1 ¿Dónde hay un hotel?

¿ _____ el _____ ? ¿Dónde está el hotel?

2 Aqui está el libro.

_____ un _____ . Aquí hay un libro.

3 Ahí hay una señorita.

_____ la _____ . Ahí está la señorita.

4 ¿Dónde hay unas sillas?

¿ _____ las _____ ? ¿Dónde están las sillas?

5 Aquí están los lápices.

_____ unos _____ . Aquí hay unos lápices.

## 6.21.22 TRANSLATION DRILL

| | | |
|---|---|---|
| 1 Where is there a cheap restaurant? | dóndeay \| ùnrrèstòrámbàrátò ↓ | ¿Dónde hay un restorán barato? |
| Where's the cheap restaurant? | dóndèstá \| elrrèstòrámbàrátò ↓ | ¿Dónde está el restorán barato? |
| 2 There's a room for you all. | àíáy \| ùŋkwártò \| pàràùstéđès ↓ | Ahí hay un cuarto para ustedes. |
| There's the room for you all. | àíestá \| elkwártò \| pàràùstéđès ↓ | Ahí está el cuarto para ustedes. |
| 3 There're the empty tables. | àíestán \| làzmésàzđèsòkùpáđàs ↓ | Ahí están las mesas desocupadas. |
| There're some empty tables. | àíáy \| ùnàzmésàzđèsòkùpáđàs ↓ | Ahí hay unas mesas desocupadas. |
| 4 There isn't a chauffeur here. | noayùnchòfér \| àkí ↓ | No hay un chofer aquí. |
| The chauffeur's not here. | noestáelchòfér \| àkí ↓ | No está el chofer aquí. |
| 5 Is the pie good? | èstáelpàstélbwénò ↑ | ¿Está el pastel bueno? |
| Is there a good pie? | áyùmpàstélbwénò ↑ | ¿Hay un pastel bueno? |
| 6 Is the hotel around the corner? | èstáelòtél \| àlàbwéltà ↑ | ¿Está el hotel a la vuelta? |
| Is there a hotel around the corner? | áyùnòtél \| àlàbwéltà ↑ | ¿Hay un hotel a la vuelta? |
| 7 The waiters are here already. | yaestán \| lòzmóṣòṣàkí ↓ | Ya están los mozos aquí. |
| There're some waiters here already. | yáy \| ùnòzmóṣòṣàkí ↓ | Ya hay unos mozos aquí. |

| | | |
|---|---|---|
| 8 Where's the apartment with two rooms? | dóndestá \| e̯làpàrtàménto \| kòndóskwártòs ↓ | ¿Dónde está el apartamento con dos cuartos? |
| Where is there an apartment with two rooms? | dónde̯áy \| ùnạpàrtàménto \| kòndóskwártòs ↓ | ¿Dónde hay un apartamento con dos cuartos? |
| 9 There's a restaurant up ahead. | áịa̯đèlánte̯ \| áyùnrrèstòrán ↓ | Ahí adelante hay un restorán. |
| The restaurant's up ahead. | áịa̯đèlánte̯ \| èstáe̯lrrèstòrán ↓ | Ahí adelante está el restorán. |

## B. DISCUSSION OF PATTERN

When a reference to the location of something is definite, /está/ is used, with the definiteness marked by the occurrence of a definite article. When the reference is not definite, the uniquely irregular form /áy/ (from the verb /abér/ ) is used, usually but not necessarily accompanied by an indefinite article.

When the definite reference occurs, the normal agreement for number between subject and verb prevails:

| | |
|---|---|
| /dóndestàlàsí(l)yà ↓/ | Where's the chair? |
| /dóndestánlà(s)sí(l)yàs ↓/ | Where're the chairs? |

but when indefinite reference occurs, there is no corresponding change in the verb form; /áy/ can appear with either singular or plural forms:

| | |
|---|---|
| /àyúnlíbro̯enlàmésà ↓/ | There's a book on the table. |
| /àyúnòslíbròs̯enlàmésà ↓/ | There're some books on the table. |

One may be definite in number, but still indefinite in reference. Thus:

| | | |
|---|---|---|
| | /àydósplúmàs \| àkí ↓/ | There're two pens here. |
| compared to: | /làsdósplúmàs \| èstánạkí ↓/ | The two pens are here. |

## 6.22 REPLACEMENT DRILLS

A ȧ(l)y̯ı́áy | u̇nȧmésȧđėsȯku̇páđȧ ↓

| | | |
|---|---|---|
| 1 | ______ kwártȯ ______ ↓ | ȧ(l)y̯ı́áy \| u̇ŋkwártȯđėsȯku̇páđȯ ↓ |
| 2 | ȧkı́ ______________ ↓ | ȧkı́áy \| u̇ŋkwártȯđėsȯku̇páđȯ ↓ |
| 3 | __________ đėsȯku̇páđȯs ↓ | ȧkı́áy \| u̇nȯskwártȯzđėsȯku̇páđȯs ↓ |
| 4 | ______ sı́(l)y̯ȧz ______ ↓ | ȧkı́áy \| u̇nȧ(s)sı́(l)y̯ȧzđėsȯku̇pádȧs ↓ |
| 5 | ______ lȧ __________ ↓ | ȧkı̯ésta \| lȧsı́(l)y̯ȧđėsȯku̇páđȧ ↓ |
| 6 | _______________ bwénȧ ↓ | ȧkı̯éstá \| lȧsı́(l)y̯ȧƀwénȧ ↓ |
| 7 | ______ u̇nȧs ________ ↓ | ȧkı́áy \| u̇nȧ(s)sı́(l)y̯ȧzƀwénȧs ↓ |

---

A Allí hay una mesa desocupada.

| | | |
|---|---|---|
| 1 | ______ cuarto ______ . | Allí hay un cuarto desocupado. |
| 2 | Aquí ______________ . | Aquí hay un cuarto desocupado. |
| 3 | __________ desocupados. | Aquí hay unos cuartos desocupados. |
| 4 | ______ sillas ______ . | Aquí hay unas sillas desocupadas. |
| 5 | ______ la ______ . | Aquí esta la silla desocupada. |
| 6 | _______________ buena. | Aquí está la silla buena. |
| 7 | ______ unas ______ . | Aquí hay unas sillas buenas. |

B bėámȯsẹlmėnú ↓

| | |
|---|---|
| 1 ______________________ kwéntȧ ↓ | bėámȯzlȧkwéntȧ ↓ |
| 2 kyérȯ ______________________ ↓ | kyérolakwéntȧ ↓ |
| 3 ______________________ mȧnşánȧs ↓ | kyérȯlȧzmȧnşánȧs ↓ |
| 4 ____________ đyéz̧ ____________ ↓ | kyérȯđyéz̧mȧnşánȧs ↓ |
| 5 ______________________ bı̇(l)y̧étės ↓ | kyérȯđyéz̧bı̇(l)y̧étės ↓ |
| 6 ____________ ménȯz____________ ↓ | kyérȯménȯzƀı̇(l)y̧étės ↓ |
| 7 téngȯ ______________________ ↓ | téŋgȯménȯzƀı̇(l)y̧étės ↓ |

---

B Veamos el menú.

| | |
|---|---|
| 1 ______________________ cuenta. | Veamos la cuenta. |
| 2 Quiero ______________________ . | Quiero la cuenta. |
| 3 ______________________manzanas. | Quiero las manzanas. |
| 4 __________ diez ______________ . | Quiero diez manzanas. |
| 5 ______________________billetes. | Quiero diez billetes. |
| 6 ___________ menos ___________ . | Quiero menos billetes. |
| 7 Tengo ______________________ . | Tengo menos billetes. |

C kéđèseán | ùstéđès | sèn̮yórès ↓

| | |
|---|---|
| 1 __________ ùstéđ ___________ ↓ | kéđèsea̯ | ùstéđ | sèn̮yór ↓ |
| 2 ________ kyére̯ _____________ ↓ | kékyére̯ | ùstéđ | sèn̮yór ↓ |
| 3 _______ đíse̯ ________________ ↓ | kéđíse̯ | ùstéđ | sèn̮yór ↓ |
| 4 kómò _______________________ ↓ | kómòđíse̯ | ùstéđ | sèn̮yór ↓ |
| 5 _______ èstán _______________ ↓ | kómo̯èstán̯ùstéđès | sèn̮yórès ↓ |
| 6 ____________________ sèn̮yòrítà ↓ | kómo̯èstáu̯stéđ | sèn̮yòrítà ↓ |
| 7 dèđóndè ____________________ ↓ | dèđóndès̯ùstéđ | sèn̮yòrítà ↓ |

---

C ¿Qué desean ustedes, señores?

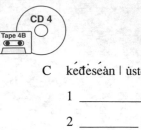

| | |
|---|---|
| 1 ¿ ________ usted, ___________ ? | ¿Qué desea usted, señor? |
| 2 ¿ _____ quiere ______, _________ ? | ¿Qué quiere usted, señor? |
| 3 ¿ _____ dice ______, ___________ ? | ¿Qué dice usted, señor? |
| 4 ¿Cómo __________, ___________ ? | ¿Cómo dice usted, señor? |
| 5 ¿ _____ están ______, __________ ? | ¿Cómo están ustedes, señores? |
| 6 ¿ ___________________ , señorita? | ¿Cómo está usted, señorita? |
| 7 ¿De dónde ________, __________ ? | ¿De dónde es usted, señorita? |

D y̱ókyéro̯ | u̇nsáŋw̱ichđėhamón ↓

1 __________ pókȯ __________ ↓ y̱ókyéro̯ | u̇mpókȯđėhamón ↓

2 ____________________ tȯmátė ↓ y̱ókyéro̯ | u̇mpókȯđėtȯmátė ↓

3 __________ sópȧ __________ ↓ y̱ókyéro̯ | u̇nȧsópȧđėtȯmátė ↓

4 __________ lȧ __________ ↓ y̱ókyérȯ | lȧsópȧđėtȯmátė ↓

5 ________ (l)y̱éƀȯ __________ ↓ y̱o(l)y̱éƀȯ | lȧsópȧđėtȯmátė ↓

6 nȯsótrȯz ____________________ ↓ nȯsótrȯz | (l)y̱ėƀámȯz | lȧsópȧđėtȯmátė ↓

7 ____________________ lėgúmbrės ↓ nȯsótrȯz | (l)y̱ėƀámȯz | lȧsópȧđėlėgúmbrės ↓

---

D Yo quiero un sandwich de jamón.

1 __________ poco __________ . Yo quiero un poco de jamón.

2 ____________________ tomate. Yo quiero un poco de tomate.

3 __________ sopa __________ . Yo quiero una sopa de tomate.

4 __________ la __________ . Yo quiero la sopa de tomate.

5 ________ llevo __________ . Yo llevo la sopa de tomate.

6 Nosotros ____________________ . Nosotros llevamos la sopa de tomate.

7 ____________________ legumbres. Nosotros llevamos la sopa de legumbres.

E béṣȧƀı̇ƀı́r | ėnẹlȯtél ↑

1 ______________ ėstáđȯṣu̇nı́đȯs ↑ — básȧƀı̇ƀı́r | ėnlȯṣėstáđȯṣu̇nı́đȯs ↑

2 ________ trȧƀȧhár ____________ ↑ — báṣȧtrȧƀȧhár | ėnlȯṣėstáđȯṣu̇nı́đȯs ↑

3 ḋeséȧn ______________________ ↑ — ḋeséȧntrȧƀȧhár | ėnlȯṣėstáđȯṣu̇nı́đȯs ↑

4 ___________________ ėmbȧháđȧ ↑ — ḋeséȧntrȧƀȧhár | ėnla̯ėmbȧháđȧ ↑

5 kyérė ________________________ ↑ — kyérėtrȧƀȧhár | ėnla̯ėmbȧháđȧ ↑

6 ________ ȧlmȯrs̯ár ____________ ↑ — kyére̯ȧlmȯrs̯ár | ėnla̯ėmbȧháđȧ ↑

7 pȯđémȯs ____________________ ↑ — pȯđémȯṣȧlmȯrs̯ár | ėnla̯ėmbȧháđȧ ↑

---

E ¿Vas a vivir en el hotel?

1 ¿ ______________ Estados Unidos? — ¿Vas a vivir en los Estados Unidos?

2 ¿ _______ trabajar______________ ? — ¿Vas a trabajar en los Estados Unidos?

3 ¿Desean ______________________ ? — ¿Desean trabajar en los Estados Unidos?

4 ¿ __________________ Embajada? — ¿Desean trabajar en la Embajada?

5 ¿Quiere _____________________ ? — ¿Quiere trabajar en la Embajada?

6 ¿ ________ almorzar ____________? — ¿Quiere almorzar en la Embajada?

7 ¿Podemos ___________________ ? — ¿Podemos almorzar en la Embajada?

F nó̇ ↓ pyénsȯƀu̇skár | u̇n̥apȧrtȧméntȯ ↓

| | | |
|---|---|---|
| 1 | _______ kyérȯ ________________ ↓ | nó̇ ↓ kyérȯƀu̇skár \| u̇n̥apȧrtȧméntȯ ↓ |
| 2 | _________________________ ȯtél ↓ | nó̇ ↓ kyérȯƀu̇skáru̇n̥ȯtél ↓ |
| 3 | ________________ ėl _________ ↓ | nó̇ ↓ kyérȯƀu̇skárėlȯtél ↓ |
| 4 | _________ pȯđémȯz___________ ↓ | nó̇ ↓ pȯđémȯzƀu̇skárėlȯtél ↓ |
| 5 | sí ↓ _________________________ ↓ | sí ↓ pȯđémȯzƀu̇skárėlȯtél ↓ |
| 6 | ___________ ėŋkȯntrár ________ ↓ | sí ↓ pȯđémȯs̥ėŋkȯntrárėlȯtél ↓ |
| 7 | __________________ ȧpȧrtȧméntȯs ↓ | sí ↓ pȯđémȯs̥ėŋkȯntrár \| lȯsȧpȧrtȧméntȯs ↓ |

---

F No, pienso buscar un apartamento.

| | | |
|---|---|---|
| 1 | _____ , quiero ________________ . | No, quiero buscar un apartamento. |
| 2 | _____ , ___________________ hotel. | No, quiero buscar un hotel. |
| 3 | _____ , ___________ el ________ . | No, quiero buscar el hotel. |
| 4 | _____ , podemos _______________ . | No, podemos buscar el hotel. |
| 5 | Si, __________________________ . | Sí, podemos buscar el hotel. |
| 6 | _____ , _____ encontrar ________ . | Sí, podemos encontrar el hotel. |
| 7 | _____ , ____________ apartamentos. | Sí, podemos encontrar los apartamentos. |

## 6.23 VARIATION DRILLS

| | | | |
|---|---|---|---|
| A | àmí \| tráygàmè \| sópađèlègúmbrès ↓ | | A mí tráigame sopa de legumbres. |
| | 1 Being *me* a sandwich. | àmí \| tráygàmeunsáŋwich ↓ | A mí tráigame un sandwich. |
| | 2 Bring *me* an apple pie. | àmí \| tráygàme \| ùmpàstéldèmànsáná ↓ | A mí tráigame un pastel de manzana |
| | 3 Bring *me* a tomato salad. | àmí \| tráygàme \| ùnaènsàláđàđètòmátè ↓ | A mí tráigame una ensalada de tomate. |
| | 4 Bring *me* a beer. | àmí \| tráygàmeùnasèrƀésà ↓ | A mí tráigame una cerveza. |
| | 5 Give *me* (some) more soup. | àmí \| đémèmá(s)sópà ↓ | A mí déme más sopa. |
| | 6 Give *me* (some) more chops. | àmí \| đémèmáschùlétàs ↓ | A mí déme más chuletas. |
| | 7 Hand *me* an apple. | àmí \| pásèmeùnamànsáná ↓ | A mí páseme una manzana. |

| | | | |
|---|---|---|---|
| B | áyùmpàstél \| dèmànsánà ↑ kézmúybwénò ↓ | | Hay un pastel de manzana que es muy bueno. |
| | 1 There's an American wine that's very good. | áyùmbíno \| àmèrikánò ↑ kézmúyƀwénò ↓ | Hay un vino americano que es muy bueno. |
| | 2 There's a school of languages that's very good. | áyùnaèskwélà \| đèléŋgwàs ↑ kézmúyƀwénà ↓ | Hay una escuela de lenguas que es muy buena. |

| | | |
|---|---|---|
| 3 There's a restaurant that's not very good. | áyúnrrėstóraŋ ↑ kėnoẹzmúyƀwénȯ ↓ | Hay un restorán que no es muy bueno. |
| 4 There are some Americans in the hotel who are from Kansas. | áyúnȯsạmérıkánȯs \| enẹlotél ↑ kėsóndėkánsȧs ↓ | Hay unos americanos en el hotel que son de Kansas. |
| 5 There's a gentleman here who doesn't speak Spanish. | áyúnsėnẹyórákı ↑ kėnọáƀlạespȧnẹyól ↓ | Hay un señor aquí que no habla español. |
| 6 There're some apartments, but they're not very good. | áyúnȯsạpȧrtȧméntȯs ↓ pérȯnósȯn \| múyƀwénȯs ↓ | Hay unos apartamentos, pero no son muy buenos. |
| 7 There're some pens on the desk, but they're not very good. | áyúnȧsplúmȧs \| ėnẹlėskritóryȯ ↓ pérȯnósȯn \| múyƀwénȧs ↓ | Hay unas plumas en el escritorio, pero no son muy buenas. |

C tráygȧ | párȧlȯzđós ↓ — Traiga para los dos.

| | | |
|---|---|---|
| 1 Bring (enough) for the three (of us). | tráygȧ \| párȧlȯstrés ↓ | Traiga para los tres. |
| 2 Bring vegetable soup. | tráygȧ \| sópȧđėlėgúmbrės ↓ | Traiga sopa de legumbres. |
| 3 Bring more ham. | tráygȧ \| máshȧmón ↓ | Traiga más jamón. |
| 4 Hand me the water. | pásėmėlágwȧ ↓ | Páseme el agua. |
| 5 Give me more wine. | démė \| mázƀínȯ ↓ | Déme más vino. |

| | | |
|---|---|---|
| 6 Give me the bill. | démėlȧkwéntȧ ↓ | Déme la cuenta. |
| 7 Let me know this afternoon. | ȧƀísėméstȧtárđė ↓ | Avíseme esta tarde. |

D kélėpȧréşė | sinȯstrȧtámȯzđėtú ↓ — ¿Qué le parece si nos tratamos de 'tú'?

| | | |
|---|---|---|
| 1 What do you say (if) we speak Spanish? | kélėpȧréşė \| si̯ȧƀlámȯşėspȧņyól ↓ | ¿Qué le parece si hablamos español? |
| 2 What do you say (if) we practice Spanish? | kélėpȧréşė \| siprȧktikámȯşėspȧņyól ↓ | ¿Qué le parece si practicamos español? |
| 3 What do you say (if) we drink wine? | kélėpȧréşė \| sitȯmámȯzbínȯ ↓ | ¿Qué le parece si tomamos vino? |
| 4 What do you say (if) we take the elevator? | kélėpȧréşė \| sitȯmámȯşėlȧs(ş)ėnsór ↓ | ¿Qué le parece si tomamos el ascensor? |
| 5 What do you say (if) we come in? | kélėpȧréşė \| sipȧsámȯşȧđėlántė ↓ | ¿Qué le parece si pasamos adelante? |
| 6 What do you say (if) we go tomorrow? | kélėpȧréşė \| siƀámȯzmȧņyánȧ ↓ | ¿Qué le parece si vamos mañana? |
| 7 What do you say (if) we eat lunch now? | kélėpȧréşė \| si̯ȧlmȯrşámȯşȧórȧ ↓ | ¿Qué le parece si almorzamos ahora? |

E tyénėzzrȧşón ↓ — Tienes razón.

| | | |
|---|---|---|
| 1 You're right, Joseph. | tyénėzrrȧşo̯ŋ \| hȯsé ↓ | Tienes razón, José. |

| | | |
|---|---|---|
| 2 You're not right, Joseph. | nótyénėzrrȧs̯óŋ \| hȯsé ↓ | No tienes razón, José. |
| 3 He's right. | tyénėrrȧs̯ón ↓ | Tiene razón. |
| 4 I'm right. | téŋgȯrrȧs̯ón ↓ | Tengo razón. |
| 5 I'm hungry. | téŋgo̯ámbrė ↓ | Tengo hambre. |
| 6 Charles and Mary are very hungry. | kárlȯsımáríȧ \| tyénėnmúchámbrė ↓ | Carlos y María tienen mucha hambre. |
| 7 You're very hungry. | ụstéđės \| tyénėnmúchámbrė ↓ | Ustedes tienen mucha hambre. |

F mós̯ȯ ↓ lȧkwéntȧ ↓ — ¡Mozo! La cuenta.

| | | |
|---|---|---|
| 1 Miss! The check. | sėn̯yȯrítȧ ↓ lȧkwéntȧ ↓ | ¡Señorita! La cuenta. |
| 2 Sir! The book. | sėn̯yór ↓ ė(l)líƀrȯ ↓ | ¡Señor! El libro. |
| 3 Joseph! The pencil. | hȯsé ↓ ė(l)lápis̯ ↓ | ¡José! El lápiz. |
| 4 Waiter! To the right. | mós̯ȯ ↓ ȧlȧđėréchȧ ↓ | ¡Mozo! A la derecha. |
| 5 Waiter! Mineral water. | mós̯ȯ ↓ ágwamınėrál ↓ | ¡Mozo! Agua mineral. |
| 6 Madam! To the left. | sėn̯yórȧ ↓ ȧlai̯s̯kyérđȧ ↓ | ¡Señora! A la izquierda. |
| 7 Gentlemen! Come in. | sėn̯yórės ↓ ȧđėlántė ↓ | ¡Señores! Adelante. |

**End of Tape 4B**
**End of CD 4**

## 6.24 REVIEW DRILL (1)

The use of the definite articles with titles

| | | |
|---|---|---|
| 1 How are you, Mr. Molina? | kómo̯ėstáu̯stéđ \| sėn̯yórmȯlínȧ ↓ | ¿Cómo está usted, Sr. Molina? |
| How's Mr. Molina? | kómo̯ėstá \| e̯lsėn̯yórmȯlínȧ ↓ | ¿Cómo está el Sr. Molina? |
| 2 How are you, Miss White? | kómo̯ėstáu̯stéđ \| sėn̯yȯrítȧhwáyt ↓ | ¿Cómo está usted, señorita White? |
| How's Miss White? | kómo̯ėstá \| lȧsėn̯yȯrítȧhwáyt ↓ | ¿Cómo está la señorita White? |
| 3 Mr. Molina, how's Miss White? | sėn̯yórmȯlínȧ ↓ kómo̯ėstá \| lȧsėn̯yȯrítȧhwáyt ↓ | Sr. Molina, ¿cómo está la señorita White? |
| 4 Miss Molina, how's Miss White? | sėn̯yȯrítȧmȯlínȧ ↓ kómo̯ėstá \| lȧsėn̯yȯrítȧhwáyt ↓ | Señorita Molina, ¿cómo está la señorita White? |
| 5 Mrs. Molina, how's Mrs. White? | sėn̯yórȧmȯlínȧ ↓ kómo̯ėstálȧsėn̯yórȧhwáyt ↓ | Sra. Molina, ¿cómo está la señora White? |
| 6 Mrs. Molina, is Mrs. White here? | sėn̯yórȧmȯlínȧ ↓ ėstálȧsėn̯yórȧhwáyt \| ȧkí ↑ | Sra. Molina, ¿está la Sra. White aquí? |
| 7 Miss Molina, is Miss White here? | sėn̯yȯrítȧmȯlínȧ ↓ ėstálȧsėn̯yórítȧhwáyt \| ȧkí ↑ | Señorita Molina, ¿está la señorita White aquí? |
| 8 Mr. Molina, is Mr. White here? | sėn̯yórmȯlínȧ ↓ ėstáe̯lsėn̯yórhwáyt \| ȧkí ↑ | Sr. Molina, ¿está el Sr. White aquí? |
| 9 Mr. Molina, where's Mr. White from? | sėn̯yórmȯlínȧ ↓ dėđóndės \| ėlsėn̯yórhwáyt ↓ | Sr. Molina, ¿de dónde es el Sr. White? |
| 10 Miss Molina, where's Miss White from? | sėn̯yȯrítȧmȯlínȧ ↓ dėđóndėz \| lȧsėn̯yȯrítȧhwáyt ↓ | Señorita Molina, ¿de dónde es la señorita White? |

(1) Review drills will be a regular part of the format of unit six and subsequent units. They will review and correlate structure points previously presented or will enlarge on structural details which were not sufficiently developed. They will usually be translation drills, though substitution and response drills will occasionally be used.

| | | |
|---|---|---|
| 11 Where're you from, Mrs. Molina? | dèđóndesụstéđ \| sènỵóràmòlínà ↓ | ¿De dónde es usted, Sra. Molina? |
| And Mrs. White? | ìlàsènỵórahwáyt ↑ | ¿Y la señora White? |
| 12 Mr. Molina, is Mr. White (an) American? | sènỵórmòlínà ↓ éṣelsènỵórhwáyt \| àmèrikánò ↑ | Señor Molina, ¿es el señor White americano? |
| 13 Miss Molina, is Miss White (an) American? | sènỵòrítàmòlínà ↓ ézlàsènỵòrítahwáyt \| àmèrikánà ↑ | Señorita Molina, ¿es la señorita White americana? |

## 6.3 CONVERSATION STIMULUS

### NARRATIVE 1

| | | |
|---|---|---|
| 1 It's eleven o'clock. | sónlàsónṣè ↓ | Son las once. |
| 2 Jose and John take a table. | hòséịhwan \| tómanụnamésà ↓ | José y Juan toman una mesa. |
| 3 They want to see the menu. | kyérembérelmènú ↓ | Quieren ver el menú. |
| 4 Jose wants to try the pork chops. | hòsékyérèpróbar \| làschùlétazđèṣérđò ↓ | José quiere probar las chuletas de cerdo. |
| 5 He's also going to have a green salad. | tàmbyémbákòmér \| ùnạènsàláđađèlègúmbrès ↓ | También va a comer una ensalada de legumbres. |
| 6 He's very hungry. | tyénèmúchámbrè ↓ | Tiene mucha hambre. |

| | | |
|---|---|---|
| 7 Juan's going to have a ham sandwich with lettuce and tomato. | hwám \| bákòmér \| ùnsáŋw̠ichđèhàmóŋ \| kònlèchúg͜aitòmátè ↓ | Juan va a comer un sandwich de jamón con lechuga y tomate. |
| 8 Jose and John want a beer. | hòsé͜ıhwáŋ \| kyérèn̩ùnàsèrbéşà ↓ | José y Juan quieren una cerveza. |

## DIALOG 1

| | | |
|---|---|---|
| Mozo, dígales 'buenos dias' a los señores y pregúnteles si desean ver el menú. | bwénòzđíàs \| sèn̩yórès ↓ dèséàmbérèlménú ↑ | Mozo: Buenos días, señores. ¿Desean ver el menú? |
| José, contéstele que sí, que por favor, y pregúntele que cúmo están las chuletas de cerdo. | sí \| pòrfàbór ↓ kómo̜están \| làschùlétàzđèşérđò ↓ | José: Sí, por favor. ¿Cómo están las chuletas de cerdo? |
| Mozo, contéstele que están muy buenas. | èstánmúybwénàs ↓ | Mozo: Están muy buenas. |
| José, preguntele a Juan que qué le parece si prueban eso, que Ud. tiene mucha hambre. | kélèpáréşè \| hwán \| sipròbámòşésò ↓ yó \| téŋgòmúchámbrè ↓ | José: ¿Qué le parece, Juan, si probamos eso? Yo tengo mucha hambre. |
| Juan, contéstele a José que no, que Ud. quiere un sandwich de cualquier cosa. | nó ↓ yókyéro̜ùnsáŋw̠ich \| đèkwàlkyérkósà ↓ | Juan: No, yo quiero un sandwich de cualquier cosa. |
| Mozo, digale al señor (Juan) que qué le parece un sandwich de jamón con lechuga y tomate. | kélèpáréşe̜ \| ùnsáŋw̠ichđèhàmóŋ \| kònlèchúg͜aitòmátè ↓ | Mozo: ¿Qué le parece un sandwich de jamón con lechuga y tomate? |

| | | |
|---|---|---|
| Juan, contestele que está bien, y que una cerveza también por favor. | èstábyén ↓ ɪùnàṣèrƀéṣàtàmbyén \| pòrfàƀór ↓ | Juan: Está bien. Y una cerveza también, por favor. |
| José, digale al mozo que a Ud. otra, con las chuletas. | àmí \| ótrà ↓ kònlàschùlétàs ↓ | José: A mí otra, con las chuletas. |

## NARRATIVE 2.

| | | |
|---|---|---|
| 1 John likes the sandwich very much. | àhwán \| lègústàmúchọèlsáŋwich ↓ | A Juan le gusta mucho el sandwich. |
| 2 It's very good. | èstámuyƀwénò ↓ | Está muy bueno. |
| 3 The pork chops are good, too. | làschùlétàzđèṣérđọ \| èstámbwénàstàmbyén ↓ | Las chuletas de cerdo están buenas también. |
| 4 Jose wants another beer. | hòsékyérẹ \| ótràṣèrƀéṣà ↓ | José quiere otra cerveza. |
| 5 So does John. | ihwántàmbyén ↓ | Y Juan también. |
| 6 Jose wants to use the familiar 'tu' with John. | hòsé \| kyérètràtáràhwán \| dètú ↓ | José quiere tratar a Juan de 'tú'. |
| 7 John says it's okay. | hwándịṣè \| kèstáƀyén ↓ | Juan dice que está bien. |

## DIALOG 2

| | | |
|---|---|---|
| José, pregúntele a Juan que qué tal el sandwich. | kétálėlsáŋw̰ich \| hwán ↓ | José: ¿Qué tal el sandwich, Juan? |
| Juan, contéstele que le gusta mucho, que está muy bueno. Pregúntele a José que qué tal las chuletas. | mėgústȧmúchȯ ↓ ėstámúyƀwénȯ ↓ ilȧschúlétȧs ↓ kétál ↓ | Juan: Me gusta mucho, está muy bueno. Y las chuletas, ¿qué tal? |
| José, contéstele que están muy buenas también. Pregúntele si quiere otra cerveza. | ėstánmúyƀwénȧs \| tȧmbyén ↓ kyérȩ óstrȧșėrƀéșȧ ↑ | José: Están muy buenas también. ¿Quiere otra cerveza? |
| Juan, dígale que Ud. cree que sí, y que si él también. | kréȯkėsí ↓ ı̯ústéđtȧmbyén ↑ | Juan: Creo que sí, ¿Y usted también? |
| José, dígale que sí, que Ud. también, pero pregúntele que qué le parece si se tratan de 'tú'. | sí \| y̧ótȧmbyén ↓ pérokélėpȧréșė \| sinȯstrȧtámȯzđėtú ↓ | José: Si, yo también. Pero, ¿qué le parece si nos tratamos de 'tú'? |
| Jose, dígale que está bien, si él quiere. | ėstáƀyén ↓ sitúkyérės ↓ | Juan: Está bien...si tú quieres... |

## NARRATIVE 3

| | | |
|---|---|---|
| 1 John needs an apartment. | hwán \| nėșėsítạunạpȧrtȧméntȯ ↓ | Juan necesita un apartmento. |
| 2 He's going to look for one. | bábúskárúnȯ ↓ | Va a buscar uno. |

| | | |
|---|---|---|
| 3 Jose's going to help John find one. | hose ǀ ƀáyuđárahwan ǀ aeŋkontrarúno ↓ | José va a ayudar a Juan a encontrar uno. |
| 4 He's going to go with him tomorrow. | bair ǀ konel ǀ manyana ↓ | Va a ir con él mañana. |
| 5 He's going to be busy in the morning, but not in the afternoon. | porlamanyana ǀ báestárokupađo ǀ péro porlatarđe ǀ nó ↓ | Por la manana va a estar ocupado, pero por la tarde no. |
| 6 John wants to go at three o'clock. | hwaŋkyereir ǀ alastrés ↓ | Juan quiere ir a las tres. |
| 7 John likes the hotel where he's staying. | ahwan ǀ legusta ǀ elotel ǀ dondestá ↓ | A Juan le gusta el hotel donde está. |
| 8 But it's cheaper to live in an apartment. | péroezmazƀarato ǀ ƀiƀirenunapartaménto ↓ | Pero es más barato vivir en un apartamento. |

## DIALOG 3

| | | |
|---|---|---|
| Juan, digale a José que Ud. necesita buscar un apartamento; y preguntele si quiere ayudarle. | hose ↓ nesesito ǀ ƀuskarunapartaménto ↓ kyeresayuđarme ↑ | Juan: José, necesito buscar un apartamento. ¿Quieres ayudarme? |
| José, dígale que cómo no, que Ud. le puede ayudar con mucho gusto. | komonó ↓ yotepweđoayuđar ǀ konmuchogústo ↓ | José: Cómo no, yo te puedo ayudar con mucho gusto. |
| Juan, pregúntele si él va a estar ocupado mañana. | tu ǀ ƀasaestar ǀ okupađomanyana ↑ | Juan: ¿Tú vas a estar ocupado mañana? |

José, contéstele que por la mañana sí, pero que pueden ir por la tarde.

pòrlàmànyánàsí ↓ péròpòđémòs | ír pòrlàtárđè ↓

José: Por la mañana sí, pero podemos ir por la tarde.

Juan, pregúntele que a qué hora.

àkẹórà ↓

Juan: ¿A qué hora?

José, dígale que a las dos o a las tres, si le parece.

àlàzđós | ọàlàstrés ↓ sitèpàréṣè ↓

José: A las dos o a las tres, si te parece.

Juan, dígale que a las tres le parece bien.

àlàstréz | mèpàréṣèƀyén ↓

Juan: A las tres me parece bien.

José, pregúntele si no le gusta el hotel donde está.

nòtègústạèlòtél | dóndèstás ↑

José: ¿No te gusta el hotel donde estás?

Juan, dígale que sí, pero que Ud. piensa que es más barato vivir en un apartamento.

sí ↓ péròpyénsò | kézmázƀàrátò | ƀiƀírènụ̀nạpàrtàméntò ↓

Juan: Sí, pero pienso que es más barato vivir en un apartamento.

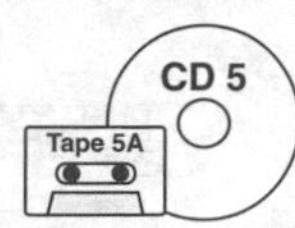




# 7.1 BASIC SENTENCES

## White and Molina look for an apartment

John White and Jose Molina leave the restaurant; on the way out they pick up a newspaper to check on apartment leads. They are walking over to Molina's car.

| English Spelling | Aid to Listening | Spanish Spelling |
|---|---|---|
| the car | èl—áwtò ↓ | el auto |
| *MOLINA* | | *MOLINA* |
| This is my car. | éstèzmịáwtò ↓ | Este es mi auto. |
| old | byéhò ↓ | viejo |
| It's old, but pretty decent. | ézƀyéhò \| péròƀwénò ↓ | Es viejo pero bueno. |
| the newspaper | èl—pèryóđikò ↓ | el periódico |
| Let's see the paper. | bámòsạƀér \| èlpèryóđikò ↓ | Vamos a ver el periódico. |
| the amount, quantity | là—kàntiđáđ ↓ | la cantidad |
| what a (large) quantity | ké—kàntiđáđ ↓ | qué cantidad |
| the advertisement | èl—ànúnṣyò ↓ | el anuncio |

| | | |
|---|---|---|
| *WHITE* | | *WHITE* |
| What a bunch of ads! | ké \| kàntiđáđẹànúnṣyòs ↓ | ¡Qué cantidad de anuncios! |
| too much | dèmàsyáđò ↓ | demasiado |
| too many | dèmàsyáđòs ↓ | demasiados |
| why | pòr—ké ↓ | por qué |
| (we) see (to see) | bémòs ↓ bér ↓ | vemos (ver) |
| the friend | èl—àmígò ↓ | el amigo |
| the agency | lạ—àhénṣyà ↓ | la agencia |
| *MOLINA* | | *MOLINA* |
| Too many. Why don't we see a friend of mine who has a (rental) agency? (1) | dèmàsyáđòs ↓ pòrkénòbémòs \| ạùnạmígòmíò \| kètyénẹùnàhénṣyà ↓ | Demasiados. ¿Por qué no vemos a un amigo mío que tiene una agencia? |

(They go to the rental agency as Molina suggested. After the introduction of White and other formalities, they inquire about apartments.)

| | | |
|---|---|---|
| to rent | àlkilár ↓ | alquilar |
| *MOLINA* | | *MOLINA* |
| Mr. White wants to rent an apartment. | èlsèñyór \| đèséàlkilár \| ùnạpàrtàméntò ↓ | El señor desea alquilar un apartamento. |

| | | |
|---|---|---|
| right now | pȯr—ȧórȧ ↓ | por ahora |
| only | sólȯ ↓ | sólo |
| available, (unoccupied), (to vacate) | dėsȯkȗpáđȯ ↓ dėsȯkupár ↓ | desocupado (desocupar) |
| *AGENT* | | *AGENTE* |
| Right now I have only two available. | pȯrȧórȧ \| sólȯteŋgȯđóz \| đėsȯkȗpáđȯs ↓ | Por ahora sólo tengo dos desocupados. |
| the building | ėl—ėđifísyȯ ↓ | el edificio |
| the field, the country | ėl—kámpȯ ↓ | el campo |
| One downtown, in the Del Campo building. | únoėnėlsentrȯ ↑ ėnėlėđifísyȯ \| đėlkámpȯ ↓ | Uno en el centro, en el edificio 'Del Campo'. |
| without | sín ↓ | sin |
| the piece of furniture (2) | ėl—mwéƀlė ↓ | el mueble |
| the furnitures | lȯz—mwéƀlės ↓ | los muebles |
| *WHITE* | | *WHITE* |
| Unfurnished? | sinmwéƀlės ↑ | ¿Sin muebles? |
| furnished (to furnish) | ȧmwėƀláđȯ ↓ ȧmwėƀlár ↓ | amueblado (amueblar) |
| *AGENT* | | *AGENTE* |
| No, furnished. | nó ↓ ȧmwėƀláđȯ ↓ | No, amueblado. |
| the month | ėl—més ↓ | el mes |

| | | |
|---|---|---|
| per month | ȧl—mé̇s ↓ | al mes |
| *WHITE* | | *WHITE* |
| How much per month? | kwántọȧlmés ↓ | ¿Cuánto al mes? |
| hundred | ṣyéntȯ ↓ | ciento |
| two hundred | dȯs(ṣ)yéntȯs ↓ | doscientos |
| to include | iŋklwí̇r ↓ | incluir |
| the light | lȧ—lúṣ ↓ | la luz |
| nor | ní̇ ↓ | ni |
| the gas | ėl—gá̇s ↓ | el gas |
| *AGENT* | | *AGENTE* |
| Two hundred not including electricity, water, or gas. | dȯs(ṣ)yéntȯs \| siniŋklwír \| lúṣ \| ágwȧ \| nıgás ↓ | Doscientos, sin incluir luz, agua ni gas. |
| *WHITE* | | *WHITE* |
| And where's the other? | iđóndėstáẹlótrȯ ↓ | ¿Y dónde está el otro? |
| that | ésė ↓ | ese |
| the outskirts | lȧs—ȧfwérȧs ↓ | las afueras |
| big, great | grándė ↓ | grande |
| *AGENT* | | *AGENTE* |
| That one's in the outskirts and it's bigger. | ésėstá \| ẹnlȧsȧfwérȧs ↑ ıézmȧzgrándė ↓ | Ese está en las afueras y es más grande. |

| | | |
|---|---|---|
| (to) me (it) suits (to suit) | mė—kȯmbyéné ↓ kȯmbėnír ↓ | me conviene (convenir) |
| *WHITE* | | *WHITE* |
| I think the first suits me better. | kréȯ I kėmėkȯmbyénėmás I ėlpriméro ↓ | Creo que me conviene más el primero. |
| Can we see it? | pȯđémȯzƀérlȯ ↑ | ¿Podemos verlo? |
| the key | lȧ—(l)y̰áƀė ↓ | la llave |
| clear, of course | kláro ↓ | claro |
| *AGENT* | | *AGENTE* |
| Yes, of course. Here's the key. | sí I kláro ↓ ȧkítyénėlȧ(l)y̰áƀė ↓ | Sí, claro; aquí tiene la llave. |

## 7.10 Notes on the basic sentences

(1) The /a/ *a* which appears in /bémos̬a̬un̬amígo/ *bemos a un amigo* is not to be translated 'to' or in any of the several other possibilities for the translation of /a/. It only indicates that the direct object of the verb is *personalized,* that is, either *is* a person or is *thought of* as a person. It will be taken up in detail in Unit 10.

(2) The Spanish word /mwébles/ *muebles* is an example of a count noun (a noun that names items customarily measured by number) which is correlated with an English word 'furniture', an example of a mass noun (one that names items customarily measured by amount). Thus /mwéble/ can be translated only in a roundabout way by saying 'a piece of furniture', since 'a furniture' is an impossible combination of 'a' directly preceding a mass noun. Further discussion and other examples will be presented in Unit 58.

# 7.2 DRILLS AND GRAMMAR

## 7.21 PATTERN DRILLS

### 7.21.1 Present tense forms of regular /—ér/ verbs

A. PRESENTATION OF PATTERN

*ILLUSTRATIONS*

| | | |
|---|---|---|
| ____________________ | 1 yókréȯkėsí ↓ | Yo *creo* que sí. |
| ____________________ | 2 kwántȯlėđébȯ ↓ | ¿Cuánto le *debo?* |
| Are you learning Spanish? | 3 ȧpréndėṣėspȧnyól ↑ | *¿Aprendes* español? |
| Do you eat in the restaurant? | 4 kómės \| ėnẹlrrėstȯrán ↑ | *¿Comes* en el restorán? |
| You eat very little. | 5 ùstéđkómė \| múypókȯ ↓ | Usted *come* muy poco. |
| How much does he owe you? | 6 kwántȯlėđébė ↓ | ¿Cuánto le *debe?* |
| We are learning a lot. | 7 ȧprėndémȯzmúchȯ ↓ | *Aprendemos* mucho. |

| | | |
|---|---|---|
| How much do we owe you? | 8 kwántȯlėđėƀémȯs ↓ | ¿Cuánto le *debemos*? |
| They eat together. | 9 é(l)y̰ȯskómėŋhúntȯs ↓ | Ellos *comen* juntos. |
| Do they believe that? | 10 kréḛṇẹ́(l)y̰ȯṣésȯ ↑ | ¿*Creen* ellos eso? |

*EXTRAPOLATION*

| | sg | pl |
|---|---|---|
| 1 | —o | —émos |
| 2 fam | —es | |
| 2-3 | —e | –en |

*NOTES*

a. Where /—ár/ verb endings have the theme /a/ recurring, /—ér/ verb endings have the theme /e/.

b. The endings are otherwise identical.

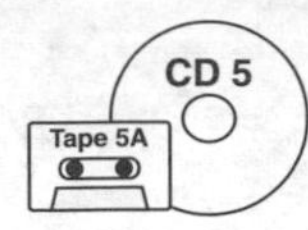




## 7.21.11 SUBSTITUTION DRILLS

Number substitution

| | |
|---|---|
| 1 ȧpréndo̮ėspȧn̮yól ↓ | ȧprėndémȯs̮ėspȧn̮yól ↓ |
| 2 kȯmémȯspȧstél ↓ | kómȯpȧstél ↓ |
| 3 déƀėƀéyntėpésȯs ↓ | débėmƀéyntėpésȯs ↓ |
| 4 kómėnmúchȯpóstrė ↓ | kómėmúchȯpóstrė ↓ |
| 5 dėƀémȯs̮ umpókȯ ↓ | déƀo̮umpókȯ ↓ |
| 6 ȧpréndė̮iŋglés ↓ | ȧpréndėn̮iŋglés ↓ |
| 7 kréȯkėsí ↓ | krė̮émȯskėsí ↓ |

---

| | |
|---|---|
| 1 *Aprendo* español. | Aprendemos español. |
| 2 *Comemos* pastel. | Como pastel. |
| 3 *Debe* veinte pesos. | Deben veinte pesos. |
| 4 *Comen* mucho postre. | Come mucho postre. |
| 5 *Debemos* un poco. | Debo un poco. |
| 6 *Aprende* inglés. | Aprenden inglés. |
| 7 *Creo* que sí. | Creemos que sí. |

Person - number substitution

1 yókómo̯a̍(l)y̯í ↓

| | |
|---|---|
| àlísya̍ ____________ ↓ | kóme̯a̍(l)y̯í ↓ |
| é(l)y̯òs ____________ ↓ | kómena̯(l)y̯í ↓ |
| àntónye̯iy̯ó ____________ ↓ | kòmémòsa̯(l)y̯í ↓ |
| ùstéđ ____________ ↓ | kóme̯a̍(l)y̯í ↓ |

2 àprèndémòzmúcho̯aí ↓

| | |
|---|---|
| y̯ó ____________ ↓ | àpréndòmúcho̯aí ↓ |

---

1 *Yo* como allí.

| | |
|---|---|
| Alicia ____________ . | Come allí. |
| Ellos ____________ . | Comen allí. |
| Antonio y yo ____________ . | Comemos allí. |
| Usted ____________ . | Come allí. |

2 Aprendemos mucho ahí.

| | |
|---|---|
| Yo ____________ . | Aprendo mucho ahí. |

ùstéđès ______________________ ↓ àpréndènmúcho̯aí ↓

àlíṣyà ______________________ ↓ àpréndèmúcho̯aí ↓

hwán ______________________ ↓ àpréndèmúcho̯aí ↓

3 àntónyòđéƀèṇèlòtél ↓

nòsótròz ______________________ ↓ dèƀémòṣèṇèlòtél ↓

páƀlò ______________________ ↓ déƀèṇèlòtél ↓

àlíṣya̯ikármèn ______________________ ↓ déƀèṇèṇèlòtél ↓

yó ______________________ ↓ déƀo̯èṇèlòtél ↓

---

Ustedes ______________________ . Aprenden mucho ahí.

Alicia ______________________ . Aprende mucho ahí.

Juan ______________________ . Aprende mucho ahí.

3 *Antonio* debe en el hotel.

Nosotros ______________________ . Debemos en el hotel.

Pablo ______________________ . Debe en el hotel.

Alicia y Carmen ______________________ . Deben en el hotel.

Yo ______________________ . Debo en el hotel.

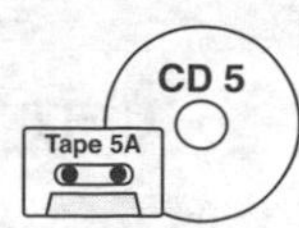




## 7.21.12 RESPONSE DRILLS

| | | |
|---|---|---|
| | 1 kómeustéđ \| enelséntrȯ ↑ oenelapartaméntȯ ↓ | kómoènèlséntrȯ ↓ |
| | 2 àpréndenustéđes \| espanyól ↑ oinglés ↓ | àprèndémȯsèspànyól ↓ |
| | 3 déƀené(l)yozmúcho ↑ ȯpókȯ ↓ | déƀèmpókȯ ↓ |
| [ènèlséntrȯ ↓] | 4 dóndekómenustéđès ↓ | kòmémȯsenelséntrȯ ↓ |
| [èspànyól ↓] | 5 keaprénde \| ùstéđakí ↓ | àpréndoespànyól ↓ |
| [dyèsiséyspésȯs ↓] | 6 kwántođéƀél ↓ | déƀe \| đyèsiséyspésȯs ↓ |

---

| | | |
|---|---|---|
| | 1 ¿Come usted en el centro o en el apartamento? | Como en el centro. |
| | 2 ¿Aprenden ustedes español o inglés? | Aprendemos español. |
| | 3 ¿Deben ellos mucho o poco? | Deben poco. |
| (en el centro) | 4 ¿Dónde comen ustedes? | Comemos en el centro. |
| (español) | 5 ¿Qué aprende usted aquí? | Aprendo español. |
| (16 pesos) | 6 ¿Cuánto debe él? | Debe 16 pesos. |

| | | |
|---|---|---|
| [lėgúmbrės ↓] | 7 kómé(l)yȧ \| hȧmón ↑ | nó ↓ kómėlėgúmbrės ↓ |
| [ėlȧpȧrtȧméntȯ ↓] | 8 kómeustéđ \| ėnėlrrėstorán ↑ | nó ↓ kómoėnėlȧpȧrtȧméntȯ ↓ |
| [múchȯ ↓] | 9 ȧpréndėné(l)yȯs \| pókoȧkí ↑ | nó ↓ ȧpréndėnmúchȯ ↓ |
| | 10 kómėnustéđėz \| múchaėnsȧláđȧ ↑ | sí ↓ kȯmémȯzmúchaėnsȧláđȧ ↓ |
| | 11 ȧpréndélėspȧnyól ↑ | sí ↓ ȧpréndėspȧnyól ↓ |

---

| | | |
|---|---|---|
| (legumbres) | 7 ¿Come ella jamón? | No, come legumbres. |
| (el apartamento) | 8 ¿Come usted en el restorán? | No, como en el apartamento. |
| (mucho) | 9 ¿Aprenden ellos poco aquí? | No, aprenden mucho. |
| | 10 ¿Comen ustedes mucha ensalada? | Sí, comemos mucha ensalada. |
| | 11 ¿Aprende él español? | Sí, aprende español. |

## 7.21.13 TRANSLATION DRILL

| | | |
|---|---|---|
| 1 *I* always eat dessert. | yósyémprė । kómȯpóstrė ↓ | Yo siempre como postre. |
| 2 *He* eats lots of pork chops. | élkómė । múchȧs । chủlétȧzđėşérđȯ ↓ | El come muchas chuletas de cerdo. |
| 3 We learn a lot here. | ȧprėndémȯzmuchǫ । ȧkí ↓ | Aprendemos mucho aquí. |
| 4 They (f) owe 21 pesos. | é(l)y̧ȧz । đéƀėm । bėyntu̯úmpésȯs ↓ | Ellas deben 21 pesos. |
| 5 *I owe* the whole (all the) bill. | y̧óđéƀȯ । tóđȧlȧkwéntȧ ↓ | Yo debo toda la cuenta. |
| 6 Where does she eat? | dóndėkómé(l)y̧ȧ ↓ | ¿Dónde come ella? |
| 7 By the way, where do you eat? | ȧprȯpósitȯ ↓ dóndėkómẹustéđ ↓ | A propósito, ¿dónde come Ud? |
| 8 They learn very well. | é(l)y̧ȯs । ȧprénděn । múyƀyén ↓ | Ellos aprenden muy bien. |
| 9 We don't believe that. | nókrẹémȯs । ésȯ ↓ | No creemos eso. |
| 10 What do you believe? | kékréẹ । ủstéđ ↓ | ¿Qué cree Ud? |
| 11 Does he eat lettuce? | kómél । lėchúgȧ ↑ | ¿Come él lechuga? |

### B. DISCUSSION OF PATTERN

As the extrapolation above shows, the pattern for /—ér/ theme class regular verbs is very similar to that of /—ár/ verbs. The only difference is the appearance of theme /—e—/ immediately after the stem and preceding the person-number indicators, the same places where the theme /—a—/ appears in /—ár/ verb form.

Stress patterns are identical for /—ér/ and /—ár/ verbs. Strong stress occurs on the stem in all forms except 1 pl, where the first syllable of the ending receives the strong stress.

## 7.21.2 The demonstratives /éste, ése, akél/

### A. PRESENTATION OF PATTERN

*ILLUSTRATIONS*

| | | |
|---|---|---|
| ______________________ | 1 éstėchékėƀyȧhérȯ ↓ | *Este* cheque viajero. |
| This soup is (tastes) good. | 2 éstȧsópa̯ \| ėstáƀwénȧ ↓ | *Esta* sopa está buena. |
| These are my cars. | 3 éstȯ(s)són \| misáwtȯs ↓ | *Estos* son mis autos. |
| I like these chairs. | 4 mėgústȧn \| éstȧ(s)sí(l)y̯ȧs ↓ | Me gustan *estas* sillas. |
| ______________________ | 5 ésė \| e̯stáe̯nlȧṣȧfwérȧs ↓ | *Ese* está en las afueras. |
| That lady is American. | 6 ésȧsėn̯yóra̯ \| ėṣȧmėrikánȧ ↓ | *Esa* señora es americana. |
| I don't want those (pieces of) furniture. | 7 nókyéro̯ \| ésȯzmwéƀlės ↓ | No quiero *esos* muebles. |

| | | |
|---|---|---|
| Those ladies are American. | 8 ésȧ(s)sėn̮yórȧs \| sónạ̇mėrikánȧs ↓ | *Esas* señoras son americanas. |
| that over there (m) | ȧkél ↓ | aquél |
| That's my car over there. | 9 ȧkelėzmȋ̯áwtȯ ↓ | *Aquél* es mi auto. |
| that over there (fem) | ȧké(l)y̱ȧ ↓ | aquélla |
| That lady there is American. | 10 ȧké(l)y̱ȧsėn̮yórạ̑ \| ėṣȧmėrikánȧ ↓ | *Aquella* señora es americana. |
| I like those cars over there. | 11 mėgústȧn \| ȧké(l)y̱ȯṣáwtȯs ↓ | Me gustan *aquellos* autos. |
| Thosc tablcs over there are empty. | 12 ȧké(l)y̱ȧzmésȧs \| ėstándėsȯkupáđȧs ↓ | *Aquellas* mesas están desocupadas. |

## *EXTRAPOLATION*

| | near me | | near you | | near him | (away from us) |
|---|---|---|---|---|---|---|
| | sg | pl | sg | pl | sg | pl |
| m | éste | éstos | ése | ésos | akél | aké(l)yos |
| f | ésta | éstas | ésa | ésas | aké(l)ya | aké(l)yas |

## *NOTES*

a. Demonstratives, which are special kinds of adjectives, have distinct forms for gender and number.

b. Spanish has one set of forms which corresponds to English 'this', two that correspond to 'that'.

**End of Tape 5A**

## 7.21.21 SUBSTITUTION DRILLS

Form substitution

1 lȧmésa̯ | ėstáđėsȯku̇páđȧ ↓

| | |
|---|---|
| éstȧ ____________________ ↓ | éstȧmésa̯ | ėstáđėsȯku̇páđȧ ↓ |
| ésȧ ____________________ ↓ | ésȧmésa̯ | ėstáđėsȯku̇páđȧ ↓ |
| ȧké(l)y̯ȧ ____________________ ↓ | ȧké(l)y̯ȧmésa̯ | ėstáđėsȯku̇páđȧ ↓ |

2 ėlkwárto̯ėzƀwénȯ ↓

| | |
|---|---|
| éstė ____________________ ↓ | éstėkwárto̯ | ėzƀwénȯ ↓ |
| ésė ____________________ ↓ | ésėkwárto̯ | ėzƀwénȯ ↓ |

---

1 *La* mesa está desocupada.

| | |
|---|---|
| Esta ____________________ . | Esta mesa está desocupada. |
| Esa ____________________ . | Esa mesa está desocupada. |
| Aquella ____________________ . | Aquella mesa está desocupada. |

2 *El* cuarto es bueno.

| | |
|---|---|
| Este ____________________ . | Este cuarto es bueno. |
| Ese ____________________ . | Ese cuarto es bueno. |

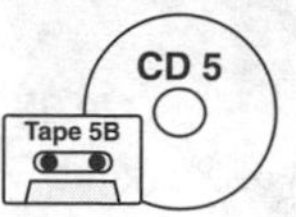

| | |
|---|---|
| ȧkél ______________________ ↓ | ȧkélkwárto̯ \| ėzƀwénȯ ↓ |
| 3 loṣapartȧméntȯs \| sómbȧrátȯs ↓ | |
| éstȯs______________________ ↓ | éstȯṣȧpȧrtȧméntȯs \| sómbȧrátȯs ↓ |
| ésȯs ______________________ ↓ | ésȯṣȧpȧrtȧméntȯs \| sómbȧrátȯs ↓ |
| ȧké(l)y̯ȯs __________________ ↓ | ȧké(l)y̯ȯṣȧpȧrtȧméntȯs \| sómbȧrátȯs ↓ |

---

| | |
|---|---|
| Aquel ______________________ . | Aquel cuarto es bueno. |
| 3 *Los* apartamentos son baratos. | |
| Estos______________________ . | Estos apartamentos son baratos. |
| Esos ______________________ . | Esos apartamentos son baratos. |
| Aquellos ___________________ . | Aquellos apartamentos son baratos. |

Number substitution

1 tráygȧmésė | s̥ėnıs̥érȯ ↓

_____________________ s̥ėnıs̥érȯs ↓ — tráygȧmésȯs | s̥ėnıs̥érȯs ↓

2 dėséó̯ır | á̯esȧhéns̥yȧ ↓

_____________________ ȧhéns̥yȧs ↓ — dėséó̯ır | á̯esȧs̥ȧhéns̥yȧs ↓

3 ȧké(l)y̯ȯs | ėđifís̥yȯs | sóŋgrándės ↓

__________ ėđıfís̥yo̯ __________ ↓ — ȧkélėđıfís̥yo̯ | ėzgrándė ↓

---

1 Tráigame ese *cenicero*.

_____________________ *ceniceros*. — Tráigame esos ceniceros.

2 Deseo ir a esa *agencia*.

_____________________ *agencias*. — Deseo ir a esas agencias.

3 Aquellos *edificios* son grandes.

__________ *edificio* __________ . — Aquel edificio es grande.

4 éstȯs̥ėskritóryȯs | sómbȧrátȯs ↓

________ ėskritóryȯ ___________ ↓ — éstėskritóryo̯ | ėzƀȧrátȯ ↓

5 bámȯs̥aƀér | ésȯspėryóđikȯs ↓

__________________ pėryóđiko ↓ — bámȯs̥aƀér | ésėpėryóđikȯ ↓

6 éstȧmésȧ | no̯ézgrándė ↓

________ mésȧz ________________ ↓ — éstȧzmésȧz | nósoŋgrándės ↓

7 ȧké(l)y̦asėn̦yóra | ės̥ėspȧn̦yólȧ ↓

_________ sėn̦yórȧs ____________ ↓ — ȧké(l)y̦ȧ(s)sėn̦yórȧs | sónės̥pȧn̦yólȧs ↓

---

4 Estos *escritorios* son baratos.

_________ *escritorio* ____________ . — Este escritorio es barato.

5 Vamos a ver esos *periódicos*.

______________________ *periódico*. — Vamos a ver ese periódico.

6 Esta *mesa* no es grande.

_________ *mesas* _______________ . — Estas mesas no son grandes.

7 Aquella *señora* es española.

_________ *señoras* ____________ . — Aquellas señoras son españolas.

Item substitution

1 kyérópresentárle | aésaseṇyórá ↓

_____________________ seṇyór ↓ kyéropresentárle | aéseseṇyór ↓

2 ésoṣapartaméntos | sómbwénos ↓

________ eskwélas _____________ ↓ ésaṣeskwélas | sómbwénas ↓

3 démeaké(l)yozlíbros ↓

_________________________ plúmas ↓ démeaké(l)yasplúmas ↓

---

1 Quiero presentarle a esa *señora*.

__________________________ *señor.* Quiero presentarle a ese señor.

2 Esos *apartamentos* son buenos.

________ *escuelas* _______________ . Esas escuelas son buenas.

3 Déme aquellos *libros*.

_________________________ *plumas*. Déme aquellas plumas.

4 pásèméséèlápiş ↓

______________________ plúmà ↓ pásèmésàplúmà ↓

5 àkélàwtọ | èstádèsòkùpádò ↓

________ mésạ ______________ ↓ àké(l)ỵàmésạ | èstádèsòkùpáđà ↓

6 éstàsèkşyón | èzgrándè ↓

_______ èđifíşyọ______________ ↓ éstèđifíşyọ | èzgrándè ↓

7 àké(l)ỵàmésạ | èstádèsòkùpáđà ↓

______ èskrıtóryọ _____________ ↓ àkélèskrıtóryọ | èstádèsòkùpáđò ↓

---

4 Páseme ese *lápiz*.

________________________ *pluma*. Páseme esa pluma.

5 Aquel *auto* está desocupado.

_________ *mesa* ______________ . Aquella mesa está desocupada.

6 Esta *sección* es grande.

________ *edificio* ______________ . Este edificio es grande.

7 Aquella *mesa* está desocupada.

_________ *escritorio* ___________ . Aquel escritorio está desocupado.

## 7.21.22 RESPONSE DRILL (1)

1 kyéréstėlápis̯ ↑ o̯éstȧplúmȧ ↓ — ésėlápis̯ ↓

2 kyéréstȯzlápis̯ės ↑ o̯éstȧsplúmȧs ↓ — ésȧsplúmȧs ↓

---

1 ¿Quiere este lápiz o esta pluma? — Ese lápiz.

2 ¿Quiere estos lápices o estas plumas? — Esas plumas.

(1) The implicit spatial reference of the demonstratives can be most effectively presented by the use of gestures to indicate position. Both tutor and the student should independently use /éste/ for items near themselves and /ése/ for items near each other or away from both.

| | | |
|---|---|---|
| [éstȯzlíƀrȯs ↓] | 3 kékyére̯ \| ůstéđ ↓ | ésȯzlíƀrȯs ↓ |
| [éstȧsplúmȧs ↓] | 4 kékyérél ↓ | ésȧsplúmȧs ↓ |
| [ésė ↓] | 5 lėgústa̯ \| éstelíƀro ↑ | ésėnó ↓ éstė ↓ |
| [ésȯs ↓] | 6 kyére̯ \| éstȯzlíƀrȯs ↑ | ésȯznó ↓ éstȯs ↓ |
| [ésȧs ↓] | 7 kyére̯ \| éstȧsplúmȧs ↑ | ésȧznó ↓ éstȧs ↓ |
| [ésȧ ↓] | 8 lėgústa̯ \| éstȧplúmȧ ↑ | ésȧnó ↓ éstȧ ↓ |

---

| | | |
|---|---|---|
| (estos libros) | 3 ¿Qué quiere Ud.? | Esos libros. |
| (estas plumas) | 4 ¿Qué quiere él? | Esas plumas. |
| (ése) | 5 ¿Le gusta este libro? | Ese no, éste. |
| (ésos) | 6 ¿Quiere estos libros? | Esos no, éstos. |
| (ésas) | 7 ¿Quiere estas plumas? | Esas no, éstas. |
| (ésa) | 8 ¿Le gusta esta pluma? | Esa no, ésta. |

9 ėzƀwéno̯ | éselíƀrȯ ↑ — éstė ↑ sí ↓ ėzmúyƀwénȯ ↓

10 ėzƀwéno̯ | éstėlíƀrȯ ↑ — ésė ↑ sí ↓ ėzmúyƀwénȯ ↓

11 ėzƀwéna̯ | éstȧplúmȧ ↑ — ésȧ ↑ sí ↓ ėzmúyƀwénȧ ↓

12 ėzƀwéna̯ | ésȧplúmȧ ↑ — éstȧ ↑ sí ↓ ėzmúyƀwénȧ ↓

13 sómbwénȯs | ésȯzlíƀrȯs ↑ — éstȯs ↑ sí ↓ sónmúyƀwénȯs ↓

---

9 ¿Es bueno ese libro? — ¿Este? Sí, es muy bueno.

10 ¿Es bueno este libro? — ¿Ese? Sí, es muy bueno.

11 ¿Es buena esta pluma? — ¿Esa? Sí, es muy buena.

12 ¿Es buena esa pluma? — ¿Esta? Sí, es muy buena.

13 ¿Son buenos esos libros? — ¿Estos? Sí, son muy buenos.

## 7.21.23 TRANSLATION DRILL

| | | | |
|---|---|---|---|
| 1 | This salad is very good. | éstạėnsȧláđạ │ ėstámúyƀwénȧ ↓ | Esta ensalada está muy buena. |
| 2 | Those (over there) gentlemen speak English. | ȧké(l)yȯ(s)sėn̦yórės │ áƀlȧn̦iŋglés ↓ | Aquellos señores hablan inglés. |
| 3 | That room to the left. | ésėkwártọȧlạịṣkyérđȧ ↓ | Ese cuarto a la izquierda. |
| 4 | That's my room over there. | ȧkélėzmıkwártȯ ↓ | Aquél es mi cuarto. |
| 5 | Can we see those pieces of furniture? | pȯđémȯzƀér │ ésȯzmwéƀlės ↑ | ¿Podemos ver esos muebles? |
| 6 | Hand me those keys. | pásėmésȧz(l)yáƀės ↓ | Páseme esas llaves. |
| 7 | That (over there) young lady is American. | ȧké(l)yȧsėn̦yórıtạ │ ėṣȧmėrıkánȧ ↓ | Aquella señorita es americana. |
| 8 | This building is large. | éstėđifíṣyọ │ ėzgrándė ↓ | Este edificio es grande. |
| 9 | In this section we are very busy. | ėn̦éstȧsėkṣyón │ ėstámȯzmúyȯkupáđȯs ↓ | En esta sección estamos muy ocupados. |
| 10 | Do you need these books? | nėṣėsítạ │ éstȯzlíƀrȯs ↑ | ¿Necesita estos libros? |
| 11 | That's Mrs. Molina. | ésạ │ ėzlȧsėn̦yórȧmȯlínȧ ↓ | Esa es la señora Molina. |

## B. DISCUSSION OF PATTERN

Demonstratives are words which designate or point out usually in terms of spatial arrangement, but sometimes in terms of time relation. They are a special kind of 'limiting' adjectives which always precede the nouns they modify. Besides the forms listed in the presentation above, demonstratives include definite articles, which have been separately presented because of special functions that they have.

English as well as Spanish has words that can be classed as demonstratives. The English demonstratives provide a relatively rare example of modifier forms which change in English for number reference, as the following chart shows:

| | near | far |
|---|---|---|
| sg | this | that |
| pl | these | those |

This change in form is called 'inflection for number', and an agreement in form with an associated noun is obligatory, i.e., we cannot say 'these book' or 'that apples'. As has already been shown in Unit 4, agreement in number between nouns and adjectives in Spanish is almost always shown by number inflection in the adjective, just as it is in this one case in English.

The spatial contrast in English demonstratives is a two-way pattern: near and not near. The Spanish demonstratives, however, have a three-way pattern: near me, near you (or a short way off), and near him (or a long way off). Thus /akél/ implies more distant in space or more remote in time. This extra distinction, coupled with three distinct gender forms, gives Spanish an inventory of 15 forms, compared to 4 in English, as follows

| | sg | pl | sg | pl |
|---|---|---|---|---|
| | this | these | that | those |
| m | éste | éstos | ése, akél | ésos, aké(1)yos |
| f | ésta | estas | ésa, aké(l)ya | ésas, aké(l)yas |
| n | ésto | | éso, (aké(l)yo) | |

Note that the pattern of the Spanish forms deviates from the normal pattern of Spanish modifiers in one important respect. The regular pattern:

| | sg | pl |
|---|---|---|
| m | —o | —os |
| f | —a | —as |

is present except in the m sg forms, where the endings are /—e/ (/éste, ése/) or zero (/akél/). A form which has a final /—o/ appears in the pattern with unmarked, or neuter, gender. The forms /ésto/ and /éso/ were presented and explained in Unit 2; /aké(l)yo/, though appearing less frequently, occurs in similar patterns.

The demonstratives can occur as modifiers (adjectives modifying nouns) or as nominalized forms (taking the place of nouns). Both uses are illustrated in the following sentence:

/éstelíbro̯ | esmásbaráto | ke̯ése ↓/ — *'This book* is cheaper than *that one'*

Note that in English the singular forms are not readily nominalized, so that 'one' replaces the noun.

The neuter forms almost always occur nominalized, since there are no neuter nouns they can modify.

Spelling conventions have established the practice of marking a written accent on the stressed vowel in masculine and feminine nominalized forms.

## 7.22 REPLACEMENT DRILLS

A ésteezmiáwtò ↓

| | |
|---|---|
| 1 àkél ______________ ↓ | àkéleezmiáwtò ↓ |
| 2 ______________ şerƀéşà ↓ | àké(l)yaezmişerƀéşà ↓ |
| 3 ésa ______________ ↓ | ésaezmişerƀéşà ↓ |
| 4 ______________ lápiş ↓ | éseezmilápiş ↓ |
| 5 ______________ mésà ↓ | ésaezmimésà ↓ |
| 6 ________ là ________ ↓ | ésaezlamésà ↓ |
| 7 ésàs ______________ ↓ | ésà(s)sónlàzmésàs ↓ |

---

A Este es mi auto.

| | |
|---|---|
| 1 Aquél ______________ . | Aquél es mi auto. |
| 2 ______________ cerveza. | Aquélla es mi cerveza. |
| 3 Esa ______________ . | Esa es mi cerveza. |
| 4 ______________ lápiz. | Ese es mi lápiz. |
| 5 ______________ mesa. | Esa es mi mesa. |
| 6 ________ la ________. | Esa es la mesa. |
| 7 Esas ______________ . | Esas son las mesas. |

B èlsèn̯yórhwáyt | dèséàlkilár | ùn̯apártaméntò ↓

| | |
|---|---|
| 1 ________ bùskár ________ ↓ | èlsèn̯yórhwáyt \| dèséàƀùskár \| ùn̯apártaméntò ↓ |
| 2 ______ sèn̯yórà ________ ↓ | làsèn̯yóràhwáyt \| dèséàƀùskár \| ùn̯apártaméntò ↓ |
| 3 ________ mwéblès ↓ | làsèn̯yóràhwáyt \| dèséàƀùskár \| ùnózmwéƀlès ↓ |
| 4 ________ ƀér ________ ↓ | làsèn̯yóràhwáyt \| dèséàƀér \| ùnózmwéƀlès ↓ |
| 5 ________ máz ________ ↓ | làsèn̯yóràhwáyt \| dèséàƀér \| mázmwéƀlès ↓ |
| 6 ________ kyérè ________ ↓ | làsèn̯yóràhwáyt \| kyérèƀér \| mázmwéƀlès ↓ |
| 7 lòs ________ ↓ | lò(s)sèn̯yórèshwáyt \| kyérèmbér \| mázmwéƀlès ↓ |

---

B El señor White desea alquilar un apartamento.

| | |
|---|---|
| 1 ________ buscar ________ . | El señor White desea buscar un apartamento. |
| 2 ________ señora ________ . | La señora White desea buscar un apartamento. |
| 3 ________ muebles. | La señora White desea buscar unos muebles. |
| 4 ________ ver ________ . | La señora White desea ver unos muebles. |
| 5 ________ más ________ . | La señora White desea ver más muebles. |
| 6 ________ quiere ________ . | La señora White quiere ver más muebles. |
| 7 Los ________ . | Los señores White quieren ver más muebles. |

C iđóndėstáe̯lótrȯ ↓

| | |
|---|---|
| 1 ______________________ mésȧ ↓ | iđóndėstálȧmésȧ ↓ |
| 2 ____________ e̯sȧ ____________ ↓ | iđóndėstáe̯sȧmésȧ ↓ |
| 3 ______________________ sí(l)y̯ȧ ↓ | iđóndėstáe̯sȧsí(l)y̯ȧ ↓ |
| 4 ____________ lȧ ____________ ↓ | iđóndėstálȧsí(l)y̯ȧ ↓ |
| 5 ____________________ sėn̯yórȧs ↓ | iđóndėstánlȧ(s)sėn̯yórȧs ↓ |
| 6 _______ kómo̯ ______________ ↓ | ikómo̯ėstánlȧ(s)sėn̯yórȧs ↓ |
| 7 __________ e̯l______________ ↓ | ikómo̯ėstáe̯lsėn̯yór ↓ |

---

C ¿Y dónde está el otro?

| | |
|---|---|
| 1 ¿ ______________________ mesa? | ¿Y dónde está la mesa? |
| 2 ¿ ___________ esa ___________ ? | ¿Y dónde está esa mesa? |
| 3 ¿ ______________________ silla? | ¿Y dónde está esa silla? |
| 4 ¿ _________ la _______________ ? | ¿Y dónde está la silla? |
| 5 ¿ _____________________señoras? | ¿Y dónde están las señoras? |
| 6 ¿ _________ cómo ___________ ? | ¿Y cómo están las señoras? |
| 7 ¿ ___________ el ___________ ? | ¿Y cómo está el señor? |

D kréȯ | kėmėkȯmbyénėmás | ėlprimérȯ ↓

| Cue | Response |
|---|---|
| 1 ______________ ótrȯ ↓ | kréȯ \| kėmėkȯmbyénėmás \| ėlótrȯ ↓ |
| 2 ______ mu̇cho̯ ______ ↓ | kréȯ \| kėmėkȯmbyénėmúcho̯ \| ėlótrȯ ↓ |
| 3 ______ gústȧ ______ ↓ | kréȯ \| kėmėgústȧmúcho̯ \| ėlótrȯ ↓ |
| 4 ______ lė ______ ↓ | kréȯ \| kėlėgústȧmúcho̯ \| ėlótrȯ ↓ |
| 5 ______ póko̯ ______ ↓ | kréȯ \| kėlėgústȧpóko̯ \| ėlótrȯ ↓ |
| 6 kréȩ ______________ ↓ | kréȩ \| kėlėgústȧpóko̯ \| ėlótrȯ ↓ |
| 7 ______________ ótrȧ ↓ | kréȩ \| kėlėgústȧpóko̯ \| la̯ótrȧ ↓ |

---

D Creo que me conviene más el primero.

| Cue | Response |
|---|---|
| 1 ______________ otro. | Creo que me conviene más el otro. |
| 2 ______ mucho ______ . | Creo que me conviene mucho el otro. |
| 3 ______ gusta ______ . | Creo que me gusta mucho el otro. |
| 4 ______ le ______ . | Creo que le gusta mucho el otro. |
| 5 ______ poco ______ . | Creo que le gusta poco el otro. |
| 6 Cree ______________ . | Cree que le gusta poco el otro. |
| 7 ______________ otra. | Cree que le gusta poco la otra. |

E pȯđémȯzƀérlȯ ↑

| | |
|---|---|
| 1 ____________________ƀu̇skárlȯ ↑ | pȯđémȯzbu̇skárlȯ ↑ |
| 2 kyérė ____________________ ↑ | kyérėƀu̇skárlȯ ↑ |
| 3 ____________________ótrȧƀés̯ ↑ | kyérė \| ƀu̇skárlo̯ \| ótrȧƀés̯ ↑ |
| 4 __________ɪ́r__________ ↑ | kyére̯ɪ́r \| ótrȧƀés̯ ↑ |
| 5 ____________________ đėspwés ↑ | kyére̯ɪ́r \| đėspwés ↑ |
| 6 __________ ƀėnɪ́r __________ ↑ | kyérėƀėnɪ́r \| đėspwés ↑ |
| 7 kyérėm ____________________ ↑ | kyérėmbėnɪ́r \| đėspwés ↑ |

---

E ¿Podemos verlo?

| | |
|---|---|
| 1 ¿ ____________________ buscarlo? | ¿Podemos buscarlo? |
| 2 ¿Quiere ____________________ ? | ¿Quiere buscarlo? |
| 3 ¿ ____________________ otra vez? | ¿Quiere buscarlo otra vez? |
| 4 ¿ __________ ir __________ ? | ¿Quiere ir otra vez? |
| 5 ¿ ____________________ después? | ¿Quiere ir después? |
| 6 ¿ __________ venir __________ ? | ¿Quiere venir después? |
| 7 ¿Quieren ____________________ ? | ¿Quieren venir después? |

F sí ↓ ȧkítyénė | lȧ(l)y̯áƀė ↓

1 ____________ lȧz______________ ↓ sí ↓ ȧkítyénė | lȧz(l)y̯áƀės ↓

2 _____________________ bı(l)y̯étės ↓ sí ↓ ȧkítyėnė | lȯzƀı(l)y̯étės ↓

3 ___________ ȧí________________ ↓ sí ↓ ȧítyénė | lȯzƀı(l)y̯étės ↓

4 ______________ u̇m ___________ ↓ sí ↓ ȧítyéne̯ | u̇mbı(l)y̯étė ↓

5 ______________________ mȯnéđȧ ↓ sí ↓ ȧítyéne̯ | u̇nȧmȯnéđȧ ↓

6 ____________ ésȧz ____________ ↓ sí ↓ ȧítyéne̯ | ésȧzmȯnéđȧs ↓

7 ________________________ chékė ↓ sí ↓ ȧítyéne̯ | ésėchékė ↓

---

F Si, aquí tiene la llave.

1 ______________ las ____________ . Sí, aquí tiene las llaves.

2 _________________________billetes. Sí, aquí tiene los billetes.

3 _________ ahí _________________ . Sí, ahí tiene los billetes.

4 ________________ un __________ . Sí, ahí tiene un billete.

5 _______________________ moneda. Sí, ahí tiene una moneda.

6 _______________ esas __________ . Sí, ahí tiene esas monedas.

7 _________________________cheque. Sí, ahí tiene ese cheque.

## 7.23 VARIATION DRILLS

| | | |
|---|---|---|
| A ėzƀyého \| péròƀwénò ↓ | | Es viejo, pero bueno. |
| 1 It's old but inexpensive. | ėzƀyého \| péròbàrátò ↓ | Es viejo, pero barato. |
| 2 It's old but excellent. | ėzƀyého \| pérọėks(ṣ)ėléntė ↓ | Es viejo, pero excelente. |
| 3 It's big but inexpensive. | ėzgrándė \| péròƀàrátò ↓ | Es grande, pero barato. |
| 4 They're old but inexpensive. | sòmbyéhòs \| péròƀàrátòs ↓ | Son viejos, pero baratos. |
| 5 They're good and inexpensive. | sòmbwénòṣıƀàrátòs ↓ | Son buenos y baratos. |
| 6 They're big and good. | sòŋgrándėṣıƀwénòs ↓ | Son grandes y buenos. |
| 7 They're inexpensive and good. | sòmbàrátòṣıƀwénòs ↓ | Son baratos y buenos. |

| | | |
|---|---|---|
| B bámòṣaƀér \| ėlpėryóđikò ↓ | | Vamos a ver el periódico. |
| 1 Let's go see the apartment. | bámòṣaƀér \| ėlapàrtàméntò ↓ | Vamos a ver el apartamento. |
| 2 Let's go see the building. | bámòṣaƀér \| ėleđıfíṣyò ↓ | Vamos a ver el edificio. |

| | | |
|---|---|---|
| 3 Let's go see the rooms. | bámos̯aƀér \| lȯskwártȯs ↓ | Vamos a ver los cuartos. |
| 4 Let's go get acquainted with the downtown section. | bámȯs̯akȯnȯs̯ér \| ėls̯éntrȯ ↓ | Vamos a conocer el centro. |
| 5 Let's go eat in the restaurant. | bámȯs̯akȯmér \| ėn̯elrrėstȯrán ↓ | Vamos a comer en el restorán. |
| 6 Let's go to work now. | bámȯs̯atrȧƀahár \| aórȧ ↓ | Vamos a trabajar ahora. |
| 7 Let's go look for an apartment. | bámȯs̯aƀuskár \| ùn̯apȧrtȧméntȯ ↓ | Vamos a buscar un apartamento. |

| | | |
|---|---|---|
| C pȯrkénȯƀémȯs \| a̯un̯amígȯmíȯ ↓ | | ¿Por qué no vemos a un amigo mío? |
| 1 Why don't we see Joseph? | pȯrkénȯƀémȯs \| ȧhósé ↓ | ¿Por qué no vemos a José? |
| 2 Why don't we eat in the restaurant? | pȯrkénȯkȯmémȯs \| ėn̯elrrėstȯrán ↓ | ¿Por qué no comemos en el restorán? |
| 3 Why don't we eat later? | pȯrkénȯkȯmémȯz \| đėspwés ↓ | ¿Por qué no comemos después? |
| 4 Why don't we go down in the elevator? | pȯrkénȯƀahámȯs \| ėn̯elas(s̯)ėnsór ↓ | ¿Por qué no bajamos en el ascensor? |
| 5 Why don't we speak Spanish? | pȯrkénȯ̯aƀlámȯs \| ėspan̯yól ↓ | ¿Por qué no hablamos español? |

| | | | |
|---|---|---|---|
| 6 | Why don't we look for another apartment? | porkénobuskámos \| ótroapartaméntȯ ↓ | ¿Por qué no buscamos otro apartamento? |
| 7 | Why don't we rent another building? | porkénoalkilámos \| ótroeđifísyȯ ↓ | ¿Por qué no alquilamos otro edificio? |

| | | | |
|---|---|---|---|
| D | | sólotéŋgȯ \| đozđesokupádȯs ↓ | Sólo tengo dos desocupados. |
| 1 | I only have five available. | sólotéŋgȯ \| síŋkođesokupáđȯs ↓ | Sólo tengo cinco desocupados. |
| 2 | I only have one available. | sólotéŋgo \| únođesokupáđȯ ↓ | Sólo tengo uno desocupado. |
| 3 | I only have one table available. | sólotéŋgo \| unamésa \| đesokupáđȧ ↓ | Sólo tengo una mesa desocupada. |
| 4 | I only have one apartment available. | sólotéŋgo \| unapartaméntȯ \| đesokúpáđȯ ↓ | Sólo tengo un apartamento desocupado. |
| 5 | I only have one desk available. | sólotéŋgo \| uneskritóryȯ \| đesokupáđȯ ↓ | Sólo tengo un escritorio desocupado. |
| 6 | I only have five chairs available. | sólotéŋgȯ \| síŋkosí(l)yaz \| đesokupáđȧs ↓ | Sólo tengo cinco sillas desocupadas. |
| 7 | He only has two rooms available. | sólotyénė \| đoskwártoz \| đesokupáđȯs ↓ | Sólo tiene dos cuartos desocupados. |

| | | | |
|---|---|---|---|
| E | | dȯs(ṣ)yéntȯs ↓ siṇiŋklwír \| lúṣ ↑ ágwȧnıgás ↓ | Doscientos, sin incluir luz, agua ni gas. |
| 1 | Three hundred, not including electricity, water or gas. | trȇs(ṣ)yéntos ↓ siṇiŋklwír \| lúṣ ↑ ágwȧnıgás ↓ | Trescientos, sin incluir luz, agua ni gas. |
| 2 | Four hundred, not including electricity, water or gas. | kwȧtroṣyéntȯs ↓ siṇiŋklwír \| lúṣ ↑ ágwȧnıgás ↓ | Cuatrocientos, sin incluir luz, agua ni gas. |
| 3 | Two hundred twenty, not including water or gas. | dȯs(ṣ)yéntȯzƀéyntė ↓ siṇiŋklwír \| ágwȧnıgás ↓ | Doscientos veinte, sin incluir agua ni gas. |
| 4 | Seven pesos, not including beer or wine. | syétėpésȯs ↓ siṇiŋklwír \| ṣėrƀéṣȧ nıƀínȯ ↓ | Siete pesos, sin incluir cerveza ni vino. |
| 5 | Fifteen dollars, not including the taxi or the tip. | kínṣėđólȧrės ↓ siṇiŋklwír \| ėl táksınılȧpropínȧ ↓ | Quince dólares, sin incluir el taxi ni la propina. |
| 6 | Two hundred dollars without furniture. | dȯs(ṣ)yéntȯzđólȧrės \| sınmwéƀlės ↓ | Doscientos dólares sin muebles. |
| 7 | Three hundred dollars furnished. | trės(ṣ)yéntȯzđólȧrės \| ȧmwėƀláđȯ ↓ | Trescientos dólares amueblado. |

| | | | |
|---|---|---|---|
| F | | ésẹ ǀ ėstáẹnlàsạfwéràs ǀ ɹėzmáz grándė ↓ | Ese está en las afueras y es más grande. |
| 1 | That one is downtown and is larger. | ésẹ ǀ ėstáẹnẹ̀lṣéntrȯ ǀ ɹėzmázgrándė ↓ | Ese está en el centro y es más grande. |
| 2 | That one is on Columbus Avenue and is less expensive. | ésẹ ǀ ėstáẹnlàƀėníđàkȯlón ǀ ɹėzmáz ƀàrátȯ ↓ | Ese está en la Avenida Colón y es más barato. |
| 3 | That one is near the American Embassy. | ésėstáṣérkà ǀ đėlạėmbàháđàmėrıkánà ↓ | Ese está cerca de la Embajada Americana. |
| 4 | That one is to the right. | ésėstálàđėréchà ↓ | Ese está a la derecha. |
| 5 | That one is to the left. | ésėstálạıṣkyérđà ↓ | Ese está a la izquierda. |
| 6 | That one is very far. | ésẹ ǀ ėstámúyléhȯs ↓ | Ese está muy lejos. |
| 7 | That one is very good. | ésẹ ǀ ėstámúyƀwénȯ ↓ | Ese está muy bueno. |

## 7.24 REVIEW DRILL

The distribution of / sér/ and /estár/

| | | |
|---|---|---|
| 1 I'm not an American but I'm in the United States. | nósóyaméríkánȯ ↓ pérọẹstóy \| ẹnlȯs̠ ẹstáđos̠uníđȯs ↓ | No soy americano, pero estoy en los Estados Unidos. |
| 2 We're not Americans, but we're in the United States. | nósómȯs \| ȧméríkánȯs ↓ pérọẹstámȯs \| ẹnlȯs̠ẹstáđos̠uníđȯs ↓ | No somos americanos, pero estamos en los Estados Unidos. |
| 3 He's not an American, but he's in the United States. | élnọés̠améríkánȯ ↓ pérọẹstá \| ẹnlȯs̠ ẹstáđos̠uníđȯs ↓ | El no es americano, pero está en los Estados Unidos. |
| 4 They're from Chile, but they're in Colombia. | é(l)y̠ȯ(s)sóndẹchílẹ ↓ pérọẹstánẹŋkȯlómbyȧ ↓ | Ellos son de Chile, pero están en Colombia. |
| 5 Carmen's from Chile, but she's in Peru. | kármẹn \| ẹzđẹchílẹ ↓ pérọẹstáẹnẹlpẹrú ↓ | Carmen es de Chile, pero está en el Perú. |
| 6 They (f) are married, and they're in California. | é(l)y̠ȧ(s)sóŋkȧsáđȧs \| i̯estánẹŋkȧlifórnyȧ ↓ | Ellas son casadas y están en California. |
| 7 She's married, and she's in California. | é(l)y̠ạẹskȧsáđȧ \| i̯estáẹŋkȧlifórnyȧ ↓ | Ella es casada y está en California. |
| 8 He's single, and he's in Cuba. | élẹ(s)sȯltérȯ \| i̯estáẹŋkúƀȧ ↓ | El es soltero y está en Cuba. |
| 9 The hotel is good, and it's not far. | ẹlȯtélẹzƀwénọ \| inọẹstáléhȯs ↓ | El hotel es bueno y no está lejos. |

| | | |
|---|---|---|
| 10 The buildings are big and they're near. | lòsèđifísyòs \| sóŋgrándès \| ịèstánsérkà ↓ | Los edificios son grandes y están cerca. |
| 11 The restaurant isn't cheap and it's very far. | èlrrèstòrán \| nọézƀàrátò ↓ ịèstámúyléhòs ↓ | El restorán no es barato y está muy lejos. |

## 7.3 CONVERSATION STIMULUS

### NARRATIVE 1

| | | |
|---|---|---|
| 1 Juan talks with the young lady that works in the cashier's office. | hwán \| áƀlàkònlàsènyórítà \| kètràƀáhạènlákáhà ↓ | Juan habla con la señorita que trabaja en la caja. |
| 2 He says he's planning to look for an apartment. | éldíse \| kèpyénsà \| ƀùskárunàpàrtàméntò ↓ | El dice que piensa buscar un apartamento. |
| 3 He likes this hotel. | lègústạéstẹòtél ↓ | Le gusta este hotel. |
| 4 But it's cheaper living in an apartment. | pérọèzmázƀàrátò ↑ ƀiƀír \| ènụ̀nàpàrtàméntò ↓ | Pero es más barato vivir en un apartamento. |
| 5 He wants it furnished. | lòkyérẹ \| àmwèƀláđò ↓ | Lo quiere amueblado. |

| | | |
|---|---|---|
| 6 But if there isn't (one) furnished he'll take one unfurnished. | pérȯsinọáy \| ȧmwėƀláđȯ ↑ tómạúnȯsınmwéƀlės ↓ | Pero si no hay amueblado, toma uno sin muebles. |
| 7 A friend who works with him in the consular section is going to help him. | unạmígȯ \| kėtrȧƀaháköṇél \| ėnlȧsėkṣyóŋkȯnsulár ↑ ƀáyụđárlė ↓ | Un amigo que trabaja con él en la sección consular, va a ayudarle. |
| 8 They're going to go this afternoon. | bánạír \| éstȧtárđė ↓ | Van a ir esta tarde. |
| 9 Juan thinks it's easy to find an apartment. | hwáŋ \| kréẹkésfáṣil \| ėŋkȯntrárȧpȧrtȧméntȯ ↓ | Juan cree que es fácil encontrar apartamento. |

## DIALOG 1

| | | |
|---|---|---|
| Juan, dígale a la Srta. que Ud. piensa buscar un apartamento. | pyénsȯƀuskár \| unạpȧrtȧméntȯ \| sėṇyȯrítȧ ↓ | Juan: Pienso buscar un apartamento, señorita. |
| Srta., pregúntele si no le gusta este hotel. | nólėgústạéstẹótel ↑ | Srta.: ¿No le gusta este hotel? |
| Juan, contéstele que sí, es excelente pero que es más barato vivir en un apartamento. | sí ↓ ėṣėks(ṣ)ėléntė ↓ péroẹzmázƀarátȯ ↑ ƀiƀír \| ėnụnạpȧrtȧméntȯ ↓ | Juan: Sí, es excelente, pero es más barato vivir en un apartamento. |

| | | |
|---|---|---|
| Srta., pregúntele si él cree que es fácil encontrar. | ùstéđkrée̯ \| kèsfáşilèŋkòntrár ↑ | Srta.: ¿Ud. cree que es fácil encontrar? |
| Juan, dígale que Ud. cree que sí. | kréò \| kèsí ↓ | Juan: Creo que sí. |
| Srta., pregúntele si lo quiere amueblado o sin muebles. | lòkyére̯ \| àmwèƀláđo̯ ↑ òsınmwéƀlès ↓ | Srta.: ¿Lo quiere amueblado o sin muebles? |
| Juan, contéstele que le conviene más amueblado, pero que si no hay, toma uno sin muebles. | mèkòmbyénèmás \| àmwèƀláđò ↓ péròsinó \| áy ↑ tómo̯unósınmwéƀlès ↓ | Juan: Me conviene más amueblado; pero si no hay, tomo uno sin muebles. |

## NARRATIVE 2

| | | |
|---|---|---|
| 1 It's almost three o'clock. | sóŋkásılástrés ↓ | Son casi las tres. |
| 2 Jose and Juan go down in the elevator. | hòséıhwám \| báhanènèlas(ş)ènsór ↓ | José y Juan bajan en el ascensor. |
| 3 Jose has yesterday's paper. | hòsétyéne̯ \| èlpèryóđıkòđe̯ayér ↓ | José tiene el periódico de ayer. |
| 4 They look at the ad section. | bén \| làsèkşyónde̯anúnşyòs ↓ | Ven la sección de anuncios. |
| 5 There are many apartments. | áymúchòşapàrtaméntòs ↓ | Hay muchos apartamentos. |

| | | |
|---|---|---|
| 6 One ad says: 'Three-room apartment, furnished, two hundred a month.' | ùnạnúnṣyȯđíṣė ↓ ȧpȧrtȧméntȯ \|<br>đėtréskwártȯs ↓ ȧmwėƀláđȯ ↓<br>dȯs(ṣ)yéntȯṣȧlmés ↓ | Un anuncio dice: 'Apartamento de tres cuartos, amueblado, doscientos al mes. |
| 7 It's too big for Juan. | ézđėmȧsyáđȯgrándė \| párȧhwán ↓ | Es demasiado grande para Juan. |

## DIALOG 2

| | | |
|---|---|---|
| Juan, dígale a José que son casi las tres. | sóŋkásılastrés \| hȯsé ↓ | Juan: Son casi las tres, José. |
| José, digale que tiene razón, que 'vamos', y que a esta hora no hay mucho movimiento. | tyénėzrrȧṣóm ↓ bámȯs ↓<br>ȧéstạórȧ \| nọáymúchȯmȯƀımyéntȯ ↓ | José: Tienes razón, vamos. A esta hora no hay mucho movimiento. |
| Juan, pregúntele a José si lleva el periódico de ayer. | (l)yéƀas \| ėlpėryóđıkȯđẹayér ↑ | Juan: ¿Llevas el periódico de ayer? |
| José, contéstele que sí, que aquí está, y que vean los anuncios. | sí ↓ ȧkíẹstá ↓ bėámȯslȯṣạnúnṣyȯs ↓ | José: Sí, aquí está. Veamos los anuncios. |
| Juan, pregúntele si ve algo. | bėṣálgȯ ↑ | Juan: ¿Ves algo? |

| | | |
|---|---|---|
| Jose, dígale que aquí hay uno: 'Apartamento de tres cuartos, amueblado, agua, luz; doscientos al mes.' | sí ↓ akịayúno ↓ apartaménto \| đetréskwártos ↑ amweƀláđo ↑ ágwa ↑ lúṣ ↑ đós(ṣ)yéntoṣalmés ↓ | José: Sí, aquí hay uno: 'Apartamento de tres cuartos, amueblado, agua, luz; doscientos al mes.' |
| Juan, dígale que no le conviene, que demasiado grande. | nómekómbyéne ↓ đemasyáđográndé ↓ | Juan: No me conviene, demasiado grande. |

## NARRATIVE 3

| | | |
|---|---|---|
| 1 Another one says: 'Unfurnished apartment, cheap....' | ótrođíṣe ↓ apartaménto \| sın mwéƀles ↑ baráto ↑ | Otro dice: 'Apartamento sin muebles, barato....' |
| 2 No, Juan wants it furnished. | nó ↓ hwánlokyérẹ \| amweƀláđo ↓ | No, Juan lo quiere amueblado. |
| 3 Here's a furnished one-room apartment. | akí \| áyunạpartaméntọ \| amweƀláđọ ↑ iđẹuŋkwárto ↓ | Aquí hay un apartamento amueblado y de un cuarto. |
| 4 But it's a long ways from downtown, almost in the outskirts. | péroẹstá \| muyléhoz \| đelṣéntro ↓ kásı \| enlaṣafwéras ↓ | Pero está muy lejos del centro, casi en las afueras. |
| 5 And Juan wants to live downtown. | ihwáŋkyéreƀíƀır \| enẹlṣéntro ↓ | Y Juan quiere vivir en el centro. |

| | | |
|---|---|---|
| 6 There are others but they're either too big or they're too far away. | áyótròs ↓ péròsónmúygrándès ↑ o̯èstánmúyléhòs ↓ | Hay otros, pero o son muy grandes o están muy lejos. |
| 7 Jose has a friend who works for an agency. | hòsétyéne̯ùnạmígò \| kètrábáha̯ ènụnàhénṣyà ↓ | José tiene un amigo que trabaja en una agencia. |
| 8 They're going to see him. | bánạbérlò ↓ | Van a verlo. |

## DIALOG 3

| | | |
|---|---|---|
| José, dígale que aquí hay otro: 'Apartamento sin muebles, barato....' | àki̯áyótrò ↓ àpàrtàméntòsin mwéblèz ↑ bàrátò \| | José: Aquí hay otro: 'Apartamento sin muebles, barato....' |
| Juan, dígale que no, que Ud. quiere uno amueblado. | nó ↓ kyéro̯úno̯ \| àmwèbládò ↓ | Juan: No, quiero uno amueblado. |
| José, dígale que aquí hay uno amueblado y de un cuarto. | àkí \| áyúno̯àmwèbládò ↑ idé̯úŋkwártò ↓ | José: Aquí hay uno amueblado y de un cuarto. |
| Juan, pregúntele si dice dónde está. | díṣè \| dóndèstá ↑ | Juan: ¿Dice dónde está? |

| | | |
|---|---|---|
| José, contéstele que sí, que en la Avenida Colón, 1621. | sí ↓ ėnlȧƀėníđȧkȯlón ↓<br>dyėş̮iséyzƀėyntyúnȯ ↓ | José: Sí, en la Avenida Colón 1621. |
| Juan, pregúntele que dónde está eso. | dóndėstáésȯ ↓ | Juan: ¿Dónde está eso? |
| Jose, contéstele que un poco lejos, que casi en las afueras. | u̇mpókȯléhȯs ↓ kásı̯ \| ėnlȧṣȧfwérȧs ↓ | José: Un poco lejos, casi en las afueras. |
| Juan, dígale que no le conviene a Ud., que Ud. quiere vivir en el centro. | nómėkȯmbyénė ↓ y̰ókyérȯƀíƀír \|<br>ėnėlș̮éntrȯ ↓ | Juan: No me conviene; yo quiero vivir en el centro. |
| José, dígale que muy bien, que Ud. tiene un amigo que trabaja en la Agencia del Valle; que pueden ir a hablar con el. | múyƀyén ↓ y̰ótéŋgo̯u̇nȧmígȯ \|<br>kėtrȧƀáha̯ \| ėnlȧhénșyȧ<br>đėlbá(l)y̰ė ↓ pȯđémȯṣır \| ȧƀlárkȯnél ↓ | José: Muy bien. Yo tengo un amigo que trabaja en la Agencia del Valle; podemos ir a hablar con él. |

**End of Tape 5B**

**End of CD 5**

# 8.1 BASIC SENTENCES

## Molina tells White about his neighbors' apartment

After having seen several apartments that were not suitable, Jose Molina and John White return to the hotel to talk it over.

| English Spelling | Aid to Listening | Spanish Spelling |
|---|---|---|
| gosh | kȧrámbȧ ↓ | caramba |
| (I) remember (to remember) | rrėkwérđȯ ↓ rrėkȯrđár ↓ | recuerdo (recordar) |
| *MOLINA* | | *MOLINA* |
| Gosh, now I remember. | kȧrámbȧ ↓ ȧórȧkėrrėkwérđȯ ↓ | ¡Caramba! Ahora que recuerdo. |
| the neighbor | ėl—bėşínȯ ↓ | el vecino |
| (they) go (to go) | bán ↓ ír ↓ | van (ir) |
| to remove | mu̇đár ↓ | mudar |
| the house | lȧ—kásȧ ↓ | la casa |
| to move (one's residence) | mu̇đársė—đė—kásȧ ↓ | mudarse de casa |
| the week | lȧ—sėmánȧ ↓ | la semana |
| My neighbors are going to move this week. | mizƀėşínȯz \| ƀánạmu̇đársė \| đėkásạ \| éstȧsėmánȧ ↓ | Mis vecinos van a mudarse de casa esta semana. |
| (they) live (to live) | bíƀėn ↓ biƀír ↓ | viven (vivir) |

| | | |
|---|---|---|
| equal to, the same as | igwál—ȧ ↓ | igual a |
| They live in an apartment just like mine. | bíƀėn \| ėn̩ún̩ȧpȧrtȧméntǫ \| igwálȧlmíȯ ↓ | Viven en un apartamento igual al mío. |
| expensive | kárȯ ↓ | caro |
| *WHITE* | | *WHITE* |
| Is it very expensive? | ézmu̇ykárȯ ↑ | ¿Es muy caro? |
| the contrary | ėl—kȯntráryȯ ↓ | el contrario |
| on the contrary | ȧl—kȯntráryȯ ↓ | al contrario |
| the price | ėl—prés̯yȯ ↓ | el precio |
| bad | mál ↓ málȯ ↓ | mal (malo) |
| *MOLINA* | | *MOLINA* |
| On the contrary, the price is not bad. | ȧlkȯntráryȯ ↓ ėlprés̯yȯ \| nǫėstámál ↓ | Al contrario, el precio no está mal. |
| (it) gives (to give) | dá ↓ dár ↓ | da (dar) |
| to face on | dár—ȧ ↓ | dar a |
| the street | lȧ—ká(l)y̰ė ↓ | la calle |
| the yard, the court, the patio | ėl—pátyȯ ↓ | el patio |
| *WHITE* | | *WHITE* |
| Does it face the street or the patio? | dálȧká(l)y̰ė ↑ ǫȧlpátyȯ ↓ | ¿Da a la calle o al patio? |

| | | |
|---|---|---|
| pretty | bȯnítȯ ↓ | bonito |
| the view | lȧ—ƀístȧ ↓ | la vista |
| *MOLINA* | | *MOLINA* |
| The street, and it has a beautiful view. | dálaká(l)y̯e̯ \| ityénė \| múyƀȯnítȧƀístȧ ↓ | Da a la calle y tiene muy bonita vista. |
| the room | la̯—ȧƀitȧs̯yón ↓ | la habitación |
| *WHITE* | | *WHITE* |
| How many rooms does it have? | kwántȧs̯ȧƀıtȧs̯yónės \| tyénė ↓ | ¿Cuántas habitaciones tiene? |
| the living room | lȧ—sálȧ ↓ | la sala |
| the kitchen | lȧ—kȯs̯ínȧ ↓ | la cocina |
| *MOLINA* | | *MOLINA* |
| A large living room, kitchen and bath. | únȧsálȧgrándė ↑ kȯs̯ína̯ \| ikwártȯđėƀán̯yȯ ↓ | Una sala grande, cocina y cuarto de baño. |
| the bedroom | ėl—dȯrmitóryȯ ↓ | el dormitorio |
| *WHITE* | | *WHITE* |
| Doesn't it have a bedroom? | nótyénė \| đȯrmitóryȯ ↑ | ¿No tiene dormitorio? |
| *MOLINA* | | *MOLINA* |
| No, but the living room is quite large. | nó ↓ pérȯlȧsála̯ \| ėzƀastántėgrándė ↓ | No, pero la sala es bastante grande. |
| the sofa | ėl—sȯfá ↓ | el sofá |

| | | |
|---|---|---|
| the bed | lȧ—kámȧ ↓ | la cama |
| the sofa-bed | ėl—sȯfá—kámȧ ↓ | el sofá cama |
| In mine I have a sofa-bed. | ėnlȧmíȧ ↑ téŋgo̯unsȯfákámȧ ↓ | En la mía tengo un sofá cama. |
| the reality | lȧ—rre̯ȧliđáđ ↓ | la realidad |
| it must be, it's probably | déƀė—sér ↓ | debe ser |
| comfortable | kómȯđȯ ↓ | cómodo |
| *WHITE* | | *WHITE* |
| Actually the apartment must be very comfortable. | ėnrre̯ȧliđáđ ↑ đéƀėsér \| múykómȯđo̯ \| ėlȧpȧrtȧméntȯ ↓ | En realidad, debe ser muy cómodo el apartamento. |
| (you) come (to come) | byénės ↓ bėnír ↓ | vienes (venir) |
| the night | lȧ—nóchė ↓ | la noche |
| tonight | éstȧ—nóchė ↓ | esta noche |
| so | ȧsí ↓ | así |
| (you) see (to see) | bés ↓ bér ↓ | ves (ver) |
| (I) live (to live) | bíƀȯ ↓ biƀír ↓ | vivo (vivir) |
| *MOLINA* | | *MOLINA* |
| Why don't you come tonight and you can see where I live? | pȯrkénóƀyénės \| éstȧnóchė \| i̯ȧsíƀéz \| đóndėƀíƀȯ ↓ | ¿Por qué no vienes esta noche y así ves dónde vivo? |

| | | |
|---|---|---|
| to leave, to let | dėhár ↓ | dejar |
| to leave me | dėhármė ↓ | dejarme |
| *WHITE* | | *WHITE* |
| O.K. Will you let me off at the hotel? | múyƀyén ↓ kyérėz ǀ đėhármę̯ ǀ ėnẹ̇lótél ↑ | Muy bien, ¿quieres dejarme en el hotel? |
| to have to | tėnér—kė ↓ | tener que |
| myself | mé ↓ | me |
| to change myself of (to change oneself) | kȧmbyármė—đė ↓ kȧmbyársė ↓ | cambiarme de (cambiarse) |
| the clothes, the clothing | lȧ—rrópȧ ↓ | la ropa |
| I have to change my clothes. | téŋgȯ ǀ kėkȧmbyármė ǀ đėrrópȧ ↓ | Tengo que cambiarme de ropa. |
| to come by | pȧsár ↓ | pasar |
| you | tí ↓ | ti |
| at eight (o'clock) | ȧ—lȧs—óchȯ ↓ | a las ocho |
| *MOLINA* | | *MOLINA* |
| Then I'll take you (to the hotel), and come by for you at eight. | ėntónṣės ǀ tė(l)y̯éƀo̯ ǀ ipásȯpȯrtí ǀ a̯lȧs óchȯ ↓ | Entonces te llevo y paso por ti a las ocho. |
| the million | ėl—mi(l)y̯ón ↓ | el millón |
| (I) hope (to hope, expect, wait for) | ėspérȯ ↓ ėspėrár ↓ | espero (esperar) |

| *WHITE* | | *WHITE* |
|---|---|---|
| Thanks a million. I'll be waiting for you. | únmı(l)y̯óndegrás̯yȧs ↓ tėsperȯ ↓ | Un millión de gracias. Te espero. |

# 8.2 DRILLS AND GRAMMAR

## 8.21 Pattern drills

### 8.21.1 Present tense forms of regular /—ír/ verbs

A. PRESENTATION OF PATTERN

*ILLUSTRATIONS*

| | | |
|---|---|---|
| ________________ | 1 ı̯àsıbéz ǀ đóndeƀíƀȯ ↓ | Y así ves donde *vivo.* |
| I live on the first floor. | 2 bíƀo̯ ǀ ėnẹlprimérpísȯ ↓ | *Vivo* en el primer piso. |
| Do you live on the first floor? | 3 bíƀės ǀ ėnẹlprimérpísȯ ↑ | ¿*Vives* en el primer piso? |
| (you) (fam.) open (to open) | áƀrės ↓ ȧƀrír ↓ | abres (abrir) |
| Why don't you open another agency? | 4 pȯrkéno̯áƀrės ǀ ótrahéns̯yȧ ↓ | ¿Por qué no *abres* otra agencia? |
| ________________ | 5 súƀe̯oƀáhȧ ↓ | ¿*Sube* o baja? |
| writes (to write) | ėskríƀė ↓ ėskriƀír ↓ | escribe (escribir) |

| | | |
|---|---|---|
| He writes too much. | 6 éleskríƀė \| đėmȧsyáđȯ ↓ | El *escribe* demasiado. |
| And so you can see where we live. | 7 ɹȧsíƀéz \| đóndėƀiƀímȯs ↓ | Y así ves donde *vivimos.* |
| (we) write (to write) | ėskriƀímȯs ↓ ėskriƀír ↓ | escribimos (escribir) |
| Why do we write so much? | 8 pȯrkéskriƀímȯstántȯ ↓ | ¿Por qué *escribimos* tanto? |
| ______________________ | 9 bíƀėn \| ėnụnạpȧrtȧméntȯ ↓ | *Viven* en un apartamento. |
| Are you going up in the elevator? | 10 súƀėn \| ėnẹlȧs(ṣ)ėnsór ↑ | ¿*Suben* en el ascensor? |

*EXTRAPOLATION*

| | sg | pl |
|---|---|---|
| 1 | —o | —ímos |
| 2 fam | —es | |
| 2-3 | —en | —en |

*NOTES*

a. The pattern for /—ír/ verbs differs from /—ér/ only in the occurrence of /—í/ as the theme vowel in 1 pl forms.

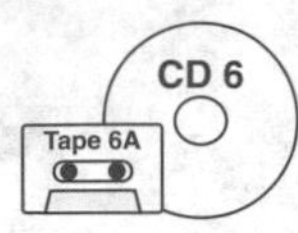




## 8.21.11 SUBSTITUTION DRILLS

Number substitution

| | |
|---|---|
| 1 ėskriƀɪ́mȯs \| ėnla̯ėskwélȧ ↓ | ėskrɪ́ƀo̯ \| ėnla̯ėskwélȧ ↓ |
| 2 bɪ́ƀėn \| léhȯzđėls̯éntrȯ ↓ | bɪ́ƀė \| léhȯzđėls̯éntrȯ ↓ |
| 3 súƀo̯ \| ėnėlȧs(s̯)ėnsór ↓ | sùƀɪ́mȯs \| ėnėlȧs(s̯)ėnsór ↓ |
| 4 no̯áƀre̯ \| ė(l)líƀrȯ ↓ | no̯áƀrėn \| ė(l)líƀrȯ ↓ |
| 5 biƀɪ́mȯs \| (s̯)érkȧđe̯ȧkí ↓ | bɪ́ƀȯ \| s̯érkȧđe̯ȧkí ↓ |
| 6 no̯ėskrɪ́ƀȯ \| múchȯ ↓ | no̯ėskriƀɪ́mȯz \| múchȯ ↓ |
| 7 súƀėn \| ménȯs̯ȧórȧ ↓ | súbė \| ménȯs̯ȧórȧ ↓ |

---

| | |
|---|---|
| 1 *Escribimos* en la escuela. | Escribo en la escuela. |
| 2 *Viven* lejos del centro. | Vive lejos del centro. |
| 3 *Subo* en el ascensor. | Subimos en el ascensor. |
| 4 No *abre* el libro. | No abren el libro. |
| 5 *Vivimos* cerca de aquí. | Vivo cerca de aquí. |
| 6 No *escribo* mucho. | No escribimos mucho. |
| 7 *Suben* menos ahora. | Sube menos ahora. |

CD 6
Tape 6A

Person - number substitution

1 y̥oƀıƀȯ | lehȯzđe̯ȧkí ↓

ȧntónyȯ ________________ ↓ — bíƀė | léhȯzđe̯ȧkí ↓

ȧlíṣyḁıyó ________________ ↓ — biƀímȯz | léhȯzđe̯ȧkí ↓

ùstéđ ________________ ↓ — bíƀė | léhȯzđe̯ȧkí ↓

é(l)y̥ȯz ________________ ↓ — bíƀėn | léhȯzđe̯ȧkí ↓

2 élėskríƀė | sólo̯ėnịŋglés ↓

y̥ó ________________ ↓ — ėskríƀȯ | sólo̯ėnịŋglés ↓

---

1 *Yo* vivo lejos de aquí.

Antonio ________________ . — Vive lejos de aquí.

Alicia y yo ________________ . — Vivimos lejos de aquí.

Ud. ________________ . — Vive lejos de aquí.

Ellos ________________ . — Viven lejos de aquí.

2 *El* escribe sólo en inglés.

Yo ________________ . — Escribo sólo en inglés.

kármėn ________________ ↓ ėskríƀė | sólo̯ėṇiŋglés ↓

nȯsótrȯs ________________ ↓ ėskriƀímȯs | sólo̯ėṇiŋglés ↓

ústéđės ________________ ↓ ėskríƀėn | sólo̯ėṇiŋglés ↓

3 é(l)y̯ȯsa̯ƀrėn | la̯ėmbȧháđȧ ↓

y̯ó ________________ ↓ áƀrȯ | la̯ėmbȧháđȧ ↓

kármėn ________________ ↓ áƀrė | la̯ėmbȧháđȧ ↓

nȯsótrȯs ________________ ↓ ȧƀrímȯz | la̯ėmbȧháđȧ ↓

ȯstéđės ________________ ↓ áƀrėn | la̯ėmbȧháđȧ ↓

---

Carmen ________________ . Escribe sólo en inglés.

Nosotros ________________ . Escribimos sólo en inglés.

Uds.________________ . Escriben sólo en inglés.

3 *Ellos* abren la Embajada.

Yo ________________ . Abro la Embajada.

Carmen ________________ . Abre la Embajada.

Nosotros ________________ . Abrimos la Embajada.

Uds.________________ . Abren la Embajada.

## 8.21.12 RESPONSE DRILL

| | | |
|---|---|---|
| | 1 ėskrı́ƀe̯ustéđ \| ėn̯espán̯yol ↑ o̯en̯iŋglés ↓ | ėskríƀo̯ėn̯iŋglés ↓ |
| | 2 bı́ƀėn̯ustéđės \| ėn̯ún̯apartaméntȯ ↑ o̯en̯únȧkásȧ ↓ | biƀı́mȯs \| ėn̯únȧkásȧ ↓ |
| | 3 ėskrı́ƀėlmúcho̯ ↑ ȯpókȯ ↓ | ėskríƀėpókȯ ↓ |
| [ėn̯ún̯ȯtél] | 4 dóndėƀı́ƀėn \| é(l)y̯ȯs ↓ | bı́ƀėn \| ėn̯ún̯ȯtél ↓ |
| [ėn̯él̯séntrȯ ↓] | 5 dóndėƀı́ƀe̯ \| ùstéđ ↓ | bı́ƀo̯ \| ėn̯él̯séntrȯ ↓ |
| [trés ↓] | 6 kwántȯschékės \| ėskrı́ƀél ↓ | ėskrı́ƀėtrés ↓ |

---

| | | |
|---|---|---|
| | 1 ¿Escribe Ud. en español o en inglés? | Escribo en inglés. |
| | 2 ¿Viven Uds. en un apartamento o en una casa? | Vivimos en una casa. |
| | 3 ¿Escribe él mucho o poco? | Escribe poco. |
| (en un hotel) | 4 ¿Dónde viven ellos? | Viven en un hotel. |
| (en el centro) | 5 ¿Dónde vive Ud.? | Vivo en el centro. |
| (tres) | 6 ¿Cuántos cheques escribe él? | Escribe tres. |

| | | | |
|---|---|---|---|
| [ėspȧn̦yó·l ↓] | 7 | ėskrı́ƀėnu̥stéđės \| ėni̥ŋglés ↑ | nó· ↓ ėskriƀı́mȯs \| ėnẹspȧn̦yó·l ↓ |
| [ȧpȧrtȧméntȯ ↓] | 8 | bı́ƀé(l)y̯a̯ \| ėnu̥ṅȧkásȧ ↑ | nó· ↓ bı́ƀe̯ \| ėnu̥ṅạpȧrtȧméntȯ ↓ |
| | | | |
| | 9 | áƀrél \| la̯ėmbȧháđȧ ↑ | sí· ↓ áƀrėla̯ėmbȧháđȧ ↓ |
| | 10 | bı́ƀėnu̥stéđės \| ėnlȧsạfwérȧs ↑ | sí· ↓ biƀı́mȯs \| ėnlȧsạfwérȧs ↓ |
| | 11 | súƀėné̥(l)y̯ȯs \| ėnẹlȧs(s)ėnsór ↑ | sí· ↓ súƀėn \| ėnẹlȧs(s̯)ėnsór ↓ |

---

| | | | |
|---|---|---|---|
| (español) | 7 | ¿Escriben Uds. en inglés? | No, escribimos en español. |
| (apartamento) | 8 | ¿Vive ella en una casa? | No, vive en un apartamento. |
| | | | |
| | 9 | ¿Abre él la Embajada? | Sí, abre la Embajada. |
| | 10 | ¿Viven Uds. en las afueras? | Sí, vivimos en las afueras. |
| | 11 | ¿Suben ellos en el ascensor? | Sí, suben en el ascensor. |

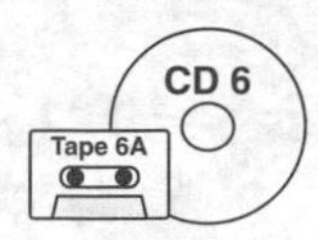




## 8.21.13 TRANSLATION DRILL

| | | | |
|---|---|---|---|
| 1 | We live in an old house. | biƀímȯs \| ėnu̯nȧkásȧƀyéhȧ ↓ | Vivimos en una casa vieja. |
| 2 | They live in a big apartment. | é(l)y̯ózƀíƀėn \| ėnu̯nȧpȧrtȧméntȯgrándė ↓ | Ellos viven en un apartamento grande. |
| 3 | What time do they open that building? | ȧke̯óráƀrėn \| ėsėđifís̯yȯ ↓ | ¿A qué hora abren ese edificio? |
| 4 | Where do you live? | dóndėƀíƀe̯ustéđ ↓ | ¿Dónde vive usted? |
| 5 | Does he write the ads? | ėskríƀél \| lȯs̯ȧnúns̯yȯs ↑ | ¿Escribe él los anuncios? |
| 6 | When do you write? | kwándo̯ėskríƀe̯ustéđ ↓ | ¿Cuándo escribe Ud.? |
| 7 | Since when have you all lived there? | dėzđėkwándȯƀíƀėn \| ustéđės̯ȧí ↓ | ¿Desde cuándo viven Uds. ahí? |
| 8 | Does he open the Embassy? | áƀrél \| la̯ėmbȧháđȧ ↑ | ¿Abre él la Embajada? |
| 9 | I go up at eight o'clock. | y̯ósúƀo̯ \| ȧlȧs̯óchȯ ↓ | Yo subo a las ocho. |
| 10 | They go up at seven. | é(l)y̯ȯ(s)súƀėn \| ȧlȧ(s)syétė ↓ | Ellos suben a las siete. |
| 11 | They live near a friend (of) mine. | bíƀėns̯érkȧ \| đe̯u̯nȧmígȯmíȯ ↓ | Viven cerca de un amigo mío. |
| 12 | I live in the United States. | bíƀȯ \| ėnlȯs̯ėstáđȯs̯uníđȯs ↓ | Vivo en los Estados Unidos. |
| 13 | I live a long ways from the language school. | bíƀȯléhȯz \| đėla̯ėskwélȧđėléŋgwȧs ↓ | Vivo lejos de la escuela de lenguas. |

## B. DISCUSSION OF PATTERN

In almost all tense forms other than present tense forms there is no distinction between /—ér/ and /—ír/ theme class verb endings, and they will be referred to as /—ér—ír/ patterns. The important differences are in the theme vowel of the infinitive and the 1 pl form of the present tense.

Below is the complete pattern for regular verbs in the present tense, illustrated with three common verbs:

| | | abl—ár | kom—ér | bıb—ír |
|---|---|---|---|---|
| 1 | sg | ábl—o | kóm—o | bíb—o |
| 2 | fam | ábl—as | kóm—es | bíb—es |
| 2-3 | sg | ábl—a | kóm—e | bíb—e |
| 1 | pl | abl—ámos | kom—émos | bıb—ímos |
| 2-3 | pl | ábl—an | kóm—en | bíb—en |

Note that theme class membership is marked by the presence of a vowel /a, e, i/ in all forms except 1 sg. All 1 sg forms have the ending /—o/ in common. Note also that the person-number endings /—s, —mos, —n/ are present in their appropriate forms regardless of what theme vowel precedes them. Note also that /—ér/ and /—ír/ verbs are distinguished only in 1 pl forms, where distinct /—e—/ and /—ı—/ theme vowels appear.

## 8.21.2 The obligatory contractions

### A. PRESENTATION OF PATTERN

*ILLUSTRATIONS*

| | | |
|---|---|---|
| ____________ | 1 kyéròprèsèntárle̯ ǀ àlsèn̯yórmòlínà ↓ | Quiero presentarle *al* señor Molina. |
| ____________ | 2 dálàká(l)y̮è ↑ o̯àlpátyò ↓ | ¿Da *a la* calle, o *al* patio? |
| of the, from the | dél ↓ | del |
| Far from the Embassy, or the hotel? | 3 léhòz ǀ đèla̯èmbàháđa̯ ↑ òđèlòtél ↓ | ¿Lejos *de la* Embajada, *o del* hotel? |
| ____________ | 4 ènẹlèđifís̯yòđèlkámpò ↓ | En el edificio *Del* Campo. |

*EXTRAPOLATION*

| | a | de |
|---|---|---|
| el | al | del |
| la | a—la | de—la |
| los | a—los | de—los |
| las | a—las | de—las |

*NOTES*

a. The contractions /al/ and /del/ are obligatory on all style levels of Spanish.

b. Many other contractions occur, but they are not obligatory.

## 8.21.21 SUBSTITUTION DRILLS

Number substitution

1 kyérèmprèsèntárlẹ | àlsèṇyór ↓

_______________ sèṇyórès ↓ — kyérèmprèsèntárlẹ | àlò(s)sèṇyórès ↓

2 là(l)ẏábédèlkwártò ↓

_______________ kwártòs ↓ — là(l)ẏábédèlòskwártòs ↓

3 làkásạ | èzđèlò(s)sèṇyórès ↓

_______________ sèṇyór ↓ — làkásạ | èzđèlsèṇyór ↓

---

1 Quieren presentarle al *señor.*

_______________ *señores.* — Quieren presentarle a los señores.

2 La llave del *cuarto*.

_______________ *cuartos*. — La llave de los cuartos.

3 La casa es de los *señores*.

_______________ *señor.* — La casa es del señor.

4 kyéro̯ȧƀlár | đėlȯs̯ȧpȧrtȧméntȯs ↓

_______________ ȧpȧrtȧméntȯ ↓ kyéro̯ȧƀlár | đėlȧpȧrtȧméntȯ ↓

5 (l)y̯éƀėnȯs | ȧlȯzrrėstȯránės ↓

_________________ rrėstȯrán ↓ (l)yéƀėnȯs | ȧlrrėstȯrán ↓

---

4 Quiero hablar de los *apartamentos*.

________________*apartamento*. Quiero hablar del apartamento.

5 Llévenos a los *restoranes*.

___________________ *restorán*. Llévenos al restorán.

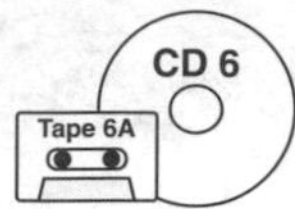




Item substitution

1 bánȧla̯ėmbȧháđȧ ↓

____________________ ȯtél ↓ bánạlȯtél ↓

2 bámȯṣa̯ls̯éntrȯ ↓

__________________ ȧhéns̯yȧ ↓ bámȯṣa̯lȧhéns̯yȧ ↓

3 ėlȯtélėzđėlȧsėn̯yórȧ ↓

__________________ sėn̯yór ↓ ėlȯtélėzđėlsėn̯yór ↓

---

1 Van a la *Embajada*.

____________________ *hotel*. Van al hotel.

2 *Vamos* al centro.

__________________ *agencia*. Vamos a la agencia.

3 El hotel es de la *señora*.

____________________ *señor*. El hotel es del señor.

4 ėlkwárto | đálaká(l)yė ↓

__________________ pátyo ↓ — ėlkwárto | đálpátyo ↓

5 kyéròprėsėntárle | àlsėnyór ↓

______________ sėnyòríta ↓ — kyéròprėsėntárle | àlàsėnyòríta ↓

---

4 El cuarto da a la *calle*.

__________________ *patio*. — El cuarto da al patio.

5 Quiero presentarle al *señor*.

__________________ *señorita*. — Quiero presentarle a la señorita.

## 8.21.22 TRANSLATION DRILL

| | | | |
|---|---|---|---|
| 1 | They want to go to the restaurant. | kyérėnı̣́r \| ȧlrrėstȯrán ↓ | Quieren ir al restorán. |
| 2 | They want to go to the agency. | kyérėnı̣́r \| ȧlȧhénşyȧ ↓ | Quieren ir a la agencia. |
| 3 | They are going to the same hotel. | bánạlmı́zmȯtél ↓ | Van al mismo hotel. |
| 4 | This is the key to (of) the house. | ésta̯ėz \| lȧ(l)y̯áƀėđėlȧkásȧ ↓ | Esta es la llave de la casa. |
| 5 | These are the keys to (of) the apartment. | éstȧ(s)són \| lȧz(l)y̯áƀėz \| đėlȧpartȧméntȯ ↓ | Estas son las llaves del apartamento. |
| 6 | Two hundred dollars a (to the) month. | dȯs(ş)yéntȯzđólȧrės \| ȧlmés ↓ | Doscientos dólares al mes. |
| 7 | This is Mr. Molina's car (the car of Mr. Molina). | éstėşėláwtȯ \| đėlsėn̮yórmȯlínȧ ↓ | Este es el auto del señor Molina. |
| 8 | This is the light bill (bill of the light). | ésta̯ėzlȧkwéntȧ \| đėlȧlúş ↓ | Esta es la cuenta de la luz. |
| 9 | This is the gas bill (bill of the gas). | ésta̯ėzlȧkwéntȧ \| đėlgás ↓ | Esta es la cuenta del gas. |

## B. DISCUSSION OF PATTERN

There are many instances of contraction, or telescoping of forms, in Spanish. This is particularly true when two vowels are brought together at word boundaries. The contraction is usually complete if the two vowels involved are the same. For example, in /dóndestá/ the final /—e/ of /dónde/ and the initial /e—/ of /está/ are telescoped in normal pronunciation. A slower pronunciation, however, would be /dóndḙ | está ↓/.

The two cases of contraction presented above are selected for special drill because they are obligatory; /de/ and /el/ will always be /del/, no matter how slowly pronounced. The two contractions /al/ and /del/ are the only ones recognized in the writing system—no others, however they are pronounced, are written as contractions. Note that it is the weak-stressed /el/ 'the' which combines with /a/ and /de/; the strong-stressed /él/ 'he' does not.

## 8.22 REPLACEMENT DRILLS

A bíƀen | ėnụnạpȧrtȧméntȯ ↓

| | | |
|---|---|---|
| 1 | ______________ kásȧ ↓ | bíƀėn \| ėnụnȧkásȧ ↓ |
| 2 | biƀímȯs ______________ ↓ | biƀímȯs \| ėnụnȧkásȧ ↓ |
| 3 | ________ éstȧ ________ ↓ | biƀímȯs \| ėnẹstȧkásȧ ↓ |
| 4 | ______________ ȯtél ↓ | biƀímȯs \| ėnẹstẹȯtél ↓ |
| 5 | trȧƀȧhámȯs ______________ ↓ | trȧƀȧhámȯs \| ėnẹstẹȯtél ↓ |
| 6 | ________ ésẹ ________ ↓ | trȧƀȧhámȯs \| ėnẹsẹȯtél ↓ |
| 7 | ______________ ėmbȧháđȧ ↓ | trȧƀȧhámȯs \| ėnẹsạėmbȧháđȧ ↓ |

---

A Viven en un apartamento.

| | | |
|---|---|---|
| 1 | ______________ casa. | Viven en una casa. |
| 2 | Vivimos ______________ . | Vivimos en una casa. |
| 3 | ________ esta ________ . | Vivimos en esta casa. |
| 4 | ______________ hotel. | Vivimos en este hotel. |
| 5 | Trabajamos______________ . | Trabajamos en este hotel. |
| 6 | ________ ese ________ . | Trabajamos en ese hotel. |
| 7 | ______________ embajada. | Trabajamos en esa embajada. |

B ėzmúykárȯ ↓

| | |
|---|---|
| 1 sȯn ______________ ↓ | sȯnmúykárȯs ↓ |
| 2 ______________ ƀȧrátȯs ↓ | sȯnmúyƀȧrátȯs ↓ |
| 3 ______________ ƀȧrátȯ ↓ | ėzmúyƀȧrátȯ ↓ |
| 4 ______________ ƀyéhȯ ↓ | ėzmúyƀyéhȯ ↓ |
| 5 sȯy ______________ ↓ | sȯymúyƀyéhȯ ↓ |
| 6 sȯn ______________ ↓ | sȯnmúyƀyéhȯs ↓ |
| 7 ______________ ƀȯnítȧ ↓ | ėzmúyƀȯnítȧ ↓ |

---

B Es muy caro.

| | |
|---|---|
| 1 Son ______________ . | Son muy caros. |
| 2 ______________ baratos. | Son muy baratos. |
| 3 ______________ barato. | Es muy barato. |
| 4 ______________ viejo. | Es muy viejo. |
| 5 Soy ______________ . | Soy muy viejo. |
| 6 Son ______________ . | Son muy viejos. |
| 7 ______________ bonita. | Es muy bonita. |

C ėlpreşyȯ | noėstámál ↓

1 éstȯs ________________ ↓ éstȯspreşyȯz | noėstánmál ↓

2 ________ kásȧ ________________ ↓ éstȧkásȧ | noėstámál ↓

3 ésȧ ________________ ↓ ésȧkásȧ | noėstámál ↓

4 ________ mwébléz ________________ ↓ ésȯzmwéblėz | noėstánmál ↓

5 ________ kȧntidád ________________ ↓ ésȧkȧntidád | noėstámál ↓

6 éstȧ ________________ ↓ éstȧkȧntidád | noėstámál ↓

7 ________ imfȯrmȧşyón ________ ↓ éstaimfȯrmȧşyón | noėstámál ↓

---

C El precio no está mal.

1 Estos ________________ . Estos precios no están mal.

2 ________ casa ________________ . Esta casa no está mal.

3 Esa ________________ . Esa casa no está mal.

4 ________ muebles ________________ . Esos muebles no están mal.

5 ________ cantidad ________________ . Esa cantidad no está mal.

6 Esta ________________ . Esta cantidad no está mal.

7 ________ información ________ . Esta información no está mal.

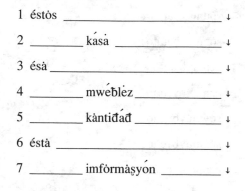

D ityénė | múyƀonítaƀístȧ ↓

| | Cue | Response |
|---|---|---|
| 1 | _______ bwénȧ _______ ↓ | ityénė \| múyƀwénaƀístȧ ↓ |
| 2 | _______________ ėntráđȧ ↓ | ityénė \| múyƀwénaėntráđȧ ↓ |
| 3 | _______________ ȧmígȯs ↓ | ityénė \| múyƀwénȯsamígȯs ↓ |
| 4 | _______ téŋgȯ _______ ↓ | itéŋgȯ \| múyƀwénȯsamígȯs ↓ |
| 5 | _______________ imfȯrmasyónės ↓ | itéŋgȯ \| múyƀwénasimfȯrmasyónės ↓ |
| 6 | _______________ mwéƀlės ↓ | itéŋgȯ \| múyƀwénȯzmwéƀlės ↓ |
| 7 | _______ málȯz _______ ↓ | itéŋgȯ \| múymálȯzmwéƀlės ↓ |

---

D Y tiene muy bonita vista.

| | Cue | Response |
|---|---|---|
| 1 | _______ buena _______ . | Y tiene muy buena vista. |
| 2 | _______________ entrada. | Y tiene muy buena entrada. |
| 3 | _______________ amigos. | Y tiene muy buenos amigos. |
| 4 | _______ tengo _______ . | Y tengo muy buenos amigos. |
| 5 | _______________ informaciones. | Y tengo muy bucnas informaciones. |
| 6 | _______________ muebles. | Y tengo muy buenos muebles. |
| 7 | _______ malos _______ . | Y tengo muy malos muebles. |

E kwántȧs | ȧƀitȧşyónėstyénė ↓

| | |
|---|---|
| 1 ______________________ són ↓ | kwántȧs \| ȧƀitȧşyónėssón ↓ |
| 2 ________ kwártȯs ____________ ↓ | kwántȯskwártȯ(s)són ↓ |
| 3 ______________________ áy ↓ | kwántȯskwártȯşáy ↓ |
| 4 ________ ágwa̯ ____________ ↓ | kwántágwáy ↓ |
| 5 ________ sėn̯yórės ____________ ↓ | kwántȯ(s)sėn̯yórėşáy ↓ |
| 6 ______________________ trȧƀáhȧn ↓ | kwántȯ(s)sėn̯yórės \| trȧƀáhȧn ↓ |
| 7 ________ sėn̯yórȧs ____________ ↓ | kwántȧ(s)sėn̯yórȧs \| trȧƀáhȧn ↓ |

---

E ¿Cuántas habitaciones tiene?

| | |
|---|---|
| 1 ¿ ______________________ son? | ¿Cuántas habitaciones son? |
| 2 ¿ ________ cuartos ____________? | ¿Cuántos cuartos son? |
| 3 ¿ ______________________ hay? | ¿Cuántos cuartos hay? |
| 4 ¿ ________ agua ____________? | ¿Cuánta agua hay? |
| 5 ¿ ________ señores ____________? | ¿Cuántos señores hay? |
| 6 ¿ ______________________ trabajan? | ¿Cuántos señores trabajan? |
| 7 ¿ ________ señoras ____________? | ¿Cuántas señoras trabajan? |

F kyérėz | đėhárme̯ | ėne̯lotél ↑

| | |
|---|---|
| 1 pwéđėz ______________ ↑ | pwéđėz \| đėhárme̯ \| ėne̯lotél ↑ |
| 2 ________ (l)y̯ėƀárme̯ ________ ↑ | pwéđėz \| (l)y̯ėƀárme̯ \| ȧlotél ↑ |
| 3 ______________ kásȧ ↑ | pwéđėz \| (l)y̯ėƀárme̯ \| ȧlȧkásȧ ↑ |
| 4 ______ ȧlkılármė ________ ↑ | pwéđės \| alkılármė \| lȧkásȧ ↑ |
| 5 ______________ȧpartaméntȯ ↑ | pwéđės \| alkılárme̯ \| ėlȧpartaméntȯ ↑ |
| 6 ______ u̇n ______________ ↑ | pwéđės \| alkılárme̯ \| u̇n̯ȧpartaméntȯ ↑ |
| 7 kyérės ______________ ↑ | kyérės \| alkılárme̯ \| u̇n̯ȧpartaméntȯ ↑ |

---

F ¿Quieres dejarme en el hotel?

| | |
|---|---|
| 1 ¿Puedes ______________? | ¿Puedes dejarme en el hotel? |
| 2 ¿ ________ llevarme ________? | ¿Puedes llevarme al hotel? |
| 3 ¿ ______________ casa? | ¿Puedes llevarme a la casa? |
| 4 ¿ ______ alquilarme________? | ¿Puedes alquilarme la casa? |
| 5 ¿ ______________ apartamento? | ¿Puedes alquilarme el apartamento? |
| 6 ¿ ________ un ________? | ¿Puedes alquilarme un apartamento? |
| 7 ¿Quieres ______________? | ¿Quieres alquilarme un apartamento? |

**End of Tape 6A**

## 8.23 VARIATION DRILLS

| | | |
|---|---|---|
| A | mizƀėṣínȯz \| ƀáṇȧmuđársė \| đėkásạ \| ėstȧsėmánȧ ↓ | Mis vecinos van a mudarse de casa esta semana. |
| 1 My friends are going to move to another apartment this week. | misȧmígȯz \| ƀáṇȧmuđársė \| đẹȧpȧrtȧméntọ \| ėstȧsėmánȧ ↓ | Mis amigos van a mudarse de apartamento esta semana. |
| 2 My neighbors are going to move to another room this week. | mizƀėṣínȯz \| ƀáṇȧmuđársė \| đėkwártọ \| ėstȧsėmánȧ ↓ | Mis vecinos van a mudarse de cuarto esta semana. |
| 3 My neighbors are going to look for another house. | mizƀėṣínȯz \| ƀáṇȧƀuskár \| ótrȧkásȧ ↓ | Mis vecinos van a buscar otra casa. |
| 4 My friends are going to rent another house. | misȧmígȯz \| ƀáṇȧlkilár \| ótrȧkásȧ ↓ | Mis amigos van a alquilar otra casa. |
| 5 My friends are going to work in an agency. | misȧmígȯz \| ƀáṇȧtrȧƀahár \| ėnụnȧhénṣyȧ ↓ | Mis amigos van a trabajar en una agencia. |
| 6 My (girl) friends are going to eat in the restaurant. | misȧmígȧz \| ƀáṇȧkȯmér \| ėnẹlrrėstȯrán ↓ | Mis amigas van a comer en el restorán. |
| 7 My (girl) friends are going to be here tomorrow. | misȧmígȧz \| ƀáṇȧėstárȧkí \| mȧṇyánȧ ↓ | Mis amigas van a estar aquí mañana. |

| | | | |
|---|---|---|---|
| B | | bíƀėn ǀ ėṇụṇạpȧrtȧméntọ̯ ǀ igwálȧlmíȯ ↓ | Viven en un apartamento igual al mío. |
| 1 | They live in a room just like mine. | bíƀėn ǀ ėṇụŋkwártọ̯ ǀ igwálȧlmíȯ ↓ | Viven en un cuarto igual al mío. |
| 2 | They live in a building just like mine. | bíƀėn ǀ ėṇụṇẹđifíṣyọ̯ ǀ igwálȧlmíȯ ↓ | Viven en un edificio igual al mío. |
| 3 | They live in a hotel. | bíƀėnẹṇụṇọtél ↓ | Viven en un hotel. |
| 4 | He lives in the United States. | bíƀẹ̯ ǀ ėnlȯṣẹstáđȯṣụníđȯs ↓ | Vive en los Estados Unidos. |
| 5 | I live in Washington. | bíƀọ̯ẹŋw̰áshiŋtȯn ↓ | Vivo en Washington. |
| 6 | We live here. | biƀímȯṣạkí ↓ | Vivimos aquí. |
| 7 | We live there. | biƀímȯṣạí ↓ | Vivimos ahí. |

| | | | |
|---|---|---|---|
| C | | dálàká(l)ẏ̰ė ↑ o̯àlpátyȯ ↓ | ¿Da a la calle o al patio? |
| 1 | Does it face the street or the avenue? | dálàká(l)ẏ̰ė ↑ o̯àlàƀėníđȧ ↓ | ¿Da a la calle o a la avenida? |
| 2 | Does it face the avenue or the court? | dálàƀėníđȧ ↑ o̯àlpátyȯ ↓ | ¿Da a la avenida o al patio? |
| 3 | Does it face 20th Street or the avenue? | dálàká(l)y̰ėƀéyntė ↑ o̯àlàƀėníđȧ ↓ | ¿Da a la Calle Veinte o a la avenida? |
| 4 | Does it face Fifth Street or Second Street? | dálàká(l)y̰ės̮íŋkȯ ↑ o̯àlàká(l)y̰ėđós ↓ | ¿Da a la Calle Cinco o a la Calle Dos? |
| 5 | Does it face the living room or the kitchen? | dálàsálȧ ↑ o̯àlàkȯs̮ínȧ ↓ | ¿Da a la sala o a la cocina? |
| 6 | Does it face the bedroom or the bathroom? | dáldȯrmitóryȯ ↑ o̯alkwártȯđėƀáñyȯ ↓ | ¿Da al dormitorio o al cuarto de baño? |
| 7 | Does it face the American Embassy? | dála̯ėmbȧháđa̯ \| ȧmėrıkánȧ ↑ | ¿Da a la Embajada Americana? |

| | English | Pronunciation | Spanish |
|---|---|---|---|
| D | | nó ↓ péròlàsálạ \| èzƀàstántė \| grándė ↓ | No, pero la sala es bastante grande. |
| 1 | No, but the kitchen is quite large. | nó ↓ péròlàkòṣínạ \| èzƀàstántė \| grándė ↓ | No, pero la cocina es bastante grande. |
| 2 | No, but the rooms are quite large. | nó ↓ péròlàsạƀitàṣyónės \| sómbàstántė \| grándės ↓ | No, pero las habitaciones son bastante grandes. |
| 3 | No, but the view is rather nice. | nó ↓ péròlàƀístạ \| èzƀàstántė \| ƀwénà ↓ | No, pero la vista es bastante buena. |
| 4 | No, but the street is rather nice. | nó ↓ péròlàká(l)yẹ \| èzƀàstántė \| ƀwénà ↓ | No, pero la calle es bastante buena. |
| 5 | Yes, and the Embassy is quite near. | sí ↓ ilạèmbàháđạ \| èstáƀàstántė \| ṣérkà ↓ | Sí, y la Embajada está bastante cerca. |
| 6 | Yes, and the restaurant is near. | sí ↓ ɪ̯èlrrèstòrán \| èstáṣérkà ↓ | Sí, y el restorán está cerca. |
| 7 | Yes, and the apartment is inexpensive. | sí ↓ ɪ̯èlàpàrtàméntọ \| èzƀàràtò ↓ | Sí, y el apartamento es barato. |

| | | | |
|---|---|---|---|
| E | | ėnlȧmíȧ ǀ téŋgo̯u̇nsȯfákámȧ ↓ | En la mía tengo un sofá cama. |
| 1 | In mine I have a bed. | ėnlȧmíȧ ǀ téŋgo̯u̇nȧkámȧ ↓ | En la mía tengo una cama. |
| 2 | In mine I have a table. | ėnlȧmíȧ ǀ téŋgo̯u̇nȧmésȧ ↓ | En la mía tengo una mesa. |
| 3 | In my room I have a desk. | ėnmikwártȯ ǀ téŋgo̯u̇nẹskritóryȯ ↓ | En mi cuarto tengo un escritorio. |
| 4 | In the living room I have four chairs. | ėnlȧsálȧ ǀ téŋgȯkwátrȯsí(l)y̯ȧs ↓ | En la sala tengo cuatro sillas. |
| 5 | In the kitchen I have a few coins. | ėnlȧkȯs̯ínȧ ǀ téŋgo̯u̇nȧzmȯnéđȧs ↓ | En la cocina tengo unas monedas. |
| 6 | In the hotel I have a few dollars. | ėnẹlȯtél ǀ téŋgo̯u̇nȯzđólȧrės ↓ | En el hotel tengo unos dólares. |
| 7 | On the table I have an ash-tray. | ėnlȧmésȧ ǀ téŋgo̯u̇ns̯ėnis̯érȯ ↓ | En la mesa tengo un cenicero. |

| | | | |
|---|---|---|---|
| F | débėsér \| múykómȯđo̯ \| ėlȧpȧrtȧméntȯ ↓ | | Debe ser muy cómodo el apartamento. |
| 1 | The room must be very comfortable. | déƀėsér \| múykómȯđo̯ \| ėlkwártȯ ↓ | Debe ser muy cómodo el cuarto. |
| 2 | The house must be very comfortable. | déƀėsér \| múykómȯđȧ \| lȧkásȧ ↓ | Debe ser muy cómoda la casa. |
| 3 | The hotel must be very good. | déƀėsér \| múyƀwéno̯ \| ėlȯtél ↓ | Debe ser muy bueno el hotel. |
| 4 | The car must be very cheap. | déƀėsér \| múyƀȧráto̯ \| ėláwtȯ ↓ | Debe ser muy barato el auto. |
| 5 | The kitchen must be very large. | déƀėsér \| múygrándė \| lȧkȯṣínȧ ↓ | Debe ser muy grande la cocina. |
| 6 | The hotels must be very cheap. | déƀėnsér \| múyƀȧrátȯz \| lȯṣȯtélės ↓ | Deben ser muy baratos los hoteles. |
| 7 | The apartments must be very nice. | déƀėnsér \| múyƀȯnítȯz \| lȯṣȧpȧrtȧméntȯs ↓ | Deben ser muy bonitos los apartamentos. |

## 8.24 REVIEW DRILL

Noun-adjective agreement

| | | |
|---|---|---|
| 1 It's a bad pen. | éṣu̇nȧplúmȧmálȧ ↓ | Es una pluma mala. |
| It's a bad book. | éṣu̇nlíƀrȯmálȯ ↓ | Es un libro malo. |
| 2 It's a good chair. | éṣu̇nȧsí(l)ỵȧƀwénȧ ↓ | Es una silla buena. |
| It's a good desk. | éṣu̇nẹ̇skritóryȯƀwénȯ ↓ | Es un escritorio bueno. |
| 3 He has an old house. | tyéne̯ \| u̇nȧkásȧƀyéhȧ ↓ | Tiene una casa vieja. |
| He has an old apartment. | tyéne̯ \| u̇nạpȧrtȧméntȯƀyéhȯ ↓ | Tiene un apartamento viejo. |
| 4 It's a good pen. | éṣu̇nȧplúmȧƀwénȧ ↓ | Es una pluma buena. |
| It's a good book. | éṣu̇nlíƀrȯƀwénȯ ↓ | Es un libro bueno. |
| 5 It's a good table. | éṣu̇nȧmésȧƀwénȧ ↓ | Es una mesa buena. |
| It's a bad desk. | és \| u̇nẹ̇skritóryȯmálȯ ↓ | Es un escritorio malo. |

| | | |
|---|---|---|
| 6 He has a pretty table. | tyénẹ̯ \| u̇nȧmésȧƀȯnítȧ ↓ | Tiene una mesa bonita. |
| He has an old desk. | tyénẹ̯ \| u̇nẹ̇skrıtóryȯƀyéhȯ ↓ | Tiene un escritorio viejo. |
| 7 He has an expensive house. | tyénẹ̯ \| u̇nȧkásȧkárȧ ↓ | Tiene una casa cara. |
| He has an expensive apartment. | tyénẹ̯ \| u̇nạ̇pȧrtȧméntȯkárȯ ↓ | Tiene un apartamento caro. |
| 8 I live in an inexpensive house. | bíƀọ̯ \| ėnụ̇nȧkásȧƀȧrátȧ ↓ | Vivo en una casa barata. |
| I live in an inexpensive apartment. | bíƀọ̯ \| ėnụ̇nạ̇pȧrtȧméntȯƀȧrátȯ ↓ | Vivo en un apartamento barato. |
| 9 I live in a comfortable house. | bíƀọ̯ \| ėnụ̇nȧkásȧkómȯđȧ ↓ | Vivo en una casa cómoda. |
| I live in a comfortable apartment. | bíƀọ̯ \| ėnụ̇nạ̇pȧrtȧméntȯkómȯđȯ ↓ | Vivo en un apartamento cómodo. |

# 8.3 CONVERSATION STIMULUS

## NARRATIVE 1

| | | |
|---|---|---|
| 1 Jose and Juan take a taxi and go see some apartments. | hòse̯ihwán ǀ tómàn̥ùntáks̯ı ǀ iƀán̥àƀér ǀ ùnòs̯àpàrtàméntòs ↓ | José y Juan toman un taxi y van a ver unos apartamentos. |
| 2 The taxi costs six pesos, more or less. | èltáksı ǀ kwéstàseyspésòz ǀ más̥òménòs ↓ | El taxi cuesta seis pesos, más o menos. |
| 3 Jose has only a ten peso bill and Juan some travelers checks. | hòsé ǀ tyénèsólo̯umbı(l)yétèđe̯ađyés̥ ↓ ihwán ǀ ùnòschékèzƀyàhéròs ↓ | José tiene sólo un billete de a diez y Juan unos cheques viajeros. |
| 4 The driver doesn't have change. | èlchófer ǀ nótyénèkámbyò ↓ | El chofer no tiene cambio. |
| 5 So he takes the ten, six for the trip and four for a tip. | èntóns̥es ǀ tóma̯èlbı(l)yétè ǀ đe̯ađyés̥ ↓ séys ǀ pòrèlbyahe̯ ǀ ikwátròđèpròpínà ↓ | Entonces toma el billete de a diez; seis por el viaje y cuatro de propina. |

## DIALOG 1

| | | |
|---|---|---|
| José, pregúntele al chofer que cuánto le debe. | kwántòlèđéƀò ↓ | José: ¿Cuánto le debo? |

| | | |
|---|---|---|
| Chofer, contéstele que son seis pesos. | sȯnséyspésȯs ↓ | Chofer: Son seis pesos. |
| José, pregúntele si tiene cambio para diez. | tyénėkámbyȯ \| párȧđyés̜ ↑ | José: ¿Tiene cambio para diez? |
| Chofer, contéstele que no, que no tiene. | nó \| sėŋyór ↓ nótéŋgȯ ↓ | Chofer: No, señor, no tengo. |
| Juan, dígale que Ud. tiene sólo cheques viajeros. | y̯ósólȯtéŋgȯ \| chékėzƀyȧhérȯs ↓ | Juan: Yo sólo tengo cheques viajeros. |
| José, dígale al chofer que tome los diez, que cuatro de propina. | tómėlȯzđyés̜ ↓ kwátrȯđėprȯpínȧ ↓ | José: Tome los diez, cuatro de propina. |
| Chofer, contéstele que un millón de gracias. | ủnmi(l)y̯óndėgrás̜yȧs ↓ | Chofer: Un millón de gracias. |

## NARRATIVE 2

| | | |
|---|---|---|
| 1 Jose and Juan talk with the agent, a friend of Jose's. | hȯsėı̯hwán \| áƀlaŋkȯnėlȧhéntė ↓ ủn̥ȧmígȯđėhȯsé ↓ | José y Juan hablan con el agente, un amigo de José. |
| 2 The three (of them) go together to the Del Campo building. | lȯstrézƀaŋhúntȯs \| ȧlėđifís̜yȯđėlkámpȯ ↓ | Los tres van juntos al edificio Del Campo. |

| | | |
|---|---|---|
| 3 They go in. | pásȧn̥ȧđėlántė ↓ | Pasan adelante. |
| 4 They like the first apartment they see very much. | ėlprimérȧpȧrtȧméntȯ \| kėƀén ↑ lėzgústȧmúchȯ ↓ | El primer apartamento que ven les gusta mucho. |
| 5 But, gosh!, it's very expensive. | pérȯ \| kȧrámbȧ ↓ ėzmúykárȯ ↓ | Pero ¡caramba!, es muy caro. |
| 6 It costs three hundred a month. | kwéstȧtrės(s̥)yéntȯs̥ȧlmés ↓ | Cuesta trescientos al mes. |
| 7 And that without including the gas and other things. | ɪ̯ésȯ \| sɪ́n̥ɪŋklwɪ́r \| ėlgás \| ɪ̯ótrȧs kósȧs ↓ | Y eso sin incluir el gas y otras cosas. |
| 8 There's another one on the same floor, but it doesn't face the street. | áyótro̯ \| ėn̥ėlmɪ́zmȯpísȯ ↓ pėrȯ ↓ nóđá \| a̯lȧká(l)y̯ė ↓ | Hay otro en el mismo piso, pero no da a la calle. |
| 9 They go see it. | bán̥ȧƀérlȯ ↓ | Van a verlo. |

## DIALOG 2

| | | |
|---|---|---|
| Agente, dígales que pasen adelante. | pásėn \| ȧđėlántė ↓ | Agente: Pasen adelante. |
| José, dígale que le gusta mucho este apartamento. Pregúntele a Juan que qué le parece a él. | mėgústa̯ \| éste̯ȧpȧrtȧméntȯ ↓ ɪ̯ȧtɪ́ ↓ kétėpȧrés̥ė \| hwán ↓ | José: Me gusta este apartamento. ¿Y a ti, qué te parece, Juan? |

| | | |
|---|---|---|
| Juan, contéstele que está bastante bonito, pero que hay que ver cuánto cuesta. | ėstá \| ƀȧstántėƀȯnítȯ ↓ pérǫ \| áykėƀér \|<br>kwántȯkwéstȧ ↓ | Juan: Está bastante bonito, pero hay que ver cuánto cuesta. |
| Agente, dígale que trescientos, sin incluir el gas y otras cosas. | trės(ș)yéntȯs ↓ sínịŋklwír \| ėlgás<br>ı̯ótrȧskósȧs ↓ | Agente: Trescientos, sin incluir el gas y otras cosas. |
| Juan, dígale que caramba, que muy caro, que no le conviene. Pregúntele si no tiene algo más barato. | kȧrámbȧ ↓ muykárȯ ↓ nómėkȯmbyénė ↓<br>nȯtyénẹ \| álgȯmázƀȧrátȯ ↑ | Juan: ¡Caramba, muy caro! No me conviene. ¿No tiene algo más barato? |
| Agente, contéstele que en este mismo piso tiene otro, pero que no da a la calle. | ėnẹ́stėmízmȯ \| písȯ \| téŋgótrȯ ↓<br>pérȯnóđá \| ạlȧká(l)yė ↓ | Agente: En este mismo piso tengo otro, pero no da a la calle. |
| Juan, pregúntele si pueden verlo. | pȯđémȯzƀérlȯ ↑ | Juan: ¿Podemos verlo? |
| Agente, contéstele que cómo no, que con mucho gusto. | kómȯnó ↓ kȯnmúchȯgústȯ ↓ | Agente: Cómo no, con mucho gusto. |

## NARRATIVE 3

| | | | |
|---|---|---|---|
| 1 | This other one costs two hundred and twenty five. | éste̯ótrȯkwéstȧ \| đós(s̯)yéntȯz ƀėyntıs̯íŋkȯ ↓ | Este otro cuesta doscientos veinticinco. |
| 2 | The bath is to the right. | ėlbáṇyo̯ \| ėstálȧđėréchȧ ↓ | El baño está a la derecha. |
| 3 | The kitchen isn't very large, but it's convenient. | lȧkȯs̯ína̯ \| no̯ézmúygrándė \| pėro̯és kómȯđȧ ↓ | La cocina no es muy grande, pero es muy cómoda. |
| 4 | Jose thinks that the price is reasonable. | ȧhȯsé ↑ lėpȧrés̯ė \| kėlprés̯yȯ \| no̯ėstámál ↓ | A José le parece que el precio no está mal. |
| 5 | But he really doesn't like it. | pėro̯ėnrre̯ȧliđáđ ↑ nólėgústȧ ↓ | Pero en realidad no le gusta. |
| 6 | The furniture looks old, and there isn't much light. | lȯzmwéƀlės \| pȧrés̯ėnmúyƀyéhȯs ↓ ı̯áypókȧlús̯ ↓ | Los muebles parecen muy viejos, y hay poca luz. |

## DIALOG 3

| | | |
|---|---|---|
| Agente, dígale a Juan que éste cuesta doscientos veinticinco. | éstė ǀ kwéstȧđóṣ(ʂ)yéntȯz ǀ ƀėyntịşíŋkȯ ↓ | Agente: Este cuesta doscientos veinticinco. |
| Juan, pregúntele dónde está el baño. | dóndėstáe̯lbáṇyȯ ↓ | Juan: ¿Dónde está el baño? |
| Agente, contéstele que ahí a la derecha. | ȧí ǀ ȧlȧđėréchȧ ↓ | Agente: Ahí a la derecha. |
| Juan, pregúntele que la cocina, dónde está. | ilȧkóşınȧ ↓ dóndėstá ↓ | Juan: Y la cocina, ¿dónde está? |
| Agente, contéstele que aquí está, que no es muy grande, pero es cómoda. | ȧkíe̯stá ↓ nóe̯zmúygrándė ǀ pėró̯es kómȯđȧ ↓ | Agente: Aquí está. No es muy grande, pero es cómoda. |
| Juan, pregúntele a José que qué cree él. | kékrée̯stú ǀ hȯsé ↓ | Juan: ¿Qué crees tú, José? |
| José, contéstele que el precio no está mal, pero que en realidad no le gusta mucho. | ėlpréşyȯ ǀ nȯe̯stámál ↓ péro̯ėn rre̯ȧliđáđ ǀ nȯmėgústȧmúchȯ ↓ | José: El precio no está mal, pero en realidad no me gusta mucho. |
| Juan, pregúntele que por qué. | pȯrké ↓ | Juan: ¿Por qué? |

| | | |
|---|---|---|
| José, contéstele que los muebles parecen muy viejos, y no hay mucha luz. | lȯzmwéƀlės \| pȧréşėnmúyƀyéhȯs ↓ inọáymúchȧlúş ↓ | José: Los muebles parecen muy viejos, y no hay mucha luz. |
| Juan, dígale a José que sí, que en realidad tiene razón. | sí ↓ ėnrrẹȧliđáđ \| tyénėzrrȧşón ↓ | Juan: Si, en realidad tienes razón. |

## NARRATIVE 1

| | | |
|---|---|---|
| 1 Mr. Richard Brown lives in this building. | ėlsėn‿yórríchȧrbráwm \| bíƀėn éstėđifíşyȯ ↓ | El Sr. Richard Brown vive en este edificio. |
| 2 He works in the American Embassy. | éltraƀáhạ \| ėnlạėmbȧháđȧmėrıkánȧ ↓ | El trabaja en la Embajada Americana. |
| 3 He has an apartment on the first floor. | tyénẹ \| ůnȧpȧrtȧméntọ \| ėnẹlprimérpísȯ ↓ | Tiene un apartamento en el primer piso. |
| 4 But he plans to move out this week. | pérȯpyénsȧmuđárşẹ \| ėstȧsėmánȧ ↓ | Pero piensa mudarse esta semana. |
| 5 The apartment is small, but comfortable and inexpensive. | ėlȧpȧrtȧméntọ \| ėspėkén‿yȯ ↑ pėrȯkómȯđọiƀarátȯ ↓ | El apartamento es pequeño pero cómodo y barato. |

| | | |
|---|---|---|
| 6 Mr. Brown isn't there now. | èlsèn̦yórƀráwn \| nọèstáíáórà ↓ | El Sr. Brown no está ahí ahora. |
| 7 But the agent has the key. | pèrọèlàhénté \| tyénélá(l)y̦ábè ↓ | Pero el agente tiene la llave. |

## DIALOG 4

| | | |
|---|---|---|
| José, pregúntele al agente que en qué piso vive el señor Richard Brown. | èŋképísóƀíƀẹ \| èlsèn̦yórríchárƀráwn ↓ | José: ¿En qué piso vive el Sr. Richard Brown? |
| Agente, pregúntele si el americano que trabaja en la Embajada. | èlàmèrikánó \| kètráƀáhạènlạèmbàháđá ↑ | Agente: ¿El americano que trabaja en la Embajada? |
| José, contéstele que sí. Que le dijeron que vive aquí, pero que piensa mudarse esta semana. | sí ↓ mèđihéróŋ \| kèƀíƀẹakí ↓ péròkè pyénsà \| múđársèstàsèmánà ↓ | José: Sí. Me dijeron que vive aquí, pero que piensa mudarse esta semana. |
| Agente, digale que caramba, que tiene razón, que ahora recuerda. | kàrámbà ↓ tyénèrràṣón ↓ àórà rrèkwérđò ↓ | Agente: ¡Caramba! Tiene razón, ahora recuerdo. |
| Que él está en el primer piso. | éléstá \| ẹnẹlprimérpísò ↓ | El está en el primer piso. |
| Y que tiene un apartamento pequeño, pero muy cómodo y barato. | ityénẹ \| ùnàpàrtàméntòpèkén̦yò \| pèròmúykómòđoiƀàrátò ↓ | Y tiene un apartamento pequeño, pero muy cómodo y barato. |
| José, pregúntclc si el Sr. Brown está ahí ahora. | èstáẹlsèn̦yórƀráwn \| áíạórà ↑ | José: ¿Está el Sr. Brown ahí ahora? |

| | | |
|---|---|---|
| Agente, contéstele que no, pero que aquí tiene Ud. la llave. | nó̇ ↓ pėro̯ȧkíténgȯlȧ(l)y̯ábė ↓ | Agente: No, pero aquí tengo la llave. |

**End of Tape 6B***
**End of CD 6***

*Tape 6B and CD 6 actually end on page 303 of this book because they cover the basic dialogues for listening and learning of Unit 9. However, Tape 7A and CD 7 start on page 299 and cover the basic dialogue for fluency of the same unit.

# 9.1 BASIC SENTENCES

## White goes to Molina's apartment

John White and Jose Molina arrive at Molina's apartment.

| English Spelling | Aid to Listening | Spanish Spelling |
|---|---|---|
| come in (to come in) | pásȧ ↓ pȧsár ↓ | pasa (pasar) |
| your (yours) | tú ↓ túyȯ ↓ | tu (tuyo) |
| *MOLINA* | | *MOLINA* |
| Come in. Make yourself at home. (1) | pásađėlántė ↓ ėstásėntukásȧ ↓ | Pasa adelante. Estás en tu casa. |
| seat (to seat) | syéntȧ ↓ sėntár ↓ | sienta (sentar) |
| seat yourself (to sit down) | syéntȧtė ↓ sėntársė ↓ | siéntate (sentarse) |
| Sit down. | syéntȧtė ↓ | Siéntate. |
| *WHITE* | | *WHITE* |
| Thanks. | grás̩yȧs ↓ | Gracias. |
| like, as | kómȯ ↓ | como |
| Will my apartment be like this one? | báser \| mi̯ȧpȧrtȧméntȯ \| kȯmo̯éstė ↑ | ¿Va a ser mi apartamento como éste? |
| just the same (equal) | igwȧlítȯ ↓ igwál ↓ | igualito (igual) |

| | | |
|---|---|---|
| *MOLINA* | | *MOLINA* |
| Just exactly. | igwàlítò ↓ | Igualito. |
| all | tóđò ↓ | todo |
| fixed, arranged (to fix, to arrange) | àrrègláđò ↓ àrrèglár ↓ | arreglado (arreglar) |
| *WHITE* | | *WHITE* |
| This is all very nicely fixed up. | ésto̯ \| èstátóđò \| múybyénàrrègláđò ↓ | Esto está todo muy bien arreglado. |
| yet, still | tòđàbíà ↓ | todavía |
| to buy | kòmprár ↓ | comprar |
| *MOLINA* | | *MOLINA* |
| I still have to buy a lot of things. | tòđàbíà \| nèşèsítòkòmprár \| múchàskósàs ↓ | Todavía necesito comprar muchas cosas. |
| the soda | là—sóđà ↓ | la soda |
| the whiskey | èl—wískì ↓ | el whiskey |
| the whiskey with soda | èl—wískì—kòn—sóđà ↓ | el whiskey con soda |
| Would you like a whiskey and soda? (2) | kyérès \| ùŋwískìkònsóđà ↑ | ¿Quieres un whiskey con soda? |
| the idea | la̯—iđéà ↓ | la idea |
| *WHITE* | | *WHITE* |
| Good idea. | bwénàiđéà ↓ | Buena idea. |

| | | |
|---|---|---|
| who | kyén ↓ | quien |
| the girl | lȧ—mu̇cháchȧ ↓ | la muchacha |
| the picture | lȧ—fótȯ ↓ | la foto |
| Who's that girl in the picture? | kyén̦ȩ́sȩsamucháchȧ \| đėlȧfótȯ ↓ | ¿Quién es esa muchacha de la foto? |
| how pretty | ké—ƀonítȯ ↓ | qué bonito |
| She sure is pretty. | kéƀȯnítȧ ↓ | ¡Qué bonita! |
| the sweetheart, the fiancée | lȧ—nóƀyȧ ↓ | la novia |
| *MOLINA* | | *MOLINA* |
| That's my fiancée. You'll have to meet her. | ėzminóƀyȧ ↓ tyénėskėkȯnoșérlȧ ↓ | Es mi novia. Tienes que conocerla. |
| (she) does (to do, to make) | áșė ↓ ȧșér ↓ | hace (hacer) |
| studying (to study) | ėstu̇đyándȯ ↓ ėstu̇đyár ↓ | estudiando (estudiar) |
| (she) is studying | ėstá—ȇstu̇đyándȯ ↓ | está estudiando |
| *WHITE* | | *WHITE* |
| What does she do? Is she studying? | kéáșė ↓ ėstáȇstu̇đyándȯ ↑ | ¿Qué hace? ¿Está estudiando? |
| working (to work) | trȧƀȧhándȯ ↓ trȧƀȧhár ↓ | trabajando (trabajar) |

| | | |
|---|---|---|
| (she) is working | ėstá—trȧƀȧhándȯ ↓ | está trabajando |
| the secretary | lȧ—sėkrėtáryȧ ↓ | la secretaria |
| *MOLINA* | | *MOLINA* |
| No, she is working as a secretary. | nó ↓ ėstátrȧƀȧhándȯ \| kȯmȯsėkrėtáryȧ ↓ | No. Está trabajando como secretaria. |
| the wedding | lȧ—ƀóđȧ ↓ | la boda |
| to have a wedding | tėnér—ƀóđȧ ↓ | tener boda |
| soon | prónto ↓ | pronto |
| *WHITE* | | *WHITE* |
| Are we going to have a wedding soon? | bámȯsatenérƀóđȧ \| prónto ↑ | ¿Vamos a tener boda pronto? |
| (we) have (to have) | émȯs ↓ ȧƀér ↓ | hemos (haber) |
| decided (to decide) | dėsiđíđȯ ↓ dėsiđír ↓ | decidido (decidir) |
| (we)'ve decided | émȯz—đėsiđíđȯ ↓ | hemos decidido |
| the date | lȧ—féchȧ ↓ | la fecha |
| *MOLINA* | | *MOLINA* |
| Yes, but we haven't set the date yet. | sí ↓ pérȯ \| noémȯzđėsiđíđȯ \| lȧféchȧ \| tȯđȧƀíȧ ↓ | Sí, pero no hemos decidido la fecha todavía. |
| the man | ėl—ómbrė ↓ | el hombre |

| | | |
|---|---|---|
| *WHITE* | | *WHITE* |
| Boy, this is a good whiskey! | ómbrė ↓ kéƀwénọėstá ǀ ẹstėw̰íski ↓ | ¡Hombre! Qué bueno está este whiskey. |
| drinking (to drink) | bėƀyéndȯ ↓ bėƀér ↓ | bebiendo (beber) |
| (you) are drinking | ėstáz—ƀėƀyéndȯ ↓ | estás bebiendo |
| What are you drinking? | itú ↑ késtázƀėƀyéndȯ ↓ | Y tú ¿qué estás bebiendo? |
| the ‘cuba libre’ | ėl—kúƀȧ—líƀrė ↓ | el ‘cuba libre’ |
| *MOLINA* | | *MOLINA* |
| A ‘cuba libre’. | u̇ŋkúƀȧlíƀrė ↓ | Un ‘cuba libre’. |
| to you | té ↓ | te |
| the | ló ↓ | lo |
| the of, the matter of (3) | ló—đė ↓ | lo de |
| your(s) | túy̰ȯ ↓ | tuyo |
| John, what do you say we go see about your apartment? | hwán ↓ kétėpárẹ̇sė ǀ siƀámȯṣȧƀér ǀ lȯđėlȧpȧrtȧméntȯtúy̰ȯ ↓ | Juan, ¿qué te parece si vamos a ver lo del apartamento tuyo? |
| (we) return (to return) | bȯlbémȯs ↓ bȯlbér ↓ | volvemos (volver) |
| Wc’ll come back later. | dėspwézbȯlbémȯs ↓ | Después volvemos. |

## 9.10 Notes on the basic sentences

(1) This expression, 'You are in your home', is paralled by dozens of similar ones. Thus if you admire a man's car, he's likely to say, 'It's yours'. This is a polite formula, of course.

(2) This expression is like many expressions referring to food combinations where in English two components are linked by *and — whiskey and soda, bacon and eggs, chicken and rice* — but in Spanish they are linked by *con — whiskey con soda, huevos con tocino, arroz con pollo.*

(3) The construction /lo–del—apartaménto—túyo/ is an example of a very important grammatical process in Spanish. This process, which will be further explained and drilled in Units 33 and 35, is called 'nominalization.' Stated in simple terms 'nominalization' means the functioning as nouns by items which normally are *not* nouns. Thus /lo/, usually a special kind of adjective, in this construction functions as a noun and is itself modified by the phrase /del—apartaménto—túyo/. A literal translation of /lo/ is very difficult to devise in English, but it implies 'the matter, the business, the idea previously mentioned'. Thus the construction /lo—del—apartaménto—túyo/ is translated in a roundabout way as 'about your apartment.'

# 9.2 DRILLS AND GRAMMAR

## 9.21 PATTERN DRILLS

### 9.21.1 The irregular verb /abér/ and regular /—do/ forms: in the present perfect construction

A. PRESENTATION OF PATTERN

*ILLUSTRATIONS*

| | | |
|---|---|---|
| | 1 y̰óy̰á \| lo̯ékȯmíđȯ ↓ | Yo ya lo *he comido.* |
| I haven't thought about the visa. | 2 no̯épėnsáđo̯ \| ėnlȧƀísȧ ↓ | No *he pensado* en la visa. |
| (you) have (to have) | ás ↓ ȧƀér ↓ | has (haber) |
| Have you already eaten it? | 3 y̰álo̯ȧskȯmíđȯ ↑ | ¿Ya lo *has comido?* |

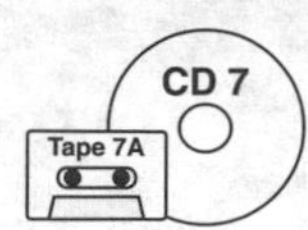




| | | |
|---|---|---|
| You haven't been here this week. | 4 no̯ásẹstáđo̯akí \| ẹstàsèmánà ↓ | No *has estado* aquí esta semana. |
| (you) have (to have) | á ↓ àƀér ↓ | a (haber) |
| Have you lived on that street? | 5 áƀiƀíđo̯ustéđ \| ènẹsàká(l)y̯è ↑ | ¿*Ha vivido* usted en esa calle? |
| Have you waited long? | 6 áẹspèràđòmúchò ↑ | ¿*Ha esperado* mucho? |
| ______________________ | 7 sí ↓ péròno̯émòzđẹsiđíđò \| là féchà \| tòđàƀíà ↓ | Sí, pero no *hemos decidido* la fecha todavía. |
| We haven't looked for a house. | 8 no̯émòz \| ƀuskáđòkásà ↓ | No *hemos buscado* casa. |
| (you) (pl.) have (to have) | án ↓ àƀér ↓ | han (haber) |
| Have you decided on the date? | 9 ándẹsiđíđò \| làféchà ↑ | ¿*Han decidido* la fecha? |
| They haven't straightened up the apartment. | 10 no̯án \| àrrèglá đo̯ \| èlàpàrtàméntò ↓ | No *han arreglado* el apartamento. |

*EXTRAPOLATION*

| | abér | /—do/ form | |
|---|---|---|---|
| | | —ár | —ér,—ír |
| | | —ádo | —ído |
| sg | | | |
| 1 | é | | |
| 2 fam | ás | | |
| 2 - 3 | á[c] | | kom—ído |
| pl | | abl—ádo | |
| 1 | émos | | bıb–ído |
| 2 -3 | án | | |

*NOTES*

a. The perfect construction consists of a conjugated form of the verb /abér/ plus the /–do/ form of the verb.

b. /—do/ forms in perfect constructions are uninflected (do not change their endings); in other constructions, functioning as modifiers, the /–do/ forms do inflect (change their endings) for number and gender.

c. A variant /áy/ occurs as a distinct form not participating in the present perfect construction.

## 9.21.11 SUBSTITUTION DRILLS

Person - number substitution

1 yo̯é | a̯prèndíđòmúcho̯ | àkí ↓

| | |
|---|---|
| kármėn ______________ ↓ | áprèndíđòmúcho̯ \| àkí ↓ |
| kármėni̯yó ______________ ↓ | émȯs \| àprèndíđòmúcho̯ \| àkí ↓ |
| ùstéđ ______________ ↓ | áprèndíđòmúcho̯ \| àkí ↓ |
| é(l)y̯ȯs ______________ ↓ | ána̯prèndíđòmúcho̯ \| àkí ↓ |

---

1 *Yo* he aprendido mucho aquí.

| | |
|---|---|
| Carmen ______________ . | Ha aprendido mucho aquí. |
| Carmen y yo ______________ . | Hemos aprendido mucho aquí. |
| Ud. ______________ . | Ha aprendido mucho aquí. |
| Ellos ______________ . | Han aprendido mucho aquí. |

2 ȧntónyȯ | no̯áe̯ŋkȯntráđȯkásȧ ↓

| | |
|---|---|
| y̯ó ______________ ↓ | no̯éŋkȯntráđȯkásȧ ↓ |
| kármėn \| i̯ȧntónyȯ ______________ ↓ | no̯án \| ėŋkȯntráđȯkásȧ ↓ |
| nȯsótrȯz ______________ ↓ | no̯émȯs \| ėŋkȯntráđȯkásȧ ↓ |
| ȯstéđėz ______________ ↓ | no̯án \| ėŋkȯntráđȯkásȧ ↓ |

3 é(l)y̯ȯsámbiƀíđo̯ | ȧ(l)y̯ítȧmbyén ↓

| | |
|---|---|
| ȧntónyo̯ \| ịy̯ó ______________ ↓ | émȯzƀiƀíđo̯ \| ȧ(l)y̯ítȧmbyén ↓ |
| ȯstéđ ______________ ↓ | áƀiƀíđo̯ \| ȧ(l)y̯ítȧmbyén ↓ |

---

2 *Antonio* no ha encontrado casa.

| | |
|---|---|
| Yo ______________ . | No he encontrado casa. |
| Carmen y Antonio ______________ . | No han encontrado casa. |
| Nosotros ______________ . | No hemos encontrado casa. |
| Uds. ______________ . | No han encontrado casa. |

3 *Ellos* han vivido allí también.

| | |
|---|---|
| Antonio y yo ______________ . | Hemos vivido allí también. |
| Ud. ______________ . | Ha vivido allí también. |

yó ______________________ ↓ éƀiƀíđo̯ | à(l)y̯ítàmbyén ↓

kármèn ______________________ ↓ áƀiƀíđo̯ | à(l)y̯ítàmbyén ↓

4 àntónyo̯ipáƀlo̯ | ántràƀàháđòpókò ↓

yó ______________________ ↓ étràƀàháđòpókò ↓

kármèn ______________________ ↓ átràƀàháđòpókò ↓

ùstéđès ______________________ ↓ ántràƀàháđòpókò ↓

nòsótròs ______________________ ↓ émòs | tràƀaháđòpókò ↓

---

Yo ______________________ . He vivido allí también.

Carmen ______________________ . Ha vivido allí también.

4 *Antonio y Pablo* han trabajado poco.

Yo ______________________ . He trabajado poco.

Carmen ______________________ . Ha trabajado poco.

Uds. ______________________ . Han trabajado poco.

Nosotros ______________________ . Hemos trabajado poco.

5 nȯsótrȯs | émȯskȯmı́đȯ | đėmȧsyáđȯ ↓

| | |
|---|---|
| lwı́sȧ ______________________ ↓ | ákȯmı́đȯ \| đėmȧsyáđȯ ↓ |
| y̯ó ______________________ ↓ | ékȯmı́đȯ \| đėmȧsyáđȯ ↓ |
| ȧntónyo̯ı̇páƀlo̯ ______________________ ↓ | áŋkȯmı́đȯ \| đėmȧsyáđȯ ↓ |
| é(l)y̯ȧs ______________________ ↓ | áŋkȯmı́đȯ \| đėmȧsyáđȯ ↓ |

---

5 *Nosotros* hemos comido demasiado.

| | |
|---|---|
| Luisa ______________________ . | Ha comido demasiado. |
| Yo ______________________ . | He comido demasiado. |
| Antonio y Pablo ______________________ . | Han comido demasiado. |
| Ellas ______________________ . | Han comido demasiado. |

Construction substitution

Problem: prònúnșyà | múyƀyén ↓

Answer: áprònùnșyáđò | múyƀyén ↓

---

Problem: *Pronuncia* muy bien.

Answer: Ha pronunciado muy bien.

| | |
|---|---|
| 1 nóƀúskȯkásȧ ↓ | no̯éƀu̇skáđȯkásȧ ↓ |
| 2 trȧƀȧhámȯz \| đėmȧsyáđȯ ↓ | émȯstrȧƀȧháđȯ \| đėmȧsyáđȯ ↓ |
| 3 nóđės̯ı́đėnẹ́sȯ ↓ | no̯ándės̯ıđı́đo̯ésȯ ↓ |
| 4 kréẹ̯tóđȯ ↓ | ákrėı́đȯtóđȯ ↓ |
| 5 ȧlkı́lo̯u̇nȧƀıtȧs̯yón ↓ | éa̯lkiláđo̯ \| u̇nȧƀıtȧs̯yón ↓ |
| 6 su̇ƀı́mȯs \| ėnėlȧs(s̯)ėnsór ↓ | émȯ(s)u̇ƀı́đo̯ \| ėnẹlȧs(s̯)ėnsór ↓ |
| 7 kómėnlȧsálȧ ↓ | ákȯmı́đo̯ \| ėnlȧsálȧ ↓ |

---

| | |
|---|---|
| 1 No *busco* casa. | No he buscado casa. |
| 2 *Trabajamos* demasiado. | Hemos trabajado demasiado. |
| 3 No *deciden* eso. | No han decidido eso. |
| 4 *Cree* todo. | Ha creído todo. |
| 5 *Alquilo* una habitación. | He alquilado una habitación. |
| 6 *Subimos* en el ascensor. | Hemos subido en el ascensor. |
| 7 *Come* en la sala. | Ha comido en la sala. |

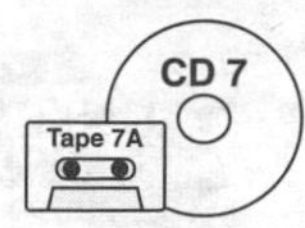




## 9.21.12 RESPONSE DRILL

| | | |
|---|---|---|
| | 1 ùstéđès ǀ ánàƀláđò ↑ ǫáŋkòmíđò ↓ | émòsàƀláđò ↓ |
| | 2 é(l)y̯òs ǀ ámbèƀíđò ↑ ǫántràƀàháđò ↓ | ámbèƀíđò ↓ |
| | 3 él ǀ áƀàháđò ↑ ǫásùƀíđò ↓ | ásùƀíđò ↓ |
| | 4 ùstéđ ǀ áƀláđò ↑ ǫátràƀàháđò ↓ | étràƀàháđò ↓ |
| [ènùnrrèstòrán ↓] | 5 dóndeákòmíđǫ ǀ é(l)y̯à ↓ | ènùnrrèstòrán ↓ |
| [làsèkrètárya ↓] | 6 kóŋkyén ǀ áƀláđǫustéđ ↓ | kònlàsèkrètárya ↓ |

---

| | | |
|---|---|---|
| | 1 ¿Uds. han hablado o han comido? | Hemos hablado. |
| | 2 ¿Ellos han bebido o han trabajado? | Han bebido. |
| | 3 ¿El ha bajado o ha subido? | Ha subido. |
| | 4 ¿Ud. ha hablado o ha trabajado? | He trabajado. |
| (en un restorán) | 5 ¿Dónde ha comido ella? | En un restorán. |
| (la secretaria) | 6 ¿Con quién ha hablado Ud.? | Con la secretaria. |

| | | |
|---|---|---|
| [káro ↓] | 7 áe̯ŋkontráđo̯ \| ustéđ \| tóđobaráto ↑ | nó ↓ éŋkontrádo \| tóđo \| múykáro ↓ |
| [apartaménto ↓] | 8 ánalkiláđo̯ \| ustéđes \| unakása ↑ | nó ↓ émos \| alkiláđo̯ \| unapartaménto ↓ |
| [iŋglés ↓] | 9 ánaƀláđo̯é(l)yos \| enespanyól ↑ | nó ↓ ánaƀláđo̯eniŋglés ↓ |
| [bwéna ↓] | 10 áe̯stáđomála \| lasópa ↑ | nó ↓ áe̯stáđo \| muyƀwéna ↓ |
| | 11 áe̯stáđo̯ustéđ \| ensamfrańsisko ↑ | sí ↓ si̯estáđo ↓ |
| | 12 ántraƀaháđo̯ustéđez \| múcho ↑ | sí ↓ émostraƀaháđo \| đemasyáđo ↓ |
| | 13 áƀiƀíđo̯el \| empanamá ↑ | sí ↓ si̯aƀiƀíđo ↓ |

---

| | | |
|---|---|---|
| (caro) | 7 ¿Ha encontrado Ud. todo barato? | No, he encontrado todo muy caro. |
| (apartamento) | 8 ¿Han alquilado Uds. una casa? | No, hemos alquilado un apartamento. |
| (inglés) | 9 ¿Han hablado ellos en español? | No, han hablado en inglés. |
| (buena) | 10 ¿Ha estado mala la sopa? | No, ha estado muy buena. |
| | 11 ¿Ha estado Ud. en San Francisco? | Sí, sí he estado. |
| | 12 ¿Han trabajado Uds. mucho? | Sí, hemos trabajado demasiado. |
| | 13 ¿Ha vivido él en Panamá? | Sí, sí ha vivido. |

## 9.21.13 TRANSLATION DRILL

| | | | |
|---|---|---|---|
| 1 | They haven't come yet. | é(l)yȯz \| nọámbėníđȯ \| tȯđȧƀíȧ ↓ | Ellos no han venido todavía. |
| 2 | We haven't remembered anything. | nọémȯz \| rrėkȯrđáđȯ \| náđȧ ↓ | No hemos recordado nada. |
| 3 | You all have left everything for tomorrow. | ủstéđės \| ándėháđȯtóđȯ \| pȧrȧmȧṇyánȧ ↓ | Uds. han dejado todo para mañana. |
| 4 | Have you been in Chile? | áẹstáđọustėđ \| ėnchílė ↑ | ¿Ha estado Ud. en Chile? |
| 5 | Has he lived in Cuba? | áƀiƀíđọel \| ėŋkúƀȧ ↑ | ¿Ha vivido él en Cuba? |
| 6 | I haven't been in that part of Peru. | nọéstáđọ \| ėnẹ́sȧpártė \| đėlpėrú ↓ | No he estado en esa parte del Perú. |
| 7 | We've rented a very pretty house. | émȯsạlkıláđọ \| ủnȧkásȧ \| múyƀónıtȧ ↓ | Hemos alquilado una casa muy bonita. |
| 8 | Where has she eaten? | dóndẹákȯmíđọ \| é(l)yȧ ↓ | ¿Dónde ha comido ella? |
| 9 | They haven't included that in the bill. | é(l)ỵȯz \| nọániŋklwíđọ \| ésọėnlȧkwéntȧ ↓ | Ellos no han incluído eso en la cuenta. |
| 10 | She hasn't gone up yet. | é(l)ỵȧ \| nọasúƀıđȯ \| tȯđȧƀíȧ ↓ | Ella no ha subido todavía. |
| 11 | I've worked here two years. | étraƀaháđọ \| akí \| đósánỵȯs ↓ | He trabajado aquí dos años. |

**B. DISCUSSION OF PATTERN**

The verb /abér/ is extremely irregular. In the present tense it has no stem, appearing only as a set of endings with erratic theme vowels /e—a / and the regular persen-number endings /—s, —mos, —n/.

/abér/ shares with /tenér/ the range of meaning covered by the English verb 'have', though they are not difficult to differentiate: /tenér/ means 'have, hold, possess', while /abér/ is the equivalent of 'have' in sentences like 'I *have* eaten'.

The /—do/ form of the verb can be constructed by adding /—ádo/ (theme /—á—/ plus /—do/) to /—ár/ verbs, and /—ído/ theme /—í—/ plus /—do/) to /—ér, —ír/ verbs. The /—do/ form is more or less equivalent to the —ed form of English verbs (peeped, begged, headed). Thus the construction equivalents are these:

yo̯-é termınádo ↓

I'*ve* finish*ed*.

There are a number of irregularly formed /—do/ forms which will be collected and drilled in Unit 44.

In the present perfect construction, as indeed in all verb constructions, only the first verb is inflected (for person, number, tense). Thus /abér/ is inflected but the /—do/ form is not. (However, see Unit 10 for other constructions the /—do/ forms appear in).

The present perfect construction in Spanish is used, although with much less frequency, in much the same way as the corresponding construction in English.

There is a variant of the 2 - 3 sg /a/ which occurs frequently without an accompanying /—do/ form. This variant, /áy/ 'there is, there are', occurs with no number agreement with the verb, as the double translation 'there is, there are' would suggest.

## 9.21.2 Possessives-full forms

### A. PRESENTATION OF PATTERN

*ILLUSTRATIONS*

| | | |
|---|---|---|
| ______________________ | 1 pòrkénòƀémòs \| ạùnạmíɡòmíò ↓ | ¿Por qué no vemos a un amigo *mío?* |
| ______________________ | 2 èlɡústọèzmíò ↓ | El gusto es *mío*. |
| our(s) | nwéstrò ↓ | nuestro |
| She's a neighbor of ours. | 3 ésùnàƀéṣìnànwéstrà ↓ | Es una vecina *nuestra*. |
| They're friends of ours. | 4 sónạmíɡòznwéstròs ↓ | Son amigos *nuestros*. |
| ______________________ | 5 bámòṣàƀér \| lòđèlàpàrtàméntòtúỵò ↓ | Vamos a ver lo del apartamento *tuyo*. |
| This is your clothing. | 6 éstạèz \| làrrópàtúỵà ↓ | Esta es la ropa *tuya*. |
| These books, Miss. Are they yours? | 7 éstòzlíƀròs \| sèṇỵòrítà ↓ sónsúỵòs ↑ | Estos libros, señorita, ¿son *suyos?* |
| This car, gentlemen. Is it yours? | 8 éstẹáwtò \| sèṇỵórès ↓ è(s)súỵò ↑ | Este auto, señores, ¿es *suyo?* |
| his | súỵò ↓ | suyo |
| Mr. Smith wants a large house; his family is coming tomorrow. | 9 èlsèṇỵórsmíṣ \| kyérẹùnàkásàɡrándè ↓ làfàmílyàsúỵà \| ƀyénè \| màṇỵánà ↓ | El señor Smith quiere una casa grande; la familia *suya* viene mañana. |

their(s) — súy̯ȯ ↓ — suyo

We don't know the Quinteros, but we have a book of theirs.

10 nókȯnȯs̯émȯs | àlȯ(s)sėn̯yórėskintérȯ ↑
pérȯtėnémȯs | u̇nlíƀrȯsúy̯ȯ ↓

No conocemos a los señores Quintero, pero tenemos un libro *suyo*.

## *EXTRAPOLATION*

| Reference: | sg | pl |
|---|---|---|
| 1 | mío(s)<br>—a(s) | nwéstro(s)<br>—a(s) |
| 2 fam | túyo(s)<br>—a(s) | |
| 2 - 3 | súyo(s)<br>—a(s) | |

## *NOTES*

a. Possessives are a special kind of adjective, and like other adjectives, they agree in number and gender with the noun they modify.

b. There are forms for singular and plural reference, both of which have singular and plural forms independently agreeing with the noun modified.

c. There are different forms that can be correlated to person; the 2 - 3 form /súyo/ is common to singular and plural reference.

## 9.21.21 SUBSTITUTION DRILLS

Form substitution

1 éste̯áwto̯ėzmío ↓

| | |
|---|---|
| ____________________ súy̯ȯ ↓ | éste̯áwto̯ \| ė(s)súy̯ȯ ↓ |
| ____________________ nwéstrȯ ↓ | éste̯áwto̯ėznwéstrȯ ↓ |

2 éstȯzmwéƀlės | sȯnmíȯs ↓

| | |
|---|---|
| ____________________ súy̯ȯs ↓ | éstȯzmwéƀlės \| sȯnsúy̯ȯs ↓ |
| ____________________ nwéstrȯs ↓ | éstȯzmwéƀlės \| sȯ(n)nwéstrȯs ↓ |

---

1 Este auto es mío.

| | |
|---|---|
| ____________________ suyo. | Este auto es suyo. |
| ____________________ nuestro. | Este auto es nuestro. |

2 Estos muebles son míos

| | |
|---|---|
| ____________________ suyos. | Estos muebles son suyos. |
| ____________________ nuestros. | Estos muebles son nuestros. |

3 éstàkásae̊zmíà ↓

| | |
|---|---|
| ______________ súyà ↓ | éstàkásae̊(s)súyà ↓ |
| ______________ nwéstrà ↓ | éstàkása | e̊znwéstrà ↓ |

4 éstàzmònéđås | so̊nmíàs ↓

| | |
|---|---|
| ______________ súyàs ↓ | éstàzmònéđås | so̊nsúyàs ↓ |
| ______________ nwéstràs ↓ | éstàzmònéđås | so̊(n)nwéstràs ↓ |

---

3 Esta casa es mía.

| | |
|---|---|
| ______________ suya. | Esta casa es suya. |
| ______________ nuestra. | Esta casa es nuestra. |

4 Estas monedas son mías.

| | |
|---|---|
| ______________ suyas. | Estas monedas son suyas. |
| ______________ nuestras. | Estas monedas son nuestras. |

5 éste̯ȯtélėzmíȯ ↓

| | |
|---|---|
| ______________________ súy̯ȯ ↓ | éste̯ȯtélė(s)súy̯ȯ ↓ |
| ______________________ nwéstrȯ ↓ | éste̯ȯtélėznwéstrȯ ↓ |

---

5 Este hotel es mío.

| | |
|---|---|
| ______________________ suyo. | Este hotel es suyo. |
| ______________________ nuestro. | Este hotel es nuestro. |

Number substitution

1 éstėƀi(l)y̯étėzmíȯ ↓

__________ ƀi(l)y̯étės ____________ ↓ — éstȯzƀi(l)y̯étės | sȯnmíȯs ↓

2 éstȧmȯnéđa̭ėzmíȧ ↓

__________ mȯnéđȧs ____________ ↓ — éstȧzmȯnéđȧs | sȯnmíȧs ↓

3 éstėchékė(s)súy̯ȯ ↓

__________ chékės ______________ ↓ — éstȯschékės | sȯnsúy̯ȯs ↓

---

1 Este *billete* es mío.

__________ billetes ______________ . — Estos billetes son míos.

2 Esta *moneda* es mía.

__________ monedas ______________ . — Estas monedas son mías.

3 Este *cheque* es suyo.

___________ cheques______________ . — Estos cheques son suyos.

4 ésèđifíşyo̯ | èznwéstrò ↓

__________ èđifíşyòs ______________ ↓ ésòşèđifíşyòs | sòn(n)nwéstròs ↓

5 éstàz(l)y̯áƀès | sònsúy̯às ↓

__________ (l)y̯áƀè ________________ ↓ éstà(l)y̯áƀè(s)súy̯à ↓

---

4 Ese *edificio* es nuestro.

__________ edificios ________________ . Esos edificios son nuestros.

5 Estas *llaves* son suyas.

__________ llave __________________ . Esta llave es suya.

6 éstȧsfótȯs | sȯ(n)nwéstrȧs ↓

__________ fóto̯ ________________ ↓ éstȧfóto̯ | ėznwéstrȧ ↓

7 éstȯs(s̯)ėnis̯érȯs | sȯnmíȯs ↓

_________ s̯ėnis̯éro̯ ______________ ↓ éstės̯ėnis̯éro̯ | ėzmíȯ ↓

---

6 Estas *fotos* son nuestras.

__________ foto ________________ . Esta foto es nuestra.

7 Estos *ceniceros* son míos.

_________ cenicero ______________ . Este cenicero es mío.

Item substitution

1 ésȧkása̯ė(s)súy̯ȧ ↓

________ ȧpȧrtȧménto̯ ______________ ↓ ése̯ȧpȧrtȧménto̯ės | súy̯ȯ ↓

2 éste̯ȯtélėznwéstrȯ ↓

__________ ȧhénsy̯a̯ ________________ ↓ éstȧhénsy̯a̯ | ėznwéstrȧ ↓

3 éstȯzmwéƀlės | sȯnsúy̯ȯs ↓

___________ kósȧs ________________ ↓ éstȧskósȧs | sȯnsúy̯ȧs ↓

4 éste̯áwto̯ėzmíȯ ↓

____________ kása̯ ________________ ↓ éstȧkása̯ėzmíȧ ↓

---

1 Esa *casa* es suya.

_________ apartamento _____________ . Ese apartamento es suyo.

2 Este *hotel* es nuestro.

__________ agencia ________________ . Esta agencia es nuestra.

3 Estos *muebles* son suyos.

__________ cosas__________________ . Estas cosas son suyas.

4 Este *auto* es mío.

__________ casa___________________ . Esta casa es mía.

5 éstàz(l)y̮áƀès | sȯnmíàs ↓

__________ pèryóđìkȯs ____________ ↓ éstȯspèryóđìkȯs | sȯnmíȯs ↓

6 éstȯzlíƀrȯs | sȯ(n)nwéstrȯs ↓

__________ sí(l)y̮ȧs ______________ ↓ éstȧ(s)sí(l)y̮ȧs | sȯ(n)nwéstrȧs ↓

7 éstȧkása̭èzmíȧ ↓

__________ èđifísyo̭ ______________ ↓ éstèđifísyo̭èzmíȯ ↓

---

5 Estas *llaves* son mías.

__________ periódicos ______________ . Estos periódicos son míos.

6 Estos *libros* son nuestros.

__________ sillas ______________ . Estas sillas son nuestras.

7 Esta *casa* es mía.

__________ edificio ______________ . Este edificio es mío.

## 9.21.22 RESPONSE DRILL

| | | |
|---|---|---|
| | 1 éstėlíƀrȯ ↓ ėzmíosúy̯ȯ ↓ | ė(s)súy̯ȯ ↓ |
| | 2 éstȧzmȯnéđȧs ↓ sȯnmíaṣosúy̯ȧs ↓ | sȯnsúy̯ȧs ↓ |
| [súy̯ȯ ↓] | 3 dėkyén \| eṣeselíƀrȯ ↓ | ėzmíȯ ↓ |
| [súy̯ȧ ↓] | 4 dėkyén \| eṣesaplúmȧ ↓ | ėzmíȧ ↓ |
| [míȯs ↓] | 5 dėkyén \| soṇestozlíbrȯs ↓ | sȯnsúy̯ȯs ↓ |
| [súy̯ȯ ↓] | 6 ėzmío̯eselíƀrȯ ↑ | nó ↓ ėzmíȯ ↓ |

---

| | | |
|---|---|---|
| | 1 Este libro, ¿es mío o suyo? | Es suyo. |
| | 2 Estas monedas, ¿son mías o suyas? | Son suyas. |
| (suyo) | 3 ¿De quién es ese libro? | Es mío. |
| (suya) | 4 ¿De quién es esa pluma? | Es mía. |
| (míos) | 5 ¿De quién son estos libros? | Son suyos. |
| (suyo) | 6 ¿Es mío ese libro? | No, es mío. |

| | | |
|---|---|---|
| [míȧ ↓] | 7 ė(s)súy̯ȧėstȧplúmȧ ↑ | nó ↓ ė(s)súy̯ȧ ↓ |
| [míȧs ↓] | 8 sȯnsúy̯ȧs \| éstȧzmȯnéđȧs ↑ | nó ↓ sȯnsúy̯ȧs ↓ |
| | 9 ė(s)súy̯ȯėsėáwtȯ ↑ | sí ↓ ėzmíȯ ↓ |
| | 10 sȯnsúy̯ȯs \| ésȯzlíƀrȯs ↑ | sí ↓ sȯnmíȯs ↓ |
| | 11 sȯnsúy̯ȧs \| ésȧzmȯnéđȧs ↑ | sí ↓ sȯnmíȧs ↓ |
| | 12 sȯnmíȧs \| éstȧzmȯnéđȧs ↑ | sí ↓ sȯnsúy̯ȧs ↓ |
| | 13 sȯnmíȯs \| éstȯzlíƀrȯs ↑ | sí ↓ sȯnsúy̯ȯs ↓ |

---

| | | |
|---|---|---|
| (mía) | 7 ¿Es suya esta pluma? | No, es suya. |
| (mías) | 8 ¿Son suyas estas monedas? | No, son suyas. |
| | 9 ¿Es suyo ese auto? | Sí, es mío. |
| | 10 ¿Son suyos esos libros? | Sí, son míos. |
| | 11 ¿Son suyas esas monedas? | Sí, son mías. |
| | 12 ¿Son mías estas monedas? | Sí, son suyas. |
| | 13 ¿Son míos estos libros? | Sí, son suyos. |

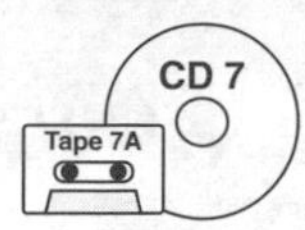




## 9.21.23 TRANSLATION DRILL

| | | | |
|---|---|---|---|
| 1 | These books are ours. | ėstȯzlíƀrȯs \| só(n)nwéstrȯs ↓ | Estos libros son nuestros. |
| 2 | That old house is ours. | ėsákasáƀyéha̯ \| ėznwéstrȧ ↓ | Esa casa vieja es nuestra. |
| 3 | This apartment is ours. | ésteapȧrtaménto̯ \| ėznwéstrȯ ↓ | Este apartamento es nuestro. |
| 4 | Whose (of whom) is this book? Is it yours? | dėkyéne̯s̯ėstelíƀrȯ ↓ ė(s)súyȯ ↑ | ¿De quién es este libro? ¿Es suyo? |
| 5 | Is that pencil his? | ė(s)súyo̯ \| ésėlápis̯ ↑ | ¿Es suyo ese lápiz? |
| 6 | Is this pencil mine? | ėzmío̯ \| éstėlápis̯ ↑ | ¿Es mío este lápiz? |
| 7 | Those books are mine. | ésȯzlíƀrȯs \| sȯnmíȯs ↓ | Esos libros son míos. |
| 8 | These books are his. | éstȯzlíƀrȯs \| sȯnsúyȯs ↓ | Estos libros son suyos. |
| 9 | These coins are mine. | éstȧzmȯnéđȧs \| sȯnmíȧs ↓ | Estas monedas son mías. |
| 10 | These things are ours. | éstȧskósȧs \| sȯ(n)nwéstrȧs ↓ | Estas cosas son nuestras. |
| 11 | That pen is yours. | ésȧplúma̯ \| ė(s)súyȧ ↓ | Esa pluma es suya. |

## B. DISCUSSION OF PATTERN

Possessives differ in meaning and association from other adjectives in that they have reference to person and number. No other adjectives have these features of similarity to pronouns and verb forms. Yet the possessives are definitely adjectives, because each form inflects for number and gender to agree with the noun modified. One should not confuse the *number of reference,* which involves selection of one form or another (/mío /—/nwéstro/) with the *number of agreement,* which involves the omission or addition of an ending (mío/—míos/). The first choice is a matter of what one wishes to say; the second is a matter of adjective agreement, and given the noun there is no choice in the number and gender of the possessive (or any other adjective). Likewise /líbro—súyo/ can mean 'his book' or '*her* book' (or 'your book'). The form /súyo/ does not change to /súya/ when it means 'her,' rather only when it modifies a feminine noun, as /kása—súya/, which can mean '*his* house' *or* 'her house' (or 'your house'). As in the case of any other adjective, the appropriately agreeing form is obligatory.

The possessives usually appear in their full forms in a position immediately after the noun they modify, or after the verb /sér/. Both variant form and a special construction in other positions are presented in Unit 11.

The forms of /súyo/ can refer to the English equivalents 'your (sg or pl), his, her, its, their'. Unless the context clearly indicates another reference, however, the most frequent reference is 'your (sg)'. If the contextual reference is not obvious other constructions are usually used (presented in Unit 13) to avoid any ambiguity. Thus the chart in A above could be modified as follows:

<table>
<tr><th>Reference</th><th>sg</th><th>pl</th></tr>
<tr><td>1</td><td>mío</td><td>nwéstro</td></tr>
<tr><td>2 fam</td><td>túyo</td><td rowspan="2">(súyo)</td></tr>
<tr><td>2 for</td><td>súyo</td></tr>
<tr><td>3</td><td>(súyo)</td><td>(súyo)</td></tr>
</table>

When these forms follow a noun they are similar to, and translated by, an English construction consisting of noun plus 'of' plus the long form of the possessive. In the equivalent Spanish construction there is no relator corresponding to 'of' . Thus 'a book of mine' is translated to /un—líbro—mío/ and English speakers have to remember not to translate the English 'of'

## 9.22 REPLACEMENT DRILLS

A básér | mi̯àpàrtàméntȯ | kómo̯estė ↑

| | |
|---|---|
| 1 __________ kásȧ ______________ ↑ | básér \| mikásȧ \| kómo̯éstȧ ↑ |
| 2 _________ sù ________________ ↑ | básér \| sùkásȧ \| kómo̯éstȧ ↑ |
| 3 bán__________________________ ↑ | bánạsér \| sùskásȧs \| kómo̯ésta ↑ |
| 4 _________ èskritóryó ___________ ↑ | básér \| su̯èskritóryȯ \| kómo̯éstė ↑ |
| 5 ___________________________ ésė ↑ | básér \| su̯èskritóryȯ \| kómo̯ésė ↑ |
| 6 __________ ƀèṣínȯs ____________ ↑ | bánạsér \| sùzƀèṣínȯs \| kómo̯ésė ↑ |
| 7 _________ sèkrètáryȧ__________ ↑ | básér \| sùsèkrètáryȧ \| kómo̯ésȧ ↑ |

---

A ¿Va a ser mi apartamento como este?

| | |
|---|---|
| 1 ¿ _________ casa ______________ ? | ¿Va a ser mi casa como ésta? |
| 2 ¿ _________ su ________________ ? | ¿Va a ser su casa como ésta? |
| 3 ¿Van __________________________ ? | ¿Van a ser sus casas como ésta? |
| 4 ¿ _________ escritorio __________ ? | ¿Va a ser su escritorio como éste? |
| 5 ¿ __________________________ ése? | ¿Va a ser su escritorio como ése? |
| 6 ¿ ________ vecinos ____________ ? | ¿Van a ser sus vecinos como ése? |
| 7 ¿ ________ secretaria ___________ ? | ¿Va a ser su secretaria como ésa? |

CD 7
Tape 7A

B tȯđȧƀı́ȧ | nės̯ėsı́tȯ | kȯmprár | múchȧskósȧs ↓

1 ____________ u̇nȧ ____________ ↓ tȯđȧƀı́ȧ | nės̯ėsı́tȯ | kȯmprár | u̇nȧkósȧ ↓

2 ___________ ƀér ______________ ↓ tȯđȧƀı́ȧ | nės̯ėsı́tȯƀér | u̇nȧkósȧ ↓

3 _________ áykė ______________ ↓ tȯđȧƀı́a̯ | áykėƀér | u̇nȧkósȧ ↓

4 ___________ ȧs̯ér______________ ↓ tȯđȧƀı́a̯ | áyke̯ȧs̯ér | u̇nȧkósȧ ↓

5 ______________________ trȧƀáhȯ ↓ tȯđȧƀı́a̯ | áyke̯ȧs̯ér | u̇ntrȧƀáhȯ ↓

6 ____________ múchȯ __________ ↓ tȯđȧƀı́a̯ | áyke̯ȧs̯ér | múchȯtrȧƀáhȯ ↓

7 ________ pwéđo̯ ______________ ↓ tȯđȧƀı́ȧ | pwéđo̯ȧs̯ér | múchȯtrȧƀáhȯ ↓

---

B Todavía necesito comprar muchas cosas.

1 ____________ una ____________ . Todavía necesito comprar una cosa.

2 ___________ ver ______________ . Todavía necesito ver una cosa.

3 _________ hay que _____________ . Todavía hay que ver una cosa.

4 __________ hacer ______________ . Todavía hay que hacer una cosa.

5 ________________________ trabajo. Todavía hay que hacer un trabajo.

6 ____________ mucho __________ . Todavía hay que hacer mucho trabajo.

7 _________ puedo_______________ . Todavía puedo hacer mucho trabajo.

| | |
|---|---|
| C ėstátrȧƀȧhándȯ \| kómȯsėkrėtáryȧ ↓ | |
| 1 ______________________ u̇stéđės ↓ | ėstátrȧƀȧhándȯ \| kómo̯u̇stéđės ↓ |
| 2 _____________ kȯn __________ ↓ | ėstátrȧƀȧhándȯ \| kȯnụstéđės ↓ |
| 3 ________ ȧƀlándȯ ______________ ↓ | ėstáƀlándȯ \| kȯnụstéđės ↓ |
| 4 ėstóy ________________________ ↓ | ėstóyȧƀlándȯ \| kȯnụstéđės ↓ |
| 5 ______________________ u̇stéđ ↓ | ėstóyȧƀlándȯ \| kȯnu̇stéđ ↓ |
| 6 ________________ đe̯ __________ ↓ | ėstóyȧƀlándȯ \| đe̯u̇stéđ ↓ |
| 7 ___________________ su̇zƀės̯ínȯs ↓ | ėstóyȧƀlándȯ \| đėsu̇zƀės̯ínȯs ↓ |

---

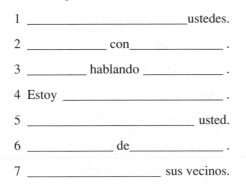

| | |
|---|---|
| C Está trabajando como secretaria. | |
| 1 ______________________ustedes. | Está trabajando como ustedes. |
| 2 ___________ con_____________ . | Está trabajando con ustedes. |
| 3 _________ hablando ___________ . | Está hablando con ustedes. |
| 4 Estoy _______________________ . | Estoy hablando con ustedes |
| 5 ________________________ usted. | Estoy hablando con usted. |
| 6 ____________ de_____________ . | Estoy hablando de usted. |
| 7 ___________________ sus vecinos. | Estoy hablando de sus vecinos. |

D bámȯṣȧtėnér | ƀóđȧpróntȯ ↑

1 bás ____________________ ↑ — báṣȧtėnér | ƀóđȧpróntȯ ↑

2 __________ kásȧ __________ ↑ — báṣȧtėnér | kásȧpróntȯ ↑

3 _______ kȯmprár __________ ↑ — báṣȧkȯmprár | kásȧpróntȯ ↑

4 ____________________ ȧórȧ ↑ — báṣȧkȯmprár | kásȧórȧ ↑

5 bán ____________________ ↑ — báṇȧkȯmprár | kásȧórȧ ↑

6 __________ álgo̯ __________ ↑ — báṇȧkȯmprár | álgo̯ȧórȧ ↑

7 ________ ȧs̯ér ____________ ↑ — báṇȧs̯érálgo̯ | ȧórȧ ↑

---

D ¿Vamos a tener boda pronto?

1 ¿Vas ____________________? — ¿Vas a tener boda pronto?

2 ¿ __________ casa ________? — ¿Vas a tener casa pronto?

3 ¿ ________ comprar ________? — ¿Vas a comprar casa pronto?

4 ¿ ____________________ ahora? — ¿Vas a comprar casa ahora?

5 ¿Van ____________________? — ¿Van a comprar casa ahora?

6 ¿ __________ algo ________? — ¿Van a comprar algo ahora?

7 ¿ ________ hacer __________? — ¿Van a hacer algo ahora?

E no̯émȯz | đè̯siđíđȯ | lȧféchȧ | tȯđȧƀíȧ ↓

1 __________ náđȧ ______________ ↓ no̯émȯz | đè̯siđíđȯnáđȧ | tȯđȧƀíȧ ↓

2 ________ trȧƀȧháđȯ ____________ ↓ no̯émȯs | trȧƀȧháđȯnáđȧ | tȯđȧƀíȧ ↓

3 ________ é __________________ ↓ no̯é | trȧƀȧháđȯnáđȧ | tȯđȧƀíȧ ↓

4 ___________ múchȯ____________ ↓ no̯é | trȧƀȧháđȯmúchȯ | tȯđȧƀíȧ ↓

5 ________ e̯stùđyáđȯ____________ ↓ no̯é | e̯stùđyáđȯmúchȯ | tȯđȧƀíȧ ↓

6 ________ án __________________ ↓ no̯an | e̯stùđyáđȯmúchȯ | tȯđȧƀíȧ ↓

7 ________ kȯmíđȯ______________ ↓ no̯áŋ | kȯmíđȯmúchȯ | tȯđȧƀíȧ ↓

---

E No hemos decidido la fecha todavía.

1 ____________ nada ____________ . No hemos decidido nada todavía.

2 _________ trabajado ____________ . No hemos trabajado nada todavía.

3 _______ he____________________ . No he trabajado nada todavía.

4 ____________ mucho __________ . No he trabajado mucho todavía.

5 _________ cstudiado____________ . No he estudiado mucho todavía.

6 ________ han__________________ . No han estudiado mucho todavía.

7 _________ comido _____________ . No han comido mucho todavía.

F  kéƀwéno̯ėstá | e̯stėw̰íski ↓

| | |
|---|---|
| 1 ______________________ kásȧ ↓ | kéƀwéna̯ėstá \| e̯stȧkásȧ ↓ |
| 2 ______________ éstȧs _________ ↓ | kéƀwénȧṣėstán \| éstȧskásȧs ↓ |
| 3 ________ són _______________ ↓ | kéƀwénȧ(s)són \| éstȧskásȧs ↓ |
| 4 _______ málȧs _______________ ↓ | kémálȧ(s)són \| éstȧskásȧs ↓ |
| 5 ______________________ líƀrȯ ↓ | kémálo̯ės \| éstėlíƀrȯ ↓ |
| 6 ___________ ésȯz ___________ ↓ | kémálȯ(s)són \| ésȯzlíƀrȯs ↓ |
| 7 ____________________ sėks̯yón ↓ | kémála̯ės \| ésȧsėks̯yón ↓ |

---

F  ¡Qué bueno está este whisky!

| | |
|---|---|
| 1 ¡ ______________________ casa! | ¡Qué buena está esta casa! |
| 2 ¡ ____________ estas _________ ! | ¡Qué buenas están estas casas! |
| 3 ¡ _________ son _____________ ! | ¡Qué buenas son estas casas! |
| 4 ¡ ________ malas ____________ ! | ¡Qué malas son estas casas! |
| 5 ¡ _____________________ libro! | ¡Qué malo es este libro! |
| 6 ¡ ____________ esos _________ ! | ¡Qué malos son esos libros! |
| 7 ¡ ____________________ sección! | ¡Qué mala es esa sección! |

**End of Tape 7A**

## 9.23 VARIATION DRILL

| | | |
|---|---|---|
| A | ėstás \| ėntukásȧ ↓ | Estás en tu casa. |
| 1 You're in your bedroom. | ėstásėntuđȯrmitóryȯ ↓ | Estás en tu dormitorio. |
| 2 You're in your room. | ėstás \| ėntukwártȯ ↓ | Estás en tu cuarto. |
| 3 You're in your hotel. | ėstás \| ėntu̯ȯtél ↓ | Estás en tu hotel. |
| 4 You're in your apartment. | ėstásėntu̯apȧrtȧméntȯ ↓ | Estás en tu apartamento. |
| 5 You're in your building. | ėstásėntu̯ėđifís̯yȯ ↓ | Estás en tu edificio. |
| 6 You're in your restaurant. | ėstásėnturrėstȯrán ↓ | Estás en tu restorán. |
| 7 You're in your car. | ėstásėntu̯áwtȯ ↓ | Estás en tu auto. |

| | | |
|---|---|---|
| B | tóđo̯ \| ėstáƀyéṇarrėgláđȯ ↓ | Todo está bien arreglado. |
| 1 The patio looks very neat. | ėlpátyo̯ \| ėstáƀyéṇarrėgláđȯ ↓ | El patio está bien arreglado. |
| 2 The apartment is unoccupied. | ėlȧpȧrtȧménto̯ \| ėstáđėsȯkůpáđȯ ↓ | El apartamento está desocupado. |
| 3 The desk is unoccupied. | ėlėskritóryo̯ \| ėstáđėsȯkůpáđȯ ↓ | El escritorio está desocupado. |
| 4 The kitchen looks very neat. | lȧkóṣiṇa̯ \| ėstáƀyéṇarrėgláđȧ ↓ | La cocina está bien arreglada. |
| 5 The house looks very neat. | lȧkásḁ \| ėstáƀyéṇarrėgláđȧ ↓ | La casa está bien arreglada. |
| 6 The rooms are unoccupied. | lȯskwártȯs \| ėstándėsȯkůpáđȯs ↓ | Los cuartos están desocupados. |
| 7 The houses are unoccupied. | lȧskásȧs \| ėstándėsȯkůpáđȧs ↓ | Las casas están desocupadas. |

| | | | |
|---|---|---|---|
| C | | kyérėṣuŋw̰ı́ski \| kȯnsóđȧ ↑ | ¿Quieres un whisky con soda? |
| 1 | Would you like a whisky and sparkling water? | kyérėṣuŋw̰ı́ski \| kȯṇágwȧmınėrál ↑ | ¿Quieres un whisky con agua mineral? |
| 2 | Would you like a 'cuba libre'? | kyérės \| u̇ŋkúƀalı́ƀrė ↑ | ¿Quieres un cuba libre? |
| 3 | Would you like a ham sandwich? | kyérės \| u̇nsáŋw̰ich \| đėhȧmón ↑ | ¿Quieres un sandwich de jamón? |
| 4 | Would you like a beer? | kyérės \| u̇nȧs̯ėrƀés̯ȧ ↑ | ¿Quieres una cerveza? |
| 5 | Would you like a bowl of vegetable soup? | kyérės \| u̇nȧsópȧ \| đėlėgúmƀrės ↓ | ¿Quieres una sopa de legumbres? |
| 6 | Would you like a pork chop? | kyérės \| u̇nȧchu̇létȧ \| đės̯érđȯ ↑ | ¿Quieres una chuleta de cerdo? |
| 7 | Would you like a tomato salad? | kyérės \| u̇na̯ėnsȧláđȧ \| đėtȯmátė ↑ | ¿Quieres una ensalada de tomate? |

| | | |
|---|---|---|
| D | kyénẹs \| ésȧmucháchȧ \| đėlafótȯ ↓ | ¿Quién es esa muchacha de la foto? |
| 1 Who is that young lady in the consular section? | kyénẹs \| ésȧmucháchȧ \| đėlasėkṣyóŋkȯŋsulár ↓ | ¿Quién es esa muchacha de la sección consular? |
| 2 Who is that young lady from the Embassy? | kyénẹs \| ésȧmucháchȧ \| đėlaembȧháđȧ ↓ | ¿Quién es esa muchacha de la Embajada? |
| 3 Who is that young lady in room seven? | kyénẹs \| ésȧmucháchȧ \| đėlkwártȯsyétė ↓ | ¿Quién es esa muchacha del cuarto siete? |
| 4 Who is that young lady with the car? | kyénẹs \| ésȧmucháchȧ \| đėláwtȯ ↓ | ¿Quién es esa muchacha del auto? |
| 5 Who is that young lady from the agency? | kyénẹs \| ésȧsenyóritȧ \| đėlahénṣyȧ ↓ | ¿Quién es esa señorita de la agencia? |
| 6 Who is that gentleman from the first floor? | kyénẹs \| ésėsenyór \| đėlprimérpísȯ ↓ | ¿Quién es ese señor del primer piso? |
| 7 Who is that gentleman from the hotel? | kyénẹs \| ésėsenyór \| đėlȯtél ↓ | ¿Quién es ese señor del hotel? |

| | | | |
|---|---|---|---|
| E | | ėzminóƀyȧ ↓ tyénėskėkȯnȯṣérlȧ ↓ | Es mi novia. Tienes que conocerla. |
| 1 | It's my girl friend. You'll have to see her. | ėzminóƀyȧ ↓ tyénėskėƀérlȧ ↓ | Es mi novia. Tienes que verla. |
| 2 | It's my friend. You'll have to see her. | ėzmi̯ȧmígȧ ↓ tyénėskėƀérlȧ ↓ | Es mi amiga. Tienes que verla. |
| 3 | It's Mrs. Molina. You have to meet her. | ėzlȧsėn̦yórȧ \| đėmȯlínȧ ↓ tyénės kėkȯnȯṣérlȧ ↓ | Es la señora de Molina. Tienes que conocerla. |
| 4 | It's Miss Molina. I have to see her. | ėzlȧsėn̦yȯrítȧmȯlínȧ ↓ téŋgȯkėƀérlȧ ↓ | Es la señorita Molina. Tengo que verla. |
| 5 | It's the secretary. I have to help her. | ėzlȧsėkrėtáryȧ ↓ téŋgȯkẹȧy̯úđárlȧ ↓ | Es la secretaria. Tengo que ayudarla. |
| 6 | It's Louise. We'll have to wait for her. | ėzlwísȧ ↓ tėnémȯskėspėrárlȧ ↓ | Es Luisa. Tenemos que esperarla. |
| 7 | It's Carmen. We'll have to take her. | ėskármėn ↓ tėnémȯskė(l)y̯ėƀárlȧ ↓ | Es Carmen. Tenemos que llevarla. |

| | | |
|---|---|---|
| F | ké \| ás̯ė ↓ ėstáe̯stùđyándȯ ↑ | ¿Qué hace? Está estudiando? |
| 1 What's she doing? Is she working? | ké \| ás̯ė ↓ ėstátrȧƀȧhándȯ ↑ | ¿Qué hace ? ¿Está trabajando? |
| 2 What are you doing? Are you speaking? | ké \| ás̯ė ↓ ėstáƀlándȯ ↑ | ¿Qué hace? ¿Está hablando? |
| 3 What are you doing? Are you thinking? | ké \| ás̯ė ↓ ėstápėnsándȯ ↑ | ¿Qué hace? ¿Está pensando? |
| 4 What are you doing? Are you going down? | ké \| ás̯ė ↓ ėstáƀȧhándȯ ↑ | ¿Qué hace? ¿Está bajando? |
| 5 What are you doing? Are you practicing? | ké \| ás̯ė ↓ ėstáprȧktikándȯ ↑ | ¿Qué hace? ¿Está practicando? |
| 6 What are you doing? Are you waiting? | ké \| ás̯ė ↓ ėstáe̯spėrándȯ ↑ | ¿Qué hace? ¿Está esperando? |
| 7 What are you doing? Are you buying something? | ké \| ás̯ė ↓ ėstákȯmprándȯ ↑ | ¿Qué hace? ¿Está comprando? |

## 9.24 REVIEW DRILL

Adjective position

| | | |
|---|---|---|
| 1 I have little furniture. | téŋgȯ \| pókȯzmwéƀlės ↓ | Tengo pocos muebles. |
| I have expensive furniture. | téŋgȯ \| mwéƀlėskárȯs ↓ | Tengo muebles caros. |
| 2 I have too many clothes. | téŋgȯ \| đėmȧsyáđȧrrópȧ ↓ | Tengo demasiada ropa. |
| I have cheap clothes. | téŋgȯ \| rrópȧƀȧrátȧ ↓ | Tengo ropa barata. |
| 3 I have many checks. | téŋgȯ \| múchȯschékės ↓ | Tengo muchos cheques. |
| I have travelers checks. | téŋgȯ \| chékėzƀyȧhérȯs ↓ | Tengo cheques viajeros. |
| 4 I have a lot of clothes. | téŋgȯ \| múchȧrrópȧ ↓ | Tengo mucha ropa. |
| I have American clothes. | téŋgȯ \| rrópȧmėrikánȧ ↓ | Tengo ropa americana. |
| 5 I have other furniture | téŋgo̯ \| ótrȯzmwéƀlės ↓ | Tengo otros muebles. |
| I have cheap furniture. | téŋgȯ \| mwéƀlėzƀȧrátȯs ↓ | Tengo muebles baratos. |
| 6 I want a lot of water. | kyérȯ \| múchágwȧ ↓ | Quiero mucha agua. |
| I want carbonated water. | kyéro̯ \| ágwȧminėrál ↓ | Quiero agua mineral. |

| | | | |
|---|---|---|---|
| 7 | I want enough clothes. | kyérȯ \| ƀȧstántėrrópȧ ↓ | Quiero bastante ropa. |
| | I want expensive clothes. | kyérȯrrópȧkárȧ ↓ | Quiero ropa cara. |
| 8 | I'm in the same section. | ėstóy \| ėnlȧmízmȧsėkṣyón ↓ | Estoy en la misma sección. |
| | I'm in the consular section. | ėstóy \| ėnlȧsėkṣyóŋkȯnsúlár ↓ | Estoy en la sección consular. |
| 9 | There is the same gentleman. | áı \| e̯stáe̯lmízmȯsėṇyór ↓ | Ahí está el mismo señor. |
| | There's the English gentleman. | áı \| e̯stáe̯lsėṇyóriŋglés ↓ | Ahí está el señor inglés. |
| 10 | Here there are few young ladies. | ȧkí \| a̯ypókȧ(s)sėṇyȯrítȧs ↓ | Aquí hay pocas señoritas. |
| | Here there are Spanish girls. | ȧkí \| a̯ysėṇyȯrítȧṣėspȧṇyólȧs ↓ | Aquí hay señoritas españolas. |
| 11 | I work with the same young lady. | trȧƀáhȯ \| kȯnlȧmízmȧsėṇyȯrítȧ ↓ | Trabajo con la misma señorita. |
| | I work with the American girl. | trȧƀáhȯ \| kȯnlȧsėṇyȯrítȧmėrıkánȧ ↓ | Trabajo con la señorita americana. |

# 9.3 CONVERSATION STIMULUS

## NARRATIVE 1

| | | |
|---|---|---|
| 1 Jose has been in his neighbors' apartment. | hȯsé \| a̯ėstáđo̯ \| ėṇėlȧpȧrtȧméntȯ \| đėsùzƀėṣɪnȯs ↓ | José ha estado en el apartamento de sus vecinos. |
| 2 And it's exactly the same as his. | ɪ̯ėṣigwȧlíto̯ȧlsúy̯ȯ ↓ | Y es igualito al suyo. |
| 3 Juan wants to see it. | hwáŋkyérėƀérlȯ ↓ | Juan quiere verlo. |
| 4 Jose says that he can go any day. | hȯséđíṣė ↑ kélpwéđe̯ɪr \| kwȧlkyérđíȧ ↓ | José dice que él puede ir cualquier día. |
| 5 Juan wants to go tomorrow. | hwáŋ \| kyére̯ɪr \| mȧṇyánȧ ↓ | Juan quiere ir mañana. |
| 6 Jose's going to talk to his neighbors, then. | hȯséƀȧƀlár \| kȯnsùzƀėṣínȯs \| ėntónṣės ↓ | José va a hablar con sus vecinos, entonces. |
| 7 And he'll let Juan know. | ile̯ȧƀísȧhwán ↓ | Y le avisa a Juan. |

## DIALOG 1

| | | |
|---|---|---|
| Juan, pregúntele a José si él ha estado en el apartamento de sus vecinos. | tu̯ás̩estáđo̯ \| ėne̯làpàrtàméntȯ \| đėtúzƀes̩ínȯs ↑ | Juan ¿Tú has estado en el apartamento de tus vecinos? |
| José, contéstele que sí, que es igualito al suyo. Pregúntele que cuándo quiere verlo. | sí ↓ ės̩igwàlíto̯almíȯ ↓ kwándȯkyérėzƀérlȯ ↓ | José: Sí, es igualito al mío. ¿Cuándo quieres verlo? |
| Juan, contéstele que cualquier día, que mañana, si le parece. | kwàlkyérđíà ↓ màn̯yánà \| sitėpàrés̩ė ↓ | Juan: Cualquier día. Mañana, si te parece. |
| José, dígale que muy bien, que Ud. habla con ellos y le avisa. | múyƀyén ↓ y̯o̯áƀlȯ \| kóne̯(l)y̯ós \| ìte̯àƀísȯ ↓ | José: Muy bien. Yo hablo con ellos y te aviso. |

## NARRATIVE 2

| | | |
|---|---|---|
| 1 Juan isn't planning to do anything this evening. | hwán \| nȯpyénsàsér \| náđa̯ \| éstàtárđė ↓ | Juan no piensa hacer nada esta tarde. |
| 2 Why doesn't he go see where Jose lives, then? | pȯrkénȯƀáƀér \| đóndėƀíƀėhósė \| e̯ntóns̩ės ↓ | ¿Por qué no va a ver dónde vive José, entonces? |

| | | |
|---|---|---|
| 3 That way he can see what his apartment is going to be like. | àsípwéđèƀér \| kómòƀàsér \| sụàpàrtàméntò ↓ | Así puede ver cómo va a ser su apartamento. |
| 4 He thinks it might be an excellent idea. | élkréẹ \| kèṣùnạiđéạeks(ṣ)eléntè ↓ | El cree que es una idea excelente. |

## DIALOG 2

| | | |
|---|---|---|
| José, pregúntele a Juan que qué piensa hacer esta noche. | képyénṣạṣáṣer \| éstànóchè \| hwán ↓ | José: ¿Qué piensas hacer esta noche, Juan? |
| Juan, contéstele que nada, que por qué. | náđà ↓ pòrké ↓ | Juan: Nada, ¿por qué? |
| José, pregúntele que por qué no viene a ver dónde Ud. vive? | pòrkénòƀyénèṣạƀér \| đóndèỵóƀíƀò ↓ | José: ¿Por qué no vienes a ver donde yo vivo? |
| Juan, contéstele que le parece una idea excelente. | mèpàréṣẹ \| ùnạiđéạèks(ṣ)èléntè ↓ | Juan: Me parece una idea excelente. |
| José, digale que así puede ver cómo va a ser el apartamento suyo. | àsípwéđèzƀér \| kómòƀásér \| èlàpàrtàméntòtúỵò ↓ | José: Así puedes ver cómo va a ser el apartamento tuyo. |

## NARRATIVE 3

| | | | |
|---|---|---|---|
| 1 | Jose has everything very neat in his apartment. | hòsétyénètóđò \| muyƀyén \| arregláđo̯ \| ènsu̯àpàrtàméntò ↓ | José tiene todo muy bien arreglado en su apartamento. |
| 2 | But he's still got a million things to buy. | péròtòđàƀía \| tyéne̯ùnmi(l)y̯óndè kósàs \| kèkòmprár ↓ | Pero todavía tiene un millón de cosas que comprar. |
| 3 | He has already talked with his neighbors. | y̯àƀláđò \| kònsùzƀesínòs ↓ | Ya ha hablado con sus vecinos. |
| 4 | They told him that they're going to be home tomorrow afternoon. | lèđihéròŋ \| kèƀána̯èstárèŋkásà \| màn̯yánàpòrlàtárđè ↓ | Le dijeron que van a estar en casa mañana por la tarde. |
| 5 | Juan says that if the other apartment is like this one, he'll take it. | hwándis̯è \| kès̯ièlótro̯àpàrtàménto̯ \| èskómo̯éstè ↑ lòtómà ↓ | Juan dice que si el otro apartamento es como éste, lo toma. |

## DIALOG 3

Juan, dígale a José que qué bien arreglado tiene todo.

kéƀyén | àrrèglá đò | tyénèstóđò ↓

Juan: ¡Qué bien arreglado tienes todo!

José, dígale que gracias, pero que todavía tiene un millón de cosas que comprar.

gráşyàs ↓ pèròtòđáƀía | téŋgọ ùnmi(l)yóndekósàs | kèkòmprár ↑

José: Gracias, pero todavía tengo un millón de cosas que comprar.

Juan, pregúntele si no ha hablado con sus vecinos todavía.

nọáşàƀláđò | kòntùzƀèşínòs | tòđaƀía ↑

Juan: ¿No has hablado con tus vecinos todavía?

José, contéstele que sí, que le dijeron que van a estar en casa mañana por la tarde.

sí ↓ mèđihéròŋ | kèƀánạèstár èŋkásà | màṇyánapòrlàtárđè ↓

José: Sí, me dijeron que van a estar en casa mañana por la tarde.

Juan, dígale que está bien, y que si el apartamento de ellos es como éste, Ud. lo toma.

èstáƀyén ↓ sịèlàpàrtàméntò | đé(l)yòs ↑ èskómọéstè ↑ lòtómò ↓

Juan: Está bien. Si el apartamento de ellos es como éste, lo tomo.

## NARRATIVE 4

| | | |
|---|---|---|
| 1 Carmen is Jose's girl friend. | kármėn \| ėzlȧnóƀyȧđėhȯsé ↓ | Carmen es la novia de José. |
| 2 Juan hasn't had the pleasure of meeting her yet. | hwán \| no̯ȧṭėníđo̯ėlgústȯ \| đė kȯnȯṣ́erlȧ \| tȯđȧƀíȧ ↓ | Juan no ha tenido el gusto de conocerla todavía. |
| 3 Here's a picture of her. She sure is pretty! | ȧkı̯áy \| u̇nȧfótȯ \| đé(l)y̰ȧ ↓ kéƀȯníta̯és ↓ | Aquí hay una foto de ella. ¡Qué bonita es! |
| 4 Jose and Carmen haven't talked about the wedding yet. | hȯsé̯ıkármėn \| no̯ánạƀláđȯ \| đėlȧƀóđȧ \| tȯđȧƀíȧ ↓ | José y Carmen no han hablado de la boda todavía. |
| 5 But Jose thinks it's going to be soon. | pérȯhȯsékrée̯ \| kėƀásér \| próntȯ ↓ | Pero José cree que va a ser pronto. |

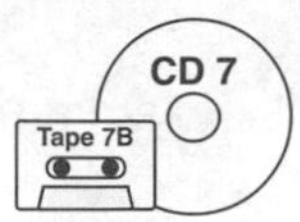



## DIALOG 4

| | | |
|---|---|---|
| José, pregúntele a Juan si él conoce a Carmen, la novia suya. | túkȯnósėsạkármėn ↑ lȧnóƀyȧmíȧ ↑ | José: ¿Tú conoces a Carmen, la novia mía? |
| Juan, contéstele que no, que todavía no ha tenido el gusto. | nó ↓ tȯđȧƀíȧ \| no̯étėníđo̯ \| ėlgústȯ ↓ | Juan: No, todavía no he tenido el gusto. |
| José, digale que aquí hay una foto de ella, y pregúntele si le gusta. | ȧki̯áy \| ủnȧfótȯ \| đé(l)y̰ȧ ↓ tėgústȧ ↑ | José: Aquí hay una foto de ella. ¿Te gusta? |
| Juan, contéstele que sí, hombre, que cómo no, que qué bonita. Y pregúntele que cuándo es la boda. | sí \| ómbrė ↓ kómȯnó ↓ kéƀȯnítȧ ↓ kwándo̯ėzlȧƀóđȧ ↓ | Juan: ¡Sí, hombre, cómo no! ¡Qué bonita! ¿Cuándo es la boda? |
| José, contéstele que todavía no han hablado de eso, pero que Ud. cree que va a ser pronto. | tȯđȧƀíȧ \| no̯émȯsạƀláđȯ \| đésȯ ↓ pérȯkréȯ \| kėƀáser \| próntȯ ↓ | José: Todavía no hemos hablado de eso, pero creo que va a ser pronto. |

# 10.1 BASIC SENTENCES

## Molina explains where he sends his laundry

After having spoken with the manager of the house and having rented the furnished apartment for John, the two friends return to Molina's apartment.

| English Spelling | Aid to Listening | Spanish Spelling |
|---|---|---|
| the end | ėl—fín ↓ | el fin |
| so, then, well | ėm—fín ↓ | en fin |
| ready | lístȯ ↓ | listo |
| *MOLINA* | | *MOLINA* |
| Well, you're all set.(1) | ėmfín ↓ yaėstálístȯ \| tóđȯ ↓ | En fin. Ya está listo todo. |
| yourself | té ↓ | te |
| yourself (you) change, move (to change, move) | tė—múđȧs ↓ mȯđársė ↓ | te mudas (mudarse) |
| When will you move? | kwándȯ \| tėmúđȧs ↓ | ¿Cuándo te mudas? |
| (they) give (to give) | dán ↓ dár ↓ | dan (dar) |
| Friday | ėl—byérnės ↓ | el viernes |
| myself (I) change, move (to change, move) | mė—múđȯ ↓ mȯđársė ↓ | me mudo (mudarse) |

| | | |
|---|---|---|
| Saturday | ėl—sáƀȧđȯ ↓ | el sábado |
| *WHITE* | | *WHITE* |
| If they give me the apartment on Friday, I'll move on Saturday. (2) | simėđán \| ėlapȧrtȧméntọ \| ėlbyérnės ↑ mėmúđọėlsáƀȧđȯ ↓ | Si me dan el apartamento el viernes, me mudo el sábado. |
| the suitcase | lȧ—mȧlétȧ ↓ | la maleta |
| *MOLINA* | | *MOLINA* |
| I can help you with your suitcases. | yótėpwéđọȧyụđár \| kȯnlȧzmȧlétȧs ↓ | Yo te puedo ayudar con las maletas. |
| the that, that which, what (3) | ló—kė ↓ | lo que |
| to bother | mȯlėstár ↓ | molestar |
| not yourself bother (to bother) | nó—tė—mȯléstės ↓ mȯlėstársė ↓ | no te molestes (molestarse) |
| *WHITE* | | *WHITE* |
| I don't have very much. You needn't bother. | éspókȯ \| lȯkėtéŋgȯ ↓ nótėmȯléstės ↓ | Es poco lo que tengo. No te molestes. |
| (you) send (to send) | mándȧs ↓ mȧndár ↓ | mandas (mandar) |
| Where do you send your laundry? | dóndėmándȧs \| tụrrópȧ ↓ | ¿Dónde mandas tu ropa? |
| the suit | ėl—tráhė ↓ | el traje |

| | | |
|---|---|---|
| them (m) | lós ↓ | los |
| the cleaner's shop | là—tintòrèrìà ↓ | la tintorería |
| in front | èmfréntè ↓ | enfrente |
| *MOLINA* | | *MOLINA* |
| I send my suits to the cleaner's across the street. (4) | lòstráhèz \| lòzmándo̯ \| àlàtintòrèríà \| kèstáe̯mfréntè ↓ | Los trajes los mando a la tintorería que está enfrente. |
| the shirt | là—kàmísà ↓ | la camisa |
| the laundry | là—làƀàndèríà | la lavandería |
| the corner | la̯—èskínà ↓ | la esquina |
| And my shirts to the laundry on the corner. (5) | ilàskàmísàs \| àlàlàƀàndèríàđèla̯èskínà ↓ | Y las camisas a la lavandería de la esquina. |
| -self | mízmò ↓ | mismo |
| I myself | y̯ó—mízmò ↓ | yo mismo |
| them (f) | lás ↓ | las |
| I take them over myself. (6) | y̯ómízmòlàz(l)y̯éƀò ↓ | Yo mismo las llevo. |
| to clean | limpyár ↓ | limpiar |

| | | |
|---|---|---|
| *WHITE* | | *WHITE* |
| Who cleans the apartment for you? | kyéntėlímpya̯ \| ėlȧpȧrtȧméntȯ ↓ | ¿Quién te limpia el apartamento? |
| (she) comes (to come) | byénė ↓ bėnír ↓ | viene (venir) |
| all, every | tóđȯ ↓ | todo |
| Thursday | ėl—hwéƀės ↓ | el jueves |
| all the Thursdays, every Thursday | tóđoz—lȯs—hwéƀės ↓ | todos los jueves |
| *MOLINA* | | *MOLINA* |
| A girl who comes every Thursday. (7) | únamúcháchȧ \| kėƀyénė \| tóđȯzlȯshwéƀės ↓ | Una muchacha que viene todos los jueves. |
| to her | lé ↓ | le |
| If you want I'll speak to her. (8) | sikyérės ↑ yóle̯áƀlȯ ↓ | Si quieres yo le hablo. |
| *WHITE* | | *WHITE* |
| Swell. | múyƀyén ↓ | Muy bien. |
| late | tárđė ↓ | tarde |
| to go myself (to go oneself, to leave) | ɪ́rmė ↓ ɪ́rsė ↓ | irme (irse) |
| Well, it's late. I've got to go. | bwénȯ ↓ ya̯éstárđė ↓ téŋgȯke̯ɪ́rmė ↓ | Bueno, ya es tarde. Tengo que irme. |
| before | ántės ↓ | antes |

| | | |
|---|---|---|
| the swallow, the drink | ėl—trágȯ ↓ | el trago |
| *MOLINA* | | *MOLINA* |
| Won't you have another drink first? [9] | ántėz \| nókyérės \| ótrȯtrágȯ ↑ | Antes, ¿no quieres otro trago? |
| *WHITE* | | *WHITE* |
| No, thanks. Tomorrow is a work day. | nó ↓ múchȧzgrás̯yȧs ↓ mȧn̡yánȧy \| kėtrȧƀȧhár ↓ | No, muchas gracias. Mañana hay que trabajar. |
| grateful (to be grateful) | ȧgrȧđės̯ıđȯ ↓ ȧgrȧđės̯ér ↓ | agradecido (agradecer) |
| Thanks a lot for everything. | múyȧgrȧđės̯íđȯ \| pȯrtóđȯ ↓ | Muy agradecido por todo. |

## 10.10 Notes on the basic sentences

(1) The utterance in Spanish says, of course, not that *you* are ready but that 'everything' is all ready already. But 'You're all set' is more probably what we would say, since the implication of the English phrase 'Everything is all ready' is that considerable packing has been completed to bring the situation into a state of readiness. The Spanish remark is much more casual in its implication.

(2) The item /mudárse / *mudarse* also means 'to change clothes.' The context and relative time sequence are all that reveal whether you should consider it as referring to a change of clothes or a change of residence. Thus /memúdo̯enmédya̯óra ↓/ *Me mudo en media hora* would mean 'I'll change clothes in half an hour,' unless, of course, the moving van were waiting out front and the context unequivocally demanded such an interpretation.

(3) The process of nominalization is represented in this construction.

(4) The only reason for the particular intonation that appears in the last part of this sentence /késtáe̯mfréntė ↓/ instead of /kėstae̯mfréntė ↓/ is to show contrast between this cleaner's store and the laundry referred to in the next utterance. The two utterances go together, and the intonation on the first one is not natural unless they do.

(5) Note the equivalence here of English *on* with Spanish *de*. It is almost impossible to state any generalized description of the differences involved here and elsewhere between English and Spanish prepositions.

(6) The form /mísmo/ *mismo* may be added to any subject pronoun or to any noun in this sense of '—self.' It agrees in respect to number and gender with the item it follows.

(7) The names of three days of the week have now appeared. It may be convenient, therefore, to list all seven here together:

| | | | |
|---|---|---|---|
| Monday | el lunes | Friday | el viernes |
| Tuesday | el martes | Saturday | el sábado |
| Wednesday | el miércoles | Sunday | el domingo |
| Thursday | el jueves | | |

When listed in series, the article is not attached.

(8) Some speakers, particularly in Madrid, might say /la/ instead of /le/.

(9) Perhaps a more literal and equally possible translation would be, 'Before you go, won't you have another drink?'

**End of Tape 7B**
**End of CD 7**

# 10.2 DRILLS AND GRAMMAR

## 10.21 PATTERN DRILLS

### 10.21.1 Personal /a/

A. PRESENTATION OF PATTERN

*ILLUSTRATIONS*

| | | |
|---|---|---|
| ____________________ | 1 pȯrkénȯƀémȯs \| a̯ůnạmígȯmíȯ ↓ | ¿Por qué no vemos *a* un amigo mío? |
| ____________________ | 2 kyérȯprėsėntárle̯ \| ȧlȧsėnyórȧ mȯlínȧ ↓ | Quiero presentarle *a* la señora Molina. |

| | | |
|---|---|---|
| Are we going to meet the family? | 3 bámȯs̥akȯnȯs̥ér \| ȧlȧfȧmílyȧ ↑ | ¿Vamos a conocer *a* la familia? |
| (I) see (to see) | béo ↓ bér ↓ | veo (ver) |
| I see the car, but l don't see the chauffer. | 4 béo̯ėláwtȯ ↑ pėrȯnóƀéo̯ȧlchȯfér ↓ | Veo el auto, pero no veo *a*l chofer. |
| anyone | álgyėn ↓ | alguien |
| Do you see anybody? | 5 bés̥álgyėn ↑ | ¿Ves *a* alguien? |
| no one | náđyė ↓ | nadie |
| No, I don't see anyone | 6 nó ↓ nóƀéo̯ȧnáđyė ↓ | No, no veo *a* nadie. |

### *EXTRAPOLATION*

| | | |
|---|---|---|
| Nonperson noun object | Verb - | object |
| Person noun object | Verb -/a/- | object |

### *NOTES*

a. When a noun referring to a person occurs as the direct object of a verb, it is marked (preceded) by the relater /a/.

b. A noun direct object is one which can be substituted for the third person direct clitic pronouns previously presented.

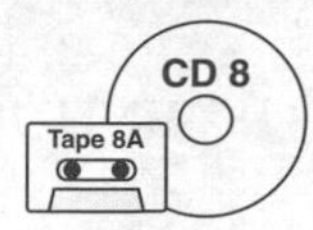



## 10.21.11 SUBSTITUTION DRILL

Personal substitution

Problem:

béolàkásà ↓

___________ kármèn ↓

Answer:

béoàkármèn ↓

---

Problem:

Veo *la casa*.

___________ Carmen.

Answer:

Veo a Carmen.

1 búskȯlȧkásȧ ↓

_________________ sėnyórȧ ↓ búskoȧlȧsėnyórȧ ↓

2 nóeŋkȯntrámȯs | ėlȧpȧrtȧméntȯ ↓

_________________ hwán ↓ nóeŋkȯntrámȯs | ȧhwán ↓

3 (l)yéƀoėláwtȯ ↓

_________________ lwísȧ ↓ (l)yéƀoȧlwísȧ ↓

---

1 Buscar *la casa.*

_________________ señora. Buscar a la señora.

2 No encontramos *el apartamento.*

_________________ Juan. No encontramos a Juan.

3 Llevo *el auto.*

_________________ Luisa. Llevo a Luisa.

4 bùskámȯs | ȧlȧsėkrėtáryȧ ↓

_________________ ėskwélȧ ↓ bùskámȯz | lȃėskwélȧ ↓

5 búskȧlȧsėnyórȧ ↓

_________________ ėđıfíşyȯ ↓ búskȃėlėđıfíşyȯ ↓

---

4 Buscamos a la *secretaria.*

_________________ escuela. Buscamos la escuela.

5 Busca a la *señora.*

_________________ edificio. Busca el edificio.

## 10.21.12 RESPONSE DRILL

| | | |
|---|---|---|
| | 1 búskàlàhénṣyà ↑ o̥àlàsèkrètáryà ↓ | àlàsèkrètáryà ↓ |
| | 2 búskànlàfótò ↑ o̥àlàmùcháchà ↓ | àlàmùcháchà ↓ |
| [àlàsèn̦yórà ↓] | 3 àkyém \| búskàn̦ùstéđès ↓ | àlàsèn̦yórà ↓ |
| [àmáryò ↓] | 4 àkyém \| búskạé(l)y̦à ↓ | àmáryò ↓ |
| [èlòtél ↓] | 5 kébúskạél ↓ | èlòtél ↓ |
| [àlmóṣò ↓] | 6 búskàn̦ùstéđès \| àlchófér ↑ | nó ↓ àlmóṣò ↓ |

---

| | | |
|---|---|---|
| | 1 ¿Busca la agencia o a la secretaria? | A la secretaria. |
| | 2 ¿Buscan la foto o a la muchacha? | A la muchacha. |
| (a la señora) | 3 ¿A quién buscan Uds.? | A la señora. |
| (a Mario) | 4 ¿A quién busca ella? | A Mario. |
| (el hotel) | 5 ¿Qué busca él? | El hotel. |
| (al mozo) | 6 ¿Buscan Uds. al chofer? | No, al mozo. |

| | | |
|---|---|---|
| [ȧkármėn ↓] | 7 búskau̯stéđ \| ȧhwán ↑ | nó ↓ ȧkármėn ↓ |
| | 8 béu̯stéđ \| ȧlȧsėn̯yórıtȧ ↑ | sí ↓ lȧƀéȯ ↓ |
| | 9 béu̯stéđ \| ȧlȧ(s)sėn̯yórȧs ↑ | sí ↓ lȧzƀéȯ ↓ |
| | 10 (l)y̯éƀan̯ustéđės \| ȧlchófer ↑ | sí ↓ lȯ(l)y̯ėƀámȯs ↓ |
| | 11 búskau̯él \| ȧlȯzmóṣȯs ↑ | sí ↓ lȯzƀúskȧ ↓ |
| | 12 bén̯ustéđės \| lȧkásȧ ↑ | sí ↓ lȧƀémȯs ↓ |
| | 13 bén̯ustéđės \| ėlȯtél ↑ | sí ↓ lȯƀémȯs ↓ |

---

| | | |
|---|---|---|
| (a Carmen) | 7 ¿Busca Ud. a Juan? | No, a Carmen. |
| | 8 ¿Ve Ud. a la señorita? | Sí, la veo. |
| | 9 ¿Ve Ud. a las señoras? | Sí, las veo. |
| | 10 ¿Llevan Uds. al chofer? | Sí, lo llevamos. |
| | 11 ¿Busca él a los mozos? | Sí, los busca. |
| | 12 ¿Ven Uds. la casa? | Sí, la vemos. |
| | 13 ¿Ven Uds. el hotel? | Sí, lo vemos. |

## 10.21.13 TRANSLATION DRILL

| | | |
|---|---|---|
| 1 We see the car, but not the chauffeur. | bémȯṣėláwtȯ ↓ pėrȯnóa̯lchȯfér ↓ | Vemos el auto pero no al chofer. |
| 2 I see the house, but not the lady. | béȯlȧkásȧ ↓ pėrȯnóa̯lȧsėn̰yórȧ ↓ | Veo la casa pero no a la señora. |
| 3 We see the building, but not the gentleman. | bémȯs \| ėlėđifíṣyȯ ↓ pėrȯnóa̯lsėn̰yór ↓ | Vemos el edificio pero no al señor. |
| 4 They see the desk, but not the secretary. | bénẹ̇lėskritóryȯ ↓ pėrȯnóa̯lȧsėkrėtáryȧ ↓ | Ven el escritorio pero no a la secretaria. |
| 5 I'm looking for the suitcases and the ladies also. | búskȯ \| lȧzmȧlétȧs ↑<br>i̯ȧlȧ(s)sėn̰yórȧstȧmbyén ↓ | Busco las maletas y a las señoras también. |
| 6 We're looking for Carmen. | bu̇skámȯṣȧkármėn ↓ | Buscamos a Carmen. |
| 7 We can't find John. | nóe̯ŋkȯntrámȯs \| ȧhwán ↓ | No encontramos a Juan. |
| 8 We can't find the house. | nóe̯ŋkȯntrámȯs \| lȧkásȧ ↓ | No encontramos la casa. |
| 9 I'm looking for the apartment. | búsko̯ėlȧpȧrtȧméntȯ ↓ | Busco el apartamento. |

## B. DISCUSSION OF PATTERN

Many Spanish verbs can be followed by a noun which is not the subject of the verb, since the usual agreement of person and number between the subject and verb is not necessary, as in /por—ké—no bémos | la kasa ↓/. If the verb is not /sér/ (as in /mi–nómbre̯ | és–hosé ↓/ in which case the noun following the verb is identified as the same as the noun preceding), the following noun is usually described as the 'direct object' of the verb.

The direct object is often thought of as in some sense 'receiving' the action of the verb; thus in /bémos—la—kása ↓/, the 'house' gets seen. There have been many examples of verbs followed by a direct object in previous units, such as /tyéne—un—lápiṣ ↑ kyére—ustéd | ágwa—minerál ↑ yo—kyéro—un—sáŋw̯ıch | de—hamón ↓ bámos—a—bér | el—peryódıko ↓/, etc.

When a noun functioning as the direct object of a verb refers to specific person, it is usually marked by the occurrence of the relater /a/ preceding the noun. The resulting phrase usually follows the verb, though it may precede: /por—ké—no—bémos | a—un—amígo—mío ↓/

The forms /kyén, álgyen, nádye/, though they do not necessarily refer to specific persons, are also included in this pattern. (Their participation in the pattern is one reason they can logically be analyzed as nouns, and not pronouns as some analysts have maintained. Also, since /kyén—kyénes/ has noun-like formation of the plural, and since none of these forms have any *case* designation in the way that the pronouns do, their analysis as a special kind of nouns, not occurring with articles, seems appropriate.)

The /a/ which marks the person noun object may or may not appear after the verb /tenér/ and minimal contrasts of the following types are possible:

| | |
|---|---|
| /téngomıfamílya̯ \| enchíle ↓/ | 'My family is in Chile.' |
| /téngo̯amıfamílya̯ \| enchíle ↓/ | 'I sent my family to Chile.' |
| /téngodóṣamígos \| akí ↓/ | 'I have two friends here.' |
| /téngo̯adóṣamígos \| akí ↓/ | 'There are two friends of mine with me.' |

The /a/ may be missing after other verbs when the reference is not to a specific person:

| | |
|---|---|
| /neṣesíto̯unchofér ↓/ | 'I need a chauffeur.' |

### 10.21.2 Direct clitic pronouns

#### A. PRESENTATION OF PATTERN

*ILLUSTRATIONS*

| | | |
|---|---|---|
| Will you take me to the hotel? | 1 mė(l)y̯éƀȧlȯtél ↑ | ¿*Me* lleva al hotel? |
| ____________ | 2 (l)y̯éƀėme̯ȧlȯtél ↓ | Llléve*me* al hotel. |
| ____________ | 3 kyéṙez \| đėhármėne̯lȯtél ↑ | ¿Quieres dejar*me* en el hotel? |
| Will you take us downtown? | 4 nȯz(l)y̯éƀȧls̯éntrȯ ↑ | ¿*Nos* lleva al centro? |
| ____________ | 5 (l)y̯éƀėnȯsȧls̯éntrȯ ↓ | Llléve*nos* al centro. |
| ____________ | 6 tėspérȯ ↓ | *Te* espero. |
| ____________ | 7 a̯u̇stéđ \| lȯ(l)y̯ámȯđėspwés ↓ | A usted *lo* llamo después. |
| ____________ | 8 ȧhwán \| lo̯ȧy̯u̇đámȯstóđȯs ↓ | A Juan *lo* ayudamos todos. |
| ____________ | 9 kómȯlȯkyérė ↓ | ¿Cómo *lo* quiere? |
| ____________ | 10 lȯsyéntȯmúchȯ ↓ | *Lo* siento mucho. |
| never | núŋkȧ ↓ | nunca |

We never can see it. — 11 núŋkȧ | pȯđémȯzbérlȯ ↓ — Nunca podemos ver*lo*.

____________________ — 12 tyénės | kėkȯnȯṣérlȧ ↓ — Tienes que conocer*la*.

____________________ — 13 lȯstráhėzlȯzmándo̯ | ȧlȧ tintȯrėríȧ ↓ — Los trajes *los* mando a la tintorería

____________________ — 14 y̰ómízmȯ | lȧz(l)y̰éƀȯ ↓ — Yo mismo *las* llevo.

*EXTRAPOLATION*

| | sg | pl |
|---|---|---|
| 1 | me | nos |
| 2 fam | te | |
| 2-3 | lo | los |
| | la | las |

*NOTES*

a. Clitic pronouns appear only with verbs, usually immediately preceding them, sometimes immediately following them.

b. Like other pronouns, clitics inflect for person, number, and in 2-3 person forms for gender.

c. A redundant construction /a—hwán, a—ustéd, los—tráhes/, restating the direct object, may be added to the sentence to clarify or emphasize the direct clitic pronoun.

## 10.21.21 SUBSTITUTION DRILLS

Form substitution

Problem: bémòzlàfótò ↓

Answer: làƀémòs ↓

| | |
|---|---|
| 1 àlkílàn̥èlàpàrtàméntò ↓ | lo̯àlkílàn ↓ |
| 2 bùskámòzlòs̥ànúns̥yòs ↓ | lòzƀùskámòs ↓ |
| 3 tyénèlàz(l)y̥áƀès ↓ | làstyénè ↓ |
| 4 kómpra̯èláwtò ↓ | lòkómprà ↓ |

---

Problem: Vemos *la foto.*

Answer: La vemos.

| | |
|---|---|
| 1 Alquilan *el apartamento.* | Lo alquilan. |
| 2 Buscamos *los anuncios.* | Los buscamos. |
| 3 Tiene *las llaves.* | Las tiene. |
| 4 Compra *el auto.* | Lo compra. |

| | |
|---|---|
| 5 ėskrı́ƀȯlȯznómbrės ↓ | lȯṣėskrı́ƀȯ ↓ |
| 6 bémȯzla̯órȧ ↓ | lȧƀémȯs ↓ |
| 7 béo̯ėlȯtél ↓ | lȯƀéȯ ↓ |
| 8 lı́mpyȧnlȧṣȧƀıtȧṣ̯yónės ↓ | lȧzlı́mpyȧn ↓ |
| 9 (l)y̰éƀȧlȧsóđȧ ↓ | lȧ(l)y̰éƀȧ ↓ |

---

| | |
|---|---|
| 5 Escribo *los nombres.* | Los escribo. |
| 6 Vemos *la hora.* | La vemos. |
| 7 Veo *el hotel.* | Lo veo. |
| 8 Limpian *las habitaciones.* | Las limpian. |
| 9 Lleva *la soda.* | La lleva. |

Person - number substitution

1 ȧnȯsótrȯz ↑ nȯs̩ȧy̭úđȧhwán ↓

| | |
|---|---|
| a̭é(l)y̭ȯz ______ ↓ | a̭é(l)y̭ȯz ↑ lȯs̩ȧy̭úđȧhwán ↓ |
| ȧmí ______ ↓ | ȧmí ↑ me̯ȧy̭úđȧhwán ↓ |
| ȧhȯsé ______ ↓ | ȧhȯsé ↑ lo̯ȧy̭úđȧhwán ↓ |
| ȧkármėn ______ ↓ | ȧkármėn ↑ lȧy̭úđȧhwán ↓ |

---

1 A nosotros *nos* ayuda Juan.

| | |
|---|---|
| A ellos ______ . | A ellos los ayuda Juan. |
| A mí ______ . | A mí me ayuda Juan. |
| A José ______ . | A José lo ayuda Juan. |
| A Carmen ______ . | A Carmen la ayuda Juan. |

2 ȧmí ↑ nómėƀúskȧnáđyė ↓

| | |
|---|---|
| ȧnȯsótrȯz ________ ↓ | ȧnȯsótrȯz ↑ nónȯzƀúskȧnáđyė ↓ |
| a̯é(l)y̱ȧz ________ ↓ | a̯é(l)y̱ȧz ↑ nónȧzƀúskȧnáđyė ↓ |
| ȧlwísȧ ________ ↓ | ȧlwísȧ ↑ nólȧƀúskȧnáđyė ↓ |
| a̯él ________ ↓ | a̯él ↑ nólȯƀúskȧnáđyė ↓ |

---

2 A mí no *me* busca nadie.

| | |
|---|---|
| A nosotros ________ . | A nosotros no nos busca nadie. |
| A ellas ________ . | A ellas no las busca nadie. |
| A Luisa ________ . | A Luisa no la busca nadie. |
| A él ________ . | A él no lo busca nadie. |

3 a̯é(l)y̯ȧ ↑ lȧ(l)y̯éƀȧntónyȯ ↓

ȧhwán ______________________ ↓

ȧmí ______________________ ↓

ȧnȯsótrȯz ______________________ ↓

a̯é(l)y̯ȯz ______________________ ↓

ȧhwán ↑ lȯ(l)y̯éƀȧntónyȯ ↓

ȧmí ↑ mė(l)y̯éƀȧntónyȯ ↓

ȧnȯsótrȯz ↑ nȯz(l)y̯éƀȧntónyȯ ↓

a̯é(l)y̯ȯz ↑ lȯz(l)y̯éƀȧntónyȯ ↓

---

3 A ella *la* lleva Antonio.

A Juan ______________________ .

A mí ______________________ .

A nosotros ______________________ .

A ellos ______________________ .

A Juan lo lleva Antonio.

A mí me lleva Antonio.

A nosotros nos lleva Antonio.

A ellos los lleva Antonio.

## 10.21.22 TRANSLATION DRILL

| | | |
|---|---|---|
| 1 The pen? I don't have it. | làplúmà ↑ nólàtéŋgò ↓ | ¿La pluma? No la tengo. |
| 2 The keys? I don't have them. | làz(l)y̰áƀès ↑ nólàstéŋgò ↓ | ¿Las llaves? No las tengo. |
| 3 The bills? You have them. | lòzƀi(l)y̰étès ↑ ùstéđlòstyénè ↓ | ¿Los billetes? Ud. los tiene. |
| 4 The coins? You have them. | làzmònéđàs ↑ ùstéđlàstyénè ↓ | ¿Las monedas? Ud. las tiene. |
| 5 The information? Here it is. | la̯imfòrmàs̬yón ↑ àkílàtyénè ↓ | ¿La información? Aquí la tiene. |
| 6 The date? I don't have it. | làféchà ↑ nólàtéŋgò ↓ | ¿La fecha? No la tengo. |
| 7 The pie? I don't want it. | èlpàstél ↑ nólòkyérò ↓ | ¿El pastel? No lo quiero. |
| 8 The apartment? I haven't rented it. | èlàpàrtàméntò ↑ nólo̯éa̯lkìláđò ↓ | ¿El apartamento? No lo he alquilado. |
| 9 The travelers checks? I haven't sent them. | lòschékèzƀyàhéròs ↑ nólòs̩émàndáđò ↓ | ¿Los cheques viajeros? No los he mandado. |

10 The soup? I haven't tried it. lȧsópȧ ↑ nóla̯éprȯƀáđȯ ↓ ¿La sopa? No la he probado.

11 She never helps me. é(l)y̯ȧnúŋkȧ | me̯ȧy̯úđȧ ↓ Ella nunca me ayuda.

12 He always takes us there. élsyémprė | nȯz(l)y̯éƀȧí ↓ El siempre nos lleva ahí.

13 They take me downtown. é(l)y̯ȯz | mė(l)y̯éƀȧṇals̯éntrȯ ↓ Ellos me llevan al centro.

14 Who's looking for her? kyénlȧƀúskȧ ↓ ¿Quién la busca?

15 Who's looking for me? kyénmėƀúskȧ ↓ ¿Quién me busca?

## B. DISCUSSION OF PATTERN

Clitic pronouns are so designated because this term describes their dependence on verbs. They can appear only with (clinging to) verbs, and then in a very close relationship: nothing can ever occur between a clitic and the verb it appears with.

There are three classes of clitic pronouns in Spanish: direct, indirect, and reflexive. All clitics have certain features in common: they are weak-stressed (except for limited patterns in some dialect areas), they are included in the intonation phrase with the verb, and they occur in the same sequence relation with regard to the verb.

Clitics *precede* conjugated verbs (those with person-number endings) except for affirmative command forms which they must follow: not /me(l)yébe̯alotél ↓/, but /(l)yébeme̯aolotél ↓/; 'Take me to the hotel'. Clitics can also appear with certain nonconjugated verb forms, the infinitives and the /—ndo/ forms (see Unit 13); the clitics *follow* these forms /podémosbérlo ↑/ 'Can we see it?' The infinitive and /—ndo/ forms, however, frequently occur in verb constructions which include conjugated verb forms. In these constructions the clitic may either precede the conjugated verb or follow the nonconjugated verb and apparently the option implies no distinction in meaning: either /mekyéresbér ↑/ or /kyéresbérme ↑/ 'Do you want to see me?' Note, however, that a clitic cannot appear between the conjugated and nonconjugated verb forms.

Direct clitic pronouns are substitutable in a frame with (can be replaced by) nouns functioning as the direct object of a verb. Direct object nouns are identifiable by the appearance of the relater /a/ before them, if the noun refers to a specific person. Thus /bémos amaría ↓/ 'We see Mary' can be restated, once we know the reference, as /labémos ↓/ 'We see her'. Nonperson nouns functioning as a direct object can usually be identified by their position after the verb. Thus /bémoslakása ↓/ 'We see the house' can be restated as /labémos ↓/ 'We see it'.

Occasionally a direct object noun and a direct clitic pronoun may both appear with one verb. With person nouns, this 'redundant construction' may occasionally be used for contrast or clarity. The sentence /labémos | amaría ↓/ 'We see Mary' may imply María, not Carmen'. With nonperson nouns, a redundant construction is less common, but may occur if the noun object precedes the verb in a different intonation phrase separated usually by a terminal-rising juncture: /lostráhes ↑ losmándo̯ | alatıntorería ↓/ 'The suits, I send to the cleaners'. The intonation phrase division between /tráhes/ and /los/ is essential as it is in an English sentence of the same type. Constructions like * /lostráheslosmándo ↓/ or * /losmándolostráhes ↓/ do not occur. The last example becomes possible by the addition of a terminal juncture after /mándo ↓/ but this gives the second phrase the character of an afterthought: /losmándo ↓ lostráhes ↓/ 'I send them, I mean the suits.' Note, of course, that the personal /a/ does not occur with nonperson direct object nouns.

Direct clitic pronouns are inflected for person and number in all forms and for gender also in 2-3 forms. Note that /lo/ can mean 'you, him, it', /la/ can mean 'you, her, it', and similarly the plurals /los, las/. If any confusion results from this multiple reference possibility, it can be clarified by a redundant phrase. Along with the inflections for person, number, and gender, a few dialects, notably in Central Spain (the dialect usually referred to as 'Castilian'), make an additional distinction in the 2-3 forms, a person-nonperson distinction:

a clitic form /le/ refers to persons (you, him—and with some speakers—her) and /les/ (you all, them), though the forms described above also appear, and are preferred in some constructions. Nonperson objects are always referred to by the clitics /lo, la, los, las/. The difference between Spain and Latin America on this point is shown in the chart below:

| | | Castilian Spain | General Latin America | Reference | |
|---|---|---|---|---|---|
| Person | sg | le—béo (lo—béo) | lo—béo | a—él | a—ustéd |
| | | la—béo (le—béo) | la—béo | a—é(l)ya | |
| | pl | lo—béo (les—béo) | los—béo | a—é(l)yos | a—ustédes |
| | | las—béo (les—béo) | las—béo | a—é(l)yas | |
| Nonperson | sg | lo—béo | | el—líbro | |
| | | la—béo | | la—plúma | |
| | pl | los—béo | | los—líbros | |
| | | las—béo | | las—plúmas | |

A student might do well to notice the similarity and correlation between direct clitic pronouns and definite articles. Both occur normally under weak stress, both frequently occur in a position that precedes the word that they are grammatically most closely associated with (articles before a noun and clitics before a verb), and three of the four forms are identical in form:

<table>
<tr><th></th><th>Definite Article</th><th>Direct Clitic</th></tr>
<tr><td>m sg</td><td>el</td><td>lo</td></tr>
<tr><td>f sg</td><td colspan="2">la</td></tr>
<tr><td>m pl</td><td colspan="2">los</td></tr>
<tr><td>f pl</td><td colspan="2">las</td></tr>
<tr><td>neuter</td><td colspan="2">lo</td></tr>
</table>

A probable answer to /tyénelaplúma ↑/ is /sí | laténgo ↓/, where the form of the article is a direct key to the selection of the form of the clitic.

Spelling conventions recognize the close relationship of verb and clitic when the clitic follows the verb by writing both as one word. Although this same close relationship prevails when the clitic precedes the verb, they are written in the spelling system as two words, that is, with space between the clitic and verb.

## 10.21.3 /—do/ forms functioning as modifiers

### A. PRESENTATION OF PATTERN

*ILLIISTRATIONS*

| | | |
|---|---|---|
| Joseph: 'Pleased to meet you'. | 1 hȯsé ↓ ėŋkȧntáđȯđėkȯnȯs̯érlȧ ↓ | José: '*Encantado* de conocerla'. |
| Mary: 'Pleased to meet you'. | 2 mȧríȧ ↓ ėŋkȧntáđȧđėkȯnȯs̯érlȯ ↓ | Maria: '*Encantada* de conocerlo'. |
| ______________________ | 3 ı̯ùstéđ ↓ éskȧsáđȯ ↑ | Y usted, ¿es *casado?* |
| And you, Mary, are you married? | 4 itú \| mȧríȧ ↓ érėskȧsáđȧ ↑ | Y tú, María, ¿eres *casada?* |
| ______________________ | 5 ȧ(l)y̰áyu̇nȧmésȧ \| đėsȯku̇páđȧ ↓ | Allá hay una mesa *desocupada.* |
| ______________________ | 6 sólȯtéŋgȯ \| đózđėsȯku̇páđȯs ↓ | Sólo tengo dos *desocupados.* |
| ______________________ | 7 kásisyémpre̯ \| ėstámozmúyȯku̇páđȯs ↓ | Casi siempre estamos muy *ocupados.* |

*EXTRAPOLATION*

| | |
|---|---|
| —ádo(s) | —ído(s) |
| —a(s) | —a(s) |

*NOTES*

a. /—do/ forms, when functioning as modifiers, are inflected for number and gender, like other regular fully inflected adjectives.

## 10.21.31 SUBSTITUTION DRILL

Item substitution

1 ái | áyùnàmésà | đèsòkùpáđà ↓

_______ ùnáwtò _______________ ↓ ái | áyùnáwtò | đèsòkùpáđò ↓

_______ ùnà(s)sí(l)yàz _______________ ↓ ái | áyùnà(s)sí(l)yàz | đèsòkùpáđàs ↓

2 ésèsènyór | èskàsáđò ↓

ésàsènyórà _______________ ↓ ésàsènyórà | èskàsáđà ↓

ésò(s)sènyórès _______________ ↓ ésò(s)sènyórès | sòŋkàsáđòs ↓

---

1 Ahí hay una mesa *desocupada*.

_______ un auto _______________ . Ahí hay un auto desocupado.

_______ unas sillas _______________ . Ahí hay unas sillas desocupadas.

2 Ese señor es *casado*.

Esa señora _______________ . Esa señora es casada.

Esos señores _______________ . Esos señores son casados.

3 ėlȧpȧrtȧménto̯ | ėstálkilá𝑑ȯ ↓

lȧkásą ________________ ↓ | lȧkásą | ėstálkilá𝑑ȧ ↓
lȯṣė𝑑ifíṣyȯs ________________ ↓ | lȯṣė𝑑ifíṣyȯs | ėstánąlkilá𝑑ȯs ↓

4 lȧsálą | ėstárrėglá𝑑ȧ ↓

lȧskámȧs ________________ ↓ | lȧskámȧs | ėstánąrrėglá𝑑ȧs ↓
ėldȯrmitóryo̯ ________________ ↓ | ėldȯrmitóryo̯ | ėstárrėglá𝑑ȯ ↓

5 lȧsėkrėtáryą | ėstáo̯kupá𝑑ȧ ↓

lȯzmóṣȯs ________________ ↓ | lȯzmóṣȯs | ėstánọkupá𝑑ȯs ↓
ėlchȯfér ________________ ↓ | ėlchȯfér | ėstáo̯kupá𝑑ȯ ↓

---

3 El apartamento está *alquilado*.

La casa ________________ . | La casa está alquilada.
Los edificios ________________ . | Los edificios están alquilados.

4 La sala está *arreglada*.

Las camas ________________ . | Las camas están arregladas.
El dormitorio ________________ . | El dormitorio está arreglado.

5 La secretaria está *ocupada*.

Los mozos ________________ . | Los mozos están ocupados.
El chofer ________________ . | El chofer está ocupado.

## 10.21.32 TRANSLATION DRILL

| | | |
|---|---|---|
| 1 I have a vacant apartment. | téŋgo̯ l ùna̯pàrtàméntȯ l đėsȯkùpáđȯ ↓ | Tengo un apartamento desocupado. |
| 2 That young lady is happy here. | ésàsėn̯yórıta̯ l ėstáeŋkàntáđa̯ l àkí ↓ | Esa señorita está encantada aquí. |
| 3 The secretaries are happy here. | là(s)sėkrėtáryȧs l ėstáne̯ŋkàntáđȧs l àkí ↓ | Las secretarias están encantadas aquí. |
| 4 At the language school they're very busy. | ėnla̯ėskwéla l đėléŋgwȧs ↑ ėstánmúy ȯkùpáđȯs ↓ | En la escuela de lenguas están muy ocupados. |
| 5 The chauffeur is busy. | ėlchȯfér l ėstáo̯kùpáđȯ ↓ | El chofer está ocupado. |
| 6 The house is rented. | làkása̯ l ėstálkıláđȧ ↓ | La casa está alquilada. |
| 7 I have a vacant house, too. | tàmbyén l téŋgo̯ùnȧkásȧ l đėsȯkùpáđȧ ↓ | También tengo una casa desocupada. |
| 8 She's not single; she's married. | é(l)y̯àno̯é(s)sȯltérȧ ↓ ėskȧsáđȧ ↓ | Ella no es soltera. Es casada. |
| 9 They're married. | é(l)y̯ȯ(s)sȯŋkȧsáđȯs ↓ | Ellos son casados. |

| | | |
|---|---|---|
| 10 The rooms are rented. | lòskwártòs \| èstánạlkiládòs ↓ | Los cuartos están alquilados. |
| 11 The apartment is quite fixed up. | èlàpàrtàméntọ \| èstámúyàrrèglá∂ò ↓ | El apartamento está muy arreglado. |

## B. DISCUSSION OF PATTERN

The /—do/ forms, when they appear in constructions other than those with /abér/, are functioning as modifiers. In this function they have full adjective inflections for number and gender. They can appear with nouns (normally following the noun): /únamésa | desokupáda ↓/; after certain verbs, most commonly /sér/ or /estár/ but also such verbs as /pareşér/:/éskasádọ ustéd ↑ estámosọkupados ↓ paréşekansádo ↓/; in the so-called 'absolute' construction: /enkantádadekonoşér la ↓/ or nominalized: /kwáleşelkasádo ↓ eldesokupádọ | estáẹnẹlşéntro ↓/. Usage has established some /—do/ forms as nouns, which now have a single gender form with no gender alternation permitted: /lạentráda ↓ lakomída ↓/. For contrast, compare /unkonoşídomío ↓ unakonoşídamía ↓/.

CD 8

Tape 8A

## 10.22 REPLACEMENT DRILLS

A mėmúđo̯ėlsáƀȧđȯ ↓

| | |
|---|---|
| 1 tė________________________ ↓ | tėmúđȧṣėlsáƀȧđȯ ↓ |
| 2 __________ ƀás ___________ ↓ | tėƀáṣėlsáƀȧđȯ ↓ |
| 3 ___________ éstė ___________ ↓ | tėƀás \| éstėsáƀȧđȯ ↓ |
| 4 _____________________ nóchė ↓ | tėƀás \| éstȧnóchė ↓ |
| 5 mė_______________________ ↓ | mėƀóy \| éstȧnóchė ↓ |
| 6 ____________________ hwéƀės ↓ | mėƀóy \| éstėhwéƀės ↓ |
| 7 ____________ ėl ____________ ↓ | mėƀóyėlhwéƀės ↓ |

---

A Me mudo el sábado.

| | |
|---|---|
| 1 Te________________________ . | Te mudas el sábado. |
| 2 _________ vas ______________ . | Te vas el sábado. |
| 3 ___________ este ___________ . | Te vas este sábado. |
| 4 ______________________ noche. | Te vas esta noche. |
| 5 Me________________________ . | Me voy esta noche. |
| 6 ______________________ jueves. | Me voy este jueves. |
| 7 __________ el ______________ . | Me voy el jueves. |

CD 8 Tape 8A

| | |
|---|---|
| B dóndėmándȧs \| tu̇rrópȧ ↓ | |
| 1 ______________ kósȧs ↓ | dóndėmándȧs \| tu̇skósȧs ↓ |
| 2 _____ (l)y̬éƀȧs ______________ ↓ | dóndė(l)y̬éƀȧs \| tu̇skósȧs ↓ |
| 3 kómȯ______________ ↓ | kómȯ(l)y̬éƀȧs \| tu̇skósȧs ↓ |
| 4 ________ éstȧs ______________ ↓ | kómȯ(l)y̬éƀȧs \| éstȧskósȧs ↓ |
| 5 ________ đės̮íđės______________ ↓ | kómȯđės̮íđės \| éstȧskósȧs ↓ |
| 6 kyén ______________ ↓ | kyéndės̮íđe̯ \| éstȧskósȧs ↓ |
| 7 ________ ás̮e̯ ______________ ↓ | kyénạ́s̮e̯ \| éstȧskósȧs ↓ |

---

| | |
|---|---|
| B Dónde mandas tu ropa? | |
| 1 ¿ ______________ cosas? | ¿Dónde mandas tus cosas? |
| 2 ¿ ________ llevas______________ ? | ¿Dónde llevas tus cosas? |
| 3 ¿Cómo ______________ ? | ¿Cómo llevas tus cosas? |
| 4 ¿ __________ estas __________ ? | ¿Cómo llevas estas cosas? |
| 5 ¿ _______ decides ___________ ? | ¿Cómo decides estas cosas? |
| 6 ¿Quién ______________ ? | ¿Quién decide estas cosas? |
| 7 ¿ _______ hace______________ ? | ¿Quién hace estas cosas? |

CD 8
Tape 8A

C y̯ómízmȯ | lȧz(l)y̯éƀȯ ↓

| | |
|---|---|
| 1 lȧnóƀyȧ ____________ ↓ | lȧnóƀyȧmízmȧ \| lȧz(l)y̯éƀȧ ↓ |
| 2 ____________ mándȧ ↓ | lȧnóƀyȧmízmȧ \| lȧzmándȧ ↓ |
| 3 nȯsótrȯz ____________ ↓ | nȯsótrȯzmízmȯz \| lȧzmȧndámȯs ↓ |
| 4 ______ tȧmbyén ______ ↓ | nȯsótrȯs \| tȧmbyénlȧzmȧndámȯs ↓ |
| 5 ____________ ȧs̯émȯs ↓ | nȯsótrȯs \| tȧmbyénlȧsȧs̯émȯs ↓ |
| 6 ȯstéđ ____________ ↓ | ȯstéđ \| tȧmbyénlȧsás̯ė ↓ |
| 7 ______ núŋkȧ ______ ↓ | ȯstéđ \| núŋkȧlȧsás̯ė ↓ |

---

C Yo mismo las llevo.

| | |
|---|---|
| 1 La novía ____________ . | La novia misma las lleva. |
| 2 ____________ manda. | La novia misma las manda. |
| 3 Nosotros ____________ . | Nosotros mismos las mandamos. |
| 4 ______ también ______ . | Nosotros también las mandamos. |
| 5 ____________ hacemos. | Nosotros también las hacemos. |
| 6 Ud. ____________ . | Ud. también las hace. |
| 7 ______ nunca ______ . | Ud. nunca las hace. |

D u̇nȧmu̇cháchȧ | kėƀyénė | tóđȯzlȯshwéƀės ↓

| | |
|---|---|
| 1 ______________ sėmánȧs ↓ | u̇nȧmu̇cháchȧ \| kėƀyénė \| tóđȧzlȧ(s)sėmánȧs ↓ |
| 2 ________ prȧktíkȧ __________ ↓ | u̇nȧmu̇cháchȧ \| kėprȧktíkȧ \| tóđȧzlȧ(s)sėmánȧs ↓ |
| 3 ________ ómbrė __________ ↓ | u̇ṇómbrė \| kėprȧktíkȧ \| tóđȧzlȧ(s)sėmánȧs ↓ |
| 4 los ______________________ ↓ | lȯṣómbrės \| kėprȧktíkȧn \| tóđȧzlȧ(s)sėmánȧs ↓ |
| 5 ______________________ díȧs ↓ | lȯṣómbrės \| kėprȧktíkȧn \| tóđȯzlȯzđíȧs ↓ |
| 6 ________ límpyȧn __________ ↓ | lȯṣómbrės \| kėlímpyȧn \| tóđȯzlȯzđíȧs ↓ |
| 7 _______ móṣȯs __________ ↓ | lȯzmóṣȯs \| kėlímpyȧn \| tóđȯzlȯzđíȧs ↓ |

---

D Una muchacha que viene todos los jueves.

| | |
|---|---|
| 1 ____________________ semanas. | Una muchacha que viene todas las semanas. |
| 2 __________ practica __________ . | Una muchacha que practica todas las semanas. |
| 3 ________ hombre ____________ . | Un hombre que practica todas las semanas. |
| 4 Los ________________________ . | Los hombres que practican todas las semanas. |
| 5 _______________________ días. | Los hombres que practican todos los días. |
| 6 ___________ limpian _________ . | Los hombres que limpian todos los días. |
| 7 _______ mozos ______________ . | Los mozos que limpian todos los días. |

E sikyérėz ↑ y̯óle̯áƀlȯ ↓

| | |
|---|---|
| 1 ____________ ėskríƀȯ ↓ | sikyérėz ↑ y̯ólėskríƀȯ ↓ |
| 2 ______ nȯsótrȯz ______ ↓ | sikyérėz ↑ nȯsótrȯzlėskribímȯs ↓ |
| 3 ____ tėpáre̥sė ________ ↓ | sitėpáre̥sė ↑ nȯsótrȯzlėskribímȯs ↓ |
| 4 ________ tú ______ ↓ | sitėpáre̥sė ↑ túlėskríƀės ↓ |
| 5 ____________ áƀlȧs ↓ | sitėpáre̥sė ↑ túle̯áƀlȧs ↓ |
| 6 ____ pwéđės________ ↓ | sipwéđės ↑ túle̯áƀlȧs ↓ |
| 7 ____________ đís̥ės ↓ | sipwéđės ↑ túlėđís̥ės ↓ |

---

E Si quieres, yo le hablo.

| | |
|---|---|
| 1 ______ , ________ escribo. | Si quieres, yo le escribo. |
| 2 ______ , nosotros ________ . | Si quieres, nosotros le escribimos. |
| 3 ____ te parece, ________ . | Si te parece, nosotros le escribimos. |
| 4 ________ , tú ________ . | Si te parece, tú le escribes. |
| 5 ________ , ________ hablas. | Si te parece, tú le hablas. |
| 6 _____ puedes, ________ . | Si puedes, tú le hablas. |
| 7 ________ , ________ dices. | Si puedes, tú le dices. |

F ántėz ↓ nȯkyérės | ótrȯtrágȯ ↑

| | |
|---|---|
| 1 ______________________ kósȧ ↑ | ántėz ↓ nȯkyérės \| ótrȧkósȧ ↑ |
| 2 dėspwéz ___________________ ↑ | dėspwéz ↓ nȯkyérės \| ótrȧkósȧ ↑ |
| 3 ________ ás̯ės ______________ ↑ | dėspwéz ↓ no̯ás̯ės \| ótrȧkósȧ ↑ |
| 4 ____________ ésȧs __________ ↑ | dėspwéz ↓ no̯ás̯ės \| ésȧskósȧs ↑ |
| 5 ėntóns̯ėz ___________________ ↑ | ėntóns̯ėz ↓ no̯ás̯ės \| ésȧskósȧs ↑ |
| 6 __________ syéntės__________ ↑ | ėntóns̯ėz ↓ nȯsyéntės \| ésȧskósȧs ↑ |
| 7 lwégȯ _____________________ ↑ | lwégȯ ↓ nȯsyéntės \| ésȧskósȧs ↑ |

---

F Antes, ¿no quieres otro trago?

| | |
|---|---|
| 1 _______ , ¿ _____________ cosa? | Antes, ¿no quieres otra cosa? |
| 2 Después, ¿ _________________ ? | Después, ¿no quieres otra cosa? |
| 3 ______ , ¿ ____ haces ________ ? | Después, ¿no haces otra cosa? |
| 4 ______ , ¿ ______ esas _______ ? | Después, ¿no haces esas cosas? |
| 5 Entonces, ¿ _________________ ? | Entonces, ¿no haces esas cosas? |
| 6 _______ , ¿ ____ sientes ______ ? | Entonces, ¿no sientes esas cosas? |
| 7 Luego, ¿ ___________________ ? | Luego, ¿no sientes esas cosas? |

## 10.23 VARIATION DRILLS

| | | | |
|---|---|---|---|
| A | ėmfı́n ↓ y̯áe̯stȧlı́stȯtóđȯ ↓ | | En fin, ya está listo todo. |
| | 1 Well, the pie's ready. | ėmfı́n ↓ y̯áe̯stȧlı́sto̯ \| ėlpȧstél ↓ | En fin, ya está listo el pastel. |
| | 2 Well, the clothes're ready. | ėmfı́n ↓ y̯áe̯stȧlı́stȧ \| lȧrrópȧ ↓ | En fin, ya está lista la ropa. |
| | 3 Well, the soup's ready. | ėmfı́n ↓ y̯áe̯stȧlı́stȧ \| lȧsópȧ ↓ | En fin, ya está lista la sopa. |
| | 4 Well, the pork-chops're ready. | ėmfı́n ↓ y̯áe̯stȧnlı́stȧz \| lȧschulétȧs ↓ | En fin, ya están listas las chuletas. |
| | 5 Well, the drinks're ready. | ėmfı́n ↓ y̯áe̯stȧnlı́stȯz \| lȯstrágȯs ↓ | En fin, ya están listos los tragos. |
| | 6 Well, the hotel's already old. | ėmfı́n ↓ y̯áe̯stȧƀyého̯ėlȯtél ↓ | En fin, ya está viejo el hotel. |
| | 7 Well, the car's already fixed. | ėmfı́n ↓ y̯áe̯stȧrrėgláđo̯ \| ėláwtȯ ↓ | En fin, ya está arreglado el auto. |
| B | y̯ó \| tėpwéđo̯ȧy̯ųđár \| kȯnlȧzmȧlétȧs ↓ | | Yo te puedo ayudar con las maletas. |
| | 1 I can help you with the salad. | y̯ó \| tėpwéđo̯ȧy̯ųđár \| kȯnla̯ėnsȧláđȧ ↓ | Yo te puedo ayudar con la ensalada. |
| | 2 I can help you with your dessert. | y̯ó \| tėpwéđo̯ȧy̯ųđár \| kȯne̯lpóstrė ↓ | Yo te puedo ayudar con el postre. |
| | 3 I can use 'tú' with you. | y̯ótėpwéđȯ \| trȧtárđėtú ↓ | Yo te puedo tratar de 'tú'. |

| | | |
|---|---|---|
| 4 I can rent the house to you. | y̯ótėpwéđo̯ \| ȧlkılárlȧkásȧ ↓ | Yo te puedo alquilar la casa. |
| 5 I can look for the wine for you. | y̯ótėpwéđȯ \| ƀuskárėlbínȯ ↓ | Yo te puedo buscar el vino. |
| 6 I can take you to the wedding. | y̯ótėpwéđo̯ \| (l)y̯ėƀáralȧƀóđȧ ↓ | Yo te puedo llevar a la boda. |
| 7 I can give you an idea, more or less. | y̯ótėpwéđo̯ \| đárúna̯ıđéȧ ↓ mása̯méno̧s ↓ | Yo te puedo dar una idea, más o menos. |

**End of Tape 8A**

| | | |
|---|---|---|
| C | lȯstráhėz ↑ lȯzmándo̯alȧtıntȯrėríȧ ↓ | Los trajes, los mando a la tintorería. |
| 1 I'll send the ashtrays to the living room. | lȯs(s̯)ėnis̯érȯz ↑ lȯzmándo̯alȧsálȧ ↓ | Los ceniceros, los mando a la sala. |
| 2 I'll send the desks to the consular section. | lȯs̯ėskritóryȯz ↑ lȯzmándo̯ \| ȧlȧ sėks̯yóŋkȯnsulár ↓ | Los escritorios, los mando a la sección consular. |
| 3 I'll send the books to the school of languages. | lȯzlíƀrȯz ↑ lȯzmándo̯ \| ȧla̯ėskwélȧ đėléŋgwȧs ↓ | Los libros, los mando a la escuela de lenguas. |
| 4 I'll send the drinks to the room. | lȯstrágȯz ↑ lȯzmándo̯alkwártȯ ↓ | Los tragos, los mando al cuarto. |
| 5 I'll send the 'cuba libres' to the apartment. | lȯskúƀȧlíƀrėz ↑ lȯzmándo̯al ȧpartȧméntȯ ↓ | Los cuba libres, los mando al apartamento. |

| | | |
|---|---|---|
| 6 I'll send the newspapers to the Embassy. | lȯspėryóđıkȯz ↑ lȯzmándo̯ala̯ ėmbȧháđȧ ↓ | Los periódicos, los mando a la Embajada. |
| 7 I'll send the shirts to the laundry. | lȧskȧmísȧz ↑ lȧzmándo̯alȧ lȧƀandėríȧ ↓ | Las camisas, las mando a la lavandería. |

| | | |
|---|---|---|
| D kyéntėlímpya̯ \| ėlȧpȧrtȧméntȯ ↓ | | ¿Quién te limpia el apartamento? |
| 1 Who sends you the newspaper? | kyéntėmánda̯ \| ėlpėryóđikȯ ↓ | ¿Quién te manda el periódico? |
| 2 Who buys the shirts for you? | kyéntėkómprȧ \| lȧskȧmísȧs ↓ | ¿Quién te compra las camisas? |
| 3 Who cashes the checks for you? | kyéntėkámbyȧ \| lȯschékės ↓ | ¿Quién te cambia los cheques? |
| 4 Who talks to you in Spanish? | kyénte̯áƀla̯ \| ėne̯spanyól ↓ | ¿Quién te habla en español? |
| 5 Who takes you downtown? | kyéntė(l)y̯éƀals̯éntrȯ ↓ | ¿Quién te lleva al centro? |
| 6 Who's waiting for you there? | kyéntėspérȧí ↓ | ¿Quién te espera ahí? |
| 7 Who helps you? | kyénte̯ay̯úđȧ ↓ | ¿Quién te ayuda? |

| | | | |
|---|---|---|---|
| E | | yáe̯stárđė ↓ téŋgȯke̯írmė ↓ | Ya es tarde. Tengo que irme. |
| | 1 It's late. I've got to study. | yáe̯stárđė ↓ téŋgȯkėstůđyár ↓ | Ya es tarde. Tengo que estudiar. |
| | 2 It's late. I've got to change clothes. | yáe̯stárđė ↓ téŋgȯ \| kėkȧmbyármė đėrrópȧ ↓ | Ya es tarde. Tengo que cambiarme de ropa. |
| | 3 I've got to move. | téŋgȯ \| kėmůđármėđėkásȧ ↓ | Tengo que mudarme de casa. |
| | 4 I've got to go back. | téŋgȯkėƀȯlbér ↓ | Tengo que volver. |
| | 5 He's got to go. | tyénėke̯ír ↓ | Tiene que ir. |
| | 6 We've got to go up. | tėnémȯskėsůƀír ↓ | Tenemos que subir. |
| | 7 They've got to go down. | tyénėŋkėƀȧhár ↓ | Tienen que bajar. |
| F | | mȧn̦yánáy \| kėtrȧƀȧhár ↓ | Mañana hay que trabajar. |
| | 1 You have to clean tomorrow. | mȧn̦yánáy \| kėlímpyár ↓ | Mañana hay que limpiar. |
| | 2 You have to return tomorrow. | mȧn̦yánáy \| kėƀȯlbér ↓ | Mañana hay que volver. |
| | 3 You have to decide soon. | prónto̯áy \| kėđėsiđír ↓ | Pronto hay que decidir. |

| | | |
|---|---|---|
| 4 You'll have to bring another one soon. | prónto̯ ǀ áykėtrȧėrótrȯ ↓ | Pronto hay que traer otro. |
| 5 You'll have to study on Monday. | ė(l)lúnės ǀ áykėstuđyár ↓ | El lunes hay que estudiar. |
| 6 You'll have to practice on Friday. | ėlbyérnės ǀ áykėprȧktıkár ↓ | El viernes hay que practicar. |
| 7 You won't have to work on Saturday. | ėlsáƀȧđȯ ǀ no̯áykėtrȧƀahár ↓ | El sábado no hay que trabajar. |

## 10.24 REVIEW DRILL

Theme class in present tense forms

| | | |
|---|---|---|
| 1 He talks and eats a lot. | áƀla̯ ǀ ıkómėmúchȯ ↓ | Habla y come mucho. |
| 2 He studies and lives here. | ėstúđya̯ ǀ ıƀíƀe̯akí ↓ | Estudia y vive aquí. |
| 3 He works and lives there. | trȧƀáha̯ ǀ ıƀíƀe̯aí ↓ | Trabaja y vive ahí. |
| 4 He works and eats very little. | trȧƀáha̯ ǀ ikómėmúypókȯ ↓ | Trabaja y come muy poco. |
| 5 We study and eat here. | ėstůđyámȯs ǀ ikȯmémȯs̯akí ↓ | Estudiamos y comemos aquí. |
| 6 We work and eat too much. | trȧƀȧhámȯs ǀ ikȯmémȯzđėmȧsyáđȯ ↓ | Trabajamos y comemos demasiado. |
| 7 We talk and write a lot. | ȧƀlámȯs ǀ i̯ėskriƀímȯzmúchȯ ↓ | Hablamos y escribimos mucho. |

| | | |
|---|---|---|
| 8 We work and live here. | tràƀàhámòs \| iƀiƀímòs̩akí ↓ | Trabajamos y vivimos aquí. |
| 9 We go down and come up very little. | bàhámòs \| isùƀímòzmúypókò ↓ | Bajamos y subimos muy poco. |
| 10 They go down and come up a lot. | báhàn \| ˙ısúƀènmúchò ↓ | Bajan y suben mucho. |
| 11 They work and live in the United States. | tràƀáhàn \| iƀíƀèn \| ènlòs̩èstáđòs̩ùníđòs ↓ | Trabajan y viven en los Estados Unidos. |
| 12 They talk and write very well. | áƀlàn \| ı̯èskríƀènmúyƀyén ↓ | Hablan y escriben muy bien. |
| 13 They study and eat very little. | èstúđyàn \| ikómènmúypókò ↓ | Estudian y comen muy poco. |

## 10.3 CONVERSATION STIMULUS

### NARRATIVE 1

| | | |
|---|---|---|
| 1 Juan likes the apartment. | àhwán ↑ lègúst̯a \| èlàpàrtàméntò ↓ | A Juan le gusta el apartamento. |
| 2 He's going to take it. | bátòmárlò ↓ | Va a tomarlo. |
| 3 He plans to move this week. | pyénsàmùđárs̯e \| éstàsèmánà ↓ | Piensa mudarse esta semana. |
| 4 But he hasn't decided what day. | pèròno̯áđès̩ıđíđò \| kéđíà ↓ | Pero no ha decidido qué día. |

| | | |
|---|---|---|
| 5 If the apartment is ready, he'll move on Saturday. | si̯èlàpàrtàméntọèstálísto ↑ sè múđa̯èlsáƀàđò ↓ | Si el apartamento está listo, se muda el sábado. |
| 6 Saturday is a good day. | èlsáƀàđọ \| èsùmbwéndíà ↓ | El sábado es un buen día. |
| 7 You don't have to work. | nọáykètràƀàhár ↓ | No hay que trabajar. |

## DIALOG 1

| | | |
|---|---|---|
| José, pregúntele a Juan que si le gusta el apartamento. | tèɡústa̯èlàpartàménto ↑ | José: ¿Te gusta el apartamento? |
| Juan, contéstele que sí, que va a tomarlo, que está muy bonito. | sí ↓ ƀóyàtòmárlò ↓ èstámúyƀònítò ↓ | Juan: Sí, voy a tomarlo. Está muy bonito. |
| José, pregúntele que cuándo piensa mudarse. | kwándòpyénsàzmùđártè ↓ | José: ¿Cuándo piensas mudarte? |
| Juan, contéstele que Ud. cree que esta semana. | kréòkéstàsèmánà ↓ | Juan: Creo que esta semana. |
| José, pregúntele si ha decidido qué día. | ázđèsiđíđò \| kéđíà ↑ | José ¿Has decidido qué día? |
| Juan, contéstele que si el apartamento está listo, se muda el sábado. | si̯èlàpàrtàméntọèstálísto ↑ mèmúđọèlsáƀàđò ↓ | Juan: Si el apartamento está listo, me mudo el sábado. |

| | | |
|---|---|---|
| José, dígale que sí, que el sábado es un buen día. Que no hay que trabajar. | sí ↓ ėlsáƀȧđọ \| ėṣụmbwéndíȧ ↓ nọáykėtrȧƀȧhár ↓ | José: Sí, el sábado es un buen día. No hay que trabajar. |

## NARRATIVE 2

| | | |
|---|---|---|
| 1 It seems that José and Juan are going to be neighbors, then. | pȧréṣė \| kėhȯséịhwám \| bánạsér ƀéṣınȯs \| ėntónṣės ↓ | Parece que José y Juan van a ser vecinos entonces. |
| 2 José can help Juan move his things. | hȯsé \| pwéđẹȧyụđárȧhwán \| ȧpȧsár sụskósȧs ↓ | José puede ayudar a Juan a pasar sus cosas. |
| 3 What John has isn't much. | nọézmúchȯ \| lȯkėtyénėhwán ↓ | No es mucho lo que tiene Juan. |
| 4 He can move them himself. | élmízmȯ \| pwéđėpȧsárlȧs ↓ | El mismo puede pasarlas. |
| 5 But Jose's got a car. | pėrȯhȯsé \| tyénẹáwtȯ ↓ | Pero José tiene auto. |
| 6 It's easier that way. | ėzmásfáṣil \| ȧsí ↓ | Es más fácil así. |

## DIALOG 2

| | | |
|---|---|---|
| José, dígale a Juan que parece que Uds. van a ser vecinos, entonces. | pȧréṣė ǀ kėƀámȯṣȧsér ǀ ƀėṣınȯs ǀ ėntónṣės ↓ | José: Parece que vamos a ser vecinos, entonces. |
| Juan, dígale que así parece. | ȧsípȧréṣė ↓ | Juan: Así parece. |
| José, dígale que Ud. le puede ayudar a pasar las cosas. | y̦ótėpwéđọȧy̦úđar ǀ ȧpȧsárlȧskósȧs ↓ | José: Yo te puedo ayudar a pasar las cosas. |
| Juan, dígale que no se moleste. Que Ud. mismo las puede pasar. Que no es mucho lo que tiene. | nótėmȯléstės ↓ y̦ȯmízmȯ ǀ lȧspwéđȯ pȧsár ↓ nọézmúchȯ ǀ lȯkėtéŋgȯ ↓ | Juan: No te molestes. Yo mismo las puedo pasar. No es mucho lo que tengo. |
| José, pero Ud. tiene auto, dígale. Dígale que es más fácil así. | pėrȯy̦ótéŋgọ ǀ áwtȯ ↓ ėzmásfáṣil ǀ ȧsí ↓ | José: Pero yo tengo auto. Es más fácil así. |
| Juan, dígale que bueno, que muy agradecido. | bwénȯ ↓ múyȧgrȧdėṣíđȯ ↓ | Juan: Bueno, muy agradecido. |

## NARRATIVE 3

| | | |
|---|---|---|
| 1 Another thing. Where can Juan take his clothes to be washed? | ótrȧkósȧ ↓ dóndėpwéđėhwán ǀ (l)y̦ėƀár sȯrrópȧlȧƀár ↓ | Otra cosa. ¿Dónde puede Juan llevar su ropa a lavar? |

| | | |
|---|---|---|
| 2 There's a laundry on the corner and a cleaner's around the corner. | áyùnàlàƀàndèría \| ènlàèskína ↑ ìùnàtintòrérialàƀwéltà ↓ | Hay una lavandería en la esquina y una tintorería a la vuelta. |
| 3 But he can't take his clothes there himself. | pèròèlmízmò \| nópwédè(l)yèƀár \| sùrrópàí ↓ | Pero él mismo no puede llevar su ropa ahí. |
| 4 This is not the United States. | éstònóez \| lòsèstáđòsùníđòs ↓ | Esto no es los Estados Unidos. |
| 5 The girl who cleans his apartment will take them, then. | làmùchácha \| kèlímpyàsùàpàrtàméntò ↑ lá(l)yéƀà \| èntónsès ↓ | La muchacha que limpia su apartamento la lleva, entonces. |

## DIALOG 3

| | | |
|---|---|---|
| Juan, dígale a José que otra cosa. Pregúntele que dónde puede llevar la ropa a lavar. | ótràkósà \| hòsé ↓ dóndèpwéđò(l)yèbár \| làrrópàlàƀár ↓ | Juan: Otra cosa, José. ¿Dónde puedo llevar la ropa a lavar? |
| José, contéstele que hay una lavandería en la esquina y una tintorería a la vuelta. | áyùnàlàƀàndèría \| ènlàèskína ↑ ìùnà tintòrèríalàƀwéltà ↓ | José: Hay una lavandería en la esquina y una tintorería a la vuelta. |
| Juan, pregúntele que si él mismo la lleva. | túmízmòlà(l)yéƀàs ↑ | Juan: ¿Tú mismo la llevas? |
| José, contéstele que no, hombre, que nunca. Que aquí no estamos en los Estados Unidos. | nó \| ómbrè ↓ núŋkà ↓ àkí \| nòestámòs \| ènlòsèstáđòsùníđòs ↓ | José: No, hombre, nunca. Aquí no estamos en los Estados Unidos. |

| | | |
|---|---|---|
| Juan, pregúntele que cómo hace él, entonces. | kómo͡ạ́ṣėṣ \| ėntónṣėṣ ↓ | Juan: ¿Cómo haces, entonces? |
| Jose, contéstele que la muchacha que limpia su apartamento la lleva. | lȧmu̇cháchȧ \| kėlímpyȧmı͡ȧpȧrtȧméntȯ \| lȧ(l)y̰éb̶ȧ ↓ | Jose: La muchacha que limpia mi apartamento la lleva. |

# 11.1 BASIC SENTENCES

## White interviews a maid

The woman who cleans Molina's apartment comes to be interviewed by White.

| English Spelling | Aid to Listening | Spanish Spelling |
|---|---|---|
| *MAID* | | *SIRVIENTA* |
| Good afternoon, sir. | bwénȧstárđės \| sėn̯yór ↓ | Buenas tardes, señor. |
| *WHITE* | | *WHITE* |
| Good afternoon. What can I do for you? | bwénȧstárđės ↓ kéđėséȧ ↓ | Buenas tardes, ¿qué desea? |
| the one that | lá—kė ↓ | la que |
| *MAID* | | *SIRVIENTA* |
| I'm the one that cleans Mr. Molina's apartment. | y̯osóy \| lȧkėlímpya̯ \| ėlȧpȧrtȧméntȯ \| đėlsėn̯yórmȯlínȧ ↓ | Yo soy la que limpia el apartamento del Sr. Molina. |
| *WHITE* | | *WHITE* |
| Oh, yes. Can you clean mine, too? | á ↓ múybyén ↓ pwéđėlímpyár ↑ ėlmíȯtȧmbyén ↑ | ¡Ah! Muy bien. ¿Puede limpiar el mío también? |
| the yours | ėl—súy̯ȯ ↓ | el suyo |
| isn't it?, didn't he?, haven't they?, etc. | nó ↑ | no |

| | | |
|---|---|---|
| *MAID* | | *SIRVIENTA* |
| Yours is blgger, isn't it? | ėlsúyo̯ \| ėzmázgrándė ↓ nó ↑ | El suyo es más grande, ¿no? |
| the (one) of him | ėl—dė—él ↓ | el de él |
| *WHITE* | | *WHITE* |
| No, it's the same size as his.[1] | nó ↓ ėsi̯gwál \| ȧldél ↓ | No, es igual al de él. |
| the day | ėl—díȧ ↓ | el día |
| What day can you come on? | kéđíȧs \| pwéđėƀėnír ↓ | ¿Qué días puede venir? |
| *MAID* | | *SIRVIENTA* |
| On Mondays.[2] | lȯzlúnės ↓ | Los lunes. |
| *WHITE* | | *WHITE* |
| No, on Mondays it's not convenient for me. | nó ↓ lȯzlúnėz \| nómėkȯmbyénė ↓ | No, los lunes no me conviene. |
| during the afternoon [3] | pȯr—lȧ—tárđė ↓ | por la tarde |
| Can't you come on Friday afternoon? | nópwéđėƀénír \| lȯzƀyérnėspȯrlȧtárđė ↑ | ¿No puede venir los viernes por la tarde? |
| *MAID* | | *SIRVIENTA* |
| I think so. | kréȯkėsí ↓ | Creo que sí. |

| | | |
|---|---|---|
| What do I have to do? | kétéŋgȯkḙȧṣér ↓ | ¿Qué tengo que hacer? |
| to sweep | bȧrrér ↓ | barrer |
| *WHITE* | | *WHITE* |
| Sweep the house and dust the furniture.(4) | bȧrrér \| ȧkásḁ ↑ ilimpyárlȯzmwéƀlės ↓ | Barrer la casa y limpiar los muebles. |
| to wash | lȧƀár ↓ | lavar |
| Mop up the kitchen and bathroom. | lȧƀár \| lȧkȯ́ṣınȧ \| ḭėlbáṉyȯ ↓ | Lavar la cocina y el baño. |
| the sheet | lȧ—sáƀȧnȧ ↓ | la sábana |
| the (pillow) case | lȧ—fúndȧ ↓ | la funda |
| the pillow | lḁ—ȧlmwáđȧ ↓ | la almohada |
| And change the sheets and pillow cases. | ikȧmbyár \| lȧ(s)sáƀȧnȧs \| ilȧsfúndȧzđḙalmwáđȧ ↓ | Y cambiar las sábanas y las fundas de almohada. |
| to charge | kȯƀrár ↓ | cobrar |
| How much are you going to charge me? | kwántȯƀákȯƀrármė ↓ | ¿Cuánto va a cobrarme? |
| mister (5) | dón ↓ | don |

| | | |
|---|---|---|
| *MAID* | | *SIRVIENTA* |
| The same as for Mr. Molina.(6) | lòmízmò \| kḛàđóŋhòsé ↓ | Lo mismo que a don José. |
| the party | là—fyéstà ↓ | la fiesta |
| *WHITE* | | *WHITE* |
| And if I have a party...Can you help me out? | isiténgo̰ \| ùnáfyéstà ↓ pwéđḛa̰yùđármè ↑ | Y si tengo una fiesta, ¿puede ayudarme ? |
| the time | èl—tyémpò ↓ | el tiempo |
| with time, in time enough | kòn—tyémpò ↓ | con tiempo |
| *MAID* | | *SIRVIENTA* |
| Certainly, if you let me know in time. | klárò ↓ simḛàbísà \| kòntyémpò ↓ | Claro, si me avisa con tiempo. |
| dirty | súṣyò ↓ | sucio |
| *WHITE* | | *WHITE* |
| This place is quite dirty.(7) | ésto̰ ↑ èstábàstántèsúṣyò ↓ | Esto está bastante sucio. |
| to begin | èmpèṣár ↓ | empezar |
| Can you begin this week? | pwéđèmpèṣár \| éstàsèmánà ↑ | ¿Puede empezar esta semana? |
| *MAID* | | *SIRVIENTA* |
| Yes. Then I'll see you Friday. | sí ↓ èntónṣès ↑ ásta̰èlbyérnès ↓ | Sí. Entonces hasta el viernes. |

### 11.10 Notes on the basic sentences

(1) This sentence of course literally says, 'It's equal to the one of him', contextually 'It's the same as his.' This construction is drilled in Unit 13, section 13.21.3.

(2) Note that with days of the week no word equivalent to English 'on' occurs.

(3) This is given as a unit expression because of the occurrence of the item *por* in the meaning 'during' or 'in', which it regularly has only with time-words like 'morning', 'afternoon', and so on.

(4) Note that this answer is to the question /kétéŋgokḙaṣér ↓/ *¿Qué tengo que hacer?*, which has the /—r/ form, the infinitive, of *hacer.* Consequently, the answer merely replaces *hacer* with a series of verbs all in the same /—r/ form, much as we would do in English in such a sequence as 'What do I have to do?' 'You have to eat, to wash up,' etc. But notice: the 'have to' must be present in the English answer though it does not need to be present in the Spanish answer.

(5) The item *don* is used only before the given name, the 'first' name, not the surname. It is translatable by 'mister' except that 'mister' is used only before surnames (though in the South one may hear servants talk about 'Mister Bill' or the like). It is rather formal. *Doña* is the feminine equivalent of *don.*

(6) See (5) above for explanation of why *Mr. Molina* is used to translate *don José.*

(7) *Bastante* occurs more often in this sense of 'rather' or 'quite' than it does in the more literal sense 'enough'.

# 11.2 DRILLS AND GRAMMAR

## 11.21 PATTERN DRILLS

### 11.21.1 Possessives—shortened forms

A. PRESENTATION PATTERN

*ILLUSTRATIONS*

| | | |
|---|---|---|
| ____________ | 1 éstėzmḭáwtȯ ↓ | Este es *mi* auto. |
| ____________ | 2 ézmınóƀyȧ ↓ | Es *mi* novia. |
| new | nwéƀȯ ↓ | nuevo |

| | | |
|---|---|---|
| Hand me my new books. | 3 pásemè \| mizlíƀroznwéƀòs ↓ | Páseme *mis* libros nuevos. |
| ______________________ | 4 èstásentùkásà ↓ | Estás en *tu* casa. |
| ______________________ | 5 dòndemándàstùrrópà ↓ | ¿Dónde mandas *tu* ropa? |
| Where are your things? | 6 dóndèstántùskósàs ↓ | ¿Dónde están *tus* cosas? |
| ______________________ | 7 éstè \| ƀásér \| sụèskritóryò ↓ | Este va a ser *su* escritorio. |
| ______________________ | 8 bínoụsteđ \| kònsùfàmílyà ↑ | ¿Vino usted con *su* familia? |
| his | sú ↓ súyò ↓ | su (suyo) |
| He himself takes his shirts. | 9 élmízmò \| (l)yéƀàsùskàmísàs ↓ | El mismo lleva *sus* camisas. |
| John and his ideas! | 10 hwánịsùsịđéàs ↓ | ¡Juan y *sus* ideas! |
| our | nwéstrò ↓ | nuestro |
| They're not our friends. | 11 é(l)yòs \| nóson \| nwéstròsamígòs ↓ | Ellos no son *nuestros* amigos. |
| their | sú ↓ súyò ↓ | su (suyo) |
| The Whites have their house (fixed up) very pretty. | 12 lòzhwáyt \| tyénènmúyƀónítà \| sù kásà ↓ | Los White tienen muy bonita *su* casa. |

*EXTRAPOLATION*

| Reference | sg | pl |
|---|---|---|
| 1 | mi(s) | [nwestro(s) a(s)] |
| 2 fam | tu(s) | |
| 2 - 3 | su(s) | |

*NOTES*

a. All possessives except /nwéstro/ occur in shortened forms when placed before nouns.

b. Gender distinctions are lost in shortened forms, though agreement in number remains.

## 11.21.11 SUBSTITUTION DRILLS

Number substitution

1 éltyéne | mişenişéro ↓

________________ şenişéros ↓ — éltyéne | mi(s)şenişéros ↓

2 yóteŋgo | suplúma ↓

________________ plúmas ↓ — yóteŋgo | susplúmas ↓

3 é(l)yozƀíƀen | e(n)nwéstroeđifíşyo ↓

________________ eđifíşyos ↓ — é(l)yozƀíƀen | e(n)nwéstroseđifíşyos ↓

---

1 El tiene mi *cenicero.*

________________ ceniceros. — El tiene mis ceniceros.

2 Yo tengo su *pluma.*

________________ plumas. — Yo tengo sus plumas.

3 Ellos viven en nuestro *edificio.*

________________ edificios. — Ellos viven en nuestros edificios.

4 é(l)y̯ȧskómėn | ė(n)nwéstrȧzmésȧs ↓

_________________________ mésȧ ↓ — é(l)y̯ȧskómėn | ė(n)nwéstrȧmésȧ ↓

5 é(l)y̯ȧtyénė | mızmȧlétȧs ↓

_________________________ mȧlétȧ ↓ — é(l)y̯ȧtyénė | mımȧlétȧ ↓

6 tėnémȯs | sủzlíƀrȯs ↓

_________________________ líƀrȯ ↓ — tėnémȯs | sủlíƀrȯ ↓

7 é(l)y̯ȯz | ƀáṇȧmıfyéstȧ ↓

_________________________ fyéstȧs ↓ — é(l)y̯ȯz | ƀáṇȧmısfyéstȧs ↓

---

4 Ellas comen en nuestras *mesas*.

_________________________ mesa. — Ellas comen en nuestra mesa.

5 Ella tiene mis *maletas*.

_________________________ maleta. — Ella tiene mi maleta.

6 Tenemos sus *libros*.

_________________________ libro. — Tenemos su libro.

7 Ellos van a mi *fiesta*.

_________________________ fiestas. — Ellos van a mis fiestas.

Form substitution

1 ésta̯ėzlȧmȧlétȧ ↓

| | |
|---|---|
| ____________ mi ____________ ↓ | ésta̯ėzmi̇mȧlétȧ ↓ |
| ____________ su̇ ____________ ↓ | ésta̯ė(s)su̇mȧlétȧ ↓ |
| ____________ nwéstrȧ __________ ↓ | ésta̯ \| ėznwéstrȧmȧlétȧ ↓ |

2 éstėse̯lkwártȯ ↓

| | |
|---|---|
| ____________ mi ____________ ↓ | éstėzmi̇kwártȯ ↓ |
| ____________ su̇ ____________ ↓ | éstė(s)su̇kwártȯ ↓ |
| ____________ nwéstrȯ __________ ↓ | éstėz \| nwéstrȯkwártȯ ↓ |

---

1 Esta es *la* maleta.

| | |
|---|---|
| ____________ mi ____________ . | Esta es mi maleta. |
| ____________ su ____________ . | Esta es su maleta. |
| ____________ nuestra __________ . | Esta es nuestra maleta. |

2 Este es *el* cuarto.

| | |
|---|---|
| ____________ mi ____________ . | Este es mi cuarto. |
| ____________ su ____________ . | Este es su cuarto. |
| ____________ nuestro __________ . | Este es nuestro cuarto. |

3 éstȯs | sȯnlȯzƀėşínȯs ↓

| | |
|---|---|
| ____________ miz ____________ ↓ | éstȯs \| sȯnmizƀėşínȯs ↓ |
| ____________ su̇z ____________ ↓ | éstȯs \| sȯnsu̇zƀėşínȯs ↓ |
| ____________ nwéstrȯz ________ ↓ | éstȯs \| sȯ(n)nwéstrȯzƀėşínȯs ↓ |

---

3 Estos son *los* vecinos.

| | |
|---|---|
| ____________ mis ____________ . | Estos son mis vecinos. |
| ____________ sus ____________ . | Estos son sus vecinos. |
| ____________ nuestros ________ . | Estos son nuestros vecinos. |

**End of Tape 8B**

**End of CD 8**

## 11.12.12 TRANSLATION DRILL

| | | |
|---|---|---|
| 1 This is my agency. | ésta̯ėzmɪ̯ȧhénṣyȧ ↓ | Esta es mi agencia. |
| 2 This is our building. | éste̯ ǀ ėznwéstro̯ėđɪfíṣyȯ ↓ | Este es nuestro edificio. |
| 3 They are my friends. | é(l)y̱ȯs ǀ sónmɪṣȧmígȯs ↓ | Ellos son mis amigos. |
| 4 Our house is vacant. | nwéstrȧkása̯ ǀ ėstáđėsȯku̇páđȧ ↓ | Nuestra casa está desocupada. |
| 5 These are my suits. | éstȯ(s)sȯnmɪstráhės ↓ | Estos son mis trajes. |
| 6 Our cleaner's is across (the street). | nwéstrȧtintȯrėrɪ́a̯ ǀ ėstáe̯mfréntė ↓ | Nuestra tintorería está enfrente. |
| 7 Your house is very big. | su̇kása̯ ǀ ėzmúygrándė ↓ | Su casa es muy grande. |
| 8 I never send my suits there. | núŋkȧmándȯ ǀ mɪstráhėṣaí ↓ | Nunca mando mis trajes ahí. |
| 9 My car is on the corner. | mɪ̯áwtȯ ǀ e̯stáe̯nla̯ėskínȧ ↓ | Mi auto está en la esquina. |
| 10 Someone has my books. | álgyėn ǀ tyénėmɪzlíƀrȯs ↓ | Alguien tiene mis libros. |

| | | |
|---|---|---|
| 11 Nobody lives in our house. | náđyėƀíƀe̯ ǀ ė(n)nwéstrȧkásȧ ↓ | Nadie vive en nuestra casa. |
| 12 Our family is here. | nwéstrȧfȧmílya̯ ǀ ėstákí ↓ | Nuestra familia está aquí. |
| 13 It's (just) that my Spanish isn't very good. | ėskemi̯espanyól ǀ no̯ézmu̇yƀwénȯ ↓ | Es que mi español no es muy bueno. |
| 14 We always speak with your (girl) friends a little bit. | syémpre̯ȧƀlámȯsu̇mpókȯ ǀ kȯnsu̇sȧmígȧs ↓ | Siempre hablamos un poco con sus amigas. |
| 15 Bring me my thirteen dollars. | tráygȧmė ǀ mistrése̯ėđólȧrės ↓ | Tráigame mis trece dólares. |

## B. DISCUSSION OF PATTERN

Some adjectives of two or more syllables in Spanish, including the possessives /mío, túyo, súyo/, are subject to shortening when they occur in a position before the nouns they modify. This shortening involves the loss of the final syllable of the adjective. A complete discussion of the patterns of shortening, including all adjectives affected, how much is removed in taking the final syllable off, and what position-agreement requirements control the shortening, are presented in the appendix.

The shortening of possessives is characterized by the loss of their final syllable whether singular or plural and in both gender forms. This shortening in chart form is:

| | Full | Shortened |
|---|---|---|
| 1 sg | mío(s)<br>mía(s) | mi(s) |
| 2 fam | túyo(s)<br>túya(s) | tu(s) |
| 2-3 | súyo(s)<br>súya(s) | su(s) |
| 1 pl | nwéstro(s)<br>nwéstra(s) | ———— |

The full forms always carry a strong stress: the shortened forms may, especially if they appear in a contrastive construction, though they are normally weak stressed. The construction with shortened forms appearing before the noun occurs much more frequently than the construction with full forms appearing after the noun.

The range of possible meaning is the same for /su/ as for /súyo/, namely all 2-3 forms. Hence / su / may be translated 'your (referring to one or more than one), his, her, its, their'. However, in the absence of contextual evidence to the contrary, it will refer only to 2 sg, that is, meaning 'your' (referring to one person). Thus thc chart presented previously could be modified as follows:

<table>
<tr><th>Reference</th><th>sg</th><th>pl</th></tr>
<tr><td>1</td><td>mi(s)</td><td>nwéstro(s)<br>—a(s)</td></tr>
<tr><td>2 fam</td><td>tu(s)</td><td rowspan="2">[su(s)]</td></tr>
<tr><td>2 for</td><td>su(s)</td></tr>
<tr><td>3</td><td>[su(s)]</td><td>[su(s)]</td></tr>
</table>

## 11.21.2 The negative particle with verbs

### A. PRESENTATION OF PATTERN

*ILLUSTRATIONS*

| | | |
|---|---|---|
| ______________ | 1 ėlpréşyȯ ǀ nóe̯stámál ↓ | El precio *no* está mal. |
| ______________ | 2 no̯émȯz ǀ đėşiđíđȯláféchȧ ↓ | *No* hemos decidido la fecha. |
| ______________ | 3 pȯrkénȯƀyénės ǀ éstȧnóchė ↓ | ¿Por qué *no* vienes esta noche? |
| ______________ | 4 ántėz ǀ nókyérės ǀ ótrȯtrágȯ ↑ | Antes, ¿*no* quieres otro trago? |
| ______________ | 5 nómėđígȧ ǀ sėn̦yórmȯlínȧ ↓ | *No* me diga señor Molina. |
| ______________ | 6 nótėmȯléstės ↓ | *No* te molestes. |
| ______________ | 7 nó ↓ ėstáléhȯs ↓ | *No,* está lejos. |
| ______________ | 8 ėlsúy̯o̯ ǀ ėzmázgrándė ↓ nó ↑ | El suyo es más grande, ¿*no*? |

*EXTRAPOLATION*

| | |
|---|---|
| Affirmative— | Verb |
| Negative— | /nó/ Verb |

*NOTES*

a. Used as a verb modifier, /nó/ appears immediately before the verb, or the verb along with any preposed clitics.

## 11.21.21 SUBSTITUTION DRILL

Construction substitution

Problem:

téŋgo̯ámbrė ↓

Answer:

nóténgo̯ámbrė ↓

| | |
|---|---|
| 1 pråktíkåm \| båstántė ↓ | nópråktíkåm \| båstántė ↓ |
| 2 låsėn̯yóra̯ \| áb̄la̯espån̯yól ↓ | låsėn̯yórå \| no̯áb̄la̯espån̯yól ↓ |
| 3 mėgústa̯éső ↓ | nómėgústa̯éső ↓ |

---

Problem:

Tengo hambre.

Answer:

No tengo hambre.

| | |
|---|---|
| 1 Practican bastante. | No practican bastante. |
| 2 La señora habla español. | La señora no habla español. |
| 3 Me gusta eso. | No me gusta eso. |

4 ėlsáƀȧđo̯ | ėstóyȯkupáđȯ ↓

5 hwán | ėstámúyȧgrȧđḙsíđȯ ↓

6 ėlhwéƀės | trȧƀȧhámȯsȧkí ↓

7 lȧkáha̯ | ėstála̯ėntráđȧ ↓

8 étrȧƀȧháđȯ | đėmȧsyáđȯ ↓

9 kómėnlėchúgȧ ↓

ėlsáƀȧđȯ | no̯éstóyȯkupáđȯ ↓

hwán | no̯éstá | múyȧgrȧđḙsíđȯ ↓

ėlhwéƀėz | nótrȧƀȧhámȯsȧkí ↓

lȧkáhȧ | no̯éstála̯ėntráđȧ ↓

no̯étrȧƀȧháđȯ | đėmȧsyáđȯ ↓

nókómėnlėchúgȧ ↓

---

4 El sabado estoy ocupado.

5 Juan está muy agradecido.

6 El jueves trabajamos aquí.

7 La caja está a la entrada.

8 He trabajado demasiado.

9 Comen lechuga.

El sábado no estoy ocupado.

Juan no está muy agradecido.

El jueves no trabajamos aquí.

La caja no está a la entrada.

No he trabajado demasiado.

No comen lechuga.

## 11.21.22 TRANSLATION DRILL

| | | |
|---|---|---|
| 1 I don't work on the first floor. | nótràbáho̯ \| èn̯èlprìmérpísò ↓ | No trabajo en el primer piso. |
| 2 He hasn't been here before. | èlno̯áe̯stáđo̯akí \| ántès ↓ | El no ha estado aquí antes. |
| 3 Gosh, I don't remember anything. | kàrámbà ↓ nórrèkwérđònáđà ↓ | ¡Caramba! No recuerdo nada. |
| 4 Well, she's not coming. | èmfín ↓ é(l)y̯ànóbyénè ↓ | En fin, ella no viene. |
| 5 They're not going to move. | nóbán \| àmùđársèđèkásà ↓ | No van a mudarse de casa. |
| 6 By the way, I don't remember your name. | àpròpósitò ↓ nórrèkwérđò \| sùnómbrè ↓ | A propósito, no recuerdo su nombre. |
| 7 They're not very grateful. | é(l)y̯òzno̯éstán \| múyàgràđès̯íđòs ↓ | Ellos no están muy agradecidos. |
| 8 She doesn't sweep very well. | nóbárrè \| múybyén ↓ | No barre muy bien. |
| 9 They don't clean the whole house. | nólímpyàn \| tóđàlàkásà ↓ | No limpian toda la casa. |

## B. DISCUSSION OF PATTERN

The particle /nó/ is uninflectable, that is, it does not change for person, number, or any other grammatical category. It is most commonly used as a complete sentence followed by a terminal juncture, / ↓ / (often marked with a comma in the writing system) answering a query in the negative, or followed by / ↑ / after a statement, which means the speaker is asking for corroboration:

/nó ↓ estáléhos ↓/

/elsúyo | esmásgránde ↓ nó ↑/

When /nó/ appears in an intonation phrase with other words, it is usually placed directly before the verb, or before the verb and any preceding clitic pronouns that accompany it, since the clitics become part of the verb.

In the case of verb phrases, /nó/ comes before the first verb, not between the two as it does in English:

| | |
|---|---|
| /no̯émosdes̯idído ↓/ | We have*n't* decided. |

The occurrence of / ↓ / between /nó/ and the verb is, of course, of the utmost importance, because it can totally change the meaning of the sentence:

| | |
|---|---|
| /nó ↓ estáléhos ↓/ | No, it's very far off. |
| /nóestáléhos ↓/ | It's not very far off. |

Both /nó/'s can occur in a single utterance, like this:

| | |
|---|---|
| /nó ↓ nóe̯stáléhos ↓/ | No, it's not very far off. |

You will note that the first /nó/ translates the English 'no', but the second one, the one which immediately precedes the verb, translates English 'not'. Examine especially these utterances, which are of very high frequency and great utility, answering the question 'Do you have it?'

| | |
|---|---|
| /nó ↓ nótéŋgo ↓/ | No, I don't. |
| /sí ↓ sítéŋgo ↓/ | Yes, I do. |

The pattern of negative usage in Spanish includes what in English is called a 'double negative', i. e. the appearance of two negative words in the same construction. 'I don't have nothing' is criticized as socially unacceptable in English, but /nó–téngo–náda/ *No tengo nada* is a normal, regular pattern in Spanish. The general pattern in Spanish is: some negative precedes the verb in a negative sentence. Thus:

| | | |
|---|---|---|
| /nádye—byéne ↓/ | or | /nó—byéne—nádye ↓/ |
| /núnka—bóy/ | | /nó—bóy—núnka ↓/ |

## 11.22 REPLACEMENT DRILLS

A pwéđėlımpyár | ėlmíȯ | tȧmbyén ↑

| | |
|---|---|
| 1 ______________ ȧórȧ ↑ | pwéđėlımpyár \| ėlmío̯ \| ȧórȧ ↑ |
| 2 ________ kwárto̯ ______ ↑ | pwéđėlımpyár \| ėlkwárto̯ \| ȧórȧ ↑ |
| 3 ________ mı ________ ↑ | pwéđėlımpyár \| mıkwárto̯ \| ȧórȧ ↑ |
| 4 ________ ƀȧrrér ________ ↑ | pwéđėƀȧrrér \| mıkwárto̯ \| ȧórȧ ↑ |
| 5 ________ ėstė ________ ↑ | pwéđėƀȧrrér \| ėstėkwárto̯ \| ȧórȧ ↑ |
| 6 ______________ đėspwés ↑ | pwéđėƀȧrrér \| ėstėkwártȯ \| đėspwés ↑ |
| 7 ________ su̇ ________ ↑ | pwéđėƀȧrrér \| su̇kwártȯ \| đėspwés ↑ |

---

A ¿Puede limpiar el mío también?

| | |
|---|---|
| 1 ¿ ______________ ahora? | ¿Puede limpiar el mío ahora? |
| 2 ¿ ________ cuarto ______ ? | ¿Puede limpiar el cuarto ahora? |
| 3 ¿ ________ mi ________ ? | ¿Puede limpiar mi cuarto ahora? |
| 4 ¿ ________ barrer ________ ? | ¿Puede barrer mi cuarto ahora? |
| 5 ¿ ________ este ________ ? | ¿Puede barrer este cuarto ahora? |
| 6 ¿ ______________ después? | ¿Puede barrer este cuarto después? |
| 7 ¿ ________ su ________ ? | ¿Puede barrer su cuarto después? |

B ėlsúyo̰ | ėzmázgrándė ↓ nó ↑

| | |
|---|---|
| 1 lȯs ________________ ↑ | lȯ(s)súyȯs \| sȯnmázgrándėz ↓ nó ↑ |
| 2 ________ ƀȯnítȧz ______ ↑ | lȧ(s)súyȧs \| sȯnmázƀȯnítȧz ↓ nó ↑ |
| 3 ______ míȧs __________ ↑ | lȧzmíȧs \| sȯnmázƀȯnítȧz ↓ nó ↑ |
| 4 _______ ėz __________ ↑ | lȧmíḁ \| ėzmázƀȯnítȧ ↓ nó ↑ |
| 5 ________ súşyȯ ________ ↑ | ėlmío̰ \| ėzmá(s)súşyȯ ↓ nó ↑ |
| 6 ______ ótro̰ __________ ↑ | ėlótro̰ \| ėzmá(s)súşyȯ ↓ nó ↑ |
| 7 lȧs ________________ ↑ | lȧsótrȧs \| sȯnmá(s)súşyȧs ↓ nó ↑ |

---

B El suyo es más grande, ¿no?

| | |
|---|---|
| 1 Los ____________, ¿ ___ ? | Los suyos son más grandes, ¿no? |
| 2 ____________ bonitas, ¿ ___ ? | Las suyas son más bonitas, ¿no? |
| 3 ______ mías ________, ¿ ___ ? | Las mías son más bonitas, ¿no? |
| 4 ______ es __________, ¿ ___ ? | La mía es más bonita, ¿no? |
| 5 ____________ sucio, ¿ ___ ? | El mío es más sucio, ¿no? |
| 6 ______ otro ________, ¿ ___ ? | El otro es más sucio, ¿no? |
| 7 Las ____________, ¿ ___ ? | Las otras son más sucias, ¿no? |

C ḱeteŋgȯkeȧşér ↓

| | |
|---|---|
| 1 ________________ kȯmprár ↓ | ḱeteŋgȯkėkȯmprár ↓ |
| 2 áy ________ ↓ | keáykėkȯmprár ↓ |
| 3 kwánto ________________ ↓ | kwántoáykėkȯmprár ↓ |
| 4 ________ tėnémȯs ________ ↓ | kwántȯtėnémȯs \| kėkȯmprár ↓ |
| 5 ________________ kȧmbyár ↓ | kwántȯtėnémȯs \| kėkȧmbyár ↓ |
| 6 ________ áykė ________ ↓ | kwántoáykėkȧmbyár ↓ |
| 7 ke ________________ ↓ | keáykėkȧmbyár ↓ |

---

C ¿Qué tengo que hacer?

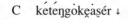

| | |
|---|---|
| 1 ¿ ________________ comprar? | ¿Qué tengo que comprar? |
| 2 ¿ ________ hay ________ ? | ¿Qué hay que comprar? |
| 3 ¿Cuánto ________________ ? | ¿Cuánto hay que comprar? |
| 4 ¿ ________ tenemos ________ ? | ¿Cuánto tenemos que comprar? |
| 5 ¿ ________________ cambiar? | ¿Cuánto tenemos que cambiar? |
| 6 ¿ ________ hay que ________ ? | ¿Cuánto hay que cambiar? |
| 7 ¿Qué ________________ ? | ¿Qué hay que cambiar? |

D kwántȯƀákȯƀrármė ↓

| | |
|---|---|
| 1 kwándȯ ______________ ↓ | kwándȯƀákȯƀrármė ↓ |
| 2 ______________ ȧƀlármė ↓ | kwándȯƀáƀlármė ↓ |
| 3 ________ ƀás __________ ↓ | kwándȯ \| ƀás̩ȧƀlármė ↓ |
| 4 ______________ mu̇đártė ↓ | kwándȯ \| ƀás̩amu̇đártė ↓ |
| 5 pȯrké ______________ ↓ | pȯrké \| ƀás̩amu̇đártė ↓ |
| 6 ________ pyénsȧz ________ ↓ | pȯrké \| pyénsȧzmu̇đártė ↓ |
| 7 ȧđóndė ______________ ↓ | ȧđóndė \| pyénsȧzmu̇đártė ↓ |

---

D ¿Cuánto va a cobrarme?

| | |
|---|---|
| 1 ¿Cuándo ______________ ? | ¿Cuándo va a cobrarme? |
| 2 ¿ ______________ hablarme? | ¿Cuándo va a hablarme? |
| 3 ¿ ________ vas __________ ? | ¿Cuándo vas a hablarme? |
| 4 ¿ ______________ mudarte? | ¿Cuándo vas a mudarte? |
| 5 ¿Por qué ______________ ? | ¿Por qué vas a mudarte? |
| 6 ¿ ________ piensas ________ ? | ¿Por qué piensas mudarte? |
| 7 ¿Adónde ______________ ? | ¿Adónde piensas mudarte? |

E ésto̯ | ėstáƀȧstántėsúşyȯ ↓

| | |
|---|---|
| 1 mikása̯ ____________________ ↓ | mikása̯ \| ėstáƀȧstántėsúşyȧ ↓ |
| 2 _______ tráhės _____________ ↓ | mistráhės \| ėstámbȧstántėsúşyȯs ↓ |
| 3 __________ múy ____________ ↓ | mistráhės \| ėstánmúysúşyȯs ↓ |
| 4 ____________________ nwéƀȯs ↓ | mistráhės \| ėstánmúynwéƀȯs ↓ |
| 5 su̇s________________________ ↓ | su̇stráhės \| ėstánmúynwéƀȯs ↓ |
| 6 _______ kȧmísȧs ____________ ↓ | su̇skȧmísȧs \| ėstánmúynwéƀȧs ↓ |
| 7 ____________________ súşyȧs ↓ | su̇skȧmísȧs \| ėstánmúysúşyȧs ↓ |

---

E Esto está bastante sucio.

| | |
|---|---|
| 1 Mi casa ____________________ . | Mi casa está bastante sucia. |
| 2 ________ trajes______________ . | Mis trajes están bastante sucios. |
| 3 __________ muy ____________ . | Mis trajes están muy sucios. |
| 4 _____________________ nuevos. | Mis trajes están muy nuevos. |
| 5 Sus________________________ . | Sus trajes están muy nuevos. |
| 6 _______ camisas ____________ . | Sus camisas están muy nuevas. |
| 7 ______________________ sucias. | Sus camisas están muy sucias. |

F pwéđėmpėşár | éstasėmánȧ ↑

| | |
|---|---|
| 1 pwéđės ________________ ↑ | pwéđėsėmpėşár \| éstasėmánȧ ↑ |
| 2 ________________ ƀyérnės ↑ | pwéđėsėmpėşár \| éstėƀyérnės ↑ |
| 3 ______ trȧƀahár __________ ↑ | pwéđėstrȧƀahár \| éstėƀyérnės ↑ |
| 4 kyérės ________________ ↑ | kyérėstrȧƀahár \| éstėƀyérnės ↑ |
| 5 ________________ đíȧs ↑ | kyérėstrȧƀahár \| éstȯzđíȧs ↑ |
| 6 __________ ůnȯz __________ ↑ | kyérėstrȧƀahár \| ůnȯzđíȧs ↑ |
| 7 ________ ƀėnír __________ ↑ | kyérėzƀėnír \| ůnȯzđíȧs ↑ |

---

F ¿Puede empezar esta semana?

| | |
|---|---|
| 1 ¿Puedes________________ ? | ¿Puedes empezar esta semana? |
| 2 ¿ ________________ viernes? | ¿Puedes empezar este viernes? |
| 3 ¿ ______ trabajar __________ ? | ¿Puedes trabajar este viernes? |
| 4 ¿Quieres ________________ ? | ¿Quieres trabajar este viernes? |
| 5 ¿ ________________ días? | ¿Quieres trabajar estos días? |
| 6 ¿ __________ unos ________ ? | ¿Quieres trabajar unos días? |
| 7 ¿ ________ venir __________ ? | ¿Quieres venir unos días? |

## 11.23 VARIATION DRILLS

A kéđías | pwéđeb̄enír ↓ ¿Qué días puede venir?

| | | |
|---|---|---|
| 1 What days can you clean? | kéđías | pwéđelimpyár ↓ | ¿Qué días puede limpiar? |
| 2 What days can you sweep? | kéđías | pwéđeb̄arrér ↓ | ¿Qué días puede barrer? |
| 3 What days can you wash? | kéđías | pwéđelab̄ár ↓ | ¿Qué días puede lavar? |
| 4 What days can you study? | kéđías | pwéđestuđyár ↓ | ¿Qué días puede estudiar? |
| 5 What days do you want to practice? | kéđías | kyérepraktikár ↓ | ¿Qué días quiere practicar? |
| 6 What days do you want to work? | kéđías | kyéretrab̄ahár ↓ | ¿Qué días quiere trabajar? |
| 7 What days do you want to return? | kéđías | kyéreb̄olbér ↓ | ¿Qué días quiere volver? |

B nópwéđėƀénır | lȯzƀyérnės | pȯrlȧtárđė ↑ — ¿No puede venir los viernes por la tarde?

| | | |
|---|---|---|
| 1 Can't you come Friday evenings? | nópwéđėƀénır \| lȯzƀyérnės \| pȯrlȧnóchė ↑ | ¿No puede venir los viernes por la noche? |
| 2 Can't you come Monday mornings? | nópwéđėƀénır \| lȯzlúnės \| pȯrlȧmaṇyánȧ ↑ | ¿No puede venir los lunes por la mañana? |
| 3 Can't you go at three o'clock? | nópwéđẹír \| ȧlȧstrés ↑ | ¿No puede ir a las tres? |
| 4 Can't you eat at six o'clock? | nópwéđekómer \| ȧlȧ(s)séys ↑ | ¿No puede comer a las seis? |
| 5 Don't you want to eat in that restaurant? | nókyérėkómér \| ėṇésėrrėstórán ↑ | ¿No quiere comer en ese restorán? |
| 6 Don't you want to come back tomorrow? | nókyérėƀólbér \| mȧṇyánȧ ↑ | ¿No quiere volver mañana? |
| 7 Don't you want to speak Spanish? | nókyérẹȧƀlár \| ėspȧṇyól ↑ | ¿No quiere hablar español? |

| | | | |
|---|---|---|---|
| C | | tyénė \| kėƀarrérlȧkásḁ ↑ ılımpyárlȯzmwéƀlės ↓ | Tiene que barrer la casa y limpiar los muebles. |
| 1 | You have to sweep the kitchen and the bathroom. | tyénė \| kėƀarrérlȧkȯsína ↑ ịėlbáṇyȯ ↓ | Tiene que barrer la cocina y el baño. |
| 2 | You have to change the sheets and the plliow cases. | tyénė \| kėkambyárlȧ(s)sáƀanȧs ↑ ılȧsfúndȧs ↓ | Tiene que cambiar las sábanas y las fundas. |
| 3 | You have to clean the entrance and the patio. | tyénė \| kėlımpyárlḁentráđȧ ↑ ịėlpátyȯ ↓ | Tiene que limpiar la entrada y el patio. |
| 4 | I have to study and to work. | téŋgȯkėstuđyár \| ıtrȧƀahár ↓ | Tengo que estudiar y trabajar. |
| 5 | I have to wait for Jose and Carmen. | téŋgȯ \| kėspėrárȧhȯsé \| ịakármėn ↓ | Tengo que esperar a José y a Carmen. |
| 6 | We have to see Jose and Mr. Molina. | tėnémȯs \| kėƀérȧhȯsé \| ịȧlsėṇyórmȯlínȧ ↓ | Tenemos que ver a José y al señor Molina. |
| 7 | They have to send the suits to the cleaner's. | tyéneŋ \| kėmȧndár \| lȯstráhesȧlȧ tıntȯrėríȧ ↓ | Tienen que mandar los trajes a la tintorería. |

| | | | |
|---|---|---|---|
| D | siteŋgo̯unȧfyéstȧ ↓ pwéđe̯ȧyu̇đárme ↑ | | Si tengo una fiesta, ¿puede ayudarme? |
| 1 | If I change the sheets, can you help me? | sikámbyo̯lȧ(s)sáƀȧnȧs ↓ pwéđe̯ȧyu̇đárme ↑ | Si cambio las sábanas, ¿puede ayudarme? |
| 2 | If I sweep the house, can you help me? | siƀárro̯lȧkásȧ ↓ pwéđe̯ȧyu̇đárme ↑ | Si barro la casa, ¿puede ayudarme? |
| 3 | If I wash the kitchen, can you help me? | siláƀo̯lȧko̯s̤ínȧ ↓ pwéđe̯ȧyu̇đárme ↑ | Si lavo la cocina, ¿puede ayudarme? |
| 4 | If I have something to do, can you help me? | siteŋgo̯álgo̯ke̯ȧs̤ér ↓ pwéđe̯ȧyu̇đárme ↑ | Si tengo algo que hacer, ¿puede ayudarme? |
| 5 | If you want a house, can you let me know? | siđėsée̯ȧunȧkásȧ ↓ pwéđe̯ȧƀisárme ↑ | Si desea una casa, ¿puede avisarme? |
| 6 | If you need a maid, can you let me know? | sinės̤ėsíta̯unȧmu̇cháchȧ ↓ pwéđe̯ȧƀisárme ↑ | Si necesita una muchacha, ¿puede avisarme? |
| 7 | If I go downtown, can you wait for me? | siƀóyȧls̤éntro̯ ↓ pwéđėspėrárme ↑ | Si voy al centro, ¿puede esperarme? |

E klárȯ ↓ simẹȧƀísȧkȯntyémpȯ ↓ — Claro, si me avisa con tiempo.

| | | |
|---|---|---|
| 1 Sure, if you let me know tomorrow. | klárȯ ↓ simẹȧƀísȧmȧnyánȧ ↓ | Claro, si me avisa mañana. |
| 2 Sure, if you let me know at three o'clock. | klárȯ ↓ simẹȧƀísȧlȧstrés ↓ | Claro, si me avisa a las tres. |
| 3 Sure, if you let me know at seven fifteen. | klárȯ ↓ simẹȧƀísạ \| ȧlȧ(s)syétẹikínṣė ↓ | Claro, si me avisa a las siete y quince. |
| 4 Sure, if you wait for me. | klárȯ ↓ simėsperȧ ↓ | Claro, si me espera. |
| 5 Sure, if you look for me. | klárȯ ↓ simėƀúskȧ ↓ | Claro, si me busca. |
| 6 Sure, if you take me. | klárȯ ↓ simė(l)yéƀȧ ↓ | Claro, si me lleva. |
| 7 Sure, if you speak to me in Spanish. | klárȯ ↓ simẹáƀlạenėspȧnyól ↓ | Claro, si me habla en español. |

| | | | |
|---|---|---|---|
| F | | ėntóns̯ės ↑ ásta̯ėlbyérnės ↓ | Entonces, hasta el viernes. |
| 1 | Well, I'll be seeing you Monday. | ėntóns̯ės ↑ ásta̯ė(l)lúnės ↓ | Entonces, hasta el lunes. |
| 2 | Well, I'll be seeing you Saturday. | ėntóns̯ės ↑ ásta̯ėlsáƀȧđȯ ↓ | Entonces, hasta el sábado. |
| 3 | Well, I'll be seeing you Thursday. | ėntóns̯ės ↑ ásta̯ėlhwéƀės ↓ | Entonces, hasta el jueves. |
| 4 | Well, I'll be seeing you tomorrow. | ėntóns̯ės ↑ ástȧmȧn̯yánȧ ↓ | Entonces, hasta mañana. |
| 5 | Well, I'll see you afterwards. | ėntóns̯ės ↑ ástȧđėspwés ↓ | Entonces, hasta después. |
| 6 | Well, I'll see you some other day. | ėntóns̯ės ↑ ásta̯ótrȯđíȧ ↓ | Entonces, hasta otro día. |
| 7 | Well, I'll see you later. | ėntóns̯ės ↑ ástȧmástárđė ↓ | Entonces, hasta más tarde. |

## 11.24 REVIEW DRILL

Unemphatic 'some, any' from English

| | | |
|---|---|---|
| 1 Give me some soup. | démėsópȧ ↓ | Déme sopa. |
| 2 Give me some salad. | démėnsȧláđȧ ↓ | Déme ensalada. |
| 3 Give me some water. | déme̯ágwȧ ↓ | Déme agua. |
| 4 Give me some wine. | démėƀínȯ ↓ | Déme vino. |
| 5 Give me some pie. | démėpȧstél ↓ | Déme pastel. |
| 6 Give me some dessert. | démėpóstrė ↓ | Déme postre. |
| 7 Give me some beer. | démėṣėrƀéṣȧ ↓ | Déme cerveza. |
| 8 Do you have any tomatoes? | tyénėtȯmátės ↑ | ¿Tiene tomates? |

| | | |
|---|---|---|
| 9 Do you have any vegetables? | tyénėlėgúmbrės ↑ | ¿Tiene legumbres? |
| 10 Do you have any pork chops? | tyénėchúlétaz \| đėserđó ↑ | ¿Tiene chuletas de cerdo? |
| 11 Do you have any beer? | tyénėserƀésȧ ↑ | ¿Tiene cerveza? |
| 12 Do you have any soup? | tyénėsópȧ ↑ | ¿Tiene sopa? |
| 13 Do you have any coffee? | tyénėkafé ↑ | ¿Tiene café? |

## 11.3 CONVERSATION STIMULUS

### NARRATIVE 1

| | | |
|---|---|---|
| 1 The girl who cleans Molina's apartment is excellent. | lȧmúchȧchȧ \| kėlímpya̯ \| ėlȧpȧrtȧméntȯ đėmȯlína̯ \| ėsėks(s)ėléntė ↓ | La muchacha que limpia el apartamento de Molina es excelente. |
| 2 And she charges very little, ten pesos a day. | ikóƀrȧmúypókȯ ↓ dyéspésȯsȧldíȧ ↓ | Y cobra muy poco, diez pesos al día. |
| 3 That's six dollars and a quarter, more or less. | éso̯ \| ėsséisdólȧrėsƀėyntisíŋkȯ \| másȯménȯs ↓ | Eso es seis dólares veinticinco, más o menos. |

| | | |
|---|---|---|
| 4 Mr. Molina is going to talk with her. | èlsèn̯yórmòlína \| ƀáƀlárkòn̩é(l)y̯à ↓ | El Sr. Molina va a hablar con ella. |
| 5 He's going to talk with her to see if she wants to clean Mr. White's apartment also. | ƀáƀlárkòn̩é(l)y̯à ↑ páràƀér \| sikyérè limpyár \| èlàpàrtàméntòđèlsèn̯yór hwáyt \| tàmbyén ↓ | Va a hablar con ella para ver si quiere limpiar el apartamento del Sr. White también. |
| 6 He'll talk with her tomorrow. | màn̯yánáƀlàkòn̩é(l)yà ↓ | Mañana habla con ella. |

## DIALOG 1

| | | |
|---|---|---|
| Juan, pregúntele a José que qué tal es la muchacha que le limpia su apartamento. | kétál \| èzlàmúchácha \| kètèlímpyàtu̯ àpàrtàméntò \| hòsé ↓ | Juan: ¿Qué tal es la muchacha que te limpia tu apartamento, José? |
| José, contéstele que es excelente. Y que cobra muy poco, diez pesos al día. | èsèks(s̩)èléntè ↓ ikóƀràmúypókò ↓ đyésp̩ésòs̩àldíà ↓ | José: Es excelente. Y cobra muy poco, diez pesos al día. |
| Juan, pregúntele que cuánto es eso en dólares. | kwántọèsẹsọ \| èndólàrès ↓ | Juan: ¿Cuánto es eso en dólares? |
| José, dígale que seis veinticinco, más o menos. | séisƀèyntìs̩íŋkò \| más̩òménòs ↓ | José: Seis veinticinco, más o menos. |

| | | |
|---|---|---|
| Juan, pregúntele que por qué no habla con ella. | pȯrkénọ̑áƀlȧs \| kȯnẹ́(l)y̰ȧ ↓ | Juan: ¿Por qué no hablas con ella? |
| José, pregúntele que para qué. | párȧké ↓ | José: ¿Para qué? |
| Juan, dígale que para ver si quiere limpiar el suyo también. | pȧrȧƀér \| sikyérėlimpyárėlmíȯ \| tȧmbyén ↓ | Juan: Para ver si quiere limpiar el mío también. |
| José, contéstele que muy bien. Que mañana habla con ella, entonces. | múyƀyén ↓ mȧn̮yánȧƀlȯkȯnẹ́(l)y̰a̯ \| ėntónṣ̆ės ↓ | José: Muy bien, mañana hablo con ella, entonces. |

## NARRATIVE 2

| | | |
|---|---|---|
| 1 The girl comes to see Mr. White in the afternoon. | lȧmu̇cháchȧ \| ƀyénẹ̑ȧƀér \| ȧlsėn̮yórhwáyt \| ėnlȧtárđė ↓ | La muchacha viene a ver al Sr. White en la tarde. |
| 2 She's the one who cleans Mr. Molina's apartment. | é(l)y̰a̯ \| ėzlȧkėlímpya̯ \| ėlȧpȧrtȧméntȯ \| đėlsėn̮yórmȯlínȧ ↓ | Ella es la que limpia el apartamento del Sr. Molina. |
| 3 She goes over there on Thursdays. | báılȯshwéƀės ↓ | Va ahí los jueves. |

| | | |
|---|---|---|
| 4 She can't come here on Saturdays, only on Fridays. | é(l)y̯ȧnópwéđė \| ƀėnírȧkílȯ(s)sáƀȧđȯs ↓ sólȯlȯzƀyérnės ↓ | Ella no puede venir aquí los sábados, sólo los viernes. |
| 5 The other days she has to go to other homes. | lȯs̩ótrȯzdías \| tyénėkḙír \| ḁótrȧskásȧs ↓ | Los otros días tiene que ir a otras casas. |

## DIALOG 2

| | | |
|---|---|---|
| Srta., dígale 'buenas tardes' al Sr. White, y que dice don José que aquí necesitan una muchacha. | bwénȧstárđės ↓ dís̩ėđȯŋhósé \| kḙȧkí \| nės̩ėsítȧn̩ụnȧmụchâchȧ ↓ | Srta.: Buenas tardes. Dice don José que aquí necesitan una muchacha. |
| Juan, pregúntele si ella es la que limpia su (de él) apartamento. | ės̩ústéđ \| lȧkėlímpyḁ \| ėlȧpȧrtȧméntȯ đél ↑ | Juan: ¿Es Ud. la que limpia el apartamento de él? |
| Srta., contéstele al señor que sí. Que Ud. va ahí los jueves. | sí \| sėn̩yór ↓ bóyáílȯshwéƀės ↓ | Srta.: Sí, señor. Voy ahí los jueves. |
| Juan, pregúntele si puede venir aquí los sábados. | pwéđėƀėníráki \| lȯ(s)sáƀȧđȯs ↑ | Juan: ¿Puede venir aquí los sábados? |

| | | |
|---|---|---|
| Srta., dígale que no, que sólo los viernes. Que los otros días tíene que ir a otras casas. | nó \| sėṇyór ↓ sólȯlȯzƀyérnės ↓<br>lȯṣótrȯzđíȧs \| téŋgȯke̯ír \| a̯ótrȧskásȧs ↓ | Srta: No, señor, sólo los viernes. Los otros días tengo que ir a otras casas. |
| Juan, contéstele que está bien. | ėstáƀyén ↓ | Juan: Está bien. |

## NARRATIVE 3

| | | |
|---|---|---|
| 1 The girl wants to see the apartment. | lȧmu̇cháchȧ \| kyérėƀérėlȧpȧrtȧménto ↓ | La muchacha quiere ver el apartamento. |
| 2 She wants to see what work there is to be done. | kyérėƀér \| kétrȧƀáho̯ \| áyke̯ȧṣér ↓ | Quiere ver qué trabajo hay que hacer. |
| 3 She's got to do all the housework. | tyénėke̯ȧṣér \| tóđo̯ėltrȧƀáhȯđėkásȧ ↓ | Tiene que hacer todo el trabajo de casa. |
| 4 That is to say, sweep the floors, wash the bathroom, make the bed... | ėzđéṣɪr ↑ bȧrrérlȯspísȯs ↑ lȧƀárėl ↑<br>báṇyȯ ↑ ȧṣérlȧkámȧ ↑ | Es decir, barrer los pisos, lavar el baño, hacer la cama... |
| 5 But she doesn't have to wash clothes. | pėrȯnótyénė \| kėlȧƀárrópȧ ↓ | Pero no tiene que lavar ropa. |

| | | |
|---|---|---|
| 6 He sends all his clothes to the laundry. | èlmándàtóđàlàrrópa̯ \| àlàlàƀàndèríà ↓ | El manda toda la ropa a la lavandería. |

## DIALOG 3

| | | |
|---|---|---|
| Srta., pregúntele al señor si puede ver el apartamento. | pwéđòƀér \| élàpàrtàméntò \| sènyór ↑ | Srta: ¿Puedo ver el apartamento, señor? |
| Juan, contéstele que sí, cómo no, que pase adelante. | sí \| kómònó ↓ pásḙàđèlántè ↓ | Juan: Sí, cómo no, pase adelante. |
| Srta., pregúntele que qué trabajo hay que hacer. | kétràƀáho̯ \| áykḙàṣér ↓ | Srta: ¿Qué trabajo hay que hacer? |
| Juan, contéstele que todo el trabajo de casa. Que es decir, barrer los pisos, lavar el baño, hacer la cama.... | tóđo̯èltràƀáhòđèkásà ↓ èzđèṣír \| ƀàrrérlòspísòs ↑ làƀárèlbányò ↑ àṣérlàkámà ↑ | Juan: Todo el trabajo de casa. Es decir, barrer los pisos, lavar el baño, hacer las camas... |
| Srta., pregúntele si tiene que lavar ropa. | téŋgòkèlàƀárrópà ↑ | Srta: ¿Tengo que lavar ropa? |

| | | |
|---|---|---|
| Juan, contéstele que no. Que la ropa hay que mandarla a la lavandería. | nó˙ ↓ lȧrrópáykėmȧndárla̯ \| ȧlȧ lȧƀȧndėríȧ ↓ | Juan: No. La ropa hay que mandarla a la lavandería. |

## NARRATIVE 4

| | | |
|---|---|---|
| 1 Now, (speaking of) another thing. | ȧóra̯ ↑ ȧƀlándȯđe̯ótrȧkósȧ ↓ | Ahora, hablando de otra cosa. |
| 2 The girl charges ten pesos for cleaning Mr. Molina's apartment. | lȧmuchácha \| kóƀrȧđyéspésos \| pȯr lïmpyár \| ėlȧpȧrtȧméntȯđėlsėnyórmȯlínȧ ↓ | La muchacha cobra diez pesos por limpiar el apartamento del Sr. Molina. |
| 3 And now she wants to charge fourteen for this one. | i̯ȧórȧ \| kyérėkȯƀrár \| kȧtórșėpȯréstė ↓ | Y ahora quiere cobrar catorce por éste. |
| 4 But she's right. This one is larger. | pėrȯtyénėrrașón ↓ éstėzmázgrándė ↓ | Pero tiene razón. Este es más grande. |
| 5 She can start tomorrow. Tomorrow is Friday. | pwéđėmpėșármȧnyánȧ ↓ mȧnyána̯ėzƀyérnės ↓ | Puede empezar mañana. Mañana es viernes. |

## DIALOG 4

| | | |
|---|---|---|
| Juan, dígale que ahora, hablando de otra cosa, cuánto cobra ella. | àóra̯ ↓ àƀlándòđe̯ótràkósà ↓ kwántò kóƀra̯ùstéđ ↓ | Juan: Ahora, hablando de otra cosa, ¿cuánto cobra Ud.? |
| Srta., contéstele que catorce pesos. | kàtórs̯èpésòs ↓ | Srta: Catorce pesos. |
| Juan, pero a don José le cobra diez, dígale. | pèro̯àđóŋhòsé \| lèkóƀràđyés̯ ↓ | Juan: Pero a don José le cobra diez. |
| Srta., dígale que sí, pero que este apartamento es más grande. | sí ↓ pèro̯éste̯àpàrtàménto̯ \| èzmáz grándè ↓ | Srta: Sí, pero este apartamento es más grande. |
| Juan, dígale que bueno, que muy bien. Que mañana es viernes. Que si puede empezar mañana. | bwénò ↓ múyƀyén ↓ màn̯yána̯èzƀyérnès ↓ pwéđèmpès̯àrmàn̯yánà ↑ | Juan: Bueno, muy bien. Mañana es viernes. ¿Puede empezar mañana? |
| Srta., contéstele que sí, y pregúntele que a qué hora? | sí \| sèn̯yór ↓ àke̯órà ↓ | Srta: Sí, señor. ¿A qué hora? |
| Juan, dígale que por la tarde, a la una o a las dos. | pòrlàtárđè ↓ àla̯únà \| o̯àlàzđós ↓ | Juan: Por la tarde, a la una o a las dos. |

**End of Tape 9A***

*Tape 9A actually ends on page 444 of this book because it covers the dialogue for listening of Unit 12. However, Tape 9B starts on page 440 and covers the dialogues for learning and fluency of the same Unit.

# 12.1 BASIC SENTENCES

## No water in White's apartment

John comes into Molina's apartment looking upset.

| English Spelling | Aid to Listening | Spanish Spelling |
|---|---|---|
| (it) happens (to happen) | pásȧ ↓ pȧsár ↓ | pasa (pasar) |
| *MOLINA* | | *MOLINA* |
| What's the matter, John? | kéteṗásȧ \| hwán ↓ | ¿Qué te pasa, Juan? |
| (I) know (to know) | sé ↓ sȧƀér ↓ | sé (saber) |
| *WHITE* | | *WHITE* |
| I don't know. There's no water in my apartment. | nósé ↓ n̯oáyágwa̯ \| ėnm̯ıȧpȧrtȧméntȯ ↓ | No sé. No hay agua en mi apartamento. |
| don't tell (to tell) | nȯ—đígȧs ↓ dės̯ír ↓ | no digas (decir) |
| *MOLINA* | | *MOLINA* |
| Don't tell me! Again? | nómėđígȧs ↓ ótrȧƀés̯ ↑ | ¡No me digas! ¿Otra vez? |
| to bathe | bȧn̯yár ↓ | bañar |
| to bathe myself (to bathe oneself) (1) | bȧn̯yármė ↓ bȧn̯yársė ↓ | bañarme (bañarse) |
| to shave | ȧfėytár ↓ | afeitar |

<table>
<tr><td>to shave myself (to shave oneself)</td><td>ȧfėytármė ↓ ȧfėytársė ↓</td><td>afeitarme (afeitarse)</td></tr>
<tr><td>And here I am without having bathed or shaved! (2)</td><td>iyó | kėstóysimbȧn̥yármė̯ | ısın̥ȧfėytármė ↓</td><td>¡Y yo que estoy sin bañarme y sin afeitarme!</td></tr>
<tr><td>(I) was (to be)</td><td>ėstáƀȧ ↓ ėstár ↓</td><td>estaba (estar)</td></tr>
<tr><td>cleaning myself (to clean oneself) (3)</td><td>limpyandȯmė ↓ limpyarsė ↓</td><td>limpiándome (limpiarse)</td></tr>
<tr><td>(I) was cleaning (myself)</td><td>ėstáƀȧ—limpyándȯmė ↓</td><td>estaba limpiándome</td></tr>
<tr><td>the tooth</td><td>ėl—dyéntė ↓</td><td>el diente</td></tr>
<tr><td>WHITE</td><td></td><td>WHITE</td></tr>
<tr><td>I was brushing my teeth.</td><td>y̯ó | e̯stáƀalımpyándȯmė | lȯzđyéntės ↓</td><td>Yo estaba limpiándome los dientes.</td></tr>
<tr><td>went, was going (to go)</td><td>íƀȧ ↓ ír ↓</td><td>iba (ir)</td></tr>
<tr><td>was going to give myself</td><td>íƀa̯—ȧ—đármė ↓</td><td>iba a darme</td></tr>
<tr><td>the shower</td><td>lȧ—đúchȧ ↓</td><td>la ducha</td></tr>
<tr><td>I was going to take a shower, too.</td><td>íƀađármeu̯nađúchȧ | tȧmbyén ↓</td><td>Iba a darme una ducha también.</td></tr>
<tr><td>the joke</td><td>lȧ—ƀrómȧ ↓</td><td>la broma</td></tr>
<tr><td>the boy</td><td>ėl—chíkȯ ↓</td><td>el chico</td></tr>
</table>

| | | |
|---|---|---|
| *MOLINA* | | *MOLINA* |
| What a fix, chum! | ké̇ƀrómȧ \| chíkȯ ↓ | ¡Qué broma, chico! |
| The party is at seven! | lȧfyéstḁ \| ėsḁlȧ(s)syétė ↓ | La fiesta es a las siete. |
| scarcely, barely | ȧpénȧs ↓ | apenas |
| (we) have (to have) | tėnémȯs ↓ tėnér ↓ | tenemos (tener) |
| half | méđyȯ ↓ | medio |
| to, in order to | párȧ ↓ | para |
| to dress | bėstír ↓ | vestir |
| to dress ourselves (to dress oneself) | bėstírnȯs ↓ bėstírsė ↓ | vestirnos (vestirse) |
| *WHITE* | | *WHITE* |
| We barely have half an hour to get dressed. | ȧpénȧs \| tėnémȯzméđyḁórȧ \| párȧbėstírnȯs ↓ | Apenas tenemos media hora para vestirnos. |
| the moment | ėl—mȯméntȯ ↓ | el momento |
| just a minute (4) | ȯn—mȯméntȯ ↓ | un momento |
| (I) go (to go) | bóy ↓ ír ↓ | voy (ir) |
| (it) arrived (to arrive) | (l)y̰ėgó ↓ (l)y̰ėgár ↓ | llegó (llegar) |

| | | |
|---|---|---|
| *MOLINA* | | *MOLINA* |
| Just a minute. I'm going to see if the water has come on. (5) | únmòméntò ↓ bóyàđér \| si(l)y̨ègóe̦lágwà ↓ | Un momento. Voy a ver si llegó el agua. |
| Yes, it has. (6) | sí ↓ y̨aáy ↓ | Sí, ya hay. |
| the haste | là—prísà ↓ | la prisa |
| to hurry myself (to hurry oneself) | dármè—prísà ↓ dársè—prísà ↓ | darme prisa (darse prisa) |
| *WHITE* | | *WHITE* |
| I'm going, then. I've got to hurry. | mèđóyèntónșès ↓ téŋgòkèđármèprísà ↓ | Me voy entonces. Tengo que darme prisa. |
| listen (to listen) | óy̨è ↓ óír ↓ | oye (oir) |
| at last | pòr—fín ↓ | por fin |
| *MOLINA* | | *MOLINA* |
| Hey, who did you finally decide to take? (7) | óy̨è ↓ pòrfín ↑ àkyémbáșà(l)y̨èđár ↓ | Oye, por fin, ¿a quién vas a llevar? |
| a little fat (fat) | gòrđítò ↓ górđò ↓ | gordito (gordo) |
| the chubby girl | là—gòrđítà ↓ | la gordita |
| the eye glasses | làz—gáfàs ↓ | las gafas |
| *WHITE* | | *WHITE* |
| The chubby gal with the glasses. | àlàgòrđítàđèlàzgáfàs ↓ | A la gordita de las gafas. |

| | | |
|---|---|---|
| to leave, to go out | sȧlír ↓ | salir |
| on leaving | ȧl—sȧlír ↓ | al salir |
| to call | (l)y̦ȧmár ↓ | llamar |
| *MOLINA* | | *MOLINA* |
| Fine. I'll call you when I leave. (8) | bwénȯ ↓ ȧlsȧlírtė(l)y̦ámȯ ↓ | Bueno, al salir te llamo. |

## 12.10 Notes on the basic sentences

(1) Reflexive verbs such as this one are not discussed and drilled in detail until Unit 24, but it is impossible to so arrange the dialogs that reflexive forms will not appear before then with some frequency. It will therefore be necessary to build up each one before that unit in the rather full form shown here: first the non-reflexive verb, then the reflexive form which appears in the utterance, and finally the reflexive citation form.

(2) This sentence is unusually difficult to approximate in a translation that reflects adequately both the structure and the meaning. The actual meaning is best paralleled by a translation like 'And I haven't bathed or shaved yet!', but structurally, the *cited* translation is somewhat closer and more subject to variation drill later in this Unit.

(3) To be examined in detail in Unit 25, this use of certain clitics in a fashion that can only be translated as possessive in English is rather common. Literally, of course, the utterance is roughly this: 'I was cleaning for myself the teeth'.

(4) The 'just' of 'just a moment' is not stated in the Spanish, nor need it be in the English: 'One moment' would be a satisfactory, though rather formal, translation.

(5) One of the striking differences between Spanish syntax and English syntax is illustrated in this sentence: the occurrence in Spanish of the Past I form [(l)y̦egó] *llegó* in a situation where only the English present perfect construction can satisfactorily occur.

(6) Here the occurrence of the present perfect construction in the English of the preceding utterance requires that the confirmation utterance (whether negative or affirmative—here it happens to be affirmative) continue in the same way. The Spanish does not require continuation in this situation, so that the complete shift, from 'arrived' to 'already there is (some)', is not startling.

(7) [porfín] *por fin* in this utterance means 'Finally after all that deliberation you were going through' or something similar. The translation is therefore not as literal as 'Hey, who are you finally going to take?'

(8) The phrase relator [a] *a* in [alsalír] *al salir* does not imply 'when' or 'before' or 'as' in itself; but the context indicates that 'On leaving' is equivalent to 'When I leave', since the more literal 'On leaving' is much too formal an English equivalent.

# 12.2 DRILLS AND GRAMMAR

## 12.21 PATTERN DRILLS

### 12.21.1 Subject pronouns

A. PRESENTATION OF PATTERN

*ILLUSTRATIONS*

| | | |
|---|---|---|
| ____________________ | 1 yókyéro̯unsáŋw̯ich \| đėhȧmón ↓ | *Yo* quiero un sandwich de jamón. |
| ____________________ | 2 itú ↑ késtázƀėƀyéndȯ ↓ | Y *tú* ¿qué estás bebiendo? |
| ____________________ | 3 kómo̯ėstáu̯stéđ ↓ | ¿Cómo está *usted?* |
| He's coming this week. | 4 élbyénėstȧsėmánȧ ↓ | *El* viene esta semana. |
| She washes very well. | 5 é(l)y̯ȧláƀȧ \| múyƀyén ↓ | *Ella* lava muy bien. |
| We're American. | 6 nȯsótrȯs \| sómos̯ȧmėrikánȯs ↓ | *Nosotros* somos americanos. |
| We're American (f). | 7 nȯsótrȧs \| sómos̯ȧmėrikánȧs ↓ | *Nosotras* somos americanas. |
| ____________________ | 8 kéđėséȧnu̯stéđės ↓ | ¿Qué desean *ustedes?* |
| They're not in the street. | 9 é(l)y̯ȯz \| no̯ėstáne̯nlȧká(l)y̯ė ↓ | *Ellos* no están en la calle. |
| They (f) want pillowcases. | 10 é(l)y̯ȧskyérėm \| fúndȧzđe̯ȧlmwáđȧ ↓ | *Ellas* quieren fundas de almohada. |

*EXTRAPOLATION*

| | sg | | pl | |
|---|---|---|---|---|
| | m | f | m | f |
| 1 | yó | | nosótros | nosótras |
| 2 fam<br>2 for | tú<br>ustéd | | ustédes | |
| 3 | él | é(l)ya | é(l)yos | é(l)yas |

*NOTES*

a. Spanish subject pronouns are usually used only for contrastive emphasis, when the reference of the pronoun is otherwise clear from the context.

b. Spanish /tú/ is the structural equivalent of English ‘thou’, but is much more frequently used.

c. English has distinct gender forms in 3 sg; Spanish has distinct gender forms in 3 sg *and* pl, and also in l pl.

d. English 3 sg ‘it’, which is neither masculine nor feminine, is very rarely translated in Spanish.

## 12.21.11 TRANSLATION DRILL

| | | |
|---|---|---|
| 1 She's American, but I'm Spanish. | é(l)yaesamerikána ↓ peroyósoyespanyól ↓ | Ella es americana, pero yo soy español. |
| 2 I'm single, but he's married. | yósoysoltéro ↓ peroéleskasádo ↓ | Yo soy soltero, pero él es casado. |
| 3 They're from here, but we're from Chile. | é(l)yo(s)sondeakí ↓ peronosótros \| sómozdechíle ↓ | Ellos son de aquí, pero nosotros somos de Chile. |
| 4 She drinks water and I drink whisky and soda. | é(l)yabébeágwa ↑ iyó \| wískikonsóda ↓ | Ella bebe agua y yo whisky con soda. |
| 5 He's in the patio, and she's in the kitchen. | élestáenelpátyo ↑ ié(l)yaenlakosína ↓ | El está en el patio, y ella en la cocina. |
| 6 They're (f) Spanish, and we are too. | é(l)ya(s)sonespanyólas ↑ inosótros tambyén ↓ | Ellas son españolas y nosotros también. |
| 7 Are we going, or are they? | bámoznosótros ↑ obané(l)yos ↓ | ¿Vamos nosotros o van ellos? |
| 8 Am I going, or are you all? | bóyyó ↑ obanustédes ↓ | ¿Voy yo o van Uds.? |

| | | |
|---|---|---|
| 9 Are they going, or are we? | bánẹ́(l)y̯ȯs ↑ ȯƀámȯznȯsótrȯs ↓ | ¿Van ellos o vamos nosotros? |
| 10 Who wants ham, you or he? | kyéŋkyérėhȧmón ↓ ùstéđ ↑ o̯él ↓ | ¿Quién quiere jamón? ¿Ud. o él? |
| 11 Who works in the consular section, you all or she? | kyéntrȧƀáhḁ \| ėnlȧsėkṣyóŋkȯnsùlár ↓ ùstéđės ↑ o̯é(l)y̯ȧ ↓ | ¿Quién trabaja en la sección consular? ¿Uds. o ella? |
| 12 Who wants something else, you or they? | kyéndėséḁ \| álgȯmás ↓ ùstéđ ↑ o̯é(l)y̯ȯs ↓ | ¿Quién desea algo más? ¿Ud. o ellos? |
| 13 What does *he* want? | kéđėséḁ \| él ↓ | ¿Qué desea él? |
| 14 What do *they* need? | kénėṣėsítan \| é(l)y̯ȯs ↓ | ¿Qué necesitan ellos? |
| 15 What does *she* want? | kékyérẹ \| é(l)y̯ȧ ↓ | ¿Qué quiere ella? |

## B. DISCUSSION OF PATTERN

In Unit 4 (4.21.1) the concept of person was discussed as it applies to the proper selection of verb forms, and person-number categories were illustrated by English pronouns. The same classification—that of first, second, and third categories, each occurring in both singular and plural forms, constituting a set of six categories for Spanish verbs—can be used to describe Spanish pronouns. In addition there are distinct gender forms in the 1 pl and 3 sg and pl categories and two 2nd person forms distinguishing formal and familiar.

This means that there are several areas of overlap between pronoun and verb patterns, as the charts below illustrate:

| | | | |
|---|---|---|---|
| yó | | nosótros | nosótras |
| tú | | ustédes | |
| ustéd | | | |
| él | é(l)ya | é(l)yos | é(l)yas |

| | |
|---|---|
| ábl—o | abl—ámos |
| ábl—as | |
| ábl—a | ábl—an |

Note that the pattern discrepancies of Spanish, though they exist, are relatively minor compared to English.

| | | | |
|---|---|---|---|
| I | | | we |
| you | | | |
| he | she | it | they |

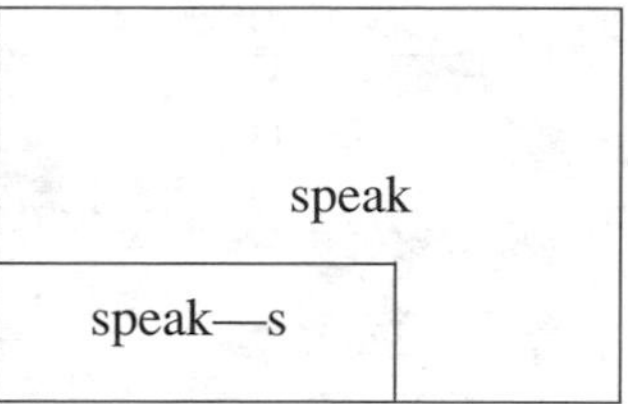


As the chart shows, only the English pronouns which are marked for gender (he, she, it) require a verb form that is different from the name form or infinitive form which all other English pronouns occur with. The Spanish pronoun and verb patterns coincide except for a distinction between 2nd formal and 3rd person forms.

Since verbs in Spanish carry person-number distinctions in their structure, pronouns that carry the same information are frequently considered redundant and unnecessary, and a student's tendency to translate all English pronouns into Spanish pronouns is very conspicuous to a Spanish speaker. Spanish pronouns are usually used only for emphasis or contrast as in /yónolokyéro ↓/ '*I* don't want it', /itú ↑ késtásbebyéndo ↓/ 'And what are *you* drinking', /yómebóy ↓ péroélsekéda ↓/ '*I*'m going, but *he's* staying', or when they are needed to distinguish forms, as between /él/ and /ustéd/ with a verb form like / ábla/.

The regional American 'you all' is often used in drills in this book to signal the distinction between /ustéd/ and /ustédes/ that 'you' alone does not show.

Very commonly used abbreviations of *usted* and *ustedes* are *Ud.* and *Uds.*

## 12.21.2 Pronouns after phrase relators

### A. PRESENTATION OF PATTERN

*ILLUSTRATIONS*

| | | |
|---|---|---|
| ______________________ | 1 àmí ↑ tráygàmè \| spóàđèlègúmbrès ↓ | *A mí* tráigame sopa de legumbres. |
| with me | kònmígò ↓ | conmigo |
| He's going to work with me. | 2 bátràƀàhár \| kònmígò ↓ | Va a trabajar *conmigo.* |
| ______________________ | 3 pásopòrtí \| àlàsóchò ↓ | Paso *por ti* a las ocho. |
| with you (fam.) | kòntígò ↓ | contigo |
| He's going to work with you. | 4 bátràƀàhár \| kòntígò ↓ | Va a trabajar *contigo.* |
| the letter | là—kártà ↓ | la carta |
| The letter is for you. | 5 làkárta \| èspárausté đ ↓ | La carta es *para usted.* |

| | | |
|---|---|---|
| ______________ | 6 nó ↓ ėṣigwál \| ȧlde̯él ↓ | No, es igual al *de él*. |
| ______________ | 7 bátrȧƀȧhár \| kȯ(n)nȯsótrȯs ↓ | Va a trabajar *con nosotros*. |
| He's going without you all. | 8 élbá \| sınụstéđės ↓ | El va *sin ustedes*. |
| Sit down with them. | 9 syéntėsė \| kȯnẹ́(l)y̱ȯs ↓ | Siéntese *con ellos*. |

*EXTRAPOLATION*

| | sg | pl |
|---|---|---|
| 1 | mí | nosótros, —as |
| 2 fam | tí | |
| 2 for | ustéd | ustédes |
| 3 | él, é(l)ya | é(l)yos, —as |

*NOTES*

a. Pronouns after phrase relators differ from subject pronouns only in 1 sg and 2 fam sg forms.

b. When the two distinct forms mentioned in (a) occur with the phrase relator /kon/, the special combinations /konmígo/ and /kontígo/ appear.

## 12.21.21 RESPONSE DRILL

| | | |
|---|---|---|
| | 1 éstoesparamí ↑ opáraustéđ ↓ | paraustéđ ↓ |
| | 2 ésoezđé(l)ya ↑ ođél ↓ | dél ↓ |
| | 3 éstoezđé(l)yas ↑ ođenosótros ↓ | denosótros ↓ |
| | 4 lozmwéƀles \| sómparanosótros ↑ | |
| | opáraé(l)yos ↓ | paraé(l)yos ↓ |
| [nosótros ↓] | 5 koŋkyém \| bané(l)yos ↓ | ko(n)nosótros ↓ |
| [é(l)ya ↓] | 6 koŋkyém \| baél ↓ | koné(l)ya ↓ |
| [él ↓] | 7 parakyén \| eséstasí(l)ya ↓ | paraél ↓ |

---

| | | |
|---|---|---|
| | 1 ¿Esto es para mí o para Ud.? | Para Ud. |
| | 2 ¿Eso es de ella o de él? | De él. |
| | 3 ¿Esto es de ellas o de nosotros? | De nosotros. |
| | 4 ¿Los muebles son para nosotros o para ellos? | Para ellos. |
| (nosotros) | 5 ¿Con quién van ellos? | Con nosotros. |
| (ella) | 6 ¿Con quién va él? | Con ella. |
| (él) | 7 ¿Para quién es esta silla? | Para él. |

| | | |
|---|---|---|
| [é(l)y̰às ↓] | 8 làzmònéđàs ↓ sómpàrànòsótròs ↑ | nó ↓ párąé(l)y̰às ↓ |
| [él ↓] | 9 ùstéđbá \| kònę́(l)y̰òs ↑ | nó ↓ kònę́l ↓ |
| [é(l)y̰à ↓] | 10 éstèskrıtóryǫ \| èspàrąél ↑ | nó ↓ pàrąé(l)y̰à ↓ |
| | 11 éstàƀıtàşyón \| èspàrąustéđ ↑ | sí ↓ pàràmí ↓ |
| | 12 éstèkwártǫ \| èspàrànòsótròs ↑ | sí ↓ pàrànòsótròs ↓ |
| | 13 é(l)y̰àƀàkònmígò ↑ | sí ↓ kònųstéđ ↓ |

---

| | | |
|---|---|---|
| (ellas) | 8 Las monedas, ¿son para nosotros? | No, para ellas. |
| (él) | 9 ¿Ud. va con ellos? | No, con él. |
| (ella) | 10 ¿Este escritorio es para él? | No, para ella. |
| | 11 ¿Esta habitación es para Ud.? | Sí, para mí. |
| | 12 ¿Este cuarto es para nosotros? | Sí, para nosotros. |
| | 13 ¿Ella va conmigo? | Sí, con Ud. |

## 12.21.22 TRANSLATION DRILL

| | | | |
|---|---|---|---|
| 1 | She's going with me. | é(l)y̯ȧƀákȯnmɪ́gȯ ↓ | Ella va conmigo. |
| 2 | This sandwich is for me. | éstėsáŋw̰ich \| ėspárȧmí ↓ | Este sandwich es para mí. |
| 3 | After them, John eats. | dėspwézđé(l)y̯ȯs \| kómėhwán ↓ | Después de ellos, come Juan. |
| 4 | They live near us. | é(l)y̯ȯzƀɪ́ƀėn \| s̩érkȧđėnȯsótrȯs ↓ | Ellos viven cerca de nosotros. |
| 5 | He doesn't work with me. | él \| nótrȧƀáhȧkȯnmígȯ ↓ | El no trabaja conmigo. |
| 6 | Carmen lives with us. | kármėn \| bɪ́ƀėkȯ(n)nȯsótrȯs ↓ | Carmen vive con nosotros. |
| 7 | John lives with them. | hwám \| bɪ́ƀėkȯné̩(l)y̯ȯs ↓ | Juan vive con ellos. |
| 8 | The sheets are for us. | lȧ(s)sáƀȧnȧs \| sómpȧrȧnȯsótrȯs ↓ | Las sábanas son para nosotros. |
| 9 | There's eleven dollars for you and ten for us. | áyóns̩ėđólȧrės \| párḁustéđ ↑ iđyés̩ \| párȧnȯsótrȯs ↓ | Hay once dólares para Ud. y diez para nosotros. |
| 10 | There's two hundred dollars for me and two hundred for them. | áyđȯs(s̩)yéntȯzđólȧrės \| párȧmí ↑ iđȯs(s̩)yéntȯs \| párḁé(l)y̯ȯs ↓ | Hay doscientos dólares para mí y doscientos para ellos. |
| 11 | There's nine dollars for him and four for her. | áynwéƀėđólȧrės \| párḁel ↑ ikwátrȯ \| párḁé(l)y̯ȧ ↓ | Hay nueve dólares para él y cuatro para ella. |

## B. DISCUSSION OF PATTERN

The forms of pronouns that are used after phrase relators are essentially subject pronouns, except that /mí/ and /tí/ replace /yó/and /tú/ in the pattern. The subject and phrase-relator pronouns can be classed as nonclitic, in contrast to the clitic pronouns that can appear only with verbs. Thus the nonclitic pronouns can be charted as follows:

| | Subject | Phrase relator |
|---|---|---|
| 1 sg | yó | mí |
| 2 fam sg | tú | tí |
| 2 for sg | ustéd | |
| 3 sg | él, é(l)ya | |
| 1 pl | nosótros, —as | |
| 2 pl | ustédes | |
| 3 pl | é(l)yos, —as | |

The significance of the relation of the subject and phrase relator function in essentially a single set of forms can be seen by comparing Spanish and English usage. The Spanish classification on nonclitic and clitic case forms is partly paralleled by the English pattern of subject and object case forms. However, as the following chart shows, there is an area of overlap in appearance after a phrase relator. In the examples, /él/ is nonclitic, /lo/ is clitic; 'he' is subject-form, and 'him' is object-form.

| Subject of verb | Object of phrase relator | Object of verb |
|---|---|---|
| élestákí ↓ | ésparaél ↓ | nópwédobérlo ↓ |
| *He's* here. | It's for *him.* | I can't see *him.* |

More will be said about the concept of 'nominalization' in the next discussion of pattern and elsewhere. The concept assumes, in substance, that a form that is not a noun behaves as if it were. An interesting example of 'pronoun nominalization' occurs in Unit 6 in the sentence /kéleparéṣe | sinosostratámosdetú ↓/, where a subject pronoun appears after a phrase relator: /tú/ appears where we might expect /tí/. In this case /tú/ has been nominalized, it is behaving as a noun, a form which has no case forms: nouns do not change in form when used as subject of a verb or object of a phrase relator.

### 12.21.3 Components of phrases

#### A. PRESENTATION OF PATTERN

*ILLUSTRATIONS*

| | | |
|---|---|---|
| ______________________ | 1 bínǫustéđ \| kònsùfàmílyà ↑ | ¿Vino usted *con su familia?* |
| ______________________ | 2 bátràƀàhár \| kò(n)nòsótròs ↓ | Va a trabajar *con nosotros.* |
| By talking so much, you don't learn anything. | 3 kòn̩àƀlártánto ↑ nǫapréndèznáđà ↓ | *Con hablar* tanto, no aprendes nada. |
| ______________________ | 4 sinịŋklwírlúṣ \| ágwà \| nıgás ↓ | *Sin incluir* luz, agua, ni gas. |
| What do you do after studying? | 5 kẹ́àṣez \| đèspwézđèstùđyár ↓ | ¿Qué haces *después de estudiar?* |
| Before translating, repeat. | 6 ántèz \| đètràđúṣır \| rèpítà ↓ | *Antes de traducir,* repita. |

*EXTRAPOLATION*

| | |
|---|---|
| phrase relator | noun<br>pronoun<br>nominalized form |

*NOTES*

a. Phrase relators introduce nominal forms.

b. The infinitive is the nominalized form of verbs that normally occurs after phrase relators.

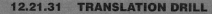

## 12.21.31 TRANSLATION DRILL

| | | |
|---|---|---|
| 1 He always studies before going out. | élsyémprestúđyą \| ántezđesalír ↓ | El siempre estudia antes de salir. |
| 2 She always cleans after eating. | é(l)yąsyémprelímpyą \| đespwézđekomér ↓ | Ella siempre limpia después de comer. |
| 3 I'm going downtown before eating lunch. | bóyalşéntrǫ \| ántezđęalmorşár ↓ | Voy al centro antes de almorzar. |
| 4 We're going after eating. | nosótrozbámoz \| đespwézđekomér ↓ | Nosotros vamos después de comer. |
| 5 Repeat this before writing it (down). | rrepítąéstǫ ↑ ántezđeskriбírlo ↓ | Repita esto antes de escribirlo. |
| 6 I don't have time for studying. | notéŋgotyémpo \| parąestuđyár ↓ | No tengo tiempo para estudiar. |
| 7 She always comes without calling. | é(l)yąsyémprebyéne \| sin(l)yamár ↓ | Ella siempre viene sin llamar. |
| 8 You can't learn without studying. | nopwéđęaprendér \| sinęstuđyár ↓ | No puede aprender sin estudiar. |
| 9 Two hundred a month without including the electricity. | dos(ş)yéntos \| almés ↑ siniŋklwírlalúş ↓ | Doscientos al mes sin incluir la luz. |

| | | |
|---|---|---|
| 10 Because of (for) talking so much, you don't learn. | pȯrȧƀlártántȯ \| no̯apréndė ↓ | Por hablar tanto no aprende. |
| 11 She charges four dollars for sweeping the whole house. | é(l)y̯ȧkóƀrȧ \| kwátrȯđólarės ↑ pȯrƀȧrrér \| tóđalȧkásȧ ↓ | Ella cobra cuatro dólares por barrer toda la casa. |
| 12 I don't like the idea of going now. | nómėgústalai̯đéa \| đe̯iraórȧ ↓ | No me gusta la idea de ir ahora. |
| 13 What do you think of the idea of buying the house? | kélėparése̯lai̯đéa \| đėkȯmprárlȧkásȧ ↓ | ¿Qué le parece la idea de comprar la casa? |

## B. DISCUSSION OF PATTERN

A phrase is a subordinate construction consisting of a phrase relator and its object (plus any modifiers of the object). The phrase normally modifies some other item (noun, verbs, etc.) in an utterance, though it may stand alone as in /atrabahár ↓/ 'Let's get to work'.

The term 'preposition' is often employed to designate phrase relators. In the structural discussions in this text it has been omitted in favor of the term 'phrase relator' to help point up structural and distributional parallels with analogous forms such as clause relators (see appendix).

The object of a phrase relator is a nominal form: either a noun, a pronoun, or a nominalized form. 'Nominalization' means the selection and appearance of an item from another form-class (an adjective, modifier, verb, etc.) in a function that is normally occupied by a noun. A nominalized form may be the subject of a sentence /elbyéhoestáki ↓/ 'The *old man* is here', the object of a verb /béo̯ún amerikáno ↓/ 'I see one *American*' or the object of a phrase relator /ástalwégo ↓/ 'See you *later*'. It may be modified by adjectives /elotrobyého ↓/ 'The *other* old man', which agree in number and gender with the nominalized form /losótrosbyéhos ↓/ 'The *other* old men.' In short, nominalized forms are functionally nouns, even though they do not have the defining morphological characteristics of nouns (inflection for gender only).

The form of the verb which is most readily nominalized is the infinitive, and this is the form which follows phrase relators. The equivalent English construction very often shows an '—ing' form of the verb where the Spanish infinitive occurs, and the

tendency to follow the English pattern is responsible for many mistakes of English speakers learning Spanish. Thus, /konablártánto ↑.../ and /sininklwírlúş ↑.../ are equivalent to 'By talking so much...' and 'without including electricity....'

The regular exception to this generalization is the English phrase relator 'to', which takes the infinitive form, just as in Spanish. The Spanish equivalent to English 'to' is /a, pára, de, ke/, and other phrase relators, varying in different constructions. Note the following correspondences:

| | |
|---|---|
| /bánatrabahár ↓/ | They're going *to work*. |
| /téngoúnaóra \|párakomér ↓/ | I have an hour *to eat*. |
| /ésfáşıl \| denkontrár ↑/ | Is it easy *to find?* |
| /tyéneskekonoşérla ↓/ | You have *to meet* her. |

In all cases the Spanish construction is always *'phrase relator* plus infinitive'. In English, it is '*to* plus *infinitive'*, but '*any other phrase relator* plus *—ing-form.*'

In most cases the Spanish infinitive immediately follows the phrase relator. Sometimes, however, the nominalized infinitive can be modified by an adjective such as the definite article, as in /alsalír | te(l)yámo ↓/, though /a/ is normally translated 'to', in this construction it is not: 'On leaving (when I leave), I'll call you.'

Many phrase relators are single words. Often, however, a verb modifier may itself be modified by a phrase in a construction which appears to include a compound phrase relator. In the utterance /elotél | estáşérka ↓/, the form /şérka/ is a verb modifier. In /elotél | estáşérka | deakí ↓/, the phrase /deakí/ modifies /şérka/. It is nevertheless convenient sometimes to consider /şérkade/ as a kind of compound phrase relator which takes the nominalized modifier /akí/ as its object.

The phrase relators so far introduced into this text include: /a, ásta, de, désde, en, ke, kómo, kon, ménos, pára, por, sin/. Compounds include: /antes—de, despwés—de, léhos—de, sérka—de/.

Tape 9B

## 12.21.4 Statement intonation patterns—normal and contrastive statements

### A. PRESENTATION OF PATTERN

*ILLUSTRATION*

| | | |
|---|---|---|
| It's near. | 1 ėstásérkȧ ↓ | 1 2 1 1 ↓<br>Está cerca. |
| ________________ | nó ↓ ėstáléhȯs ↓ | 21 1 2 3 1 ↓<br>No, está lejos. |
| ________________ | 2 ėzmúykárȯ ↓ | 1 2 1 1 ↓<br>Es muy caro. |
| ________________ | ȧlkȯntráryȯ ↓ | 1 3 1 ↓<br>Al contrario. |
| ________________ | 3 tántȯgústȯ ↓ | 2 1 1 ↓<br>Tanto gusto. |
| ________________ | ėlgústȯezmíȯ ↓ | 1 2 31 ↓<br>El gusto es mío. |

*EXTRAPOLATION*

| Statement | |
|---|---|
| Uncolored | Contrastive |
| /1211 ↓/ | /1231 ↓/ |

*NOTES*

a. The uncolored Spanish pattern resembles an English pattern that is often associated with expressions of disinterest or boredom.

b. The contrastive (or emphatic) pattern resembles an English uncolored pattern.

## 12.21.41 SUBSTITUTION DRILLS

Problem:

ėstóyėŋkȯlómbyȧ ↓

Answer:

ėstóyėŋkȯlómbyȧ ↓

---

Problem:

1 2 1 1 ↓
Estoy en Colombia.

Answer:

1 2 3 1 ↓
Estoy en Colombia.

| | |
|---|---|
| 1 trȧƀáho̯ėŋkȧrákȧs ↓ | trȧƀáho̯ėŋkȧrákȧs ↓ |
| 2 isóyđėchílė ↓ | isóyđėchílė ↓ |
| 3 kȯmémȯzmúchȯ ↓ | kȯmémȯzmúchȯ ↓ |
| 4 ėstáo̯ku̇páđȯ ↓ | ėstáo̯ku̇páđȯ ↓ |
| 5 prȯnúnsyȧstóđȯ ↓ | prȯnúnsyȧstóđȯ ↓ |
| 6 ėŋkȯntrámȯskásȧ ↓ | ėŋkȯntrámȯskásȧ ↓ |

---

```
   1  2           1  1 ↓              1  2          3 1 ↓
1  Trabajo en Caracas.                Trabajo en Caracas.

   1  2         1 1 ↓                 1  2         3 1 ↓
2  Y soy de Chile.                    Y soy de Chile.

   1  2        1   1 ↓                1  2        3   1 ↓
3  Comemos mucho.                     Comemos mucho.

   1  2       1 1 ↓                   1  2       3  1 ↓
4  Está ocupado.                      Está ocupado.

   1  2         1  1 ↓                1  2         3  1 ↓
5  Pronuncias todo.                   Pronuncias todo.

   1       2      1 1 ↓               1       2      3 1 ↓
6  Encontramos casa.                  Encontramos casa.
```

| | |
|---|---|
| 7 àlkilámȯṣèlkwártò ↓ | àlkilámȯṣèlkwártò ↓ |
| 8 èstúđyȧmpókò ↓ | èstúđyȧmpókò ↓ |
| 9 èmpèṣámȯzmȧn̯yánȧ ↓ | èmpèṣámȯzmȧn̯yánȧ ↓ |
| 10 nèṣèsítạunlíƀrò ↓ | nèṣèsítạunlíƀrò ↓ |
| 11 pròƀámȯṣèlpóstrè ↓ | pròƀámȯṣèlpóstrè ↓ |

---

| | |
|---|---|
| 1 2 1 1 ↓<br>7 Alquilamos el cuarto. | 1 2 3 1 ↓<br>Alquilamos el cuarto. |
| 1 2 1 1 ↓<br>8 Estudian poco. | 1 2 3 1 ↓<br>Estudian poco. |
| 1 2 1 1 ↓<br>9 Empezamos mañana. | 1 2 3 1 ↓<br>Empezamos mañana. |
| 1 2 1 1 ↓<br>10 Necesita un libro. | 1 2 3 1 ↓<br>Necesita un libro. |
| 1 2 1 1 ↓<br>11 Probamos el postre. | 1 2 3 1 ↓<br>Probamos el postre. |

## 12.21.42 RESPONSE DRILL

Problem 1:

dėđóndės̩u̇stéđ ↓

Answer:

sóyđėchílė ↓

Problem 2:

dėđóndė ↑

Answer:

dėchílė ↓

---

Problem 1:

¿De dónde es Ud.?

Answer:

1 21 ↓
Soy de Chile.

Problem 2:

¿De dónde?

Answer:

1 31 ↓
De Chile.

| | | |
|---|---|---|
| [dóṣė ↓] | 1 kwántȯskwártȯṣáy ↓ | ȧyđóṣė ↓ |
| | kwántȯs ↑ | đóṣė ↓ |
| [ȧ(l)y̱í ↓] | 2 dóndėstáe̱(l)líƀrȯ ↓ | ėstá(l)y̱í ↓ |
| | dóndė ↑ | ȧ(l)y̱í ↓ |

---

| | | |
|---|---|---|
| (doce) | 1 ¿Cuántos cuartos hay? | 1 2 1 ↓<br>Hay doce. |
| | ¿Cuántos? | 3 1 ↓<br>Doce. |
| (allí) | 2 ¿Dónde está el libro? | 1 2 11 ↓<br>Está allí. |
| | ¿Dónde? | 1 31 ↓<br>Allí. |

| | | |
|---|---|---|
| [byáhė ↓] | 3 pȧrȧkéșėstėchékė ↓ | pȧrạėlbyáhė ↓ |
| | pȧrȧké ↑ | pȧrạėlbyáhė ↓ |
| [ámbrė ↓] | 4 kétyénė ↓ | téŋgọámbrė ↓ |
| | ké ↑ | ámbrė ↓ |
| [w̰ískịkȯnsóđȧ ↓] | 5 kékyérė ↓ | w̰ískịkȯnsóđȧ ↓ |
| | kȯŋké ↑ | kȯnsóđȧ ↓ |

---

| | | |
|---|---|---|
| (viaje) | 3 ¿Para qué es este cheque? | 1 2 1 ↓<br>Para el viaje. |
| | ¿Para qué? | 1 3 1 ↓<br>Para el viaje. |
| (hambre) | 4 ¿Qué tiene? | 2 1 1 ↓<br>Tengo hambre. |
| | ¿Qué ? | 3 1 ↓<br>Hambre. |
| (whisky con soda) | 5 ¿Qué quiere? | 2 2 1 ↓<br>Whisky con soda. |
| | ¿Con qué? | 1 3 1 ↓<br>Con soda. |

| | | |
|---|---|---|
| [ėnlȧtintȯrėríȧ ↓] | 6 dóndėtrȧƀáh͜ȧél ↓ | ėnlȧtintȯrėríȧ ↓ |
| | dóndė ↑ | ėnlȧtintȯrėríȧ ↓ |
| [ėn̯ėlėskritóryȯ ↓] | 7 dóndėstálȧplúmȧ ↓ | ėn̯ėlėskritóryȯ ↓ |
| | dóndė ↑ | ėn̯ėlėskritóryȯ ↓ |
| [bámȯs̯ȧkȯmér ↓] | 8 pȧrȧđóndėƀán ↓ | bámȯs̯ȧkȯmér ↓ |
| | pȧrȧđóndė ↑ | ȧkȯmér ↓ |

---

| | | |
|---|---|---|
| (en la tintorería) | 6 ¿Dónde trabaja él? | 1 21 ↓<br>En la tintorería. |
| | ¿Dónde? | 1 31 ↓<br>En la tintorería. |
| (en el escritorio) | 7 ¿Dónde está la pluma? | 1 2 1 ↓<br>En el escritorio. |
| | ¿Dónde? | 1 3 1 ↓<br>En el escritorio. |
| (vamos a comer) | 8 ¿Para dónde van? | 1 21 ↓<br>Vamos a comer. |
| | ¿Para dónde? | 1 31 ↓<br>A comer. |

| | | |
|---|---|---|
| [àtràƀàhár ↓] | 9 àđóndèƀán ↓ | àtràƀàhár ↓ |
| | àđóndè ↑ | àtràƀàhár ↓ |
| [ótràkàmísà ↓] | 10 kékyérè ↓ | ótràkàmísà ↓ |
| | ké ↑ | ótràkàmísà ↓ |
| [ènlàkòşínà ↓] | 11 dóndẹaẹstáđò ↓ | ènlàkòşínà ↓ |
| | dóndè ↑ | ènlàkòşínà ↓ |

---

| | | |
|---|---|---|
| (a trabajar) | 9 ¿Adónde van? | 1 21 ↓<br>A trabajar. |
| | ¿Adónde? | 1 31 ↓<br>A trabajar. |
| (otra camisa) | 10 ¿Qué quiere? | 1 21 ↓<br>Otra camisa. |
| | ¿Qué? | 2 31 ↓<br>Otra camisa. |
| (en la cocina) | 11 ¿Dónde ha estado? | 1 2 1 ↓<br>En la cocina. |
| | ¿Dónde? | 1 3 1 ↓<br>En la cocina. |

## B. DISCUSSION OF PATTERN

Intonation patterns are arrangements of stress /´ ˙/, pitch /1, 2, 3/, and terminal junctures / |, ↑, ↓/. These patterns are different in English and Spanish, first of all because the number of available counters in the systems of the two languages is different: Spanish has two stresses, English four; Spanish has three pitches, English four.

In this text intonation patterns have been shown by /´/ and /˙/ placed at varying heights over each syllable to represent pitch. This is an effective pedagogical device to present these patterns. However, Spanish intonations can most efficiently be described by marking all real or potential pitch changes, followed by the terminal juncture. It has been determined that normally the points of potential pitch change in any single phrase are all strong stressed syllables plus the first and last syllables, when these are weak stressed. Thus the intonation pattern of /ėstaşérkȧ ↓/, /tėnémoslȧbísa ↓/ can be abstracted as /1211 ↓/ for both sentences, even though the formula has to account for a different number of syllables in each case. The sentences can then be rewritten
1 2 1 1     1 2     1 1
/estáşérka ↓/, /tenémoslabísa ↓/, writing the significant numbers above each appropriate syllable and marking only strong stress.

When the first syllable is strong-stressed, the first number of the pattern formula does not actually occur: /tyénėnọ́trȯ ↓/,
2 1 1     2 1 1
/dóndėstámȯs ↓/ or /tyénenọtro ↓/, /dóndestámos ↓/. When the last syllable is strong-stressed, both numbers are written over the
1 2 11     1 2 31
last vowel, since a glide in this position can be significant; /ėstákí ↓ /, /ėstákí ↓/then are written /estákí ↓/, /estákí ↓/. The last /1/ on the first sentence may seem to be superfluous, but is needed in the analysis to contrast with the last /1/ on the second
1 2 33
sentence, which cannot be omitted; /ėstákı ↓/ can occur, analyzed as /estákí ↓/, where final /3/ is significantly and minimally different from final /1/ of the previous sentence.

The two patterns drilled in this section, /1211 ↓/ and /1231 ↓/, are important because they resemble English patterns which have very different meanings. A pattern very much like /1211 ↓/, unlike the Spanish normal, uncolored connotation, means
2 1 1     2 1
disinterested or discourteous: /Whât's for dínner ↓/, /Whŷ nót ↓/, and unless a student realizes that it has no such meaning in Spanish, he will avoid using it, even though he may be unaware of his aversion to the pattern.

On the other hand, /1231 ↓/, which is contrastive in Spanish, used only for special emphasis, is very similar to a pattern that
2 31 ↓ 3 3 1 ↓
means normal or uncolored in English. Thus the pattern of /I'm gôing hóme /, /Hê's frôm Kánsas /, if transferred to Spanish
2 3 1 2 3 1
/bóyakása ↓/ /ésdekánsas ↓/ is likely to sound over-insistent in Spanish where /1231 ↓/ means emphatic.

One other feature related to intonation that needs to be brought to the attention of students, since it is notably different in the structure of the two languages, is rhythm. Rhythm is syllable-centered in Spanish, phrase-centered in English. This means that the recurring tempo unit in Spanish is the syllable—each is of approximately the same length; in English the recurring tempo unit is the phrase, and also each is of approximately the same length. But Spanish phrases and English syllables are of differing lengths, and English phrases usually arrange syllables so that two long (stronger stressed) do not occur together nor more than two short (weaker stressed) occur in uninterrupted sequence. Imposing the English pattern of alternate long and short syllables on Spanish produces a distortion which will immediately come to the attention of any Spanish speaker, even though he may not be able to explain exactly what it is that 'sounds funny'. This feature of rhythm was discussed with illustrations in Section 1.22.4.

One of the important purposes of this and of subsequent intonation drills is to bring the patterns that are involved to the awareness of the learner. In some cases the patterns are similar to English patterns; in some cases they are very different. It is most important that the student master the differences, but in all cases the manipulation of the patterns, with the proper correlation to the meaning significance of their use, is valuable practice.

## 12.22 REPLACEMENT DRILLS

A nósé ↓ noayáagwa | enmiapartaménto ↓

| | | |
|---|---|---|
| 1 | ______ pwéđo ______________ ↓ | nópwéđo ↓ noayáagwa | enmiapartaménto ↓ |
| 2 | ____________ el ___________ ↓ | nópwéđo ↓ noayáagwa | enelapartaménto ↓ |
| 3 | ______________________ kása ↓ | nópwéđo ↓ noayáagwa | enlakása ↓ |
| 4 | __________ náđye ___________ ↓ | nópwéđo ↓ noaynáđye | enlakása ↓ |
| 5 | ______ kréo ________________ ↓ | nókréo ↓ noaynáđye | enlakása ↓ |
| 6 | _____________ aké(l)ya ______ ↓ | nókréo ↓ noaynáđye | enaké(l)yakása ↓ |
| 7 | _______________________ otél ↓ | nókréo ↓ noaynáđye | enakelotél ↓ |

---

A No sé, no hay agua en mi apartamento.

| | | |
|---|---|---|
| 1 | _______ puedo, ______________ . | No puedo, no hay agua en mi apartamento. |
| 2 | ______ , ______ el __________ . | No puedo, no hay agua en el apartamento. |
| 3 | ______ , ________________casa. | No puedo, no hay agua en la casa. |
| 4 | ______ , ____ nadie __________ . | No puedo, no hay nadie en la casa. |
| 5 | ______ creo, ________________ . | No creo, no hay nadie en la casa. |
| 6 | ______ , _______ aquella______ . | No creo, no hay nadie en aquella casa. |
| 7 | ______ , ________________hotel. | No creo, no hay nadie en aquel hotel. |

B yo̯éstáƀȧ | l̇impyándȯmėlȯzđyéntės ↓

| | |
|---|---|
| 1 ____________________ rrópȧ ↓ | yo̯éstáƀȧ \| l̇impyándȯmėlȧrrópȧ ↓ |
| 2 _____ kȯmprándȯmė _______ ↓ | yo̯éstáƀȧ \| kȯmprándȯmėlȧrrópȧ ↓ |
| 3 ____________________ áwtȯ ↓ | yo̯éstáƀȧ \| kȯmprándȯmėláwtȯ ↓ |
| 4 ____________ u̇n _______ ↓ | yo̯éstáƀȧ \| kȯmprándȯme̯u̇ná̯wtȯ ↓ |
| 5 __________________ mwéƀlės ↓ | yo̯éstáƀȧ \| kȯmprándȯme̯u̇nȯzmwéƀlės ↓ |
| 6 _______ ȧsyéndȯme̯ _________ ↓ | yo̯éstáƀa̯ \| ȧsyéndȯme̯u̇nȯzmwéƀlės ↓ |
| 7 ___________________ trágȯs ↓ | yo̯éstáƀa̯ \| ȧsyéndȯme̯u̇nȯstrágȯs ↓ |

---

B Yo estaba limpiándome los dientes.

| | |
|---|---|
| 1 ______________________ ropa. | Yo estaba limpiándome la ropa. |
| 2 _______ comprándome _______ . | Yo estaba comprándome la ropa. |
| 3 ______________________ auto. | Yo estaba comprándome el auto. |
| 4 _______________ un ________ . | Yo estaba comprándome un auto. |
| 5 ___________________ muebles. | Yo estaba comprándome unos muebles. |
| 6 ________ haciéndome _______ . | Yo estaba haciéndome unos muebles. |
| 7 ____________________ tragos. | Yo estaba haciéndome unos tragos. |

| | |
|---|---|
| C ȧpénȧstėnémȯz \| méđyȧórȧ \| pȧrȧƀėstírnȯs ↓ | |
| 1 ________________ ƀȧn̰yarnȯs ↓ | ȧpénȧstėnémȯz \| médyȧórȧ \| pȧrȧƀȧn̰yárnȯs ↓ |
| 2 __________ únȧ ____________ ↓ | ȧpénȧstėnémȯs \| únȧórȧ \| pȧrȧƀȧn̰yárnȯs ↓ |
| 3 syémprė____________________ ↓ | syémprėtėnémȯs \| únȧórȧ \| pȧrȧƀȧn̰yárnȯs ↓ |
| 4 __________________ ȧfėytárnȯs ↓ | syémprėtėnémȯs \| únȧórȧ \| pȧrȧfėytárnȯs ↓ |
| 5 _________ mȯméntȯ _________ ↓ | syémprėtėnémȯs \| unmȯméntȯ \| pȧrȧfėytárnȯs ↓ |
| 6 núŋkȧ____________________ ↓ | núŋkȧtėnémȯs \| unmȯméntȯ \| pȧrȧfėytárnȯs ↓ |
| 7 ȧórȧ _____________________ ↓ | ȧórȧtėnémȯs \| unmȯméntȯ \| pȧrȧfėytárnȯs ↓ |

---

| | |
|---|---|
| C Apenas tenemos media hora para vestirnos. | |
| 1 ___________________ bañarnos. | Apenas tenemos media hora para bañarnos. |
| 2 __________ una ____________ . | Apenas tenemos una hora para bañarnos. |
| 3 Siempre ____________________ . | Siempre tenemos una hora para bañarnos. |
| 4 __________________ afeitarnos. | Siempre tenemos una hora para afeitarnos. |
| 5 __________ momento _________ . | Siempre tenemos un momento para afeitarnos. |
| 6 Nunca_____________________ . | Nunca tenemos un momento para afeitarnos. |
| 7 Ahora _____________________ . | Ahora tenemos un momento para afeitarnos. |

**End of Tape 9B**

**End of CD 9**

| | | |
|---|---|---|
| D | mėƀóy ǀ ėntónşės ↓ téŋgȯkėđármėprísȧ ↓ | |
| 1 | ____________________ kȯmér ↓ | mėƀóy ǀ ėntónşės ↓ téŋgȯkėkȯmér ↓ |
| 2 | ___________ áykė ___________ ↓ | mėƀóy ǀ ėntónşės ↓ áykėkȯmér ↓ |
| 3 | ____________________ traƀȧhár ↓ | mėƀóy ǀ ėntónşės ↓ áykėtraƀȧhár ↓ |
| 4 | ________ tėnémȯskė ________ ↓ | mėƀóy ǀ ėntónşės ↓ tėnémȯskėtraƀȧhár ↓ |
| 5 | ____________________ ƀėstírnȯs ↓ | mėƀóy ǀ ėntónşės ↓ tėnémȯskėƀėstírnȯs ↓ |
| 6 | ____________________ ėstuđyár ↓ | mėƀóy ǀ ėntónşės ↓ tėnémȯskėstuđyár ↓ |
| 7 | __________ téŋgȯkẹ __________ ↓ | mėƀóy ǀ ėntónşės ↓ téŋgȯkėstuđyár ↓ |

---

| | | |
|---|---|---|
| D | Me voy entonces, tengo que darme prisa. | |
| 1 | __________ , ___________ comer. | Me voy entonces, tengo que comer. |
| 2 | __________ , hay que _________ . | Me voy entonces, hay que comer. |
| 3 | __________ , ___________ trabajar. | Me voy entonces, hay que trabajar. |
| 4 | __________ , tenemos que _____ . | Me voy entonces, tenemos que trabajar. |
| 5 | __________ , _________ vestirnos. | Me voy entonces, tenemos que vestirnos. |
| 6 | __________ , __________ estudiar. | Me voy entonces, tenemos que estudiar. |
| 7 | __________ , tengo que ________ . | Me voy entonces, tengo que estudiar. |

E óy̦ė ↓ pȯrfín | ȧkyémbȧṣa(l)y̦ėƀár ↓

| | |
|---|---|
| 1 ____________________(l)y̦ȧmár ↓ | óy̦ė ↓ pȯrfín \| ȧkyémbȧṣa(l)y̦ȧmár ↓ |
| 2 ________ ėntónṣės ___________ ↓ | óy̦ė ↓ ėntónṣės \| ȧkyémbȧṣa(l)y̦ȧmár ↓ |
| 3 ___________ kwándȯ_________ ↓ | óy̦ė ↓ ėntónṣės \| kwándȯƀȧṣa(l)y̦ȧmár ↓ |
| 4 ____________________ trȧƀȧhár ↓ | óy̦ė ↓ ėntónṣės \| kwándȯƀȧṣatrȧƀȧhár ↓ |
| 5 ___________ đóndė __________ ↓ | óy̦ė ↓ ėntónṣez \| đóndėƀȧṣatrȧƀȧhár ↓ |
| 6 chíkȯ ______________________ ↓ | chíkȯ ↓ ėntónṣez \| đóndėƀȧṣatrȧƀȧhár ↓ |
| 7 ___________ kȯŋkyém _______ ↓ | chíkȯ ↓ ėntónṣės \| kȯŋkyémbȧṣatrȧƀȧhár ↓ |

---

E Oye, ¿por fin a quién vas a llevar?

| | |
|---|---|
| 1 _____ , ¿ _______________ llamar? | Oye, ¿por fin a quién vas a llamar? |
| 2 _____ , ¿entonces _____________ ? | Oye, ¿entonces a quién vas a llamar? |
| 3 _____ , ¿ ________ cuándo ______ ? | Oye, ¿entonces cuándo vas a llamar? |
| 4 _____ , ¿ _______________trabajar? | Oye, ¿entonces cuándo vas a trabajar? |
| 5 _____ , ¿ ________ dónde _______ ? | Oye, ¿entonces dónde vas a trabajar? |
| 6 Chico, ¿ ______________________ ? | Chico, ¿entonces dónde vas a trabajar? |
| 7 _____ , ¿ ______ con quién ______ ? | Chico, ¿entonces con quién vas a trabajar? |

F bwénȯ ↓ ȧlsȧlírtė(l)y̯ámȯ ↓

| | |
|---|---|
| 1 óy̯ė ______________________ ↓ | óy̯ė ↓ ȧlsȧlírtė(l)y̯ámȯ ↓ |
| 2 ________ (l)y̯ėgár ______________ ↓ | óy̯ė ↓ ȧl(l)y̯ėgártė(l)y̯ámȯ ↓ |
| 3 ______________________ ȧy̯úđȯ ↓ | óy̯ė ↓ ȧl(l)y̯ėgártẹȧy̯úđȯ ↓ |
| 4 ėntónṣės ______________________ ↓ | ėntónṣės ↑ ȧl(l)y̯ėgártẹȧy̯úđȯ ↓ |
| 5 ______________________ ȧƀísȯ ↓ | ėntónṣės ↑ ȧl(l)y̯ėgártẹȧƀísȯ ↓ |
| 6 ___________ ėmpėṣár __________ ↓ | ėntónṣės ↑ ȧlėmpėṣártẹȧƀísȯ ↓ |
| 7 byén ______________________ ↓ | byén ↓ ȧlėmpėṣártẹȧƀísȯ ↓ |

---

F Bueno, al salir te llamo.

| | |
|---|---|
| 1 Oye, ______________________ . | Oye, al salir te llamo. |
| 2 ______ , _______ llegar _________ . | Oye, al llegar te llamo. |
| 3 ______ , _________________ ayudo. | Oye, al llegar te ayudo. |
| 4 Entonces, ____________________ . | Entonces, al llegar te ayudo. |
| 5 __________ , ______________ aviso. | Entonces, al llegar te aviso. |
| 6 ___________ , empezar__________ . | Entonces, al empezar te aviso. |
| 7 Bien, ______________________ . | Bien, al empezar te aviso. |

## 12.23 VARIATION DRILLS

| | | |
|---|---|---|
| A kétėpásȧ \| hwán ↓ | | ¿Qué te pasa, Juan? |
| 1 What's the matter, Jose? | kétėpásȧ \| hȯsé ↓ | ¿Qué te pasa, José? |
| 2 What do you think of it, Jose? | kétėpȧréş̣ė \| hȯsé ↓ | ¿Qué te parece, José? |
| 3 What do you think of it, boy? | kétėpȧréş̣ė \| chíkȯ ↓ | ¿Qué te parece, chico? |
| 4 What do you like, Carmen? | kétėgústȧ \| kármėn ↓ | ¿Qué te gusta, Carmen? |
| 5 What do you want, Carmen? | kékyérės \| kármėn ↓ | ¿Qué quieres, Carmen? |
| 6 What are you writing, Carmen? | késkríƀės \| kármėn ↓ | ¿Qué escribes, Carmen? |
| 7 What are you studying, Carmen? | késtúđyȧs \| kármėn ↓ | ¿Qué estudias, Carmen? |

B iy̯ó | kėstóysimbàn̯yárme̯ | isin̯afėytármė ↓ — ¡Y yo que estoy sin bañarme y sin afeitarme!

| | | | |
|---|---|---|---|
| 1 | And here I am without having brushed my teeth! | iy̯ó \| kėstóysinlimpyármė \| lozđyéntės ↓ | ¡Y yo que estoy sin limpiarme los dientes! |
| 2 | And here I am without having changed my clothes! | iy̯ó \| kėstóysiŋkàmbyármė \| đėrrópà ↓ | ¡Y yo que estoy sin cambiarme de ropa! |
| 3 | And here I am without having worked! | iy̯ó \| kėstóysintràƀàhár ↓ | ¡Y yo que estoy sin trabajar! |
| 4 | And here I am without having eaten! | iy̯ó \| kėstóysiŋkòmér ↓ | ¡Y yo que estoy sin comer! |
| 5 | And here I am without having had lunch! | iy̯ó \| kėstóysin̯àlmòrs̯ár ↓ | ¡Y yo que estoy sin almorzar! |
| 6 | And here's John without any dollars! | ihwáŋ \| kėstásindólàrės ↓ | ¡Y Juan que está sin dólares! |
| 7 | And here's John without a car. | ihwáŋ \| kėstásin̯áwtò ↓ | ¡Y Juan que está sin auto! |

| | | | |
|---|---|---|---|
| C | íƀàđármẹùnàđúchà \| tàmbyén ↓ | | Iba a darme una ducha también. |
| | 1 I was going to clean my teeth. | íƀàlimpyármė \| lòzđyéntės ↓ | Iba a limpiarme los dientes. |
| | 2 I was going to change my shirt. | íƀàkàmbyármė \| làkàmísà ↓ | Iba a cambiarme la camisa. |
| | 3 I was going to sit there. | íƀàsèntármẹàí ↓ | Iba a sentarme ahí. |
| | 4 I was going to move. | íƀàmùđármė \| đèkásà ↓ | Iba a mudarme de casa. |
| | 5 I was going to hire a taxi. | íƀàlkilár \| ùntáksi ↓ | Iba a alquilar un taxi. |
| | 6 I was going to wait for Jose. | íƀạèspèrár \| àhòsé ↓ | Iba a esperar a José. |
| | 7 I was going to practice Spanish. | íƀàpràktikár \| èspàñyól ↓ | Iba a practicar español. |

| | | |
|---|---|---|
| D | ilȧfyésta̯ \| ėṣȧlȧ(s)syétė ↓ | Y la fiesta es a las siete. |
| 1 And the party is at nine o'clock. | ilȧfyésta̯ \| ėṣȧlȧznwéƀė ↓ | Y la fiesta es a las nueve. |
| 2 And the party is tomorrow. | ilȧfyésta̯ \| ėzmȧṉyánȧ ↓ | Y la fiesta es mañana. |
| 3 And the party is later. | ilȧfyésta̯ \| ėzđėspwés ↓ | Y la fiesta es después. |
| 4 And the party is before. | ilȧfyésta̯ \| ėṣántės ↓ | Y la fiesta es antes. |
| 5 And the party is in my apartment. | ilȧfyésta̯ \| ėṣėnmi̯ȧpȧrtȧméntȯ ↓ | Y la fiesta es en mi apartamento. |
| 6 And there'll be whiskey at the party. | ilȧfyésta̯ \| ėskȯŋw̯íski ↓ | Y la fiesta es con whisky. |
| 7 And there'll be 'cuba libre' at the party. | ilȧfyésta̯ \| ėskȯŋkúƀȧlíƀrė ↓ | Y la fiesta es con cuba libre. |

E únmȯméntȯ ↓ bóyȧƀér | si(l)y̯ėgóe̯lágwȧ ↓ — Un momento, voy a ver si llegó el agua.

| | | |
|---|---|---|
| 1 Just a minute, I'll see if the car has arrived. | únmȯméntȯ ↓ bóyȧƀér \| si(l)y̯ėgóe̯láwtȯ ↓ | Un momento, voy a ver si llegó el auto. |
| 2 Just a minute, I'll see if my neighbor has arrived. | únmȯméntȯ ↓ bóyȧƀér \| si(l)y̯ėgómiƀėșínȯ ↓ | Un momento, voy a ver si llegó mi vecino. |
| 3 Just a minute, I'll see if Miss Molina has arrived. | únmȯméntȯ ↓ bóyȧƀér \| si(l)y̯ėgó \| lȧsėn̯yȯrítamȯlínȧ ↓ | Un momento, voy a ver si llegó la señorita Molina. |
| 4 Just a minute, I'll see if the taxi has arrived. | únmȯméntȯ ↓ bóyȧƀér \| si(l)y̯ėgóe̯ltáksi ↓ | Un momento, voy a ver si llegó el taxi. |
| 5 Just a minute, I'll see if the lady who cleans the apartment has arrived. | únmȯméntȯ ↓ bóyȧƀér \| si(l)y̯ėgó \| lȧkėlímpya̯ ėlȧpȧrtȧméntȯ ↓ | Un momento, voy a ver si llegó la que limpia el apartamento. |
| 6 Just a minute, I'll see if the wash-woman has arrived. | únmȯméntȯ ↓ bóyȧƀér \| si(l)y̯ėgó \| lȧkėláƀȧlȧrrópȧ ↓ | Un momento, voy a ver si llegó la que lava la ropa. |
| 7 Just a minute, I'll see if the girl who studies Spanish has arrived. | únmȯméntȯ ↓ bóyȧƀér \| si(l)y̯ėgó \| lȧ kėstúđya̯ėspȧn̯yól ↓ | Un momento, voy a ver si llegó la que estudia español. |

| | English | Transcription | Spanish |
|---|---|---|---|
| F | | lȧgȯrđíṫa \| đėlȧzgáfȧs ↓ | La gordita de las gafas. |
| | 1 The chubby girl at the cashier's desk. | lȧgȯrđíṫa \| đėlȧkáhȧ ↓ | La gordita de la caja. |
| | 2 The young lady at the cleaners'. | lȧsėn̜yȯríṫa \| đėlȧtıntȯrėríȧ ↓ | La señorita de la tintorería. |
| | 3 The young lady who has the car. | lȧsėn̜yȯríṫa \| đėláwtȯ ↓ | La señorita del auto. |
| | 4 The girl at the hotel. | lȧmu̇cháchȧ \| đėlȯtél ↓ | La muchacha del hotel. |
| | 5 The lady on the first floor. | lȧsėn̜yórȧ \| đėlprimérpísȯ ↓ | La señora del primer piso. |
| | 6 The gentleman in the ad. | ėlsėn̜yór \| đėlȧnúnșyȯ ↓ | El señor del anuncio. |
| | 7 The man in the elevator. | ėlómbrė \| đėlȧs(ș)ėnsór ↓ | El hombre del ascensor. |

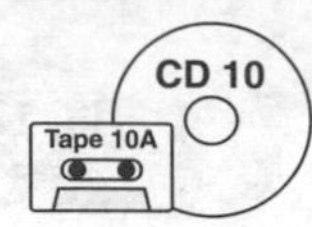




## 12.24 REVIEW DRILL

Adjective agreement in remote position

| | | | |
|---|---|---|---|
| 1 | The house is pretty. | lȧkása̯ėzƀȯnítȧ ↓ | La casa es bonita. |
| 2 | The school is good. | la̯ėskwéla̯ėzƀwénȧ ↓ | La escuela es buena. |
| 3 | The books are expensive. | lȯzlíƀrȯ(s)sȯŋkárȯs ↓ | La libros son caros. |
| 4 | The agency is no good. | lȧhéns̯ya̯ėzmálȧ ↓ | La agencia es mala. |
| 5 | The apartments are comfortable. | lȯṣȧpȧrtȧméntȯs \| sȯŋkómȯđȯs ↓ | Los apartamentos son cómodos. |
| 6 | The secretary is pretty. | lȧsėkrėtárya̯ėzƀȯnítȧ ↓ | La secretaria es bonita. |
| 7 | The lady is Spanish. | lȧsėn̯yóra̯ \| ėṣėspȧn̯yólȧ ↓ | La señora es española. |
| 8 | The cars are American. | lȯṣáwtȯs \| sóṇȧmėrıkánȯs ↓ | Los autos son americanos. |
| 9 | The suitcases are expensive. | lȧzmȧlétȧs \| sȯŋkárȧs ↓ | Las maletas son caras. |
| 10 | The buildings are pretty. | lȯṣėđifís̯yȯs \| sȯmbȯnítȯs ↓ | Los edificios son bonitos. |
| 11 | The shirts are cheap. | lȧskȧmísȧs \| sȯmbȧrátȧs ↓ | Las camisas son baratas. |
| 12 | The furniture is no good. | lȯzmwéƀlės \| sȯnmálȯs ↓ | Los muebles son malos. |
| 13 | The ladies are English. | lȧ(s)sėn̯yórȧs \| sȯṇıŋglésȧs ↓ | Las señoras son inglesas. |

## NARRATIVE 1

| | | |
|---|---|---|
| 1 Tonight there's a party at the Harris' (home). | éstȧnóchẹ ↑ áyu̇nȧfyéstạ \| ėnlȧ kásȧđėlȯshárris ↓ | Esta noche hay una fiesta en la casa de los Harris. |
| 2 Jose and Juan are going (to go). | hȯsé̯ıhwám \| bána̯ír ↓ | José y Juan van a ir. |
| 3 They have to be there at seven. | tyénėŋkėstárȧ(l)y̰í \| a̯lȧ(s)syétė ↓ | Tienen que estar allí a las siete. |
| 4 Juan is going to take that chubby girl. | hwám \| bá(l)y̰ėƀár \| ȧké(l)y̰ȧgȯrđítȧ ↓ | Juan va a llevar a aquella gordita. |
| 5 She isn't very pretty, but he likes her very much. | no̯ézmu̇yƀonítȧ ↓ pėro̯ȧé(l)lėgústȧ múchȯ ↓ | No es muy bonita, pero a él le gusta mucho. |
| 6 Jose is going to take his fiancée. | hȯsé \| ƀá(l)y̰ėƀárȧsu̇nóƀyȧ ↓ | José va a llevar a su novia. |
| 7 He's going to come by for Juan at six-thirty. | élbȧpȧsárpȯrhwán \| ȧlȧ(s)séys ı̇méđyȧ ↓ | El va a pasar por Juan a las seis y media. |

8 Then they'll pick up the girls. — lwégȯ ↑ pásampȯrlȧschíkȧs ↓ — Luego pasan por las chicas.

9 Jose doesn't want another drink, now. — hȯsé | nókyérȩ | ótrȯtrágọ | ȧórȧ ↓ — José no quiere otro trago ahora.

10 He's got to leave. — tyénėkẹ́irsė ↓ — Tiene que irse.

11 He barely has time to shave and dress. — ȧpénȧstyénėtyémpȯ | pȧrȧfėytársẹ ịƀestírsė ↓ — Apenas tiene tiempo para afeitarse y vestirse.

## DIALOG 1

José, dígale a Juan que esta noche hay una fiesta en la casa de los Harris, que si recuerda. — éstȧnóchẹ | áyunȧfyéstạ | ėnlȧkásȧ đėlȯshárris ↓ rrėkwérđȧs ↑ — José: Esta noche hay una fiesta en la casa de los Harris, ¿recuerdas?

Juan, contéstele que sí, que cómo no. Pregúntele que a qué hora hay que estar allí. — sí ↓ kómȯnó ↓ ȧkẹóraykėstárȧ(l)yí ↓ — Juan: Sí, cómo no. ¿A qué hora hay que estar allí?

José, contéstele que a las siete, y pregúntele si va a llevar a alguien. — ȧlȧ(s)syétė ↓ básạ(l)yėƀáralgyėn ↑ — José: A las siete. ¿Vas a llevar a alguien?

| | | |
|---|---|---|
| Juan, dígale que sí, que a la gordita. Que no es muy bonita pero que a Ud. le gusta mucho. Y pregúntele que a quién va a llevar él. | sí ↓ àlàgórđità ↓ no̯ézmùyƀónità \| pèro̯àmímègústàmúchò ↓ itú ↓ àkyémbàsa̯(l)y̯èƀár ↓ | Juan: Sí, a la gordita. No es muy bonita pero a mí me gusta mucho. Y tú, ¿a quién vas a llevar? |
| José, contéstele que a su novia. Dígale que si quiere, Ud. pasa por él a las seis y media y luego pasan por las chicas. | àminóƀyà ↓ sikyérès \| pásòpórtì ↑ a̯là(s)sèys̯iméđyà ↓ ilwégò \| pàsámòs pòrlàschíkàs ↓ | José: A mi novia. Si quieres, paso por ti a las seis y media y luego pasamos por las chicas. |
| Juan, dígale que muy bien, y pregúntele si no quiere otro trago. | múyƀyén ↓ nòkyérès̯ótròtrágò ↑ | Juan: Muy bien. ¿No quieres otro trago? |
| José, contéstele que no, gracias, que Ud. ya se va. Que apenas tiene tiempo para afeitarse y vestirse. Que adiós. | nògrás̯yàs ↓ y̯ámèƀóy ↓ àpénàs téŋgòtyémpò \| pàràféytàrme̯iƀèstírmè ↓ àđyós ↓ | José: No, gracias, ya me voy. Apenas tengo tiempo para afeitarme y vestirme. Adiós. |

## NARRATIVE 2

| | | |
|---|---|---|
| 1 Juan isn't ready yet. | hwá(n)no̯èstálístò \| tòđàƀíà ↓ | Juan no está listo todavía. |
| 2 He doesn't look like an American. | nó \| pàrés̯e̯àmèrìkánò ↓ | No parece americano. |
| 3 It's already twenty to seven. | y̯ásònlà(s)syétè \| ménòzƀéyntè ↓ | Ya son las siete menos veinte. |

| | | |
|---|---|---|
| 4 And they've got to go pick up the girls. | ɹáykėpȧsár \| pȯrlȧschíkȧs ↓ | Y hay que pasar por las chicas. |
| 5 Juan says there's (plenty of) time. | hwán \| dísėkẹáytyémpȯ ↓ | Juan dice que hay tiempo. |
| 6 Here it's not like in the United States. | ȧkínọés \| kómọènlȯṣėstáđȯṣúnıđȯs ↓ | Aquí no es como en los Estados Unidos. |
| 7 One's got to arrive late to parties. | áykė(l)yėgártárđẹ \| ȧlȧsfyéstȧs ↓ | Hay que llegar tarde a las fiestas. |
| 8 'But the party is at an American home', says José. | pėrȯlȧfyéstạ \| ėṣėŋkásȧđẹȧmėrikanȯz \| đíṣėhȯsé ↓ | Pero la fiesta es en casa de americanos—dice José. |
| 9 It's the same as being in the United States. | ėzlȯmízmȯ \| kėstárėnlȯṣėstáđȯs uníđȯs ↓ | Es lo mismo que estar en los Estados Unidos. |
| 10 Jose's right. Juan's going to hurry, then. | hȯsétyénėrráṣón ↓ hwám \| báđársė prísạ \| ėntónṣės ↓ | José tiene razón. Juan va a darse prisa, entonces. |
| 11 He'll be ready in a minute. | ėnúnmȯméntọ ↑ ėstálístȯ ↓ | En un momento está listo. |

---

## DIALOG 2

---

| | | |
|---|---|---|
| Juan, digale a José que qué tal, que pase adelante, y dígale que Ud. no está listo todavía. | kėtál \| hȯsé ↓ pásáđėlántė ↓ nọėstóylístȯ \| tȯđȧƀíȧ ↓ | Juan: ¿Qué tal José? Pasa adelante. No estoy listo todavía. |

| | | |
|---|---|---|
| José, dígale a José que *¿Qué?* Dígale que no parece americano. Que ya son las siete menos veinte. Y que hay que pasar por las chicas. | ké ↑ nopárẹ̱ses \| àmèrikánò ↓<br>yásònlà(s)syétè \| ménòzƀéyntè ↑<br>ıáykèpàsár \| pòrlàschíkàs ↓ | José: ¿¡Qué!? No pareces americano. Ya son las siete menos veinte. Y hay que pasar por las chicas. |
| Juan, dígale que hay tiempo, hombre, que hay tiempo. Que aquí no es como en los Estados Unidos. Que aquí hay que llegar tarde a las fiestas. | áytyémpo̱ \| ómbrè ↓ áytyémpò ↓<br>àkínọes \| kómọenlòsẹstáđọsụníđòs ↓<br>àkí ↑ áykè(l)yègártarđẹ \| àlàsfyéstàs ↓ | Juan: Hay tiempo, hombre, hay tiempo. Aquí no es como en los Estados Unidos. Aquí hay que llegar tarde a las fiestas. |
| José, dígale que sí, pero que la fiesta es en casa de americanos. Que es lo mismo que estar en los Estados Unidos. | sí \| pèròlàfyéstạ \| èsẹŋkásàđẹ<br>àmèrikánòs ↓ èzlòmízmò \|<br>kèstár \| ènlòsẹstáđòsụníđòs ↓ | José: Sí, pero la fiesta es en casa de americanos. Es lo mismo que estar en los Estados Unidos. |
| Juan, dígale que tiene razón, que Ud. va a darse prisa, entonces. Y que en un momento está listo. | tyénezrrạsón ↓ bóyađármèprísạ \|<br>èntónṣès ↓ ènụnmòméntọ \| èstóylístò ↓ | Juan: Tienes razón. Voy a darme prisa, entonces. En un momento estoy listo. |

## NARRATIVE 3

| | | |
|---|---|---|
| 1 Juan has to bathe, shave, and get dressed, that's all. | hwán \| tyénèkèƀàṇyársẹ ↑ àfèytársẹ<br>ìƀestírsè ↓ ésọestóđò ↓ | Juan tiene que bañarse, afeitarse, y vestirse, eso es todo. |
| 2 But, gosh! What's wrong now? There isn't any water. | péròi \| kàrámbà ↓ képásàórà ↓<br>nọayágwà ↓ | Pero ¡caramba! ¿Qué pasa ahora? No hay agua. |
| 3 He can't shave or bathe. | nòpwéđẹàfèytársè \| níƀàṇyársè ↓ | No puede afeitarse ni bañarse. |

| | | |
|---|---|---|
| 4 They'll never get to the party. | nȯƀánạ̇(l)y̯ėgár \| núŋkạ \| ȧlȧfyéstȧ ↓ | No van a llegar nunca a la fiesta. |
| 5 Jose can do one thing, then. | hȯsé \| pwéđẹȧṣérunȧkósạ \| ėntónṣės ↓ | José puede hacer una cosa, entonces. |
| 6 He can go pick up the girls first. | pwéđėpȧsár \| pȯrlȧschíkȧs \| priméṙȯ ↓ | Puede pasar por las chicas primero. |
| 7 And then he'll come by for Juan. | ilwégȯ \| pásȧpȯrhwán ↓ | Y luego pasa por Juan. |
| 8 If Juan isn't ready then, Jose won't wait. | sihwán \| nóẹstálístọ \| ėntónṣes ↑<br>hȯsé \| nóẹspérȧ ↓ | Si Juan no está listo entonces, José no espera. |

## DIALOG 3

| | | |
|---|---|---|
| José, pregúntele a Juan que qué tiene que hacer. | kétyénėskẹȧṣér ↓ | José: ¿Qué tienes que hacer? |
| Juan, contéstele que tiene que bañarse, afeitarse y vestirse, que eso es todo.<br>Pero ahora diga: ¡Ay, caramba! | téŋgȯkėƀȧn̯yármẹ ↑<br>ȧfėytármẹıƀėstírmė ↓<br>ésọėstóđȯ ↓ áy ↓ kȧrámbȧ ↓ | Juan: Tengo que bañarme, afeitarme y vestirme, eso es todo...<br>¡Ay, caramba! |
| José, pregúntele que qué le pasa ahora. | kétėpásȧorá ↓ | José: ¿Qué te pasa ahora? |

Juan, contéstele que Ud. no puede bañarse ni afeitarse. Que no hay agua.

ṅȯpwéđȯƀȧṇ̃yárṁe | ṇ̑ịȧfėytármė ↓
nọ̑áyágwȧ ↓

Juan: No puedo bañarme ni afeitarme. No hay agua.

José, dígale que ¡no puede ser! Que Uds. no van a llegar nunca a la fiesta.

nópwéđėsér ↓ nȯƀámȯs | ȧ(l)y̰ėgárnúŋkạ̑ |
ȧlȧfyéstȧ ↓

José: ¡No puede ser! No vamos a llegar nunca a la fiesta.

Juan, pregúntele que por qué no hace una cosa.

pȯrkénọ̑ásẹ̆ṡụnȧkósȧ ↓

Juan: ¿ Por qué no haces una cosa?

José, pregúntele que qué cosa.

kékósȧ ↓

José: ¿Qué cosa?

Juan, dígale que por qué no pasa por las chicas primero y luego pasan por usted.

pȯrkénȯpásȧs | pȯrlȧschíkȧs | priméṙo ↑
ilwégȯpásȧmpȯrmí ↓

Juan: ¿Por qué no pasas por las chicas primero y luego pasan por mí?

José, digale que está bien, pero si él no está listo entonces, que Ud. no espera, que lo siente mucho.

ėstáƀyén pėrȯsinóẹ̑stázlístọ̑ |
ėntónṣ̆ės ↑ nóẹ̑spérȯ ↓ lȯsyéntȯmúchȯ ↓

José: Está bien, pero si no estás listo entonces, no espero, lo siento mucho.

# 13.1 BASIC SENTENCES

## White and Molina go to a party

After being introduced to Carmen, Jose's fiancee, and meeting his own date, John goes with the others to the party which a Latin American official is giving in honor of the newly arrived Americans.

| English Spelling | Aid to Listening | Spanish Spelling |
|---|---|---|
| often | ȧ—mėnúđȯ | a menudo |
| *WHITE* | | *WHITE* |
| Hey, do they throw these parties here very often? (1) | óyė ↓ dán \| éstȧsfyéstȧṣȧkí \| múyȧmėnúđȯ ↑ | Oye, ¿dan estas fiestas aquí muy a menudo? |
| from time to time | dė—ƀéṣ—ėŋ—kwándȯ ↓ | de vez en cuando |
| *MOLINA* | | *MOLINA* |
| No, just every now and then. Why? | nó ↓ sólȯ \| đėƀėṣėŋkwándȯ ↓ pȯrké ↓ | No, sólo de vez en cuando, ¿por qué? |
| terrific | ėstu̇péndȯ ↓ | estupendo |
| *WHITE* | | *WHITE* |
| I think this one's terrific. | éstȧ \| mėpȧréṣẹ \| ėstu̇péndȧ ↓ | Esta me parece estupenda. |
| to fix | fihár ↓ | fijar |
| fix yourself, notice (to pay attention) | fíhȧtė ↓ fihársė ↓ | fíjate (fijarse) |
| dancing (to dance) | bȧylándȯ ↓ bȧylár ↓ | bailando (bailar) |

| | | |
|---|---|---|
| brunette | mȯrénȯ ↓ | moreno |
| Look how that brunette's dancing! | fíhȧtė \| kómo̯estáƀaylándo̯ \| ésȧmȯrénȧ ↓ | ¡Fíjate cómo está bailando esa morena! |
| the care | ėl—kwiđáđȯ ↓ | el cuidado |
| don't go (to go) | nȯ—ƀáy̯ȧs ↓ ír ↓ | no vayas (ir) |
| to put in | mėtér ↓ | meter |
| the paw | lȧ—pátȧ ↓ | la pata |
| to put your foot in your mouth | mėtér—lȧ—pátȧ ↓ | meter la pata |
| *MOLINA* | | *MOLINA* |
| Careful. Don't go making any cracks! | kwiđáđȯ ↓ nóƀáy̯ȧs \| ȧmėtérlȧpátȧ ↓ | ¡Cuidado, no vayas a meter la pata! |
| the daughter | la̯—íhȧ ↓ | la hija |
| the owner of the house | ėl—sėn̯yór—đė—lȧ—kásȧ ↓ | el señor de la casa |
| That's the daughter of our host. | ėzla̯íhȧ \| đėlsėn̯yórđėlȧkásȧ ↓ | Es la hija del señor de la casa. |
| look (to look) | mírȧ ↓ mirár ↓ | mira (mirar) |
| (I) believed (to believe) | krėíȧ ↓ krėér ↓ | creía (creer) |
| (they) were, were being (to be) [2] | érȧn ↓ sér ↓ | eran (ser) |
| quiet | trȧŋkílȯ ↓ | tranquilo |

| | | |
|---|---|---|
| *CARMEN* | | *CARMEN* |
| Say! I thought Americans were more reserved.[3] | mírȧ ↓ y̠ókrėíȧ \| kėlȯṣạmėrikánȯs \| érȧnmástrȧŋkílȯs ↓ | Mira. Yo creía que los americanos eran más tranquilos. |
| that way | pȯr—ȧí ↓ | por ahí |
| the colonel | ėl—kȯrȯnél ↓ | el coronel |
| *MOLINA* | | *MOLINA* |
| That man going that way is Colonel Harris. | ésėkėpásȧ \| pȯrȧí ↑ ėṣėlkȯrȯnélhárris ↓ | Ese que pasa por ahí, es el Coronel Harris. |
| come (to come) | bén ↓ bėnír ↓ | ven (venir) |
| Come on over and I'll introduce you.[4] | bén ↑ itėlȯprėséntȯ ↓ | Ven y te lo presento. |
| the goblet | lȧ—kópȧ ↓ | la copa |
| *WHITE* | | *WHITE* |
| Let's take our drinks.[5] | bámȯṣạ(l)y̠ėƀárnȯz \| lȧskópȧs ↓ | Vamos a llevarnos las copas. |
| yours | lȧ—túy̠ȧ ↓ | la tuya |
| Here's yours. | ȧkítyénėzlȧtúy̠ȧ ↓ | Aquí tienes la tuya. |
| to confuse | kȯmfu̇ndír ↓ | confundir |
| don't yourself confuse (to confuse oneself) | nó—tė—kȯmfúndȧs ↓ kȯmfu̇ndírsė ↓ | no te confundas (confundirse) |

| | | |
|---|---|---|
| hers | lȧ—đe̯—é(l)y̯ȧ ↓ | la de ella |
| Carmen's | lȧ—đė—kármėn ↓ | la de Carmen |
| *MOLINA* | | *MOLINA* |
| Don't get them mixed; that's hers, Carmen's. | nótėkómfúndȧs ↓ ėzlȧđé(l)y̯ȧ ↓ lȧđėkármėn ↓ | No te confundas. Es la de ella, la de Carmen. |
| *WHITE* | | *WHITE* |
| Oh, sorry. | á ↓ sí ↓ pėrđón ↓ | Ah, sí, perdón. |
| the girl | lȧ—chɪ́kȧ ↓ | la chica |
| at once, right away | ėn—sėgɪ́đȧ ↓ | en seguida |
| Will you girls excuse us? | bwénȯ \| chíkȧs ↓ kȯmpėrmɪ́sȯ ↓ | Bueno, chicas. Con permiso. |
| We'll be right back. | ėnsėgɪ́đȧ \| ƀolbémȯs ↓ | En seguida volvemos. |

## 13.10 Notes on the basic sentences

(l) 'Hey' is not a very good translation of /óye/ *oye,* but neither is anything else. /óye/ is an attention-attracter whose equivalent in English is usually some sort of gesture, such as raised eye-brows, an upward lift of the head to call for attention—something to indicate that a remark of importance, however slight, is to be made.

(2) Note that the verb form here, an irregular Past II form (to be dealt with in Unit 18), is indicated as being Past II rather than Past I by the presence of *two translations:* simple past, 'were', and what may be called *durative past,* 'were being'.

(3) /míra/ *mira,* like the equivalent given here, 'Say', is essentially an empty exclamation of mild surprise. It may also be used like *oye* as an attention-attracter to be sure the audience is paying attention to what one is about to say.

(4) The occurrence of two clitics in succession will be treated in Unit 20; for the moment, be certain you realize that /telo preséntoˈ ↓/ *te lo presento* means 'I'll present him to you' and *not* 'I'll present you to him'.

(5) The reflexive clitics will be treated in Unit 24. Literally this sentence means 'Let's take the cups for ourselves'—i.e., 'which belong to us.'

# 13.2 DRILLS AND GRAMMAR

## 13.21 PATTERN DRILLS

### 13.21.1 /—ndo/ forms and the present progressive construction

#### A. PRESENTATION OF PATTERN

*ILLUSTRATIONS*

| | | |
|---|---|---|
| I'm thinking about that. | 1 ėstóy \| pėnsándo̯ėnẹ́sȯ ↓ | *Estoy pensando* en eso. |
| I'm not drinking as much now. | 2 nó̯estóyƀėƀyéndȯ \| tánto̯ȧórȧ ↓ | No *estoy bebiendo* tanto ahora. |
| ________________ | 3 itú ↓ kéẹstázƀėƀyéndȯ ↓ | Y tú, ¿qué *estás bebiendo?* |
| You're finally translating. | 4 pȯrfín \| ėstástrȧđụsyéndȯ ↓ | Por fin *estás traduciendo.* |
| ________________ | 5 ėstáẹstụ̇đyándȯ ↑ | *¿Está estudiando?* |
| ________________ | 6 ėstátrȧƀȧhándȯ \| kómȯsėkrėtáryȧ ↓ | *Está trabajando* como secretaria. |

| | | |
|---|---|---|
| We're waiting for that moment. | 7 ėstámȯṣėspėrándo̯ \| ésėmȯméntȯ ↓ | *Estamos esperando* ese momento. |
| We're just now arriving. | 8 y̯áe̯stámȯz \| (l)y̯ėgándȯ ↓ | Ya *estamos llegando.* |
| How long have you been living here? | 9 dézđėkwándo̯ \| ėstámbiƀyéndo̯akí ↓ | ¿Desde cuándo *están viviendo* aquí? |
| How those brunettes are dancing! | 10 kómo̯ėstámbȧylándo̯ \| ésȧzmȯrénȧs ↓ | ¡Cómo *están bailando* esas morenas! |

*EXTRAPOLATION*

| | | estár | /—ndo/ form | |
|---|---|---|---|---|
| | | | —ár | —ér, —ír |
| | | | —ándo | —yéndo |
| sg | | | | |
| | 1 | estóy | | |
| | 2 fam | estás | | kom—yéndo |
| | 2-3 | está | abl—ándo | |
| pl | | | | |
| | 1 | estámos | | bib—yéndo |
| | 2-3 | están | | |

*NOTES*

a. The progressive construction consists of a conjugated form of the verb /estár/ plus the /—ndo/ form of the verb.

b. /—ndo/ forms are invariable, that is, they never inflect for number, gender, etc.

**End of Tape 10A**

## 13.21.11 SUBSTITUTION DRILLS

Person-number substitution

1 é(l)y̯ȯs | ėstámbu̇skándo̯ | ȧpȧrtȧméntȯ ↓

| | |
|---|---|
| y̯ó ______ ↓ | ėstóyƀu̇skándo̯ | ȧpȧrtȧméntȯ ↓ |
| hwán ______ ↓ | ėstáƀu̇skándo̯ | ȧpȧrtȧméntȯ ↓ |
| kármėni̯y̯ó ______ ↓ | ėstámȯz | búskándo̯ | ȧpȧrtȧméntȯ ↓ |
| u̇stéđės ______ ↓ | ėstámbu̇skándo̯ | ȧpȧrtȧméntȯ ↓ |

2 y̯ó | e̯stóytrȧƀȧhándo̯ | ȧórȧ ↓

| | |
|---|---|
| nȯsótrȯs ______ ↓ | ėstámȯstrȧƀȧhándo̯ | ȧórȧ ↓ |
| tú ______ ↓ | ėstástrȧƀȧhándo̯ | ȧórȧ ↓ |

---

1 *Ellos* están buscando apartamento.

| | |
|---|---|
| Yo ______ . | Estoy buscando apartamento. |
| Juan ______ . | Está buscando apartamento. |
| Carmen y yo ______ . | Estamos buscando apartamento. |
| Uds. ______ . | Están buscando apartamento. |

2 *Yo* estoy trabajando ahora.

| | |
|---|---|
| Nosotros ______ . | Estamos trabajando ahora. |
| Tú ______ . | Estás trabajando ahora. |

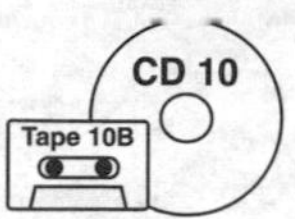




| | |
|---|---|
| ùstéđ ________________ ↓ | èstátràƀàhándo̯ ǀ aórà ↓ |
| kármèn ________________ ↓ | èstátràƀàhándo̯ ǀ àórà ↓ |

3 kármèn ǀ èstáprèndyéndòmúchò ↓

| | |
|---|---|
| yó ________________ ↓ | èstóy ǀ àprèndyéndòmúchò ↓ |
| ùstéđès ________________ ↓ | èstán ǀ àprèndyéndòmúchò ↓ |
| tú ________________ ↓ | èstás ǀ àprèndyéndòmúchò ↓ |
| nòsótròs ________________ ↓ | èstámòs ǀ àprèndyéndòmúchò ↓ |

---

| | |
|---|---|
| Ud. ________________ . | Está trabajando ahora. |
| Carmen ________________ . | Está trabajando ahora. |

3 *Carmen* está aprendiendo mucho.

| | |
|---|---|
| Yo ________________ . | Estoy aprendiendo mucho. |
| Uds. ________________ . | Están aprendiendo mucho. |
| Tú ________________ . | Estás aprendiendo mucho. |
| Nosotros ________________ . | Estamos aprendiendo mucho. |

4 hwáṇịkármėn | ėstáŋkȯmyéndȯ ↓

| | |
|---|---|
| él ________________ ↓ | ėstákȯmyéndȯ ↓ |
| yó ________________ ↓ | ėstóykȯmyéndȯ ↓ |
| é(l)yȧs ________________ ↓ | ėstáŋkȯmyéndȯ ↓ |
| ůstéđ ________________ ↓ | ėstákȯmyéndȯ ↓ |

5 hwáṇėstáėskrịƀyéndȯ ↓

| | |
|---|---|
| é(l)yȯs ________________ ↓ | ėstán \| ėskrịƀyéndȯ ↓ |
| éḷiyó ________________ ↓ | ėstámos \| ėskrịƀyéndȯ ↓ |
| kármėṇịhwán ________________ ↓ | ėstán \| ėskrịƀyéndȯ ↓ |
| yó ________________ ↓ | ėstóy \| ėskrịƀyéndȯ ↓ |

---

4 *Juan y Carmen* están comiendo.

| | |
|---|---|
| El ________________ . | Está comiendo. |
| Yo ________________ . | Estoy comiendo. |
| Ellas ________________ . | Están comiendo. |
| Ud. ________________ . | Está comiendo. |

5 *Juan* está escribiendo.

| | |
|---|---|
| Ellos ________________ . | Están escribiendo. |
| El y yo ________________ . | Estamos escribiendo. |
| Carmen y Juan ________________ . | Están escribiendo. |
| Yo ________________ . | Estoy escribiendo. |

Construction substitution

| | |
|---|---|
| 1 tómo̯ágwȧ ↓ | ėstóytȯmándo̯ágwȧ ↓ |
| 2 prȯnúnṣyȧzƀyén ↓ | ėstásprȯnùnṣyándȯƀyén ↓ |
| 3 límpyane̯ldȯrmitóryȯ ↓ | ėstánlimpyándo̯ \| ėldȯrmitóryȯ ↓ |
| 4 biƀímose̯nlaṣafwérȧs ↓ | ėstámȯz \| ƀiƀyéndo̯enlaṣafwérȧs ↓ |
| 5 ėskríƀo̯enlȧsálȧ ↓ | ėstóyėskriƀyéndo̯ \| ėnlȧsálȧ ↓ |
| 6 béƀen \| ágwȧminerál ↓ | ėstámbėƀyéndo̯ \| ágwȧminerál ↓ |
| 7 kómėpókȯ ↓ | ėstákȯmyéndȯpókȯ ↓ |

---

| | |
|---|---|
| 1 *Tomo* agua. | Estoy tomando agua. |
| 2 *Pronuncias* bien. | Estás pronunciando bien. |
| 3 *Limpian* el dormitorio. | Están limpiando el dormitorio. |
| 4 *Vivimos* en las afueras. | Estamos viviendo en las afueras. |
| 5 *Escribo* en la sala. | Estoy escribiendo en la sala. |
| 6 *Beben* agua mineral. | Están bebiendo agua mineral. |
| 7 *Come* poco. | Está comiendo poco. |

## 13.21.12 RESPONSE DRILL

| | | |
|---|---|---|
| | 1 ėstáņůstéđės ǀ tråƀåháṅdȯ ↑ o̯ėstůđyándȯ ↓ | ėstámȯșėstůđyándȯ ↓ |
| | 2 ėstáņẹ́(l)y̯ȯzƀåhándo̯ ↑ ȯsůƀyéndȯ ↓ | ėstánsůƀyéndȯ ↓ |
| | 3 ėsta̯é(l)y̯ålåƀándo̯ ↑ ȯlímpyándȯ ↓ | ėstálimpyándȯ ↓ |
| | 4 ėstáu̯stéđbėƀyéndo̯ ↑ ȯkȯmyéndȯ ↓ | ėstóykȯmyéndȯ ↓ |
| [bėƀyéndȯ ↓] | 5 késtȧșyéndo̯él ↓ | ėstáƀėƀyéndȯ ↓ |
| [tråƀåhándȯ ↓] | 6 késtȧņạșyéndo̯é(l)y̯ȯs ↓ | ėstántråƀåhándȯ ↓ |
| [ėskriƀyéndȯ ↓] | 7 késtȧșyéndo̯ůstéđ ↓ | ėstóyėskriƀyéndȯ ↓ |

---

| | | |
|---|---|---|
| | 1 ¿Están Uds. trabajando o estudiando? | Estamos estudiando. |
| | 2 ¿Están ellos bajando o subiendo? | Están subiendo. |
| | 3 ¿Está ella lavando o limpiando? | Está limpiando. |
| | 4 ¿Está Ud. bebiendo o comiendo? | Estoy comiendo. |
| (bebiendo) | 5 ¿Qué está haciendo él? | Está bebiendo. |
| (trabajando) | 6 ¿Qué están haciendo ellos? | Están trabajando. |
| (escribiendo) | 7 ¿Qué está haciendo Ud.? | Estoy escribiendo. |

| | | |
|---|---|---|
| [kȯmyéndȯ ↓] | 8 ėstánụstéđėzƀėƀyéndȯ ↑ | nó ↓ ėstámȯskȯmyéndȯ ↓ |
| [tràƀȧhándȯ ↓] | 9 ėstánẹ́(l)y̯ȧṣėstůđyándȯ ↑ | nó ↓ ėstántràƀȧhándȯ ↓ |
| | 10 ėstáu̯stéđȧlmȯrṣándȯ ↑ | sí ↓ ėstóyȧlmȯrṣándȯ ↓ |
| | 11 ėstáél \| ȧƀlándo̭ėspȧṇyól ↑ | sí ↓ estáƀlándo̭ėspȧṇyól ↓ |
| | 12 ėstástú \| a̭prėndyéndȯmúchȯ ↑ | sí ↓ ėstóy \| ȧprėndyéndȯmúchȯ ↓ |
| | 13 ėstáƀȧrryéndo̭é(l)y̯ȧ ↑ | sí ↓ ėstáƀȧrryéndȯ ↓ |

---

| | | |
|---|---|---|
| (comiendo) | 8 ¿Están Uds. bebiendo? | No, estamos comiendo. |
| (trabajando) | 9 ¿Están ellas estudiando? | No, están trabajando. |
| | 10 ¿Está Ud. almorzando? | Sí, estoy almorzando. |
| | 11 ¿Está él hablando español? | Sí, está hablando español. |
| | 12 ¿Estás tú aprendiendo mucho? | Sí, estoy aprendiendo mucho. |
| | 13 ¿Está barriendo ella? | Sí, está barriendo. |

## 13.21.13 TRANSLATION DRILL

| | | |
|---|---|---|
| 1 I'm working at the Embassy. | ėstóytrȧƀȧhándo̥ \| ėnlḁėmbȧháđȧ ↓ | Estoy trabajando en la Embajada. |
| 2 We're living downtown. | ėstámȯzƀiƀyéndo̥ \| ėnėl̥séntrȯ ↓ | Estamos viviendo en el centro. |
| 3 They're writing now. | ėstánėskribyéndo̥ \| ȧórȧ ↓ | Están escribiendo ahora. |
| 4 I'm looking at the glasses. | ėstóyƀyéndȯlȧzgáfȧs ↓ | Estoy viendo las gafas. |
| 5 Who's calling? | kyénėstá(l)yȧmándȯ ↓ | ¿Quién está llamando? |
| 6 Where're you living? | dóndėstáƀiƀyéndȯ ↓ | ¿Dónde está viviendo? |
| 7 What are you all learning? | késtánȧprėndyéndȯ ↓ | ¿Qué están aprendiendo? |
| 8 What time are they arriving (these days)? | ȧkeórḁ \| ėstán(l)yėgándȯ ↓ | ¿A qué hora están llegando? |
| 9 The girl is making (fixing) the beds. | lȧmu̇cháchḁ \| ėstárrėgléndȯlȧskámȧs ↓ | La muchacha está arreglando las camas. |
| 10 We're speaking less English. | ėstámȯsȧƀlándȯ \| ménȯsiŋglés ↓ | Estamos hablando menos inglés. |
| 11 I'm not giving (any) tips (these days). | no̥ėstóyđándȯ \| prȯpínȧs ↓ | No estoy dando propinas. |

| | | |
|---|---|---|
| 12 They're always studying. | syémpre | estánestudyándo ↓ | Siempre están estudiando. |
| 13 He's going up in the elevator. | estásubyéndo | enelas(s)ensór ↓ | Está subiendo en el ascensor. |

## B. DISCUSSION OF PATTERN

The progressive construction in Spanish is closely paralleled by a similar construction in English, composed of a form of the verb *be* plus the *—ing* form of a verb: 'I'm going, he's going,' etc.

In Spanish the progressive construction consists of a form of the verb /estár/ and the /—ndo/ form of a verb, arranged together in a close construction which only rarely admits the appearance of any form intervening between them. In the comparable English construction, the relationship of the constituents is not so close; 'He's just now eating' in Spanish would be /yáestákomyéndo ↓/, rather then * /estáyá komyéndo ↓/.

The English *—ing* form can be made plural, as in 'his comings and goings', but the /—ndo/ form in Spanish is invariable—it never changes or inflects for number, gender, etc. Analytically the /—ndo/ form is classed as a verb element in verb constructions, or as a verb modifier, a function class of words which typically do not inflect: /estudyándomúcho | seapréndemúcho ↓/.

While /estár/ is most frequently the conjugated verb that appears in the construction 'verb plus /—ndo/', others, such as /andár, /benír, (l)yegár, ír, segír/, appear with /—ndo/ forms with different but related meanings. Thus:

| | |
|---|---|
| /están—aprendyéndo ↓/ | 'They're learning'. |
| /bán—aprendyéndo ↓/ | 'They're beginning to learn'. |
| /ándan—aprendyéndo ↓/ | 'They're (out) learning'. |
| /sígen—aprendyéndo ↓/ | 'They're still learning'. |

Usually the Spanish construction appears in contexts where the same English construction would be appropriate. One important exception is the use of the progressive construction in English with reference to future time. It's quite normal in English to say 'He's coming tonight,' but in Spanish */estábinyéndo̯ | éstanóche ↓/ would never occur (simple present would); the construction is limited to present or customary actions.

## 13.21.2 Possessive constructions with /de/

### A. PRESENTATION OF PATTERN

*ILLUSTRATIONS*

| | | |
|---|---|---|
| This is our part. | 1 éstaėzlápartė \| đėnósótrȯs ↓ | Esta es la parte *de nosotros.* |
| Pardon, is this your book? | 2 pėrđónė ↓ ėsėstėlíƀrȯ \| đeųstéđ ↑ | Perdone, ¿es éste el libro *de usted?* |
| Come in; that's your table. | 3 ȧđėlántė ↓ ȧké(l)yaėzlamésȧ \| đeųstéđės ↓ | Adelante; aquélla es la mesa *de ustedes.* |
| His car is excellent. | 4 ėláwtȯđél \| ėsėks(s)ėléntė ↓ | El auto *de él* es excelente. |
| small | pėkéṇyȯ ↓ | pequeño |
| Her room is very small. | 5 ėlwártȯđé(l)ya \| ėzmúypėkéṇyȯ ↓ | El cuarto *de ella* es muy pequeño. |
| Their furniture is expensive. | 6 lȯzmwéƀlėzđé(l)yȯs \| sȯŋkárȯs ↓ | Los muebles *de ellos* son caros. |

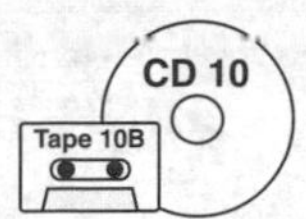



| | | |
|---|---|---|
| Please hand me their (f) glasses (goblets). | 7 pȯrfȧƀór ↓ pásėmėlȧskópȧzđé(l)y̰ȧs ↓ | Por favor, páseme las copas *de ellas*. |
| ____________________ | 8 ėlȧpȧrtȧméntȯ \| đėlsėn̰yórmȯlínȧ ↓ | El apartamento *del señor* Molina. |
| ____________________ | 9 ėzlá̯ıhȧ \| đėlsėn̰yórđėlȧkásȧ ↓ | Es la hija *del señor* de la casa. |

## *EXTRAPOLATION*

| Possessives | |
|---|---|
| Forms | Constructions |
| la—kása—mía [c]<br>la—kása—nwéstra | ______ [a]<br>la—kása—de—nosótros [b] |
| la—kása—túya | ______ [a] |
| la—kása—súya | la—kása—de—ustéd<br>la—kása—de—ustédes<br>la—kása—de—él<br>la—kása—de—é(l)ya<br>la—kása—de—é(l)yos<br>la—kása—de—é(l)yas |

## *NOTES*

a. Possessive constructions equivalent to /mío/ and /túyo/ do not occur.

b. The phrase /de—nosótros/ as part of a possessive construction occurs more frequently than /nwéstro/ in certain dialect areas.

c. For /la—kása—mía/ etc., read also /el—líbro—mío/, /las—kásas—mías/, and /los—líbros—míos/.

## 13.21.21 SUBSTITUTION DRILL

Construction substitution

Problem:

ésa̯ezlȧmígȧsúyȧ ↓ [de̯él ↓]

ésta̯ė(s)sụkwéntȧ ↓ [de̯ụstéđ ↓]

Answer:

ésa̯ezlȧmígȧđél ↓

ésta̯ | ėzlȧkwéntȧđe̯ụstéđ ↓

---

Problem:

Esa es la amiga *suya*. (de él)

Esta es *su* cuenta. (de Ud.)

Answer:

Esa es la amiga de él.

Esta es la cuenta de Ud.

1 ésta̯ėzlȧrrópȧsúy̯ȧ ↓ [de̯ùstéđės ↓] ésta̯ | ėzlȧrrópȧđe̯ustéđės ↓

2 ėlȧpȧrtȧméntȯsúy̯o̯ | ėzgrándė ↓ [dé(l)y̯ȧ ↓] ėlȧpȧrtȧméntȯđé(l)y̯a̯ | ėzgrándė ↓

3 lȧnóƀyȧsúy̯a̯ | ėzƀȯnítȧ ↓ [de̯ùstéđ ↓] lȧnóƀyȧđe̯ustéđ | ėzƀȯnítȧ ↓

4 ésta̯ė(s)sụmȧlétȧ ↓ [de̯ùstéđės ↓] ésta̯ | ėzlȧmȧlétȧđe̯ustéđės ↓

5 ésa̯ė(s)sụfȧmílyȧ ↓ [dé(l)y̯ȧ ↓] ésa̯ | ėzlȧfȧmílyȧđé(l)y̯ȧ ↓

---

1 Esta es la ropa *suya*. (de Uds.) — Esta es la ropa de Uds.

2 El apartamento *suyo* es grande. (de ella) — El apartamento de ella es grande.

3 La novia *suya* es bonita. (de Ud.) — La novia de Ud. es bonita.

4 Esta es *su* maleta. (de Uds.) — Esta es la maleta de Uds.

5 Esa es *su* familia. (de ella) — Esa es la familia de ella.

| | | |
|---|---|---|
| 6 éstȧs \| sȯ(n)nwéstrȧsfótȯs ↓ | [dėnȯsótrȯs ↓] | éstȧs \| sȯnlȧsfótȯzđėnȯsótrȯs ↓ |
| 7 su̯ȧmíga̯ėskȧsáđȧ ↓ | [dél ↓] | lȧmígȧđélėskȧsáđȧ ↓ |
| 8 su̇ṣȧmígȯ(s)sȯnsȯltérȯs ↓ | [dé(l)y̯ȧ ↓] | lȯṣȧmígȯzđé(l)y̯ȧ \| sȯnsȯltérȯs ↓ |
| 9 su̇táksi̯ \| ėstálȧđėréchȧ ↓ | [dé(l)y̯ȯs ↓] | ėltáksiđé(l)y̯ȯs \| ėstálȧđėréchȧ ↓ |

---

| | |
|---|---|
| 6 Estas son *nuestras* fotos. (de nosotros) | Estas son las fotos de nosotros. |
| 7 *Su* amiga es casada. (de él) | La amiga de él es casada. |
| 8 *Sus* amigos son solteros. (de ella) | Los amigos de ella son solteros. |
| 9 *Su* taxi está a la derecha. (de ellos) | El taxi de ellos está a la derecha. |

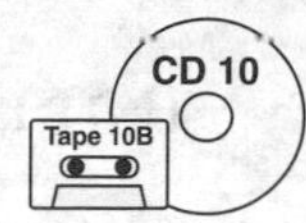




## 13.21.22 TRANSLATION DRILL

| | | |
|---|---|---|
| 1 Their apartment is nice. | ėlȧpȧrtȧméntȯ \| đé(l)y̯as \| ėzƀonítȯ ↓ | El apartamento de ellas es bonito. |
| 2 Her family is very large. | lȧfȧmílyȧ \| đé(l)y̯a̯ \| ėzmúygrándė ↓ | La familia de ella es muy grande. |
| 3 His room (number) is fifteen. | ėlkwártȯđél \| ėse̯lkínse̯ ↓ | El cuarto de él es el quince. |
| 4 All your friends are Americans. | tóđoz \| los̯amígozđe̯ustéđes \| sȯn amėrikánȯs ↓ | Todos los amigos de Uds. son americanos. |
| 5 Your suitcases are very good. | lȧzmȧlétȧz \| đe̯ȯstéđ \| sȯnmúyƀwénȧs ↓ | Las maletas de Ud. son muy buenas. |
| 6 His girl friend is Spanish. | lȧnóƀyȧđél \| ėse̯spȧn̯yólȧ ↓ | La novia de él es española. |
| 7 We can't find her house. | nóe̯ŋkȯntrámȯz \| lȧkásȧđé(l)yȧ ↓ | No encontramos la casa de ella. |
| 8 Their bedroom is small. | ėldȯrmitóryȯđé(l)yȯs \| ėspėkén̯yȯ ↓ | El dormitorio de ellos es pequeño. |
| 9 You should see his car. | áykėƀér \| ėláwtȯđél ↓ | Hay que ver el auto de él. |

### B. DISCUSSION OF PATTERN

A possessive construction is a phrase which consists of the phrase relator /de/ plus a noun or a pronoun. This phrase appears immediately after a noun (or sometimes after the verb /sér/) and indicates the possessor or owner of the modified noun.

In units 9 and 11 possessive forms were presented. In the present extrapolation the full forms are listed along with the equivalent possessive constructions which occur. As can be seen in the chart, the 2-3 form /súya/ is listed as the equivalent of at least six constructions. The fact that /súya/ can be the equivalent of six different constructions implies that the constructions give the more definite information. The phrases /de—ustéd, de—él/ etc. are used when the context does not supply all the information needed to identify the reference of the possessive. Since /súyo—su/ most often means /de—ustéd/, the constructions /de—ustédes, de—él, de—é(l)ya, de—é(l)yos, de—é(l)yas/ are more frequently used to refer to 'yours, his, hers, theirs' than is /súyo—su/ with these meanings.

The construction /de—nosótros/ is not used extensively in some dialects, but in others, as in Chile, it is used to the almost complete exclusion of /nwéstro/.

## 13.21.3 Nominalized possessive constructions

### A. PRESENTATION OF PATTERN

*ILLUSTRATIONS*

| | | |
|---|---|---|
| ______________________ | 1 ėlmío̯ėshwán ↓ | *El mío* es Juan. |
| Can you clean ours too? | 2 pwéđėlímpyár \| ėlnwéstrȯtȧmbyén ↑ | ¿Puede limpiar *el nuestro* también? |
| ______________________ | 3 ȧkítyénėzlȧtúy̰ȧ ↓ | Aquí tienes *la tuya*. |
| ______________________ | 4 ėlsúy̰o̯ėzmázgrándė ↓ nó ↑ | *El suyo* es más grande, ¿no? |

each — káđȧ ↓ — cada

Every (man) to his own (taste).
5 káđaúnȯ | kȯnlȯsúyȯ ↓
Cada uno con *lo suyo*.

In ours there isn't much activity.
6 ėnlȧđėnȯsótrȯz | noáymúchȯmoƀımyéntȯ ↓
En *la de nosotros* no hay mucho movimiento.

Yours is bigger, isn't it?
7 ėldeústéđ | ėzmázgrándė ↓ nó ↑
*El de usted* es más grande, ¿no?

In yours there's almost no activity.
8 ėnlȧzđeústéđės | kásinoáymóƀımyéntȯ ↓
En *las de ustedes* casi no hay movimiento.

______________________
9 nó ↓ ėsigwálȧldél ↓
No, es igual *al de él.*

______________________
10 ėzlȧđé(l)yȧ ↓ lȧđėkármėn ↓
Es *la de ella, la de Carmen.*

No, it's just like theirs (m).
11 nó ↓ ėsigwálȧldé(l)yȯs ↓
No, es igual *al de ellos.*

They're theirs, the girls'.
12 sȯnlȧzđé(l)yȧs ↓ lȧzđėlȧschíkȧs ↓
Son *las de ellas, las de las chicas.*

## *EXTRAPOLATION*

| Possessive forms and constructions | | Nominalized [a] | |
|---|---|---|---|
| la—kása—mía[c]<br>la—kása—nwéstra | ________ [b]<br>la—kása—de—nosótros | la—mía[c]<br>la—nwéstra | ________ [b]<br>la—de—nosótros |
| la—kása—túya | ________ [b] | la—túya | ________ [b] |
| la—kása—súya | la—kása—de—ustéd<br>la—kása—de—ustédes | la—súya | la—de—ustéd<br>la—de—ustédes |
| | la—kása—de—él<br>la—kása—de—é(l)ya<br>la—kása—de—é(l)yos<br>la—kása—de—é(l)yas | | la—de—él<br>la—de—é(l)ya<br>la—de—é(l)yos<br>la—de—é(l)yas |
| | | lo—súyo | |

## *NOTES*

a. Nominalization of these constructions is accomplished by omitting the noun.

b. Combinations which do not occur are marked by a dash.

c. For /la—kása—mía/, /la—mía/, etc., read also /el—mío/, /las—mías/, /los—míos/ etc.

## 13.21.31 SUBSTITUTION DRILL

Construction substitution

Problem:

làz(l)y̰áƀèzmíàz | nóe̯stáṇakí ↓

Answer:

làzmíàz | nóe̯stáṇakí ↓

| | | |
|---|---|---|
| 1 | làkásàsúy̰a̰ \| èstáşérkà ↓ | làsúy̰a̰èstáşérkà ↓ |
| 2 | èlàpàrtàméntòsúy̰ò \| tyénèđóẓƀáṇyòs ↓ | èlsúy̰ò \| tyénèđóẓƀáṇyòs ↓ |

---

Problem:

*Las llaves mías* no están aquí.

Answer:

Las mías no están aquí.

| | | |
|---|---|---|
| 1 | *La casa suya* está cerca. | La suya está cerca. |
| 2 | *El apartamento suyo* tiene dos baños. | El suyo tiene dos baños. |

| | |
|---|---|
| 3 lȧnóƀyȧmíȧ \| no̯ézƀȯnítȧ ↓ | lȧmíȧ \| no̯ézƀȯnítȧ ↓ |
| 4 lȧ(s)sí(l)y̯ȧ(s)súy̯ȧs \| ėstáṇȧla̯ɪ̯ṣkyérđȧ ↓ | lȧ(s)súy̯ȧs \| ėstáṇȧla̯ɪ̯ṣkyérđȧ ↓ |
| 5 ėlsȯfásúy̯o̯ \| ėskómȯđȯ ↓ | ėlsúy̯o̯ėskómȯđȯ ↓ |
| 6 la̯íhȧtúy̯a̯ \| ėzmúyƀȯnítȧ ↓ | lȧtúy̯a̯ \| ėzmúyƀȯnítȧ ↓ |
| 7 lȯzmwéƀlėstúy̯ȯs \| sȯnmúyƀȯnítȯs ↓ | lȯstúy̯ȯs \| sȯnmúyƀȯnítȯs ↓ |

---

| | |
|---|---|
| 3 *La novia mía* no es bonita. | La mía no es bonita. |
| 4 *Las sillas suyas* están a la izquierda. | Las suyas están a la izquierda. |
| 5 *El sofá suyo* es cómodo. | El suyo es cómodo. |
| 6 *La hija tuya* es muy bonita. | La tuya es muy bonita. |
| 7 *Los muebles tuyos* son muy bonitos. | Los tuyos son muy bonitos. |

## 13.21.32 TRANSLATION DRILL

| | | |
|---|---|---|
| 1 There's *my* car; and there's *yours*, too. | ȧi̯está \| e̯láwtȯmíȯ ↓ i̯ėlde̯ȯstéđestȧmbyén ↓ | Ahí está el auto mío y el de Uds. también. |
| 2 *My* family isn't large. What about *yours*? | lȧfȧmílyȧmíȧ \| no̯ézgrándė ↓ ilȧđe̯ȯstéđ ↑ | La familia mía no es grande. ¿Y la de Ud.? |
| 3 This is our table. (Which is) theirs? | ésta̯eznwéstrȧmésȧ ↓ ilađé(l)y̯ȯs ↑ | Esta es nuestra mesa. ¿Y la de ellos? |
| 4 This is John's check. (Which is) hers ? | éste̯ \| ėse̯lchékėđėhwán ↓ i̯ėldé(l)y̯ȧ ↑ | Este es el cheque de Juan. ¿Y el de ella? |
| 5 My daughter is single. What about theirs? | la̯íhȧmía̯e(s)sȯltérȧ ↓ ilȧđé(l)y̯ȯs ↑ | La hija mía es soltera. ¿Y la de ellos? |
| 6 Carmen's family arrives on Friday. What about yours? | lȧfȧmílyȧđėkármėn \| (l)y̯éga̯ėlbyérnės ↓ ilȧđe̯ȯstéđės ↑ | La familia de Carmen llega el viernes. ¿Y la de Uds.? |
| 7 *My* friends are arriving on Saturday. What about *yours*? | lȯsȧmígȯzmíȯz \| (l)y̯éganėlsáƀȧđȯ ↓ ilȯzđe̯ȯstéđ ↑ | Los amigos míos llegan el sábado. ¿Y los de Ud.? |
| 8 John's apartment doesn't have (any) gas. Does hers? | ėlȧpȧrtȧméntȯđėhwán \| nȯtyénėgás ↓ i̯ėldé(l)y̯ȧ ↑ | El apartamento de Juan no tiene gas. ¿Y el de ella? |
| 9 *My* girl friend is staying at the American Hotel. Where's *yours* staying? | lȧnóƀyȧmía̯ \| ėstáe̯nėlȯtélȧmėrikánȯ ↓ ilȧtúy̯ȧ ↑ | La novia mía está en el Hotel Americano. ¿Y la tuya? |

### B. DISCUSSION OF PATTERN

Possessive forms (full forms only) as well as possessive constructions can occur nominalized. These nominalized constructions serve to make a second reference to a noun which has just been mentioned or is readily understood from the context.

The nominalization can be viewed as the simple omission of the noun from the construction. Thus /el—líbro—mío/ becomes /el—mío/, where /mío/, now nominalized, is the head of the phrase. Note that the English equivalent 'mine' never occurs preceded by 'the.' In the possessive construction /el—líbro—de—ustéd/, the nominalized version is /el—de—ustéd/, where /el/ is the nominalized form, modified by the phrase /de—ustéd/.

One nominalized possessive, /lo—súyo/, may but usually does not occur as a possessive form; that is, it usually appears only nominalized. This is not surprising, since the neuter /lo—súyo/ cannot modify a noun, there being no neuter nouns in Spanish. Thus /tódos | bánạtraér | losúyo ↓/ probably refers to a group of things thought of as a composite whole, translating 'They're all going to bring their own stuff.'

## 13.21.4 Question intonation patterns—Information questions

### A. PRESENTATION OF PATTERN

*ILLUSTRATIONS*

| | | |
|---|---|---|
| ______________ | 1 késẹésȯ ↓ | 2 1 1 ↓<br>¿Qué es eso? |
| ______________ | késẹésȯ ↓ | 2 3 1 ↓<br>¿Qué es eso? |
| ______________ | 2 dóndestálakáhȧ ↓ | 2 2 1 1 ↓<br>¿Dónde está la caja? |
| ______________ | dóndestálakáhȧ ↓ | 2 2 3 1 ↓<br>¿Dónde está la caja? |

| | | |
|---|---|---|
| ______________ | 3 àkómọèstáẹlkámbyò ↓ | 1 2 2 1 1 ↓<br>¿A cómo está el cambio? |
| ______________ | àkómọèstáẹlkambyò ↓ | 1 2 2 3 1 ↓<br>¿A cómo está el cambio? |

*EXTRAPOLATION*

| Information question uncolored | Information question emphatic |
|---|---|
| /1211 ↓/ | /1231 ↓/ |

*NOTES*

a. The intonation patterns of information questions parallel those of statements.

## 13.21.41 SUBSTITUTION DRILL

Pattern substitution

Problem:

ȧđóndėƀámȯs ↓

Answer:

ȧđóndėƀ́amȯs ↓

---

Problem:

1 2 1 1 ↓
¿A dónde vamos?

Answer:

1 2 3 1 ↓
¿A dónde vamos?

| | | |
|---|---|---|
| 1 | pȧrȧkétrȧƀȧhámȯs ↓ | pȧrȧkétrȧƀȧhámȯs ↓ |
| 2 | dėđóndėƀyénėn ↓ | dėđóndėƀyénėn ↓ |
| 3 | dėđóndérės ↓ | dėđóndérės ↓ |
| 4 | pȯrkéstúđyȧn ↓ | pȯrkéstúđyȧn ↓ |
| 5 | ikwándȯlo̯ȧrréglȧn ↓ | ikwándȯlo̯ȧrréglȧn ↓ |

---

| | | |
|---|---|---|
| 1 | 1 2 1 1 ↓<br>¿Para qué trabajamos? | 1 2 3 1 ↓<br>¿Para qué trabajamos? |
| 2 | 1 2 1 1 ↓<br>¿De dónde vienen? | 1 2 3 1 ↓<br>¿De dónde vienen? |
| 3 | 1 2 1 1 ↓<br>¿De dónde eres? | 1 2 3 1 ↓<br>¿De dónde eres? |
| 4 | 1 2 1 1 ↓<br>¿Por qué estudian? | 1 2 3 1 ↓<br>¿Por qué estudian? |
| 5 | 1 2 1 1 ↓<br>¿Y cuándo lo arreglan? | 1 2 3 1 ↓<br>¿Y cuándo lo arreglan? |

| | | |
|---|---|---|
| 6 | iđóndėlȯzmándȧs ↓ | iđóndėlȯzmándȧs ↓ |
| 7 | ikómȯlo̯kyérės ↓ | ikómȯlȯkyérės ↓ |
| 8 | ikwándȯlo̯ȧlkílȧn ↓ | ikwándȯlo̯ȧlkílȧn ↓ |
| 9 | ikwándȯlȯƀémȯs ↓ | ikwándȯlȯƀémȯs ↓ |
| 10 | iđóndėkómėn ↓ | iđóndėkómėn ↓ |
| 11 | ikwántȯđėƀémȯs ↓ | ikwántȯđėƀémȯs ↓ |

---

| | | |
|---|---|---|
| | 1 2 1 1 ↓ | 1 2 3 1 ↓ |
| 6 | ¿Y dónde los mandas? | ¿Y dónde los mandas? |
| | 1 2 1 1 ↓ | 1 2 3 1 ↓ |
| 7 | ¿Y cómo lo quieres? | ¿Y cómo lo quieres? |
| | 1 2 1 1 ↓ | 1 2 3 1 ↓ |
| 8 | ¿Y cuándo lo alquilan? | ¿Y cuándo lo alquilan? |
| | 1 2 1 1 ↓ | 1 2 3 1 ↓ |
| 9 | ¿Y cuándo lo vemos? | ¿Y cuándo lo vemos? |
| | 1 2 1 1 ↓ | 1 2 3 1 ↓ |
| 10 | ¿Y dónde comen? | ¿Y dónde comen? |
| | 1 2 1 1 ↓ | 1 2 3 1 ↓ |
| 11 | ¿Y cuánto debemos? | ¿Y cuánto debemos? |

## B. DISCUSSION OF PATTERN

Information questions are those which cannot be answered by a simple yes or no, but rather must be answered by a statement. Information questions normally begin with a question word, equivalent to 'who, what, when, why, where,' etc. in English.

The intonation patterns appropriate for information questions are the same ones used for statements:/1211 ↓/is normal, and /1231 ↓/ adds special emphasis, or in some cases adds the idea of politeness. When a contrast is additionally implied by the occurrence of /entónses ↓/ after an information question, the /1231 ↓/ pattern is almost compulsory:

| | |
|---|---|
| 1 2 3 1 1 1 1<br>/parakétrabahámos \| entónses ↓/ | What are we working for, then? |
| 1 2 3 1 1 1 1<br>/dedóndéres \| entónses ↓/ | Where're you from, then? |

Since these questions very often begin with the stressed syllable of the question word, the first number of the intonation pattern formula is often lost.

## 13.22 REPLACEMENT DRILLS

A dán | éstȧsfyéstȧṣȧkí | a̯mėnúđȯ ↑

| | |
|---|---|
| 1 ______________ đėƀéṣėŋkwándȯ ↑ | dán \| éstȧsfyéstȧṣȧkí \| đėƀéṣėŋkwándȯ ↑ |
| 2 ______________ ȧí ______________ ↑ | dán \| éstȧsfyéstȧṣȧí \| đėƀéṣėŋkwándȯ ↑ |
| 3 ___________ trágȯs ______________ ↑ | dán \| éstȯstrágȯṣȧí \| đėƀéṣėŋkwándȯ ↑ |
| 4 __________ ésȯs ________________ ↑ | dán \| ésȯstrágȯṣȧí \| đėƀéṣėŋkwándȯ ↑ |
| 5 áṣėn __________________________ ↑ | áṣėn \| ésȯstrágȯṣȧí \| đėƀéṣėŋkwándȯ ↑ |
| 6 __________ traƀáhọ ______________ ↑ | áṣėn \| ésėtraƀáhọȧí \| đėƀéṣėŋkwándȯ ↑ |
| 7 ______________________ syémprė ↑ | áṣėn \| ésėtraƀáhọȧí \| syémprė ↑ |

---

A ¿Dan estas fiestas aquí a menudo?

| | |
|---|---|
| 1 ¿ _____________ de vez en cuando? | ¿Dan estas fiestas aquí de vez en cuando? |
| 2 ¿ __________ ahí ________________ ? | ¿Dan estas fiestas ahí de vez en cuando? |
| 3 ¿ ________ tragos ______________ ? | ¿Dan estos tragos ahí de vez en cuando? |
| 4 ¿ ________ esos ________________ ? | ¿Dan esos tragos ahí de vez en cuando? |
| 5 ¿Hacen ______________________ ? | ¿Hacen esos tragos ahí de vez en cuando? |
| 6 ¿ _________ trabajo _____________ ? | ¿Hacen ese trabajo ahí de vez en cuando? |
| 7 ¿ ______________________ siempre? | ¿Hacen ese trabajo ahí siempre? |

CD 10
Tape 10B



B éstȧ | mėpȧréşėstu̇péndȧ ↓

1 éstȧz ______________________ ↓ — éstȧz | mėpȧrėşėnẹstu̇péndȧs ↓

2 ______________________ bwénȧs ↓ — éstȧz | mėpȧréşėmbwénȧs ↓

3 éstė ______________________ ↓ — éstė | mėpȧréşėƀwénȯ ↓

4 ______________________ málȯ ↓ — éstė | mėpȧréşėmálȯ ↓

5 ȧké(l)y̱ȧ ______________________ ↓ — ȧké(l)y̱ȧ | mėpȧréşėmálȧ ↓

6 ______________________ ėks(ş)ėléntės ↓ — ȧké(l)y̱ȧz | mėpȧréşėnẹks(ş)ėléntės ↓

7 ȧkél ______________________ ↓ — ȧkél | mėpȧréşėks(ş)ėléntė ↓

---

B Esta me parece estupenda.

1 Estas ______________________ . — Estas me parecen estupendas.

2 ______________________ buenas. — Estas me parecen buenas.

3 Este ______________________ . — Este me parece bueno.

4 ______________________ malo. — Este me parece malo.

5 Aquélla ______________________ . — Aquélla me parece mala.

6 ______________________ excelentes. — Aquéllas me parecen excelentes.

7 Aquél ______________________ . — Aquél me parece excelente.

CD 10 Tape 10B

C fíhȧtė | kómo̯ėstáƀȧylȧndo̯ | ėsȧmȯrénȧ ↓

| | | |
|---|---|---|
| 1 | ____________ chíkȧs ↓ | fíhȧtė \| kómo̯ėstámbȧyláṅdo̯ \| ėsȧschíkȧs ↓ |
| 2 | ________ ȧké(l)y̯ȧs ____ ↓ | fíhȧtė \| kómo̯ėstámbȧyláṅdo̯ \| ȧké(l)y̯ȧschíkȧs ↓ |
| 3 | ________ ƀėƀyéndo̯ ____ ↓ | fíhȧtė \| kómo̯ėstámbėƀyéndo̯ \| ȧké(l)y̯ȧschíkȧs ↓ |
| 4 | ____________ sėn̯yór ↓ | fíhȧtė \| kómo̯ėstábėbyéndo̯ \| ȧkélsėn̯yór ↓ |
| 5 | ________ ȧƀlándo̯ ____ ↓ | fíhȧtė \| kómo̯ėstáƀlándo̯ \| ȧkélsėn̯yór ↓ |
| 6 | ____ kȯŋkyén ________ ↓ | fíhȧtė \| kȯŋkyén̯ėstáblándo̯ \| ȧkélsėn̯yór ↓ |
| 7 | ____________ sėn̯yórės ↓ | fíhȧtė \| kȯŋkyén̯ėstán̯ȧblándo̯ \| ȧké(l)y̯ȯ(s)sėn̯yórės ↓ |

---

C Fíjate cómo está bailando esa morena.

| | | |
|---|---|---|
| 1 | ____________ chicas. | Fíjate cómo están bailando esas chicas. |
| 2 | ________ aquellas ____ . | Fíjate cómo están bailando aquellas chicas. |
| 3 | ________ bebiendo ________ . | Fíjate cómo están bebiendo aquellas chicas. |
| 4 | ____________ señor. | Fíjate cómo está bebiendo aquel señor. |
| 5 | ________ hablando ________ . | Fíjate cómo está hablando aquel señor. |
| 6 | ____ con quién ________ . | Fíjate con quién está hablando aquel señor. |
| 7 | ____________ señores. | Fíjate con quién están hablando aquellos señores. |

D ėzlá̯ihȧ | đėlsėn̯yórđėlȧkásȧ ↓

| | |
|---|---|
| 1 ______ íhȧz ______________ ↓ | sȯnlȧs̯íhȧz \| đėlsėn̯yórđėlȧkásȧ ↓ |
| 2 _________ sėn̯yórȧ _________ ↓ | sȯnlȧs̯íhȧz \| đėlȧsėn̯yórȧđėlȧkásȧ ↓ |
| 3 ______ ȧmígȯ ______________ ↓ | ės̯ėlȧmígȯ \| đėlȧsėn̯yórȧđėlȧkásȧ ↓ |
| 4 _____ ótro̯ ________________ ↓ | ės̯ótro̯ȧmígȯ \| đėlȧsėn̯yórȧđėlȧkásȧ ↓ |
| 5 sómȯs ____________________ ↓ | sómȯs̯ótrȯs \| ȧmígȯz \| đėlȧsėn̯yórȧđėlȧkásȧ ↓ |
| 6 _________ sėn̯yórėz _________ ↓ | sómȯs̯ótrȯs \| ȧmígȯz \| đėlȯ(s)sėn̯yórėzđėlȧkásȧ ↓ |
| 7 sóy ______________________ ↓ | sóyótro̯ȧmígȯ \| đėlȯ(s)sėn̯yórėzđėlȧkásȧ ↓ |

---

D Es la hija del señor de la casa.

| | |
|---|---|
| 1 ______ hijas _______________ . | Son las hijas del señor de la casa. |
| 2 _________ señora ___________ . | Son las hijas de la señora de la casa. |
| 3 ______ amigo _______________ . | Es el amigo de la señora de la casa. |
| 4 ______ otro ________________ . | Es otro amigo de la señora de la casa. |
| 5 Somos _____________________ . | Somos otros amigos de la scñora dc la casa. |
| 6 __________ señores _________ . | Somos otros amigos de los señores de la casa. |
| 7 Soy _______________________ . | Soy otro amigo de los señores de la casa. |

E éṣekėpásȧ | pȯrȧí ↑ éṣėlkȯrȯnélhárris ↓

1 __________ sėṇyórȧ ________ ↓ — ésȧkėpásȧ | pȯrȧí ↑ ézlȧsėṇyórȧhárris ↓

2 ______________________ míȧ ↓ — ésȧkėpásȧ | pȯrȧí ↑ ézlȧsėṇyórȧmíȧ ↓

3 ____________ ȧmígȯ ________ ↓ — ésėkėpásȧ | pȯrȧí ↑ éṣėlȧmígȯmíȯ ↓

4 ȧké(l)ẏȯs __________________ ↓ — ȧké(l)ẏȯs | kėpásȧn | pȯrȧí ↑ sónlȯṣȧmígȯzmíȯs ↓

5 ____________ ùnȯs __________ ↓ — ȧké(l)ẏȯs | kėpásȧn | pȯrȧí ↑ sóṇụnȯṣȧmígȯzmíȯs ↓

6 ______________________ súẏȯs ↓ — ȧké(l)ẏȯs | kėpásȧn | pȯrȧí ↑ sóṇụnȯṣȧmígȯ(s)súẏȯs ↓

7 __________ ȧmígȧ __________ ↓ — ȧké(l)ẏȧ | kėpásȧ | pȯrȧí ↑ éṣụnȧmígȧsúẏȧ ↓

---

E Ese que pasa por ahí es el Coronel Harris.

1 __________ señora __________ . — Esa que pasa por ahí es la señora Harris.

2 ______________________ mía. — Esa que pasa por ahí es la señora mía.

3 __________ amigo __________ . — Ese que pasa por ahí es el amigo mío.

4 Aquéllos __________________ . — Aquéllos que pasan por ahí son los amigos míos.

5 ____________ unos __________ . — Aquéllos que pasan por ahí son unos amigos míos.

6 ______________________ suyos. — Aquéllos que pasan por ahí son unos amigos suyos.

7 ____________ amiga ________ . — Aquélla que pasa por ahí es una amiga suya.

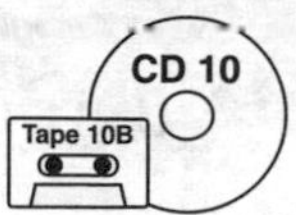


F àkɪ́tyénėzlȧtúy̯à ↓

1 ____________________ túy̯ȯ ↓ — àkɪ́tyénėsėltúy̯ȯ ↓

2 __________ e̯stá __________ ↓ — àkɪ́e̯stáe̯ltúy̯ȯ ↓

3 ____________________ míȧs ↓ — àkɪ́e̯stánlȧzmíȧs ↓

4 àɪ́ ____________________ ↓ — àɪ́e̯stánlȧzmíȧs ↓

5 __________ ótrȧz __________ ↓ — àɪ́e̯stán | ótrȧzmíȧs ↓

6 __________________ nwéstrȯs ↓ — àɪ́e̯stán | ótrȯznwéstrȯs ↓

7 ________ e̯l ______________ ↓ — àɪ́e̯stáe̯lnwéstrȯ ↓

---

F Aquí tienes la tuya.

1 ______________________ tuyo. — Aquí tienes el tuyo.

2 __________ está ______________ . — Aquí está el tuyo.

3 ______________________ mías. — Aquí están las mías.

4 Ahí ______________________ . — Ahí están las mías.

5 ____________ otras __________ . — Ahí están otras mías.

6 ____________________ nuestros. — Ahí están otros nuestros.

7 ______________ el ____________ . — Ahí está el nuestro.

**End of Tape 10B**

**End of CD 10**

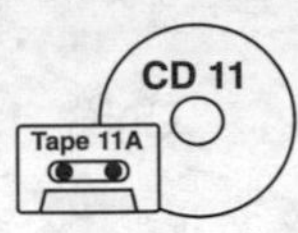




## 13.23 VARIATION DRILLS

| | | | |
|---|---|---|---|
| A | | nó ↓ sólȯđėƀéşėŋkwándȯ ↓ pȯrké ↓ | No, sólo de vez en cuando, ¿Por qué? |
| 1 | No, just on Sundays. Why? | nó ↓ sólȯlȯzđȯmíŋgȯs ↓ pȯrké ↓ | No, sólo los domingos. ¿Por qué? |
| 2 | No, just on Fridays. Why? | nó ↓ sólȯlȯzƀyérnės ↓ pȯrké ↓ | No, sólo los viernes. ¿Por qué? |
| 3 | No, just on Saturdays. Why? | nó ↓ sólȯlȯ(s)sáƀȧđȯs ↓ pȯrké ↓ | No, sólo los sábados. ¿Por qué? |
| 4 | No, just in the morning. Why? | nó ↓ sólo̯ėnlȧmȧnyánȧ ↓ pȯrké ↓ | No, sólo en la mañana. ¿Por qué? |
| 5 | No, just at night. Why? | nó ↓ sólo̯ėnlȧnóchė ↓ pȯrké ↓ | No, sólo en la noche. ¿Por qué? |
| 6 | No, just in the afternoon. Why? | nó ↓ sólo̯ėnlȧtárđė ↓ pȯrké ↓ | No, sólo en la tarde. ¿Por qué? |
| 7 | No, just in the room. Why? | nó ↓ sólo̯ėnėlkwártȯ ↓ pȯrké ↓ | No sólo en el cuarto. ¿Por qué? |

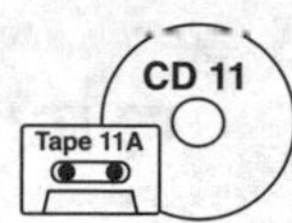




| | | |
|---|---|---|
| B | kwiđáđȯ ↓ nóƀáy̯ȧs \| ȧmėtérlȧpátȧ ↓ | ¡Cuidado, no vayas a meter la pata! |
| 1 Careful, don’t go eat that! | kwiđáđȯ ↓ nóƀáy̯ȧs \| ȧkȯméréső ↓ | ¡Cuidado, no vayas a comer eso! |
| 2 Careful, don’t go see that! | kwiđáđȯ ↓ nóƀáy̯ȧs \| ȧƀéréső ↓ | ¡Cuidado, no vayas a ver eso! |
| 3 Careful, don’t go drink that! | kwiđáđȯ ↓ nóƀáy̯ȧs \| ȧƀėƀéréső ↓ | ¡Cuidado, no vayas a beber eso! |
| 4 Careful, don’t go do that! | kwiđáđȯ ↓ nóƀáy̯ȧs \| ȧs̯éréső ↓ | ¡Cuidado, no vayas a hacer eso! |
| 5 Careful, don’t go say that! | kwiđáđȯ ↓ nóƀáy̯ȧs \| ȧđės̯íréső ↓ | ¡Cuidado, no vayas a decir eso! |
| 6 Careful, don’t go buy that! | kwiđáđȯ ↓ nóƀáy̯ȧs \| ȧkȯmpráréső ↓ | ¡Cuidado, no vayas a comprar eso! |
| 7 Careful, don’t go try that! | kwiđáđȯ ↓ nóƀáy̯ȧs \| ȧprȯƀáréső ↓ | ¡Cuidado, no vayas a probar eso! |

C mı́rȧ ↓ y̭ókrėı́ȧ | kėlȯs̭ȧmėrikánȯs | érȧnmástrȧŋkílȯs ↓ — Mira, yo creía que los americanos eran más tranquilos.

| | | |
|---|---|---|
| 1 Say, I thought (the) apartments were more expensive. | mı́rȧ ↓ y̭ókrėı́ȧ \| kėlȯs̭ȧpȧrtȧméntȯs \| érȧnmáskárȯs ↓ | Mira, yo creía que los apartamentos eran más caros. |
| 2 Say, I thought (the) hotels were more expensive. | mı́rȧ ↓ y̭ókrėı́ȧ \| kėlȯs̭ȯtélės \| érȧn máskárȯs ↓ | Mira, yo creía que los hoteles eran más caros. |
| 3 Say, I thought (the) restaurants were less expensive. | mı́rȧ ↓ y̭ókrėı́ȧ \| kėlȯzrrėstȯránės \| érȧnmázƀȧrátȯs ↓ | Mira, yo creía que los restoranes eran más baratos. |
| 4 Say, I thought (the) houses were cheaper. | mı́rȧ ↓ y̭ókrėı́ȧ \| kėlȧskásȧs \| érȧn mázƀȧrátȧs ↓ | Mira, yo creía que las casas eran más baratas. |
| 5 Say, I thought the rooms were bigger. | mı́rȧ ↓ y̭ókrėı́ȧ \| kėlȯskwártȯs \| érȧn mázgrándės ↓ | Mira, yo creía que los cuartos eran más grandes. |
| 6 Say, I thought the embassy was prettier. | mı́rȧ ↓ y̭ókrėı́ȧ \| kėla̭èmbȧháđa̭ \| érȧ mázƀȯnítȧ ↓ | Mira, yo creía que la embajada era más bonita. |
| 7 Say, I thought the downtown was nicer. | mı́rȧ ↓ y̭ókrėı́ȧ \| kėls̭éntro̭ \| érȧ mázƀȯnítȯ ↓ | Mira, yo creía que el centro era más bonito. |

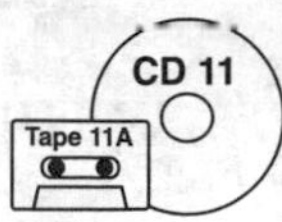




| | | |
|---|---|---|
| D | bámȯs \| ȧ(l)y̯ėƀárnȯzlȧskópȧs ↓ | Vamos a llevarnos las copas. |
| 1 Let's take our chair. | bámȯs \| ȧ(l)y̯ėƀárnȯzlȧsí(l)y̯ȧ ↓ | Vamos a llevarnos la silla. |
| 2 Let's take our pen. | bámȯs \| ȧ(l)y̯ėƀárnȯzlȧplúmȧ ↓ | Vamos a llevarnos la pluma. |
| 3 Let's take our newspaper. | bámȯs \| ȧ(l)y̯ėƀárnȯs̯ėlpėryóđikȯ ↓ | Vamos a llevarnos el periódico. |
| 4 Let's take our car. | bámȯs \| ȧ(l)y̯ėƀárnȯs̯ėláwtȯ ↓ | Vamos a llevarnos el auto. |
| 5 Let's take our shirts. | bámȯs \| ȧ(l)y̯ėƀárnȯzlȧskȧmísȧs ↓ | Vamos a llevarnos las camisas. |
| 6 Let's take our suits. | bámȯs \| ȧ(l)y̯ėƀárnȯzlȯstráhės ↓ | Vamos a llevarnos los trajes. |
| 7 Let's take our furniture. | bámȯs \| ȧ(l)y̯ėƀárnȯzlȯzmwéƀlės ↓ | Vamos a llevarnos los muebles. |

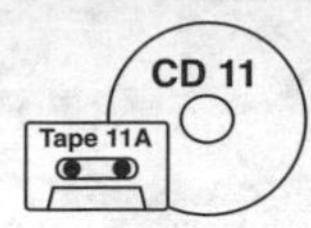



| | | | |
|---|---|---|---|
| E | nótėkȯmfúndȧs ↓ ėzlȧđé(l)y̲ȧ ↓ lȧđėkármėn ↓ | | No te confundas. Es la de ella, la de Carmen. |
| 1 | Don't get them mixed. That's hers, Bertha's. | nótėkȯmfúndȧs ↓ ėzlȧđé(l)y̲ȧ ↓ lȧđėƀértȧ ↓ | No te confundas. Es la de ella, la de Berta. |
| 2 | Don't get them mixed. That's his, Jose's. | nótėkȯmfúndȧs ↓ ėzlȧđél ↓ lȧđėhósé ↓ | No te confundas. Es la de él, la de José. |
| 3 | Don't get them mixed. That's John's. | nótėkȯmfúndȧs ↓ ėzlȧđėhwán ↓ | No te confundas. Es la de Juan. |
| 4 | Don't get them mixed. That's (m) hers. | nótėkȯmfúndȧs ↓ ėṣėldé(l)y̲ȧ ↓ | No te confundas. Es el de ella. |
| 5 | Don't get them mixed. That's (m) theirs (f). | nótėkȯmfúndȧs ↓ ėṣėldé(l)y̲ȧs ↓ | No te confundas. Es el de ellas. |
| 6 | Don't get them mixed. That's (m) theirs (m). | nótėkȯmfúndȧs ↓ ėṣėldé(l)y̲ȯs ↓ | No te confundas. Es el de ellos. |
| 7 | Don't get them mixed. They're (m) theirs. | nótėkȯmfúndȧs ↓ sȯnlȯzđé(l)y̲ȯs ↓ | No te confundas. Son los de ellos. |

| | | | |
|---|---|---|---|
| F | | bwénȯ \| chíkȧs ↓ kȯmpėrmísȯ ↓ ėnsėgíđȧƀȯlbémȯs ↓ | Bueno, chicas. Con permiso. En seguida volvemos. |
| 1 | Will you girls excuse us? We'll be back tomorrow. | bwénȯ \| chíkȧs ↓ kȯmpėrmísȯ ↓ mȧnyánȧƀȯlbémȯs ↓ | Bueno, chicas. Con permiso. Mañana volvemos. |
| 2 | Will you girls excuse us? We'll be back Monday. | bwénȯ \| chíkȧs ↓ kȯmpėrmísȯ ↓ ėlúnezƀȯlbémȯs ↓ | Bueno, chicas. Con permiso. El lunes volvemos. |
| 3 | Will you girls excuse us? We'll be back some other day. | bwénȯ \| chíkȧs ↓ kȯmpėrmísȯ ↓ ótrȯ đíȧƀȯlbémȯs ↓ | Bueno, chicas. Con permiso. Otro día volvemos. |
| 4 | Will you boys excuse us? We'll be back later. | bwénȯ \| mȯcháchȯs ↓ kȯmpėrmísȯ ↓ dėspwézƀȯlbémȯs ↓ | Bueno, muchachos. Con permiso. Después volvemos. |
| 5 | Well gentlemen, we'll be back tonight. | bwénȯ \| sėnyórės ↓ éstȧnóchėƀȯlbémȯs ↓ | Bueno, señores. Esta noche volvemos. |
| 6 | Well ladies, we'll be back this afternoon. | bwénȯ \| sėnyórȧs ↓ éstȧtárđėƀȯlbémȯs ↓ | Bueno, señoras. Esta tarde volvemos. |
| 7 | Well Charles, we'll be back in the morning. | bwénȯ \| kárlȯs ↓ ėnlȧmȧnyánȧƀȯlbémȯs ↓ | Bueno, Carlos. Mañana volvemos. |

## 13.24 REVIEW DRILL

Placement of negative particle

| | | | |
|---|---|---|---|
| 1 | I'm not married. | nósóykȧsáđȯ ↓ | No soy casado. |
| 2 | I'm not single. | nósóysȯltérȯ ↓ | No soy soltero. |
| 3 | I'm not Spanish. | nósóyėspȧn̯yól ↓ | No soy español. |
| 4 | I'm not American. | nósóyȧmėrıkánȯ ↓ | No soy americano. |
| 5 | I'm not English. | nósóyıŋglés ↓ | No soy inglés. |
| 6 | I'm not ready. | nóe̯stóylístȯ ↓ | No estoy listo. |
| 7 | I'm not fat (now). | nóe̯stóygórđȯ ↓ | No estoy gordo. |
| 8 | I'm not comfortable. | nóe̯stóykómȯđȯ ↓ | No estoy cómodo. |
| 9 | I'm not busy. | nóe̯stóyȯku̇páđȯ ↓ | No estoy ocupado. |
| 10 | I'm not helping. | nóe̯stóyȧy̯u̇đándȯ ↓ | No estoy ayudando. |
| 11 | I'm not studying. | nóe̯stóyėstu̇đyándȯ ↓ | No estoy estudiando. |
| 12 | I'm not learning. | nóe̯stóyȧprėndyéndȯ ↓ | No estoy aprendiendo. |
| 13 | I'm not writing. | nóe̯stóyėskrıƀyéndȯ ↓ | No estoy escribiendo. |

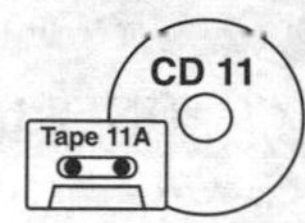




# 13.3 CONVERSATION STIMULUS

## NARRATIVE 1

| | | |
|---|---|---|
| 1 This is not Juan's glass. | éstȧ \| no̯ézlȧkópȧđėhwán ↓ | Esta no es la copa de Juan. |
| 2 If it isn't Juan's, it must be Jose's. | sino̯ézlȧđėhwán ↑ débėsérlȧđėhȯsé ↓ | Si no es la de Juan, debe ser la de José. |
| 3 Yes, it's his. | sí ↓ ėzlȧđél ↓ | Sí, es la de él. |
| 4 Juan is drinking 'cuba libre.' | hwán \| ėstáƀėƀyéndȯ \| kúƀȧlíƀrė ↓ | Juan está bebiendo cuba libre. |
| 5 He isn't dancing. | nóe̯stáƀȧylándȯ ↓ | No está bailando. |
| 6 He's waiting for his little chubby girl. | ėstáe̯spėrándo̯ \| ȧsu̇gȯrđítȧ ↓ | Está esperando a su gordita. |
| 7 She's in the kitchen helping the hostess fix some drinks. | é(l)y̯a̯ėstáe̯nlȧkȯs̯ína̯ ↓ ȧy̯u̇đándo̯ \| ȧlȧsėn̯yórȧđėlȧkása̯ \| ȧs̯éru̇nȯstrágȯs ↓ | Ella está en la cocina, ayudando a la señora de la casa a hacer unos tragos. |

## DIALOG 1

| | | |
|---|---|---|
| José, pregúntele a Juan sí ésta es su copa o la de él. | ėsėstȧtuḱopa ↑ ȯlamíȧ ↓ | José: ¿Es ésta tu copa o la mía? |
| Juan, contéstele que debe ser la de él. Que Ud. está bebiendo cuba libre. | déƀėsérlȧtúyȧ ↓ yóestóyƀėƀyéndȯ \| kúƀȧlíƀrė ↓ | Juan: Debe ser la tuya. Yo estoy bebiendo cuba libre. |
| José, pregúntele a Juan que por qué no está bailando. | pȯrkénoėstázƀȧyláṅdȯ ↓ | José: ¿Por qué no estás bailando? |
| Juan, contéstele que Ud. está esperando a su gordita. | ėstóyėspėrándoȧmigȯrđítȧ ↓ | Juan: Estoy esperando a mi gordita. |
| José, pregúntele que dónde está ella. | dóndėstaé(l)yȧ ↓ | José: ¿Dónde está ella? |
| Juan, contéstele que está en la cocina ayudando a la señora de la casa a hacer unos tragos. | ėstáenlȧkóṡinȧ ↓ ȧyuđándo \| ȧlȧsėnyórȧ đėlȧkásȧ \| aséruṅostrágȯs ↓ | Juan: Está en la cocina ayudando a la señora de la casa a hacer unos tragos. |

## NARRATIVE 2

| | | |
|---|---|---|
| 1 There's a brunette dancing in front of Juan and Jose. | áyu̇nȧmȯrénȧ \| ƀȧylȧndo̮ \| ėmfréntė đėhwȧni̮hȯsé ↓ | Hay una morena bailando enfrente de Juan y José. |
| 2 She's Colonel Harris' secretary. | ėzlȧsėkrėtȧryȧ \| đėlkȯrȯnėlhárris ↓ | Es la secretaria del Coronel Harris. |
| 3 Juan likes her. He thinks she's terrific. | ȧhwȧnlėgústȧ ↓ lėpȧrėṣėstu̇péndȧ ↓ | A Juan le gusta. Le parece estupenda. |
| 4 Jose doesn't know her very well. | hȯsé \| nólȧkȯnóṣė \| mu̇yƀyén ↓ | José no la conoce muy bien. |
| 5 But she's a friend of Carmen's, Jose's fiancée. | pėro̮é(l)ya̮ \| ėṣȧmígađėkármėn ↓ lȧnóƀyȧđėhȯsé ↓ | Pero ella es amiga de Carmen, la novia de José. |
| 6 Her name is Cecilia. | su̇nómbrės(ṣ)ėṣílyȧ ↓ | Su nombre es Cecilia. |
| 7 Juan wants to meet her. | hwáŋkyérėkȯnȯṣérlȧ ↓ | Juan quiere conocerla. |
| 8 But he can't now. | pėro̮ȧórȧ \| nópwéđė ↓ | Pero ahora no puede. |
| 9 He's waiting for his little chubby girl. | ėstáe̮spėrándo̮ \| ȧsu̇gȯrđítȧ ↓ | Está esperando a su gordita. |

10 Shhh...Careful...Here she comes.

shh | kwiđáđo ↓ akíƀyéne ↓

¡Shhh!...cuidado...aquí viene.

## DIALOG 2

Juan, pregúntele a José que quién es esa morena que está bailando enfrente de Uds.

kyénesésamoréna | kestáƀaylándo | emfréntedenosótros ↓

Juan: ¿Quién es esa morena que está bailando enfrente de nosotros?

José, contéstele que es la secretaria del Coronel Harris. Pregúntele que por qué, que si le gusta.

ezlasekretárya | đelkoronélhárris ↓ porké ↓ tegústa ↑

José: Es la secretaria del Coronel Harris. ¿Por qué?, ¿te gusta?

Juan, contéstele que le parece estupenda. Pregúntele si él la conoce.

meparése | estupénda ↓ túlakonóses ↑

Juan: Me parece estupenda. ¿Tú la conoces?

José, dígale que no muy bien. Pero que Carmen es amiga de ella. Pregúntele a Carmen si no es así.

nomúyƀyém ↓ pérokármen | esamígađé(l)ya ↓ noésasí | kármen ↑

José: No muy bien. Pero Carmen es amiga de ella. ¿No es así, Carmen?

Carmen, pregúntele a José que quién.

kyén ↑

Carmen: ¿Quién?

José, dígale que Cecilia, la morena que está bailando enfrente de Uds.

ṣẹṣıḷyȧ ↓ lȧmȯréṅȧ | kėstáƀȧyláṇdo̤ |
ėmfréṅteđenȯsótrȯs ↓

José: Cecilia, la morena que está bailando enfrente de nosotros.

Carmen, contéstele que claro, que ella y Ud. son muy buenas amigas. Pregúntele a Juan que si quiere conocerla.

kláṙȯ ↓ é(l)y̯a̤iy̯ó | sȯmȯzmúyƀwéṅȧṣ
ȧmígȧs ↓ kyéṙėkȯṅo̤ṣérlȧ | hwán ↑

Carmen: Claro, ella y yo somos muy buenas amigas.
¿Quiere conocerla, Juan?

Juan, contéstele que sí, pero que ahora no puede. Dígale que está esperando a su gordita.

sí ↓ pėro̤ȧóṙȧnopwéđȯ ↓ ėstóy
ėspėrándo̤ȧmıgȯrđítȧ ↓

Juan: Sí, pero ahora no puedo.
Estoy esperando a mi gordita.

José, dígale a Juan que Ud. lo siente mucho.

lȯsyéṇtȯmúchȯ ↓

José: Lo siento mucho.

Juan, dígale que Ud. también. Ahora dígale que shh... que cuidado...que aquí viene.

y̯ótȧmbyén ↓ sh | kwiđáđo̤ ↓
ȧkíƀyéṅė ↓

Juan: Yo también. Shh...
cuidado...aquí viene.

Carmen, dígale a José que no vaya a meter la pata.

nóƀáy̯ȧs | ȧmėtérlȧpátȧ | hósė ↓

Carmen: No vayas a meter la pata, José.

## NARRATIVE 3

| | | |
|---|---|---|
| 1 The little fat gal's name is Luz. | ėlnómbrė \| đėlȧgȯrđɪ́ta̯ \| ėzlús̬ ↓ | El nombre de la gordita es Luz. |
| 2 Luz wants to know what Juan,<br>Jose, and Carmen are talking about. | lús̬kyérėsȧƀér \| đėkéstánạƀlándȯ \|<br>hwán \| hȯsé̯ɪkármėn ↓ | Luz quiere saber de qué están<br>hablando Juan, José y Carmen. |
| 3 They're talking about...the party,<br>says Juan. He thinks it's very nice. | ėstánạƀlándȯđė \| lȧfyéstȧ \| đís̬ė<br>hwán ↓ lėpȧrés̬ė \| kėstámúybȯnítȧ ↓ | Están hablando de ...la fiesta,<br>dice Juan. Le parece que está<br>muy bonita. |
| 4 And it's really terrific. | ɪ̯ėnrr̯ėȧliđáđ ↑ ėstáe̯stu̇péndȧ ↓ | Y en realidad está estupenda. |
| 5 Juan wants to dance this one with Luz. | hwáŋ \| kyérėƀȧylárėstȧ \| kȯnlús̬ ↓ | Juan quiere bailar ésta con Luz. |
| 6 They'll be back right away. | ėnsėgíđȧƀwélbėn ↓ | En seguida vuelven. |

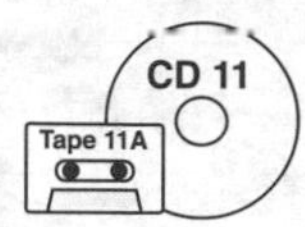



## DIALOG 3

Luz, dígales 'hola' a ellos. Pregúnteles si Ud. puede saber de qué están hablando.

ólȧ ↓ pwéđȯsȧƀér | đėkéstánȧblándȯ ↑

Luz: Hola. ¿Puedo saber de qué están hablando?

Juan, contéstele que están hablando de...la fiesta. Dígale que está bonita, que si no le parece.

ėstámȯsȧbláṇdȯđė | lȧfyéstȧ ↓
ėstábȯnítȧ ↓ nȯtėpȧréṣė ↑

Juan: Estamos hablando de...la fiesta. Está bonita, ¿no te parece?

Luz, contéstele que sí, que en realidad está estupenda.

sí ↓ ėnrrėȧliđáđ | ėstáėstȯpéndȧ ↓

Luz: Sí, en realidad está estupenda.

Juan, pregúntele si quiere bailar ésta.

kyérėzƀȧyláréstȧ ↑

Juan: ¿Quieres bailar ésta?

Luz, dígale que encantada.

ėŋkȧntáđȧ ↓

Luz: Encantada.

Juan, digales a José y a Carmen que con permiso. Que en seguida vuelven.

kȯmpėrmísȯ ↓ ėnsėgíđȧƀȯlbémȯs ↓

Juan: Con permiso. En seguida volvemos.

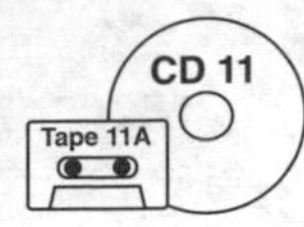




# 14.1 BASIC SENTENCES

## Colonel Harris talks about his family's arrival

Colonel Harris is speaking to Molina and White after the introductions.

| English Spelling | Aid to Listening | Spanish Spelling |
|---|---|---|
| satisfied, contented | kȯnténtȯ ↓ | contento |
| *WHITE* | | *WHITE* |
| Are you enjoying it here, Colonel? (1) | ėstákȯnténtọȧkí \| kȯrȯnél ↑ | ¿Está contento aquí, coronel? |
| *HARRIS* | | *HARRIS* |
| Yes, very much so. | sí ↓ múy \| kȯnténtȯ ↓ | Sí, muy contento. |
| besides | ȧđėmás ↓ | además |
| Besides, my family arrives tomorrow. | ȧđėmás ↑ mȧnyánȧ \| (l)yégȧmifȧmílyȧ ↓ | Además, mañana llega mi familia. |
| (they) come (to come) | byénėn ↓ bėnír ↓ | vienen (venir) |
| the boat | ėl—bárkȯ ↓ | el barco |
| by boat | ėm—bárkȯ ↓ | en barco |
| *WHITE* | | *WHITE* |
| Are they coming by boat? | byénėnėmbárkȯ ↑ | ¿Vienen en barco? |

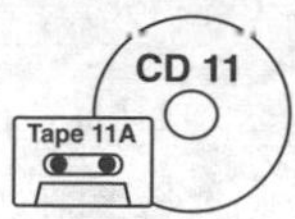



<table>
<tr><td>(they're) go(ing) to come</td><td>bán̦aƀėnír ↓</td><td>van a venir</td></tr>
<tr><td>the plane</td><td>ėl—ȧƀyón ↓</td><td>el avión</td></tr>
<tr><td>by plane</td><td>pȯr—ȧƀyón ↓</td><td>por avión</td></tr>
<tr><td>HARRIS</td><td></td><td>HARRIS</td></tr>
<tr><td>No, they're coming by plane.</td><td>nó ↓ bán̦aƀėnír | pȯrȧƀyón ↓</td><td>No, van a venir por avión.</td></tr>
<tr><td>the mother-in-law</td><td>lȧ—swégrȧ ↓</td><td>la suegra</td></tr>
<tr><td>to make dizzy</td><td>mȧrėár ↓</td><td>marear</td></tr>
<tr><td>herself (she) gets seasick (to get seasick)</td><td>sė—mȧréa̧ ↓ mȧrėársė ↓</td><td>se marea (marearse)</td></tr>
<tr><td>My mother-in-law gets seasick in a ship.</td><td>miswégrȧ | sėmȧréa̯embárkȯ ↓</td><td>Mi suegra se marea en barco.</td></tr>
<tr><td>WHITE</td><td></td><td>WHITE</td></tr>
<tr><td>Oh, your mother-in-law's coming too?</td><td>á ↓ byénė | sȯswégrȧtȧmbyén ↑</td><td>Ah, ¿viene su suegra también?</td></tr>
<tr><td>the wife</td><td>lȧ—e̯spósȧ ↓</td><td>la esposa</td></tr>
<tr><td>the child</td><td>ėl—nínyȯ ↓</td><td>el niño</td></tr>
<tr><td>HARRIS</td><td></td><td>HARRIS</td></tr>
<tr><td>Yes, she's coming with my wife and the children. (2)</td><td>sí ↓ byénė | kȯnmi̯ėspósa̯ | ikȯnlȯzníny̯ȯs ↓</td><td>Sí, viene con mi esposa y con los niños.</td></tr>
<tr><td>the son</td><td>ėl—íhȯ ↓</td><td>el hijo</td></tr>
</table>

| | | |
|---|---|---|
| *WHITE* | | *WHITE* |
| How many children do you have? | kwántosíhos \| tyénė ↓ | ¿Cuántos hijos tiene? |
| the male | ėl—bȧrón ↓ | el varón |
| the (small) girl | lȧ—nínyȧ ↓ | la niña |
| *HARRIS* | | *HARRIS* |
| Three, two boys and a girl. | trés ↓ dózƀarónės \| ụnȧnínyȧ ↓ | Tres. Dos varones y una niña. |
| *MOLINA* | | *MOLINA* |
| Do you have a house yet? (3) | ỵátyénėkásȧ ↑ | ¿Ya tiene casa? |
| Bellavista | bė(l)ỵȧƀístȧ ↓ | Bellavista |
| behind | dėtrás ↓ | detrás |
| in back of, behind, beyond | dėtráz—đė ↓ | detrás de |
| the park | ėl—párkė ↓ | el parque |
| *HARRIS* | | *HARRIS* |
| Yes, in Bellavista, on the other side of the park. | sí ↓ ėmbė(l)ỵȧƀístȧ \| đėtrázđėlpárkė ↓ | Sí, en Bellavista detrás del parque. |
| really (real) | rrẹ̄almḗntė ↓ rrẹ̄ál ↓ | realmente (real) |
| (it) is worth (to be worth) | bálė ↓ bȧlér ↓ | vale (valer) |
| the sorrow, grief | lȧ—pénȧ ↓ | la pena |
| (it) is worthwhile | bálė—lȧ—pénȧ ↓ | vale la pena |
| the section (of a town) | ėl—bárryȯ ↓ | el barrio |

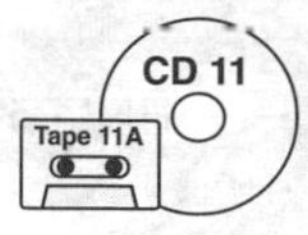




| | | |
|---|---|---|
| *MOLINA* | | *MOLINA* |
| It's really worthwhile to live in that section. | rẹȧlméntė \| ƀálėlápénȧ ↑ ƀiƀír \| ėnẹ́sėƀárryȯ ↓ | Realmente vale la pena vivir en ese barrio. |
| It's very quiet. | ézmúytrȧŋkílȯ ↓ | Es muy tranquilo. |
| above | sóƀrė ↓ | sobre |
| above all, especially | sóbrė—tóđȯ ↓ | sobre todo |
| *HARRIS* | | *HARRIS* |
| And it's an especially good place for kids. | isóbrėtóđȯ ↑ ƀwénȯpȧrȧlȯzníṉyȯs ↓ | Y sobre todo, bueno para los niños. |
| the sister | lạ—ėrmánȧ ↓ | la hermana |
| *MOLINA* | | *MOLINA* |
| A married sister of mine lives there. | ùnạėrmánȧmía \| kȧsáđȧ \| ƀíƀẹȧ(l)ẏí ↓ | Una hermana mía casada vive allí. |
| the airport | ėl—ạėrȯpwértȯ ↓ | el aeropuerto |
| (you're) go(ing) to go | bá—ạ—ír ↓ | va a ir |
| What time are you going to the airport? | ȧkẹórȧ \| ƀáirustéđ \| ȧlạėrȯpwértȯ ↓ | ¿A qué hora va a ir usted al aeropuerto? |
| *HARRIS* | | *HARRIS* |
| At one. | ȧlạúnȧ ↓ | A la una. |

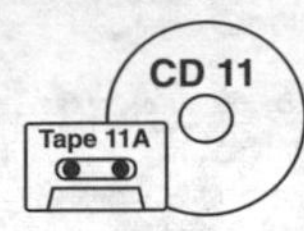




| | | |
|---|---|---|
| the order | là—órđèn ↓ | la orden |
| at your service | à—sùs—órđènès ↓ | a sus órdenes |
| *MOLINA* | | *MOLINA* |
| Let me know if I can help you. | èstóy \| àsùsórđénès \| pàràyùđárlè ↓ | Estoy a sus órdenes para ayudarle. |
| the car | èl—kárrò ↓ | el carro |
| the disposition | là—đispòsisyón ↓ | la disposición |
| at your disposal | à—sù—đispòsisyón ↓ | a su disposición |
| My car is at your disposal. | mikárro \| èstásuđispòsisyón ↓ | Mi carro está a su disposición. |
| look (to look) | míre ↓ mirár ↓ | mire (mirar) |
| *HARRIS* | | *HARRIS* |
| Thanks, Molina. Look, the girls are waiting for you all. | grásyàz \| mòlínà ↓ míre \| làzmùchácház \| lòsèstánèspèrándò ↓ | Gracias, Molina. Mire, las muchachas los están esperando. |
| (we're) go(ing) to talk | bámòs—a—àblár ↓ | vamos a hablar |
| *MOLINA* | | *MOLINA* |
| So long. We'll talk later. (4) | ástàlwégò ↓ bámosablárđespwés ↓ | Hasta luego. Vamos a hablar después. |

## 14.10 Notes on the basic sentences

(1) The translation of /konténto/ *contento* in this sentence is far from literal, but there is no very satisfactory literal translation possible. It does not mean 'contented' or 'satisfied' or even 'happy' in the sense that English speakers would mean in a sentence like 'Are you happy?', which implies something like 'Well, you *were* having problems; have things straightened out now?' The sentence just means, 'Are things going smoothly, is life treating you right?'

(2) Note that English does not normally repeat the preposition before a double object; Spanish does: cf. 'with my wife and the children' and *con mi esposa y con los niños*.

(3) The word /yá/ *ya* has been seen in Spanish utterances that have received a variety of translations into English: 'already,' 'still,' 'yet,' 'right away,' etc. A list of those equivalents that it is most likely to have may be useful:

'already' as in *Ya está aquí*. 'He's already here'.

'yet' as in *¿Ya está aquí?* 'Is he here yet?'

'right away' as in *Ya voy*. 'I'm coming right away'.

'now' as in *Ya estamos llegando*. 'We're arriving now'.

'any longer' as in *Ya no*. 'Not any longer'.

(4) It should be noted that /bámoṣablár/ *vamos a hablar* could mean 'Let's talk' instead of 'We'll talk.' That is, the form /bámoṣa__r/ *vamos a -r* is also used in the hortatory sense. It will be examined more closely and drilled in Unit 28.

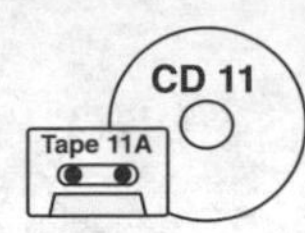




# 14.2 DRILLS AND GRAMMAR

## 14.21 PATTERN DRILLS

### 14.21.1 Present tense forms of the irregular verbs /ír, dár, bér/

A. PRESENTATION OF PATTERN

*ILLUSTRATIONS*

| | | |
|---|---|---|
| ______________________ | 1 mėƀóy \| ėntónșės ↓ | Me *voy*, entonces. |
| Are you going to the party? | 2 bás̯ạlȧfyéstȧ ↑ | ¿*Vas* a la fiesta? |
| ______________________ | 3 kómȯlėƀá ↓ | ¿Cómo le *va?* |
| Let's go that way. | 4 bámȯspȯraí ↓ | *Vamos* por ahí. |
| Are they going downtown? | 5 bánạls̯éntrȯ ↑ | ¿*Van* al centro? |
| | | |
| ______________________ | 6 lėđóytrés ↓ únȯđėprȯpínȧ ↓ | Le *doy* tres, uno de propina. |
| How much are you giving him, then? | 7 kwántȯlėđás \| ėntónșės ↓ | ¿Cuánto le *das,* entonces? |
| ______________________ | 8 dálȧká(l)y̯ė ↑ o̯ȧlpátyȯ ↓ | ¿*Da* a la calle, o al patio? |

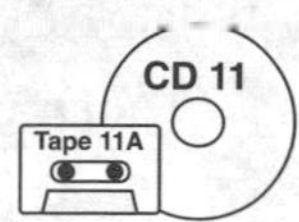



| | | |
|---|---|---|
| We'll give you (an) hour and a half. | 9 lėđámȯs \| óra̯ımėđyȧ ↓ | Le *damos* hora y media. |
| ______________________ | 10 simėđán \| ėlȧpȧrtȧméntȯ ↓ | Sí me *dan* el apartamento. |
| It's just that I don't see too well. | 11 és \| kėnóƀéȯmúyƀyén ↓ | Es que no *veo* muy bien. |
| ______________________ | 12 ȧsíƀéz \| đóndėƀíƀȯ ↓ | Así *ves* donde vivo. |
| Who do you see? | 13 ȧkyémbéu̯stéđ ↓ | ¿A quién *ve* usted? |
| ______________________ | 14 pȯrkénȯƀémȯs \| a̯uṇamígȯmíȯ ↓ | ¿Por qué no *vemos* a un amigo mío? |
| Do you all see that brunette? | 15 bén \| a̯ésȧmȯrénȧ ↑ | ¿*Ven* a esa morena? |

*EXTRAPOLATION*

| | ír | dár | bér |
|---|---|---|---|
| sg | | | |
| 1 | b—óy | d—óy | bé—o |
| 2 fam | b—ás | d—ás | b—és |
| 2 – 3 | b—á | d—á | b—é |
| pl | | | |
| 1 | b—ámos | d—ámos | b—émos |
| 2 – 3 | b—án | d—án | b—én |

*NOTES*

a. These verbs are irregular in their 1 sg forms.

b. /ír/ has a stem /b—/ appearing in the present tense.

c. The monosyllabic forms are stressed on their endings.

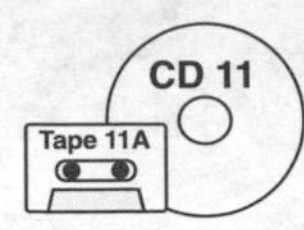




## 14.21.11 SUBSTITUTION DRILLS

Number substitution

1 dámȯsprȯpínȧ ↓ — dóyprȯpínȧ ↓

2 béȯlȯṣanúnṣyȯs ↓ — bémȯzlȯṣanúnṣyȯs ↓

3 bámȯṣalatıntȯrėríȧ ↓ — bóyalatıntȯrėríȧ ↓

4 dóyđėmȧsyáđȯ ↓ — dámȯzđėmȧsyáđȯ ↓

5 bénẹlpėryóđikȯ ↓ — bélpėryóđikȯ ↓

6 bóyėnạ́wtȯ ↓ — bámȯṣenạ́wtȯ ↓

---

1 Damos propina. — Doy propina.

2 Veo los anuncios. — Vemos los anuncios.

3 Vamos a la tintorería. — Voy a la tintorería.

4 Doy demasiado. — Damos demasiado.

5 Ven el periódico. — Ve el periódico.

6 Voy en auto. — Vamos en auto.

| | |
|---|---|
| 7 dámpėrmísȯ ↓ | dápėrmísȯ ↓ |
| 8 bémȯzlȧstáşȧs ↓ | béȯlȧstáşȧs ↓ |
| 9 báláƀóđȧ ↓ | báṇȧláƀóđȧ ↓ |
| 10 dánchékės ↓ | dáchékės ↓ |
| 11 bámpróntȯ ↓ | bápróntȯ ↓ |

---

| | |
|---|---|
| 7 Dan permiso. | Da permiso. |
| 8 Vemos las tazas. | Veo las tazas. |
| 9 Va a la boda. | Van a la boda. |
| 10 Dan cheques. | Da cheques. |
| 11 Van pronto. | Va pronto. |

**End of Tape 11A**

Person - number substitution

1 y̯óđóy | lȧrrópȧƀyéhȧ ↓

| | |
|---|---|
| mȧríȧ ______________ ↓ | dálȧrrópȧƀyéhȧ ↓ |
| hwáṇy̯ó ______________ ↓ | dámȯzlȧrrópȧƀyéhȧ ↓ |
| ȯstéđėz ______________ ↓ | dánlȧrrópȧƀyéhȧ ↓ |
| tú ______________ ↓ | dázlȧrrópȧƀyéhȧ ↓ |

2 hwán | nóƀélȯsȧnúnșyȯs ↓

| | |
|---|---|
| ȯstéđėz ______________ ↓ | nóƀénlȯsȧnúnșyȯs ↓ |
| y̯ó ______________ ↓ | nóƀéȯlȯsȧnúnșyȯs ↓ |

---

1 *Yo* doy la ropa vieja.

| | |
|---|---|
| María ______________ . | Da la ropa vieja. |
| Juan y yo ______________ . | Damos la ropa vieja. |
| Uds. ______________ . | Dan la ropa vieja. |
| Tú ______________ . | Das la ropa vieja. |

2 *Juan* no ve los anuncios.

| | |
|---|---|
| Uds. ______________ . | No ven los anuncios. |
| Yo ______________ . | No veo los anuncios. |

mȧría̯ikármėn ____________________ ↓ — nóƀénlȯs̯anún̯syȯs ↓

é(l)y̯ȯz ____________________ ↓ — nóƀénlȯs̯anún̯syȯs ↓

3 nȯsótrȯz | ƀámȯs̯éstȧnóchė ↓

é(l)y̯ȧ ____________________ ↓ — báe̯stȧnóchė ↓

y̯ó ____________________ ↓ — bóyėstȧnóchė ↓

hwáni̯kármėn ____________________ ↓ — bán̯ėstȧnóchė ↓

ùstéđ ____________________ ↓ — báe̯stȧnóchė ↓

---

Maria y Carmen ____________________ . — No ven los anuncios.

Ellos ____________________ . — No ven los anuncios.

3 *Nosotros* vamos esta noche.

Ella ____________________ . — Va esta noche.

Yo ____________________ . — Voy esta noche.

Juan y Carmen ____________________ . — Van esta noche.

Ud. ____________________ . — Va esta noche.

4 é(l)y̯ȯz | đánmúchȧsprȯpínȧs ↓

| | |
|---|---|
| ȯstéđ ______ ↓ | dámúchȧsprȯpínȧs ↓ |
| mȧríạihwán ______ ↓ | dánmúchȧsprȯpínȧs ↓ |
| y̯ó ______ ↓ | dóymúchȧsprȯpínȧs ↓ |
| é(l)y̯ȧ ______ ↓ | dámúchȧsprȯpínȧs ↓ |

---

4 *Ellos* dan muchas propinas.

| | |
|---|---|
| Ud. ______ . | Da muchas propinas. |
| María y Juan ______ . | Dan muchas propinas. |
| Yo ______ . | Doy muchas propinas. |
| Ella ______ . | Da muchas propinas. |

5 y̰ó | ƀéȯmúyƀyén ↓

| | |
|---|---|
| ȧntónyȯ ____________ ↓ | bémúyƀyén ↓ |
| tú ____________ ↓ | bézmúyƀyén ↓ |
| ůstéđi̯ȧntónyȯ ____________ ↓ | bénmúyƀyén ↓ |
| nȯsótrȯz ____________ ↓ | bémȯzmúyƀyén ↓ |

---

5 *Yo* veo muy bien.

| | |
|---|---|
| Antonio ____________ . | Ve muy bien. |
| Tú ____________ . | Ves muy bien. |
| Ud. y Antonio ____________ . | Ven muy bien. |
| Nosotros ____________ . | Vemos muy bien. |

## 14.21.12 RESPONSE DRLLL

| | | |
|---|---|---|
| | 1 báu̯stéđȧlsẹ́ntrȯ ↑ o̯ȧsu̇kásȧ ↓ | bóyȧlsẹ́ntrȯ ↓ |
| | 2 bén̦ustéđez \| lȯsȧnúnsyȯs ↑ ȯlȧsfótȯs ↓ | bémȯzlȧsfótȯs ↓ |
| | 3 bán̦é(l)y̯ȯs \| ȧórȧ ↑ o̯éstȧnóchė ↓ | bán̦ȧórȧ ↓ |
| | 4 béél \| lȯspėryóđi̇kȯs ↑ ȯlȯzlíƀrȯs ↓ | bélȯzlíƀrȯs ↓ |
| [lȯsȧnúnsyȯs ↓] | 5 kéƀéu̯stéđ ↓ | béȯlȯsȧnúnsyȯs ↓ |
| [y̯á ↓] | 6 kwándȯƀán̦ustéđės ↓ | bámȯzy̯á ↓ |
| [lȧsėkrėtáryȧ ↓] | 7 ȧkyémbén̦é(l)y̯ȯs ↓ | bén̦ȧlȧsėkrėtáryȧ ↓ |
| [ȧlȧskwátrȯ ↓] | 8 ȧke̯órȧƀáél ↓ | bálȧskwátrȯ ↓ |

---

| | | |
|---|---|---|
| | 1 ¿Va Ud. al centro o a su casa? | Voy al centro. |
| | 2 ¿Ven Uds. los anuncios o las fotos? | Vemos las fotos. |
| | 3 ¿Van ellos ahora o esta noche? | Van ahora. |
| | 4 ¿Ve él los periódicos o los libros? | Ve los libros. |
| (los anuncios) | 5 ¿Qué ve Ud.? | Veo los anuncios. |
| (ya) | 6 ¿Cuándo van Uds.? | Vamos ya. |
| (la secretaria) | 7 ¿A quién ven ellos? | Ven a la secretaria. |
| (a las cuatro) | 8 ¿A qué hora va él? | Va a las cuatro. |

| | | |
|---|---|---|
| [ȧlȧṣóchȯ ↓] | 9 báu̯stéđ ǀ ȧláznwébė ↑ | nó ↓ bóyȧlȧṣóchȯ ↓ |
| [ȧlȧ(s)séys ↓] | 10 bánu̯stéđės ǀ ȧlás(ṣ)íŋkȯ ↑ | nó ↓ bámȯṣȧla(s)séys ↓ |
| [lȯṣȧnúnṣyȯs ↓] | 11 béné(l)yȯz ǀ ȧsfótȯs ↑ | nó ↓ bénlȯṣȧnúnṣyȯs ↓ |
| | 12 dánustéđėz ǀ lȯstráhėzƀyéhȯs ↑ | sí ↓ lȯzđámȯs ↓ |
| | 13 dáu̯stéđ ǀ lȧskȧmísȧzƀyéhȧs ↑ | sí ↓ lȧzđóy ↓ |
| | 14 dáél ǀ múchȧspropínȧs ↑ | sí ↓ dámúchȧs ↓ |
| | 15 dáné(l)yȯz ǀ lȧrrópȧƀyéhȧ ↑ | sí ↓ lȧđán ↓ |

---

| | | |
|---|---|---|
| (a las ocho) | 9 ¿Va Ud. a las nueve? | No, voy a las ocho. |
| (a las seis) | 10 ¿Van Uds. a las cinco? | No, vamos a las seis. |
| (los anuncios) | 11 ¿Ven ellos las fotos? | No, ven los anuncios. |
| | 12 ¿Dan Uds. los trajes viejos? | Sí, los damos. |
| | 13 ¿Da Ud. las camisas viejas? | Sí, las doy. |
| | 14 ¿Da él muchas propinas? | Sí, da muchas. |
| | 15 ¿Dan ellos la ropa vieja? | Sí, la dan. |

## 14.21.13 TRANSLATION DRILL

| | | | |
|---|---|---|---|
| 1 | I'm not going now. | y̧ónȯƀóyȧórȧ ↓ | Yo no voy ahora. |
| 2 | She's going to the wedding. | é(l)y̧ȧƀálȧƀóđȧ ↓ | Ella va a la boda. |
| 3 | They never give anything. | é(l)y̧ȯznúŋkȧ ǀ đá(n)náđȧ ↓ | Ellos nunca dan nada. |
| 4 | Let's go right away. | bámȯṣėnsėgíđȧ ↓ | Vamos en seguida. |
| 5 | Why aren't you (all) going? | pȯrké ǀ nȯƀánụstéđės ↓ | ¿Por qué no van Uds.? |
| 6 | I always look at the ads. | syémprė ǀ ƀéȯlȯṣȧnúnṣyȯs ↓ | Siempre veo los anuncios. |
| 7 | From time to time I go to that restaurant | dėƀéṣẹ̇ŋkwándȯ ↑ bóya̯ésėrrėstȯrán ↓ | De vez en cuando voy a ese restorán. |
| 8 | How many ladies are going? | kwántȧ(s)sėn̦yórȧzƀán ↓ | ¿Cuántas señoras van? |
| 9 | I'm giving all my old clothes. | y̧óđóy ǀ tóđȧmirrópȧƀyéhȧ ↓ | Yo doy toda mi ropa vieja. |
| 10 | He doesn't give many tips. | él ǀ nóđá ǀ múchȧsprȯpínȧs ↓ | El no da muchas propinas. |
| 11 | We give too many tips. | dámȯz ǀ đėmȧsyáđȧsprȯpínȧs ↓ | Damos demasiadas propinas. |

## B. DISCUSSION OF PATTERN

The verb /ír/ is irregular in having a special stem /b—/ in the present tense. This stem is further irregular in that it conjugates not like an /—ír/ verb, but rather like a regular /—ár/ verb except for the added final /—y/ in /bóy/.

The verb /dár/ is irregular only in having a final /—y/ on the 1 sg form, /dóy/ shares this irregularity with /bóy/, /sóy/, and /estóy/.

The verb /bér/ has its regular stern /b—/ in all forms except 1 sg where the stem /be—/ occurs in /béo/.

All of these verbs have monosyllabic conjugated forms except in 1 pl /bámos/, /dámos/, and /bemos/, and in 1 sg /béo/. As monosyllables their lexical stress appears on their endings rather than on a preceding syllable.

# 14.21.2 The periphrastic future construction

## A. PRESENTATION OF PATTERN

*ILLUSTRATIONS*

| | | | |
|---|---|---|---|
| ___________________ | 1 | bóyȧƀér \| sı(l)y̱ėgóe̯lágwȧ ↓ | *Voy a ver* si llegó el agua. |
| I'm going to talk later. | 2 | bóyȧƀlár \| đėspwés ↓ | *Voy a hablar* después. |
| ___________________ | 3 | básạ̇ƀıbír \| ėnẹlȯtél ↑ | ¿*Vas a vivir* en el hotel? |
| ___________________ | 4 | ȧkyémbásạ̇(l)y̱ėƀár ↓ | ¿A quién *vas a llevar?* |
| ___________________ | 5 | kwántȯƀákȯƀrármė ↓ | ¿Cuánto *va a cobrarme?* |

| | | |
|---|---|---|
| ____________ | 6 bátrȧƀȧhár \| kȯ(n)nȯsótrȯs ↓ | *Va a trabajar* con nosotros. |
| ____________ | 7 bámȯsạtėnér \| ƀóđȧpróntȯ ↑ | ¿*Vamos a tener* boda pronto? |
| ____________ | 8 bámȯsạbér \| ėlpėryóđikȯ ↓ | *Vamos a ver* el periódico. |
| ____________ | 9 bánạkȧmbyársė \| đėkásȧ ↓ | *Van a cambiarse* de casa. |
| ____________ | 10 nó ↓ bánạƀėnír \| pȯrȧƀyón ↓ | No, *van a venir* por avión. |

## *EXTRAPOLATION*

| | ir | a | /—Vr/ | | |
|---|---|---|---|---|---|
| | | | —ár | —ér | —ír |
| sg | | | | | |
| 1 | bóy | | | | |
| 2 fam | bás | a | abl—ár | kom—ér | bib—ír |
| 2 – 3 | bá | | | | |
| pl | | | | | |
| 1 | bámos | | | | |
| 2 – 3 | bán | | | | |

## *NOTES*

a. The periphrastic future construction consists of a conjugated form of the verb /ír/ plus the phrase relator /a/ plus the infinitive form of the verb.

b. Before an infinitive beginning with the vowel /a/, or after the form /bá/, the phrase relator /a/ regularly fails to occur in actual pronunciation.

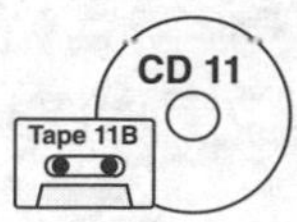



## 14.21.21 SUBSTITUTION DRILLS

Person-number substitution

1 y̰ó ƀóyȧtrȧđu̇şír ↓

| | |
|---|---|
| u̇stéđ ______ ↓ | bȧtrȧđu̇şír ↓ |
| hwániy̰ó ______ ↓ | bámȯşatrȧđu̇şír ↓ |
| é(l)y̰ȯz ______ ↓ | bánȧtrȧđu̇şír ↓ |
| kármėn ______ ↓ | bátrȧđu̇şír ↓ |

2 nȯsótrȯz | ƀámȯşȧtrȧƀȧhárȧí ↓

| | |
|---|---|
| é(l)y̰ȯz ______ ↓ | bánȧtrȧƀȧhárȧí ↓ |
| y̰ó ______ ↓ | bóyȧtrȧƀȧhárȧí ↓ |

---

1 *Yo* voy a traducir.

| | |
|---|---|
| Ud. ______ . | Va a traducir. |
| Juan y yo ______ . | Vamos a traducir. |
| Ellos ______ . | Van a traducir. |
| Carmen ______ . | Va a traducir. |

2 *Nosotros* vamos a trabajar ahí.

| | |
|---|---|
| Ellos ______ . | Van a trabajar ahí. |
| To ______ . | Voy a trabajar ahí. |

lwísạịantónẏo _______________ ↓ bánạtrȧƀȧháṙaí ↓

tú _______________ ↓ básạtrȧƀȧháṙaí ↓

3 é(l)ẏa | ƀákȯmérđėspwés ↓

ẏó _______________ ↓ bóyȧkȯmérđėspwés ↓

lwísạịantónẏo _______________ ↓ bánạkȯmérđėspwés ↓

lwísạịẏó _______________ ↓ bámȯsạkȯmérđėspwés ↓

ùstéđėz _______________ ↓ bánạkȯmérđėspwés ↓

---

Luisa y Antonio _______________ . Van a trabajar ahí.

Tú _______________ . Vas a trabajar ahí.

3 *Ella* va a comer después.

Yo _______________ . Voy a comer después.

Luisa y Antonio _______________ . Van a comer después.

Luisa y yo _______________ . Vamos a comer después.

Uds. _______________ . Van a comer después.

Construction substitution

| | |
|---|---|
| 1 kómȯƀȧstántė ↓ | bóyȧkȯmérƀȧstántė ↓ |
| 2 tȯmámȯzƀínȯ ↓ | bámȯsạtȯmárƀínȯ ↓ |
| 3 súƀėn ǀ ėnẹlȧs(s̩)ėnsór ↓ | bánạsu̇ƀír ǀ ėnẹlȧs(s̩)ėnsór ↓ |
| 4 báylȧí ↓ | báƀȧylárȧí ↓ |
| 5 bíƀo̯emfréntė ↓ | bóyȧƀiƀírėmfréntė ↓ |
| 6 mándȧnlȯstráhės ↓ | bánạmȧndárlȯstráhės ↓ |
| 7 ėstu̇đyámȯsẹnẹlkwártȯ ↓ | bámȯsạėstu̇đyár ǀ ėnẹlkwártȯ ↓ |

---

| | |
|---|---|
| 1 Como bastante. | Voy a comer bastante. |
| 2 Tomamos vino. | Vamos a tomar vino. |
| 3 Suben en el ascensor. | Van a subir en el ascensor. |
| 4 Baila ahí. | Va a bailar ahí. |
| 5 Vivo enfrente. | Voy a vivir enfrente. |
| 6 Mandan los trajes. | Van a mandar los trajes. |
| 7 Estudiamos en el cuarto. | Vamos a estudiar en el cuarto. |

## 14.21.22 RESPONSE DRILL

| | | |
|---|---|---|
| | 1 báu̯stéđ \| ȧtrȧƀahár ↑ o̯ȧe̯stu̇đyár ↓ | bóyȧtrȧƀȧhár ↓ |
| | 2 bánu̯stéđės \| a̯ėskriƀír ↑ o̯ȧsalír ↓ | bámȯsa̯sȧlír ↓ |
| | 3 báé(l)ya̯ \| ȧlȧƀár ↑ o̯aƀȧrrér ↓ | báƀȧrrér ↓ |
| [ȧe̯skribír ↓] | 4 kéƀán \| ȧse̯ré(l)yȯs ↓ | bána̯ėskribír ↓ |
| [ȧe̯stu̇ƀyár ↓] | 5 kéƀáse̯rústéđ ↓ | bóya̯ėstu̇đyár ↓ |
| [ȧbėƀér ↓] | 6 kéƀán \| ȧse̯rústéđės ↓ | bámȯsa̯bėƀér ↓ |
| [u̇ntráhė ↓] | 7 kéƀás \| ȧkȯmprártú ↓ | bóyȧkȯmprárúntráhė ↓ |

---

| | | |
|---|---|---|
| | 1 ¿Va Ud. a trabajar o a estudiar? | Voy a trabajar. |
| | 2 ¿Van Uds. a escribir o a salir? | Vamos a salir. |
| | 3 ¿Va ella a lavar o a barrer? | Va a barrer. |
| (a escribir) | 4 ¿Qué van a hacer ellos? | Van a escribir. |
| (a estudiar) | 5 ¿Qué va a hacer Ud.? | Voy a estudiar. |
| (a beber) | 6 ¿Qué van a hacer Uds.? | Vamos a beber. |
| (un traje) | 7 ¿Qué vas a comprar tú? | Voy a comprar un traje. |

| | | | |
|---|---|---|---|
| [lȯschékės ↓] | 8 | kéƀánȧkȧmbyárústéđės ↓ | bámȯsạkȧmbyár \| lȯschékės ↓ |
| [ȧe̯stúđyár ↓] | 9 | básȧlírél ↑ | nó ↓ báe̯stúđyár ↓ |
| [ȧsȧlír ↓] | 10 | bána̯ėskriƀírústéđės ↑ | nó ↓ bámȯsạsȧlír ↓ |
| | 11 | bákȯmére(l)ya̯ \| póstrė ↑ | sí ↓ é(l)ya̯ \| ƀákȯmérpóstrė ↓ |
| | 12 | bánạkȯmérústéđės \| pȧstél ↑ | sí ↓ bámȯsạkȯmérpȧstél ↓ |
| | 13 | bá(l)yėƀárústéđ \| ėláwtȯ ↑ | sí ↓ bóyȧ(l)yėƀárlȯ ↓ |

---

| | | | |
|---|---|---|---|
| (los cheques) | 8 | ¿Qué van a cambiar Uds.? | Vamos a cambiar los cheques. |
| (a estudiar) | 9 | ¿Va a salir él? | No, va a estudiar. |
| (a salir) | 10 | ¿Van a escribir Uds.? | No, vamos a salir. |
| | 11 | ¿Va a comer ella postre? | Sí, ella va a comer postre. |
| | 12 | ¿Van a comer Uds. pastel? | Sí, vamos a comer pastel. |
| | 13 | ¿Va a llevar Ud. el auto? | Sí, voy a llevarlo. |

## 14.21.23 TRANSLATION DRILL

| | | |
|---|---|---|
| 1 We're going to repeat that. | bámȯs̥àrrėpėtíréso ↓ | Vamos a repetir eso. |
| 2 I'm going to shave. | bóyȧfėytármė ↓ | Voy a afeitarme. |
| 3 What're you going to do? | kéƀás̥érústéđ ↓ | ¿Qué va a hacer Ud.? |
| 4 Where are you going to work? | dóndėƀátrȧƀahár ↓ | ¿Dónde va a trabajar? |
| 5 I'm going to take a bath. | bóyȧƀàn̥yármė ↓ | Voy a bañarme. |
| 6 He's not going to stick his foot (in his mouth) again. | él \| nóƀáméter \| lȧpát̥aótráƀés̥ ↓ | El no va a meter la pata otra vez. |
| 7 They're going to practice (some) more. | bán \| ȧpràktikármás ↓ | Van a practicar más. |
| 8 They're going to look for a house. | bán \| ȧƀùskárkásȧ ↓ | Van a buscar casa. |
| 9 We're going to take (make) a trip. | bámȯs \| ȧs̥érumbyáhė ↓ | Vamos a hacer un viaje. |

### B. PRESENTATION OF PATTERN

The periphrastic future construction has three component forms (1) a conjugated form of the verb /ír/, (2) the phrase relator /a/, and (3) an infinitive. These elements are usually not separated by any other forms, though sometimes a pronoun subject will appear after the form of /ír/.

As the name *periphrastic* indicates, this construction is a roundabout way of expressing future time. Spanish has a future tense which will be presented in Unit 53, but the periphrastic future construction seems to occur more frequently than the future tense in most dialects. It is a rather close equivalent of the 'to be going to....' construction in English.

This double English construction, combining both present progressive and periphrastic future constructions, has no exact parallel in Spanish, though its function is performed by the Spanish periphrastic future.

The periphrastic construction frequently brings into immediate sequence two and sometimes three /a/ phonemes. The normal phonetic pattern of reduction to a single /a/ in normal conversation may appear to be an omission of the relator /a/. Thus /bá—a—komér/ becomes /bákomér/ and /bá—a—ablár/ becomes /báblár/. The relator becomes quickly evident again when /bán/ is substituted for /bá/: /bána̯komér/. /bána̯blár/, showing that the reduction is purely phonological.

The periphrastic future construction in its 1 pl form can express future time (or intention) as in /bámos—a—estudyár | ésta—nóche ↓/ 'We're going to study tonight', or it can express what might be called a hortatory construction, where the speaker exhorts others to accompany him in an action. Thus /bámos—a—komér ↓/ appearing in its affirmative form can mean 'We're going to eat' or 'Let's eat'.

## 14.21.3 Question intonation patterns – Yes-no questions

### A. PRESENTATION OF PATTERN

*ILLUSTRATIONS*

| | | |
|---|---|---|
| You like the room. | 1 lėgústa̯ėlkwártȯ ↓ | 1 2 1 1 ↓<br>Le gusta el cuarto. |
| ______________ | lėgústa̯ėlkwártȯ ↑ | 1 2 2 2 ↑<br>¿Le gusta el cuarto? |

| | | |
|---|---|---|
| ________________ | 2 ėstáléhȯs ↓ | 1 2 1 1 ↓<br>Está lejos. |
| Is it far? | ėstálėhȯs ↑ | 1 2 2 2 ↑<br>¿Está lejos? |
| ________________ | 3 ėzmúykárȯ ↓ | 1 2 1 1 ↓<br>Es muy caro. |
| Is it very expensive? | ėzmúykárȯ ↑ | 1 2 2 2 ↑<br>¿Es muy caro? |

*EXTRAPOLATION*

| Statement | Yes-no question |
|---|---|
| /1211 ↓/ | /1222 ↑/ |

*NOTES*

a. One frequent Spanish yes-no question pattern is /1222 ↑/, similar to a common English pattern, but not ending as high as the English pattern does.

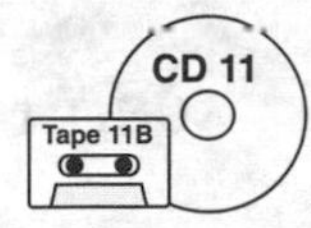




## 14.21.31 SUBSTITUTION DRILL

Pattern substitution

Problem:

tràƀáhànmúchò ↓

Answer:

tràƀáhànmúchò ↑

1 àlkílànelkwártò ↓ — àlkílànelkwártò ↑

2 lègústaelprésyò ↓ — lègústaelprésyò ↑

---

/1211 ↓/ > /1222 ↑/

Problem: 1 2 1 1 ↓
Trabajan mucho.

Answer: 1 2 2 2 ↑
¿Trabajan mucho?

1 2 1 1 ↓
1 Alquilan el cuarto. — 1 2 2 2 ↑ ¿Alquilan el cuarto?

1 2 1 1 ↓
2 Le gusta el precio. — 1 2 2 2 ↑ ¿Le gusta el precio?

| | | |
|---|---|---|
| 3 | sùƀímȯṣaórà ↓ | sùƀímȯṣȧóra ↑ |
| 4 | ėstámwėƀláđȯ ↓ | ėstámwėƀláđȯ ↑ |
| 5 | kȯmprámȯṣėláwtȯ ↓ | kȯmprámȯṣėláwtȯ ↑ |
| 6 | dėséálgȯ ↓ | dėséálgȯ ↑ |
| 7 | tȯmámȯṣụntáksi ↓ | tȯmámȯṣụntáksi ↑ |
| 8 | àlmȯrṣámȯshúntȯs ↓ | àlmȯrṣámȯshúntȯs ↑ |

---

| | | |
|---|---|---|
| 3 | 1 2 1 1 ↓<br>Subimos ahora. | 1 2 2 2 ↑<br>¿Subimos ahora? |
| 4 | 1 2 1 1 ↓<br>Está amueblado. | 1 2 2 2 ↑<br>¿Está amueblado? |
| 5 | 1 2 1 1 ↓<br>Compramos el auto. | 1 2 2 2 ↑<br>¿Compramos el auto? |
| 6 | 1 2 1 1 ↓<br>Desea algo. | 1 2 2 2 ↑<br>¿Desea algo? |
| 7 | 1 2 1 1 ↓<br>Tomamos un taxi. | 1 2 2 2 ↑<br>¿Tomamos un taxi? |
| 8 | 1 2 1 1 ↓<br>Almorzamos juntos. | 1 2 2 2 ↑<br>¿Almorzamos juntos? |

| | |
|---|---|
| 9 lėpȧréșėkárȯ ↓ | lėpȧréșėkárȯ ↑ |
| 10 bu̇skámȯșótrȯ ↓ | bu̇skámȯșótrȯ ↑ |
| 11 kȯmprámȯ(s)sáƀȧnȧs ↓ | kȯmprámȯ(s)sáƀȧnȧs ↑ |

---

| | |
|---|---|
| 1 2 1 1 ↓<br>9 Le parece caro. | 1 2 2 2 ↑<br>¿Le parece caro? |
| 1 2 1 1 ↓<br>10 Buscamos otro. | 1 2 2 2 ↑<br>¿Buscamos otro? |
| 1 2 1 1 ↓<br>11 Compramos sábanas. | 1 2 2 2 ↑<br>¿Compramos sábanas? |

## B. PRESENTATION OF PATTERN

The most common intonation pattern that occurs with yes-no questions, particularly when the questioner does not anticipate whether the answer will be 'yes' or 'no', is /1222 ↑/.

This pattern will give English speakers relatively little difficulty since it is very similar to an English pattern with the same meaning. The English pattern, however, ends somewhat higher and this extra height might be interpreted as insistence or annoyance in Spanish.

Thus /nó—tyéne—ótro ↑/ (2 2 2 2) Don't you have another?' is normal and /nó—tyéne—ótro ↑/ (2 2 2 3) could mean 'Don't you have just one more?'

## 14.22 REPLACEMENT DRILLS

A ėstákȯnténtọȧkí | kȯrȯnél ↑

| | | |
|---|---|---|
| 1 | ________________ sėn̯yórės ↑ | ėstáŋkȯnténtȯs \| ȧkí \| sėn̯yórės ↑ |
| 2 | __________ ȧórȧ __________ ↑ | ėstáŋkȯnténtȯs \| ȧórȧ \| sėn̯yórės ↑ |
| 3 | _______ ȯkůpáđȯs __________ ↑ | ėstánọ̇kůpáđȯs \| ȧórȧ \| sėn̯yórės ↑ |
| 4 | ________________ sėn̯yȯrítȧs ↑ | ėstánọ̇kůpáđȧs \| ȧórȧ \| sėn̯yȯrítȧs ↑ |
| 5 | _______ dėsȯkůpáđȧs__________ ↑ | ėstándėsȯkůpáđȧs \| ȧórȧ \| sėn̯yȯrítȧs ↑ |
| 6 | ______________________ hȯsé ↑ | ėstáđėsȯkůpáđọ \| ȧórȧ \| hȯsé ↑ |
| 7 | ____________________ kármėn ↑ | ėstáđėsȯkůpáđạ \| ȧórȧ \| kármėn ↑ |

---

A ¿Esta contento aquí, Coronel?

| | | |
|---|---|---|
| 1 | ¿ ___________________ señores? | ¿Están contentos aquí, señores? |
| 2 | ¿ __________ ahora, _________ ? | ¿Están contentos ahora, señores? |
| 3 | ¿ _______ ocupados __________ ? | ¿Están ocupados ahora, señores? |
| 4 | ¿ __________________ señoritas? | ¿Están ocupadas ahora, señoritas? |
| 5 | ¿ ______ desocupadas ________ ? | ¿Están desocupadas ahora, señoritas? |
| 6 | ¿ ______________________ José? | ¿Está desocupado ahora, José? |
| 7 | ¿ ___________________ Carmen? | ¿Está desocupada ahora, Carmen? |

B ȧđėmás ↑ mȧṇyánȧ | (l)y̯égȧmifȧmílyȧ ↓

1 ____________________ ȧmígȯs ↓ — ȧđėmás ↑ mȧṇyánȧ | (l)y̯égȧnmiṣȧmígȯs ↓

2 ________________ su̇s ________ ↓ — ȧđėmás ↑ mȧṇyánȧ | (l)y̯égȧnsu̇ṣamígȯs ↓

3 ___________ ƀyénėn _________ ↓ — ȧđėmás ↑ mȧṇyánȧ | ƀyénėnsu̇ṣȧmígȯs ↓

4 ________ ėlhwéƀėz ___________ ↓ — ȧđėmás ↑ ėlhwéƀėz | ƀyénėnsu̇ṣȧmígȯs ↓

5 _____________ ȧké(l)y̯ȯs ______ ↓ — ȧđėmás ↑ ėlhwéƀėz | ƀyénėn | ȧké(l)y̯ȯṣȧmígȯs ↓

6 ____________________ mȯrénȧ ↓ — ȧđėmás ↑ ėlhwéƀėz | ƀyénẹȧké(l)y̯ȧmȯrénȧ ↓

7 _____________________ sėṇyór ↓ — ȧđėmás ↑ ėlhwéƀėz | ƀyénẹȧkélsėṇyór ↓

---

B Además, mañana llega mi familia.

1 ______ , _______________ amigos. — Además, mañana llegan mis amigos.

2 ______ , ___________ sus ______ . — Además, mañana llegan sus amigos.

3 ______ , _________ vienen ______ . — Además, mañana vienen sus amigos.

4 ______ , el jueves _____________ . — Además, el jueves vienen sus amigos.

5 ______ , _________ aquellos ____ . — Además, el jueves vienen aquellos amigos.

6 ______ , ______________ morena. — Además, el jueves viene aquella morena.

7 ______ , ________________ señor. — Además, el jueves viene aquel señor.

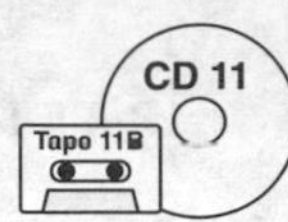

C kwántȯṣíhȯstyénė ↓

| | |
|---|---|
| 1 __________ nínỵȧs ____________ ↓ | kwántȧznínỵȧstyénė ↓ |
| 2 __________________________ áy ↓ | kwántȧznínỵȧṣáy ↓ |
| 3 ___________ tyémpo̯ __________ ↓ | kwántȯtyémpo̯áy ↓ |
| 4 _______________________ kyérės ↓ | kwántȯtyémpȯkyérės ↓ |
| 5 ____________ ágwȧ __________ ↓ | kwántágwȧkyérės ↓ |
| 6 ________________________ ƀéƀės ↓ | kwántágwȧƀéƀės ↓ |
| 7 ____________ trágȯz __________ ↓ | kwántȯstrágȯzƀéƀės ↓ |

---

C ¿Cuántos hijos tiene?

| | |
|---|---|
| 1 ¿ ___________ niñas __________ ? | ¿Cuántas niñas tiene? |
| 2 ¿ _________________________ hay? | ¿Cuántas niñas hay? |
| 3 ¿ __________ tiempo __________ ? | ¿Cuánto tiempo hay? |
| 4 ¿ ______________________ quieres? | ¿Cuánto tiempo quieres? |
| 5 ¿ __________ agua ____________ ? | ¿Cuánta agua quieres? |
| 6 ¿ _______________________ bebes? | ¿Cuánta agua bebes? |
| 7 ¿ _________ tragos ____________ ? | ¿Cuántos tragos bebes? |

D u̇na̯ėrmánȧmíȧ | kȧsáđȧ | ƀíƀe̯ȧ(l)y̱í ↓

1 _______ ėrmánȧz _____________ ↓ — u̇nȧṣėrmánȧzmíȧs | kȧsáđȧz | ƀíƀėṇȧ(l)y̱í ↓

2 ___________ súy̱ȧs ____________ ↓ — u̇nȧṣėrmánȧ(s)súy̱ȧs | kȧsáđȧz | ƀíƀėṇȧ(l)y̱í ↓

3 ________ ı́hȯ ________________ ↓ — u̇nı̣́hȯsúy̱ȯ | kȧsáđȯ | ƀíƀe̯ȧ(l)y̱í ↓

4 ______________ sȯltérȯ ________ ↓ — u̇nı̣́hȯsúy̱ȯ | sȯltérȯ | ƀíƀe̯ȧ(l)y̱í ↓

5 _______________ trȧƀáhȧ _______ ↓ — u̇nı̣́hȯsúy̱ȯ | sȯltérȯ | trȧƀáhȧ(l)y̱í ↓

6 ________ mı́ȯ _________________ ↓ — u̇nı̣́hȯmı́ȯ | sȯltérȯ | trȧƀáhȧ(l)y̱í ↓

7 ______ ȧmı́gȯz ________________ ↓ — u̇nȯṣȧmı́gȯzmı́ȯs | sȯltérȯs | trȧƀáhȧṇȧ(l)y̱í ↓

---

D Una hermana mía casada vive allí.

1 _______ hermanas _____________ . — Unas hermanas mías casadas viven allí.

2 ___________ suyas ____________ . — Unas hermanas suyas casadas viven allí.

3 _______ hijo __________________ . — Un hijo suyo casado vive allí.

4 _____________ soltero __________ . — Un hijo suyo soltero vive allí.

5 _______________ trabaja ________ . — Un hijo suyo soltero trabaja allí.

6 _____________ mío ____________ . — Un hijo mío soltero trabaja allí.

7 _______ amigos ________________ . — Unos amigos míos solteros trabajan allí.

E ȧke̯órȧ | ƀa̋ɪrústéđ | ȧla̯ėrȯpwértȯ ↓

| | |
|---|---|
| 1 ______________________ fyéstȧ ↓ | ȧke̯órȧ \| ƀa̋ɪrústéđ \| ȧlȧfyéstȧ ↓ |
| 2 __________ nȯsótrȯs __________ ↓ | ȧke̯órȧ \| ƀámȯsạ̇ɪ́rnȯsótrȯs \| ȧlȧfyéstȧ ↓ |
| 3 kȯŋkyém ____________________ ↓ | kȯŋkyém \| ƀámȯsạ̇ɪ́rnȯsótrȯs \| ȧlȧfyéstȧ ↓ |
| 4 _________ y̱ó _______________ ↓ | kȯŋkyém \| bóyȧɪ́ry̱ó \| a̯lȧfyéstȧ ↓ |
| 5 pȯrké ______________________ ↓ | pȯrké \| bóyȧɪ́ry̱ó \| a̯lȧfyéstȧ ↓ |
| 6 _________ ƀėnɪ́r ____________ ↓ | pȯrké \| ƀóyȧƀėnɪ́ry̱ó \| a̯lȧfyéstȧ ↓ |
| 7 ___________ é(l)y̱ȯs __________ ↓ | pȯrké \| ƀánạ̇bėnɪ́ré(l)y̱ȯs \| ȧlȧfyéstȧ ↓ |

---

E ¿A qué hora va a ir usted al aeropuerto?

| | |
|---|---|
| 1 ¿ ______________________ fiesta? | ¿A qué hora va a ir usted a la fiesta? |
| 2 ¿ __________ nosotros __________ ? | ¿A qué hora vamos a ir nosotros a la fiesta? |
| 3 ¿Con quién __________________ ? | ¿Con quién vamos a ir nosotros a la fiesta? |
| 4 ¿ ____________ yo ___________ ? | ¿Con quién voy a ir yo a la fiesta? |
| 5 ¿Por qué ____________________ ? | ¿Por qué voy a ir yo a la fiesta? |
| 6 ¿ __________ venir ___________ ? | ¿Por qué voy a venir yo a la fiesta? |
| 7 ¿ ___________ ellos ___________ ? | ¿Por qué van a venir ellos a la fiesta? |

F ástȧlwégȯ ↓ ƀámȯs̯aƀlárđėspwés ↓

1 múyƀyėn ____________________ ↓
múyƀyén ↓ ƀámȯs̯aƀlárđėspwés ↓

2 ________________________ ȧórȧ ↓
múyƀyén ↓ ƀámȯs̯aƀlárȧórȧ ↓

3 ______________ ėstuđyár ______ ↓
múyƀyén ↓ ƀámȯs̯ȧėstuđyárȧórȧ ↓

4 ____________ bóy ___________ ↓
múyƀyén ↓ bóya̯ėstuđyárȧórȧ ↓

5 ȧđyós ______________________ ↓
ȧđyós ↓ bóya̯ėstuđyárȧórȧ ↓

6 __________ téŋgȯke̯ __________ ↓
ȧđyós ↓ téŋgȯkėstuđyárȧórȧ ↓

7 __________ áykė ____________ ↓
ȧđyós ↓ áykėstuđyárȧórȧ ↓

---

F Hasta luego, vamos a hablar después.

1 Muy bien, ____________________ .
Muy bien, vamos a hablar después.

2 ______ , ________________ ahora.
Muy bien, vamos a hablar ahora.

3 ______ , _______ estudiar ________ .
Muy bien, vamos a estudiar ahora.

4 ______ , _____ voy _____________ .
Muy bien, voy a estudiar ahora.

5 Adiós, _______________________ .
Adiós, voy a estudiar ahora.

6 ______ , tengo que ______________ .
Adiós, tengo que estudiar ahora.

7 ______ , hay que _______________ .
Adiós, hay que estudiar ahora.

## 14.23 VARIATION DRILLS

| | | |
|---|---|---|
| A byénènèmbárkò ↑ | | ¿Vienen en barco? |
| 1 Are they coming by car? | byénènènáwtò ↑ | ¿Vienen en auto? |
| 2 Are they coming by plane? | byénènènàƀyón ↑ | ¿Vienen en avión? |
| 3 Are they coming in the evening? | byénènènlànóchè ↑ | ¿Vienen en la noche? |
| 4 Are they coming in the morning? | byénènènlàmànyánà ↑ | ¿Vienen en la mañana? |
| 5 Are they coming in the afternoon? | byénènènlàtárđè ↑ | ¿Vienen en la tarde? |
| 6 Are they coming right away? | byénènènsègíđà ↑ | ¿Vienen en seguida? |
| 7 Are they coming some other day? | byénènòtròđíà ↑ | ¿Vienen otro día? |

| | | | |
|---|---|---|---|
| B | | nó ↓ bánạƀénír \| pòráƀyón ↓ | No, van a venir por avión. |
| 1 | No, they're coming by boat. | nó ↓ bánạƀénír \| pòrƀárkò ↓ | No, van a venir por barco. |
| 2 | No, they're coming by car. | nó ↓ bánạƀénír \| pòráwtò ↓ | No, van a venir por auto. |
| 3 | No, they're coming in the evening. | nó ↓ bánạƀénír \| pòrlànóchè ↓ | No, van a venir por la noche. |
| 4 | No, they're coming in the morning. | nó ↓ bánạƀénír \| pòrlàmàṇyánạ ↓ | No, van a venir por la mañana. |
| 5 | No, they're coming in the afternoon. | nó ↓ bánạƀénír \| pòrlàtárđè ↓ | No, van a venir por la tarde. |
| 6 | Yes, they're coming for you. | sí ↓ bánạƀénír \| pòrùstéđ ↓ | Sí, van a venir por usted. |
| 7 | Yes, they're coming for me. | sí ↓ bánạƀénír \| pòrmí ↓ | Sí, van a venir por mí. |

| | English | Transcription | Spanish |
|---|---|---|---|
| C | | trés ↓ dózƀàrónès \| i̯ùnàníṇyà ↓ | Tres. Dos varones y una niña. |
| 1 | Four. Three boys and a girl. | kwátrò ↓ trézƀàrónès \| i̯ùnàníṇyà ↓ | Cuatro. Tres varones y una niña. |
| 2 | Five. One boy and four girls. | ʂíŋkò ↓ úmbàrón \| ikwátròníṇyàs ↓ | Cinco. Un varón y cuatro niñas. |
| 3 | Three. The wife, the mother-in-law, and the child. | trés ↓ la̯èspósà \| làswégrà \| i̯èlníṇyò ↓ | Tres. La esposa, la suegra y el niño. |
| 4 | Six. The wife and five children. | séys ↓ la̯èspósa̯ \| ìʂíŋko̯íhòs ↓ | Seis. La esposa y cinco hijos. |
| 5 | Two. Mr. and Mrs. Molina. | dós ↓ èlsèṇyór \| ilàsèṇyóràđèmòlínà ↓ | Dos. El señor y la señora de Molina. |
| 6 | Two. John and Joseph. | dós ↓ hwáṇihòsé ↓ | Dos. Juan y José. |
| 7 | Three. Mr. Molina, Joseph and myself. | trés ↓ èlsèṇyórmòlínà \| hòsé̯i̯yó ↓ | Tres. El señor Molina, José y yo. |

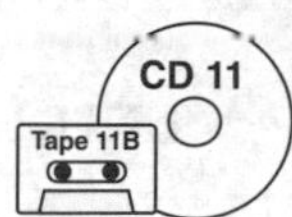




| | | |
|---|---|---|
| D | bálėlȧpénȧ \| ƀiƀírėṇéséƀárryȯ ↓ | Vale la pena vivir en ese barrio. |
| 1 That's a good building to live in. | bálėlȧpénȧ \| ƀiƀír \| ėṇéséđifíşyȯ ↓ | Vale la pena vivir en ese edificio. |
| 2 This is a good section to live in. | bálėlȧpénȧ \| ƀiƀír \| ėṇéstėƀárryȯ ↓ | Vale la pena vivir en este barrio. |
| 3 This is a good restaurant to come to for dinner. | bálėlȧpénȧ \| kȯmér \| ėṇéstėrrėstȯrán ↓ | Vale la pena comer en este restorán. |
| 4 It's worthwhile to study in this school. | bálėlȧpéna̯ \| ėstu̇đyár \| ėṇésta̯ėskwélȧ ↓ | Vale la pena estudiar en esta escuela. |
| 5 It's worthwhile to work in that school. | bálėlȧpénȧ \| trȧƀȧhár \| ėṇésa̯ėskwélȧ ↓ | Vale la pena trabajar en esa escuela. |
| 6 It's not worth the trouble to speak any more. | nóƀálėlȧpéna̯ \| ȧƀlármás ↓ | No vale la pena hablar más. |
| 7 It's not worth the trouble going there. | nóƀálėlȧpéna̯ \| írȧ(l)y̯á ↓ | No vale la pena ir allá. |

| | | | |
|---|---|---|---|
| E | | mikárro̯ ǀ ėstásu̇đispȯsi̇s̯yón ↓ | Mi carro está a su disposición. |
| 1 | You're welcome to my house. | mikása̯ ǀ ėstásu̇đispȯsi̇s̯yón ↓ | Mi casa está a su disposición. |
| 2 | You're welcome to my apartment. | mi̯ȧpȧrtȧménto̯ ǀ ėstásu̇đispȯsi̇s̯yón ↓ | Mi apartamento está a su disposición. |
| 3 | You're welcome to my room. | mikwárto̯ ǀ ėstásu̇đispȯsi̇s̯yón ↓ | Mi cuarto está a su disposición. |
| 4 | You're welcome to my plane. | mi̯ȧƀyón ǀ ėstásu̇đispȯsi̇s̯yón ↓ | Mi avión está a su disposición. |
| 5 | You're welcome to use my shower. | miđúcha̯ ǀ ėstásu̇đispȯsi̇s̯yón ↓ | Mi ducha está a su disposición. |
| 6 | You're welcome to use our kitchen. | nwéstrȧkȯs̯ína̯ ǀ ėstásu̇đispȯsi̇s̯yón ↓ | Nuestra cocina está a su disposición. |
| 7 | You're welcome to use our living-room. | nwéstrȧsála̯ ǀ ėstásu̇đispȯsi̇s̯yón ↓ | Nuestra sala está a su disposición. |

| | | | |
|---|---|---|---|
| F | | lȧzmu̇cháchȧz \| lȯṣėstánẹspėrándȯ ↓ | Las muchachas los están esperando. |
| 1 | The young ladies are waiting for you. | lȧ(s)sėn̦yȯrítȧz \| lȯṣėstánẹspėrándȯ ↓ | Las señoritas los están esperando. |
| 2 | The ladies are waiting for you. | lȧ(s)sėn̦yóȧz \| lȯṣėstánẹspėrándȯ ↓ | Las señoras los están esperando. |
| 3 | The boys are waiting for you. | lȯzmu̇cháchȯz \| lȯṣėstánẹspėrándȯ ↓ | Los muchachos los están esperando. |
| 4 | The gentlemen are waiting for us. | lȯ(s)sėn̦yórėz \| nȯṣėstánẹspėrándȯ ↓ | Los señores nos están esperando. |
| 5 | They're waiting for us. | é(l)y̦ȯz \| nȯṣėstánẹspėrándȯ ↓ | Ellos nos están esperando. |
| 6 | Mary and Joseph are waiting for me. | mȧríạihȯsé \| mėstánẹspėrándȯ ↓ | María y José me están esperando. |
| 7 | The American girls are waiting for me. | lȧṣȧmėrikánȧz \| mėstánẹspėrándȯ ↓ | Las americanas me están esperando. |

**End of Tape 11B**
**End of CD 11**

## 14.24 REVIEW DRILL

Theme class in /—do/ forms of verbs

| | | | |
|---|---|---|---|
| 1 | I've talked and eaten a lot. | éa̯ƀláđo̯ ǀ ikȯmíđȯmúchȯ ↓ | He hablado y comido mucho. |
| 2 | I've gone up and down a lot. | éƀȧháđo̯ ǀ isuƀíđȯmúchȯ ↓ | He bajado y subido mucho. |
| 3 | I've studied and translated very little. | éstu̇đyáđo̯ ǀ itrȧđu̇s̯íđȯ ǀ múypókȯ ↓ | He estudiado y traducido muy poco. |
| 4 | I've danced and gone out very little. | éƀȧyláđo̯ ǀ isȧlíđȯ ǀ múypókȯ ↓ | He bailado y salido muy poco. |
| 5 | I've studied and learned a little. | éstu̇đyáđȯ ǀ i̯ȧprėndíđo̯ ǀ úmpókȯ ↓ | He estudiado y aprendido un poco. |
| 6 | I've washed and swept everything. | élȧƀáđo̯ ǀ iƀȧrríđȯtóđȯ ↓ | He lavado y barrido todo. |
| 7 | I've eaten and drunk too much. | éa̯lmȯrs̯áđo̯ ǀ iƀėƀíđȯđėmȧsyáđȯ ↓ | He almorzado y bebido demasiado. |
| 8 | I've taken and brought back the car. | é(l)y̯ėƀáđo̯ ǀ itrȧíđo̯ėláwtȯ ↓ | He llevado y traído el auto. |
| 9 | I've arranged and swept the room. | éa̯rrėgláđo̯ ǀ iƀȧrríđo̯ėlkwártȯ ↓ | He arreglado y barrido el cuarto. |
| 10 | I've bought and brought everything. | ékȯmpráđo̯ ǀ itrȧíđȯtóđȯ ↓ | He comprado y traído todo. |
| 11 | I've worked and lived there. | éstrȧƀȧháđo̯ ǀ ibiƀíđo̯aí ↓ | He trabajado y vivido ahí. |

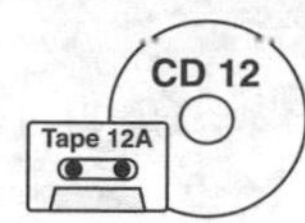




# 14.3 CONVERSATION STIMULUS

## NARRATIVE 1

| | | |
|---|---|---|
| 1 Jose introduces Colonel Harris to his fiancée. | hòsélèprèsénta̭ \| èlkòrònélhárrìs \| àsùnóƀyà ↓ | José le presenta el Coronel Harris a su novia. |
| 2 The Colonel arrived Monday from the States. | èlkòrònél(l)y̭ègó \| ḙ(l)lúnèz \| đèlòs èstáđòs̭ùníđòs ↓ | El Coronel llegó el lunes de los Estados Unidos. |
| 3 He's going to be here a long time. | él \| báḙstárákí \| múchòtyémpò ↓ | El va a estar aquí mucho tiempo. |
| 4 He's going to work with the Embassy. | bátràƀàhár \| kònla̭èmbàháđà ↓ | Va a trabajar con la Embajada. |

## DIALOG 1

| | | |
|---|---|---|
| José, dígale al Coronel que quiere presentarle a su novia, la señorita Del Valle. A Carmen dígale Carmen, el Coronel Harris. | kòrònél ↓ kyéròprèsèntárlḙ \| àmì nóƀyà \| làsèn̯yòrìtàđèlbá(l)y̭è ↓ kármèn ↓ èlkòrònélhárrìs ↓ | José: Coronel, quiero presentarle a mi novia, la señorita Del Valle. Carmen, el Coronel Harris. |
| Coronel, dígale a la señorita que tanto gusto. | tántògústò \| sèn̯yòrítà ↓ | Coronel: Tanto gusto, señorita. |

| | | |
|---|---|---|
| Carmen, dígale al Coronel que encantada. | ėŋkȧntáđȧ ↓ | Carmen: Encantada. |
| José, dígale a Carmen que el Coronel llegó el lunes de los Estados Unidos. | ėlkȯrȯnél ǀ (l)y̯ėgóe̯(l)lúnėz ǀ đėlȯs ėstáđȯs̯ųníđȯs ↓ | José: El Coronel llegó el lunes de los Estados Unidos. |
| Carmen, diga 'ah, ¿sí?,' y pregúntele al Coronel si va a estar aquí mucho tiempo. | á ǀ sí ↑ báe̯stárȧkí ǀ múchȯtyémpȯ ↑ | Carmen: Ah, ¿sí? ¿Va a estar aquí mucho tiempo? |
| Coronel, contéstele que Ud. cree que sí. Que va a trabajar con la Embajada. | kréȯkėsí ↓ bóyȧtrȧƀȧhár ǀ kȯn la̯ėmbȧháđȧ ↓ | Coronel: Creo que sí. Voy a trabajar con la Embajada. |

## NARRATIVE 2

| | | |
|---|---|---|
| 1 The Colonel's family is arriving tomorrow. | lȧfȧmílyȧ ǀ đėlkȯrȯnél ǀ (l)y̯égȧ manyánȧ ↓ | La familia del Coronel llega mañana. |
| 2 The airport, isn't it quite a distance? | ėla̯ėrȯpwértȯ ↓ nóe̯stá ǀ múylėhȯs ↑ | El aeropuerto, ¿no está muy lejos? |
| 3 It's half an hour from here by car, more or less. | ėstá ǀ a̯méđya̯órađe̯aki ǀ e̯náwtȯ ǀ máșȯménȯs ↓ | Está a media hora de aquí en auto, más o menos. |
| 4 But he doesn't know how he's going to (do) manage. | péro̯el ǀ nósáƀė ǀ kómȯƀa̯sér ↓ | Pero él no sabe cómo va a hacer. |

| | | |
|---|---|---|
| 5 He's got so many things to do. | tyénė \| tántaskósȧkḙaṣér ↓ | Tiene tantas cosas que hacer. |
| 6 Jose says his car is at the Colonel's disposal. | hȯséđíṣė \| kesukárrǫ \| ėstálȧ đispȯsiṣyón \| dėlkȯrȯnél ↓ | José dice que su carro está a la disposición del coronel. |
| 7 'Thanks a million', says the Colonel. | ùnmi(l)y̯óndėgráṣyȧz \| đíṣėlkȯrȯnél ↓ | Un millón de gracias -dice el Coronel. |
| 8 Jose isn't going to be at the Embassy tomorrow. Tomorrow is Saturday. | hȯsé \| nóbáḙstár \| ėnlḁémbȧháđȧ \| mȧnyánȧ ↓ mȧnyánḁe(s)sábȧđȯ ↓ | José no va a estar en la Embajada mañana. Mañana es sábado. |
| 9 But the Colonel can call him at home. | péroėlkȯrȯnél \| pwéđė(l)y̯ȧmárlǫ ȧlakásȧ ↓ | Pero el Coronel puede llamarlo a la casa. |
| 10 The Colonel says that if he needs him, he'll call him. | ėlkȯrȯnéldíṣė \| kėsilȯnėṣėsítȧ \| lȯ(l)y̯ámȧ ↓ | El Coronel dice que si lo necesita, lo llama. |

## DIALOG 2

| | | |
|---|---|---|
| Carmen, pregúntele al Coronel si vino con su familia. | bínǫustéđ \| kȯnsufamílyȧ ↑ | Carmen: ¿Vino usted con su familia? |
| Coronel, contéstele que no. Que su familia llega mañana. Pregúntele a José, a propósito, si el aeropuerto está muy lejos. | nó ↓ mifȧmílyȧ \| (l)y̯égamȧnyánȧ ↓ ȧprȯpósitȯ \| hȯsé ↓ ėstámuylé hȯs \| ėlḁeropwértȯ ↑ | No. Mi familia llega mañana. A propósito, José, ¿está muy lejos el aeropuerto? |

| | | |
|---|---|---|
| José, contéstele que no, que a media hora de aquí en auto, más o menos. | nó ↓ àmédyao̯ráđe̯akí \| e̯ná̦wtò \| másòménòs ↓ | José: No, a media hora de aquí en auto, más o menos. |
| Coronel, dígale que Ud. no sabe cómo va a hacer. Que tiene tantas cosas que hacer mañana. | nòsé \| kómòƀóyàṣér ↓ téŋgò \| tántàs kósàske̯àṣér \| màn̡yánà ↓ | Coronel: No sé cómo voy a hacer. Tengo tantas cosas que hacer mañana. |
| José, dígale que su carro está a la disposición de él. | mikárro̯ \| èstásùđispòsiṣyón ↓ | José: Mi carro está a su disposición. |
| Coronel, dígale que un millón de gracias. Pregúntele si él va a estar en la Embajada mañana. | ùnmi(l)y̰óndègráṣyàs ↓ ùstéđbá e̯stár \| ènla̯èmbàháđà \| màn̡yánà ↑ | Coronel: Un millón de gracias. ¿Usted va a estar en la Embajada mañana? |
| Jose, dígale que no, que mañana es sábado. Pero puede llamarlo a su casa, dígale. | nó ↓ màn̡yána̯è(s)sáƀàđò ↓ pèrò pwéđè \| (l)y̰àmármе̯àmikásà ↓ | José: No, mañana es sábado. Pero puede llamarme a mi casa. |
| Coronel, dígale que muy bien, que si lo necesita lo llama. Y que muchas gracias. | múyƀyén ↓ silònèṣèsítò \| lò(l)y̰ámò ↓ múchàzgráṣyàs ↓ | Coronel: Muy bien. Si lo necesito, lo llamo. Muchas gracias. |

## NARRATIVE 3

| | | |
|---|---|---|
| 1 His wife, three children and his mother-in-law are coming. | byénėnsu̇sėn̥yórȧ ↑ trésíhȯs \| i̇su̇swégrȧ ↓ | Vienen su señora, tres hijos y su suegra. |
| 2 His whole family. | tóđȧsu̇famílyȧ ↓ | Toda su familia. |
| 3 He's going to have to rent a house. | bátėnér \| ke̯ȧlkilárŭnȧkásȧ ↓ | Va a tener que alquilar una casa. |
| 4 But he doesn't know if it's worth the trouble. | péro̯él \| nósáƀė \| siƀálėlȧpénȧ ↓ | Pero él no sabe si vale la pena. |
| 5 They say that houses here cost a lot. | díṣėŋ \| kėlȧskȧsȧṣȧkí \| kwéstȧn múchȯ ↓ | Dicen que las casas aquí cuestan mucho. |
| 6 But Carmen lives in the Bellavista section. | pėrȯkármėm \| bíƀėnẹlbárryȯ bė(l)y̭ȧƀístȧ ↓ | Pero Carmen vive en el barrio Bellavista. |
| 7 And the houses there are very nice and inexpensive. | ilȧskásȧṣȧ(l)y̭í \| sȯnmúyƀȯnítȧs i̇ƀȧrátȧs ↓ | Y las casas allí son muy bonitas y baratas. |
| 8 The Colonel is going to talk to his wife (about it) to see what she says. | ėlkȯrȯnél \| báƀlárkȯnsu̯ėspósȧ \| pȧrȧƀér \| kéđíṣé(l)yȧ ↓ | El Coronel va a hablar con su esposa para ver qué dice ella. |

## DIALOG 3

| | | |
|---|---|---|
| Carmen, pregúntele al Coronel si viene toda su familia. | byénėtóđȧsúfȧmílyȧ ↑ | Carmen: ¿Viene toda su familia? |
| Coronel, contéstele que sí, que su señora y tres hijos. Que también viene su suegra. | sí ↓ misėn̯yóra̯ \| ı̇trésı̣hȯs ↓<br>tȧmbyémbyénėmiswégrȧ ↓ | Coronel: Sí, mi señora y tres hijos. También viene mi suegra. |
| Carmen, dígale que entonces va a tener que alquilar una casa. | ėntónṣėz ↑ ƀátėnér \| ke̯ȧlkilár<br>u̇nȧkásȧ ↓ | Carmen: Entonces va a tener que alquilar una casa. |
| Coronel, dígale que Ud. no sabe si vale la pena. Que dicen que aquí las casas cuestan mucho. | nósé \| siƀálėlȧpénȧ ↓ dı̯ṣėŋke̯ȧkí \|<br>lȧskásȧskwéstȧnmuchȯ ↓ | Coronel: No sé si vale la pena. Dicen que aquí las casas cuestan mucho. |
| Carmen, dígale que en el barrio Bellavista, donde Ud. vive, hay casas muy baratas y bonitas. | ėn̯ėlbárryȯƀė(l)y̯ȧƀístȧ \| đóndėy̯ó<br>ƀíƀo̯ ↑ ȧykásȧz \| múyƀȧrátȧṣı̯ƀȯnítȧs ↓ | Carmen: En el barrio Bellavista, donde yo vivo, hay casas muy baratas y bonitas. |
| Coronel, dígale que Ud. va a hablar con su esposa para ver qué dice ella. | bóyȧƀlár \| kȯnmı̯ėspósȧ \| pȧrȧƀér \| ké<br>đíṣé(l)y̯ȧ ↓ | Coronel: Voy a hablar con mi esposa para ver qué dice ella. |

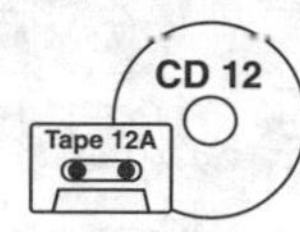




# 15.1 BASIC SENTENCES

## Mrs. Harris goes through customs

Mr. and Mrs. Harris and Molina are going to the customs office while the mother-in-law and children stay behind and wait for them.

| English Spelling | Aid to Listening | Spanish Spelling |
|---|---|---|
| rigorous, strict | rrigurósȯ ↓ | riguroso |
| the customs office | la̯—ȧđwánȧ ↓ | la aduana |
| *MRS. HARRIS* | | *SRA. HARRIS* |
| Are they very strict at the customs office here? | sónmúyrrigurósos \| ėnlađwánaki ↑ | ¿Son muy rigurosos en la aduana aquí? |
| sure | sėgúrȯ ↓ | seguro |
| *MOLINA* | | *MOLINA* |
| No, I'm sure that they won't bother you. | nó ↓ ėstóysėgúrȯ \| đėke̯ȧu̯stéđ \| nólabána̯ molėstár ↓ | No. Estoy seguro de que a usted no la van a molestar. |
| the baggage | ėl—ėkipáhė ↓ | el equipaje |
| *MRS. HARRIS* | | *SRA. HARRIS* |
| Right here. My baggage is here now. | ȧkí ↓ sėnyór ↓ y̯áe̯stákí \| mi̯ėkipáhė ↓ | Aquí, señor. Ya está aquí mi equipaje. |
| which | kwál ↓ | cuál |
| *CLERK* | | *EMPLEADO* |
| Which is it? | kwálés ↓ | ¿Cuál es? |
| green | bérđė ↓ | verde |

| | | |
|---|---|---|
| the trunk | èl—bàúl ↓ | el baúl |
| *MRS. HARRIS* | | *MRS. HARRIS* |
| It's these green suitcases and this small trunk. (1) | són \| éstàzmàlétàzƀérđès ↑ ı̯éstèƀàúl pèkéṇyò ↓ | Son estas maletas verdes y este baúl pequeño. |
| have (to have) | téŋgà ↓ tènér ↓ | tenga (tener) |
| the kindness, goodness | là—bòndáđ ↓ | la bondad |
| be so kind as to, please | téŋgà—là—bòndáđ—đè ↓ | tenga la bondad de |
| *CLERK* | | *EMPLEADO* |
| Please open the trunk first. | téŋgàlàƀòndáđ \| đẹàbrírèlbàúl \| primérò ↓ | Tenga la bondad de abrir el baúl primero. |
| This thing—what is it? | éstò ↓ ké \| és ↓ | Esto, ¿qué es? |
| the gift | èl—rrègálò ↓ | el regalo |
| to declare | dèklàrár ↓ | declarar |
| *MRS. HARRIS* | | *SRA. HARRIS* |
| It's some gifts. Everything's declared. | sónụ̀nòzrrègálòs ↓ tóđọ̀estáđèklàráđò ↓ | Son unos regalos. Todo está declarado. |
| the list | là—lístà ↓ | la lista |
| *CLERK* | | *EMPLEADO* |
| Oh, yes. Here it is on the list. | á \| sí ↓ àkíẹstáẹnlàlístà ↓ | Ah, sí. Aquí está en la lista. |
| the overnight case, handbag | èl—màlètín ↓ | el maletín |

| | | |
|---|---|---|
| (for) me | mé ↓ | me |
| to examine, inspect | rrebisár ↓ | revisar |
| *MRS. HARRIS* | | *SRA. HARRIS* |
| This handbag, aren't you going to check it? (2) | éstemaletín ↓ nómelobárrebisár ↑ | Este maletín, ¿no me lo va a revisar? |
| necessary | neşesáryo ↓ | necesario |
| *CLERK* | | *EMPLEADO* |
| No ma'am, it's not necessary. | nóseñyóra ↓ noéznesesáryo ↓ | No señora, no es necesario. |
| to you (it) lacks (to lack) | le—fálta ↓ faltár ↓ | le falta (faltar) |
| *MOLINA* | | *MOLINA* |
| Are you missing anything, Mrs. Harris? | nóléfaltanáđa \| señyóra ↑ | ¿No le falta nada, señora? |
| complete | kompléto ↓ | completo |
| *MRS. HARRIS* | | *SRA. HARRIS* |
| No, everything's here. | nó ↓ tóđoestákompléto ↓ | No. Todo está completo. |
| (Later, in the lobby) | | |
| to take care of, assist | atendér ↓ | atender |
| the immigration | la—inmigraşyón ↓ | la inmigración |
| *MOLINA* | | *MOLINA* |
| Did they take good care of you in Immigration? (3) | lánatendíđobyén \| eninmigraşyón ↑ | ¿La han atendido bien en Inmigración? |

| | | |
|---|---|---|
| to complain myself (to complain oneself) | kėhármė ↓ kėhársė ↓ | quejarme (quejarse) |
| *MRS. HARRIS* | | *SRA. HARRIS* |
| I can't complain. | yó \| nómėpwéđokėhár ↓ | Yo no me puedo quejar. |
| kind, nice, courteous | àmáƀlė ↓ | amable |
| They've been very nice to me. | kònmígo ↑ ànsíđòmúyàmáƀlės ↓ | Conmigo han sido muy amables. |
| for us | nós ↓ | nos |
| that (he) may carry (to carry) | kė—(l)yéƀė ↓ (l)yėƀár ↓ | que lleve (llevar) |
| *HARRIS* | | *HARRIS* |
| I'll go look for a taxi and someone to carry the suitcases for us. | bóyàƀùskárùntáksi ↑ ịálgyėŋ \| kėnòz(l)yéƀė làzmàlétàs ↓ | Voy a buscar un taxi y a alguien que nos lleve las maletas. |
| (I) said (to say) | díhė ↓ dėṣír ↓ | dije (decir) |
| last night | ànóchė ↓ | anoche |
| the car | ėl—kóchė ↓ | el coche |
| to fit | kàƀér ↓ | caber |
| *MOLINA* | | *MOLINA* |
| As I said last night, there's room in my car for all of us *and* the luggage. | kómòlėđíhėànóchė ↑ ėnmikóchė \| kàƀémòstóđos \| ịėlėkipáhė ↓ | Como le dije anoche, en mi coche cabemos todos y el equipaje. |
| great (large) | grán ↓ grándė ↓ | gran (grande) |
| the help | la—àyúđà ↓ | la ayuda |

| | | |
|---|---|---|
| to us | nós ↓ | nos |
| to lend, to provide | prėstár ↓ | prestar |
| *HARRIS* | | *HARRIS* |
| You're being a great help to us. Thanks a lot, Molina. | nȯs̥ėstáprėstándo̯ \| ủnȧgránȧy̯úđȧ ↓ múchȧzgrás̥yȧz \| mȯlínȧ ↓ | Nos está prestando una gran ayuda. Muchas gracias, Molina. |

## 15.10 Notes on the basic sentences

(1) It is perhaps worth calling to your attention thc fact that in this Spanish utterance the number of the verb (plural) rigorously agrees with the number of the subject (plural) even though the subject is positioned *after* the verb. In English the 'logical' subject is plural, but the grammatical subject is *it*, which is singular and requires the singular verb form *is*. The same situation occurs below, 'It's some gifts'.

(2) The occurrence of both direct and indirect clitics in the same phrase will be examined closely in Unit 20. In the meanwhile all that need be pointed out is that the indirect clitic is the first of the two. Note, however, that no equivalent to the indirect /me/ appears in the English translation.

(3) Notice that the Spanish present perfect construction /án—atendído/ is translated by the English past tense *'did* they take good care of' in this sentence. This is a not infrequent translation pattern.

# 15.2 DRILLS AND GRAMMAR

## 15.21 PATTERN DRILLS

### 15.21.1 Indirect clitic pronouns—one object

**A. PRESENTATION OF PATTERN**

*ILLUSTRATIONS*

| | | |
|---|---|---|
| ____________ | 1 sí ↓ mėgústȧ ↓ | Sí, *me* gusta. |
| ____________ | 2 mėkȯmbyénemás \| ėlprimérȯ ↓ | *Me* conviene más el primero. |
| ____________ | 3 kétėpásȧ ↓ | ¿Qué *te* pasa? |

| | | |
|---|---|---|
| What do you need (lack)? | 4 ké̇tefáltȧ ↓ | ¿Qué *te* falta? |
| ____________________ | 5 lėgústa̯ėlkwártȯ ↑ | ¿*Le* gusta el cuarto? |
| ____________________ | 6 kómȯlėƀá ↓ | ¿Cómo *le* va? |
| We like the room. | 7 nȯzgústa̯ėlkwártȯ ↓ | *Nos* gusta el cuarto. |
| It looks small to us. | 8 nȯspȧré̦sėpėkéṉyȯ ↓ | *Nos* parece pequeño. |
| What do you all think? | 9 kélėspȧré̦sė ↓ | ¿Qué *les* parece? |
| Does it look all right to you? | 10 lėspȧré̦sėƀyén ↑ | ¿*Les* parece bien? |

*EXTRAPOLATION*

| | sg | pl |
|---|---|---|
| 1 | me | nos |
| 2 fam | te | |
| 2 – 3 | le | les |

*NOTES*

a. Indirect clitic pronouns inflect for person and number, but not for gender.

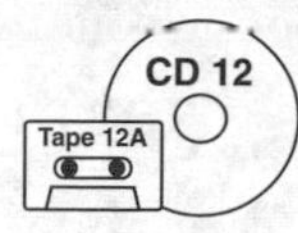



## 15.21.11 SUBSTITUTION DRILL

Number substitution

| | |
|---|---|
| 1 mėgústalȧkásȧ ↓ | nȯzgústalȧkásȧ ↓ |
| 2 nȯsfáltanlȧskȧmísȧs ↓ | mėfáltanlȧskȧmísȧs ↓ |
| 3 lėzgústa̯ėlėđifísyȯ ↓ | lėgústa̯ėlėđifísyȯ ↓ |
| 4 lėfálta̯úndólȧr ↓ | lėsfálta̯úndólȧr ↓ |
| 5 nȯzgústanlȧzlėgúmbrės ↓ | mėgústanlȧzlėgúmbrės ↓ |
| 6 lėskȯmbyénėmása̯ėlótrȯ ↓ | lėkȯmbyénėmása̯ėlótrȯ ↓ |
| 7 mėbámúybyén ↓ | nȯzbámúybyén ↓ |

---

| | |
|---|---|
| 1 *Me* gusta la casa. | Nos gusta la casa. |
| 2 *Nos* faltan las camisas. | Me faltan las camisas. |
| 3 *Les* gusta el edificio. | Le gusta el edificio. |
| 4 *Le* falta un dólar. | Les falta un dólar. |
| 5 *Nos* gustan las legumbres. | Me gustan las legumbres. |
| 6 *Les* conviene más el otro. | Le conviene más el otro. |
| 7 *Me* va muy bien. | Nos va muy bien. |

## 15.21.12 RESPONSE DRILL

| | | |
|---|---|---|
| | 1 lėgústȧlȧṣėrbéṣȧ ↑ o̯elkúƀȧlíbrė ↓ | mėgústȧlȧṣėrƀéṣȧ ↓ |
| | 2 lėzgústa̯ėlȧpȧrtȧménto̯ ↑ ȯlȧkásȧ ↓ | nȯzgústa̯ėlȧpȧrtȧméntȯ ↓ |
| | 3 lėfáltȧlȧsópa̯ ↑ ȯla̯ėnsȧláđȧ ↓ | lėfáltȧlȧsópȧ ↓ |
| | 4 lėzƀáƀyén ↑ ȯmál ↓ | lėzƀáƀyén ↓ |
| [grándė ↓] | 5 kétėpȧréṣe̯ \| ėla̯éreo̯pwértȯ ↓ | mėpȧréṣėgrándė ↓ |
| [pėkényȯ ↓] | 6 kélėspȧréṣe̯ \| ėlėđifíṣyȯ ↓ | nȯspȧréṣėpėkényȯ ↓ |
| [bȧrátȯs ↓] | 7 kélėspȧréṣėn \| lȯstráhės ↓ | lėspȧréṣėmbȧrátȯs ↓ |
| [dóṣė ↓] | 8 kwántȧ(s)sėmánaz \| lėfáltȧn ↓ | mėfáltȧndóṣė ↓ |

---

| | | |
|---|---|---|
| | 1 ¿Le gusta la cerveza o el cuba libre? | Me gusta la cerveza. |
| | 2 ¿Les gusta el apartamento o la casa? | Nos gusta el apartamento. |
| | 3 ¿Le falta la sopa o la ensalada? | Le falta la sopa. |
| | 4 ¿Les va bien o mal? | Les va bien. |
| (grande) | 5 ¿Qué te parece el aeropuerto? | Me parece grande. |
| (pequeño) | 6 ¿Qué les parece el edificio? | Nos parece pequeño. |
| (baratos) | 7 ¿Qué les parecen los trajes? | Les parecen baratos. |
| (doce) | 8 ¿Cuántas semanas le faltan? | Me faltan doce. |

| | | |
|---|---|---|
| [múyƀyén ↓] | 9 kómòlèzƀá ↓ | nòzƀámúyƀyén ↓ |
| | | |
| [èlàƀyón ↓] | 10 lèzgústạèlbárkò ↑ | nó ↓ lèzgústạèlàƀyón ↓ |
| [làkásà ↓] | 11 lègústạèlàpàrtàméntò ↑ | nó ↓ lègústàlàkásà ↓ |
| [bwénà ↓] | 12 tèpàréṣèmálà \| làlàƀàndèríà ↑ | nó ↓ mèpàréṣèƀwénà ↓ |
| | | |
| | 13 lègústà \| lạèskwéláđèléŋgwàs ↑ | sí ↓ mègústàmúchò ↓ |
| | 14 lèspàréṣèƀyén \| àlà(s)syétè ↑ | sí ↓ nòspàréṣèbyén ↓ |
| | 15 lèƀàƀyénạkí ↑ | sí ↓ lèƀámúyƀyén ↓ |

---

| | | |
|---|---|---|
| (muy bien) | 9 ¿Cómo les va? | Nos va muy bien. |
| | | |
| (el avión) | 10 ¿Les gusta el barco? | No, les gusta el avión. |
| (la casa) | 11 ¿Le gusta el apartamento? | No, le gusta la casa. |
| (bucna) | 12 ¿Te parece mala la lavandería? | No, me parece buena. |
| | | |
| | 13 ¿Le gusta la escuela de lenguas? | Sí, me gusta mucho. |
| | 14 ¿Les parece bien a las siete? | Sí, nos parece bien. |
| | 15 ¿Le va bien aquí? | Si, le va muy bien. |

## 15.21.13 TRANSLATION DRILL

| | | | |
|---|---|---|---|
| 1 | The suits seem inexpensive to us. | lȯstráhėz ǀ nȯspȧréşėmbȧrátȯs ↓ | Los trajes nos parecen baratos. |
| 2 | He likes this suburb very much. | lėgústȧmúcho̯ ǀ ėstėƀárryȯ ↓ | Le gusta mucho este barrio. |
| 3 | I don't like that name. | nómėgústa̯ ǀ ésėnómbrė ↓ | No me gusta ese nombre. |
| 4 | Does she need (lack) anything? | lėfáltálgȯ ↑ | ¿Le falta algo? |
| 5 | Don't you like the house? | nólėgústȧlȧkásȧ ↑ | ¿No le gusta la casa? |
| 6 | On the contrary, I like it very much. | ȧlkȯntráryȯ ↓ mėgústȧmúchȯ ↓ | Al contrario, me gusta mucho. |
| 7 | Besides, it seems inexpensive to us. | ȧđėmás ↑ nȯspȧréşėƀȧrátȧ ↓ | Además, nos parece barata. |
| 8 | We're thirteen dollars short. | nȯsfáltȧn ǀ tréşėđólȧrės ↓ | Nos faltan trece dólares. |
| 9 | How's it going with you all? | komolezƀá ↓ | ¿Cómo les va? |
| 10 | What do they think of the laundry on the corner? | kélėspȧréşė ǀ lȧlȧƀȧndėríȧ ǀ đėla̯ėskínȧ ↓ | ¿Qué les parece la lavandería de la esquina? |
| 11 | Does she like the new building? | lėgústa̯ėlėđifísyȯnwéƀȯ ↑ | ¿Le gusta el edificio nuevo? |
| 12 | It doesn't suit me, it's too expensive. | nómėkȯmbyénė ↓ ėzmúykárȯ ↓ | No me conviene, es muy caro. |
| 13 | Does the other one suit you? | lėkȯmbyénėlótrȯ ↑ | ¿Le conviene el otro? |

**B. DISCUSSION OF PATTERN**

As stated in Unit 10, clitics are pronoun forms which occur with verbs. Clitics are of three kinds, direct (presented in Unit 10), indirect (presented here), and reflexive (to be presented in Unit 24).

The selection of the clitic depends on the verb it accompanies. Some verbs may appear only with direct clitics, some only with indirect, some only with reflexive, and some with various combinations. There is some overlap; some verbs may appear with direct or indirect (/lo—ayúdo/ vs /le—ayúdo/, /lo—espéro/ vs /le—espéro/, /lo—(l)yámo/ vs /le—(l)yámo/), and some verbs have a different semantic content when used with direct or indirect clitics (/páselo ↓/ 'Pass it' vs /ké—le—pása ↓/ 'What's the matter with him').

The presentation in this section has been of constructions where a single clitic, an indirect, appears with a verb. The clitic will often be translated by 'to—'; for example, /mé/= 'to me', though sometimes the English sentence must be rearranged for this to be true: /legústa̯elkwárto ↑/ = 'Does the room please you?' or 'Is the room pleasing to you?' or more freely, 'Do you like the room?'

## 15.21.2 Indirect clitic pronouns—two objects (indirect clitic pronoun object and direct noun object)

**A. PRESENTATION OF PATTERN**

*ILLUSTRATIONS*

| | | |
|---|---|---|
| ____________________ | 1 mėđihérȯŋ ǀ kėsėríandós ↓ | *Me* dijeron que serían dos. |
| Will you lend me your pencil? | 2 mėpréstȧs ǀ tulápiș ↑ | *¿Me* prestas tu lápiz? |
| ____________________ | 3 kyéntėlímpya̯ ǀ ėlapȧrtȧméntȯ ↓ | ¿Quién *te* limpia el apartamento? |
| Who sends you the newspapers? | 4 kyéntėmándȧ ǀ lȯspėryóđikȯs ↓ | ¿Quién *te* manda los periódicos? |
| ____________________ | 5 lėđóytrés ↓ únȯđėprȯpínȧ ↓ | *Le* doy tres, uno de propina. |
| What has Mario brought you? | 6 kéle̯ȧtráíđȯmáryȯ ↓ | ¿Qué *le* ha traído Mario? |

| | | |
|---|---|---|
| | 7 álgyėŋ ǀ kėnȯz(l)y̰éƀėlȧzmȧlétȧs ↓ | Alguien que *nos* lleve las maletas. |
| They told us it would be two. | 8 nȯzđihérȯŋ ǀ kėsėrı́ȧndós ↓ | *Nos* dijeron que serían dos. |
| Who cleans your apartment for you? | 9 kyénlėzlı́mpya̭ ǀ ėlȧpȧrtȧméntȯ ↓ | ¿Quién *les* limpia el apartamento? |
| Someone to carry the suitcases for them. | 10 álgyėŋ ǀ kėlėz(l)y̰éƀėlȧzmȧlétȧs ↓ | Alguien que *les* lleve las maletas. |

*EXTRAPOLATION*

| | sg | pl |
|---|---|---|
| 1 | me | nos |
| 2 fam | te | |
| 2 – 3 | le | les |

*NOTES*

a. This is a repetition of the forms presented in the preceding drill point, appearing here in a different construction.

## 15.21.21 SUBSTITUTION DRILL

Item translation substitution

Problem:

hwán | memándalosperyóđikos ↓

(her) ____________________

Answer:

hwán | lemándalosperyóđikos ↓

---

Problem:

Juan *me* manda los periódicos.

(her) ____________________

Answer:

Juan le manda los periódicos.

1 élnȯstrá͜elȧrrópȧ ↓

| | | |
|---|---|---|
| (him) | ____________________ ↓ | é(l)lėtrá͜elȧrrópȧ ↓ |
| (me) | ____________________ ↓ | élmėtrá͜elȧrrópȧ ↓ |
| (her) | ____________________ ↓ | é(l)lėtrá͜elȧrrópȧ ↓ |
| (them) | ____________________ ↓ | é(l)lėstrá͜elȧrrópȧ ↓ |
| (you) | ____________________ ↓ | é(l)lėtrá͜elȧrrópȧ ↓ |

---

1 El *nos* trae la ropa.

| | | |
|---|---|---|
| (him) | ____________________ . | El le trae la ropa. |
| (me) | ____________________ . | El me trae la ropa. |
| (her) | ____________________ . | El le trae la ropa. |
| (them) | ____________________ . | El les trae la ropa. |
| (you) | ____________________ . | El le trae la ropa. |

2 é(l)yalesęskríbe | loznómbres

| | | |
|---|---|---|
| (us) | ________ ↓ | é(l)yanosęskríbe | loznómbres ↓ |
| (him) | ________ ↓ | é(l)yaleskríbe | loznómbres ↓ |
| (me) | ________ ↓ | é(l)yameskríbe | loznómbres ↓ |
| (you) | ________ ↓ | é(l)yaleskríbe | loznómbres ↓ |
| (them) | ________ ↓ | é(l)yalesęskríbe | loznómbres ↓ |

---

2 Ella *les* escribe los nombres.

| | | |
|---|---|---|
| (us) | ________ . | Ella nos escribe los nombres. |
| (him) | ________ . | Ella le escribe los nombres. |
| (me) | ________ . | Ella me escribe los nombres. |
| (you) | ________ . | Ella le escribe los nombres. |
| (them) | ________ . | Ella les escribe los nombres. |

3 é(l)y̱ȯz | lėđámpėrmísȯ ↓

| | | |
|---|---|---|
| (them) | ______________ ↓ | é(l)y̱ȯz \| lėzđámpėrmísȯ ↓ |
| (me) | ______________ ↓ | é(l)y̱ȯz \| mėđámpėrmísȯ ↓ |
| (her) | ______________ ↓ | é(l)y̱ȯz \| lėđámpėrmísȯ ↓ |
| (us) | ______________ ↓ | é(l)y̱ȯz \| nȯzđámpėrmísȯ ↓ |
| (you pl) | ______________ ↓ | é(l)y̱ȯz \| lėzđámpėrmísȯ ↓ |

---

3 Ellos *le* dan permiso.

| | | |
|---|---|---|
| (them) | ______________ . | Ellos les dan permiso. |
| (me) | ______________ . | Ellos me dan permiso. |
| (her) | ______________ . | Ellos le dan permiso. |
| (us) | ______________ . | Ellos nos dan permiso. |
| (you pl) | ______________ . | Ellos les dan permiso. |

4 meánrrebisado | lazmalétas ↓

| | | |
|---|---|---|
| (her) | ______ ↓ | leánrrebisado | lazmalétas ↓ |
| (us) | ______ ↓ | nosánrrebisado | lazmalétas ↓ |
| (him) | ______ ↓ | leánrrebisado | lazmalétas ↓ |
| (them) | ______ ↓ | lesánrrebisado | lazmalétas ↓ |
| (you) | ______ ↓ | leánrrebisado | lazmalétas ↓ |

---

4 *Me* han revisado las maletas.

| | | |
|---|---|---|
| (her) | ______ . | Le han revisado las maletas |
| (us) | ______ . | Nos han revisado las maletas. |
| (him) | ______ . | Le han revisado las maletas. |
| (them) | ______ . | Les han revisado las maletas. |
| (you) | ______ . | Le han revisado las maletas. |

5 lwísȧ | lèzláƀȧlȧskȧmísȧs ↓

| | | |
|---|---|---|
| (me) | ____________ ↓ | lwísȧ \| mèláƀȧlȧskȧmísȧs ↓ |
| (him) | ____________ ↓ | lwísȧ \| lèláƀȧlȧskȧmísȧs ↓ |
| (us) | ____________ ↓ | lwísȧ \| nȯzláƀȧlȧskȧmísȧs ↓ |
| (you) | ____________ ↓ | lwísȧ \| lèláƀȧlȧskȧmísȧs ↓ |
| (them) | ____________ ↓ | lwísȧ \| lèzláƀȧlȧskȧmísȧs ↓ |

---

5 Luisa *les* lava las camisas.

| | | |
|---|---|---|
| (me) | ____________. | Luisa me lava las camisas. |
| (him) | ____________. | Luisa le lava las camisas. |
| (us) | ____________. | Luisa nos lava las camisas. |
| (you) | ____________. | Luisa le lava las camisas. |
| (them) | ____________. | Luisa les lava las camisas. |

**End of Tape 12A**

## 15.21.22 TRANSLATION DRILLS

Paired sentences

| | | |
|---|---|---|
| 1 When do you send them the newspapers?<br>When do you send the newspapers to them? | kwándȯ \| lėzmándau̯stéđ \| lȯspėryóđikȯs ↓ | ¿Cuándo les manda Ud. los periódicos? |
| 2 What have you sent them?<br>What have you sent to them? | kéléṣamȧndáđo̯ \| ustéđa̯é(l)y̯ȯs ↓ | ¿Qué les ha mandado Ud. a ellos? |
| 3 She never sends us anything.<br>She never sends anything to us. | é(l)y̯ȧ \| núŋkȧnȯzmándȧnáđȧ ↓ | Ella nunca nos manda nada. |
| 4 What has John brought you all?<br>What has John brought to you all? | kéléṣatraíđȯ \| hwánạu̯stéđės ↓ | ¿Qué les ha traído Juan a Uds.? |
| 5 Miy sister always brings me a new shirt.<br>My sister always brings a new shirt to me. | mi̯ėrmánȧ \| syémprėmėtráe̯ \| ůnȧkȧmísȧnwéƀȧ ↓ | Mi hermana siempre me trae una camisa nueva. |
| 6 My mother-in-law always gives me wine.<br>My mother-in-law always gives wine to me. | miswégrȧ \| syémprėmėđaƀínȯ ↓ | Mi suegra siempre me da vino. |

| | | |
|---|---|---|
| 7 I've given him my pen.<br>I've given my pen to him. | yólėđáđȯ ǀ miplúmȧél ↓ | Yo le he dado mi pluma a él. |
| 8 The Molinas haven't rented him the apartment.<br>The Molinas haven't rented the apartment to him. | lȯzmȯlína ǀ nólé̯anạlkıláđo̯ ǀ ėlȧpartȧméntȯ ↓ | Los Molina no le han alquilado el apartamento. |
| 9 I write her very little.<br>I write very little to her. | yólėskríƀȯmúypóko̯ ǀ ȧé(l)y̯ȧ ↓ | Yo le escribo muy poco a ella. |
| 10 My girl friend writes me a lot.<br>My girl friend writes a lot to me. | minóƀyȧ ǀ mėskríƀėmúchȯ ↓ | Mi novia me escribe mucho. |
| 11 When are you going to write him?<br>When are you going to write to him? | kwándȯlėbáe̯skrıbír ǀ ústéđ ↓ | ¿Cuándo le va a escribir Ud? |

## SENTENCE TRANSLATIONS

| | | | |
|---|---|---|---|
| 1 | When does he give us their names? | kwándȯnȯzđá \| lȯznómbrėzđé(l)y̰ȯs ↓ | ¿Cuándo nos da los nombres de ellos? |
| 2 | Are you going to help her work? | ustéđ \| lėƀáy̰uđáratraƀahár ↑ | ¿Ud. me va a ayudar a trabajar? |
| 3 | Is she going to rent you (all) the house? | lėzƀálkilárlakása ↑ | ¿Les va a alquilar la casa? |
| 4 | I don't owe him anything. | yónoleđéƀonáđa ↓ | Yo no le debo nada. |
| 5 | How much do you owe me? | kwántomeđéƀe̯ustéđ | ¿Cuánto me debe Ud.? |
| 6 | The Harrises always speak to us in English. | lȯshárris \| syémprė \| nȯsáƀlanėniŋglés ↓ | Los Harris siempre nos hablan en inglés. |
| 7 | The Garcías haven't rented the apartment to him. | lȯzgarsía \| nóle̯análkiláđo̯ \| ėlapartaméntȯ ↓ | Los García no le han alquilado el apartamento. |
| 8 | They're going to write to me. | é(l)y̰ȯz \| mėƀána̯eskriƀír ↓ | Ellos me van a escribir. |
| 9 | Why don't you write to them? | pȯrkénȯlėseskríƀe̯ \| ustéđ ↓ | ¿Por qué no les escribe Ud.? |

| | | |
|---|---|---|
| 10 The girl cleans the furniture for them. | lȧmu̇cháchȧ \| lėzlímpyȧlȯzmwéƀlės ↓ | La muchacha les limpia los muebles. |
| 11 The chauffer always carries the suitcases for us. | ėlchȯfér \| syémprė \| nȯz(l)y̯ébȧlȧzmȧlétȧs ↓ | El chofer siempre nos lleva las maletas. |
| 12 My wife doesn't wash my (the) shirts for me. | mi̯ėspósȧ \| nómėláƀȧlȧskȧmísȧs ↓ | Mi esposa no me lava las camisas. |
| 13 Nobody sweeps the apartment for them. | náđyė \| lėzƀárrėlȧpȧrtȧméntȯ ↓ | Nadie les barre el apartamento. |
| 14 Mr. Miranda has bought the furniture from us. | ėlsėn̯yórmirándȧ \| nȯṣákȯmpráđȯlȯzmwéƀlės ↓ | El Sr. Miranda nos ha comprado los muebles. |
| 15 I have bought the sofa bed from them. | yólėṣėkȯmpráđo̯ \| ėlsȯfákámȧ ↓ | Yo les he comprado el sofá-cama. |
| 16 A man has bought the house from them. | u̇nsėn̯yór \| lėṣákȯmpráđȯ \| lȧkásȧé(l)y̯ȯs ↓ | Un señor les ha comprado la casa a ellos. |

## B. DISCUSSION OF PATTERN

In the earlier drill sections on indirect clitics, one indirect clitic appeared as the single pronoun object of the verb. In the present drill section, two objects appear. They could both be clitics, but since complicating changes occur among the clitics when two appear together, a drill on such combined sequences is reserved for a later unit (Unit 20). In this section one pronoun object (expressed by an indirect clitic) and one noun object appear, controlled by the same verb.

Notice that the indirect relationship of Spanish is expressed in English with object pronouns in two positions: alone after a verb: 'He writes us a letter every day'; or with the relator 'to': 'He sent the book to us'. Notice also that the indirect clitic construction in Spanish translates several English relators other than 'to'; they seem to mean quite different things in English, though they are classified as similar by their common participation in the Spanish indirect clitic construction: /metráelos líbros ↓/

'He brings the books *to* me'; /me(l)yéba | lamaléta ↓/ He carries the suitcase *for* me'; /mekómpra̯ | elkárro ↓/ 'He's buying the car *from* me'. *To, for,* and *from* can all be translated by the Spanish indirect clitic.

## 15.21.3 Question intonation patterns—Yes questions

### A. PRESENTATION OF PATTERN

*ILLUSTRATIONS*

| | | |
|---|---|---|
| ______________ | 1 tyéne̯unlápis̥ ↑ | 2 2 2 ↑<br>¿Tiene un lápiz? |
| ______________ | tyéne̯unlápis̥ \| | 2 3 1 \|<br>¿Tiene un lápiz? |
| ______________ | 2 pȯđémȯzƀérlȯ ↑ | 1 2 2 2 ↑<br>¿Podemos verlo? |
| ______________ | pȯđémȯzƀérlȯ \| | 1 2 3 1 \|<br>¿Podemos verlo? |
| ______________ | 3 ėzmúykárȯ ↑ | 1 2 2 2 ↑<br>¿Es muy caro? |
| ______________ | ėzmúykarȯ \| | 1 2 3 1 \|<br>¿Es muy caro? |

*EXTRAPOLATION*

| Yes-no question | Yes question |
|---|---|
| /1222 ↑/ | /1231 \|/ |

*NOTES*

a. The /1231 |/ pattern signals, in appropriate contexts, a yes-no question in which a 'yes' answer is more or less expected. Note that it differs from the emphatic or contrasting statement pattern of units 12 and 13 (/1231 ↓/) only in the extent and abruptness of the final fade-out. This difference is transcribed by / | / vs / ↓ /.

## 15.21.31 SUBSTITUTION DRILL

Pattern substitution

Problem:

lèpáreşèƀáratò ↑

Answer:

lèpáreşèƀáratò |

| | | |
|---|---|---|
| 1 | èstálaƀwélta ↑ | èstálaƀwéltà \| |
| 2 | lègústalaıđéa ↑ | lègústalaıđéà \| |
| 3 | èstáđesokúpađo ↑ | èstáđesokúpađò \| |
| 4 | nèşèsítalmwáđas ↑ | nèşèsítalmwađàs \| |

---

Problem: 1 2 2 2 ↑
¿Le parece barato?

Answer: 1 2 3 1 |
¿Le parece barato?

| | | |
|---|---|---|
| 1 | 1 2 2 2 ↑<br>Está a la vuelta? | 1 2 3 1 \|<br>¿Está a la vuelta? |
| 2 | 1 2 22 ↑<br>¿Le gusta la idea? | 1 2 31 \|<br>¿Le gusta la idea? |
| 3 | 1 2 2 2 ↑<br>¿Está desocupado? | 1 2 3 1 \|<br>¿Está desocupado? |
| 4 | 1 2 2 2 ↑<br>¿Necesita almohadas? | 1 2 3 1 \|<br>¿Necesita almohadas? |

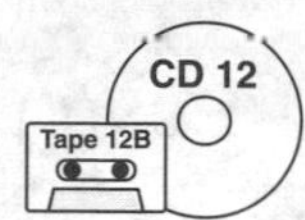


| | | |
|---|---|---|
| 5 | tȯđȧƀíȧhúntȯs ↑ | tȯđȧƀíȧhúntȯs \| |
| 6 | syémprėtrȧƀȧhándȯ ↑ | syémprėtrȧƀȧhándȯ \| |
| 7 | ėstáe̯nlȧkásȧ ↑ | ėstáe̯nlȧkásȧ \| |
| 8 | ėnla̯ėmbȧháđȧmėrɪkánȧ ↑ | ėnla̯ėmbȧháđȧmėrɪkánȧ \| |
| 9 | ėnlȧƀėnɪđánwéƀė ↑ | ėnlȧƀėnɪđánwéƀė \| |

---

| | | |
|---|---|---|
| 5 | 1 2 2 2 ↑<br>¿Todavía juntos? | 1 2 3 1 \|<br>¿Todavía juntos? |
| 6 | 2 2 2 ↑<br>¿Siempre trabajando? | 2 3 1 \|<br>¿Siempre trabajando? |
| 7 | 1 2 2 2 ↑<br>¿Está en la casa? | 1 2 3 1 \|<br>¿Está en la casa? |
| 8 | 1 2 2 2 ↑<br>¿En la Embajada Americana? | 1 2 3 1 \|<br>¿En la Embajada Americana? |
| 9 | 1 2 2 2 ↑<br>¿En la Avenida Nueve? | 1 2 3 1 \|<br>¿En la Avenida Nueve? |

| | |
|---|---|
| 10 ityéne̯ámbrė ↑ | ityéne̯ámbrė \| |
| 11 ibébėbínȯ ↑ | ibébėbínȯ \| |

---

| | |
|---|---|
| 1 2 2 2 ↑<br>10 ¿Y tiene hambre? | 1 2 3 1 \|<br>¿Y tiene hambre? |
| 1 2 2 2 ↑<br>11 ¿Y bebe vino? | 1 2 3 1 \|<br>¿Y bebe vino? |

## B. DISCUSSION OF PATTERN

A yes-no question, particularly in an informal situation, to which a 'yes' answer is more or less expected, is frequently uttered with the intonation pattern /1231 |/.

The statement of /1231 |/ on a question anticipating a 'yes' answer can have additional meaning. For instance /tyéne̯unlápiṣ |/ (2 3 1) may really mean, 'Can I borrow a pencil' if uttered in an appropriate context, such as with the hand of the speaker extended toward the person addressed.

As a generalization, however, it is not inappropriate to say that 'yes' is the anticipated reply to such a question.

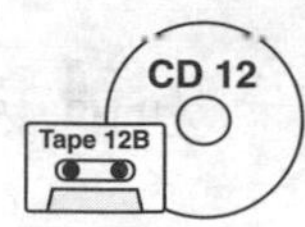




## 15.22 REPLACEMENT DRILLS

A sónmúyrrigurósos | enladwána ↑

1 ________________ ésa _______ ↑ sónmúyrrigurósos | enesadwána ↑

2 ________________________ kása ↑ sónmúyrrigurósos | enesakása ↑

3 _________ amábles ____________ ↑ sónmúyamábles | enesakása ↑

4 _________ trankílos ____________ ↑ sónmúytrankílos | enesakása ↑

5 _________ súsyos _____________ ↑ sónmúysúsyos | enesakása ↑

6 _______________________ otéles ↑ sónmúysúsyos | enesosotéles ↑

7 ______________ akél __________ ↑ sónmúysúsyos | enakelotél ↑

---

A ¿Son muy rigurosos en la aduana?

1 ¿ ________________ esa _______ ? ¿Son muy rigurosos en esa aduana?

2 ¿ ________________________ casa? ¿Son muy rigurosos en esa casa?

3 ¿ ________ amables ____________ ? ¿Son muy amables en esa casa?

4 ¿ ________ tranquilos___________ ? ¿Son muy tranquilos en esa casa?

5 ¿ ________ sucios_____________ ? ¿Son muy sucios en esa casa?

6 ¿ ______________________ hoteles? ¿Son muy sucios en esos hoteles?

7 ¿ ______________ aquel ________ ? ¿Son muy sucios en aquel hotel?

B y̯áe̯stákı | mi̯ekipáhė ↓

| | |
|---|---|
| 1 ____________________ ƀȧúlės ↓ | y̯áe̯stánạkí | mızƀȧúlės ↓ |
| 2 ________ ȧ(l)y̯í____________ ↓ | y̯áe̯stánạ(l)y̯í | mızƀȧúlės ↓ |
| 3 ____________ sụ ___________ ↓ | y̯áe̯stá(l)y̯í | sụƀȧúl ↓ |
| 4 ____________________ kósȧs ↓ | y̯áe̯stánạ(l)y̯í | sụskósȧs ↓ |
| 5 tòđȧƀíạ ____________________ ↓ | tòđȧƀíạ | ėstánạ(l)y̯í | sụskósȧs ↓ |
| 6 ____________ ésȧs __________ ↓ | tòđȧƀíạ | ėstánạ(l)y̯í | e̯sȧskósȧs ↓ |
| 7 ____________________ mȧlėtínės ↓ | tòđȧƀíạ | ėstánạ(l)y̯í | e̯sȯzmȧlėtínės ↓ |

---

B Ya está aquí mi equipaje.

| | |
|---|---|
| 1 ______________________ baúles. | Ya están aquí mis baúles. |
| 2 ___________ allí ___________ . | Ya están allí mis baúles. |
| 3 _____________ su ___________ . | Ya está allí su baúl. |
| 4 ______________________ cosas. | Ya están allá sus cosas. |
| 5 Todavía ____________________ . | Todavía están allí sus cosas. |
| 6 ______________ esas _______ . | Todavía están allí esas cosas. |
| 7 ____________________ maletines. | Todavía están allí esos maletines. |

C són | u̇nȧzmȧlétȧzƀérđės ↓

| | |
|---|---|
| 1 és ____________________ ↓ | és \| u̇nȧmȧlétȧƀérđė ↓ |
| 2 ________ bȧúl ________ ↓ | és \| u̇mbȧúlbérđė ↓ |
| 3 ________________ pėkén̯yȯ ↓ | és \| u̇mbȧúlpėkén̯yȯ ↓ |
| 4 _____ éstė ______________ ↓ | és \| éstėƀȧúlpėkén̯yȯ ↓ |
| 5 _______ mésȧs _________ ↓ | són \| éstȧzmésȧspėkén̯yȧs ↓ |
| 6 _____ ótrȧz ____________ ↓ | són \| ótrȧzmésȧpėkén̯yȧs ↓ |
| 7 áy ____________________ ↓ | áy \| ótrȧzmésȧspėkén̯yȧs ↓ |

---

C Son unas maletas verdes.

| | |
|---|---|
| 1 Es ____________________ . | Es una maleta verde. |
| 2 ________ baúl ________ . | Es un baúl verde. |
| 3 ________________ pequeño. | Es un baúl pequeño. |
| 4 _____ este ______________ . | Es este baúl pequeño. |
| 5 _______ mesas _________ . | Son estas mesas pequeñas. |
| 6 _____ otras ____________ . | Son otras mesas pequeñas. |
| 7 Hay ____________________ . | Hay otras mesas pequeñas. |

D ȧkı́e̯stálȧlístȧ ↓

| | |
|---|---|
| 1 __________ éstȧ __________ ↓ | ȧkı́e̯stá \| e̯stȧlístȧ ↓ |
| 2 ________________ mȧlėtínės ↓ | ȧkı́e̯stán \| éstȯzmȧlėtínės ↓ |
| 3 __________ lȯz____________ ↓ | ȧkı́e̯stán \| lȯzmȧlėtínės ↓ |
| 4 _____ áy ________________ ↓ | ȧkı́áy \| u̇nȯzmȧlėtínės ↓ |
| 5 ____________________ kósȧs ↓ | ȧkı́áy \| u̇nȧskósȧs ↓ |
| 6 __________ ótrȧs __________ ↓ | ȧkı́áy \| ótrȧskósȧs ↓ |
| 7 __________________ ómbrės ↓ | ȧkı́áy \| ótrȯsómbrės ↓ |

---

D Aquí está la lista.

| | |
|---|---|
| 1 __________ esta __________ . | Aquí está esta lista. |
| 2 __________________ maletines. | Aquí están estos maletines. |
| 3 ___________ los __________ . | Aquí están los maletines. |
| 4 ________ hay______________ . | Aquí hay unos maletines. |
| 5 ____________________ cosas. | Aquí hay unas cosas. |
| 6 _______ otras ____________ . | Aquí hay otras cosas. |
| 7 __________________ hombres. | Aquí hay otros hombres. |

E tóđo̯ėstákȯmplétȯ ↓

| | |
|---|---|
| 1 __________ đėsȯkupáđȯ ↓ | tóđo̯ėstáđėsȯkupáđȯ ↓ |
| 2 lȧzmésȧs __________ ↓ | lȧzmésȧs \| ėstándėsȯkupáđȧs ↓ |
| 3 __________ lístȧ ↓ | lȧmésa̯ėstálístȧ ↓ |
| 4 ėlsėn̯yór __________ ↓ | ėlsėn̯yórėstálístȯ ↓ |
| 5 __________ kȯnténtȯs ↓ | lȯ(s)sėn̯yórės \| ėstáŋkȯnténtȯs ↓ |
| 6 nȯsótrȯs __________ ↓ | nȯsótrȯs \| ėstámȯskȯnténtȯs ↓ |
| 7 _____ e̯stóy __________ ↓ | yóe̯stóykȯnténtȯ ↓ |

---

E Todo está completo.

| | |
|---|---|
| 1 __________ desocupado. | Todo está desocupado. |
| 2 Las mesas __________ . | Las mesas están desocupadas. |
| 3 __________ lista. | La mesa está lista. |
| 4 El señor __________ . | El señor está listo. |
| 5 __________ contentos. | Los señores están contentos. |
| 6 Nosotros __________ . | Nosotros estamos contentos. |
| 7 _____ estoy __________ . | Yo estoy contento. |

F bóyȧƀuskáru̇ntáksi ↓

| | |
|---|---|
| 1 ________ trȧér ________________ ↓ | bóyȧtrȧéru̇ntáksi ↓ |
| 2 ________________________ líƀrȯs ↓ | bóyȧtrȧéru̇nȯzlíƀrȯs ↓ |
| 3 bámȯs ________________________ ↓ | bámȯs \| ȧtrȧéru̇nȯzlíƀrȯs ↓ |
| 4 _________ kȯmprár ___________ ↓ | bámȯs \| ȧkȯmprárụnȯzlíƀrȯs ↓ |
| 5 ______________ ésȯz __________ ↓ | bámȯs \| ȧkȯmprár \| ésȯzlíƀrȯs ↓ |
| 6 ________________________ kósȧs ↓ | bámȯs \| ȧkȯmprár \| ésȧskósȧs ↓ |
| 7 tėnémȯs \| kė __________________ ↓ | tėnémȯs \| kėkȯmprár \| ésȧskósȧs ↓ |

---

F Voy a buscar un taxi.

| | |
|---|---|
| 1 ___________ traer ______________ . | Voy a traer un taxi. |
| 2 _________________________ libros. | Voy a traer unos libros. |
| 3 Vamos ________________________ . | Vamos a traer unos libros. |
| 4 _________ comprar _____________ . | Vamos a comprar unos libros. |
| 5 ___________________ esos ______ . | Vamos a comprar esos libros. |
| 6 _________________________ cosas. | Vamos a comprar esas cosas. |
| 7 Tenemos que __________________ . | Tenemos que comprar esas cosas. |

## 15.23 VARIATION DRILLS

| | | |
|---|---|---|
| A | ėstóysėgúrȯ \| đėkḙȧu̯stéđ \| nólȯƀán̦ȧmȯléstár ↓ | Estoy seguro de que a usted no lo van a molestar. |
| 1 I'm sure they're not going to send *you*. | ėstóysėgúrȯ \| đėkḙȧu̯stéđ \| nólȯƀán̦ȧmȧndár ↓ | Estoy seguro de que a usted no lo van a mandar. |
| 2 I'm sure they're not going to wait for *him*. | ėstóysėgúrȯ \| đėkḙȧél \| nólȯbán̦ȧespėrár ↓ | Estoy seguro de que a él no lo van a esperar. |
| 3 I'm sure they're not going to take *her*. | ėstóysėgúrȯ \| đėkḙȧé(l)y̦ȧ \| nólȧƀán̦ȧ(l)y̦ėƀár ↓ | Estoy seguro de que a ella no la van a llevar. |
| 4 He's sure they're going to need *me*. | ėstásėgúrȯ \| đėkḙȧmí \| mėƀán̦ȧneșesıtár ↓ | Está seguro de que a mí me van a necesitar. |
| 5 He's sure they're going to need *them*. | ėstásėgurȯ \| đėkḙȧe(l)y̦óz \| lozƀán̦ȧneșesıtár ↓ | Está seguro de que a ellos los van a necesitar. |
| 6 We're sure they're going to send John and Jose. | ėstámȯ(s)sėgúrȯz \| đėkḙȧhwán \| ɹ̯ahȯsé \| lȯzƀán ȧmȧndár ↓ | Estamos seguros de que a Juan y a José los van a mandar. |
| 7 We're sure they're going to send Mary and Carmen. | ėstámȯ(s)sėgúrȯz \| đėkḙȧmȧría \| ɹ̯akármėn \| láz ƀán̦ȧmȧndár ↓ | Estamos seguros de que a María y a Carmen las van a mandar. |

| | | | |
|---|---|---|---|
| B | téŋgàlaƀòndáđ \| đe̯àƀrírèlbàúl \| primérò ↓ | | Tenga la bondad de abrir el baúl primero. |
| 1 | Please open the green suitcase. | téŋgàlaƀòndáđ \| đe̯àƀrír \| làmàlétaƀérđè ↓ | Tenga la bondad de abrir la maleta verde. |
| 2 | Please dress right away. | téŋgàlaƀòndáđ \| đèƀèstírsènsègíđà ↓ | Tenga la bondad de vestirse en seguida. |
| 3 | Please wait a moment. | téŋgàlaƀòndáđ \| đèspèrárunmòméntò ↓ | Tenga la bondad de esperar un momento. |
| 4 | Please wait around the corner. | téŋgàlaƀòndáđ \| đèspèráralaƀwéltà ↓ | Tenga la bondad de esperar a la vuelta. |
| 5 | Please speak English. | téŋgàlaƀòndáđ \| đe̯àƀláriŋglés ↓ | Tenga la bondad de hablar inglés. |
| 6 | Please come alone. | téŋgàlaƀòndáđ \| đèƀènírsólò ↓ | Tenga la bondad de venir solo. |
| 7 | Please come (pl.) together. | téŋganlaƀòndáđ \| đèƀènírhúntòs ↓ | Tengan la bondad de venir juntos. |

| | | | |
|---|---|---|---|
| C | sónu̯nòzrrègálòs ↓ tóđo̯estáđèklàráđò ↓ | | Son unos regalos. Todo está declarado. |
| 1 | They're some books. Everything's bought. | sónu̯nòzlíƀròs ↓ tóđo̯estákòmpráđò ↓ | Son unos libros. Todo está comprado. |
| 2 | They're some shirts. Everything's washed. | sónu̯nàskàmísàs ↓ tóđo̯estálàƀáđò ↓ | Son unas camisas. Todo está lavado. |

| | | |
|---|---|---|
| 3 It's whisky. It's in the declaration. | ėzw̲ískі ↓ ėstáđėklȧráđȯ ↓ | Es whiskey. Está declarado. |
| 4 The shirt is washed. | lȧkȧmísa̯ėstálȧƀáđȧ ↓ | La camisa está lavada. |
| 5 The car is fixed. | ėlawtọestȧrreglȧ́đȯ ↓ | El auto está arreglado. |
| 6 The rooms are rented. | lȯskwártȯs \| ėstána̯lkıláđȯs ↓ | Los cuartos están alquilados. |
| 7 The shirts are washed. | lȧskȧmísȧs \| ėstánlȧƀáđȧs ↓ | Las camisas están lavadas. |
| D lána̯tėndíđȯƀyén \| ėn̯inmigrasyón ↑ | | ¿La han atendido bien en inmigración? |
| 1 Have they taken good care of you (f) in the hotel? | lána̯tėndíđȯƀyén \| ėn̯elótėl ↑ | ¿La han atendido bien en el hotel? |
| 2 Have they included you (m) in the list? | lọánin̯ŋklwíđọ \| ėnlálista ↑ | ¿Lo han incluído en la lista? |
| 3 Have they seen much of Washington? | áŋkȯnȯsíđȯmúchọ \| ėŋw̲áshıŋtȯn ↑ | ¿Han conocido mucho en Washington? |
| 4 Have you (pl) eaten in that restaurant? | áŋkȯmíđọ \| ėn̯ésėrrėstȯrán ↑ | ¿Han comido en ese restorán? |
| 5 Have you (pl) learned much Spanish? | ána̯prėndíđȯ \| múchọėspan̯yól ↑ | ¿Han aprendido mucho español? |

| | | |
|---|---|---|
| 6 Have you (sg) waited a long time? | áe̯spèráđò \| múchòtyémpò ↑ | ¿Ha esperado mucho tiempo? |
| 7 Have you (sg) spoken with them? | áƀláđò \| kòné̩(l)y̩òs ↑ | ¿Ha hablado con ellos? |

E kònmígo̯ ↑ ànsíđòmúyàmáƀlès ↓ — Conmigo han sido muy amables.

| | | |
|---|---|---|
| 1 They've been very nice to you (fam). | kòntígo̯ ↑ ànsíđòmúyàmáƀlès ↓ | Contigo han sido muy amables. |
| 2 They've been very nice to you (form). | kònu̩stéđ ↑ ànsíđòmúyàmáƀlès ↓ | Con usted han sido muy amables. |
| 3 They've been very nice to him. | kòné̩l ↑ ànsíđòmúyàmáƀlès ↓ | Con él han sido muy amables. |
| 4 He's been very nice to her. | kòné̩(l)y̩a̯ ↑ àsíđòmúyàmáƀlè ↓ | Con ella ha sido muy amable. |
| 5 He hasn't spoken with us. | kò(n)nòsótròz ↑ no̯áƀláđò ↓ | Con nosotros no ha hablado. |
| 6 He hasn't worked with us. | kò(n)nòsótròz ↑ no̯átràƀàhàđò ↓ | Con nosotros no ha trabajado. |
| 7 He hasn't been out with us. | kò(n)nòsótròz ↑ no̯ásàlíđò ↓ | Con nosotros no ha salido. |

F nȯṣėstápréstándǫ | ùnàgránạyúđà ↓ — Nos está prestando una gran ayuda.

| | | |
|---|---|---|
| 1 He's waiting for us in the rear of the building. | nȯṣėstáẹspėrándȯ \| đėtrázđėlėđıfíṣyȯ ↓ | Nos está esperando detrás del edificio. |
| 2 He's waiting for us in the park. | nȯṣėstáẹspėrándȯ \| ėnẹlpárkė ↓ | Nos está esperando en el parque. |
| 3 The lady is speaking to you (fam). | tėstáƀlándȯlàsėn̩yórȧ ↓ | Te está hablando la señora. |
| 4 He's fixing the car for you (fam). | tėstárrėglándǫėláwtȯ ↓ | Te está arreglando el auto. |
| 5 He's sending me two hundred dollars a month. | mėstámȧndándȯ \| đȯs(ṣ)yéntȯzđólȧrės \| ȧlmés ↓ | Me está mandando doscientos dólares al mes. |
| 6 He's giving me twenty dollars a week. | mėstáđándȯ \| ƀéyntėđólȧrės \| ȧlȧsėmánȧ ↓ | Me está dando veinte dólares a la semana. |
| 7 It's bothering me a lot. | mėstámȯlėstándȯmúchȯ ↓ | Me está molestando mucho. |

## 15.24 REVIEW DRILL

Possessive constructions

| | | | |
|---|---|---|---|
| 1 | Juan's sister is here. | la̯ėrmánȧ \| đėhwán \| ėstákí ↓ | La hermana de Juan está aquí. |
| 2 | Antonio's wife is here. | la̯ėspósȧ \| đe̯ȧntónyȯ \| e̯stákí ↓ | La esposa de Antonio está aquí. |
| 3 | Carmen's mother-in-law is here. | lȧswégrȧ \| đėkármėn \| ėstákí ↓ | La suegra de Carmen está aquí. |
| 4 | Antonio's son is here. | ėlíhȯ \| đe̯ȧntónyȯ \| e̯stákí ↓ | El hijo de Antonio está aquí. |
| 5 | Carmen's cup is here. | lȧtáṣȧ \| đėkármėn \| ėstákí ↓ | La taza de Carmen está aquí. |
| 6 | Antonio's girl is here. | lȧnínyȧ \| đe̯ȧntónyȯ \| e̯stákí ↓ | La niña de Antonio está aquí. |
| 7 | Antonio's boy is here. | ėlnínyȯ \| đe̯ȧntónyȯ \| e̯stákí ↓ | El niño de Antonio está aquí. |
| 8 | Carmen's friend is here. | lȧmígȧ \| đėkármėn \| ėstákí ↓ | La amiga de Carmen está aquí. |
| 9 | Carmen's things are here. | lȧskósȧz \| đėkármėn \| ėstánạkí ↓ | Las cosas de Carmen están aquí. |
| 10 | Jose's furniture is here. | lȯzmwéƀlėz \| đėhósė \| ėstánạkí ↓ | Los muebles de José están aquí. |
| 11 | Juan's desk is here. | ėlėskritóryȯ \| đėhwán \| ėstákí ↓ | El escritorio de Juan está aquí. |

# 15.3 CONVERSATION STIMULUS

## NARRATIVE 1

| | | |
|---|---|---|
| 1 The immigration people have taken good care of Colonel Harris' family. | lȯ(s)sėn̦yórėz \| đėl̦ainmigràșyón ↑ àn̦àtėndíđȯ múyƀyén \| àlàfàmílyà \| đėlkȯrȯnélhárris ↓ | Los señores de la inmigración han atendido muy bien a la familia del coronel Harris. |
| 2 They've been very nice to them. | ánsıđȯ \| múyamáƀlės \| kȯn̦é(l)y̦ȯs ↓ | Han sido muy amables con ellos. |
| 3 Mrs. Harris' name is Jean. | ėlnómbrė \| đėlàsėn̦yóraharrıs \| ėzy̦ín ↓ | El nombre de la señora Harris es Jean. |
| 4 Jean has to go to customs now. | y̦ín \| tyénėkėir \| àlàđwanàórà ↓ | Jean tiene que ir a la aduana ahora. |
| 5 The colonel thinks that they are very strict there. | ėkȯrȯnél ↑ kréėkėsón \| muyrrıgurósȯs \| àí ↓ | El coronel cree que son muy rigurosos ahí. |
| 6 But he isn't sure. | pėrȯn̦ȯėstásėgúrȯ ↓ | Pero no está seguro. |
| 7 Jean has the list of all the things she's bringing. | y̦ín \| tyénėlàlístà \| đėtóđazlàskósàskėtráė ↓ | Jean tiene la lista de todas las cosas que trae. |
| 8 The colonel can't go in. | ėlkȯrȯnél \| nópwéđėpàsár ↓ | El coronel no puede pasar. |
| 9 He'll wait for them here. | àkílȯșėspérà ↓ | Aquí los espera. |

## DIALOG 1

Coronel, pregúntele a Jean si la han atendido bien en inmigración.

tẹánạtėndıđȯƀyén | ėnịnmigrȧṣyón | ỵín ↑

Coronel: ¿Te han atendido bien en inmigración, Jean?

Jean, contéstele que sí, que los señores ahí han sido muy amables con ustedes.

sí ↓ lȯ(s)sėṇyórės | ȧí ↑ ȧnsíđȯmúyȧmáƀlės | kȯ(n)nȯsótrȯs ↓

Jean: Sí, los señores ahí han sido muy amables con nosotros.

Coronel, dígale que ahora tiene que ir a la aduana.

ȧórȧ | tyénėskẹírȧlȧđwánȧ ↓

Coronel: Ahora tienes que ir a la aduana.

Jean, dígale que sí, y pregúntele si son muy rigurosos ahí.

sí ↓ sónmúyrrigúrósȯs | ȧí ↑

Jean: Sí. ¿Son muy rigurosos ahí?

Coronel, contéstele que Ud. cree que sí, que no está seguro. Pregúntele si tiene la lista de todas las cosas que trae.

kréȯkėsí ↓ nóẹstóysėgúrȯ ↓ tyénėzlȧlístȧ | đėtóđȧslȧskósȧs | kėtráės ↑

Coronel: Creo que sí, no estoy seguro. ¿Tienes la lista de todas las cosas que traes?

Jean, contéstele que sí, que aquí está. Que todo está declarado. Pregúntele si no viene con Uds.

sí ↓ ȧkíẹstá ↓ tóđọ | ėstáđėklȧráđȯ ↓ nȯƀyénėskȯ(n)nȯsótrȯs ↑

Jean: Sí, aquí está. Todo está declarado. ¿No vienes con nosotros?

Coronel, contéstele que no, que Ud. no puede pasar. Que aquí los espera.

nó ↓ ỵónȯpwéđȯpȧsár ↓ ȧkílȯṣėspérȯ ↓

Coronel: No, yo no puedo pasar. Aquí los espero.

## NARRATIVE 2

| | | |
|---|---|---|
| 1 They're ready now. | y̰áȩstánlístȯs ↓ | Ya están listos. |
| 2 Jean looks very happy. | y̰ín \| pȧréșėmúykȯnténtȧ ↓ | Jean parece muy contenta. |
| 3 And why shouldn't she? They didn't charge her anything. | ipȯrkenó ↓ nȯlȩáŋkȯƀráđȯnađȧ ↓ | ¿Y por qué no? No le han cobrado nada. |
| 4 She doesn't know why. | é(l)y̰ȧ \| nósáƀėpȯrké ↓ | Ella no sabe por qué. |
| 5 They didn't tell her. | nóleđıhérȯn ↓ | No le dijeron. |
| 6 And she isn't going to ask them. | i̯é(l)y̰ȧ \| nóƀápreguntárlės ↓ | Y ella no va a preguntarles. |
| 7 The colonel (just) can't believe it! | ėlkȯrȯnél \| nópwéđėkreérlȯ ↓ | ¡El coronel no puede creerlo! |
| 8 He thought they were very strict here. | élkréıȧ \| kérȧnmúyrrigúrósȯs \| ȧkí ↓ | El creía que eran muy rigurosos aquí. |

## DIALOG 2

| | | |
|---|---|---|
| Jean, dígale a su esposo que ya están listos ustedes. | yá \| e̯stámòzlístòs ↓ | Jean: Ya estamos listos. |
| Coronel, dígale que ella parece muy contenta. Que por qué. | pàréşez \| múy \| kònténtà ↓ pòrké ↓ | Coronel: Pareces muy contenta. ¿Por qué? |
| Jean, contéstele que no le han cobrado nada. | nó \| me̯àŋkòƀráđònáđà ↓ | Jean: No me han cobrado nada. |
| Coronel, dígale que no puede creerlo. Que por qué. | nópwéđòkrèérlò ↓ pòrké ↓ | Coronel: No puedo creerlo, ¿por qué? |
| Jean, contéstele que Ud. no sabe por qué. Que no le dijeron, y que Ud. no va a preguntarles. | nó \| sé \| pòrké ↓ nómèđìhéròn \| iy̯ónóƀóy \| àpregùntárlès ↓ | Jean: No sé por qué. No me dijeron y yo no voy a preguntarles. |
| Coronel, dígale que estupendo. Y que Ud. creía que eran rigurosos aquí. | èstùpéndò ↓ iy̯ókrèíà \| kéràn̄rrigùrósòs \| àkí ↓ | Coronel: ¡Estupendo! Y yo creía que eran rigurosos aquí. |

## NARRATIVE 3

| | | |
|---|---|---|
| 1 A friend of the colonel's is going to take them in his car. | ùnàmígò \| đèlkòrònél \| bá(l)y̯èbárlòşènsùkárrò ↓ | Un amigo del coronel va a llevarlos en su carro. |
| 2 But with so much baggage there won't be room for all. | pèròkòntántọ \| èkipáhè \| nóƀánàkaƀér \| tóđòs ↓ | Pero con tanto equipaje no van a caber todos. |

| | | |
|---|---|---|
| 3 They'll make two trips, then. | áșèndózƀyáhès \| èntónșès ↓ | Hacen dos viajes, entonces. |
| 4 But good gosh! Just a moment! | péròkáràmbà ↓ únmòméntò ↓ | ¡Pero caramba!, ¡un momento! |
| 5 Something's wrong. | álgòpásà ↓ | Algo pasa. |
| 6 Jean's missing the suitcase with the gifts. | àyín \| lèfáltà \| làmàlátàkònlózrrègálòs ↓ | A Jean le falta la maleta con los regalos. |
| 7 She may have left it in the customs (office). | pwéđȩ \| àƀérlà \| đèháđǫ \| ènlàđwánà ↓ | Puede haberla dejado en la aduana. |
| 8 She's going to go look for it there. | báír \| àƀùskárlàí ↓ | Va a ir a buscarla ahí. |

## DIALOG 3

| | | |
|---|---|---|
| Coronel, dígale a su esposa que listos, entonces, y que un amigo suyo va a llevarlos a Uds. en su carro. | lístòs \| èntónșès ↓ ùn̥àmígòmíò \| bá(l)yèƀárnòs \| ènsùkárrò ↓ | Coronel: Listos, entonces. Un amigo mío va a llevarnos en su carro. |
| Jean, dígale que con tanto equipaje no van a caber todos. | kòntántǫèkìpáhè \| nóƀámòșàkàƀér \| tóđòs ↓ | Jean: Con tanto equipaje no vamos a caber todos. |

Coronel, dígale que hacen dos viajes, entonces.

àṣémȯzđózƀyáhės | ėntónṣės ↓

Coronel: Hacemos dos viajes entonces.

Jean, dígale que ¡ay, caramba! que un momento.

áy | kȧrámbȧ ↓ únmȯméntȯ ↓

Jean: ¡Ay, caramba! Un momento.

Coronel, pregúntele que qué le pasa.

kétėpásȧ ↓

Coronel: ¿Qué te pasa?

Jean, contéstele que le falta la maleta con los regalos.

mėfáltȧ | lȧmȧlétȧ | kȯnlȯzrrėgálȯs ↓

Jean: Me falta la maleta con los regalos.

Coronel, dígale que debe haberla dejado en la aduana.

déƀės | ȧƀérlȧ | đėháđo̯ | ėnlȧđwánȧ ↓

Coronel: Debes haberla dejado en la aduana.

Jean, dígale que puede ser. Que Ud. va a ir a buscarla ahí.

pwéđėsér ↓ bóya̯ír | ȧƀúskárlȧí ↓

Jean: Puede ser. Voy a ir a buscarla ahí.

**End of Tape 12B**
**End of CD 12**

# AI.1 VOCABULARY

## Units 1–15

The following vocabulary list includes all words presented in Units 1–15. The entries are in a respelling which makes it possible to find any item for which the pronunciation is known without being acquainted with the irregularities of the Spanish spelling system.

The first indentations under the main entry are constructions in which the entry item (or a variant form of the entry item) appears, which are felt to be idiomatic from the point of view of English translation.

The second indentations under the main entry consist of inflected forms which are irregular or which have not been treated yet in the drills or discussion.

Main entries are alphabetized according to the English alphabet with the following modifications: /(l)y/ follows /ly/, /n̦y/ follows /ny/, and /ș/ follows /s/. The respelling used in the vocabulary is the same as that used in the extrapolations and discussions, technically referred to as a 'phonemic transcription.' This differs from the respelling in the 'aid to listening' column of the basic sentences only in omitting certain details of pronunciation which can also be determined by the position of the 'phoneme' in a sequence of sounds (for example, the phoneme /d/ is [d ] initially in an utterance, or after /n/ or /l/; it is [đ] elsewhere; both are listed /d/ in the vocabulary.)

Nouns are identified for gender class membership by their appearance with the appropriate form of the definite article. A few nouns which ordinarily do not appear with articles (as some names of persons and places, names of the months, and some indefinites) are identified by empty parentheses instead of by articles.

Adjectives are identified by one of two ways. Those which have two gender endings are listed in their masculine form, with the feminine ending following: /byého , —a/. Those which have a common gender (both masculine and feminine agreement by a single form) are shown with a zero following: /gránde, —ø /.

Verbs can be identified by the /—Vr/ (i.e./—ár, —ér, —ír/) ending and the English translation 'to ______ ,' Forms of irregular verbs and unfamiliar forms are given (as described above) at the second indentation after the main entry. Second person verb forms are formal unless marked (fam) for familiar. Command forms appear without an indicated subject. Verb forms which are so irregular as to alphabetize differently from the main entry of the infinitive are cross-referenced.

Clitic pronouns are marked by a following dash, which indicates their dependence on accompanying verbs in an utterance: /les—/. Other pronouns are not marked, but can be identified by their English translations.

/a/

The second column gives the traditional Spanish orthography of the main entries, in parentheses.

The third column gives the English translations of all the entry items.

The fourth (right hand) column gives the unit and section of the first appearance of each entry. Thus 10.1 indicates the item first appears in the basic dialogs of Unit 10; 10.2, in an illustration drill of the drills and grammar section in Unit 10.

In Unit 16 and after, new vocabulary also appears in the reading selections, so 16.4 would indicate that the first appearance was in the readings section, and a second reference of 21.1 would indicate a subsequent entry in the basic dialogs. Two 'first' entries are necessary because an 'active' knowledge is presumed for all items presented in basic sentences and drills, and only a 'passive' knowledge or recognition is presumed for items presented in readings. So, items presented in the readings are not used in drills until or unless they appear later in basic dialogs.

The following abbreviations are used:

| | |
|---|---|
| (f) | feminine |
| (fam) | familiar |
| (n) | neuter |
| (pl) | plural |
| (sg) | singular |

/a/

| | | | | |
|---|---|---|---|---|
| a | | (a) | to | 1.1 |
| | | | at | 2.1 |
| | a—kómo—está—(el—kámbyo) | | what's the rate (of exchange) | 3.1 |
| | al | | to the | 1.1 |
| | a—la—bwélta | | around the corner | 5.1 |
| | al—kontráryo | | on the contrary | 8.1 |
| | al—(més) | | per (month) | 7.1 |

| | | | | |
|---|---|---|---|---|
| | a—menúdo | | often | 13.1 |
| | a—propósito | | by the way | 4.1 |
| | a—su—disposisyón | | at your disposal | 14.1 |
| | a—sus—órdenes | | at your service | 14.1 |
| | á | (ah) | oh | 4.1 |
| | á (see abér) | | | |
| la | abenída | (avenida) | avenue | 3.1 |
| | abér | (haber) | there to be | 1.1 |
| | | | to have | 6.1 |
| | á | | (you) have | 9.2 |
| | án | | (you) have (pl) | 9.2 |
| | ás | | (you) have (fam) | 9.2 |
| | áy | | there is, there are | 1.1 |
| | é | | (I) have | 6.1 |
| | émos | | (we) have | 9.1 |
| | áy—ke | | it's necessary to | 3.1 |
| | nó—áy—de—ké | | don't give it a thought | 1.1 |
| | abisár | (avisar) | to notify | 5.1 |
| la | abitasyón | (habitación) | room | 8.1 |
| | ablár | (hablar) | to speak, to talk | 4.1 |
| | abrír | (abrir) | to open | 8.2 |
| el | abyón | (avión) | plane | 14.1 |
| | por—abyón | | by plane | 14.1 |
| | adelánte | (adelante) | straight ahead, forward; come (on) in | 2.1 |
| | pasár—adelánte | | to come in | 9.1 |

/ade/

| | | | | |
|---|---|---|---|---|
| | además | (además) | besides | 14.1 |
| | administratíbo, —a | (administrativo) | administrative | 4.1 |
| la | adwána | (aduana) | customs office | 15.1 |
| | adyós | (adiós) | goodbye | 1.1 |
| el | a̯eropwérto | (aeropuerto) | airport | 14.1 |
| | afeytár | (afeitar) | to shave | 12.1 |
| | afeytárse | | to shave oneself | 12.1 |
| las | afwéras | (afueras) | outskirts | 7.1 |
| | agradeşér | (agradecer) | to be grateful | 10.1 |
| | agradeşído, —a | (agradecido) | grateful | 10.1 |
| | múy—agradeşído—por—tódo | | thanks a lot for everything | 10.1 |
| el | ágwa (f) | (agua) | water | 3.1 |
| la | ahénşya | (agencia) | agency | 7.1 |
| el | ahénte | (agente) | agent | 7.1 |
| | aí | (ahí) | there | 2.1 |
| | por—aí | | that way | 13.1 |
| | akél | (aquél) | that (over there) | 7.2 |
| | aké(l)ya (f) | | that (over there) | 7.2 |
| | aké(l)yos, —as | | those | 7.2 |
| | akí | (aquí) | here | 3.1 |
| | akí—tyéne | | here you are | 3.1 |
| | | | here is (are) | 7.1 |
| | álgo | (algo) | anything, something | 3.1 |
| | álgo—mas | | anything else | 3.1 |
| ( ) | álgyen | (alguien) | anyone | 10.2 |
| | alkilár | (alquilar) | to rent | 7.1 |

| | | | | |
|---|---|---|---|---|
| | almorsár | (almorzar) | to lunch | 5.1 |
| la | almwáda | (almohada) | pillow | 11.1 |
| | a(l)yí | (allí) | there (in that place) | 6.1 |
| | amáble, —ø | (amable) | kind, nice, courteous | 15.1 |
| el | ámbre (f) | (hambre) | hunger | 5.1 |
| | tenér—ámbre | | to be hungry | 5.1 |
| | amerikáno, —a | (americano) | American | 2.1 |
| el | amígo | (amigo) | friend | 7.1 |
| | amwebládo, —a | (amueblado) | furnished | 7.1 |
| | amweblár | (amueblar) | to furnish | 7.1 |
| | án (see abér) | | | |
| | anóche | (anoche) | last night | 15.1 |
| | ántes | (antes) | before | 10.1 |
| el | anúnşyo | (anuncio) | advertisement | 7.1 |
| | aóra | (ahora) | now | 3.1 |
| | aóra—mísmo | | right now | 3.1 |
| | por—aóra | | right now | 7.1 |
| el | apartaménto | (apartamento) | apartment | 6.1 |
| | apénas | (apenas) | scarcely, barely | 12.1 |
| | aprendér | (aprender) | to learn | 4.1 |
| | arregládo, —a | (arreglado) | fixed, arranged | 9.1 |
| | arreglár | (arreglar) | to fix, to arrange | 9.1 |
| | ás (see abér) | | | |
| | así | (así) | so | 8.1 |
| el | as(ş)ensór | (ascensor) | elevator | 3.1 |

/ast/

| | | | | |
|---|---|---|---|---|
| | ásta | (hasta) | until | 1.1 |
| | ásta—lwégo | | so long | 1.1 |
| | ásta—man̯yána | | see you tomorrow | 1.1 |
| | aşér | (hacer) | to do, to make | 9.1 |
| | atendér | (atender) | to take care of, to assist | 15.1 |
| el | áwto | (auto) | car | 7.1 |
| | áy (see abér) | | | |
| | ayér | (ayer) | yesterday | 4.1 |
| la | ayúda | (ayuda) | help | 15.1 |
| | ayudár | (ayudar) | to help | 6.1 |

/b/

| | | | | |
|---|---|---|---|---|
| | bá (see ír) | | | |
| | bahár | (bajar) | to go down | 2.1 |
| | bahér | (valer) | to be worth | 14.1 |
| | balér—la—péna | | to be worthwhile | 14.1 |
| | bámos (see ír) | | | |
| | bán (see ír) | | | |
| | ban̯yár | (bañar) | to bathe | 12.1 |
| | ban̯yárse | | to bathe oneself | 12.1 |
| el | bányo | (baño) | bathroom | 2.1 |
| | baráto, —a | (barato) | cheap, inexpensive | 5.1 |
| el | bárko | (barco) | boat | 14.1 |
| | em—bárko | | by boat | 14.1 |
| el | barón | (varón) | male | 14.1 |
| | barrér | (barrer) | to sweep | 11.1 |

| | | | | |
|---|---|---|---|---|
| el | bárryo | (barrio) | section (of town) | 14.1 |
| | bás (see ír) | | | |
| | bastántes, —ø | (bastante) | enough, quite (a bit) | 5.1 |
| el | baúl | (baúl) | trunk | 15.1 |
| | báyas (see ír) | | | |
| | baylár | (bailar) | to danee | 13.1 |
| | bé (see bér) | | | |
| | beámos (see bér) | | | |
| | bebér | (beber) | to drink | 9.1 |
| ( ) | be(l)yabísta | (Bellavista) | Bellavista | 14.1 |
| | bén (see benír, bér) | | | |
| | benír | (venir) | to come | 5.1 |
| | bén | | come (fam) | 13.1 |
| | bíno | | (you) came | 5.1 |
| | byéne | | (she) comes | 10.1 |
| | byénen | | (they) come | 14.1 |
| | byénes | | (you) come (fam) | 8.1 |
| | béo (see bér) | | | |
| | bér | (ver) | to see | 6.1 |
| | bé | | (you) see | 14.2 |
| | beámos | | let's see | 6.1 |
| | bén | | (you) see (pl) | 14.2 |
| | béo | | (I) see | 10.2 |
| | bés | | (you) see (fam) | 14.2 |
| | bérde, —ø | (verde) | green | 15.1 |

/bes/

| | | | | |
|---|---|---|---|---|
| | bés (see bér) | | | |
| | bestír | (vestir) | to dress | 12.1 |
| | bestírse | | to dress oneself | 12.1 |
| la | béș | (vez) | time | 2.1 |
| | de—béș—en—kwándo | | from time to time | 13.1 |
| | ótra—béș | | again | 2.1 |
| el | beșíno | (vecino) | neighbor | 8.1 |
| | béynte, —ø | (veinte) | twenty | 2.1 |
| | bibír | (vivir) | to live | 6.1 |
| el | bi(l)yéte | (billete) | bill | 3.1 |
| | bíno (see benír) | | | |
| el | bíno | (vino) | wine | 6.1 |
| la | bísta | (vista) | view | 8.1 |
| la | bóda | (boda) | wedding | 9.1 |
| | bolbér | (volver) | to return | 9.1 |
| la | bondád | (bondad) | kindness, goodness | 15.1 |
| | tenér—la—bondád—de | | to be so kind as to, please | 15.1 |
| | boníto, —a | (bonito) | pretty | 8.1 |
| | bóy (see ír) | | | |
| la | bróma | (broma) | joke | 12.1 |
| | ké—bróma | | what a fix | 12.1 |
| | buskár | (buscar) | to look for | 6.1 |
| la | bwélta | (vuelta) | turn | 5.1 |
| | a—la—bwélta | | around the corner | 5.1 |
| | bwéno, —a | (bueno) | good | 1.1 |

| | | | | |
|---|---|---|---|---|
| | | | OK | 4.1 |
| | bwén | | good | 5.1 |
| | bwénos—días | | good morning | 1.1 |
| | bwénas—nóches | | good evening | 1.1 |
| | bwénas—tárdes | | good afternoon | 1.1 |
| el | byáhe | (viaje) | trip | 4.1 |
| | byahéro, —a | (viajero) | traveler | 3.1 |
| | byého, —a | (viejo) | old | 7.1 |
| | byén | (bien) | well, fine | 1.1 |
| | está—byén | | that's O.K., OK | 1.1 |
| | byéne (see benír) | | | |
| | byénen (see benír) | | | |
| | byénes (see benír) | | | |
| el | byérnes | (viernes) | Friday | 10.1 |

/ch/

| | | | | |
|---|---|---|---|---|
| el | chéke | (cheque) | check | 3.1 |
| la | chíka | (chica) | girl | 13.1 |
| el | chíko | (chico) | boy | 12.1 |
| el | chofér | (chofer) | chauffeur | 4.1 |
| la | chuléta | (chuleta) | chop | 6.1 |

/d/

| | | | | |
|---|---|---|---|---|
| | dá(n) (see dár) | | | |
| | dár | (dar) | to give | 2.1 |
| | dá | | (it) gives | 8.1 |
| | dán | | (they) give | 10.1 |
| | dás | | (you) give (fam) | 14.2 |
| | dé | | give | 2.1 |
| | dóy | | (I) give | 4.1 |
| | dár—a—(la—ká(l)ye) | | to face on (the street) | 8.1 |
| | dárse—prísa | | to hurry (oneself) | 12.1 |
| | dárse—una—dúcha | | to take a shower | 12.1 |
| | dás (see dár) | | | |
| | de | (de) | of, from | 1.1 |
| | de—béṣ—en—kwándo | | from time to time | 13.1 |
| | del | | of the, from the | 8.2 |
| | de—náda | | you're welcome | 1.1 |
| | lo—de | | the matter of, about | 9.1 |
| | dé (see dár) | | | |
| | debér | (deber) | to owe, must, ought | 4.1 |
| | débe(n)—sér | | must be, probably is (are) | 8.1 |
| | dehár | (dejar) | to leave, to let | 8.1 |
| | deklarár | (declarar) | to declare | 15.1 |
| | demasyádo, —a | (demasiado) | too much | 7.1 |
| | demasyádos, —as | | too many | 7.1 |
| la | derécha | (derecha) | right | 2.1 |
| | désde | (desde) | since | 4.1 |
| | désde—kwándo | | since when (how long) | 4.1 |

| | | | | |
|---|---|---|---|---|
| | deseár | (desear) | to wish | 6.1 |
| | desokupádo, —a | (desocupado) | empty, unoccupied | 6.1 |
| | desokupár | (desocupar) | to vacate, to empty | 6.1 |
| | despwés | (después) | later | 3.1 |
| | deșidír | (decidir) | to decide | 9.1 |
| | deșír | (decir) | to say, to tell | 2.1 |
| | díga | | say | 4.1 |
| | dígas | | tell (fam) | 12.1 |
| | díhe | | (I) said | 15.1 |
| | dihéron | | (they) told | 4.1 |
| | díșe | | (you) say | 2.1 |
| | deșírse | | to say itself, to be said | 2.1 |
| | kerér—deșír | | to mean | 2.1 |
| | detrás | (detrás) | behind | 14.1 |
| | detrás—de | | in back of, behind, beyond | 14.1 |
| el | día | (día) | day | 1.1 |
| | bwénos—días | | good morning | 1.1 |
| | díga (see deșír) | | | |
| | dígas (see deșír) | | | |
| | díhe (see deșír) | | | |
| | dihéron (see deșír) | | | |
| | dispensár | (dispensar) | to excuse | 1.1 |
| la | disposișyón | (disposición) | disposition | 14.1 |
| | a—su—disposișyón | | at your disposal | 14.1 |

/diş/

| | | | | |
|---|---|---|---|---|
| | díşe (see deşír) | | | |
| el | dólar | (dólar) | dollar | 3.1 |
| el | domíngo | (domingo) | Sunday | 10.1 |
| | dón | (don) | mister | 11.1 |
| | dónde | (dónde) | where | 2.1 |
| el | dormitóryo | (dormitorio) | bedroom | 8.1 |
| | dós, —ø | (dos) | two | 2.1 |
| | dóşe, —ø | (doce) | twelve | 2.1 |
| | dóy (see dár) | | | |
| la | dúcha | (ducha) | shower | 12.1 |
| | dárse—una—dúcha | | to take a shower | 12.1 |
| el | dyénte | (diente) | tooth | 12.1 |
| | limpyárse—los—dyéntes | | to brush one's teeth | 12.1 |
| | dyéş, —ø | (diez) | ten | 2.1 |

/e/

| | | | | |
|---|---|---|---|---|
| | é (see abér) | | | |
| el | edifíşyo | (edificio) | building | 7.1 |
| el | ekipáhe | (equipaje) | baggage | 15.1 |
| | eks(ş)elénte, —ø | (excelente) | excellent | 4.1 |
| | el | (el) | the | 1.1 |
| | la | | the (f) | 1.1 |
| | los, las | | the (pl) | 2.1 |
| | al | | to the | 1.1 |

| | | | | |
|---|---|---|---|---|
| | él | (él) | he | 4.2 |
| | é(l)ya | | she | 4.2 |
| | é(l)yos, (é(l)yas) | | they | 4.2 |
| la | embaháda | (embajada) | embassy | 2.1 |
| | emfrénte | (enfrente) | in front (across the street) | 10.1 |
| | émos (see abér) | | | |
| | empeşár | (empezar) | to begin | 11.1 |
| el | empleádo | (empleado) | clerk | 15.1 |
| | en | (en) | in | 2.1 |
| | | | on | 3.1 |
| | | | at | 4.1 |
| | en—bárko | | by boat | 14.1 |
| | en—rrȩalidád | | actually | 8.1 |
| | en—segída | | at once, right away | 13.1 |
| | enkantádo, —a | (encantado) | enchanted | 1.1 |
| | enkantádo—de—konoşérla | | delighted to meet you | 1.1 |
| | enkantár | (encantar) | to enchant | 1.1 |
| | enkontrár | (encontrar) | to find | 6.1 |
| la | ensaláda | (ensalada) | salad | 6.1 |
| | entónşes | (entonces) | then | 3.1 |
| la | entráda | (entrada) | entrance | 3.1 |
| | éran (see sér) | | | |
| | éres (see sér) | | | |
| la | ermána | (hermana) | sister | 14.1 |

/es/

| | | | | |
|---|---|---|---|---|
| | és (see sér) | | | |
| | ése, —a | (ese) | that | 7.1 |
| la | eskína | (esquina) | corner | 10.1 |
| | eskribír | (escribir) | to write | 8.2 |
| el | eskritóryo | (escritorio) | desk | 5.1 |
| la | eskwéla | (escuela) | school | 4.1 |
| | éso (n) | (eso) | that | 2.1 |
| el | espanyól | (español) | (the) Spanish (language) | 2.1 |
| | esperár | (esperar) | to hope, expect, wait for | 8.1 |
| la | espósa | (esposa) | wife | 14.1 |
| | está (see estár) | | | |
| el | estádo | (estado) | state | 4.1 |
| los | estádos—unídos | (Estados Unidos) | United States | 4.1 |
| | están (see estár) | | | |
| | estár | (estar) | to be | 1.1 |
| | está | | (you) are | 1.1 |
| | están | | (they) are | 2.1 |
| | estás | | (you) are (fam) | 4.2 |
| | estóy | | (I) am | 1.1 |
| | está—byén | | that's O.K., O.K. | 1.1 |
| | estás—en—tu—kása | | make yourself at home | 9.1 |
| | estás (see estár) | | | |
| | éste, —a | (este) | this | 3.1 |
| | ésta—nóche | | tonight | 8.1 |
| | ésto (n) | (esto) | this | 2.1 |
| | estóy (see estár) | | | |

| | | | | |
|---|---|---|---|---|
| | estudyár | (estudiar) | to study | 9.1 |
| | estupéndo, —a | (estupendo) | terrific | 13.1 |

/f/

| | | | | |
|---|---|---|---|---|
| el | fabór | (favor) | favor | 2.1 |
| | por—fabór | | please | 2.1 |
| | faltár | (faltar) | to lack | 15.1 |
| la | famílya | (familia) | family | 5.1 |
| | fásil, —ø | (fácil) | easy | 6.1 |
| la | fécha | (fecha) | date | 9.1 |
| | fihár | (fijar) | to fix | 13.1 |
| | fihárse | | to pay attention | 13.1 |
| el | fín | (fin) | end | 10.1 |
| | em—fín | | so, then, well | 10.1 |
| | por—fín | | at last | 12.1 |
| la | fóto | (foto) | picture | 9.1 |
| la | fúnda | (funda) | the (pillow) case | 11.1 |
| la | fyésta | (fiesta) | party | 11.1 |

/g/

| | | | | |
|---|---|---|---|---|
| las | gáfas | (gafas) | eye glasses | 12.1 |
| el | gás | (gas) | gas | 7.1 |

/gor/

| | | | | |
|---|---|---|---|---|
| | górdo, —a | (gordo) | fat | 12.1 |
| | gordíto, —a | | a little fat | 12.1 |
| | gránde, —ø | (grande) | big, great | 7.1 |
| | grán | | great, large | 15.1 |
| | grás̜yas | (gracias) | thanks | 1.1 |
| | múchas—grás̜yas | | thanks a lot | 1.1 |
| | gustár | (gustar) | to please | 3.1 |
| el | gústo | (gusto) | pleasure | 1.1 |
| | múcho—gústo—(de—konos̜érlo) | | glad to meet you | 1.1 |
| | tánto—gústo—de—konos̜érlo | | I'm very glad to know (meet) you | 4.1 |

/h/

| | | | | |
|---|---|---|---|---|
| el | hamón | (jamón) | ham | 6.1 |
| ( ) | hosé | (José) | Joseph, Joe | 4.1 |
| | húntos, —as | (juntos) | together | 5.1 |
| ( ) | hwán | (Juan) | John | 4.1 |
| el | hwébes | (jueves) | Thursday | 10.1 |

/i/

| | | | | |
|---|---|---|---|---|
| | i | (y) | and | 1.1 |
| | íba (see ír) | | | |
| la | idéa | (idea) | idea | 9.1 |

| | | | | |
|---|---|---|---|---|
| | igwál, —ø | (igual) | equal | 1.1 |
| | igwál—a | | the same as | 8.1 |
| | igwalménte | | equally; same here | 1.1 |
| | igwalíto, —a | | just the same | 9.1 |
| la | íha | (hija) | daughter | 13.1 |
| el | ího | (hijo) | son | 14.1 |
| la | imformaşyón | (información) | information | 3.1 |
| el | inglés | (inglés) | (the) English (language) | 2.1 |
| | inklwír | (incluir) | to include | 7.1 |
| la | inmigraşyón | (inmigración) | immigration | 15.1 |
| | ir | (ir) | to go | 1.1 |
| | bá | | (it) goes | 1.1 |
| | bámos | | let's go, (we) go | 5.1 |
| | bán | | (they) go | 8.1 |
| | bás | | (you) go (fam) | 6.1 |
| | báyas | | go (fam) | 13.1 |
| | bóy | | (I) go | 12.1 |
| | íba | | (I) went, was going | 12.1 |
| | írse | | to leave | 10.1 |
| | kómo—le bá | | how are you getting along | 1.1 |
| la | işkyérda | (izquierda) | left | 2.1 |

/k/

| | | | | |
|---|---|---|---|---|
| | kabér | (caber) | to fit | 15.1 |
| | káda, —ø | (cada) | each | 13.2 |
| la | káha | (caja) | box, cashier's desk | 3.1 |
| el | kahéro | (cajero) | cashier | 3.1 |
| la | ká(l)ye | (calle) | street | 8.1 |
| la | káma | (cama) | bed | 8.1 |
| | kambyár | (cambiar) | to change, exchange | 3.1 |
| | kambyárse | | to change (oneself) | 8.1 |
| | kambyárse—(de—rrópa) | | to change (clothes) | 8.1 |
| el | kámbyo | (cambio) | change, exchange | 3.1 |
| la | kamísa | (camisa) | shirt | 10.1 |
| el | kámpo | (campo) | field, country | 7.1 |
| la | kantidád | (cantidad) | amount, quantity | 7.1 |
| | karámba | (caramba) | gosh | 8.1 |
| ( ) | kármen | (Carmen) | Carmen | 13.1 |
| | káro, —a | (caro) | expensive | 8.1 |
| el | kárro | (carro) | car | 14.1 |
| la | kárta | (carta) | letter | 12.2 |
| la | kása | (casa) | house | 8.1 |
| | el—senyór—de—la—kása | | the owner of the house | 13.1 |
| | estás—en—tu—kása | | make yourself at home | 9.1 |
| | kasádo, —a | (casado) | married | 5.1 |
| | kasár | (casar) | to marry | 5.1 |
| | kási | (casi) | almost | 4.1 |

| | | | |
|---|---|---|---|
| katórs̩e, —ø | (catorce) | fourteen | 2.1 |
| ke | (que) | that | 3.1 |
| | | who | 7.1 |
| áy—ke | | it's necessary to | 3.1 |
| lo—ke | | the that, that which, what | 10.1 |
| tenér—ke | | to have to | 8.1 |
| ké, —ø | (qué) | what | 1.1 |
| | | how | 9.1 |
| ké—bróma | | what a fix | 12.1 |
| ké—le—parés̩e | | what do you say | 6.1 |
| ké—óra—és | | what time is it | 5.1 |
| ké—tál | | how goes it | 1.1 |
| | | how | 4.1 |
| ké—te—pása | | what's the matter | 12.1 |
| nó—áy—de—ké | | don't give it a thought | 1.1 |
| por—ké | | why | 7.1 |
| kehár | | | |
| kehárse | (quejarse) | to complain | 15.1 |
| kerér | (querer) | to want | 1.1 |
| kyére | | (it) wants | 2.1 |
| kyéren | | (you) want (pl) | 6.1 |
| kyéres | | (you) want (fam) | 6.1 |
| kyéro | | (I) want | 1.1 |
| kerér—des̩ír | | to mean | 2.1 |
| kíns̩e, —ø | (quince) | fifteen | 2.1 |

/kla/

| | | | | |
|---|---|---|---|---|
| | kláro, —a | (claro) | clear | 7.1 |
| | kláro | | of course | 7.1 |
| | kobrár | (cobrar) | to charge | 11.1 |
| el | kóche | (coche) | car | 15.1 |
| ( ) | kolón | (Colón) | Columbus | 3.1 |
| | kombenír | (convenir) | to suit | 7.1 |
| | kombyéne | | (it) suits | 7.1 |
| | komér | (comer) | to eat | 6.1 |
| | komfundír | (confundir) | to confuse | 13.1 |
| | komfundírse | | to be confused | 13.1 |
| | komo | (como) | like, as | 9.1 |
| | kómo | (cómo) | how | 1.1 |
| | a—kómo—está—el—kámbyo | | what's the rate of exchange | 3.1 |
| | kómo—le—bá | | how are you getting along | 1.1 |
| | kómo—nó | | certainly | 1.1 |
| | kómodo, —a | (cómodo) | comfortable | 8.1 |
| | kompléto, —a | (completo) | complete | 15.1 |
| | komprár | (comprar) | to buy | 9.1 |
| | kón | (con) | with | 1.1 |
| | kom—permíso | | excuse me | 1.1 |
| | konmígo | | with me | 12.2 |
| | kontígo | | with you (fam) | 12.2 |
| | kon—tyémpo | | in time | 11.1 |
| | konoşér | (conocer) | to meet, get acquainted, to know | 1.1 |
| | enkantádo—de—konoşérla | | delighted to meet you | 1.1 |

| | | | | |
|---|---|---|---|---|
| | múcho—gústo—de—konoşérla | | glad to meet you | 1.1 |
| | tánto—gústo—de—conoşérlo | | I'm very glad to know you | 4.1 |
| | konsulár, —ø | (consular) | consular | 4.1 |
| | konténto, —a | (contento) | satisfied, contented | 14.1 |
| el | kontráryo | (contrario) | contrary | 8.1 |
| | al—kontráryo | | on the contrary | 8.1 |
| la | kópa | (copa) | goblet | 13.1 |
| el | koronél | (coronel) | colonel | 13.1 |
| la | kósa | (cosa) | thing | 4.1 |
| | kostár | (costar) | to cost | 3.1 |
| | kwésta | | (it) costs | 3.1 |
| la | koşína | (cocina) | kitchen | 8.1 |
| | kreér | (creer) | to believe | 6.1 |
| | kreér—ke—sí | | to think so | 6.1 |
| el | kúba—líbre | (cuba libre) | cuba libre | 9.1 |
| | kwál, —ø | (cuál) | which (one) | 15.1 |
| | kwalkyéra, —ø | (cualquiera) | whatever | 5.1 |
| | kwalkyér | | whatever | 5.1 |
| | kwándo | (cuando) | when | 4.1 |
| | | (cuándo) | when | 4.1 |
| | de—béş—en—kwándo | | from time to time | 13.1 |
| | désde—kwándo | | since when (how long) | 4.1 |
| | kwánto, —a | (cuánto) | how much | 2.1 |
| | kwántos, —as | | how many | 3.1 |
| el | kwárto | (cuarto) | room | 3.1 |
| el | kwárto | (cuarto) | quarter | 5.1 |

/kwa/

| | | | | |
|---|---|---|---|---|
| | kwátro, —ø | (cuatro) | four | 2.1 |
| la | kwénta | (cuenta) | check, bill | 6.1 |
| | kwésta (see kostár) | | | |
| el | kwidádo | (cuidado) | care | 13.1 |
| | | | (be) careful | 13.1 |
| | kyén | (quién) | who | 9.1 |
| | kyére (see kerér) | | | |
| | kyéren (see kerér) | | | |
| | kyéres (see kerér) | | | |
| | kyéro (see kerér) | | | |

/l/

| | | | | |
|---|---|---|---|---|
| | la(—) (see el, lo—) | | | |
| la | labandería | (lavandería) | laundry | 10.1 |
| | labár | (lavar) | to wash | 11.1 |
| el | lápiș | (lápiz) | pencil | 2.1 |
| | le— | (le) | (to) you | 1.1 |
| | | | (to) him | 4.1 |
| | | | (to) her | 10.1 |
| la | lechúga | (lechuga) | lettuce | 6.1 |
| la | legúmbre | (legumbre) | vegetable | 6.1 |
| | léhos | (lejos) | far | 3.1 |
| la | léngwa | (lengua) | language, tongue | 4.1 |
| el | líbro | (libro) | book | 2.1 |

| | | | | |
|---|---|---|---|---|
| | limpyár | (limpiar) | to clean | 10.1 |
| | limpyárse | | to clean oneself | 12.1 |
| | limpyárse—los—dyéntes | | to brush one's teeth | 12.1 |
| la | lísta | (lista) | list | 15.1 |
| | lísto, —a | (listo) | ready | 10.1 |
| | lo (n) | (lo) | the | 9.1 |
| | lo—de | | the matter of, about | 9.1 |
| | lo—ke | | the that, that which, what | 10.1 |
| | lo—, la— | (lo, la) | you | 1.1 |
| | | | it | 1.1 |
| | | | him (her) | 4.1 |
| | los—, las— | | them | 10.1 |
| | los, las (see el) | | | |
| el | lúnes | (lunes) | Monday | 10.1 |
| la | lús | (luz) | light | 7.1 |
| | lwégo | (luego) | then, later | 1.1 |
| | asta—lwégo | | so long | 1.1 |

/(l)y/

| | | | | |
|---|---|---|---|---|
| la | (l)yábe | (llave) | kcy | 7.1 |
| | (l)yamár | (llamar) | to call | 12.1 |
| | (l)yebár | (llevar) | to take, carry | 2.1 |
| | (l)yegár | (llegar) | to arrive | 12.1 |

/m/

| | | | | |
|---|---|---|---|---|
| la | maléta | (maleta) | suitcase | 10.1 |
| el | maletín | (maletín) | overnight case, handbag | 15.1 |

/mal/

| | | | | |
|---|---|---|---|---|
| | málo, —a | (malo) | bad | 8.1 |
| | mál | | bad | 8.1 |
| | mandár | (mandar) | to send | 10.1 |
| la | mans̯ána | (manzana) | apple | 6.1 |
| | man̯yána | (mañana) | tomorrow | 1.1 |
| | asta—man̯yána | | see you tomorrow | 1.1 |
| | mareár | (marear) | to make dizzy | 14.1 |
| | mareárse | | to get seasick | 14.1 |
| el | mártes | (martes) | Tuesday | 10.1 |
| | más | (más) | more | 3.1 |
| | álgo—más | | anything else | 3.1 |
| | me— | (me) | me | 1.1 |
| | | | (to) me | 2.1 |
| | | | myself | 8.1 |
| | médyo, —a | (medio) | half | 12.1 |
| | ménos | (menos) | less | 3.1 |
| el | menú | (menú) | menu | 6.1 |
| | menúdo | (menudo) | | |
| | a—menúdo | | often | 13.1 |
| el | més | (mes) | month | 7.1 |
| | al—més | | per month | 7.1 |
| la | mésa | (mesa) | table | 2.1 |
| el | meséro | (mesero) | waiter | 6.1 |
| | metér | (meter) | to put in | 13.1 |
| | metér—la—páta | | to put your foot in your mouth | 13.1 |

| | | | | |
|---|---|---|---|---|
| | mi, —ø | (mi) | my | 4.1 |
| | mí | (mí) | me | 6. 1 |
| | konmígo | | with me | 12.2 |
| el | mi(l)yón | (millón) | million | 8.1 |
| | minerál, —ø | (mineral) | mineral | 3.1 |
| | mío, —a | (mío) | mine (my) | 4.1 |
| | mi, —ø | | my | 4.1 |
| | mirár | (mirar) | to look | 13.1 |
| | místmo, —a | (mismo) | same | 3.1 |
| | | | —self | 10.1 |
| | aóra—mísmo | | right now | 3.1 |
| el | mobimyénto | (movimiento) | movement, activity | 4.1 |
| | molestár | (molestar) | to bother | 10.1 |
| | molestárse | | to bother | 10.1 |
| el | moménto | (momento) | moment | 12.1 |
| | un—moménto | | just a minute | 12.1 |
| la | monéda | (moneda) | coin, change | 3.1 |
| el | mós̥o | (mozo) | porter | 3.1 |
| | | | waiter | 6.1 |
| | moréno, —a | (moreno) | brunette | 13.1 |
| la | muchácha | (muchacha) | girl | 9.1 |
| | múcho, —a | (mucho) | much, a lot, lots | 1.1 |
| | múchos, —as | | many | 1.1 |
| | múchas—grás̥yas | | thanks a lot | 1.1 |
| | múcho—gústo—(de—konos̥érlo) | | glad to meet you | 1.1 |

/much/

| | | | | |
|---|---|---|---|---|
| | muchísimo, —a | | very much | 5.1 |
| | mudár | (mudar) | to move | 8.1 |
| | mudárse | | to change, to move | 10.1 |
| | mudárse—de—kása | | to move (one's residence) | 8.1 |
| | múy | (muy) | very | 1.1 |
| el | mwéble | (mueble) | (piece of) furniture | 7.1 |
| | sin—mwébles | | unfurnished | 7.1 |
| el | myérkoles | (miércoles) | Wednesday | 10.1 |

/n/

| | | | | |
|---|---|---|---|---|
| | náda | (nada) | nothing | 1.1 |
| | de—náda | | you're welcome | 1.1 |
| ( ) | nádye | (nadie) | no one | 10.2 |
| | neşesáryo, —a | (necesario) | necessary | 15.1 |
| | neşesitár | (necesitar) | to need | 3.1 |
| | ni | (ni) | nor, (or) | 7.1 |
| la | níɳya | (niña) | (small) girl | 14.1 |
| el | níɳyo | (niño) | child | 14.1 |
| | nó | (no) | no, not | 1.1 |
| | | (¿no?) | isn't it, didn't he, etc. | 11.1 |
| | kómo—nó | | certainly | 1.1 |
| | nó—áy—de—ké | | don't give it a thought | 1.1 |
| la | nóbya | (novia) | sweetheart, fiancée | 9.1 |
| la | nóche | (noche) | night, evening | 1.1 |

| | | | | |
|---|---|---|---|---|
| | bwénas—nóches | | good evening | 1.1 |
| | ésta—nóche | | tonight | 8.1 |
| el | nómbre | (nombre) | name | 4.1 |
| | nos— | (nos) | us | 2.1 |
| | | | ourselves | 6.1 |
| | | | to us | 15.1 |
| | nosótros | (nosotros) | we, us | 4.1 |
| | nosótras | | we, us (f) | 12.2 |
| | núnka | (nunca) | never | 10.2 |
| | nwébe, —ø | (nueve) | nine | 2.1 |
| | nwébo, —a | (nuevo) | new | 11.1 |
| | nwéstro, —a | (nuestro) | our(s) | 9.2 |

/o/

| | | | | |
|---|---|---|---|---|
| | o | (o) | or | 2.1 |
| | ócho, —ø | (ocho) | eight | 2.1 |
| el | ofişyál | (oficial) | officer | 4.1 |
| | oír | (oír) | to listen | 12.1 |
| | óye | | listen (fam) | 12.1 |
| | okupádo, —a | (ocupado) | busy | 4.1 |
| | okupár | (ocupar) | to occupy | 4.1 |
| | óla | (hola) | hello, hi | 1.1 |
| el | ómbre | (hombre) | man | 9.1 |
| | ónşe, —ø | (once) | eleven | 2.1 |

/ora/

| | | | | |
|---|---|---|---|---|
| la | óra | (hora) | hour | 5.1 |
| | ké—óra—és | | what time is it | 5.1 |
| la | órden | (orden) | order | 14.1 |
| | a—sus—órdenes | | at your service | 14.1 |
| el | otél | (hotel) | hotel | 2.1 |
| | ótro, —a | (otro) | another | 2.1 |
| | ótra—béș | | again | 2.1 |
| | óye (see oír) | | | |

/p/

| | | | | |
|---|---|---|---|---|
| | pára | (para) | for | 6.1 |
| | | | to, in order to | 12.1 |
| | pareșér | (parecer) | to seem | 5.1 |
| | ké—le—paréșe | | what do you say | 6.1 |
| | le—paréșe—byén | | OK with you | 5.1 |
| el | párke | (parque) | park | 14.1 |
| la | párte | (parte) | part | 5.1 |
| | pasár | (pasar) | to pass, to hand | 2.1 |
| | | | to come by | 8.1 |
| | | | to come in | 9.1 |
| | | | to happen | 12.1 |
| | ké—te—pása | | what's the matter | 12.1 |
| | pasár—adelánte | | to come in | 9.1 |
| el | pastél | (pastel) | pie | 6.1 |
| la | páta | (pata) | paw | 13.1 |

| | | | | |
|---|---|---|---|---|
| | metér—la—páta | | to put your foot in your mouth | 13.1 |
| el | pátyo | (patio) | yard, court, patio | 8.1 |
| | pekényo, —a | (pequeño) | small | 13.2 |
| la | péna | (pena) | sorrow, grief | 14.1 |
| | balér—la—péna | | to be worthwhile | 14.1 |
| | pensár | (pensar) | to think, plan | 6.1 |
| | pyénso | | (I) think | 6.1 |
| el | perdón | (perdón) | pardon; excuse me | 2.1 |
| el | permíso | (permiso) | permission | 1.1 |
| | kom—permíso | | excuse me | 1.1 |
| | péro | (pero) | but | 4.1 |
| el | peryódiko | (periódico) | newspaper | 7.1 |
| el | péso | (peso) | peso | 3.1 |
| el | píso | (piso) | floor | 3.1 |
| la | plúma | (pluma) | pen | 2.1 |
| | podér | (poder) | to be able | 3.1 |
| | pwéde | | (you) can | 3.1 |
| | pwédo | | (I) can | 6.1 |
| | póko, —a | (poco) | little | 4.1 |
| | por | (por) | for, in exchange for | 2.1 |
| | | | during | 11.1 |
| | por—abyón | | by plane | 14.1 |
| | por—aí | | that way | 13.1 |
| | por—aóra | | right now | 7.1 |
| | por—fabór | | please | 2.1 |

/por/

| | | | | |
|---|---|---|---|---|
| | por—fín | | at last | 12.1 |
| | por—ké | | why | 7.1 |
| | por—la—tárde | | during the afternoon | 11.1 |
| el | póstre | (postre) | dessert | 6.1 |
| | praktikár | (practicar) | to practice | 4.1 |
| | presentár | (presentar) | to present | 1.1 |
| | prestár | (prestar) | to lend, to provide | 15.1 |
| el | préşyo | (precio) | price | 8.1 |
| | priméro, —a | (primero) | first | 3.1 |
| | primér | | first | 3.1 |
| la | prísa | (prisa) | haste | 12.1 |
| | dárse—prísa | | to hurry oneself | 12.1 |
| | probár | (probar) | to try, to taste | 6.1 |
| | prónto | (pronto) | soon | 9.1 |
| | pronunşyár | (pronunciar) | to pronounce | 4.1 |
| la | propína | (propina) | tip | 4.1 |
| el | propósito | (propósito) | purpose | 4.1 |
| | a—propósito | | by the way | 4.1 |
| | pwéde (see podér) | | | |
| | pwéden (see podér) | | | |
| | pwédo (see podér) | | | |
| | pyénso (see pensár) | | | |

/r/

| | | | | |
|---|---|---|---|---|
| la | rraṣón | (razón) | reason | 6.1 |
| | tenér—rraṣón | | to be right | 6.1 |
| | rre̯al, —ø | (real) | real | 14.1 |
| | rre̯álménte | | really | 14.1 |
| la | rre̯alidád | (realidad) | reality | 8.1 |
| | en—rre̯alidád | | actually | 8.1 |
| | rrebisár | (revisar) | to examine, inspect | 15.1 |
| el | rregálo | (regalo) | gift | 15.1 |
| | rrekordár | (recordar) | to remember | 8.1 |
| | rrekwérdo | | (I) remember | 8.1 |
| | rrepetír | (repetir) | to repeat | 2.1 |
| | rrepíta | | repeat, say it again | 2.1 |
| el | rrestorán | (restorán) | restaurant | 5.1 |
| | rrigurós0, —a | (riguroso) | rigorous, strict | 15.1 |
| la | rrópa | (ropa) | clothes, clothing | 8.1 |

/s/

| | | | | |
|---|---|---|---|---|
| el | sábado | (sábado) | Saturday | 10.1 |
| la | sábana | (sábana) | sheet | 11.1 |
| | sabér | (saber) | to know | 12.1 |
| | sé | | (I) know | 12.1 |
| la | sála | (sala) | living room | 8.1 |
| | salír | (salir) | to leave, to go out | 12.1 |
| el | sánwich | (sandwich) | sandwich | 6.1 |

/se/

| | | | | |
|---|---|---|---|---|
| | se— | (se) | —self (3rd person, sg and pl) | 2.1 |
| | sé (see sabér) | | | |
| | segída | | | |
| | en—segída | | at once, right away | 13.1 |
| | segúro, —a | (seguro) | sure | 15.1 |
| la | sekretárya | (secretaria) | secretary | 9.1 |
| la | sekṣyón | (sección) | section | 4.1 |
| la | semána | (semana) | week | 8.1 |
| | sentár | (sentar) | to seat | 2.1 |
| | syénta | | seat (fam) | 9.1 |
| | syénte | | seat | 2.1 |
| | sentárse | | to sit down | 2.1 |
| | sentír | (sentir) | to regret, to feel | 1.1 |
| | syénto | | (I) feel | 1.1 |
| | sentírlo—múcho | | to be very sorry | 1.1 |
| el | seṇyór | (señor) | sir, mister | 1.1 |
| | el—seṇyór—de—la—kása | | the owner of the house | 13.1 |
| la | seṇyóra | (señora) | madam, Mrs. | 1.1 |
| la | seṇyoríta | (señorita) | miss | 1.1 |
| | sér | (ser) | to be | 2.1 |
| | éran | | (they) were | 13.1 |
| | éres | | (you) are (fam) | 5.2 |
| | és | | (it) is | 2.1 |
| | sómos | | (we) are | 5.2 |

| | | | | |
|---|---|---|---|---|
| | són | | (they) are | 4.1 |
| | sóy | | (I) am | 5.1 |
| | débe(n)—sér | | must be, probably is (are) | 8.1 |
| | séys, —ø | (seis) | six | 2.1 |
| | si | (si) | if | 6.1 |
| | sí | (sí) | yes | 2.1 |
| | kre̯ér—ke—sí | | to think so | 6.1 |
| la | sí(l)ya | (silla) | chair | 2.1 |
| | sín | (sin) | without | 7.1 |
| | sin—mwébles | | unfurnished | 7.1 |
| la | sirbyénta | (sirvienta) | maid | 11.1 |
| | sóbre | (sobre) | above | 14.1 |
| | sóbre—tódo | | above all, especially | 14.1 |
| la | sóda | (soda) | soda | 9.1 |
| el | sofá | (sofá) | sofa | 8.1 |
| el | sofá—káma | (sofá cama) | sofa-bed | 8.1 |
| | sólo | (sólo) | only | 7.1 |
| | soltéro, —a | (soltero) | unmarried (bachelor) | 5.1 |
| | sómos (see sér) | | | |
| | són (see sér) | | | |
| la | sópa | (sopa) | soup | 6.1 |
| | sóy (see sér) | | | |
| | sú, —ø | (su) | your (sg and pl) | 5.1 |
| | | | his, their | 11.2 |
| | subír | (subir) | to go up | 2.1 |

/sus/

| | | | | |
|---|---|---|---|---|
| | súşyo, —a | (sucio) | dirty | 11.1 |
| | súyo, —a | (suyo) | your(s) (sg and pl) | 5.1 |
| | | | his, their(s) | 9.2 |
| | sú, —ø | | your (sg and pl) | 5.1 |
| | | | his, their | 11.2 |
| la | swégra | (suegra) | mother—in—law | 14.1 |
| | syémpre | (siempre) | always | 4.1 |
| | syénta (see sentár) | | | |
| | syénte (see sentár) | | | |
| | syénto (see sentír) | | | |
| | syéte, —ø | (siete) | seven | 2.1 |

/ş/

| | | | | |
|---|---|---|---|---|
| el | şenişéro | (cenicero) | ashtray | 2.1 |
| el | şéntro | (centro) | center (of town), downtown | 2.1 |
| la | şerbéşa | (cerveza) | beer | 6.1 |
| el | şérdo | (cerdo) | pork, pig | 6.1 |
| | şérka | (cerca) | near | 3.1 |
| | şérka—de | | near to | 3.1 |
| | şínko, —ø | (cinco) | five | 2.1 |
| | şyento, —ø | (ciento) | hundred | 7.1 |
| | şyéntos, —as | | hundreds | 7.1 |

/t/

| | | | | |
|---|---|---|---|---|
| el | táksi | (taxi) | taxi | 3.1 |
| | tál, —ø | (tal) | such | 1.1 |
| | ké—tál | | how goes it | 1.1 |
| | | | how | 4.1 |
| | tambyén | (también) | also, too | 5.1 |
| | tánto, —a | (tanto) | so much | 4.1 |
| | tánto—gústo—dc—konoşérlo | | I'm very glad to know (meet) you | 4.1 |
| | tárde | (tarde) | late | 10.1 |
| la | tárde | (tarde) | afternoon | 1.1 |
| | bwénas—tárdes | | good afternoon | 1.1 |
| | por—la—tárde | | during the afternoon | 11.1 |
| | te | (te) | you, (to) you (fam) | 6.1 |
| | | | to you | 9.1 |
| | | | yourself | 9.1 |
| | tenér | (tener) | to have | 2.1 |
| | ténga | | have | 15.1 |
| | téngo | | (I) have | 2.1 |
| | tyéne | | (you) have | 2.1 |
| | tyénes | | (you) have (fam) | 6.1 |
| | akí—tyéne | | here you are | 3.1 |
| | | | here is (are) | 7.1 |
| | tenér—ámbre | | to be hungry | 5.1 |
| | tenér—ke | | to have to | 8.1 |
| | tenér—la—bondád—de | | to be so kind as to, please | 15.1 |

/ten/

| | | | | |
|---|---|---|---|---|
| | tenér—rraşón | | to be right | 6.1 |
| | ténga (see tenér) | | | |
| | téngo (see tenér) | | | |
| | tí | (ti) | you (fam) | 8.1 |
| | kontígo | | with you | 12.2 |
| la | tintorería | (tintorería) | cleaner's shop | 10.1 |
| | todabía | (todavía) | yet, still | 9.1 |
| | tódo, —a | (todo) | all | 9.1 |
| | | | every | 10.1 |
| | sóbre—tódo | | above all, especially | 14.1 |
| | tomár | (tomar) | to take | 3.1 |
| el | tomáte | (tomate) | tomato | 6.1 |
| | trabahár | (trabajar) | to work | 4.1 |
| | traduşír | (traducir) | to translate | 2.1 |
| | tradúşka | | translate | 2.1 |
| | traér | (traer) | to bring | 6.1 |
| | tráyga | | bring | 6.1 |
| el | trágo | (trago) | swallow, drink | 10.1 |
| el | tráhe | (traje) | suit | 10.1 |
| | trankílo, —a | (tranquilo) | quiet | 13.1 |
| | tratár | (tratar) | to treat | 6.1 |
| | tratárse—de | | to address as | 6.1 |
| | tráyga (see traér) | | | |
| | trés, —ø | (tres) | three | 2.1 |
| | tréşe, —ø | (trece) | thirteen | 2.1 |

| | | | | |
|---|---|---|---|---|
| | tu, —ø | (tu) | your (fam) | 9.1 |
| | tú | (tú) | you (fam) | 4.2 |
| | túyo, —a | (tuyo) | your(s) (fam) | 9.1 |
| | tu, —ø | | your (fam) | 9.1 |
| el | tyémpo | (tiempo) | time | 11.1 |
| | kon—tyémpo | | in time | 11.1 |
| | tyéne (see tenér) | | | |
| | tyénes (see tenér) | | | |

/u/

| | | | | |
|---|---|---|---|---|
| | unído, —a | (unido) | united | 4.1 |
| | unír | (unir) | to unite | 4.1 |
| | úno, —a | (uno) | one | 2.1 |
| | | | a, an | 2.3 |
| | un | | a, an | 2.1 |
| | únos, —as | | some, a few | 3.1 |
| | ustéd | (usted) | you | 1.1 |

/w/

| | | | | |
|---|---|---|---|---|
| el | wíski | (whiskey) | whiskey | 9.1 |

/y/

| | | | | |
|---|---|---|---|---|
| | yá | (ya) | already | 5.1 |
| | | | yet | 14.1 |
| | | | now | 15.1 |
| | yó | (yo) | I | 4.2 |

# AI.2 INDEX

# NOTES